Dear Friend,

You're just the one we had in mind as we planned
this new book. To begin with, we know there are
lots of ways you use a cookbook. You read it—
simply because you like to read about food.
Or you use it to "look up a recipe." Someone
brought you a brace of pheasants, or there was
a special at the market . . . so you look up a
specific recipe. You use a cookbook to learn
to cook—or as a refresher course, to become a
better, more up-to-the-minute cook. You use it to
plan a party leafing through the whole book to
get ideas, to start your mind working.

We kept you in mind when we tested and tasted
each recipe, and when we asked our home testers
to tell us how the recipes fit into their lives. We
know you're busy, so we've used convenience
foods and shortcuts wherever we could. We know
you demand quality, so every recipe is our
taste-tempting best.

In short, we've given you a cookbook to cook with,
to be comfortable with. We hope it will become
a friendly member of your kitchen family, that
it will answer your questions, help solve your
problems and make the eating and living in your
house just a little easier, a lot more fun.

Betty Crocker

Betty Crocker's
COOKBOOK

BANTAM BOOKS
TORONTO · NEW YORK · LONDON

BETTY CROCKER'S COOKBOOK

*A Bantam Book / published by arrangement with
Western Publishing Company, Inc.*

PRINTING HISTORY

*Golden Press edition published September 1969
22 printings through 1974*

*Literary Guild edition published December 1969
13 printings through 1974*

Bantam edition / November 1974

2nd printing . . November 1974	4th printing . . . . January 1975
3rd printing . . December 1974	5th printing . . November 1975
	6th printing . . . October 1976	

Contents

The Betty Crocker Difference-

Betty Crocker used to say, "You get a perfect cake every time you bake—cake after cake after cake." Today we can say it about Paella or Quiche Lorraine or Cinnamon Rolls or any one of the hundreds of recipes in this book. We can make this statement with complete confidence—and this is the Betty Crocker difference.

No one sat down and "wrote" this cookbook. No one clipped and snipped and borrowed from old books and said, "Here's one that will do." We work our recipes out—and we do mean work! Work that starts with the first idea or need for a recipe. Work that leads to a recipe developed by one of our home economists and taste tested by a small but critical group of staff members who take the recipe apart, ask questions, suggest changes and possible variations.

When the dish has been prepared again and again, when we have tried it with you in mind—to see what happens if you add a little more or a little less liquid, if you use eggs that are larger or smaller than ours, if your oven temperature is set a bit high or low—when we have made it as cook-proof as we can, what happens?

Then the recipe goes to a new group of home economists and tasters. And if it works for them, and if they like it, then it's ready to go to our test panel of 1300 homemakers in all parts of the country.

We ask these women to use the recipe and tell us how their families liked it. "Did it seem too expensive?" "Was it too much trouble?" "Could you find all the ingredients?" "Were the directions clear?" "Will you make it again?" Then—tested! . . . re-tested! . . . people-tested!—and only then does the recipe go into our cookbook.

And it is because of all this work—what we call the Betty Crocker difference—that we can say, "if you follow the recipes exactly, you can be sure of perfect results—every time!"

For this you can trust Betty Crocker!

TERMS—WHAT YOU NEED TO KNOW

FOR PREPARING INGREDIENTS

Crush: Press to extract juice with garlic press, mallet or side of knife (garlic).

Mince: Cut into very small pieces (garlic, onion).

Snip: Cut into very small pieces with a scissors (parsley, chives).

Chop: Cut into pieces with a knife or other sharp tool (hold end of knife tip on the board with one hand; move the blade up and down with the other).

Dice: Cut into small cubes (less than ½ inch).

Cube: Cut into cubes ½ inch or larger.

Sliver: Cut into long thin pieces (almonds).

Julienne: Cut into matchlike sticks (cooked meat, cheese).

Grate: Cut into tiny particles using small holes of grater (lemon peel).

Shred: Cut into thin pieces using large holes on grater or shredder (cheese).

Pare: Cut off outer covering with a knife or other sharp tool (potatoes, apples).

Peel: Strip off outer covering (oranges).

FOR COMBINING INGREDIENTS

(Note: These are arranged from the gentlest action to the most vigorous.)

Toss: Tumble ingredients lightly with a lifting motion (salads).

Fold: Combine ingredients lightly by a combination of two motions: one cuts vertically through mixture, the other slides the spatula or wire whisk across the bottom of the bowl and up the side, turning over (chiffon cakes, soufflés).

Cut in: Distribute solid fat in dry ingredients by chopping with knives or pastry blender (pastry, biscuits).

Stir: Combine ingredients with circular or figure-8 motion until of uniform consistency.

Mix: Combine in any way that distributes all ingredients evenly.

Blend: Thoroughly combine all ingredients until very smooth and uniform.

Cream: Beat just until smooth, light and fluffy (the combination of sugar and shortening).

Beat: Make mixture smooth by a vigorous over and over motion with a spoon, whip or rotary beater.

Whip: Beat rapidly in order to incorporate air.

FOR COOKING

Cook and stir: Cook in small amount of shortening until tender, stirring occasionally (onion). We use this term rather than sauté.

Brown: Cook until food changes color, usually in small amount of fat over moderate heat (meat).

Simmer: Cook in liquid just below the boiling point. Bubbles form slowly and collapse *below* the surface.

Boil: Heat until bubbles rise continuously and break on the surface of liquid (rolling boil—bubbles form rapidly).

OTHER TERMS

Cool: Allow to come to room temperature.

Chill: Refrigerate to make cold.

Refrigerate: Place in refrigerator to store.

Marinate: Let food stand in liquid that will add flavor or tenderize.

Baste: Spoon a flavoring ingredient over food during cooking period.

Toast: Brown in oven or toaster (bread, nuts).

MEASURING INGREDIENTS— THE RIGHT WAY

GRADUATED SPOONS

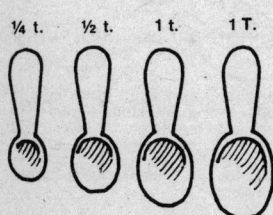

¼ t.   ½ t.   1 t.   1 T.

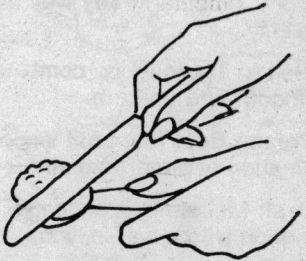

For thin liquids: Pour into appropriate spoon until full.

For dry ingredients and thick liquids: Pour or scoop into appropriate spoon until full, then level.

If your set of graduated spoons does not have a ⅛ teaspoon, measure, use the ¼ teaspoon; fill, then remove half.

A dash is less than ⅛ teaspoon.

GLASS MEASURING CUP

Used for measuring liquids. Be sure to read the measurement at eye level.

GRADUATED NESTED MEASURING CUPS

Used for measuring non-liquids.

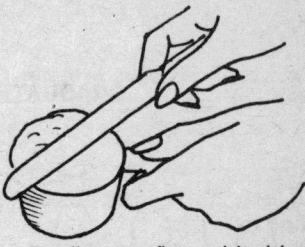

For all-purpose flour, quick-mixing flour and granulated sugar: Dip cup into ingredient to fill, then level with straight-edged spatula or knife. (We do not sift flour to measure or combine with other ingredients.)

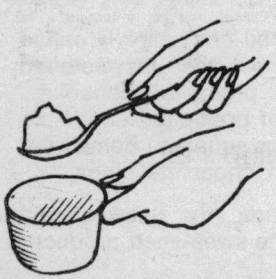

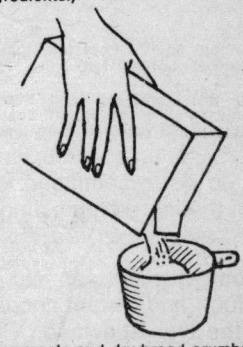

For cake flour, confectioners' sugar and buttermilk baking mix: Lightly spoon into cup, then level. (Sift confectioners' sugar only if it is lumpy.)

For nuts, coconut, shredded cheese, cut-up or small fruit and soft bread crumbs: Spoon into cup and pack down lightly.

For cereals and dry bread crumbs: Pour into cup, then level. (This method can also be used for measuring quick-mixing flour and confectioners' sugar.)

For brown sugar, fats and shortening: Spoon into cup and pack down firmly. (When a recipe calls for melted shortening, it can be measured before or after melting.)

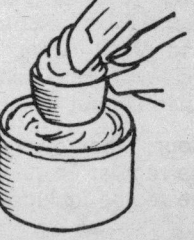

INGREDIENTS—HINTS TO HELP YOU

Ascorbic Acid: The Vitamin C ingredient used to preserve the color of fruits and vegetables (usually sold with canning supplies).

Baking Powder: All our testing has been done with double-action baking powder. Do not use a single-action baking powder.

Cheese: Many of our recipes call for natural or process cheese; be sure to use the type specified. They vary in fat and moisture content as well as in texture and flavor.

Chocolate: Our recipes call for unsweetened, semisweet and sweet cooking chocolate; be sure to use the type specified.

When 1 ounce melted unsweetened chocolate is called for, you can either melt and cool the unsweetened squares or use the envelopes of premelted chocolate. (We do not recommend the use of premelted chocolate when the ingredient listing specifies squares.) Semisweet chocolate pieces are often called chocolate chips.

Cocoa: Our recipes call for cocoa (the unsweetened product) and instant cocoa mix (the sweetened product); use the type specified.

Cream: Whipping (30 to 35% butterfat), coffee (about 20% butterfat), half and half (10 to 12% butterfat), dairy sour (20% butterfat). Do not substitute one for another. Our recipes do not call for cream which has been soured.

Eggs: The eggs used in our bakings are medium to large grade A eggs. (When the exact size is essential to the success of a recipe, as in the case of cakes, we have also given a cup measurement.) If you use larger or smaller eggs, measure them—1 medium to large egg equals about ¼ cup.

Flour: When our recipes call for all-purpose flour, either the regular or quick-mixing type can be used . . . unless the recipe includes another recommendation.

Specific directions for the use of self-rising flour are included in each recipe using more than ¼ cup. With lesser amounts, you may substitute self-rising flour without other recipe adjustments. Cake flour should be used when it is called for in recipes. (See Measuring Ingredients, page 8; we do not recommend sifting flour.)

Gelatin: Unflavored gelatin is packaged in envelopes, each containing about 1 tablespoon. (We usually call for the entire package.) Flavored gelatin contains sugar, color and flavoring. (Our recipes call for the 3-ounce package.)

Herbs and Spices: Ground herbs should be used in the recipes unless another form is specified. If you substitute fresh herbs, increase the amount.

Milk: Our testing has been done with fresh whole milk. When buttermilk is called for, use commercial-cultured buttermilk. (Do not substitute soured milk for buttermilk.) To substitute evaporated milk for fresh milk, mix with an equal amount of water.

Mixes: Our recipes have been perfected with *our* mixes only. Follow package directions carefully, with the exceptions noted in individual recipes. When a mix is listed in the recipe with "(dry)," use the mix just as it comes from the package.

Pudding: Be sure to use the type called for in the recipe. It may be canned, instant (the type which is not cooked), regular or cooked (called pudding or pie filling; cooked when being prepared).

Shortening: When a recipe calls for shortening, we refer to the type sold in 1- or 3-pound cans. In baked goods, such as cakes, you may substitute butter (only) for up to half the amount.

When the shortening ingredient is listed as "butter or margarine, softened," use only butter or stick-type non-whipped margarine. Do not use the soft-type (tub) margarine unless the ingredient listing is "soft butter or margarine." Follow manufacturer's directions for whipped margarine.

Salad oil is any oil of vegetable origin. Use oil only when called for in recipes; do not use as a substitute for other shortenings even though they are melted.

Sugar: When "sugar" is listed in a recipe, use granulated (cane or beet) sugar. Brown sugar and confectioners' (powdered) sugar are always indicated in recipes. When more than one type of sugar is used in any recipe, all types are designated. (We do not sift any sugars unless it is necessary to remove lumps.)

EQUIPMENT—THE CORRECT CHOICES

We have used standard equipment in the preparation of all the recipes in this book. (Standard sizes are usually marked on the back of a pan; if not, measure from inside rim to inside rim.) Where applicable, choices of pans have been given. Other substitutions affect baking temperature and time and are not recommended.

Some of the equipment called for throughout the book is described below. Equipment related to specific bakings (breads, pies, cakes, cookies) is described in the pertinent chapters.

FOR COOKING AND BAKING

Baking Dish: Heat-resistant dish with low sides. If metal pans are used for baking, adjustments must be made.

Baking Pans: The standard metal pans in the sizes specified. We have given choices wherever possible; it is best not to make substitutions. If glass is used, reduce the oven temperature 25°.

Baking Sheet: Sometimes called cookie sheet; may have shallow sides.

Bundt Pan: Pan with a tube in the middle and scalloped sides (the capacity should be correct; measure by cups).

Casserole: Heat-resistant dish with deep sides.

Double Boiler: Because of advancements in the heat control of ranges, we have eliminated the use of the double boiler in many recipes. It is, however, essential in a few.

Dutch Oven: Deep cooking utensil with tight-fitting cover.

FOR PREPARATION

Measuring Cups and Spoons: See page xi.

Rotary Beater: Standard electric mixer, hand electric mixer or hand (non-electric) beater. In some cases, only one type of beater is suitable, and it is so specified in the recipe.

Mixer Bowl: The sturdy bowl that is sold with standard electric mixers. When our recipes call for a mixing bowl, use any container in which you can combine the necessary ingredients.

Appetizers

*First courses are friendly, first courses are fun.
Nibbles in the living room, to take the edge off
early-bird appetites. A curtain-raiser at the table,
to set the stage for the good meal to come. Or
just a "special little something" any old night—
to tell your favorite family, "I'm so glad you came
home!" Here they are. Help yourself, and then
make up a few more all your own.*

Dips

What do you dip in a dip? Something crisp! Surprises like raw asparagus, sliced mushrooms, thin strips of turnip or zucchini; or old friends like carrot and celery sticks, cauliflowerets, radishes. And something crunchy! Not just chips—but pretzels, snacks and cracker "scoops."

Dips are good do-aheads, too. But take them out of the cold in time to soften a bit. Want a bright new note? Offer at least one hot dip, in a chafing dish or on a hot-tray.

CAPE COD DIP

Something special in the traditional onion dip.

Stir 1 envelope (about 1½ ounces) dry onion soup mix into 2 cups dairy sour cream. Stir in 1 can (7 to 8 ounces) minced clams, drained. Cover; refrigerate at least 3 hours.

2½ cups.

ARTICHOKES WITH ONION DIP

Prepare 2 packages (9 ounces each) frozen artichoke hearts as directed on package except—add 2 slices lemon to the cooking water. Drain and chill artichokes.

Serve artichokes on picks to dip into Creamy Onion Dip (below).
6 servings.

CREAMY ONION DIP

⅓ cup dairy sour cream
⅓ cup mayonnaise or salad dressing

1 tablespoon dry onion soup mix

Mix all ingredients thoroughly. Refrigerate at least 1 hour.
About ⅔ cup.

PEPPERED CHEDDAR DIP

Crisp carrot and celery sticks are the perfect go-withs for this dip.

1½ cups dairy sour cream
1 cup shredded Cheddar cheese (about 4 ounces)
¼ cup finely chopped onion
3 tablespoons minced green pepper

¼ teaspoon salt
⅛ teaspoon red pepper sauce
1 tablespoon milk

Mix all ingredients. If necessary, add another tablespoon milk to make a good dipping consistency. Cover; refrigerate at least 1 hour.
2 cups.

HARLEQUIN DIP

Here's a dip that offers a change of pace—a golden color and snappy flavor that's sure to please all of your guests.

½ cup dairy sour cream
½ cup mayonnaise or salad dressing
½ cup chopped ripe olives
2 tablespoons snipped chives

1 teaspoon Worcestershire sauce
½ teaspoon prepared mustard
½ teaspoon curry powder

Blend sour cream and mayonnaise. Add remaining ingredients; mix well. Cover; refrigerate at least 1 hour.
About 1½ cups.

NIPPY BLUE CHEESE DIP

To bring out the zip in this dip, use tart red-skinned apple slices as the dunkers.

2 packages (3 ounces each) cream cheese, softened
3 tablespoons milk
1 tablespoon mayonnaise or salad dressing
½ teaspoon Worcestershire sauce
¼ cup crumbled blue cheese

Blend cream cheese, milk, mayonnaise and Worcestershire sauce. Fold in blue cheese.
About 1 cup.

DILLED SHRIMP DIP

Offer this seafood treat in an elegant shell, and garnish with whole shrimp.

¼ cup milk
1 package (8 ounces) cream cheese, softened
1 can (4½ ounces) shrimp, rinsed, drained and chopped
1 teaspoon lemon juice
1 teaspoon Worcestershire sauce
½ teaspoon garlic salt
¼ teaspoon dill weed

Blend milk gradually into cream cheese. Stir in shrimp, lemon juice, Worcestershire sauce, garlic salt and dill weed. Cover; refrigerate at least 1 hour.
About 1½ cups.

DIPSY DEVIL

1 jar (5 ounces) cream cheese with pimiento
1 can (2¼ ounces) deviled ham
¼ cup mayonnaise or salad dressing
2 tablespoons snipped parsley
1 tablespoon minced onion
4 drops red pepper sauce

Combine all ingredients in small mixer bowl. Beat until creamy.
1 cup.

DRIED BEEF DIP

1 cup creamed cottage
  cheese (small curd)
2 tablespoons skim milk
2 to 3 tablespoons
  horseradish

½ teaspoon instant minced
  onion
1 envelope (about 2½
  ounces) dried beef

Place cottage cheese and milk in blender. Blend on high speed until smooth and creamy, about 2 minutes.

Add remaining ingredients; blend on low speed until beef is shredded and evenly distributed throughout cheese mixture, about 3 minutes. Cover; refrigerate at least 1 hour.

About 1½ cups.

CALIFORNIA ONION SLIM-DIP

¼ cup skim milk
2 cups creamed cottage
  cheese (small curd)

1 envelope (about 1½
  ounces) dry onion soup
  mix

Place skim milk and cottage cheese in blender. Blend on high speed until smooth and creamy, about 4 minutes. Stir in onion soup mix. Cover; refrigerate at least 1 hour.

2 cups.

FRUIT 'N CHEESE DIP

This "mock sour cream" dip looks and tastes rich and creamy— actually it's designed for dieters.

⅓ cup skim milk
1 teaspoon lemon juice or
  vinegar
1 cup dry cottage cheese
  (large curd)
¼ cup safflower oil
½ teaspoon salt

½ teaspoon garlic salt,* if
  desired
12 soda crackers, 2x2 inches
1 large orange, pared and
  cut into cubes
1 large red apple, cut into
  wedges

Place milk, lemon juice, cottage cheese, oil and seasonings in blender; blend 15 seconds. Scrape sides with rubber spatula. Blend about 1 minute longer or until smooth. Cover; refrigerate 3 to 4 hours.

*2 teaspoons snipped chives or 1 tablespoon dry onion soup mix can be substituted for the garlic salt.

To serve, mound cheese dip in a small bowl and place on tray with crackers for dipping. Insert picks in orange cubes and apple wedges; arrange on tray.

6 servings. (195 calories and 10 grams fat for each serving, allowing about 2½ tablespoons dip per serving.)

POLYNESIAN SHRIMP DIP

Cut 1-inch slice from top of pineapple, leaving green leaves on top. Cut out and remove fruit, leaving a ½-inch wall. Remove core from fruit and cut remaining pineapple into bite-size pieces.

Place a pitted ripe olive in curve of each cooked shrimp; secure with a pick. (You will need about 1 cup shrimp.) Place pineapple pieces on picks. Attach rows of shrimp and pineapple in spiral design to shell of pineapple.

Place custard cup of Curry Dip (below) in pineapple; cover with pineapple top. To refrigerate before serving, cover completely with plastic wrap.

6 servings.

CURRY DIP

Stir together 1 cup dairy sour cream, ¾ teaspoon curry powder and ¼ teaspoon salt.

1 cup.

GUACAMOLE

Spunky avocado dip from the Southwest, traditionally served with corn-flavored chips.

2 ripe avocados, peeled and pitted	1 teaspoon salt
1 medium onion, finely chopped	½ teaspoon coarsely ground pepper
2 green chili peppers, finely chopped	½ teaspoon ascorbic acid mixture
1 tablespoon lemon juice	1 medium tomato, peeled and finely chopped

Mash avocados; add onion, peppers, lemon juice, salt, pepper and ascorbic acid mixture. Beat until creamy. Gently fold in tomato. Cover and refrigerate until served.

About 2 cups.

SANTA FE BEAN DIP

Spicy as a southwestern favorite should be. Serve hot with corn chips.

1 can (10½ ounces) condensed black bean soup (undiluted)
1 can (8 ounces) tomato sauce
½ cup shredded natural Cheddar cheese
¼ teaspoon chili powder

Combine all ingredients in small saucepan; heat through, stirring constantly. If desired, garnish with snipped parsley.

About 2 cups.

HOT CLAM DIP

¼ cup chopped onion
¼ cup chopped green pepper
¼ cup butter or margarine
1 can (7 to 8 ounces) minced clams, drained
1 cup shredded process American cheese (about 4 ounces)
¼ cup catsup
1 tablespoon Worcestershire sauce

Cook and stir onion and green pepper in butter until onion is tender. Add clams, cheese, catsup and Worcestershire sauce; cook, stirring constantly, until cheese is melted.

About 2 cups.

HOT BACON-BEAN DIP

1 can (8 ounces) red kidney beans, drained
2 slices bacon
1 cup dairy sour cream
1 tablespoon chopped green pepper
1 teaspoon instant minced onion
½ teaspoon salt
⅛ teaspoon garlic powder
⅛ teaspoon pepper

Mash beans. Fry bacon until crisp; remove and drain. Stir beans into drippings in skillet. Cook over low heat, stirring until all fat is absorbed.

Mix sour cream, green pepper, onion and seasonings; stir into bean mixture. Crumble bacon and stir in.

2 cups.

DIP "DISHES" Present your party dip in a gay little bowl or, if you have one, in a special "dip and dunk" tray. When serving seafood dips, small baking shells are especially appropriate. For a special flair, use scooped-out fruits and vegetables—green peppers, big white onions or grapefruit or cantaloupe halves.

LOBSTER FONDUE DIP

Serve this hot cheese dip in a glowing chafing dish and offer crisp cracker dippers.

2 tablespoons butter or margarine
2 cups shredded sharp process American cheese (about 8 ounces)
2 drops red pepper sauce
⅓ cup dry white wine
1 can (5 ounces) lobster, drained and broken into small pieces

Melt butter in small saucepan over low heat. Gradually stir in cheese until cheese is melted. (Cheese-butter mixture may appear separated.)

Add red pepper sauce; slowly add wine, stirring until mixture is smooth. Add lobster; stir until heated.

About 1½ cups.

Canapés

The canapé tray can be the life of the party—but not if the bread's soggy. So use firm bread and spread to the edges (some people spread before they cut). Think of your tray as a picture—vary shapes, colors, textures, tastes. Garnish with good-to-eats—ripe and green olives, Pickle Fans (page 9), Radish Canapés (page 14), crisp sprigs of watercress or parsley. (See pages 563–565 for more garnish ideas.) And be sure your party has a canapé captain to consolidate and refill the trays.

CANAPÉ TOAST BASES

Skillet Method: Remove crusts from slices of sandwich bread. Cut each slice into 4 squares or cut with round, star or other shaped cutter. Melt small amount of butter or margarine in skillet; toast bread cutouts in skillet over low heat until brown on one side. Just before serving, spread untoasted side with desired spread.

Broiler Method: Set oven control at broil and/or 550°. Remove crusts from slices of sandwich bread. Cut each slice into 4 squares or cut with round, star or other shaped cutter. Lightly brush one side with melted butter or margarine. Place 3 to 4 inches from heat; toast 3 to 4 minutes or until golden brown on buttered side. Just before serving, spread untoasted side with desired spread.

SMOKED SALMON CANAPÉS

2 packages (3 ounces each) cream cheese, softened
2 teaspoons prepared mustard
25 Canapé Toast Bases (above)

1 can (3⅔ ounces) smoked salmon, drained
Parsley

Blend cream cheese and mustard; spread part of mixture thinly on canapé bases. Place piece of salmon on each canapé; top with dot of remaining cream cheese mixture. Or, if desired, pipe all the cream cheese mixture around base. Top each canapé with sprig of parsley.

25 canapés.

PETALS 'N PICKLES

1 package (8 ounces) cream cheese, softened
1 tablespoon horseradish
40 Canapé Toast Bases (page 8)

Red food color
Pickle Fans (below)

Stir together cream cheese and horseradish. Spread canapé bases with about ⅓ of cheese mixture. Tint remaining cheese mixture pink with red food color; spoon into decorators' tube.

Pipe tinted cheese onto corner of each base in shape

of flower blossom (see page 186). Arrange a pickle fan on base to resemble stem and leaves.

40 canapés.

PICKLE FANS

For each pickle fan, use a gherkin (small pickle). Make 4 lengthwise cuts from one end to the other; spread gently to form a little fan.

CAVIAR CANAPÉS

Divide 2 jars (2 ounces each) red caviar among 20 Canapé Toast Bases (page 8); spread evenly. If desired, cut lemon into ⅛-inch slices. Make very tiny lemon wedges by cutting along membrane lines. Place 2 wedges on each canapé.

20 canapés.

QUICK PIZZA CANAPÉS

4 dozen Melba or cracker rounds	1 package (4 ounces) shredded mozzarella cheese
¾ cup catsup	Oregano
Thinly sliced pepperoni (about 2 ounces)	

Heat oven to 400°. Spread rounds with catsup; top with pepperoni slices. Sprinkle cheese and oregano over pepperoni. Place on ungreased baking sheet. Bake 3 to 5 minutes or until cheese is melted.

4 dozen canapés.

GREEN LEAF CANAPES

1 package (3 ounces) cream cheese, softened	1 to 2 drops green food color
1 ounce blue cheese, crumbled	50 Canapé Toast Bases (page 8)
1 teaspoon light cream	Capers or tiny pearl onions

Blend cheeses, cream and food color in blender until smooth. Spoon mixture into decorators' tube with leaf point attached. Form about 3 leaves on each Canapé Toast Base (see page 186). Garnish with capers or tiny pearl onions.

About 50 canapés.

Note: Cream cheese and blue cheese can be put through a fine sieve, then blended with mixer.

ROSETTE CANAPÉS

1 package (3 ounces) cream cheese, softened
1½ teaspoons anchovy paste
1 to 2 drops red food color

75 Canape Toast Bases (page 8)
Mint sprigs

In blender or in small mixer bowl, blend cheese, anchovy paste and food color until smooth. Spoon mixture into decorators' tube with rosette point attached. Form a rosette on each Canapé Toast Base (see page 186). Garnish with sprig of mint.

About 75 canapés.

Pâtés and Spreads

As with dips, pâtés and spreads give you a happy headstart on your party. These self-service appetizers can be prepared well in advance of the arrival of your guests, leaving you time for last-minute canapés and hot finger foods.

Don't stick to the same old spread forever. Look around. Experiment. Try curried seafood; smoked salmon, chopped and mixed to a paste with cream and capers; mashed sardines with sour cream. Collect your own seasoning secrets—a few drops of Worcestershire, a favorite seasoning salt, English mustard. Start with the party-proved recipes that follow—and let your imagination take it from there.

APPETIZER PÂTÉ

1 package (8 ounces) frozen chicken livers, thawed
½ cup water
1 chicken bouillon cube or 1 teaspoon instant chicken bouillon
¼ cup chopped onion
¼ teaspoon thyme leaves

3 slices bacon, crisply fried and crumbled
¼ cup butter or margarine, softened
¼ teaspoon dry mustard
⅛ teaspoon garlic salt
Dash pepper

Combine chicken livers, water, bouillon cube, onion and thyme in small saucepan. Heat to boiling; reduce heat and simmer 15 minutes or until chicken livers are done. Cool mixture; drain and reserve ¼ cup broth.

In small mixer bowl or in blender, combine chicken livers, reserved broth and the remaining ingredients. Blend on low speed of mixer and then beat on high speed until creamy, or beat on blender 30 seconds or until smooth. Divide mixture among eight 1½-inch paper nut cups. Cover; refrigerate at least 3 hours.

At serving time, remove paper cups and invert molded pâté on individual plates. If desired, garnish each with parsley.

8 servings.

FROSTED LIVERWURST PÂTÉ

A pretty addition to the hors d'oeuvre table. Or slice and serve as the first course, with toast.

1 pound liverwurst	⅛ teaspoon red pepper
1 clove garlic, crushed	sauce
½ teaspoon basil	1 teaspoon mayonnaise or
¼ cup minced onion	salad dressing
1 package (8 ounces) cream	Red or black caviar or
cheese, softened	anchovy paste
1 clove garlic, crushed	Parsley

Mash liverwurst with fork; thoroughly mix in 1 clove garlic, the basil and onion. Mound on plate and form into igloo shape. Cover and chill.

Blend cream cheese, 1 clove garlic, the red pepper sauce and mayonnaise; spread over liverwurst. Refrigerate at least 8 hours.

Just before serving, garnish top with circle of caviar or spread top with anchovy paste. Garnish with parsley.

12 to 16 servings.

GOUDA BURST

1 Gouda cheese (about 8 ounces)	1 teaspoon prepared mustard
1 tablespoon milk	2 drops red pepper sauce
1 tablespoon dry white wine or, if desired, apple juice	

Unwrap cheese; let stand at room temperature until softened. To form petals, make four 2½-inch intersecting cuts in top of cheese ball. Be sure to cut completely through plastic casing. Carefully pull back each section of casing, curling point over the index finger. Scoop out cheese, leaving a ¼-inch wall. Refrigerate casing shell.

Mash cheese with fork; blend in milk, wine, mustard and red pepper sauce. Fill shell with cheese mixture. Cover; refrigerate at least 3 hours. Before serving, let cheese stand at room temperature about 1 hour to soften.

6 to 8 servings.

PARTY CHEESE BALL

Adapt our holiday versions to any special occasion.

2 packages (8 ounces each)
  cream cheese
¾ cup crumbled blue cheese
  (about 4 ounces)
1 cup shredded sharp
  Cheddar cheese (about
  4 ounces)

¼ cup minced onion
1 tablespoon Worcestershire
  sauce
Finely snipped parsley

Place cheeses in small mixer bowl; let stand at room temperature until softened. Add onion and Worcestershire sauce; blend on low speed. Beat on medium speed until fluffy, scraping side and bottom of bowl. Cover; chill at least 8 hours.

Shape mixture into 1 large ball or into thirty to thirty-six 1-inch balls. Roll in parsley; place on serving plate. Cover; chill 2 hours or until firm.

Arrange small crisp crackers around large ball and serve as a spread. To serve small balls, insert a pick in each and serve with crackers.

About 12 servings.

VARIATIONS

■ *Holiday Cheese Ball:* Shape mixture into 1 large ball; do not roll in parsley. Decorator ball as desired with cuts of pimiento, green pepper and sliced pimiento-stuffed olives. Trim base of ball with tiny cocktail onions or pimiento-stuffed olives. For Christmas top ball with green pepper star or a gay ribbon bow.

■ *Christmas Tree:* Do not shape mixture into ball(s). Cover; chill only until mixture is firm enough to mold. Mound on inverted flat-bottomed bowl, about 5 inches in diameter. With 2 spatulas or knives, shape mixture to form peaked Christmas tree. Cover and chill.

When ready to serve, place tree and bowl in center of large tray; sprinkle tree with snipped parsley. Arrange crackers and snacks around bowl. If desired, use strips of green pepper and pimiento to form candles (or cut with canapé cutter to form other ornamental shapes); press gently into tree. Cut 2 star shapes from green pepper; arrange back to back at the top of the tree.

Pick-up Nibbles

Put your guests at ease with a light snack—before dinner, as the grand finale to an evening at the theater, with bridge. Remember these rules:

Finger foods should not be messy,
particularly when the guests are dressy;
the rule that says what size is right
is keep it down to just one bite.
Color is for eye delight,
taste and texture, appetite.
Another rule we're often told
is vary foods from hot to cold.

TOASTED CEREAL SNACKS

Warm or cool, this crunchy combo disappears by the handful. You'll want to have plenty for the holidays—for gift-giving as well as for guests.

2 cups corn puffs cereal	1 tablespoon Worcestershire
2 cups O-shaped puffed oat cereal	sauce
2½ cups pretzel sticks	½ teaspoon garlic salt
1½ cups mixed nuts	½ teaspoon celery salt
⅓ cup butter or margarine, melted	

Heat oven to 250°. Mix cereals, pretzels and nuts in baking pan, 13x9x2 inches. Blend butter and seasonings. Pour over cereal mixture. Bake 30 minutes, stirring gently with wooden spoon after 15 minutes.

About 8 cups.

GINGERED ALMONDS

1 cup blanched almonds
2 tablespoons butter or
  margarine

1 teaspoon salt
½ teaspoon ginger

Heat oven to 350°. Place almonds and butter in shallow baking pan. Bake 20 minutes or until golden brown, stirring occasionally. Drain on paper towels. Sprinkle salt and ginger over nuts; toss. Serve warm.

1 cup.

VARIATION

■ *Garlic Almonds:* Omit salt and substitute garlic salt for the ginger.

PARMESAN-GLAZED WALNUTS

1½ cups walnut halves
  1 tablespoon butter or
    margarine, melted
¼ teaspoon hickory-smoked
    salt

¼ teaspoon salt
¼ cup shredded Parmesan
    cheese

Heat oven to 350°. Spread walnuts in shallow baking pan; toast in oven 10 minutes. Stir together butter and salts; toss lightly with walnuts. Sprinkle cheese over top; stir. Return to oven and heat 3 to 4 minutes or until cheese is melted.

1½ cups.

RADISH CANAPÉS

Add crunch and color to an hors d'oeuvre tray with these dressed-up vegetables.

10 large radishes
  1 package (3 ounces) cream
    cheese, softened

1 teaspoon celery seed
1 teaspoon light cream

Wash, trim and dry radishes; cut each in half lengthwise. If necessary, cut thin slice from rounded side of radish to make level. Mix cream cheese, celery seed and light cream. Mound cream cheese mixture onto cut side of each radish.

20 appetizers.

VARIATION

■ *Beet Canapés:* Substitute 1 jar (1 pound) pickled whole beets for the radishes; drain beets, reserving

1 teaspoon beet juice. Pat beets dry and cut each in half. If necessary, cut thin slice from rounded side of beet to make level. Substitute horseradish for the celery seed and the reserved beet juice for the light cream.

18 appetizers.

RUMAKI

6 chicken livers	6 slices bacon
4 water chestnuts	Brown sugar
Teriyaki Sauce (below)	

Cut chicken livers in half; cut each water chestnut into 3 pieces. Pour Teriyaki Sauce over chicken livers and water chestnuts in bowl; refrigerate about 4 hours. Drain.

Cut bacon slices in half. Wrap a piece of chicken liver and a piece of water chestnut in each bacon slice. Secure with wooden pick; roll in brown sugar.

Set oven control at broil and/or 550°. Broil, turning occasionally, 3 to 4 inches from heat 10 minutes or until bacon is crisp.

12 appetizers.

Note: To cook on a hibachi, place over hot coals; cook 15 to 20 minutes, turning frequently.

TERIYAKI SAUCE

¼ cup salad oil	1 tablespoon vinegar
¼ cup soy sauce	¼ teaspoon pepper
2 tablespoons catsup	2 cloves garlic, crushed

Mix all ingredients thoroughly.

NIPPY SHRIMP

1 cup cleaned cooked shrimp*	½ cup chili sauce
½ clove garlic, slivered	8 to 10 slices bacon

Combine shrimp and garlic; pour chili sauce over. Cover; refrigerate several hours, stirring occasionally.

Cut bacon slices in half. Fry bacon until partially cooked; drain. Wrap each shrimp in bacon piece; secure with wooden pick. Set oven control at broil and/or 550°. Broil 2 to 3 inches from heat until bacon is crisp.

16 to 20 appetizers.

*From ¾ pound fresh or frozen raw shrimp (in shells). 1 package (7 ounces) frozen peeled shrimp or 1 can (4½ or 5 ounces) shrimp.

CAVIAR CLASSIC

Mound crushed ice in large glass bowl; place dish of chilled black or red caviar in center of ice. (Or leave caviar in original container.) If desired, sprinkle caviar with sieved hard-cooked egg yolks and egg whites, minced onion or snipped chives. Serve with lemon wedges and crisp toast triangles or black bread.

Allow 1 tablespoon caviar per serving.

COCKTAIL MEATBALLS

1 pound ground beef	⅛ teaspoon pepper
½ cup dry bread crumbs	½ teaspoon Worcestershire
⅓ cup minced onions	sauce
¼ cup milk	¼ cup shortening
1 egg	1 bottle (12 ounces) chili
1 tablespoon snipped	sauce
parsley	1 jar (10 ounces) grape jelly
1 teaspoon salt	

Mix ground beef, bread crumbs, onion, milk, egg and next 4 ingredients; gently shape into 1-inch balls.

Melt shortening in large skillet; brown meatballs. Remove meatballs from skillet; pour off fat. Heat chili sauce and jelly in skillet, stirring constantly, until jelly is melted. Add meatballs and stir until thoroughly coated. Simmer uncovered 30 minutes.

5 dozen appetizers.

VARIATION

■ *Cocktail Sausages:* Substitute 4 jars (4½ ounces each) cocktail sausages for the meatballs; simmer in jelly mixture 20 minutes.

SPIEDINI

Hot hors d'oeuvres from Italy. Buttery bread slices drip with melted cheese and smack of anchovy.

1 loaf (1 pound) French	½ cup butter or margarine,
bread	melted
1 package (6 ounces)	Snipped parsley
mozzarella cheese slices	
1 can (2 ounces) anchovy	
fillets, drained	

Heat oven to 350°. Cut bread into ¾-inch slices, cutting to within ½ inch of bottom crust. Place a piece of cheese slice into each cut; tuck tiny bits of anchovy fillet between cheese and bread.

Place loaf on ungreased baking sheet; pour melted butter over loaf. Heat 10 to 15 minutes or until cheese melts. Sprinkle with parsley.

About 20 appetizers.

MUSHROOMS ROYALE

Each mushroom cap holds a spicy golden stuffing.

1 pound medium mushrooms (about 3 dozen)	1½ cups soft bread crumbs
	½ teaspoon salt
3 tablespoons butter or margarine	½ teaspoon thyme
	¼ teaspoon turmeric
¼ cup finely chopped green pepper	¼ teaspoon pepper
	1 tablespoon butter or margarine
¼ cup finely chopped onion	

Heat oven to 350°. Wash, trim and dry mushrooms thoroughly. Remove stems; finely chop enough stems to measure ⅓ cup.

Melt 3 tablespoons butter in skillet. Cook and stir chopped mushroom stems, green pepper and onion in butter about 5 minutes or until tender. Remove from heat; stir in remaining ingredients except mushroom caps and 1 tablespoon butter.

Melt 1 tablespoon butter in shallow baking dish. Fill mushroom caps with stuffing mixture; place mushrooms filled side up in baking dish. Bake 15 minutes.

Set oven control at broil and/or 550°. Broil mushrooms 3 to 4 inches from heat 2 minutes.

About 3 dozen appetizers.

FRANKO CORN THINS

Serve these warm to bring out all the flavor.

2 eggs	½ cup grated Parmesan cheese
¾ cup milk	
1 package (14 ounces) corn muffin mix	5 frankfurters
	1 teaspoon celery seed
¾ teaspoon salt	¼ teaspoon garlic salt

Heat oven to 400°. Grease jelly roll pan, 15½ x 10½ x 1 inch. Mix eggs and milk. Stir in muffin mix (dry), salt and half the cheese. Pour into pan.

Cut each frankfurter into 9 slices; arrange slices evenly over batter. Sprinkle with remaining cheese, the celery seed and garlic salt. Bake 15 to 20 minutes or until golden. Cut into squares.

45 appetizers.

OLIVE-CHEESE BALLS

2 cups shredded sharp natural Cheddar cheese (about 8 ounces)
1¼ cups all-purpose flour*

½ cup butter or margarine, melted
About 36 pimiento-stuffed small olives, drained

Mix cheese and flour. Add butter and mix thoroughly. (If dough seems dry, work with hands.) Mold 1 teaspoon dough around each olive; shape into ball. Place 2 inches apart on ungreased baking sheet. Cover; chill at least 1 hour. Heat oven to 400°. Bake 15 to 20 minutes.

3 to 4 dozen appetizers.

*Do not use self-rising flour in this recipe.

COCKTAIL BUNS

Serve warm with a meat and cheese platter or split for little sandwiches. You can make the dough well ahead of time.

2 packages active dry yeast
2 cups warm water (105 to 115°)
½ cup sugar
¼ cup shortening
1 egg
2 teaspoons salt

6½ to 7 cups all-purpose flour*
1 egg yolk
2 tablespoons water
Poppy seed or sesame seed

Dissolve yeast in warm water. Stir in sugar, shortening, 1 egg, the salt and 3½ cups of the flour. Beat until smooth. Mix in enough remaining flour to make dough easy to handle.

Place dough in greased bowl; turn greased side up. Cover; refrigerate at least 2 hours. When dough rises, punch it down. Cut off amount of dough needed and return remaining dough to refrigerator. Dough can be kept 3 to 4 days.

*If using self-rising flour, omit salt.

About 2 hours before baking, shape bits of dough into 1- to 1¼-inch balls. Blend egg yolk and 2 tablespoons water; brush tops of balls with mixture and dip into poppy seed. Place 1 inch apart on lightly greased baking sheet. Cover; let rise until double, 1 to 1½ hours. Heat oven to 400°. Bake 10 minutes or until golden brown.

About 5 dozen buns.

PARMESAN FANS

1 cup butter	¾ cup shredded Parmesan
1½ cups all-purpose flour*	cheese
½ cup dairy sour cream	

Cut butter into flour thoroughly. Blend in sour cream. Divide dough into 4 equal parts; wrap each part and chill at least 8 hours.

Self-rising flour can be used; reduce baking time slightly.

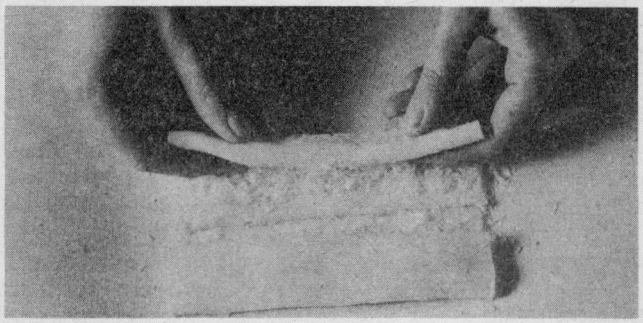

Fold in the folded edges to meet in the center.

Fold rectangle as if closing a book; flatten, repeat.

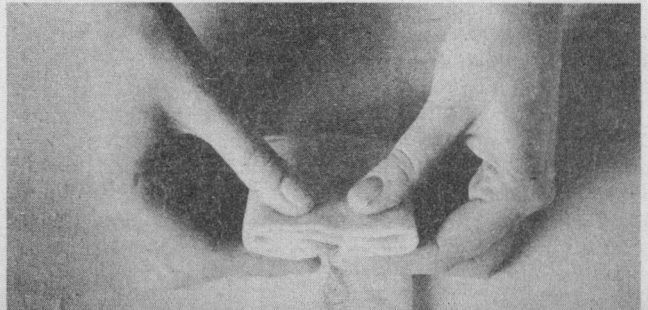

Heat oven to 350°. On well-floured cloth-covered board, roll each part of pastry into rectangle, 12x6 inches. Sprinkle with 2 tablespoons of the cheese. Fold ends to meet in center, forming a square. Sprinkle with 1 tablespoon of the cheese. Fold in folded edges to meet in center. Fold in half lengthwise (as if you were closing a book). Flatten lightly; fold again lengthwise.

On the folded edge, cut ³⁄₁₆-inch slices. Place on ungreased baking sheet; bring the ends together to form a fan. Bake 20 to 25 minutes.

About 4 dozen appetizers.

CHEESE PENNIES

Good warm or cold. An appetizer that you handle like refrigerator cookie dough—and like its sweet cousin, just slice and bake as needed.

1 jar (5 ounces) pasteurized process sharp American cheese spread*

¼ cup shortening
⅔ cup all-purpose flour

In small mixer bowl, mix all ingredients on medium speed 20 to 30 seconds. On lightly floured surface, mold dough into 2 rolls, 1 inch in diameter and about 8 inches long. (Dough will be soft but not sticky.) Wrap; chill at least 2 hours.

Heat oven to 375°. Cut rolls into ¼-inch slices. Place on ungreased baking sheet. Bake 10 to 12 minutes or until light brown.

About 5 dozen appetizers.

*Pasteurized process cheese spread with bacon, garlic or with added hickory smoke flavor can be substituted.

VARIATIONS

■ *Cheese Strips:* Heat oven to 350°. After mixing dough, place in cookie press with star plate attached. Form long strips on ungreased baking sheet; cut into 3-inch lengths. Bake 10 minutes or until light brown. Immediately remove strips to wire rack.

About 4 dozen appetizers.

■ *Penny Surprises:* Divide dough into 4 equal parts. Roll each part into rectangle, about 8x2 inches. Place a row of small pimiento-stuffed olives, anchovies, cocktail wieners or ¼-inch salami strips lengthwise down center of rectangle. Mold edges of dough together to form a roll. Wrap, refrigerate and bake as directed.

About 7 dozen appetizers.

COOKING WITH COALS An appetizer hibachi, just large enough to hold 2 or 3 charcoal briquets and small enough to perch on an end table near a window, makes for fun, conversation and mixing at a party. Soak tooth-pick-thin wooden skewers in water; thread with Rumaki (page 15), Nippy Shrimp (page 15), Mushrooms Royale (page 17), cocktail franks and bacon-wrapped olives. Arrange pin-wheel fashion on a platter; accompany with a tray holding mustard, plum jelly and picks. Sit back and watch the fun. Better yet, join in!

First Course Appetizers

Sometimes you want the formality of a first course at the table. Sometimes it seems friendlier to have the first course in the living room—to get the good talk started. Either way, the recipes in this section can be spectacularly successful.

Oysters or Clams on the Half Shell (page 24), arranged on a platter of crushed ice and garnished with lemon wedges, can be served in the living room. Just provide each guest with a plate, oyster fork, napkin and sauce container. Oysters Rockefeller (page 26) can go straight from the oven to a hot-dish tile on the coffee table.

SPRING GRAPEFRUIT CUP

2 grapefruit	¼ cup sugar
1 pint strawberries	1 teaspoon aromatic bitters

Cut each grapefruit in half. Cut around edges and membranes to remove grapefruit sections. Place sections in bowl. Remove membrane from grapefruit shells and reserve shells.

Wash and hull strawberries; cut in half and place in bowl with grapefruit sections. Sprinkle sugar and bitters over fruit; toss. Cover and chill.

At serving time, fill grapefruit shells with fruit mixture. If desired, trim with mint leaves.

4 servings.

TAHITIAN FRUIT CUP

3 small coconuts
1 medium pineapple
¼ cup orange-flavored
   liqueur or, if desired,
   orange juice

Whole strawberries
Mint sprigs

Break each coconut in half crosswise. (You'll need a hammer for this job.) Remove coconut meat; reserve shells. Cover and refrigerate half the coconut meat for future use. Cut remaining coconut meat into bite-size pieces.

Remove rind from pineapple and cut fruit into bite-size pieces as directed on page 557. Stir together coconut meat and pineapple; add orange liqueur and toss. Cover; chill several hours.

At serving time, fill coconut shells with fruit mixture. Garnish each with whole strawberries and a mint sprig.

6 servings.

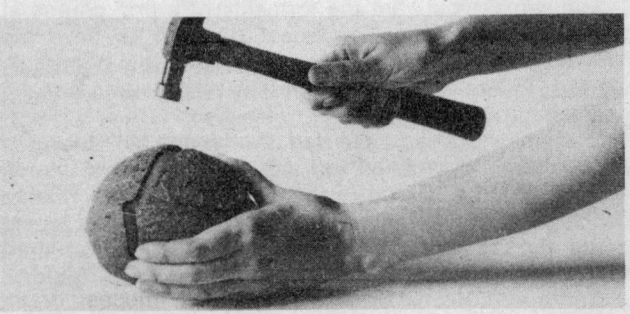

Tap around middle of coconut with hammer. When you reach starting point give an extra tap (or use saw).

Pry out coconut meat with a sturdy knife.

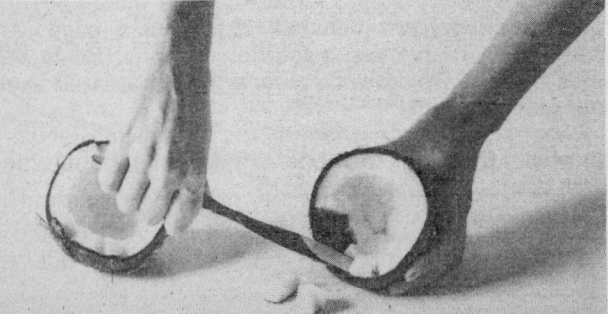

SPARKLING FRUIT COMPOTE

What better way to salute the welcome season of summer.

3 medium peaches
2 cups sliced strawberries
2 cups blueberries
2 cups melon balls

3 medium bananas
1 bottle (1 pint 9 ounces)
pink sparkling catawba
grape juice, chilled

Peel peaches and slice into bowl. Top peach slices with strawberries, blueberries and melon balls. Cover tightly and chill.

Just before serving, peel bananas and slice into fruit mixture. Pour juice over fruit.

8 to 10 servings.

GRAPEFRUIT-SEAFOOD COCKTAIL

Grapefruit halves make unusual holders for dips and melon balls as well as fruit cocktails. Cut the grapefruit in half first, then carefully remove sections. Refrigerate the halves upside down until ready to use.

½ cup chili sauce
¼ cup mayonnaise or salad
dressing
1 teaspoon instant minced
onion
½ teaspoon sugar
¼ teaspoon Worcestershire
sauce
⅛ teaspoon salt

1 grapefruit, pared and
sectioned
1 can (7½ ounces) crabmeat,
drained and cartilage
removed
1 cup cleaned cooked
shrimp*
⅓ cup chopped green pepper
Bibb or leaf lettuce

Stir together chili sauce, mayonnaise, onion, sugar, Worcestershire sauce and salt; chill.

Cut grapefruit sections into bite-size pieces; drain. Combine grapefruit, crabmeat, shrimp and green pepper; toss.

Arrange seafood mixture in lettuce-lined shells or cocktail sherbets. Chill thoroughly. Just before serving, top each serving with mayonnaise mixture.

6 servings.

*From ¾ pound fresh or frozen raw shrimp (in shells), 1 package (7 ounces) frozen peeled shrimp or 1 can (4½ or 5 ounces) shrimp.

MELON AND PROSCIUTTO

A sweet 'n spicy appetizer borrowed from the Italian cuisine.

Cut a ripe cantaloupe, casaba, honeydew or Spanish melon (about 3 pounds) in half; scoop out seeds and fibers. Cut each half into 6 lengthwise wedges. Remove outside rind. Cut crosswise slits 1½ inches apart in each melon wedge.

Cut ¼ pound sliced prosciutto (Italian ham) into 1-inch strips. Place several strips of ham over each wedge; push ham into slits.

12 servings.

VARIATION

■ *Bite-size Melon and Prosciutto:* Cut pared melon into bite-size pieces. Wrap each piece in strips of prosciutto; secure with picks.

SHRIMP COCKTAIL

Everyone's favorite starter course! If serving buffet style, better plan on seconds for everybody. For some reason, they disappear twice as fast.

1 bottle (12 ounces) chili sauce	¼ teaspoon salt Dash pepper
1 to 2 tablespoons horseradish	36 cleaned cooked medium shrimp, chilled
1 tablespoon lemon juice	
½ teaspoon Worcestershire sauce	

Combine all ingredients except shrimp; chill sauce thoroughly. To serve as individual appetizers, mix shrimp with sauce and serve in lettuce-lined cocktail sherbets.

For a party snack, fill a large bowl with crushed ice and place a dish of sauce in center; arrange shrimp over ice. Serve with picks for dipping shrimp into sauce.

6 servings.

CLAMS ON THE HALF SHELL

36 shell clams (littlenecks or cherrystones)	Cocktail Sauce (page 580) Lemon wedges

Wash clams thoroughly, discarding any broken-shell or open (dead) clams. Hold clam in palm of one hand with the shell's hinge against the palm. Insert a slender, strong, sharp knife between the halves of the shell and carefully cut around the clam, twisting the knife slightly to pry open the shell.

Cut both muscles from shells. Remove only half of the shell. Arrange a bed of crushed ice in 6 shallow bowls or plates. Place 6 half-shell clams on ice with small container of Cocktail Sauce in center. Garnish with lemon wedges.

6 servings.

OYSTERS ON THE HALF SHELL

For each serving, scrub 5 or 6 medium oysters in shell under running cold water. Break off thin end of shell with hammer. Force a table knife or shucking knife between shell at broken end; pull apart. Cut oyster at muscle to separate from shell. Remove any bits of shell. Place oyster on deep half of shell; discard other half.

Arrange filled shells on crushed ice. Garnish with parsley and lemon wedges. Serve with rye bread and spicy cocktail sauce.

SHRIMP REMOULADE

An elegant beginning for an important dinner party. Colorful, zesty and sure to satisfy even the most discriminating diner.

½ cup plus 2 tablespoons salad oil
¼ cup prepared mustard
3 tablespoons vinegar
1 teaspoon salt
¼ teaspoon red pepper sauce
2 tablespoons paprika
1 hard-cooked egg yolk
½ cup minced celery

2 tablespoons grated onion
2 tablespoons snipped parsley
2 tablespoons minced green pepper
1 hard-cooked egg white, chopped
1 pound cleaned cooked medium shrimp*
Crisp lettuce leaves

Beat oil, mustard, vinegar, salt, red pepper sauce, paprika and egg yolk with rotary beater until thick and blended. Fold in celery, onion, parsley, green pepper and egg white. Gently stir in shrimp. Cover; chill, stirring occasionally.

Just before serving, spoon shrimp mixture into lettuce-lined cocktail sherbets.

4 or 5 servings.

*From 2 pounds fresh or frozen raw shrimp (in shells), 2 packages (7 ounces each) frozen peeled shrimp or 3 cans (4½ or 5 ounces each) shrimp.

OYSTERS ROCKEFELLER

Rock salt	¼ cup butter or margarine
12 medium oysters in shell	½ cup chopped fresh spinach
2 tablespoons finely chopped onion	⅓ cup dry bread crumbs
2 tablespoons snipped parsley	¼ teaspoon salt
	7 drops red pepper sauce
2 tablespoons finely chopped celery	Dash ground anise

Fill two 9-inch glass pie pans with rock salt to ½-inch depth; sprinkle with water.

Scrub and prepare oysters as directed for Oysters on the Half-Shell (page 25). Arrange filled shells on rock salt base.

Heat oven to 450°; Cook and stir onion, parsley and

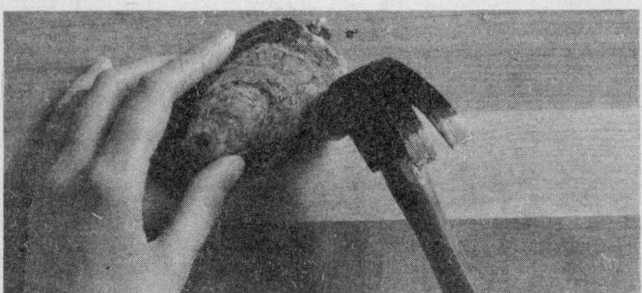

Gently chip away the thin end of the oyster shell with a hammer. (This process is called "billing" an oyster).

Force a table knife (or a shucking knife, if you have one) between shell at broken end; pull the halves of shell apart.

celery in butter until onion is tender. Mix in remaining ingredients. Spoon about 1 tablespoon spinach mixture onto oyster in each shell. Bake 10 minutes.

2 servings.

VARIATION

■ *Oysters Parmesan:* Omit spinach mixture; spoon 1 teaspoon dairy sour cream onto oyster in each shell. Mix ½ cup shredded Parmesan cheese, ¼ cup cracker crumbs, ¼ cup butter or margarine, melted, and ½ teaspoon dry mustard. Spoon about 2 teaspoons cheese mixture over sour cream and oyster in each shell.

SEAFOOD COQUILLE

An elegant preliminary that can be started well ahead of time.

⅓ cup minced onion
1 clove garlic, crushed
⅓ cup butter or margarine
¼ cup all-purpose flour
½ teaspoon salt
¼ teaspoon pepper
1⅓ cups milk
⅔ cup sauterne or, if desired, apple juice

1 can (7½ ounces) crabmeat, drained and cartilage removed
1 cup cleaned cooked shrimp*
6 tablespoons shredded Swiss cheese or 6 teaspoons grated Parmesan cheese

Cook and stir onion and garlic in butter until onion is tender. Remove from heat. Blend in flour, salt and pepper. Cook over low heat, stirring until mixture is bubbly. Remove from heat. Stir in milk and wine. Heat to boiling, stirring constantly. Boil and stir 1 minute. Stir in crabmeat and shrimp.

Divide mixture among 6 baking shells or individual baking dishes; top each with 1 tablespoon Swiss cheese or 1 teaspoon Parmesan cheese.

Set oven control at broil and/or 550°. Broil 4 to 5 inches from heat 3 to 4 minutes or until cheese is golden.

6 servings.

Do-ahead Note: Fill the shells early in day; cover and refrigerate. At serving time, broil about 5 minutes or until mixture is heated through.

*From ¾ pound fresh or frozen raw shrimp (in shells), 1 package (7 ounces) frozen peeled shrimp or 1 can (4½ or 5 ounces) shrimp.

APPETIZER VS. ENTREE If you start with a rich, creamy coquille, follow it with a simple main course. If your meat is substantial, choose a gentle first course, like melon or consommé. Many of the more elaborate first courses are equally at home as main courses for light meals—bridge, lunch, Sunday brunch, late-evening supper.

ESCARGOTS (SNAILS)

Canned snails and packages of snail shells are available in specialty food stores—as are snail holders, long slender forks and specially grooved plates designed to prevent the shells from rattling and tipping as they're baked and served. (You may, of course, improvise with standard equipment.)

⅔ cup butter or margarine, softened
2 cloves garlic, crushed
1 teaspoon parsley flakes
1 teaspoon finely chopped green onion
½ teaspoon salt
⅛ teaspoon pepper

1 package (2 dozen) snail shells
1 can (4½ ounces) natural snails, drained and rinsed
2 tablespoons dry white wine or, if desired, apple juice

Heat oven to 400°. Mix thoroughly butter, garlic, parsley flakes, onion, salt and pepper. Spoon small amount of butter mixture into each snail shell; insert snail and top each with remaining butter mixture.

Pour wine into baking dish, 8x8x2 inches, or into each section of snail plates; arrange filled shells open end up in dish or plates. Bake 10 minutes or until butter is bubbly.

4 to 6 servings.

Appetizers That Make a Meal

Party perfect! When you want something a little different, good to eat, festive, for easy entertainment—try the meal-in-itself appetizer. For small groups, you can choose foods that require forks and plates; for larger groups, stick to finger foods.

Take Quick Lorraine Tarts (page 32) and accompany them with Spiced Coffee (page 39)—there's your afternoon party. Team them with Mulled Tomato Juice (page 52) and you're set for late evening. Serve them for Sunday brunch. London Broil (page 32) can turn up happily at an eggnog party on a cold New Year's Day. For your bridge club, Rye Ribbon Round (page 33). For a poker party, Sausage Smorgasbord (below). Cut down on your work and enjoy your own party. Here are the recipes to help you!

SAUSAGE SMORGASBORD

The perfect and complete "after-anything" supper.

Salami Wedges (below)	½ pound Swiss cheese
Cream Cheese Balls (page 30)	½ pound caraway cheese
Sausage Frills (page 30)	¾ pound hard summer sausage, sliced
½ pound natural Cheddar cheese	Lettuce

Prepare Salami Wedges, Cream Cheese Balls and Sausage Frills; cover and refrigerate until ready to arrange platter.

Cut cheeses in ½-inch cubes. Cover large serving platter with lettuce; arrange wedges, balls, frills, cheese cubes and sliced summer sausage in attractive pattern on lettuce. Cover platter and chill until serving time. If desired, serve with assorted breads and crackers.

8 to 10 servings.

SALAMI WEDGES

Soften 1 package (3 ounces) cream cheese; spread cheese over 9 slices salami (4½ inches in diameter). Stack spread slices and top with a plain slice salami. Cover and chill. Before arranging on platter, cut stack into 12 wedges.

CREAM CHEESE BALLS

1 package (8 ounces) cream
  cheese, softened
1 teaspoon horseradish
  Chopped radishes
½ teaspoon curry powder
  Chopped pitted ripe olives
½ teaspoon celery seed
  Chopped sweet pickles

Divide cream cheese into 3 equal parts. To one part, stir in horseradish; shape into 1-inch balls and roll in chopped radishes. To second part cream cheese, stir in curry powder; shape into 1-inch balls and roll in chopped ripe olives. Stir remaining cream cheese with the celery seed; shape into 1-inch balls and roll in chopped pickles.

SAUSAGE FRILLS

Spread your favorite cheese spread in a strip across center of each of 6 slices large bologna. Fold meat in half lengthwise through center of cheese. Keeping rounded edges of folded meat together, "pleat" into S-shape into thirds. Secure end with a pick.

PARMESAN APPETIZER LOAF

1 package active dry yeast
¼ cup warm water (105 to
  115°)
¾ cup lukewarm milk
  (scalded then cooled)
¼ cup sugar
1 teaspoon salt
1 egg
¼ cup butter or margarine
3½ to 3¾ cups all-purpose
  flour*
½ cup butter or margarine,
  melted
2 jars (2½ ounces each)
  shredded Parmesan
  cheese
  Guacamole (page 5)
  Sliced cooked ham

Dissolve yeast in warm water. Stir in milk, sugar, salt, egg, ¼ cup butter and 2 cups of the flour. Beat until smooth. Mix in enough remaining flour to make dough easy to handle.

Turn dough onto lightly floured board; knead until smooth and elastic, about 5 minutes. Place in greased bowl; turn greased side up. Cover; let rise in warm place until double, about 2 hours.

Line tube pan, 10x4 inches, with aluminum foil; grease. Punch down dough. Turn onto lightly floured board; divide into 24 equal pieces. Dip each piece into

*If using self-rising flour, omit salt.

melted butter; roll in cheese. Place 12 pieces in pan in one layer. Arrange second layer of 12 pieces on top of first. Cover; let rise until double.

Heat oven to 375°. Bake 35 minutes. Remove from pan. Serve warm with Guacamole and thin slices of ham. If desired, serve mustard sauce as a dip for the ham.

12 servings.

DECORATE WITH FOOD A shining apothecary jar filled with cereal snacks. A bowl of red, red apples. A pretty ginger jar with fresh toasted gingered almonds. A brandy snifter abrim with cherry tomatoes. An easy-going mixture of popular snacks in a great wooden bowl or in a foil-lined, ribbon-tied basket. Decorate with food—it makes your rooms come alive with a warm and friendly welcome.

DEVILED PUFFS ✳

Prepare puffs and filling early in the day. Fill at party time.

1 cup water	1 tablespoon horseradish
½ cup butter or margarine	¾ teaspoon pepper
1 cup all-purpose flour	¾ teaspoon onion salt
4 eggs	⅓ cup dairy sour cream
3 cans (4½ ounces each) deviled ham	

Heat oven to 400°. Heat water and butter to a rolling boil in large saucepan. Stir in flour. Stir vigorously over low heat until mixture forms a ball, about 1 minute. Remove from heat. Beat in eggs (all at once) until smooth and glossy.

Drop dough by slightly rounded teaspoonfuls onto ungreased baking sheet. Bake about 25 minutes or until puffed, golden brown and dry. Remove puffs to wire rack; cool slowly away from draft.

Blend deviled ham, horseradish, pepper, onion salt and sour cream; refrigerate. Just before serving, cut off tops of puffs with sharp knife; remove any filaments of soft dough. Fill each puff with slightly rounded teaspoonful of ham mixture.

6 dozen appetizers.

QUICK LORRAINE TARTS

Speedy miniatures of Quiche Lorraine. And these tarts are easy for a party when you bake them the day before.

2 sticks or 1 packet pie
   crust mix
1 tablespoon poppy seed
1⅓ cups coarsely shredded
   Swiss cheese (about
   ⅓ pound)
⅔ cup chopped salami

⅓ cup sliced green onions
4 eggs
1⅓ cups dairy sour cream
1 teaspoon salt
1 teaspoon Worcestershire
   sauce

Heat oven to 375°. Prepare pastry for Two-crust Pie as directed on package except—stir poppy seed into mix. Roll ¹⁄₁₆ inch thick on lightly floured cloth-covered board; cut into 3-inch rounds. Fit rounds into muffin cups.

Combine cheese, salami and onion; spoon into pastry-lined muffin cups. Beat eggs slightly; stir in sour cream, salt and Worcestershire sauce. Pour about 1 tablespoon sour cream mixture into each muffin pan. Bake 20 to 25 minutes or until light brown. Cool in pans 5 minutes before serving.

3 dozen tarts.

Do-ahead Note: Cool baked tarts and wrap in aluminum foil; refrigerate. At serving time, heat wrapped tarts in 350° oven for 10 minutes.

LONDON BROIL

Hearty appetizers to serve on crackers or small rounds of rye bread.

1-pound flank steak, scored
1 cup rosé wine or, if
   desired, cranberry cocktail

1 teaspoon salt
½ teaspoon rosemary leaves
¼ teaspoon pepper

Place steak in shallow glass dish. Combine remaining ingredients; pour over meat. Cover; refrigerate several hours, turning meat occasionally.

Set oven control at broil and/or 550°. Remove steak from marinade. Broil 2 to 3 inches from heat 4 minutes. Turn; broil 3 to 4 minutes longer. Cut meat diagonally across grain into thin slices. If desired, salt before serving.

6 to 8 servings.

RYE RIBBON ROUND

2 cans (4½ ounces each)
deviled ham
1 teaspoon instant minced
onion
¼ cup chopped pitted ripe
olives
1 package (3 ounces) cream
cheese, softened.
2 ounces blue cheese
1 drop green food color
1 can (7¾ ounces) crabmeat,
drained and cartilage
removed

1 jar (5 ounces) pasteurized
Neufchâtel cheese with
pineapple
¼ cup chopped celery
1 round loaf (2 pounds)
unsliced rye bread, about
8 inches in diameter*
3 cartons (4 ounces each)
whipped cream cheese
¼ cup slivered blanched
almonds, toasted
½ cup sliced pitted ripe
olives

Combine deviled ham, minced onion and chopped
olives; cover. With electric mixer, blend cream cheese,
blue cheese and green food color; cover. Flake the crabmeat; stir in cheese with pineapple and the chopped
celery; cover.

Remove crust from loaf; cut loaf horizontally into 4
slices. Spread bottom slice with ham filling; top with
second slice. Spread with blue cheese mixture; top with
third slice. Spread with crabmeat mixture; top with
fourth slice. Cover loaf tightly; refrigerate at least 3
hours.

Allow whipped cream cheese to come to room temperature. An hour before serving, frost loaf with cream
cheese. Press almonds and sliced olives into cheese
frosting around side and top of loaf. Refrigerate until
serving time. Cut into wedges.

8 to 10 servings.

*Available on special order from a bakery.

SWISS CHEESE TARTS

Easy Foil Tarts (below)
½ cup water
¼ cup butter or margarine
½ cup all-purpose flour*
2 eggs
6 cups water

1 tablespoon salt
Cream Sauce (below)
1 cup shredded Swiss or
Gruyère cheese (about
4 ounces)

Prepare Easy Foil Tarts.

Heat oven to 425°. Heat ½ cup water and the butter
to rolling boil. Stir in flour. Stir vigorously over low heat

*Do not use self-rising flour in this recipe.

about 1 minute or until mixture forms a ball. Remove from heat. Beat in eggs (all at once) until smooth and glossy.

Heat 6 cups water and the salt to boiling in medium saucepan. Drop dough by rounded half-teaspoonfuls into water. Cook about 4 minutes or until puffy. Drain. Divide puffs among tart shells.

Pour Cream Sauce over puffs; sprinkle cheese over tops. Bake 20 minutes or until cheese is melted and light brown.

6 servings.

EASY FOIL TARTS

Prepare pastry for 8- or 9-inch One-crust Pie (page 501) except—divide pastry into 6 equal parts. Place each part on 6-inch square of heavy-duty aluminum foil; roll each into 6-inch circle. Trim edges to make even. Shape foil and pastry together into tart by turning up 1½-inch edge; flute. Place on baking sheet.

CREAM SAUCE

¼ cup butter or margarine	½ teaspoon salt
¼ cup all-purpose flour	2 cups light cream (20%)

Melt butter in saucepan over low heat. Blend in flour and salt. Cook over low heat, stirring until mixture is smooth and bubbly. Remove from heat. Stir in light cream. Heat to boiling, stirring constantly. Boil and stir 1 minute.

TRIPLE-CHEESE APPETIZER WHEEL

1 cup all-purpose flour*	⅓ cup plus 1 tablespoon shortening
½ cup shredded Swiss cheese	2 tablespoons water
½ teaspoon salt	Cheese Filling (right)

Heat oven to 475°. Stir together flour, cheese and salt. Cut in shortening thoroughly. Sprinkle water over mixture, 1 tablespoon at a time, mixing with fork until flour is moistened.

Gather dough into a ball; divide in half. Roll one half into 9-inch circle. Place on baking sheet; turn under

*If using self-rising flour, omit salt.

½ inch all around. Crimp edge and prick pastry with fork. Bake 8 to 10 minutes or until golden brown.

Roll other half into 7-inch circle; place on baking sheet. Score into 16 sections, cutting only part way through pastry. Cut around rim of each section to form scalloped edge. Cut 2-inch hole in middle of circle. Bake about 10 minutes or until golden brown. Cool.

Just before serving, spread Cheese Filling evenly to edge of 9-inch circle; place scalloped circle on top. If desired, small candles can be inserted in Cheese Filling around scalloped circle. Garnish with parsley and olives if desired. To serve, cut into wedges.

16 servings.

CHEESE FILLING

Soften 4 ounces cream cheese; beat in 2 ounces blue cheese and 1 tablespoon horseradish until smooth. Add 1 tablespoon milk; beat until fluffy. Fold in ¼ cup sliced pimiento-stuffed olives.

Beverages

What can take the place of a good cup of coffee?
To wake you up, to warm you up, to cheer you
up, to share with a friend. Only one thing, some
people would argue—a good cup of tea! Here are
a few tips to brighten coffee-time, tea-time,
cocoa-time, any time someone needs
a friendly little lift.

Coffee and Coffee Drinks

No two people quite agree on how strong a good cup of coffee should be—or the one and only way to make it. One thing is sure. It's hard to make a bad cup if you remember these things:

■ Start with a coffee maker that is thoroughly clean. Wash after each use with soapy hot water and rinse well with hot water; never scour with an abrasive pad. When washing an automatic coffee maker, follow the manufacturer's directions.

■ Always use fresh coffee and freshly drawn cold water. Never use hot water, especially in automatic coffee makers; it changes the percolating time. Keep your coffee tightly covered—air dries out coffee and causes it to lose flavor.

■ Serve steaming hot coffee as soon as possible after brewing. If necessary to let coffee stand any length of time, remove grounds and hold coffee at serving temperature over very low heat. Keep coffee hot but do not boil.

COFFEE CHART

	For each serving . . .
Weak Coffee	1 level tablespoon ground coffee to ¾ cup water
Medium Coffee*	2 level tablespoons ground coffee to ¾ cup water
Strong Coffee	3 level tablespoons ground coffee to ¾ cup water

Best general recommendation

Methods of Preparation

Automatic: Follow manufacturer's directions for selecting grind of coffee, measuring and brewing the coffee and holding the coffee at serving temperature. Special grinds of coffee are available for automatic coffee makers.

Drip: Measure cold water into kettle and heat to boiling. Meanwhile, preheat coffeepot by rinsing with very hot water. Measure drip-grind coffee into cone holding filter paper or into filter section of coffeepot, depending on the type of drip pot used. Pour measured fresh boiling water into upper container; cover. When dripping is completed, remove upper container and filter section and simply pour the coffee.

Vacuum: Measure fresh cold water into lower bowl and heat to boiling. Place filter in upper bowl; add fine or drip-grind coffee. Remove boiling water from heat; reduce heat. Insert upper bowl with a slight twist. Return to heat. Let water rise into upper bowl; stir. Remove from heat. Coffee should return to lower bowl within 2 minutes. Remove upper bowl and serve coffee.

INSTANT COFFEE

Make it right and no one will care whether your coffee's regular or instant. It's good—that's all that really matters.

In the cup: Measure 1 to 2 teaspoons instant coffee into each cup. Fill with boiling water; stir.

In the pot: Measure 2 to 4 tablespoons instant coffee into heatproof container. Stir in part of 4 cups cold water; add remaining water. Heat *just* to boiling but do not boil. Serve immediately. (Or, heat water to boiling; remove from heat and stir in the instant coffee. Cover and let stand 3 minutes.)

6 servings (⅔ cup each).

ICED COFFEE

Prepare Strong Coffee (page 36). Fill tall glass with crushed ice. Pour hot coffee over ice. If desired, serve with sugar and light cream or whipped cream.

Or, prepare Medium Coffee (page 36). Cool. Pour into divided freezer trays; freeze. To serve, pour freshly brewed Medium Coffee over coffee cubes in tall glass.

CAFÉ AU LAIT

Serve in gay ceramic mugs for a Gallic plus.

Prepare coffee as directed on page 37, using ¾ cup ground coffee and 3 cups water.

Heat 3 cups milk. Pour equal amounts of hot coffee and hot milk *simultaneously* from separate pots into each cup.

8 servings (¾ cup each).

IRISH COFFEE

An extra-rich, extra-special after-dinner beverage.

1 cup chilled whipping cream	3 cups water
¼ cup confectioners' sugar	4 ounces (½ cup) Irish whiskey or brandy
1 teaspoon vanilla	4 to 8 teaspoons granulated sugar
¾ cup ground coffee	

In chilled bowl, beat cream, confectioners' sugar and vanilla until stiff. Refrigerate.

Prepare coffee as directed on page 37, using the ¾ cup ground coffee and the 3 cups water.

Heat mugs by rinsing with boiling water; drain. Add 1 ounce (2 tablespoons) whiskey and 1 to 2 teaspoons granulated sugar to each mug; stir. Pour hot coffee into each mug. Top with the whipped cream. Serve immediately.

4 servings (¾ cup each).

DEMITASSE

From the French "demi-tasse," meaning half a cup. This classic, strong after-dinner coffee is always, but always, served in small cups. True devotees make it a daily treat.

Prepare coffee as directed on page 37, using 2 tablespoons ground coffee for each ⅓ cup water. (Each demitasse serving should be about ⅓ cup.) Demitasse is often served with a twist of lemon peel. Sugar may be offered but cream is usually shunned.

INSTANT DEMITASSE

Measure ½ cup instant coffee into heatproof container. Stir in 1 quart boiling water. Cover; let stand 5 minutes.
12 servings (⅓ cup each).

Note: For smaller amounts, use 2 teaspoons instant coffee and ⅓ cup boiling water for each serving.

SPICED COFFEE

A change of taste for demitasse service.

2 cups water	Peel of 1 orange
1 tablespoon brown sugar	¼ teaspoon whole allspice
2 three-inch cinnamon sticks	1 tablespoon instant coffee

Combine all ingredients except coffee in saucepan; heat to boiling. Strain mixture; pour liquid over coffee in heatproof container and stir until coffee is dissolved. If desired, serve with twist of lemon peel or a cinnamon stick.
6 servings (⅓ cup each).

Coffee Italian Style

The first must for good Italian coffee is dark roasted Italian coffee beans. In the Neapolitan drip pot (left) hot water drips down through the basket of fine coffee grains. In the espresso machine (right) pressure forces steam and boiling water up through the grains.

MOCHA DESSERT COFFEE

The classic combination of chocolate and coffee for after dinner or a between-meal warm-up.

For each serving, place 1 to 2 tablespoons canned chocolate frosting in cup. Fill with hot coffee; stir until blended. If desired, garnish with whipped cream. Serve immediately.

INTERNATIONAL COFFEE

⅓ cup instant cocoa mix   4 cups boiling water
¼ cup instant coffee   Sweetened whipped cream

Mix cocoa mix and coffee in heatproof container. Pour in boiling water; stir. Top each serving with whipped cream.
6 servings (about ⅔ cup each).

CALIFORNIA COFFEE

An after-dinner beverage that doubles as dessert.

For each serving, pour 1 ounce (2 tablespoons) brandy into mug. Fill ⅔ full with hot Strong Coffee (page 36). Top with 1 scoop (about ¼ cup) chocolate ice cream. Serve immediately.

Tea

Would it surprise you to know that tea is the world's favorite beverage? It shouldn't. Even in our own United States, iced tea and hot tea have become round-the-year, round-the-clock refreshers. And afternoon tea, once associated with silver tea services and starched maids, has now become a friendly custom.

Types of Tea

As you learned in your schoolbooks, there are literally hundreds of varieties of tea. The quality varies according to the soil, climate and altitude in which it is grown and the age and size of the leaves when they are picked.

The tea you buy is a delicate blend of some 20 to 30 varieties, carefully selected by expert tea-tasters to maintain the high quality of color, flavor, aroma or body of each brand.

Despite all these varieties, tea can be classified into three broad types: black, oolong or green.

■ Black tea undergoes a special processing treatment in which the leaves are allowed to oxidize. This turns the leaves black and produces a rich brew. Over 97% of the tea consumed in the United States is the black type.

■ Oolong tea is semi-oxidized. Its leaves are partly brown and partly green. It brews light in color, and a growing number of Americans have come to prefer its delicate flavor.

■ Green tea is not oxidized, so the leaves remain green. The brew is pale green in color.

Loose, Teabag or Instant?

Loose tea is the classic and, to connoisseurs, the preferred form to use in brewing tea. Following package directions, 1 pound makes about 200 cups.

The teabag was "accidentally" invented at the turn of the century when a tea merchant distributed his samples in small silk bags. Today the "bags" are made of special filter paper, each bag holding about a teaspoonful of tea.

Instant tea is commercially prepared by removing the water from a highly concentrated brew. It comes in both powdered and liquid forms, sometimes flavored with lemon and sugar or low-calorie sweeteners.

Method of Preparation

Whether you use loose tea or teabags, the method of preparation is the same:

■ Start with a spotlessly clean teapot, made of glass, china or earthenware. Add rapidly boiling water; allow to stand a few minutes and pour out.

■ Heat cold water to a full rolling boil.

■ Add tea or teabags to the warm pot, allowing 1 teaspoon of loose tea or 1 teabag for each cup of tea desired. Pour boiling water over the tea (¾ cup for each cup of tea); let steep 3 to 5 minutes to bring out the full flavor. Stir the tea once to ensure uniform strength.

■ Strain the tea or remove teabags. If desired, serve with sugar and milk or lemon.

■ Do not judge the strength of tea by its color; you must taste it.

Instant tea, a concentrate, should be prepared according to the directions on the jar.

ICED TEA

Follow directions for preparation of tea (above) except—double the amount of tea. Strain tea over ice in pitcher or into ice-filled glasses.

Note: Tea that has been steeped too long or that has been refrigerated will become cloudy. Pour a small amount of boiling water into tea pitcher to make clear again.

DO-AHEAD ICED TEA

A speedy way to make your own on-call iced tea. When you need it, it will always be there.

Use 2 teaspoons loose tea or 2 teabags for each cup of cold water. Place tea in glass container; add water. Cover; refrigerate at least 24 hours. To serve, pour over crushed ice.

SPICED TEA

4 cups boiling water	½ teaspoon dried orange
4 teaspoons loose tea	peel
6 whole cloves, broken into pieces	⅛ teaspoon cinnamon

Pour boiling water over tea, cloves, orange peel and cinnamon in heatproof container. Cover; let steep 3 to 5 minutes. Stir and strain.

6 servings (⅔ cup each).

Chocolate Drinks
and Cocoa

Who's for chocolate? Families, that's who! Cocoa at breakfast, shared with the children; hot chocolate after skating or skiing. And a rich, stimulating brew of chocolate—full, strong, bitter—is beginning to be understood as an adult beverage, too.

HOT CHOCOLATE

2 ounces unsweetened   Pinch salt
  chocolate   ¼ cup sugar
1 cup water   3 cups milk

In large saucepan, heat chocolate and water, stirring until chocolate is melted and mixture is smooth. Stir in salt and sugar. Heat to boiling; reduce heat and simmer 4 minutes, stirring mixture constantly.

Stir in milk; cover and heat through but do not boil. Just before serving, beat with rotary beater until foamy.

6 servings (⅔ cup each).

FRENCH CHOCOLATE

Prepare the chocolate mixture ahead of time. And serve in your best china cups for a note of elegance on a special day.

⅓ cup semisweet chocolate   ½ teaspoon vanilla
  pieces   1 cup chilled whipping
¼ cup light corn syrup   cream
 3 tablespoons water   4 cups milk

Heat chocolate pieces, corn syrup and water over low heat, stirring until chocolate is melted and mixture is smooth. Stir in vanilla. Chill.

In chilled bowl, beat cream until stiff, adding chilled chocolate gradually. Continue beating until mixture mounds when dropped from a spoon. Refrigerate.

Just before serving, heat milk through but do not boil. Fill cups ½ full with whipped cream mixture. Fill cups with milk; blend.

8 servings.

MEXICAN CHOCOLATE

3 ounces unsweetened chocolate	½ teaspoon nutmeg
½ cup sugar	¼ teaspoon salt
3 tablespoons instant coffee	1½ cups water
1 teaspoon cinnamon	4 cups milk
	Whipped cream

In large saucepan, heat chocolate, sugar, coffee, spices, salt and water over low heat, stirring until mixture is smooth. Heat to boiling; reduce heat and simmer 4 minutes, stirring constantly.

Stir in milk; heat. Beat with rotary beater until foamy. Top with whipped cream.

8 servings (about ⅔ cup each).

COLOMBIAN CHOCOLATE

1 package (6 ounces) semisweet chocolate pieces	1 teaspoon cinnamon
	Pinch salt
1 cup Strong Coffee (page 36)	6 cups milk
	½ teaspoon vanilla

In large saucepan, heat chocolate pieces, coffee, cinnamon and salt over medium heat, stirring until chocolate is melted and mixture is smooth.

Add milk; heat through, stirring occasionally, but do not boil. Stir in vanilla. Just before serving, beat with rotary beater until foamy.

10 servings (about ⅔ cup each).

HOT COCOA

⅓ cup sugar	1½ cups water
⅓ cup cocoa	4½ cups milk
¼ teaspoon salt	

Mix sugar, cocoa and salt in large saucepan. Add water. Heat to boiling, stirring constantly. Boil and stir 2 minutes. Stir in milk; heat through but do not boil. If desired, add ¼ teaspoon vanilla.

Just before serving, beat with rotary beater until foamy or stir until smooth.

9 servings (⅔ cup each).

Dairy Drinks

Drinks you never outgrow! A Suzy-special for somebody small. A build-you-up for a tired man. A happy-after-school for a boy and his gang. You can say a lot with a milk drink—a lot of good nutrition, a lot of goodwill. Do say it often—with great drinks like these.

FLAVORED MILKS

For each serving, add one of the following to an 8-ounce glass of milk and stir thoroughly. Serve immediately.

Cactus Juice: 2 drops red or yellow food color.

Creamy Caramel: 2 tablespoons caramel syrup.

Cheery Cherry: 1 maraschino cherry and 2 tablespoons maraschino cherry juice.

Choc-O-Nut: 1 tablespoon chocolate syrup and 1 tablespoon chunky peanut butter.

Fudgy Chocolate: 1 to 2 tablespoons chocolate syrup, cocoa mix or ice-cream topping.

Honeysuckle Nectar: 1 tablespoon honey and 1 tablespoon grape juice, orange juice, lemonade or limeade concentrate.

Monkey Juice: ½ banana, mashed.

Woodsman's Special: 2 tablespoons maple syrup; sprinkle with cinnamon.

MILK SHAKES

For each serving, measure ¾ cup milk and ingredients for any Flavored Milk (above) into blender; add 1 scoop of your favorite ice cream. Blend until smooth. (Or, beat all ingredients with rotary beater.)

ICE-CREAM SODAS

Chocolate reigns supreme!

For each soda, place 2 to 3 tablespoons any flavor syrup (or ice-cream topping) or ¼ cup crushed fruit with 1 teaspoon sugar in tall glass. Fill glass ½ full with chilled sparkling water. Add 1 scoop of your favorite ice cream; stir vigorously, scraping syrup from side and bottom of glass. Fill glass with sparkling water.

ORANGE-BUTTERMILK SHAKE

1 cup buttermilk
1 scoop vanilla ice cream
(about ½ cup)

½ cup orange juice
2 tablespoons brown sugar

Measure all ingredients into blender, mix on high speed until smooth. (Or, beat all ingredients with rotary beater.)

2 servings (about ¾ cup each).

MOCHA COOLER

1 cup Strong Coffee (page 36), chilled
1 pint chocolate ice cream

1 teaspoon vanilla
½ teaspoon cinnamon
¼ teaspoon salt

Pour coffee into blender. Spoon in ice cream, vanilla, cinnamon and salt. Blend 10 to 15 seconds. (Or beat all ingredients with rotary beater.) Serve immediately over ice cubes in tall glasses.

3 or 4 servings.

HOT CHOCOLATE MILK

Heat 1 quart chocolate-flavored milk over medium-low heat until small bubbles form around edge of pan. Beat with rotary beater until foamy. Serve immediately.

6 servings (⅔ cup each).

SPOON-UP EGGNOG

Can eggnog be elegant? Just try this one and see.

4 eggs, separated
½ cup sugar
⅛ teaspoon salt
½ cup golden rum or, if
desired, 1 to 2 tablespoons
rum flavoring

2 cups whipping cream,
whipped

Beat egg whites until stiff. Beat egg yolks, sugar and salt until very thick and lemon colored; stir in rum.

Fold egg yolk mixture into whipped cream. Fold egg whites into egg yolk-cream mixture. Chill thoroughly.

Serve in cups, with spoons. If desired, sprinkle with nutmeg.

12 servings (about ½ cup each).

Punches and Fruit Drinks

Heat got everyone down? Cool things off with a frosty fruit drink. Be sure to chill the glasses while you measure and stir; pour the makings over ice and garnish with a citrus slice. Watch the troops revive! And for parties, weddings, banquets—pick a punch. They're here, too.

CRANBERRY-APPLE PUNCH

3 quarts water
2 cups sugar
2 cups strong tea
2 cans (6 ounces each)
  frozen lemonade
  concentrate, thawed

2 quarts cranberry cocktail
1 quart apple juice
2 cups orange juice

Heat water and sugar to boiling, stirring constantly until sugar is dissolved. Cool.

Prepare tea as directed on page 41, using 3 teaspoons loose tea or 3 teabags and 2 cups boiling water. Cool.

Chill all ingredients. Just before serving, stir together in large punch bowl.

60 servings (about ½ cup each).

ROSÉ PUNCH

A colorful wine punch.

2 bottles (⅘ quart each)
  rosé, chilled
½ cup grenadine syrup

½ cup lemon juice
1 quart ginger ale, chilled

In large punch bowl, combine wine, grenadine syrup and lemon juice: Stir in ginger ale. Serve immediately.

22 servings (about ½ cup each).

VARIATION

■ *Creamy Rosé Punch:* Spoon 1 pint raspberry sherbet into punch. Do not use ice.

TAHITIAN PUNCH

Citrus slices and a sprig of mint garnish this punch.

1 can (46 ounces) pineapple
juice, chilled

1 can (46 ounces) orange-
grapefruit juice, chilled

2 quarts carbonated lemon-
lime beverage, chilled

1 pint lemon or lime sherbet

In large punch bowl, stir together juices and carbonated beverage. Spoon sherbet into bowl. Serve immediately.

38 servings (about ½ cup each).

SPARKLING CRANBERRY PUNCH

2 quarts cranberry cocktail,
chilled

1 can (6 ounces) frozen pink
lemonade concentrate,
thawed

1 quart sparkling water,
chilled

In large punch bowl, combine cranberry cocktail and
lemonade concentrate. Stir in sparkling water. Serve
immediately.

25 servings (about ½ cup each).

FRUIT GLOW PUNCH

1 can (6 ounces) frozen
orange juice concentrate,
thawed.

1 can (6 ounces) frozen
lemonade concentrate,
thawed

1 quart apple juice, chilled

2 quarts ginger ale, chilled

1 pint lemon or orange
sherbet

In large punch bowl, combine concentrates and apple
juice. Stir in ginger ale. Spoon sherbet into bowl. Serve
immediately.

28 servings (about ½ cup each).

DAIQUIRI PUNCH

1 bottle (⅘ quart) white
rum, chilled

1¼ cups (12 ounces) daiquiri
mix, chilled

2 quarts carbonated lemon-
lime beverage, chilled

In large punch bowl, combine rum and daiquiri mix. Stir in carbonated lemon-lime beverage. Serve immediately.

25 servings (about ½ cup each).

HOT APPLE CIDER PUNCH

1 gallon apple cider
2 teaspoons whole cloves
2 teaspoons whole allspice
2 three-inch cinnamon sticks

⅔ cup water
2 oranges, studded with cloves

Heat cider, cloves, allspice, cinnamon and sugar to boiling; cover and simmer 20 minutes. Strain punch and pour into punch bowl. Float oranges in bowl.

32 servings (about ½ cup each).

ICE RING FOR PUNCH BOWL

In 6- to 6½-cup ring mold, arrange thin citrus slices and maraschino cherries or strawberries in an attractive design. Pour water into mold to partially cover fruit. Freeze.

When frozen, add water to fill mold ¾ full; freeze. At serving time, unmold and float fruit slice up in punch bowl.

If you prefer, freeze ring without decoration. Or, instead of freezing water, freeze part of a non-sparkling punch recipe itself; this will keep punch cold without diluting it.

HOLIDAY EGGNOG

6 eggs
1 cup sugar
½ teaspoon salt
1 cup golden rum or, if desired, 1 to 2 tablespoons rum flavoring

1 quart light cream (20%)
Nutmeg

In large bowl, beat eggs until light and foamy. Add sugar and salt, beating until thick and lemon colored. Stir in rum and cream. Chill at least 3 hours. Just before serving, sprinkle with nutmeg.

12 servings (about ½ cup each).

SPARKLING ORANGE EGGNOG

2 quarts orange juice, chilled
½ cup lemon juice
6 eggs
¼ cup sugar
¼ teaspoon cinnamon
¼ teaspoon ginger
¼ teaspoon cloves
1 quart vanilla ice cream
1 quart ginger ale, chilled
Nutmeg

Into large bowl, measure 3 cups of the orange juice, the lemon juice, eggs, sugar, cinnamon, ginger and cloves. Blend with rotary beater. Stir in remaining orange juice; cover and refrigerate.

Just before serving, pour eggnog mixture into large punch bowl. Spoon ice cream into bowl; add ginger ale. Blend with rotary beater. Sprinkle with nutmeg.

30 servings (about ½ cup each).

RASPBERRY SHRUB

A foamy-topped cooler.

4 packages (10 ounces each) frozen raspberries, thawed
1 can (6 ounces) frozen lemonade concentrate, thawed
2 quarts ginger ale, chilled

Cook raspberries 10 minutes. Rub through strainer with wooden spoon; cool.

Add concentrate; stir in ginger ale. Serve immediately in tall glasses with ice cubes or crushed ice.

12 servings (1 cup each).

LEMONADE

Stir together 3 cups water, 1 cup lemon juice (about 4 lemons) and ½ cup sugar. Pour over ice.

5 servings (about ¾ cup each).

VARIATIONS

■ *Minted Lemonade:* Place bruised mint leaves in glasses before pouring Lemonade. Garnish each serving with a sprig of mint.

■ *Pink Lemonade:* Add 2 tablespoons grenadine syrup and 2 to 3 drops red food color. Or, add only the red food color.

LIMEADE

Stir together 3 cups water, 1 cup lime juice (about 10 limes) and ¾ cup sugar. Pour over ice.

5 servings (about ¾ cup each).

ORANGE SWIZZLE

Serve as a tall drink or in punch cups.

1 can (12 ounces) frozen orange juice concentrate	Orange half-slices Maraschino cherries
1 quart ginger ale, chilled	

Reconstitute orange juice with ginger ale. Pour over crushed ice. Serve with an orange slice and cherry on each swizzle stick.

6 servings (about 1 cup each).

Appetizer Beverages

These delicious drinks lead a double life: They can be served at the table as the first course or, more casually; enjoyed in the living room, allowing you to slip away for those last-minute touches in the kitchen.

Don't forget tomato juice, clam juice, vegetable juice and orange juice—they're all good to keep on hand for quick wake-up-the-appetite drinks.

SPARKLING RED ROUSER

Just before serving, mix gently 1 can (8 ounces) tomato sauce and 2 bottles (7 ounces each) carbonated lemon-lime beverage. Serve over ice.

6 servings.

TANGY FRUIT COCKTAIL

Chill 1 quart cranberry cocktail and 1 cup grape juice. Just before serving, pour chilled juices over cracked ice. If desired, garnish with maraschino cherries, lemon slices and orange slices.

10 servings (about ½ cup each).

MOCK CHAMPAGNE COCKTAIL

1 bottle (7 ounces) lemon-
 lime carbonated beverage,
 chilled

½ cup apple juice, chilled
3 thin slices lemon

Just before serving, mix carbonated beverage and apple juice. Serve in stemmed glasses with lemon slice in each.
3 servings.

POW!

A hot and spicy bouillon drink. You'll want to have plenty on hand for those cold and blustery days of winter.

3 cans (10½ ounces each)
 condensed beef broth
 (bouillon)

1½ cups water
 2 teaspoons horseradish
 ½ teaspoon dill weed

Heat all ingredients to simmering, stirring occasionally. Serve hot.
10 servings (about ½ cup each).

TOMATO BOUILLON

A pre-dinner drink with plenty of zest. Try serving it in the living room before guests come to the table.

4 cups tomato juice
3 cans (10½ ounces each)
 condensed beef broth
 (bouillon)
1 tablespoon lemon juice

½ teaspoon Worcestershire
 sauce
½ teaspoon horseradish
½ cup sherry, if desired

Measure all ingredients except wine into saucepan. Heat slowly 30 minutes, stirring occasionally. Just before serving, stir in wine.
15 servings (about ½ cup each).

MULLED TOMATO JUICE

2 cans (46 ounces each)
 tomato juice
1 tablespoon Worcestershire
 sauce
1 teaspoon salt

1 teaspoon celery salt
½ teaspoon oregano
5 drops red pepper sauce
½ cup soft butter

Combine all ingredients in Dutch oven or large kettle.

Cover and heat to boiling. Reduce heat; simmer 10 to 15 minutes, stirring occasionally. Serve in small mugs.

15 servings (about ¾ cup each).

Note: A 15-cup automatic percolator (with basket removed) can be used. Measure ingredients into percolator and let it perk one cycle.

SPICED CRANBERRY CIDER

A good starter for holiday parties.

2 quarts apple cider	1½ teaspoons whole cloves
1½ quarts cranberry cocktail	1 lemon, thinly sliced
¼ cup brown sugar (packed)	
4 three-inch cinnamon sticks	

Combine all ingredients in large kettle. Heat to boiling; reduce heat and simmer 15 to 20 minutes.

With slotted spoon, remove cinnamon, cloves and lemon slices. If desired, float fresh lemon slice in each cup.

25 servings (about ½ cup each).

Crowd-size Beverages

Happy crowds trooping in after the game for hot bouillon, sliced turkey, relishes and crusty breads. Children warming up after skating with fragrant mugs of Hot Cocoa (page 55) and cookies. Old friends sharing an afternoon with French Chocolate (page 55) tea sandwiches and pretty pastel Petits Fours (page 143). Young daughters learning to be grown up—pouring tea or coffee at opposite ends of a flower-centered tea table. A flickering campfire and old songs mingling with the fragrance of sizzling franks and brewing coffee. Beautiful moments that turn into memories.

It's fun to have a crowd—fun to have the kind of house the crowd likes to come to. And with crowd-size things to drink like these—and easy-going foods to keep them company (or maybe even a crowd-size dinner, pages 495 to 500)—you can make a happy memory often.

LARGE QUANTITY COFFEE

A mammoth percolator-urn is perfect for brewing coffee for a crowd. But you can do the job just as well with one or more kettles.

Measure regular-grind coffee into a clean cloth sack; fill only ½ full to allow for expansion of coffee and free circulation of water. (Before using sack, soak and rinse thoroughly.) Tie sack, allowing enough cord for fastening to pan handle.

Heat measured amount of fresh cold water to a full rolling boil in kettle. Reduce heat to simmer. Fasten sack to pan handle; submerge into water. Keep kettle over low heat. Brew 6 to 8 minutes, pushing sack up and down frequently to get proper extraction. When coffee is ready, remove sack, permitting all extract to drain into kettle.

COFFEE-MAKING CHART

People	Servings (⅔ cup each)	Ground Coffee	Water
12	23	2 cups	4 quarts
25	46	4 cups	8 quarts

EGG COFFEE

An old-fashioned recipe for up-to-date goodness. At home or over a crackling campfire, its so easy to do—and without special equipment.

10 quarts water	2 eggs
3 cups regular-grind coffee	1½ cups water

Heat 10 quarts water to boiling. Mix coffee, eggs and 1½ cups water; pour into boiling water. Heat to rolling boil (coffee mixture will sink to bottom). Remove from heat; add 1 cup cold water to settle coffee.

60 servings (about ⅔ cup each).

INSTANT COFFEE

Measure 1 cup (2 ounces) instant coffee into large pot or kettle. Stir in part of 6 quarts (24 cups) cold water; add remaining water.

Heat *just* to boiling but do not boil. Serve immediately. (Or heat water to boiling; remove from heat and stir in the instant coffee. Cover and let stand 3 minutes.)

36 servings (⅔ cup each).

INSTANT TEA

Make a concentrate by measuring 1 cup (2 ounces) instant tea into large stainless steel or glass container; stir in 2½ quarts (10 cups) boiling water. Just before serving, pour 1 part concentrate and 2 parts boiling water into teapot.

45 servings (⅔ cup each).

HOT COCOA

1 cup sugar	4 cups water
1 cup cocoa	3 quarts milk
½ teaspoon salt	

In large kettle or Dutch oven, mix sugar, cocoa and salt. Add water. Heat to boiling, stirring constantly. Boil and stir 2 minutes. Stir in milk; heat through but do not boil. If desired, add ½ teaspoon vanilla.

Just before serving, beat with rotary beater until foamy or stir until smooth.

24 servings (about ⅔ cup each).

FRENCH CHOCOLATE

⅔ cup semisweet chocolate pieces	1 teaspoon vanilla
½ cup light corn syrup	2 cups chilled whipping cream
¼ cup plus 2 tablespoons water	8 cups milk

Heat chocolate pieces, corn syrup and water over low heat, stirring until chocolate is melted and mixture is smooth. Stir in vanilla. Chill.

In chilled bowl, beat cream until stiff, adding chilled chocolate gradually. Continue beating until mixture mounds when dropped from a spoon. Refrigerate.

Just before serving, heat milk through but do not boil. Fill cups ½ full with whipped cream mixture. Fill cups with milk; blend.

16 servings.

Quick Breads

*The nicest quality about quick breads is that they
are just that—quick! A quick way to make any
breakfast Sunday-special! Something quick to
pop in the oven when a new neighbor drops in
for coffee. A quick treat to bake and share with
a friend who has a problem. And a quick way,
any time, to say without words to anybody,
"I 'specially wanted to have something nice,
for you!"*

Biscuits

Picture this: Golden, flaky biscuits with crisp fried
chicken; hot buttered biscuits with glazed baked ham;
biscuits, in fact, with almost everything. There's something about a basket of piping-hot biscuits that's too
good to save for special days—especially when it's so
easy to make them any time.

And variety? Make your biscuits large or small, flat or
high, crisp or soft, buttermilk or plain, with or without
additions. They can be dropped from a spoon or cut with
a knife or biscuit cutter. In short, there's a recipe for
every taste. And here are the tips to make them even
easier:

■ For tender, flaky biscuits, cut the shortening in
thoroughly, using two knives, a fork or a pastry blender.
The dough, before the addition of the liquid, should resemble meal.

■ To get soft dough, stir the liquid into the dry ingredients just until the dough leaves the side of the bowl and
rounds up into a ball.

■ Knead the dough gently, but do knead it. This ensures a fine-textured biscuit.

Biscuits—and a prepared biscuit mix—make a good
beginning for a junior cook. With the easy recipes on

the box, she'll be making drop biscuits, rolled biscuits and shortcake in no time. A minute-saver for you, too.

But don't use biscuits just as bread. Make a meat or fruit pie with a biscuit topping. Or make a shortcake—with creamed chicken, beef or salmon or with any fruit. Or a bubbling stew—chicken, meat or fruit—with biscuit dumplings. Whatever you're planning to serve today, biscuits could make it better.

BAKING POWDER BISCUITS

2 cups all-purpose flour*	¼ cup shortening
3 teaspoons baking powder	¾ cup milk
1 teaspoon salt	

Heat oven to 450°. Measure flour, baking powder and salt into bowl. Cut in shortening thoroughly, until mixture looks like meal. Stir in almost all the milk. If dough is not pliable, add just enough milk to make a soft, puffy, easy-to-roll dough. (Too much milk makes dough sticky, not enough makes biscuits dry.)

Round up dough on lightly floured cloth-covered board. Knead lightly 20 to 25 times, about ½ minute. Roll ½ inch thick. Cut with floured biscuit cutter. Place on ungreased baking sheet. Bake 10 to 12 minutes or until golden brown.

About sixteen 1¾-inch biscuits.

*If using self-rising flour, omit baking powder and salt.

VARIATIONS

■ *Bacon Biscuits:* Stir in ⅓ cup crumbled crisply fried bacon with the milk.

■ *Buttermilk Biscuits:* Substitute buttermilk for the milk; decrease baking powder to 2 teaspoons and add ¼ teaspoon soda to flour mixture. (If using self-rising flour, omit baking powder and salt and increase buttermilk to 1 cup).

■ *Cheese Biscuits:* Stir in ½ cup shredded sharp Cheddar cheese with the milk.

■ *Drop Biscuits:* Increase milk to 1 cup. Drop dough by spoonfuls onto greased baking sheet.

■ *Herb Biscuits:* Add 1¼ teaspoons caraway seed, ½ teaspoon crumbled leaf sage and ¼ teaspoon dry mustard to flour mixture.

1. Cut in shortening until mixture resembles meal.

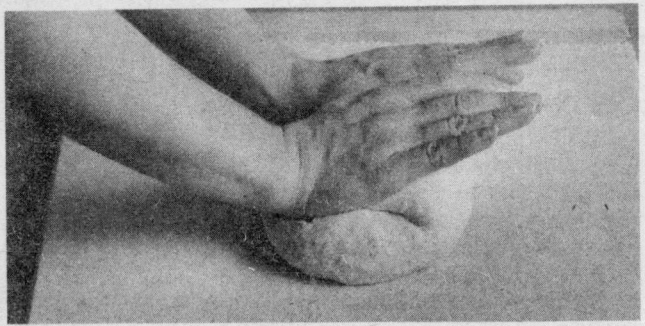

2. Round up dough; knead 20 to 25 times about ½ minute.

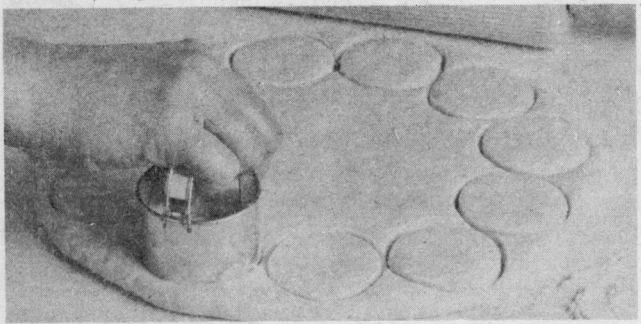

3. Cut with floured cutter; keep rounds close together.

4. For crusty sides, bake biscuits 1 to 2 inches apart.

SOUTHERN BISCUITS

2 cups all-purpose flour*
2 teaspoons sugar
2 teaspoons baking powder
1 teaspoon salt
½ teaspoon soda
⅓ cup shortening
⅔ cup buttermilk

Heat oven to 450°. Measure flour, sugar, baking powder, salt and soda into bowl. Cut in shortening thoroughly, until mixture looks like meal.

Stir in almost all the buttermilk. If dough is not pliable, add just enough milk to make a soft, puffy, easy-to-roll dough.

Round up dough on lightly floured cloth-covered board. Knead lightly 20 to 25 times, about ½ minute. Roll a little less than ½ inch thick. Cut with floured biscuit cutter. Place on ungreased baking sheet. Bake 10 to 12 minutes or until golden brown.

About 2 dozen 1¾-inch biscuits.

*If using self-rising flour, omit baking powder and salt.

BUTTER DIPS

¼ cup butter or margarine
1¼ cups all-purpose flour*
2 teaspoons sugar
2 teaspoons baking powder
1 teaspoon salt
⅔ cup milk

Heat oven to 450°. In square pan, 9x9x2 inches, melt butter in oven. Remove pan from oven.

Measure flour, sugar, baking powder and salt into bowl. Add milk; stir just until dough forms.

Turn dough onto well-floured cloth-covered board. Roll dough around to coat with flour. Knead lightly about 10 times. Roll into 8-inch square. With floured knife, cut dough in half, then cut each half into nine 4-inch strips. Dip each strip into melted butter, coating both sides; arrange strips close together in 2 rows in pan. Bake 15 to 20 minutes or until golden brown.

18 sticks.

*Do not use quick-mixing flour in this recipe. If using self-rising flour, omit baking powder and salt.

STIR 'N ROLL BISCUITS

REGULAR BISCUITS

2 cups all-purpose flour*	⅓ cup salad oil
3 teaspoons baking powder	⅔ cup milk
1 teaspoon salt	

BUTTERMILK BISCUITS

2 cups all-purpose flour*	¼ teaspoon soda
2 teaspoons baking powder	⅓ cup salad oil
1 teaspoon salt	⅔ cup buttermilk

Heat oven to 450°. Measure dry ingredients into bowl. Pour oil and milk into measuring cup (do not stir together); pour all at once into flour mixture. Stir until mixture cleans side of bowl and forms a ball.

To knead dough: turn onto waxed paper, lift paper by one corner and fold dough in half; press down firmly and pull paper back. Repeat until dough looks smooth. Pat or roll ½ inch thick between 2 sheets of waxed paper. Cut dough with unfloured biscuit cutter. Place on ungreased baking sheet. Bake 10 to 12 minutes or until golden brown.

About sixteen 1¾-inch biscuits.

*If using self-rising flour, omit baking powder, salt and soda.

Muffins

Hot muffins to warm the inner man—a wonderful addition to any breakfast, brunch or coffee break. They're good served with supper, too.

One of the nicest things about muffins is you don't even need a mixer to make them. Just put all the liquid ingredients in a bowl, add the dry ingredients all at once and stir just a little. You can mix muffins from scratch in two or three minutes—what a fun first-baking for a five-year-old, if an adult puts the pan in the oven.

For more speed, try a muffin mix—the easy directions are on the package. They come in several delicious flavors. They make quick and good coffee cakes, too, baked in square pans and topped with cinnamon-sugar.

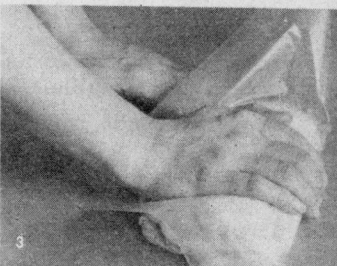

1. Pour salad oil onto milk; do not stir liquids together.

2. Stir until mixture cleans side of bowl and forms a ball.

3. To knead, lift waxed paper over dough and press down.

4. Pat or roll dough between 2 sheets of waxed paper.

FAVORITE MUFFINS

Make it a point to serve muffins hot—right from the oven or split and reheated in the broiler.

POPULAR MUFFINS

1 egg
1 cup milk
¼ cup salad oil
2 cups all-purpose flour*

¼ cup sugar
3 teaspoons baking powder
1 teaspoon salt

SWEET MUFFINS

1 egg
½ cup milk
¼ cup salad oil
1½ cups all-purpose flour*

½ cup sugar
2 teaspoons baking powder
½ teaspoon salt

Heat oven to 400°. Grease bottoms of 12 medium muffin cups (2¾ inches in diameter). Beat egg; stir in milk and oil. Mix in remaining ingredients *just* until flour is moistened. Batter should be lumpy.

Fill muffin cups ⅔ full. Bake 20 to 25 minutes or until golden brown. Immediately remove from pan.

12 muffins.

*If using self-rising flour, omit baking powder and salt.

VARIATIONS

■ *Apple Muffins:* Stir in 1 cup grated apple with the oil and add ½ teaspoon cinnamon with the flour. Sprinkle with Nut-Crunch Topping: Mix ⅓ cup brown sugar (packed), ⅓ cup broken nuts and ½ teaspoon cinnamon. Bake 25 to 30 minutes.

■ *Blueberry Muffins:* Fold 1 cup fresh blueberries or ¾ cup well-drained frozen blueberries (thawed) into batter.

■ *Buttermilk Muffins:* Follow recipe for Popular Muffins, except—substitute buttermilk for the milk, decrease baking powder to 2 teaspoons and add ½ teaspoon soda.

■ *Cereal Muffins:* Follow recipe for Popular Muffins except—decrease flour to 1 cup and milk to ½ cup; fold 2 cups whole wheat flakes cereal into batter.

■ *Cranberry-Orange Muffins:* Fold 1 tablespoon grated orange peel and 1 cup cranberries, cut in half, into batter.

■ *Surprise Muffins:* Fill muffin cups only ½ full; drop 1 teaspoon jelly in center of each and add batter to fill cups ⅔ full.

■ *Whole Wheat Muffins:* Follow recipe for Popular Muffins except—decrease flour to 1 cup and baking powder to 2 teaspoons; add 1 cup whole wheat flour.

PUMPKIN MUFFINS

1½ cups all-purpose flour*	½ cup milk
½ cup sugar	½ cup canned pumpkin
2 teaspoons baking powder	¼ cup butter or margarine,
½ teaspoon salt	melted
½ teaspoon cinnamon	1 egg
½ teaspoon nutmeg	½ cup raisins

Heat oven to 400°. Grease bottoms of 12 medium muffin cups (2¾ inches in diameter). Mix all ingredients *just* until flour is moistened. Batter should be lumpy.

Fill muffin cups ⅔ full. Sprinkle ¼ teaspoon sugar over batter in each cup. Bake 18 to 20 minutes. Immediately remove from pan.

12 muffins.

If using self-rising flour, omit baking powder and salt.

FRENCH BREAKFAST MUFFINS

Rich but airy. Elegant enough for a special brunch or coffee-time treat.

⅓ cup shortening	¼ teaspoon nutmeg
½ cup sugar	½ cup milk
1 egg	½ cup sugar
1½ cups all-purpose flour* or cake flour	1 teaspoon cinnammon
	½ cup butter or margarine,
1½ teaspoons baking powder	melted
½ teaspoon salt	

Heat oven to 350°. Grease 15 medium muffin cups (2¾ inches in diameter). Mix thoroughly shortening, ½ cup sugar and the egg. Stir in flour, baking powder, salt and nutmeg alternately with milk.

Fill muffin cups ⅔ full. Bake 20 to 25 minutes. Mix ½ cup sugar and the cinnamon. Immediately after baking, roll puffs in melted butter, then in cinnamon-sugar mixture. Serve hot.

15 muffins.

If using self-rising flour, omit baking powder and salt.

OATMEAL MUFFINS

1 egg	1 cup all-purpose flour*
1 cup buttermilk	1 teaspoon baking powder
½ cup brown sugar (packed)	1 teaspoon salt
⅓ cup shortening	½ teaspoon soda
1 cup quick-cooking oats	

Heat oven to 400°. Grease bottoms of 12 medium muffin cups (2¾ inches in diameter). Beat egg; stir in buttermilk, brown sugar and shortening. Mix in remaining ingredients *just* until flour is moistened. Batter should be lumpy.

Fill muffin cups ⅔ full. Bake 20 to 25 minutes or until light brown. Immediately remove from pan.

12 muffins.

If using self-rising flour, omit baking powder and salt.

BLUEBERRY-NUT MUFFINS

1 package (13.5 ounces) wild blueberry muffin mix	½ cup milk
	½ cup chopped nuts
1 egg	

Heat oven to 400°. Grease bottoms of 12 medium muffin cups (2¾ inches in diameter). Drain blueberries; rinse and set aside.

Blend egg and milk. Stir in muffin mix (dry) just until blended. Batter should be lumpy. Fold in blueberries and nuts. Fill muffin cups ½ full. Bake 15 to 20 minutes. Immediately remove from pan.

12 muffins.

RASPBERRY TOPHATS

Heat oven to 450°. Prepare biscuit dough as directed on package of buttermilk baking mix except—after rolling dough ½ inch thick, cut 10 rounds with floured 2-inch cutter. Place each round in ungreased medium muffin cup (2¾ inches in diameter). Make a depression in center of each; place 1 teaspoon raspberry jam in each depression. Shape remaining dough into 10 balls; place on jam. Bake 10 minutes or until light brown.

10 muffins.

Dinner Breads

Breads like these go 'way back into American history —back to the first settlers who learned from the Indians the good things you can do with corn, back to the South where spoon bread flourished (and isn't it good?), to thrifty New England where brown bread steamed right along with the crocks of Saturday-night-supper beans.

CORN STICKS

Be sure to serve piping hot, with plenty of butter.

1½ cups cornmeal
½ cup all-purpose flour*
3 teaspoons baking powder
1 teaspoon sugar
1 teaspoon salt
½ teaspoon soda
¼ cup shortening
1½ cups buttermilk
1 egg

Heat oven to 450°. Grease corn stick pans; place in oven to heat. Stir together all ingredients; beat vigorously ½ minute. Fill pans ⅔ full. Bake 12 to 15 minutes or until golden brown.
About 18 sticks.

*If using self-rising flour, decrease baking powder to 2 teaspoons and omit salt.

CHEESE-CORN BREAD

2 cups all-purpose flour*
¼ cup sugar
3 teaspoons baking powder
1 teaspoon salt
1 egg, slightly beaten
1 cup milk
½ cup shredded Cheddar cheese
1 can (7 ounces) whole kernel corn, drained (1 cup)
¼ cup shortening, melted, or salad oil

Heat oven to 400°. Grease square pan, 8x8x2 or 9x9x2 inches. Measure all ingredients in order listed into bowl; stir *just* until flour is moistened. Batter should be lumpy.
Spread evenly in pan. Bake 8-inch pan 45 minutes, 9-inch pan 35 minutes or until golden brown.
9 to 12 servings.

*If using self-rising flour, omit baking powder and salt.

CORN BREAD

1 cup yellow cornmeal	½ teaspoon salt
1 cup all-purpose flour*	1 cup milk
2 tablespoons sugar	¼ cup shortening
4 teaspoons baking powder	1 egg

Heat oven to 425°. Grease square pan, 8x8x2 or 9x9x2 inches. Blend all ingredients about 20 seconds. Beat vigorously 1 minute. Pour into pan. Bake 20 to 25 minutes or until golden brown.

9 to 12 servings.

*If using self-rising flour, decrease baking powder to 2 teaspoons and omit salt.

VARIATIONS

■ *Corn Muffins:* Fill 12 greased medium muffin cups (2¾ inches in diameter) ⅔ full. Bake 15 minutes. 12 muffins.

■ *Double Corn Bread:* Prepare the 9x9x2-inch pan; use 2 eggs and stir 1 can (7 or 8 ounces) whole kernel corn, well drained, into batter.

POPOVERS

A bread spectacular that pops up while baking, forming crusty hollow shells. Break and spread with butter or fill with creamed seafood or meat.

4 eggs	2 cups all-purpose flour*
2 cups milk	1 teaspoon salt

Heat oven to 450°. Grease 12 deep custard cups (5 ounces) or 16 medium muffin cups. With hand beater, beat eggs slightly; add milk, flour and salt and beat just until smooth. Do not overbeat.

Fill custard cups ½ full, muffin cups ⅔ full. Bake 25 minutes. Lower oven temperature to 350° and bake 15 to 20 minutes longer or until deep golden brown. Immediately remove from pan; serve hot.

12 to 16 popovers.

*Do not use self-rising flour in this recipe.

Yorkshire Pudding: The traditional English accompaniment for roast beef is simply popover batter baked in the meat drippings. Complete directions for preparing it with the meat are on page 368.

FLUFFY SPOON BREAD

A light soufflé-type bread that is spooned onto the plate and eaten with a fork

1½ cups boiling water	1 cup buttermilk
1 cup cornmeal	1 teaspoon salt
1 tablespoon butter or margarine, softened	1 teaspoon sugar
	1 teaspoon baking powder
3 eggs, separated	¼ teaspoon soda

Heat oven to 375°. Grease 2-quart casserole. In large bowl, stir boiling water into cornmeal; to prevent lumping, continue stirring until mixture is cool. Blend in butter and egg yolks. Stir in buttermilk, salt, sugar, baking powder and soda.

Beat egg whites just until soft peaks form; fold into batter. Pour into casserole. Bake 45 to 50 minutes. Serve hot with butter.

8 to 10 servings.

DUMPLINGS

Perfect accompaniment for chicken or beef stew.

1½ cups all-purpose flour*	3 tablespoons shortening
2 teaspoons baking powder	¾ cup milk
¾ teaspoon salt	

Measure flour, baking powder and salt into bowl. Cut in shortening thoroughly, until mixture looks like meal. Stir in milk.

Drop dough by spoonfuls onto hot meat or vegetables in boiling stew. (Do not drop directly into liquid.) Cook uncovered 10 minutes. Cover; cook about 10 minutes longer or until dumplings are fluffy.

8 to 10 dumplings.

*If using self-rising flour, omit baking powder and salt.

VARIATIONS

■ *Cheese Dumplings:* Add ¼ cup shredded sharp cheese to flour mixture.

■ *Parsley, Chive or Herb Dumplings:* Add 3 tablespoons snipped parsley or chives or ½ teaspoon dried herbs (sage, celery seed or thyme) to flour mixture.

Suggested Foods for Fritters (Fritter Batter)

MAIN DISH: Chopped cooked shrimp or ham, cubed luncheon meat.
VEGETABLES: Corn.
FRUITS: Chopped apple, banana, pineapple cubes.

Suggested Foods to Deep-fry (Thin Batter)

APPETIZER OR MAIN DISH: Whole shrimp, scallops, oysters, fish fillets, chicken pieces (partially cooked), cutlets.
VEGETABLES: Eggplant slices, cauliflowerets, onion rings, zucchini slices.
FRUITS: Pineapple slices, bananas (quartered), apple slices, apricot halves.

FRITTERS AND DEEP-FRIED FOODS

Use Fritter Batter with chopped or shredded foods; use Thin Batter when you want to retain shape of food to be deep-fried.

FRITTER BATTER

1 cup all-purpose flour*	2 eggs
1 teaspoon baking powder	½ cup milk
1 teaspoon salt**	1 teaspoon salad oil

THIN BATTER (FOR DEEP-FRYING)

1 cup all-purpose flour*	1 egg
1 teaspoon baking powder	1 cup milk
½ teaspoon salt**	¼ cup salad oil

Prepare food to be fried (see suggested foods above). Thaw frozen foods completely before frying. Dry food thoroughly before dipping into batter. Heat fat or oil (3 to 4 inches) to 375° in deep fat fryer or kettle. Measure all ingredients for choice of batter into bowl; beat with rotary beater until smooth.

To prepare fritters: Stir about 1 cup suggested food into Fritter Batter; drop level tablespoonfuls into hot fat and fry about 5 minutes or until thoroughly cooked. Drain.

To deep-fry foods: Coat prepared food with flour. With tongs or fork, dip food into Thin Batter, allowing excess batter to drip into bowl; fry in hot fat until golden brown. Drain.

*If using self-rising flour, omit baking powder and salt.
**If adding salted foods to the batter, omit salt.

STEAMED BROWN BREAD

A moist brown bread usually served with baked beans. Whatever you serve it with, serve it hot and with plenty of butter.

1 cup all-purpose flour*
  or medium rye flour
1 cup cornmeal
1 cup whole wheat flour
2 teaspoons soda

1 teaspoon salt
2 cups buttermilk
¾ cup molasses
1 cup raisins, if desired

Grease four 1-pound cans or one 7-inch tube mold. Measure all ingredients into large mixer bowl. Beat ½ minute, scraping bowl constantly. Fill cans or mold ⅔ full; cover tightly with aluminum foil.

Place rack in Dutch oven and pour boiling water into pan up to level of rack. Place filled cans on rack. Cover Dutch oven. Keep water boiling over low heat to steam bread 3 hours or until wooden pick inserted in center comes out clean. (If it is necessary to add water during steaming, lift lid and quickly add boiling water.) Immediately remove from cans.

**If using self-rising flour, decrease soda to 1 teaspoon and omit salt.*

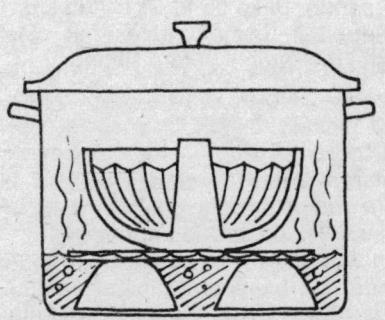

Steaming Equipment

If you don't have a regular steamer pan, you can improvise one quite easily using a Dutch oven or large saucepan with a tight-fitting cover. Place a wire rack in pan about 1 or 2 inches from the bottom. If rack is not adjustable, simply balance it on custard cups as shown here.

Tea Breads

Thin-sliced tea breads, spread with butter, are naturals for teas and parties. But have you ever thought of them as gifts? We know people who bake them by the dozens in foil pans for holidays, birthdays or neighborly greetings. (And they freeze so well!) Wrap a pretty little package and take it to your hostess. (Tip to bazaar committees: They sell well, too!)

NUT BREAD

For tea sandwiches, spread thin slices with cream cheese or butter. Try some of the unusual spreads on pages 664–666, too. And you'll love the looks of the colorful variations.

2½ cups all-purpose flour*	3 tablespoons salad oil
1 cup sugar	1¼ cups milk
3½ teaspoons baking powder	1 egg
1 teaspoon salt	1 cup finely chopped nuts

Heat oven to 350°. Grease and flour 9x5x3-inch loaf pan or two 8½x4½x2½-inch loaf pans. Measure all ingredients into large mixer bowl; beat on medium speed ½ minute, scraping side and bottom of bowl constantly.

Pour into pan(s). Bake 55 to 65 minutes or until wooden pick inserted in center comes out clean. Remove from pan; cool thoroughly before slicing.

*If using self-rising flour, omit baking powder and salt.

VARIATIONS

■ *Apricot Nut Bread:* Decrease milk to ½ cup; add 4 teaspoons grated orange peel, ¾ cup orange juice and 1 cup finely chopped dried apricots.

■ *Banana Nut Bread:* Decrease milk to ¾ cup; add 1 cup mashed ripe bananas (2 to 3 medium).

■ *Date Nut Bread:* Add 1 cup cut-up dates.

■ *Orange Nut Bread:* Decrease milk to ½ cup; add 4 teaspoons grated orange peel and ¾ cup orange juice.

■ *Prune Nut Bread:* Decrease milk to ½ cup; add ¾ cup prune juice and 1 cup drained chopped cooked prunes.

CRANBERRY-CHEESE BREAD

2 cups all-purpose flour*	2 tablespoons shortening
1 cup sugar	Juice from 1 orange
1½ teaspoons baking powder	1½ cups shredded Cheddar
½ teaspoon soda	cheese (about 6 ounces)
½ teaspoon salt	1 egg, beaten
2 teaspoons grated orange	1 cup cranberries, halved
peel	½ cup finely chopped walnuts

Heat oven to 350°. Grease loaf pan, 9x5x3 inches. Measure flour, sugar, baking powder, soda, salt and peel into bowl. Cut in shortening. Add water to juice to measure ¾ cup; mix in with cheese and egg. Stir in cranberries and nuts.

Pour into pan. Bake 60 to 70 minutes or until wooden pick inserted in center comes out clean. Remove from pan; let loaf stand at least 8 hours.

*If using self-rising flour, omit baking powder, soda and salt.

PUMPKIN BREAD

⅔ cup shortening	1½ teaspoons salt
2⅔ cups sugar	½ teaspoon baking powder
4 eggs	1 teaspoon cinnamon
1 can (1 pound) pumpkin	1 teaspoon cloves
⅔ cup water	⅔ cup coarsely chopped
3⅓ cups all-purpose flour*	nuts
2 teaspoons soda	⅔ cup raisins

Heat oven to 350°. Grease two 9x5x3-inch loaf pans or three 8½x4½x2½-inch loaf pans. In large bowl, cream shortening and sugar until fluffy. Stir in eggs, pumpkin and water. Blend in flour, soda, salt, baking powder, cinnamon and cloves. Stir in nuts and raisins.

Pour into pans. Bake about 70 minutes or until wooden pick inserted in center comes out clean.

*If using self-rising flour, omit baking powder, soda and salt.

Breakfast Specials

Mary's sleeping over! Jim's bringing a *girl* home from college! You've asked friends to come for brunch after church. Or you just woke up this morning so full of goodwill that you wanted to make the day special. That's the day for any one of the good things in this section. (Our testers tell us they're delicious!) Spread this morning sunshine all through the day—any time's a good time for these coffee companions. And they're just as good with a glass of milk, a cup of tea or even a mug of soup!

GOLDEN PUFFS

2 cups all-purpose flour*	¼ cup salad oil
¼ cup sugar	¾ cup milk
3 teaspoons baking powder	1 egg
1 teaspoon salt	½ cup sugar
1 teaspoon nutmeg or mace	1 teaspoon cinnamon

Heat fat or oil (3 to 4 inches) to 375° in deep fat fryer or kettle. Measure flour, ¼ cup sugar, the baking powder, salt and nutmeg into bowl. Add oil, milk and egg; beat until smooth.

Drop batter by teaspoonfuls (too large puffs will not cook through) into hot fat. Fry four or five at a time about 3 minutes or until golden brown on both sides. Drain.

Stir together ½ cup sugar and the cinnamon. Roll warm puffs in sugar-cinnamon mixture.

2½ dozen puffs.

*If using self-rising flour, omit baking powder and salt.

VARIATION

■ *Buttermilk Nut Puffs:* Decrease baking powder to 1 teaspoon, add ½ teaspoon soda and substitute buttermilk for the milk. Blend 1 cup confectioners' sugar and ⅓ cup boiling water. Glaze puffs with warm mixture and roll in finely chopped nuts. If desired, omit glaze and roll warm puffs in sugar. (Do not use self-rising flour.)

BUTTONS AND BOWKNOTS

2 cups buttermilk baking mix	1 egg
2 tablespoons sugar	¼ cup butter or margarine, melted
1 teaspoon nutmeg	
⅛ teaspoon cinnamon	½ cup sugar
⅓ cup milk	

Heat oven to 400°. Mix thoroughly baking mix, 2 tablespoons sugar, the nutmeg, cinnamon, milk and egg. Beat vigorously 20 strokes.

Round up dough on lightly floured cloth-covered board; knead 5 times. Roll ½ inch thick. Cut with floured doughnut cutter.

To make Bowknots, hold opposite sides of each ring with fingers and twist to form figure "8." Place "holes" (Buttons) and Bowknots on ungreased baking sheet. Bake 8 to 10 minutes. Immediately after baking, dip each Button and Bowknot into melted butter, then into sugar.

About 10 buns.

CARAMEL STICKY BUNS

Something new. Sticky buns in muffin cups.

½ cup butter or margarine	1 teaspoon nutmeg
½ cup brown sugar (packed)	⅛ teaspoon cinnamon
2 cups buttermilk baking mix	⅔ cup light cream (20%)
2 tablespoons granulated sugar	1 egg
	36 pecan halves

Heat oven to 400°. In each of 12 medium muffin cups (2¾ inches in diameter), place 2 teaspoons each butter and brown sugar. Place in oven to melt. Mix remaining ingredients except pecan halves; beat vigorously ½ minute.

Remove muffin cups from oven; place 3 pecan halves on butter-sugar mixture in each muffin cup. Divide batter evenly among muffin cups (cups should be about ½ full). Bake about 15 minutes. Immediately invert pan and gently remove buns to prevent sticking.

12 buns.

CHOCOLATE SWIRL COFFEE CAKE

⅓ cup flaked coconut	¼ cup sugar
¼ cup chopped nuts	1 egg
¼ cup sugar	¾ cup milk
3 tablespoons butter or margarine, melted	⅓ cup semisweet chocolate pieces, melted
2 cups buttermilk baking mix	

Heat oven to 400°. Grease square pan, 8x8x2 inches. Stir together coconut, nuts, ¼ cup sugar and 1 tablespoon of the melted butter; set aside.

Mix baking mix, ¼ cup sugar, remaining melted butter, the egg and milk. Beat vigorously ½ minute. Pour into pan.

Spoon chocolate over batter; with knife, cut through batter several times for a marble effect. Sprinkle coconut mixture evenly over top. Bake 20 to 25 minutes. Serve warm.

9 servings.

FAVORITE COFFEE CAKE

1½ cups all-purpose flour*	¼ cup shortening
¾ cup sugar	¾ cup milk
2½ teaspoons baking powder	1 egg
¾ teaspoon salt	Topping (below)

Heat oven to 375°. Grease round layer pan, 9x1½ inches, or square pan, 8x8x2 or 9x9x2 inches. Blend all ingredients except Topping; beat vigorously ½ minute. Spread in pan.

Sprinkle Topping over batter. Bake 25 to 30 minutes or until wooden pick inserted in center comes out clean. Serve warm.

9 to 12 servings.

*If using self-rising flour, omit baking powder and salt.

TOPPING

Mix ⅓ cup brown sugar (packed), ¼ cup all-purpose flour, ½ teaspoon cinnamon and 3 tablespoons firm butter until crumbly.

VARIATIONS

■ *Blueberry Buckle:* Increase flour to 2 cups, carefully stir 2 cups well-drained blueberries into batter and omit Topping. Mix ½ cup sugar, ⅓ cup all-purpose flour, ½ teaspoon cinnamon and ¼ cup soft butter; sprinkle over batter in pan. Bake 45 to 50 minutes.

■ *Jam-Raisin Coffee Cake:* Decrease sugar to ¼ cup and omit Topping; spread batter in prepared square pan, 8x8x2 or 9x9x2 inches. Mix ¼ cup brown sugar (packed), ½ cup raisins and ¼ teaspoon cinnamon; sprinkle over batter. Spoon ⅔ cup cherry or apricot jam or orange marmalade over brown sugar mixture.

While warm, spread with Confectioners' Sugar Icing: Blend 1 cup confectioners' sugar, ½ teaspoon vanilla and about 1 tablespoon water.

■ *Streusel-filled Coffee Cake:* Omit Topping; spread half the batter in prepared pan. Mix ½ cup brown sugar (packed), 2 teaspoons cinnamon, ½ cup finely chopped nuts and 2 tablespoons butter, melted; sprinkle half the mixture over batter in pan. Top with remaining batter, then remaining brown sugar mixture.

COCONUT-PINEAPPLE COFFEE CAKE

⅓ cup butter or margarine, softened
⅓ cup brown sugar (packed)
½ cup flaked coconut
1 package (13.5 ounces) wild blueberry muffin mix
1 can (8½ ounces) crushed pineapple, well drained

Heat oven to 400°. Grease square pan, 9x9x2 inches. Mix butter, sugar and coconut; set aside.

Prepare muffin mix as directed on package except— fold in crushed pineapple. Pour into pan. Spoon coconut mixture evenly over batter. Bake 25 to 30 minutes or until golden brown.

9 servings.

SOUR CREAM COFFEE CAKE

¾ cup butter or margarine, softened
1½ cups sugar
3 eggs
1½ teaspoons vanilla
3 cups all-purpose flour*
1½ teaspoons baking powder
1½ teaspoons soda
¼ teaspoon salt
1½ cups dairy sour cream
Filling (page 76)

Heat oven to 350°. Grease tube pan, 10x4 inches, or 2 loaf pans, 9x5x3 inches. Combine butter, sugar, eggs and vanilla in large mixer bowl. Beat on medium speed 2 minutes or 300 vigorous strokes by hand. Mix in flour, baking powder, soda and salt alternately with sour cream.

For tube pan, spread ⅓ of batter (about 2 cups) in pan and sprinkle with ⅓ of Filling (about 6 tablespoons); repeat 2 times. For loaf pans, spread ¼ of batter (about 1½ cups) in each pan and sprinkle each with ¼ of Filling (about 5 tablespoons); repeat.

*If using self-rising flour, omit baking powder, soda and salt.

Bake about 60 minutes or until wooden pick inserted in center comes out clean. Cool slightly in pan(s) before removing.

14 to 16 servings.

FILLING

Mix ½ cup brown sugar (packed), ½ cup finely chopped nuts and 1½ teaspoons cinnamon.

SHOO-FLY COFFEE CAKE

A coffee cake with the flavors of the famous Pennsylvania Dutch Shoo-fly Pie. It's really a molasses version of our favorite Sour Cream Coffee Cake.

¾ cup butter or margarine, softenend	3 cups all-purpose flour*
1 cup sugar	1½ teaspoons baking powder
3 eggs	2 teaspoons soda
1½ teaspoons vanilla	¼ teaspoon salt
½ cup light molasses	1⅓ cups dairy sour cream
	Filling (below)

Heat oven to 350°. Grease tube pan, 10x4 inches, or 2 loaf pans, 9x5x3 inches. Combine butter, sugar, eggs, vanilla and molasses in large mixer bowl. Beat on medium speed 2 minutes or 300 vigorous strokes by hand. Mix in flour, baking powder, soda and salt alternately with sour cream.

For tube pan, spread ⅓ of batter (about 2 cups) in pan. Sprinkle with ⅓ of Filling (about 6 tablespoons). Repeat 2 times. For loaf pans, spread ¼ of batter (about 1½ cups) in each pan. Sprinkle each with ¼ of Filling (about 5 tablespoons). Repeat.

Bake 55 to 60 minutes or until wooden pick inserted in center comes out clean. Cool slightly in pan(s) before removing.

14 to 16 servings.

*If using self-rising flour, omit baking powder and salt and decrease soda to 1 teaspoon. Bake about 60 minutes.

FILLING

Mix ½ cup brown sugar (packed), ½ cup finely chopped nuts and 1½ teaspoons cinnamon.

HELP YOURSELF BRUNCHES Just set up a pitcher of juice on crushed ice and a pitcher of pancake or waffle batter beside an electric skillet or a waffle iron. Small bowls of blueberries, chopped cooked ham and the like allow "diner's choice"; simply drop a spoonful on top of the batter as it cooks. Place cold toppings to one side, hot ones on a hot tray along with crispy bacon or sausages. Your coffee maker keeps the coffee hot. A brunch like than can go on into the afternoon. Great for poolside parties!

DANISH PUFF

½ cup butter or margarine, softened
1 cup all-purpose flour*
2 tablespoons water
½ cup butter or margarine
1 cup water

1 teaspoon almond extract
1 cup all-purpose flour*
3 eggs
Confectioners' Sugar Glaze (below)
Chopped nuts

Heat oven to 350°. Cut ½ cup butter into 1 cup flour. Sprinkle 2 tablespoons water over mixture; mix. Round into ball; divide in half. On ungreased baking sheet, pat each half into strip, 12x3 inches. Strips should be about 3 inches apart.

Heat ½ cup butter and 1 cup water to rolling boil in medium saucepan. Remove from heat and quickly stir in almond extract and 1 cup flour. Stir vigorously over low heat until mixture forms a ball, about 1 minute. Remove from heat. Beat in eggs (all at once) until smooth and glossy.

Divide in half; spread each half evenly over strips. Bake about 60 minutes or until topping is crisp and brown. Cool. (Topping will shrink and fall, forming the custardy top of this puff.) Frost with Confectioners' Sugar Glaze and sprinkle generously with nuts.

10 to 12 servings.

*Self-rising flour can be used in this recipe.

CONFECTIONERS' SUGAR GLAZE

Mix 1½ cups confectioners' sugar, 2 tablespoons butter or margarine, softened, 1½ teaspoons vanilla and 1 to 2 tablespoons warm water until smooth and of spreading consistency.

VARIATION

■ *Individual Danish Puffs:* Pat dough into 3-inch circles, using a rounded teaspoonful (1½ teaspoons) for each. Spread rounded tablespoonful (1½ tablespoons) batter over each circle, extending it just beyond edge of circle. Bake 30 minutes. (Topping will shrink and fall slightly when baked.) Cool slightly. Frost puffs with glaze and sprinkle with nuts. 2 dozen.

FAVORITE PANCAKES

Is there a better way to start any day? Plus enough variations to please any taste.

1 egg
1 cup buttermilk
2 tablespoons shortening, melted, or salad oil
1 cup all-purpose flour*

1 tablespoon sugar
1 teaspoon baking powder
½ teaspoon soda
½ teaspoon salt

Beat egg; add remaining ingredients in order listed and beat with rotary beater until smooth. Grease heated griddle if necessary. To test griddle, sprinkle with few drops of water. If bubbles skitter around, heat is just right.

Pour batter from tip of large spoon or from pitcher onto hot griddle. Turn pancakes as soon as they are puffed and full of bubbles but before bubbles break. Bake other side until golden brown.

Ten 4-inch pancakes.

*If using self-rising flour, omit baking powder and salt and decrease soda to ¼ teaspoon.

VARIATIONS

■ *Apple Pancakes:* Decrease buttermilk to ½ cup and stir ½ cup applesauce into batter.

■ *Blueberry Pancakes:* Fold ½ cup fresh or well-drained frozen blueberries (thawed) into batter.

■ *Buckwheat Pancakes:* Decrease flour to ½ cup and add ½ cup buckwheat flour.

■ *Cheese Pancakes:* Omit sugar and stir 1 cup shredded Cheddar cheese into batter.

■ *Cornmeal Pancakes:* Decrease flour to ½ cup and add ½ cup cornmeal.

■ *Ham Pancakes:* Omit sugar and stir ⅓ to ½ cup ground or chopped cooked ham into batter.

■ *Nut Pancakes:* Stir ¼ to ½ cup broken or chopped nuts into batter.

■ *Polka Dot Pancakes:* Omit sugar. Cut 3 or 4 frankfurters into ⅛-inch slices. Group 6 slices together on griddle; pour ¼ cup batter over slices.

■ *Silver Dollar Pancakes:* Pour batter by tablespoonfuls onto hot griddle to form small pancakes (about 2 inches in diameter). Eighteen 2-inch pancakes.

PANCAKE SPECIALS

Make your favorite pancakes, then dress up with one or several toppings. Take your pick!

HAWAIIAN PANCAKES

Top pancakes with Pineapple-Sour Cream Topping, (below). Pour on Pineapple Syrup (below) and sprinkle with chopped macadamia nuts.

Pineapple-Sour Cream Topping: Drain 1 can (8¾ ounces) crushed pineapple, reserving syrup. Stir crushed pineapple (about ½ cup) into 1 cup dairy sour cream. About 1⅓ cups.

Pineapple Syrup: Heat to boiling reserved pineapple syrup (about ½ cup) and ¼ cup maple-flavored syrup. About ¾ cup.

PIGS 'N BLANKET

Spread pancakes with soft butter or margarine. Top each with cooked pork sausage link and pour on maple syrup.

CHERRY-TOPPED PANCAKES

Spread dairy sour cream over pancakes. Spoon cherry pie filling over cream.

WOODSMAN'S SPECIAL

Spread pancakes with Orange Butter (below). Drain 1 can (14 ounces) blueberries, reserving liquid. Top pancakes with blueberries and Blueberry Syrup (below).

Orange Butter: Beat 1 cup soft butter or margarine and 2 teaspoons grated orange peel until fluffy.

Blueberry Syrup: Heat to boiling reserved blueberry liquid and ½ cup maple-flavored syrup. About 1¼ cups.

DENVER PANCAKES

Spread pancakes with Mustard Butter (below). Fill each 2 pancakes with Denver Filling (below). Pour maple syrup over pancake sandwiches.

Mustard Butter: Beat 1 cup soft butter or margarine and 2 tablespoons prepared mustard.

Denver Filling: Cook and stir ½ cup minced onion and ½ cup minced green pepper in 2 tablespoons butter or margarine until onion is tender. Stir in 1 cup diced cooked ham; heat through. Serve warm. About 1½ cups.

WAFFLES

POPULAR WAFFLES

2 eggs
2 cups buttermilk
2 cups all-purpose flour*
2 teaspoons baking powder

1 teaspoon soda
½ teaspoon salt
¼ cup plus 2 tablespoons shortening

RICHER WAFFLES

3 eggs
1½ cups buttermilk
1¾ cups all-purpose flour*
2 teaspoons baking powder

1 teaspoon soda
½ teaspoon salt
½ cup shortening

Heat waffle iron. Beat eggs; beat in remaining ingredients with rotary beater until smooth.

Pour batter from cup or pitcher onto center of hot waffle iron. Bake about 5 minutes or until steaming stops. Remove waffle carefully.

About eight 7-inch waffles.

If using self-rising flour, omit baking powder and salt.

Note: To substitute milk for buttermilk, separate eggs, beating egg whites until stiff; increase baking powder to 4 teaspoons; omit soda and fold egg whites into batter.

VARIATIONS

■ *Blueberry Waffles:* Sprinkle 2 tablespoons blueberries over batter for each waffle as soon as it has been poured onto iron.

■ *Cheese and Bacon Waffles:* Follow recipe for Popular Waffles except—stir 1 cup shredded Cheddar cheese into batter. After pouring batter onto iron, place 4 short strips of lightly browned bacon on batter for each waffle.

■ *Nut Waffles:* Sprinkle 2 tablespoons coarsely chopped nuts over batter for each waffle as soon as it has been poured onto iron.

■ *Western Waffles:* Slice 1 quart strawberries or use 2 packages (16 ounces each) frozen sliced strawberries, thawed and drained. In chilled bowl, beat 1 cup chilled whipping cream and 2 tablespoons confectioners' sugar until stiff. Top baked waffles with strawberries and whipped cream.

RAISED WAFFLES

1 package active dry yeast
¼ cup warm water (105 to 115°)
1¾ cups lukewarm milk (scalded then cooled)
2 tablespoons sugar
1 teaspoon salt
3 eggs
¼ cup butter or margarine, softened
2 cups all-purpose flour*

In large mixer bowl, dissolve yeast in warm water. Add remaining ingredients; beat until smooth. Cover; let rise in warm place 1½ hours. Stir down batter. Cover again; refrigerate 8 to 12 hours.

Stir down batter. Pour from cup or pitcher onto center of hot waffle iron. Bake about 5 minutes or until steaming stops. Remove waffle carefully.

About eight 7-inch waffles.

*If using self-rising flour, omit salt.

VARIATIONS

■ *Raised Pancakes:* Pour batter from ¼-cup measuring cup or from tip of large spoon onto hot griddle. (Grease griddle lightly if necessary.) Turn pancakes as soon as they are puffed and full of bubbles—but before bubbles break. Bake other side until golden brown.

■ *Mock Belgian Waffles:* Break waffles into sections. In chilled bowl, beat 1 cup chilled whipping cream and 2 tablespoons confectioners' sugar until stiff; fold in

1 cup sliced fresh strawberries or 1 package (16 ounces) frozen sliced strawberries, thawed and well drained.

Put waffle sections together in pairs with strawberry-whipped cream mixture. Sprinkle confectioners' sugar over each waffle sandwich.

■ *Pecan Waffles:* For each waffle, sprinkle ¼ cup chopped pecans on heated waffle grids. Close iron; heat about 3 minutes or until nuts are golden brown. Pour batter over nuts and bake as directed above. Serve waffles with maple syrup and Honey Butter: Whip ½ cup soft butter and ½ cup honey until fluffy.

FAVORITE DOUGHNUTS

Tender and light—a favorite with everyone. And don't forget to fry the "holes" as a special treat for the children.

3⅓ cups all-purpose flour*	¼ teaspoon nutmeg
1 cup sugar	2 tablespoons shortening
3 teaspoons baking powder	2 eggs
½ teaspoon salt	¾ cup milk
½ teaspoon cinnamon	

*If using self-rising flour, omit baking powder and salt.

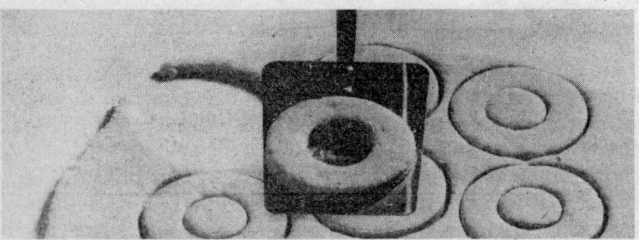

To keep shape, lift with wide spatula.

Do not prick when removing from fat.

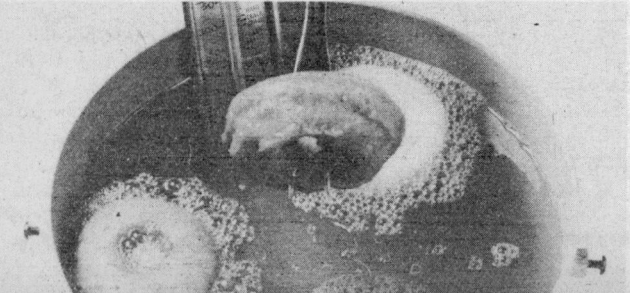

Heat fat or oil (3 to 4 inches) to 375° in deep fat fryer or kettle. Measure 1½ cups flour and the remaining ingredients into large mixer bowl. Blend ½ minute on low speed, scraping bowl constantly. Beat 2 minutes medium speed, scraping bowl occasionally. Stir in remaining flour.

Turn dough onto well-floured cloth-covered board; roll around lightly to coat with flour. Roll dough gently ⅜ inch thick. Cut with floured doughnut cutter.

With wide spatula, slide doughnuts into hot fat. Turn doughnuts as they rise to surface. Fry 2 to 3 minutes or until golden brown on both sides. Carefully remove from fat; do not prick the surface. Drain. Serve plain, sugared or frosted.

2 dozen doughnuts.

VARIATION

■ *Buttermilk Doughnuts:* Decrease baking powder to 2 teaspoons, add 1 teaspoon soda and substitute buttermilk for the milk. (Do not use self-rising flour.)

RAISED DOUGHNUTS

1 package active dry yeast	1 teaspoon salt
¼ cup warm water (105 to 115°)	1 egg
	¼ cup shortening
¾ cup lukewarm milk (scalded then cooled)	3½ to 3¾ cups all-purpose flour*
¼ cup sugar	

Dissolve yeast in warm water. Stir in milk, ¼ cup sugar, the salt, egg, shortening and 2 cups of the flour. Beat until smooth. Mix in enough remaining flour to make dough easy to handle.

Turn dough onto lightly floured cloth-covered board; knead until smooth and elastic, about 5 minutes. Place in greased bowl; turn greased side up. Cover; let rise in warm place until double, about 1½ hours.

Punch down dough; let rise again until almost double, about 30 minutes.

Roll dough ⅜ inch thick on lightly floured cloth-covered board. Cut dough with floured doughnut cutter. Let rise on board until double and very light, 30 to 45

*If using self-rising flour, omit salt.

minutes (leave uncovered so crust will form on dough).

Heat fat or oil (3 to 4 inches) to 375° in deep fat fryer or kettle. Drop doughnuts into hot fat. Turn doughnuts as they rise to surface. Fry 2 to 3 minutes or until golden brown on both sides.

Carefully remove from fat; do not prick the surface. Drain. While warm, roll doughnuts in sugar or, if desired, frost or glaze.

2 dozen doughnuts.

DRESSED-UP DOUGHNUTS

To sugar: Roll warm Raised Doughnuts in granulated sugar. Shake Favorite Doughnuts one at a time in a bag with a little confectioners' sugar.

To glaze: Blend ⅓ cup boiling water into 1 cup confectioners' sugar. Dip warm doughnuts into warm glaze.

To garnish: Sprinkle glazed doughnuts with chopped nuts, colored sugar or confetti candies.

CUSTARDY FRENCH TOAST

4 slices white bread	¼ teaspoon salt
3 eggs	2 tablespoons butter or
¾ cup milk	margarine
1 tablespoon sugar	

Arrange bread in baking dish, 13½x9x2 inches. Beat eggs, milk, sugar and salt until fluffy. Pour over bread; turn each slice to coat well. Cover; refrigerate overnight. (If desired, bread can be dipped into egg mixture and cooked immediately. And you'll find the egg mixture will cover more bread slices.)

Heat butter in skillet. Carefully transfer each bread slice to skillet. (Use a pancake turner to avoid tearing the saturated bread.) Cook over medium heat 4 minutes on each side or until golden brown.

4 slices.

VARIATION

■ *Oven French Toast:* Heat oven to 500°. Arrange dipped bread on greased baking sheet. Bake about 8 minutes on each side or until golden brown.

FLUFFY FRENCH TOAST

Thick French bread slices are transformed into a company brunch treat. Serve with butter and offer a choice of syrup, jam or confectioners' sugar.

½ cup all-purpose flour*	18 slices day-old French
1½ tablespoons sugar	bread, 1 inch thick
¼ teaspoon salt	1 tablespoon butter or
2 cups milk	margarine
6 eggs	

Beat flour, sugar, salt, milk and eggs with rotary beater until smooth. Soak bread in batter until saturated.

Heat butter in skillet. Carefully transfer each bread slice to skillet; do not overcrowd. Cook bread over medium heat 12 minutes on each side or until golden brown.

18 slices.

*If using self-rising flour, omit salt.

Bakery Breads

Bakery bread—but very personally yours! You serve it warm. You add interesting flavors to the butter. You turn French bread into cheese bread. Just because you're you. Tuck away these ideas for the next time you need them!

HOT BREADS IN FOIL

Heat oven to 400°. Cut 1 loaf (1 pound) French bread into 1-inch slices, cut Vienna, rye or pumpernickel bread into ½-inch slices or split 8 large individual club rolls in half horizontally. Spread generously with ½ cup soft butter or margarine or one of the Butter Spreads (page 86).

Reassemble loaf or rolls; wrap securely in 28x18-inch piece of heavy-duty aluminum foil. Heat loaf 15-20 minutes, rolls 10 to 12 minutes.

BUTTER SPREADS

Cream ½ cup soft butter or margarine with one of the following—

Garlic: 1 medium clove garlic, minced.

Herb-Cheese: 2 teaspoons snipped parsley, ½ teaspoon oregano leaves, 2 tablespoons grated Parmesan cheese and ⅛ teaspoon garlic salt.

Onion: 2 tablespoons minced onion or snipped chives.

Seeded: 1 to 2 teaspoons celery, poppy, dill or sesame seed.

Tarragon: 1 teaspoon tarragon leaves and ¼ teaspoon paprika.

BLUE CHEESE FRENCH BREAD

1 loaf (1 pound) French bread
½ cup soft butter or margarine
¼ cup crumbled blue cheese
2 tablespoons grated Parmesan cheese

Heat oven to 350°. Cut loaf diagonally into 1-inch slices. Mix thoroughly butter and blue cheese; spread part of butter mixture on slices.

Reassemble loaf; spread top of loaf with remaining butter mixture and sprinkle with Parmesan cheese. Wrap loaf securely in 28x18-inch piece of heavy-duty aluminum foil. Heat 20 minutes.

About 24 slices.

HICKORY FRENCH BREAD

1 loaf (1 pound) French bread
½ cup soft butter or margarine
1 cup shredded natural sharp Cheddar cheese (about 4 ounces)
1 tablespoon snipped parsley
½ teaspoon hickory-smoked salt
2 teaspoons Worcestershire sauce

Heat oven to 350°. Cut loaf diagonally into 1-inch slices. Mix remaining ingredients; spread on slices. Reassemble loaf; wrap securely in 28x18-inch piece of heavy-duty aluminum foil. Heat 20 minutes.

About 24 slices.

HOT CHILI FRENCH BREAD

1 loaf (1 pound) French
  bread
½ cup soft butter or
  margarine
1 cup shredded natural
  sharp Cheddar cheese
  (about 4 ounces)

1 to 2 teaspoons chopped
  hot chili peppers
1 teaspoon Worcestershire
  sauce

Heat oven to 350°. Cut loaf diagonally into 1-inch slices. Mix remaining ingredients; spread on slices. Reassemble loaf; wrap securely in 28x18-inch piece of heavy-duty aluminum foil. Heat 20 minutes.

About 24 slices.

TOAST CUPS

For your favorite creamed dishes.

Heat oven to 375°. Trim crusts from thinly sliced fresh bread; spread with soft butter or margarine. Press buttered side down into muffin cups. Bake 12 minutes or until lightly toasted.

VARIATION

■ *Poppy Seed Cups:* Sprinkle buttered side of bread with poppy seed before pressing into cups.

TOASTED PARTY RYE

Heat oven to 325°. Spread slices of snack rye bread with soft butter or margarine; place on ungreased baking sheet. Heat 10 to 12 minutes or until crusty.

HOT CURRIED RAISIN BREAD

Pair with barbecued chicken for an unusual duo.

⅓ cup crunchy peanut butter
¼ cup mayonnaise
¾ teaspoon curry powder

1 loaf (1 pound) sliced
  raisin bread

Heat oven to 350°. Mix peanut butter, mayonnaise and curry powder; spread mixture on one side of each slice of bread.

Reassemble loaf with spread sides together; wrap securely in 18x15-inch piece of heavy-duty aluminum foil. Heat 15 to 20 minutes.

About 8 servings.

CHEESE BRIOCHES

Heat oven to 350°. Thaw 1 package (8 ounces) frozen brioches. Cut around topknot of each brioche and remove. Place about 1 teaspoon of your favorite pasteurized process cheese spread in each brioche; replace topknot. Return brioches to foil package; heat uncovered 10 minutes.

6 brioches.

CHEESE AND DILL ROLLS

Heat oven to 350°. Mix thoroughly 1 teaspoon dill weed and 2 packages (3 ounces each) cream cheese, softened. Spread cheese mixture in breaks of 12 butterfly rolls or in Parker House rolls. Wrap rolls securely in single thickness heavy-duty aluminum foil. Heat 10 to 15 minutes.

12 rolls.

MUSTARD SLICES

1 package (10 ounces) brown and serve French bread
¼ cup soft butter or margarine
2 tablespoons snipped parsley
1 tablespoon prepared mustard
1 teaspoon instant minced onion
1 teaspoon lemon juice

Heat oven to 400°. Cut bread diagonally into 1-inch slices. Mix remaining ingredients; spread on slices. Reassemble loaf; place on ungreased baking sheet. Bake about 15 minutes.

About 24 slices.

SEASONED BROWN AND SERVE ROLLS

Heat oven to 450°. Cut 12 brown and serve rolls in half horizontally. Place bottom halves on ungreased baking sheet. Melt ¼ cup butter or margarine; blend in 1 tablespoon of your favorite salad dressing mix. Brush butter mixture over bottom halves. Replace top halves and brush butter mixture over tops. Bake 8 to 10 minutes.

12 rolls.

JUMBO BREAD STICKS

Heat oven to 375°. In baking pan, 13x9x2 inches, melt ½ cup butter or margarine in oven. Remove from oven as soon as butter is melted.

Cut two 1¼-inch slices from a 1-pound unsliced loaf of white bread (do not remove crust). Cut each slice crosswise into six 1-inch strips. Roll each stick in melted butter until coated on all sides. Arrange sticks in pan; sprinkle garlic salt, grated Parmesan cheese, sesame or poppy seed over top.

Toast in oven 20 to 25 minutes, turning sticks to brown on all sides. Serve hot.

12 sticks.

SPICY ENGLISH MUFFINS

Sensational with a seafood or chicken salad.

½ cup soft butter or margarine	½ teaspoon onion salt
1 teaspoon chili powder	4 large English muffins, split

Mix thoroughly butter and seasonings; spread on cut surfaces of muffins. Place muffins buttered side up on rack in broiler pan. Broil 3 inches from heat 2 to 3 minutes or until golden brown.

8 halves.

Yeast Breads

Does anything in the world ever smell quite so
good as a just-baked loaf of bread? Does
anything make you feel so pleased with yourself
as baking bread? Why not try it? For here they
all are—white bread, brown bread, in-between
bread. Hot rolls. Cinnamon buns. Coffee cakes.
Doughs you knead, doughs that don't need it.
This is a chapter to work your way through—
you'll never forget it, never regret it.

About the Ingredients

On the following pages you'll find white bread, wheat
bread, rye and others. Hot rolls, sweet rolls, cinnamon
buns, coffee cakes. They all begin with the same basic
ingredients. And if bread baking is a new art to you, it
will help to understand just what these ingredients are
and what each one does.

Yeast is made up of thousands of tiny living plants
which, when given moisture, warmth and "food," will
grow and give off a gas (carbon dioxide); it is that gas
that makes dough rise. Yeast is available in active dry
and in compressed forms. One package or 1 scant tablespoon of dry yeast is equivalent to 1 cake (⅗ ounce) of
compressed. Our recipes call for active dry yeast. No-
dissolve and instant blend yeasts can be used according
to manufacturers' general directions (blending undis-
solved yeast with flour) or can be used in the traditional
way (dissolving yeast in warm water). Our recipes follow
the traditional methods.

Flour, the all-purpose type, contains gluten, which
builds the structure in bread and traps gas formed by
the yeast. Special flavor flours (rye, oatmeal) do not
have enough gluten themselves so are used in combination with all-purpose flour.

Liquids used are usually water or milk. Breads made

with water will have a harder crust; those made with milk, a softer one. Milk adds to the nutritive value of breads.

Sugar provides food for the yeast, helping it grow. It adds flavor and helps the crust brown.

Salt controls the growth of the yeast and also adds flavor.

Fats make bread tender and soft; they, too, add flavor.

Eggs, used in some recipes, tenderize and add richness to bread; they are important for color, food value and flavor.

Tips for Yeast Breads

Take a look at pages 92–94. You'll find some helpful tips to keep in mind when working with yeast breads. And here are some others:

■ When making rolls, add the second addition of flour slowly. Add just enough so that the dough can be handled without sticking. The dough for rolls should be softer than that for plain breads.

■ Store baked yeast breads in airtight containers or wrap in plastic bags or aluminum foil and store in a cool dry place.

■ To freeze yeast breads, cool to room temperature after baking. (We do not recommend that you freeze the dough.) Do not frost. Wrap in moisture-proof paper. Breads properly cooled and wrapped will keep from 9 to 12 months. To thaw frozen breads, let stand at room temperature 2 to 3 hours or wrap with aluminum foil and heat in a 350° oven for 20 to 25 minutes.

Loaves

So you're going to bake bread! High time you tried! And you don't have to save a whole day for it. You can do it in a morning—or in an afternoon—or even in an evening—and catch up on ironing or bill-paying or watch TV in the bargain. It isn't half as hard as you thought it might be. There are new, improved ingredients and new streamlined techniques that make bread-baking easier than it was for your grandmother. But there are a few things the first-time baker should know:

TIPS FOR YEAST BREADS

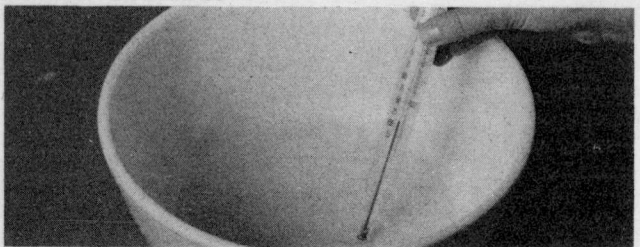

1. Water used to dissolve granular yeast should be 105 to 115°. Use a thermometer or test a drop on inside of wrist (water should feel very warm but not hot).

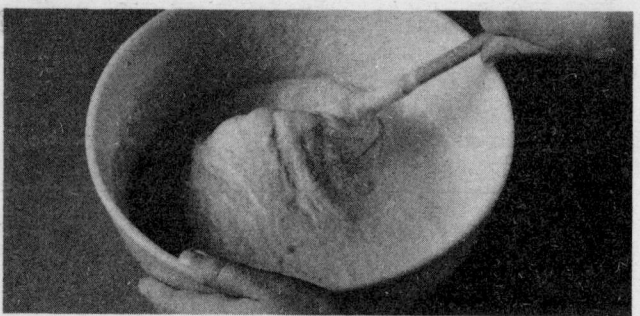

2. After the first addition of flour, beat ingredients with electric mixer or wooden spoon. Batter breads require especially vigorous beating.

3. To knead, fold dough toward you and then push away with heel of hand in a rocking motion; rotate dough a quarter turn. Repeat until dough is smooth and blistered.

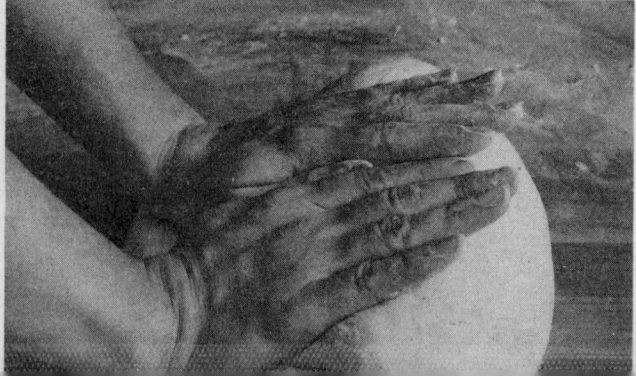

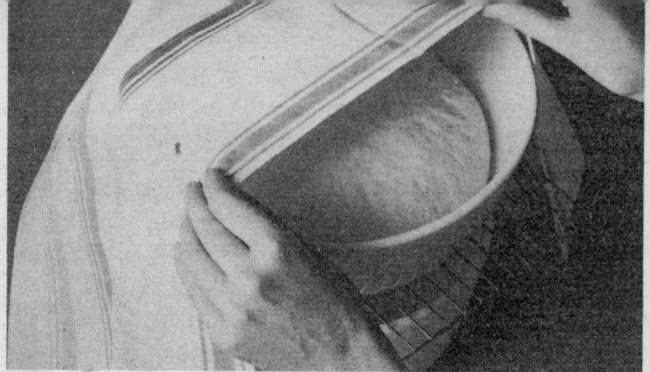

4. To let dough rise, cover and keep in a warm, draft-free place. If necessary, place bowl of dough on a wire rack over a bowl of warm water.

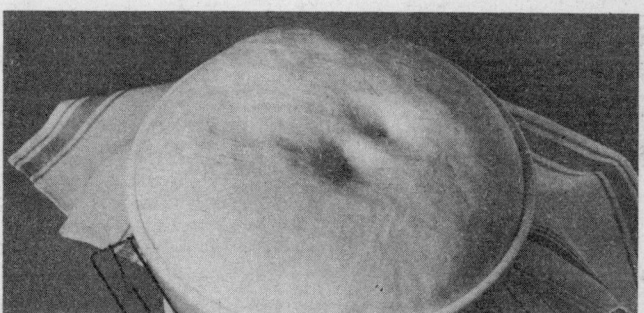

5. To test for doubled bulk, stick fingertips ½ inch into dough; impressions will remain if dough has doubled.

6. To punch down dough, plunge fist into center of dough. (Batter breads are stirred down).

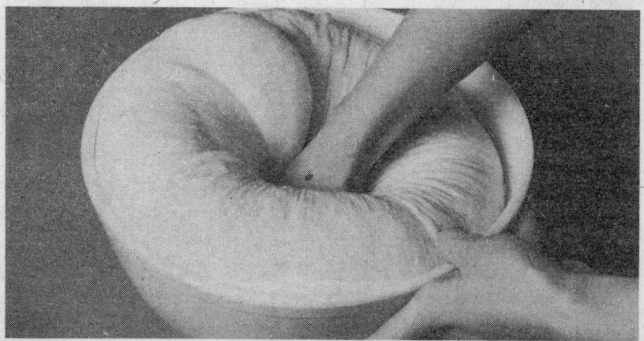

TIPS FOR REGULAR LOAVES

TIPS FOR ROUND LOAVES

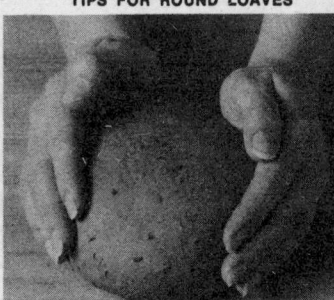

1. Roll dough into rectangle, 18x9 inches. Roll up from short side.

1. Shape and round the dough into slightly flattened ball. Do not "tear" the dough by pulling.

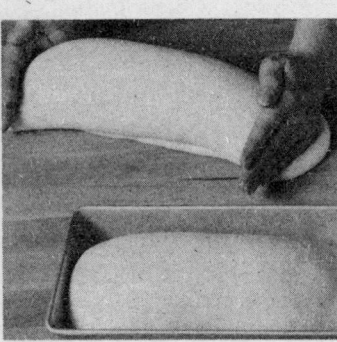

2. Press ends to seal; fold ends under. Place seam side down in greased pan.

2. Place rounds on opposite corners of baking sheet. Place sheet on center rack in oven.

3. Bake loaf with the top of pan in the middle of the oven.

3. To test for doneness, tap top crust. It should have a hollow sound. Regular loaves are tested the same way.

■ Use loaf plans of the size specified in the recipe. The pans should have anodized aluminum or darkened metal exteriors to help absorb heat and give loaves a good brown crust. (A non-stick coating on the inside will not change the baking characteristics of the pan.) A shiny metal pan can be darkened by heating it about 5 hours in a 350° oven.

■ When baking, stagger the loaf pans on the bottom shelf of the oven so that they do not touch either the sides of the oven or each other. The top of each pan should be level with, or slightly above, the middle of the oven. If baking round loaves on a baking sheet, place the sheet on the center rack of the oven.

■ To test loaf for doneness, tap the crust. It will have a hollow sound when done.

■ To cool bread, remove loaves from pans *immediately* and place on wire racks away from draft. If you like a soft crust, brush the loaf with shortening and cover with a towel for a few minutes.

■ For freezing information, see page 741.

WHITE BREAD

2 packages active dry yeast	1 tablespoon salt
¾ cup warm water (105 to 115°)	3 tablespoons shortening
2⅔ cups warm water	9 to 10 cups all-purpose flour*
¼ cup sugar	Soft butter or margarine

Dissolve yeast in ¾ cup warm water. Stir in 2⅔ cups warm water, the sugar, salt, shortening and 5 cups of the flour. Beat until smooth. Mix in enough remaining flour to make dough easy to handle.

Turn dough onto lightly floured board; knead until smooth and elastic, about 10 minutes. Place in greased bowl; turn greased side up. Cover; let rise in warm place until double, about 1 hour. (Dough is ready if impression remains.)

Punch down dough; divide in half. Roll each half into rectangle, 18x9 inches. Roll up, beginning at short side. With side of hand, press each end to seal. Fold ends under loaf. Place seam side down in greased loaf pan,

*If using self-rising flour, omit salt.

9x5x3 inches. Brush loaves lightly with butter. Let rise until double, about 1 hour.

Heat oven to 425°. Place loaves on low rack so that tops of pans are in center of oven. Pans should not touch each other or sides of oven. Bake 30 to 35 minutes or until deep golden brown and loaves sound hollow when tapped. Remove from pans. Brush loaves with soft butter; cool on wire rack.

2 loaves.

Note: Three loaf pans, 8½x4½x2½ inches, can be used. Divide dough into 3 equal parts after punching it down.

VARIATION

■ *Cinnamon-Raisin Bread:* Stir in 1 cup raisins with the remaining flour. After rolling dough into rectangles, sprinkle each with 1 teaspoon water and mixture of ¼ cup sugar and 2 teaspoons cinnamon.

CRUSTY WHITE BREAD

A less-rich bread made with water and oil.

2 packages active dry yeast	1 tablespoon salt
2 cups warm water (105 to 115°)	¼ cup salad oil
2 tablespoons sugar	6 to 6½ cups all-purpose flour*

Dissolve yeast in warm water. Stir in sugar, salt, oil and 3 cups of the flour. Beat until smooth. Mix in enough remaining flour to make dough easy to handle.

Turn dough onto lightly floured board; knead until smooth and elastic, 8 to 10 minutes. Place in greased bowl; brush top with salad oil. Cover; let rise in warm place until double, about 45 minutes. (Dough is ready if impression remains.)

Punch down dough; divide in half. Roll each half into rectangle, 18x9 inches. Roll up, beginning at short side. With side of hand, press each end to seal. Fold ends under loaf. Place seam side down in greased loaf pan, 9x5x3 inches. Brush loaves with salad oil. Let rise until double, about 1 hour.

*If using self-rising flour, omit salt.

Heat oven to 400°. Bake about 35 minutes or until loaves sound hollow when tapped.

2 loaves.

VARIATION

■ *Braids:* Divide dough into fourths. Divide each fourth into 3 equal parts. Shape each part into strand, about 10 inches long. Braid each group of 3 strands on greased baking sheet, topping strands before and after braiding with ¼ of any of the following:

■ Combine 2 tablespoons poppy seed and 2 tablespoons honey.

■ Sprinkle with 1 tablespoon caraway seed and ½ cup shredded Cheddar cheese.

■ Sprinkle with ⅓ cup tiny cubes Swiss cheese and paprika.

■ Combine 1 tablespoon garlic cheese, French or Parmesan salad dressing mix (dry) and 1 tablespoon salad oil.

Let braids rise 30 minutes or until double. Bake in 375° oven 30 minutes or until done. 4 braids.

QUICK BUTTERMILK BREAD

2 packages active dry yeast	¼ cup shortening
¾ cup warm water (105 to 115°)	2 tablespoons sugar
1¼ cups buttermilk	2 teaspoons baking powder
4½ to 5 cups all-purpose flour*	2 teaspoons salt
	Soft butter or margarine

Grease loaf pan, 9x5x3 inches.** In large mixer bowl, dissolve yeast in yarm water. Add buttermilk, 2½ cups of the flour, the shortening, sugar, baking powder and salt. Blend ½ minute on low speed, scraping bowl constantly. Beat 2 minutes medium speed, scraping bowl occasionally. Stir in remaining flour. (Dough should remain soft and slightly sticky.)

Turn dough onto well-floured board; knead 5 minutes or about 200 turns. Roll dough into rectangle, 18x9 inches. Roll up, beginning at short side. With side of

*If using self-rising flour, omit baking powder and salt.
**Two 8½x4½x2½-inch pans can be used. Divide dough in half after kneading.

hand, press each end to seal. Fold ends under loaf. Place seam side down in pan. Brush loaf lightly with butter. Let rise in warm place until double, about 1 hour. (Dough in center should be about 2 inches above pan.)

Heat oven to 425°. Oven rack should be in lowest position or bread will brown too quickly. Bake 30 to 35 minutes. Remove from pan. Brush loaf with butter; cool on wire rack.

Note: To prepare 2 large loaves, double all ingredients except yeast. Blend 1 minute on low speed, scraping bowl constantly. Beat 4 minutes medium speed, scraping bowl occasionally. Stir in remaining flour. Divide dough in half; knead each half 5 minutes.

VARIATIONS

■ *Cheese Bread:* Omit shortening; stir in 1 cup shredded sharp natural Cheddar cheese (about 4 ounces) with the second addition of flour.

■ *Cornmeal Bread:* Increase salt to 2½ teaspoons and substitute 1½ cups all-purpose flour and ¾ cup yellow cornmeal for the second addition of flour. Sprinkle additional cornmeal over loaf before baking.

■ *Garlic Bread:* Add ¾ teaspoon garlic powder to yeast-water mixture.

■ *Herb Bread:* Add 2 teaspoons caraway seed, ½ teaspoon sage and ½ teaspoon nutmeg to yeast-water mixture.

Beat yeast mixture at medium speed exactly 2 minutes.

Let dough rise until it is 2 inches above the top of pan.

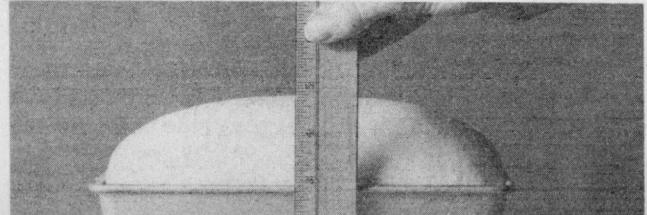

■ *Oatmeal Bread:* Substitute 1½ cups all-purpose flour and 1½ cups quick-cooking oats for the second addition of flour.

■ *Whole Wheat Bread:* Substitute 1½ cups all-purpose flour and 1 cup whole wheat flour for the first addition of flour; substitute 2 cups whole wheat flour for the second addition of flour.

RICH EGG BREAD

2 packages active dry yeast	1 tablespoon salt
½ cup warm water (105 to 115°)	3 eggs
1½ cups lukewarm milk (scalded then cooled)	¼ cup shortening or butter or margarine, softened
¼ cup sugar	7¼ to 7½ cups all-purpose flour*

Dissolve yeast in warm water. Stir in milk, sugar, salt, eggs, shortening and 4 cups of the flour. Beat until smooth. Mix in enough remaining flour to make dough easy to handle.

Turn dough onto lightly floured board; knead until smooth and elastic, about 5 minutes. Place in greased bowl; turn greased side up. Cover; let rise in warm place until double, 1½ to 2 hours.

Punch down dough; divide in half. Roll each half into rectangle, 18x9 inches. Roll up, beginning at short side. With side of hand, press each end to seal. Fold ends under loaf. Place seam side down in greased loaf pan, 9x5x3 or 8½x4½x2½ inches. Cover; let rise until double, about 1 hour.

Heat oven to 425°. Bake 25 to 30 minutes.

2 loaves.

*If using self-rising flour, omit salt.

STREAMLINED BATTER BREAD

1 package active dry yeast	2 teaspoons salt
1¼ cups warm water (105 to 115°)	2⅔ cups all-purpose flour* Melted butter, margarine or shortening
2 tablespoons shortening	
2 tablespoons sugar	

In large mixer bowl, dissolve yeast in warm water. Add shortening, sugar, salt and 2 cups of the flour. Blend

*If using self-rising flour, omit salt.

½ minute on low speed, scraping bowl constantly. Beat 2 minutes medium speed, scraping bowl occasionally. (By hand, beat 300 vigorous strokes.) Stir in remaining flour until smooth. Scrape batter from side of bowl. Cover; let rise in warm place until double, about 30 minutes.

Stir down batter by beating about 25 strokes. Spread evenly in greased loaf pan, 9x5x3 inches. Smooth out top of batter by patting into shape with floured hand. Cover; let rise until double, about 40 minutes.

Heat oven to 375°. Bake 45 minutes or until loaf sounds hollow when tapped. Brush top with melted butter. Remove loaf from pan; cool on wire rack.

VARIATIONS

■ *Cheese-Caraway Batter Bread:* Add 1 cup shredded sharp Cheddar cheese (about 4 ounces) and 1 teaspoon caraway seed to yeast-water mixture.

■ *Garlic Batter Bread:* Add ½ teaspoon garlic powder to yeast-water mixture.

■ *Herb Batter Bread:* Add 1 teaspoon caraway seed, ½ teaspoon nutmeg and ½ teaspoon sage to yeast-water mixture.

■ *Onion Batter Bread:* Add 2 to 3 tablespoons instant minced onion to yeast-water mixture.

■ *Poppy Seed Batter Bread:* Add 2 tablespoons poppy seed to yeast-water mixture. After smoothing out top of loaf, sprinkle 1 tablespoon poppy seed over top.

PUMPERNICKEL BREAD

3 packages active dry yeast	2 tablespoons caraway seed
1½ cups warm water (105 to 115°)	2¾ cups rye flour
½ cup molasses	2¾ to 3¼ cups all-purpose flour*
4 teaspoons salt	Cornmeal
2 tablespoons shortening	

Dissolve yeast in warm water. Stir in molasses, salt, shortening, caraway seed and rye flour. Beat until smooth. Mix in enough white flour to make dough easy to handle.

*If using self-rising flour, omit salt.

Turn dough onto lightly floured board. Cover; let rest 10 to 15 minutes. Knead until smooth, about 5 minutes. Place in greased bowl; turn greased side up. Cover; let rise in warm place until double, about 1 hour. Punch down dough; round up, cover and let rise again until double, about 40 minutes.

Grease baking sheet; sprinkle with cornmeal. Punch down dough; divide in half. Shape each half into round, slightly flat loaf. Place loaves in opposite corners of baking sheet. Cover; let rise 1 hour.

Heat oven to 375°. Bake 30 to 35 minutes.

2 loaves.

SWEDISH LIMPA RYE BREAD

2 packages active dry yeast	Grated peel of 1 to 2 oranges
1½ cups warm water (105 to 115°)	2½ cups medium rye flour
¼ cup molasses	2¼ to 2¾ cups all-purpose flour*
⅓ cup sugar	Cornmeal
1 tablespoon salt	
2 tablespoons shortening	

Dissolve yeast in warm water. Stir in molasses, sugar, salt, shortening, orange peel and rye flour. Beat until smooth. Mix in enough white flour to make dough easy to handle.

Turn dough onto lightly floured board. Cover; let rest 10 to 15 minutes. Knead until smooth, about 5 minutes. Place in greased bowl; turn greased side up. Cover; let rise in warm place until double, about 1 hour. Punch down dough; round up, cover and let rise until double, about 40 minutes.

Grease baking sheet; sprinkle with cornmeal. Punch down dough; divide in half. Shape each half into round, slightly flat loaf. Place loaves in opposite corners of baking sheet. Cover; let rise 1 hour.

Heat oven to 375°. Bake 30 to 35 minutes.

2 loaves.

*If using self-rising flour, omit salt.

Dinner Rolls

Want to make your dinner rolls something extra-special? You can do it with Butter Curls. It's so easy! Let butter curler stand in hot water for at least 10 minutes. Pull curler firmly across surface of ¼-pound bar of firm butter. (Butter should not be too cold or curls will break.) Drop curls into iced water; cover and refrigerate. Dip curler into hot water before you make each curl. You can teach this trick to the children—tell them about Butter Balls, page 107, too.

BROWN 'N SERVE ROLLS

Fresh homebaked have-on-hand rolls for any occasion. Dough can be formed into other shapes, too.

1 package active dry yeast	¼ cup sugar
¾ cup warm water (105 to 115°)	2¼ teaspoons salt
	¼ cup shortening
¾ cup lukewarm milk (scalded then cooled)	4½ cups all-purpose flour*

Dissolve yeast in warm water. Stir in milk, sugar, salt, shortening and 2½ cups of the flour. Beat until smooth. Mix in remaining flour to form soft dough.

Turn dough onto lightly floured board; knead until smooth and elastic, about 5 minutes. Place in greased bowl; turn greased side up. Cover; let rise in warm place until double, about 1½ hours.

Punch down dough; turn onto lightly floured board and divide into 24 equal pieces. Shape each piece into smooth ball. Place in greased muffin cups or about 3 inches apart on greased baking sheet. Cover; let rise until almost double, about 45 minutes.

Heat oven to 275°. Bake 20 to 30 minutes (do not allow rolls to brown). Remove from pans and cool at room temperature.

Place rolls in plastic bags or wrap in plastic wrap or aluminum foil. Store in refrigerator several days or freeze. At serving time, brown rolls in 400° oven 7 to 10 minutes.

2 dozen rolls.

*If using self-rising flour, omit salt.

GOLDEN CRESCENTS

2 packages active dry yeast
¾ cup warm water (105 to 115°)
½ cup sugar
1 teaspoon salt

2 eggs
½ cup shortening (part soft butter)
4 cups all-purpose flour*
Soft butter or margarine

Dissolve yeast in warm water. Stir in sugar, salt, eggs, shortening and 2 cups of the flour. Beat until smooth. Mix in remaining flour until smooth. Scrape dough from side of bowl. Cover; let rise in warm place until double, about 1½ hours.

Divide dough in half; roll each half into 12-inch circle. Spread with butter; cut into 16 wedges. Roll up each wedge, beginning at rounded edge. Place rolls, with point under, on greased baking sheet. Cover; let rise until double, about 1 hour.

Heat oven to 400°. Bake 12 to 15 minutes or until golden brown. Brush rolls with butter.

32 rolls.

*If using self-rising flour, omit salt.

CARAWAY PUFFS

2 packages active dry yeast
½ cup warm water (105 to 115°)
2 tablespoons caraway seed
2 cups creamed cottage cheese

¼ cup sugar
2 teaspoons salt
½ teaspoon soda
2 eggs, slightly beaten
4⅓ cups all-purpose flour*
Soft butter or margarine

Dissolve yeast in warm water. Add caraway seed. Heat cheese just until lukewarm. Mix cheese, sugar, salt, soda and eggs into yeast mixture. Slowly add flour, mixing until dough cleans bowl.

Let rise in warm place until double, about 1 hour. Stir down dough. Divide among 24 well-greased medium muffin cups. Cover and let rise again until double, about 45 minutes.

Heat oven to 350°. Bake about 25 minutes. Remove from cups; brush with butter.

2 dozen puffs.

*If using self-rising flour, omit salt and soda.

TRADITIONAL ROLL DOUGH

1 package active dry yeast	1 teaspoon salt
¼ cup warm water (105 to 115°)	1 egg
¾ cup lukewarm milk (scalded then cooled)	¼ cup shortening or butter or margarine, softened
¼ cup sugar	3½ to 3¾ cups all-purpose flour*

Dissolve yeast in warm water. Stir in milk, sugar, salt, egg, shortening and 2 cups of the flour. Beat until smooth. Mix in enough remaining flour to make dough easy to handle.

Turn dough onto lightly floured board; knead until smooth and elastic, about 5 minutes. Place in greased bowl; turn greased side up. Cover; let rise in warm place until double, about 1½ to 2 hours. (Dough is ready if impression remains.)

Punch down dough; divide in half. Use half the dough in each of the Variations. Let rise 20 minutes before baking. Heat oven to 400°. Bake rolls 15 to 20 minutes.

*If using self-rising flour, omit salt.

QUICK SOUR CREAM DOUGH

2 packages active dry yeast	5½ cups all-purpose flour*
¾ cup warm water (105 to 115°)	½ cup shortening
¾ cup buttermilk	2 tablespoons sugar
¾ cup dairy sour cream	2 teaspoons baking powder
	2 teaspoons salt

In large mixer bowl, dissolve yeast in warm water. Add buttermilk, sour cream, 2½ cups of the flour, the shortening, sugar, baking powder and salt. Blend ½ minute on low speed, scraping bowl constantly. Beat 2 minutes medium speed, scraping bowl occasionally. Stir in remaining flour. Turn dough onto well-floured board; knead 5 minutes or about 200 turns. (Shape immediately.)

Divide dough into 3 parts. Use ⅓ of dough in each of the Variations. Let rise 1 hour before baking. (Dough is ready if impression remains.) Heat oven to 375°. Bake rolls 20 to 25 minutes.

*If using self-rising flour, omit baking powder and salt.

Casseroles

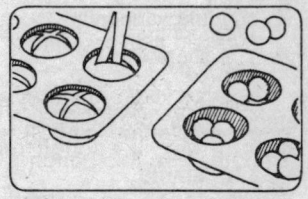

Four-leaf Clovers and Cloverleafs

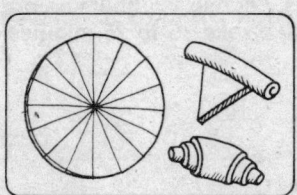

Crescents

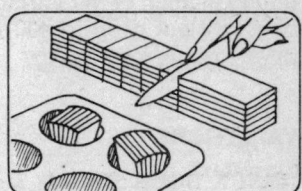

Fan Tans

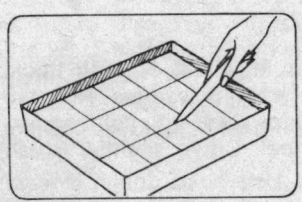

Pan Biscuits

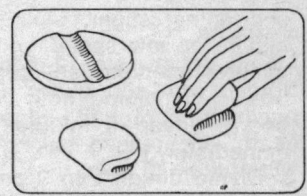

Parker House

POTATO REFRIGERATOR DOUGH

1 package active dry yeast	2 eggs
1½ cups warm water (105 to 115°)	1 cup lukewarm mashed potatoes
⅔ cup sugar	7 to 7½ cups all-purpose flour*
1½ teaspoons salt	
⅔ cup shortening	

Dissolve yeast in warm water. Stir in sugar, salt, shortening, eggs, potatoes and 4 cups of the flour. Beat until smooth. Mix in enough remaining flour to make dough easy to handle.

Turn dough onto lightly floured board; knead until smooth and elastic, about 5 minutes. Place in greased bowl; turn greased side up. Cover bowl tightly; refrigerate at least 8 hours or until ready to use. (Dough can be kept up to 5 days in refrigerator at 45° or below. Keep covered.)

Punch down dough; divide into 4 parts. Use ¼ of dough in each of the Variations. Let rise 1½ hours before baking. Heat oven to 400°. Bake rolls 15 to 25 minutes.

*If using self-rising flour, omit salt.

VARIATIONS

CASSEROLES

Shape bits of dough into 1-inch balls. Place in lightly greased round layer pan, 9x1½ inches. Brush with butter. 3 dozen rolls.

CLOVERLEAFS

Shape bits of dough in 1-inch balls. Place 3 balls in each greased muffin cup. Brush with butter. 12 rolls.

CRESCENTS

Roll dough into 12-inch circle, about ¼ inch thick. Spread with soft butter. Cut into 16 wedges. Roll up, beginning at rounded edge. Place rolls, with point underneath, on greased baking sheet. Curve slightly. Brush with butter. 16 rolls.

FAN TANS

Roll dough into rectangle, 13x9 inches. Spread with soft butter. Cut crosswise into 6 strips, 1½ inches wide.

Stack strips evenly; cut into 12 pieces, about 1 inch wide. Place cut side down in greased muffin cups; brush with butter. 12 rolls.

FOUR-LEAF CLOVERS

Shape pieces of dough into 2-inch balls. Place each ball in greased medium muffin cup (2¾ inches in diameter). With scissors, snip each ball in half, then into quarters. Brush with butter.

About 12 rolls.

PAN BISCUITS

Use ⅔ of the Quick Sour Cream Dough, half the Potato Refrigerator Dough or all of the Traditional Roll Dough.

Roll dough into rectangle, 13x9 inches, about ½ inch thick. Place in greased baking pan, 13x9x2 inches. Score dough ¼ inch deep into 15 rolls. Brush with butter. 15 rolls.

PARKER HOUSE

Roll dough into oblong, 13x9 inches, about ¼ inch thick. Cut into 3-inch circles. Brush with butter.

Make crease across each circle; fold so top half overlaps slightly. Press edges together. Place close together in greased 9-inch pan. Brush with butter. 10 rolls.

Sweet Rolls and Coffee Cakes

Watch early-morning moodiness dissolve into a sunny smile. All of these sweet breads can turn the trick—and they can do it even faster when served piping hot with plenty of butter. For company brunch, dress them up with Butter Curls (page 102) or Butter Balls. To make butter balls, scald a pair of wooden butter paddles in boiling water for 30 seconds; chill in iced water. Cut ¼-pound bar of firm butter in 1-inch squares. Cut each square in half; stand one half upright on paddle. Smack butter between paddles. Holding bottom paddle steady, rotate top paddle quickly to form ball. If butter clings to paddles, dip them into hot water, then into iced water.

Drop each finished ball into iced water; cover and refrigerate. Luckily, it's easier than it sounds.

TRADITIONAL SWEET ROLL DOUGH

2 packages active dry yeast
½ cup warm water (105 to 115°)
½ cup lukewarm milk (scalded then cooled)
½ cup sugar
1 teaspoon salt
2 eggs
½ cup shortening or butter or margarine, softened
4½ to 5 cups all-purpose flour*

Dissolve yeast in warm water. Stir in milk, sugar, salt, eggs, shortening and 2½ cups of the flour. Beat until smooth. Mix in enough remaining flour to make dough easy to handle.

Turn dough onto lightly floured board; knead until smooth and elastic, about 5 minutes. Place in greased bowl; turn greased side up. (At this point, dough can be refrigerated 3 to 4 days.) Cover; let rise in warm place until double, about 1½ hours. (Dough is ready if impression remains when touched.)

Punch down dough. Shape dough into desired rolls and coffee cakes (at right and through pages 113). Cover; let rise until double, about 30 minutes.

Heat oven to 375°. Bake as directed.

*If using self-rising flour, omit salt.

QUICK BUTTERMILK SWEET DOUGH

2 packages active dry yeast
½ cup warm water (105 to 115°)
1¼ cups buttermilk
2 eggs
5½ to 6 cups all-purpose flour*
½ cup butter or margarine, softened
½ cup sugar
2 teaspoons baking powder
2 teaspoons salt

In large mixer bowl, dissolve yeast in warm water. Add buttermilk, eggs, 2½ cups of the flour, the butter, sugar, baking powder and salt. Blend ½ minute on low speed, scraping bowl constantly. Beat 2 minutes medium speed, scraping bowl occasionally. Stir in enough remaining flour to make dough easy to handle. (Dough should remain soft and slightly sticky.)

Turn dough onto well-floured board; knead 5 minutes

*If using self-rising flour, omit baking powder and salt.

or about 200 turns. Shape dough immediately (no need to let rise) into desired rolls and coffee cakes (below and through page 113). Cover; let rise in warm place until double, about 1 hour. (Dough is ready if impression remains when touched.)

Heat oven to 375°. Bake as directed.

FROSTED ORANGE ROLLS

3 tablespoons butter or margarine, softened
1 tablespoon grated orange peel
2 tablespoons orange juice

1½ cups confectioners' sugar
½ recipe Traditional Sweet Roll Dough (left) or ½ recipe Quick Buttermilk Sweet Dough (left)

Beat butter, orange peel, juice and confectioners' sugar until creamy and smooth.

Roll dough into rectangle, 12x7 inches; spread with half the orange filling. Roll up, beginning at wide side. Pinch edge of dough into roll to seal well. Stretch roll to make even.

Cut roll into 12 slices. Place slightly apart in greased round layer pan, 9x1½ inches. Let rise until double. Bake 25 to 30 minutes. While warm, frost with remaining filling.

12 rolls.

CINNAMON ROLLS

½ recipe Traditional Sweet Roll Dough (page 108) or ½ recipe Quick Buttermilk Sweet Dough (page 108)

2 tablespoons butter or margarine, softened
¼ cup sugar
2 teaspoons cinnamon Sweet Icing (page 111)

Roll dough into rectangle, 15x9 inches; spread with butter. Mix sugar and cinnamon; sprinkle over rectangle. Roll up, beginning at wide side. Pinch edge of dough into roll to seal well. Stretch roll to make even.

Cut roll into 15 slices. Place slightly apart in greased baking pan, 13x9x2 inches, or in greased muffin cups. Let rise until double. Bake 25 to 30 minutes. While warm, frost rolls with icing.

15 rolls.

VARIATION

■ *Butterscotch-Pecan Rolls:* Before rolling dough into rectangle, melt ¼ cup butter or margarine in baking pan; stir in ½ cup brown sugar (packed), 2 tablespoons corn syrup and ½ cup pecan halves. Spread in pan. Roll, slice and bake as directed. Immediately turn pan upside down on large tray. Let pan remain a minute so butter-scotch drizzles over rolls.

CHOCOLATE CINNAMON ROLLS

Traditional Sweet Roll Dough (page 108) or Quick Buttermilk Sweet Dough (page 108)
⅔ cup cocoa

4 tablespoons butter or margarine, softened
½ cup sugar
1 tablespoon cinnamon
Icing (below)

Prepare dough as directed except—mix in cocoa with the first addition of flour.

Divide dough in half. Roll each half into rectangle, 15x9 inches. Spread each with 2 tablespoons butter. Mix sugar and cinnamon; sprinkle half the mixture over each rectangle. Roll up, beginning at wide side. Pinch edge of dough into roll to seal well. Stretch roll to make even.

Cut each roll into 15 slices. Place slightly apart in 2 greased baking pans. 13x9x2 inches, or in greased muffin cups. Let rise until double.

Bake 25 to 30 minutes. While warm, frost rolls with Icing.

2½ dozen rolls.

ICING

Mix 1½ cups confectioners' sugar, 1 tablespoon milk and ½ teaspoon vanilla until smooth.

BUTTERFLY ROLLS

½ recipe Traditional Sweet Roll Dough (page 108) or ½ recipe Quick Buttermilk Sweet Dough (page 108)
Butter or margarine, melted
½ cup sugar

1 teaspoon cinnamon
⅓ cup all-purpose flour
2 tablespoons sugar
2 tablespoons butter or margarine
1½ teaspoons cinnamon
Sweet Icing (page 111)

Roll dough into rectangle, 18x9 inches. Brush with melted butter. Mix ½ cup sugar and 1 teaspoon cin-namon; sprinkle evenly over rectangle. Roll up, beginning at wide side. Pinch edge of dough into roll to seal well. Stretch roll to make even. Cut into 1-inch slices. Place pencil in center of each slice parallel to cut sides; press almost through dough. Invert and turn cut surfaces up. Place on greased baking sheet.

Rub together flour, 2 tablespoons sugar, 2 tablespoons butter and 1½ teaspoons cinnamon until crumbly; sprinkle over rolls. Let rise until double.

Bake about 12 minutes. Drizzle rolls with icing.

1½ dozen rolls.

SWEET ICING

Mix 1 cup confectioners' sugar, 1 tablespoon milk and ½ teaspoon vanilla until smooth.

CHEESE DIAMONDS

1 package (8 ounces) cream cheese, softened	1 tablespoon lemon juice
¼ cup sugar	½ recipe Traditional Sweet Roll Dough (page 108) or ½ recipe Quick Buttermilk Sweet Dough (page 108)
3 tablespoons flour	
1 egg yolk	
½ teaspoon grated lemon peel	½ cup jam
	Chopped nuts

Beat cream cheese and sugar until light and fluffy. Stir in flour, egg yolk, lemon peel and juice.

Roll dough into 15-inch square. Cut into twenty-five 3-inch squares. Place on greased baking sheets. Place 1 tablespoon cheese mixture in center of each square. Brink 2 diagonally opposite corners to center of each square, overlapping slightly; pinch to seal. Let rise until double.

Bake 12 to 15 minutes. Heat jam until melted; brush lightly over hot rolls and sprinkle with chopped nuts.

25 rolls.

For butterfly "wings," keep pencil parallel to cut sides.

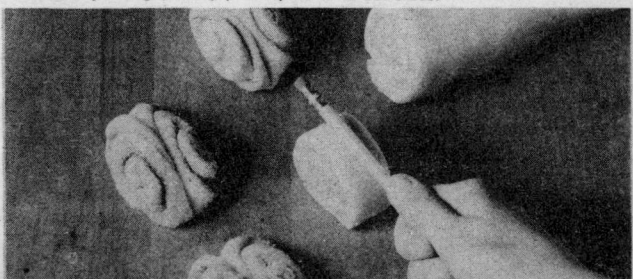

BALLOON BUNS

Surprise your guests with this hollow sweet bun. The marshmallow melts and the sweet cinnamon syrup coats the inside
of the roll.

Traditional Roll Dough   1 cup sugar
(page 104) or Quick Sour   18 to 24 large marshmallows
Cream Dough (page 104)   ½ cup butter or margarine,
1 tablespoon cinnamon   melted

Divide dough in half. Roll each half about ¼ inch thick.
Cut into 3½-inch circles. Mix cinnamon and sugar. Dip
each marshmallow into butter, then into cinnamon-sugar
mixture. Wrap each dough circle around marshmallow,
pinching together tightly at the bottom. Dip roll in butter,
then in cinnamon-sugar mixture. Place in greased medium muffin cups (2¾ inches in diameter). Let rise until
double.

Bake 20 to 25 minutes.

1½ dozen rolls with traditional roll dough; 2 dozen
rolls with quick sour cream dough.

HUNGARIAN COFFEE CAKE

High, light and handsome. Don't be surprised if it becomes a
Sunday morning special request. And let the children do the
serving—it's such fun!

Traditional Sweet Roll   ½ cup butter or margarine,
Dough (page 108) or Quick   melted
Buttermilk Sweet Dough   ¾ cup sugar
(page 108)   1 teaspoon cinnamon
                       ½ cup finely chopped nuts

Shape 1½-inch pieces of dough into balls. Dip into
butter, then into mixture of sugar, cinnamon and nuts.
Place a single layer of balls in well-greased 10-inch tube
pan so they just touch. (If pan has removable bottom,
line with aluminum foil.) Top with another layer of balls.
Let rise until double.

Bake traditional Sweet Roll Dough 35 to 40 minutes,
Quick Buttermilk Sweet Dough 60 minutes. (If coffee
cake browns too quickly, cover with aluminum foil.)
Loosen from pan. Invert pan onto serving plate so butter-
sugar mixture can drizzle down over cake. To serve,
break coffee cake apart with 2 forks.

VARIATION

■ *Toffee Coffee Cake:* Roll balls of dough in mixture of ¾ cup dark brown sugar (packed) and 1½ tablespoons instant coffee.

LATTICE COFFEE CAKE

A not-too-sweet coffee cake that's great for late-night snacking. You weave the yeast strips just as you would for a lattice-crust pie (see page 508).

Prepare Traditional Roll Dough (page 104). After rising, round up dough on board; cover and let rest 15 minutes.

Grease 2 square pans, 8x8x2 inches. Divide dough in half. Roll each half into 8-inch square; cut each square into eight 1-inch strips. Place 4 strips in each pan; to make lattice, weave in 4 cross strips.

Brush with melted butter. Mix ½ cup sugar and 2 teaspoons cinnamon; sprinkle half the mixture over each coffee cake. Let rise until double.

Bake 25 to 30 minutes.

2 coffee cakes.

SWEDISH TEA RING

A sweet wheel-like coffee ring that does double duty as the centerpiece for a special brunch.

½ recipe Traditional Sweet Roll Dough (page 108) or ½ recipe Quick Buttermilk Sweet Dough (page 108)
2 tablespoons butter or margarine, softened
½ cup brown sugar (packed)
2 teaspoons cinnamon
½ cup raisins

Roll dough into rectangle, 15x9 inches. Spread with butter and sprinkle with sugar, cinnamon and raisins. Roll up, beginning at wide side. Pinch edge of dough into roll to seal well. Stretch roll to make even.

With sealed edge down, shape into ring on lightly greased baking sheet. Pinch ends together. With scissors, make cuts ⅔ of the way through ring at 1-inch intervals. Turn each section on its side. Let rise until double.

Bake 25 to 30 minutes. If desired, frost while warm with Sweet Icing (page 111) and decorate with nuts and cherries. Serve warm.

SALLY LUNN

2 packages active dry yeast	2 tablespoons sugar
½ cup warm water (105 to 115°)	1½ teaspoons salt
	2 eggs
1½ cups lukewarm milk (scalded then cooled)	¼ cup shortening
	5½ cups all-purpose flour*

Dissolve yeast in warm water. Stir in milk, sugar, salt, eggs, shortening and flour. Beat until smooth. Cover; let rise in warm place until double, about 1 hour.

Stir down batter. Spread in greased tube pan, 10x4 inches. Let rise to within 1 inch of top of pan, 45 minutes.

Heat oven to 350°. Bake 45 to 50 minutes or until golden brown and crusty. Serve hot.

16 servings.

*If using self-rising flour, omit salt.

Holiday and Foreign Favorites

There's no time like the holidays to awake and stir memories with traditional foods. These festive breads have been adapted just for you.

BRIOCHES

Traditional French rolls that are rapidly becoming American favorites.

1 package active dry yeast	1 egg yolk (reserve white)
¾ cup warm water (105 to 115°)	½ cup butter or margarine, softened
½ cup sugar	3½ cups all-purpose flour*
½ teaspoon salt	1 tablespoon sugar
3 eggs	

In large mixer bowl, dissolve yeast in warm water. Add ½ cup sugar, the salt, eggs, egg yolk, butter and 2 cups of the flour. Blend ½ minute on low speed, scraping bowl constantly. Beat 10 minutes medium speed, scraping bowl occasionally. Stir in remaining flour until smooth. Scrape batter from side of bowl. Cover; let rise in warm place until double, about 1 hour.

*If using self-rising flour, omit salt.

Stir down batter by beating 25 strokes. Cover bowl tightly; chill at least 8 hours.

Stir down batter. Divide dough in half and place one half on lightly floured surface (keep other half chilled). Roll dough into roll, about 8 inches long. Cut into 16 slices.

Shape 12 slices into balls and place in greased medium muffin cups, working very quickly with floured hands as dough is soft and sticky. Flatten and make a deep indentation in center of each. Cut each of the remaining 4 slices into 3 equal parts. Shape each part into a small ball; place ball in each indentation. Repeat with other half of dough. Let rise until double, about 40 minutes.

Heat oven to 375°. Beat reserved egg white and 1 tablespoon sugar slightly; brush over rolls. Bake 15 to 20 minutes.

2 dozen rolls.

CROISSANTS

Impress weekend guests with a continental breakfast. It's a snap, too. Just two or three croissants, a choice of jams and plenty of coffee—or café au lait—to do it up right.

1 package active dry yeast	1 teaspoon grated lemon peel
½ cup warm water (105 to 115°)	2 eggs
1 cup lukewarm milk (scalded then cooled)	4½ to 5 cups all-purpose flour*
2 tablespoons shortening	1 cup butter or margarine, softened
2 tablespoons sugar	Light cream
1 teaspoon salt	

Dissolve yeast in warm water. Stir in milk, shortening, sugar, salt, lemon peel, eggs and 2½ cups of the flour. Beat until mixture is smooth. Mix in enough remaining flour to make dough easy to handle.

Turn dough onto lightly floured board; knead until smooth and elastic, about 5 minutes. Place in greased bowl; turn greased side up. Cover; let rise in warm place until double. Punch down dough. Cover; chill 1 hour.

Punch down dough again. Roll on lightly floured board into rectangle, 25x10 inches; spread with ⅓ cup butter.

*If using self-rising flour, omit salt.

Fold rectangle into thirds, making 3 layers; roll out. Repeat process 2 times, spreading rectangle with 1/3 cup butter each time. Divide dough in half; chill 1 hour.

Shape half the dough at a time (keep other half chilled). Roll each into rectangle, 25x10 inches, about 1/4 inch thick. Cut lengthwise in half, then crosswise into 5 squares. Cut each square diagonally into 2 triangles.

Roll up each triangle, beginning at long side. Place rolls, with point underneath, on ungreased baking sheet. Curve to form crescent. Chill 30 minutes.

Heat oven to 425°. Brush rolls with light cream; bake 15 to 18 minutes or until brown and crisp. Serve hot.

40 rolls.

HOT CROSS BUNS

2 packages active dry yeast	1/2 cup butter or margarine, softened
1/2 cup warm water (105 to 115°)	2 eggs
1/2 cup lukewarm milk (scalded then cooled)	1 teaspoon cinnamon
3/4 cup unseasoned lukewarm mashed potatoes	1/4 teaspoon nutmeg
	1 cup raisins
1/2 cup sugar	1/2 cup citron
1 1/4 teaspoons salt	4 1/2 cups all-purpose flour*
	Egg Yolk Glaze (right)
	Quick White Icing (right)

Dissolve yeast in warm water. Stir in milk, potatoes, sugar, salt, butter, eggs, cinnamon, nutmeg, raisins, citron and 2 1/2 cups of the flour. Beat until smooth. Mix in remaining flour to form soft dough.

Turn dough onto lightly floured board; knead until smooth and elastic, about 5 minutes. Place in greased bowl; turn greased side up. Cover; let rise in warm place until double, about 1 1/2 hours.

Punch down dough; divide in half. Cut each half into 16 pieces. Shape into smooth balls and place about 2 inches apart on greased baking sheet. With scissors, snip a cross on top of each bun. Cover; let rise until double, about 40 minutes.

Heat oven to 375°. Brush tops of buns with Egg Yolk Glaze. Bake about 20 minutes or until golden brown. When cool, frost crosses on tops of buns with Quick White Icing.

32 buns.

*If using self-rising flour, omit salt.

Note: Rolls can be baked in 2 greased round layer pans, 9x1½ inches (16 buns in each pan).

EGG YOLK GLAZE

Mix 1 egg yolk and 2 tablespoons cold water.

QUICK WHITE ICING

Mix 1 cup confectioners' sugar, 1 tablespoon water or milk and ½ teaspoon vanilla until smooth and of spreading consistency.

THE MEANING OF CHALLAH Dating back to Biblical times, the bread "challah" has been served as the white bread of the festive Friday evening meal of fish and wine that marks the beginning of the Jewish Sabbath. Even today, a small piece is burned in the oven in symbolic memory of the days when a portion of the bread was shared with the priests for a challah, or sacrifice.

CHALLAH BRAID

1 package active dry yeast	1 egg
¼ cup warm water (105 to 115°)	1 tablespoon shortening
½ cup lukewarm water	2½ to 2¾ cups all-purpose flour*
1 tablespoon sugar	1 egg yolk
1 teaspoon salt	2 tablespoons cold water

Dissolve yeast in warm water. Stir in lukewarm water, the sugar, salt, 1 egg, the shortening and 1¼ cups of the flour. Beat until smooth. Mix in enough remaining flour to make dough easy to handle.

Turn dough onto lightly floured board; knead until smooth and elastic, about 5 minutes. Round up dough in greased bowl; turn greased side up. Cover; let rise in warm place until double, 1½ to 2 hours.

Punch down dough; divide into 3 equal parts. Roll each part into strand, 14 inches long. Place strands close together on lightly greased baking sheet. Braid gently and loosely. Do not stretch. Fasten ends; tuck under securely. Brush braid with shortening. Let rise until double, 40 to 50 minutes.

Heat oven to 375°. Beat egg yolk and cold water until blended; brush over braid. Bake 25 to 30 minutes.

*If using self-rising flour, omit salt.

VARIATION

■ *Richer Braid:* Substitute lukewarm milk (scalded then cooled) for the ½ cup lukewarm water and butter or margarine for the shortening.

CHEESE SOUFFLÉ BREAD

1 package active dry yeast	1 egg
¼ cup warm water (105 to 115°)	½ teaspoon salt
	¼ teaspoon pepper
¼ cup lukewarm milk (scalded then cooled)	⅔ cup finely shredded Cheddar cheese
⅓ cup butter or margarine, softened	1½ cups all-purpose flour*
	Soft butter or margarine

In large mixer bowl, dissolve yeast in warm water. Add milk, ⅓ cup butter, the egg, salt, pepper, cheese and ½ cup of the flour. Blend ½ minute on low speed, scraping bowl constantly. Beat 2 minutes medium speed, scraping bowl occasionally. Stir in remaining flour until smooth. Scrape batter from side of bowl. Cover dough; let rise in warm place until double, about 30 minutes. (Dough is ready if impression remains.)

Stir down batter by beating about 25 strokes. Spread evenly in greased 1-quart casserole. Cover; let rise until double, about 40 minutes.

Heat oven to 375°. Bake 40 to 45 minutes or until brown and loaf sounds hollow when tapped. Immediately remove from pan; place on wire rack. Brush top with butter. Serve hot or cool. To serve, cut into wedges with serrated knife.

*If using self-rising flour, omit salt.

KULICH

2 packages active dry yeast	½ cup shortening
½ cup warm water (105 to 115°)	4½ to 5 cups all-purpose flour*
½ cup lukewarm milk (scalded then cooled)	½ cup raisins
½ cup sugar	¼ cup chopped blanched almonds
1 teaspoon salt	½ teaspoon vanilla
2 eggs	Lemon Icing (right)

Dissolve yeast in warm water. Stir in milk, sugar, salt, eggs, shortening, 2½ cups of the flour, the raisins, al-

*If using self-rising flour, omit salt.

monds and vanilla. Beat until smooth. Mix in enough
remaining flour to make dough easy to handle.

Turn dough onto lightly floured board; knead until
smooth and elastic, about 5 minutes. Place in greased
bowl; turn greased side up. Cover; let rise in warm place
until double, about 1½ hours. (Dough is ready if impression remains when touched.)

Punch down dough; let rise again until almost double,
30 to 40 minutes.

Divide dough in half. Shape each half into well-
rounded bun-like shape; place in well-greased 1-pound
coffee can (can will be about ½ full). Cover; let rise until
dough begins to puff over top of can, 40 to 50 minutes.

Heat oven to 375°. Place cans on low rack so that
midpoint of each is in center of oven. Bake 40 to 45
minutes or until brown. Remove kulichs from cans.

Spoon Lemon Icing over tops, allowing some to drizzle
down sides. If desired, trim with tiny decorating candies.

2 loaves.

LEMON ICING

Mix ½ cup confectioners' sugar, 1½ teaspoons warm
water, ½ teaspoon grated lemon peel and ½ teaspoon
lemon juice.

CANDY CANE COFFEE CAKES

This recipe makes three cakes—one for the brunch table and
two for gift-giving.

2 cups dairy sour cream	About 6 cups all-purpose
2 packages active dry yeast	flour*
½ cup warm water (105 to	1½ cups finely chopped dried
115°)	apricots
¼ cup butter or margarine,	1½ cups drained finely
softened	chopped maraschino
⅓ cup sugar	cherries
2 teaspoons salt	Soft butter or margarine
2 eggs	Thin Icing (page 120)

Heat sour cream over low heat just until lukewarm.
Dissolve yeast in warm water. Stir in sour cream, ¼ cup
butter, the sugar, salt, eggs and 2 cups of the flour. Beat
until smooth. Mix in enough remaining flour to make
dough easy to handle.

*If using self-rising flour, omit salt.

Turn dough onto well-floured board; knead until smooth, about 10 minutes. Place in greased bowl; turn greased side up. Cover; let rise in warm place until double, about 1 hour.

Heat oven to 375°. Punch down dough; divide into 3 equal parts. Roll each part into rectangle, 15x6 inches; place on greased baking sheet. With scissors, make 2-inch cuts at ½-inch intervals on long sides of rectangles.

Combine apricots and cherries; spread ⅓ of mixture down center of each rectangle. Crisscross strips over filling. Stretch dough to 22 inches. Curve to form cane.

Bake 15 to 20 minutes or until golden brown. While warm, brush with butter and drizzle canes with Thin Icing. If desired, decorate with cherry halves or pieces.

3 coffee cakes.

THIN ICING

Blend 2 cups confectioners' sugar with about 2 tablespoons water. If icing is too stiff, stir in few drops water.

HANDS ACROSS THE SEA The delicate croissants and brioches of sunny breakfasts on the Continent, the hot cross buns of Merrie Olde England, the Russian kulich, Sweden's Saint Lucia buns and Italy's panettone—these are but a few of the festive breads that generations of immigrants and visitors have brought to our shores. And we've borrowed them—and adapted them—for these pages.

Enjoy these traditional favorites from far-flung lands— use them to build new family traditions in your house.

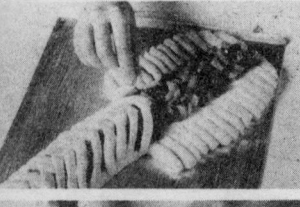

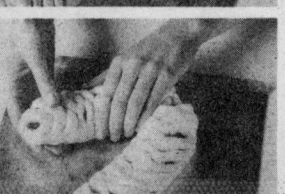

Left: Arrange strips in crisscross pattern.

Bottom: Curve top of dough to form a cane.

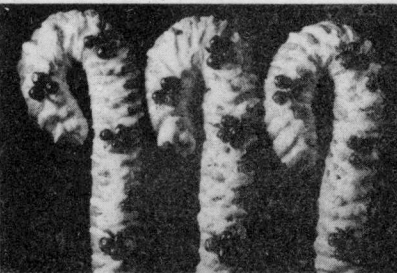

SAINT LUCIA CROWN

2 packages active dry yeast
½ cup warm water (105 to 115°)
Pinch saffron,* crushed
½ cup lukewarm milk (scalded then cooled)
½ cup sugar
1 teaspoon salt
2 eggs, beaten
¼ cup butter or margarine, softened

4½ to 5 cups all-purpose flour**
½ cup chopped citron
¼ cup chopped blanched almonds
1 tablespoon grated lemon peel
Icing (below)
Green and red candied cherries

Dissolve yeast in warm water. Stir saffron into milk. Mix saffron-milk, sugar, salt, eggs, butter and 2½ cups of the flour into yeast mixture. Beat until smooth. Stir in citron, almonds, lemon peel and enough remaining flour to make dough easy to handle.

Turn dough onto lightly floured board; knead until smooth, about 10 minutes. Place in greased bowl; turn greased side up. Cover; let rise in warm place until double, about 1½ hours.

Punch down dough; cut off ⅓ of dough for top braid and reserve. Divide remaining dough into 3 equal parts; roll each part into strand, 25 inches long. Place close together on greased baking sheet. Braid strands; shape into circle and pinch ends to seal.

Divide reserved dough into 3 equal parts; roll each part into strand, 16 inches long. Place close together on another greased baking sheet. Braid strands; shape into circle and pinch ends to seal. Cover; let rise until double, about 45 minutes.

Heat oven to 375°. Bake 20 to 25 minutes. When cool, make holes for 6 candles in small braid. Drizzle braid with Icing; garnish with cherries. Insert candles. Place small braid on large braid.

*2 or 3 drops yellow food color can be substituted for the saffron.

**If using self-rising flour, omit salt and substitute 2 or 3 drops yellow food color for the saffron.

ICING

Blend 1 cup confectioners' sugar and 1 tablespoon water. If icing is too stiff, mix in few drops water.

VARIATION

■ *Lucia Buns:* When ready to shape dough, cut into

pieces about 2½ inches in diameter. Shape each piece into roll, 15 inches long; form into tightly coiled "S" shape. Place on greased baking sheet; cover and let rise until double, about 45 minutes. Bake 15 minutes. 12 to 18 buns.

STOLLEN

1 package active dry yeast	¼ cup cut-up citron
¾ cup warm water (105 to 115°)	¼ cup cut-up candied cherries, if desired
½ cup sugar	¼ cup raisins
½ teaspoon salt	1 tablespoon grated lemon peel
3 eggs	
1 egg yolk (reserve white)	¼ cup plus 2 tablespoons soft butter
½ cup butter or margarine, softened	Quick White Icing (page 123)
3½ cups all-purpose flour*	Blanched almond halves
½ cup chopped blanched almonds	Pieces of citron
	Candied cherry halves

In large mixer bowl, dissolve yeast in warm water. Add sugar, salt, eggs, egg yolk, ½ cup butter and 1½ cups of the flour. Blend ½ minute low speed, scraping bowl constantly. Beat 10 minutes medium speed, scraping bowl occasionally.

Stir in remaining flour, ½ cup almonds, ¼ cup each citron, cherries, raisins and the lemon peel. Scrape batter from side of bowl. Cover; let rise in warm place until double, about 1½ hours.

Stir down batter by beating 25 strokes. Cover bowl tightly; refrigerate at least 8 hours.

Turn dough onto well-floured board; turn to coat with flour. Divide dough in half. Press each half into oval, about 10x7 inches. Spread each with 3 tablespoons butter. Fold lengthwise in half; press only folded edge firmly. Place on greased baking sheet. Beat reserved egg white slightly; beat in 1 tablespoon water and brush over stollen. Let rise until double, 45 to 60 minutes.

Heat oven to 375°. Bake 20 to 25 minutes or until golden brown. While warm, frost with Quick White Icing; decorate with almond halves, pieces of citron and cherry halves to resemble poinsettias. Or, if desired, dust with confectioners' sugar.

2 stollen.

*Do not use self-rising flour in this recipe.

QUICK WHITE ICING

Mix 1½ cups confectioners' sugar and 1½ tablespoons milk until smooth.

FRUITED WREATH

2 packages active dry yeast	½ cup sugar
½ cup warm water (105 to 115°)	2 teaspoons baking powder
1¼ cups buttermilk	2 teaspoons salt
2 eggs	½ cup chopped pecans
5½ cups all-purpose flour*	1 tablespoon grated lemon peel
½ cup butter or margarine, softened	1 cup chopped mixed candied fruit

In large mixer bowl, dissolve yeast in warm water. Add buttermilk, eggs, 2½ cups of the flour, the butter, sugar, baking powder and salt. Blend ½ minute on low speed, scraping bowl constantly. Beat 2 minutes medium speed, scraping bowl occasionally. Stir in remaining flour, the pecans, lemon peel and candied fruit. (Dough should remain soft and slightly sticky.)

Turn dough onto floured board; knead 5 minutes or about 200 turns. Roll dough into strip, 24x6 inches. Cut into 3 strips, each 24x2 inches; braid loosely. On greased baking sheet, twirl braid into wreath shape and pinch ends to seal. Let rise in warm place until double, about 1 hour.

Heat oven to 375°. Bake about 30 minutes. If desired, brush wreath with Thin Glaze: Mix ½ cup confectioners' sugar and 1 tablespoon milk; decorate with candied cherries and leaf shapes made from angelica.

*If using self-rising flour, omit baking powder and salt.

CHRISTMAS TREE COFFEE CAKE

Prepare Quick Buttermilk Sweet Dough (page 108). Divide dough in half. Shape one half at a time into seventeen 2-inch balls. On each of 2 lightly greased baking sheets, form tree shape with balls in rows of 5, 4, 3, 2, 1; roll 2 balls together to form trunk of tree. Let rise until double, about 1 hour.

Heat oven to 375°. Bake 20 to 25 minutes or until golden brown. Decorate trees with Quick Icing: Mix 2 cups confectioners' sugar, 2 to 3 tablespoons water or milk and 1 teaspoon vanilla until smooth. Trim with colored sugar.

2 coffee cakes.

KUGELHUPF

A crusty, tender Alsatian bread delicately flavored with lemon . . . easy to mix, no kneading. Keep an eye out for interestingly shaped kugelhupf molds when browsing through gourmet shops.

1 package active dry yeast	2½ cups all-purpose flour*
¾ cup warm water (105 to 115°)	½ cup raisins
	Grated peel of 1 lemon
½ cup sugar	¼ cup very finely chopped almonds or dry bread crumbs
½ teaspoon salt	
¼ cup butter or margarine, softened	
2 eggs	12 to 16 blanched almonds

In large mixer bowl, dissolve yeast in warm water. Add sugar, salt, butter, eggs and 1¼ cups of the flour. Blend ½ minute on low speed, scraping bowl constantly. Beat 4 minutes medium speed, scraping bowl occasionally. Stir in raisins, lemon peel and remaining flour. Scrape batter from side of bowl. Cover; let rise in warm place until double, about 1½ hours.

Grease side and bottom of bundt pan or 6½-cup anodized ring mold; sprinkle with chopped almonds. Arrange blanched almonds evenly on bottom of pan.

Stir down batter by beating 25 strokes. Spoon batter evenly into pan (batter will be sticky). Let rise until double, about 1 hour.

Heat oven to 350°. Bake about 50 minutes. Immediately remove from pan.

*Do not use self-rising flour in this recipe.

PANETTONE

A glossy, golden brown fruited Italian bread.

2 packages active dry yeast
½ cup warm water (105 to 115°)
½ cup lukewarm milk (scalded then cooled)
½ cup sugar
1 teaspoon salt
2 eggs
½ cup butter or margarine, softened

4½ to 5 cups all-purpose flour*
½ cup raisins
½ cup cut-up citron
1 tablespoon anise seed
2 tablespoons pine nuts, if desired
1 egg
1 tablespoon water

Dissolve yeast in warm water. Stir in milk, sugar, salt, 2 eggs, the butter and 2½ cups of the flour. Beat until smooth. Mix in fruit, anise seed, nuts and enough remaining flour to make dough easy to handle.

Turn dough onto lightly floured board; knead until smooth and elastic, about 5 minutes. Place in greased bowl; turn greased side up. Cover; let rise in warm place until double, 1½ to 2 hours.

Punch down dough; divide in half. Shape each half into round, slightly flat loaf. Place loaves in opposite corners of greased baking sheet. Cut a cross ½ inch deep on top of each loaf. Let rise until double, about 1 hour.

Heat oven to 350°. Blend 1 egg and 1 tablespoon water; brush on loaves. Bake 35 to 45 minutes.

2 loaves.

*Do not use self-rising flour in this recipe.

Cakes and Frostings

Make somebody happy today—bake a cake! A chocolate cake for that someone special. Or a white cake with peppermint frosting for a sweet snack after bridge. Bake a sponge cake for Grandma, as lovely-light as the kind she used to bake. Bake a cake—have a party. Bake a cake to take to a party. Bake a cake just because you feel good today.

Look through this section. Bake a brand-new, magnificent, splendiferous, high, light 'n handsome cake! Here they all are—the "shortening-type" cakes and the "foam-type" cakes, as the cooking-class textbooks call them. Shortening-type cakes are the classic cakes— white, yellow, chocolate and spice—made with solid shortening. Chiffons, angel foods and sponge cakes are called foam-type cakes because it's the foam of beaten egg whites that accounts for their light, fluffy, open texture. (Pages 131 and 160 will tell you more.)

But cake baking can be considered an art as well as a pleasure—and, like any art, it is exacting. Because you are working with a delicately balanced formula, the ingredients must be measured exactly (with no substitutions), the directions followed carefully and the correct pans used. Stick to these few rules and you can be sure of success.

Begin at the Beginning

Read through the recipe carefully; assemble *all* utensils and ingredients; heat the oven; prepare the pans. Be sure all ingredients are at room temperature. (Please forgive us if we insist—don't make changes in the recipes!)

Pointers on Pans

■ For good size, shape and texture, always use pans of the size called for in your recipe. A cake baked in a pan that is too large will be pale, flat and shrunken. A cake baked in too small or too shallow a pan will bulge over and lose its shape. Layer pans should be at least 1½ inches deep; square or oblong, 2 inches deep; pound or loaf, more than 2 inches deep.

■ Shiny metal pans are preferred for cake-baking because they reflect heat away from the cake and produce a light brown, tender crust. Heatproof glass pans are also acceptable; if you use them, set the oven temperature 25° lower than specified in the recipe but bake for the same amount of time. Do *not* use darkened metal or enamel pans.

■ Never fill cake pans more than half full. If you are using an odd-shaped pan (lamb, bell, star, heart, Christmas tree), measure the capacity of the pan by filling with water, then measure the water and use only half that amount of batter. You can always use the rest for cupcakes.

Preparing the Pans

■ For butter-type cakes, sheet cakes (Petits Fours, page 143) and two-egg chiffon cakes, grease bottoms and sides of pans generously with shortening. (Do not use butter, margarine or oil.) Dust each greased pan with flour, shaking pan until bottom and sides are well coated. Shake out excess flour. When using pans with a non-stick coating, follow the manufacturer's directions.

■ For *classic* angel food and chiffon cakes, do not grease and flour the pans. The batter must cling to the side and tube to rise properly.

■ For fruit cakes, line pans with aluminum foil, then grease. Leave short "ears" so you can "lift" the cake out easily. If you intend to store the fruit cake, extend the foil well over the sides of the pan. When cake has cooled, bring foil up and over the top and seal.

■ Jelly roll pans should first be lined with waxed paper or aluminum foil, then greased.

Storing Cakes

■ Cool unfrosted cakes thoroughly before storing. If covered warm, they become sticky.

■ Keep cake with a creamy-type frosting under a cake safe (or large inverted bowl) or cover loosely with aluminum foil, plastic wrap or waxed paper.

■ Serve cake with a fluffy-type frosting the day it's made. If you must store the cake overnight, use a cake safe or inverted bowl, but slip a knife under the edge so the container *is not* airtight.

■ Cakes with whipped cream toppings or cream fillings should be kept in the refrigerator.

Freezing Cakes

■ Unfrosted cakes and cupcakes freeze better than frosted cakes. Allow the cakes to cool thoroughly; place on cardboard, then cover with aluminum foil or plastic wrap. Properly packaged, unfrosted cakes can be kept frozen 4 to 5 months.

■ Of the frosted cakes, those with creamy-type frostings freeze best. Fluffy-type and whipped cream frostings freeze well but they tend to stick to the covering. To avoid some of the stickiness, freeze the cake before wrapping it. Or insert wooden picks around the top and side of the cake to hold the wrapping away from the frosting. Frozen frosted cakes keep for 2 to 3 months.

■ Do not freeze cakes with custard or fruit fillings. They tend to become soggy while thawing.

■ Do not freeze cake batter.

Thawing Cakes

■ Let the *wrapped* frozen cake stand at room temperature as follows: 2 hours for frosted cakes, 1 hour for unfrosted layers, 30 minutes for cupcakes. (Do *not* thaw in oven.) Cakes with whipped cream toppings or fillings should be thawed in the refrigerator about 3 to 4 hours.

■ If you do not need the whole cake, cut individual pieces; they will thaw in about 5 minutes.

Cutting Cakes

Use a sharp, thin knife to cut shortening-type cakes, a long serrated knife for angels and chiffons. If the frosting sticks, dip the knife in hot water and wipe with a damp paper towel after cutting each slice.

Why not try one of these special cuts next time you serve cake to your guests.

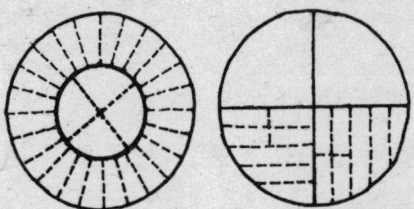

1. To cut layer cakes into smaller pieces, cut a circle as shown. First cut pieces from the outer circle; then cut center. (28 pieces)

2. Or, cut cake into quarters. Then cut quarters into slices. Pieces near the center only can be cut in half. (28 pieces)

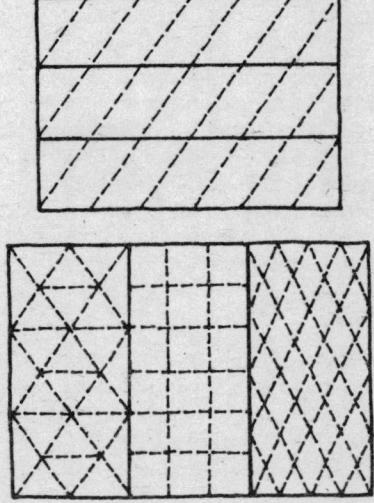

3. To cut a 9x13 inch cake into smaller pieces, cut lengthwise into thirds. Cut diagonally into diamonds and triangles as shown. (21 pieces)

4. To cut a 15x10 inch cake into more pieces, cut crosswise into thirds. Cut each section as shown or cut all the same way.

SPECIAL FLAVORS FOR CAKE MIXES *Don't miss these easy flavor variations for basic white, chocolate and yellow layer cake mixes.*

Prepare 1 package (18.5 ounces) layer cake mix as directed except—		Yellow Cake	Chocolate Cake	White Cake
Cherry-Nut	Fold ½ cup finely chopped nuts and ½ cup finely chopped maraschino cherries, well drained, into batter.	■	■	■
Chocolate Chip	Fold 2 squares (1 ounce each) shaved sweet, semi-sweet or unsweetened chocolate (about ½ cup) into batter.	■		■
Maple-Nut	Add 2 teaspoons maple flavoring before mixing. Fold ½ cup finely chopped nuts into batter.	■		■
Mint	Add ¼ teaspoon peppermint extract before mixing. If desired, tint white cake batter with red or green food color.	■	■	■
Mocha	Stir 2 tablespoons powdered instant coffee into mix.	■	■	■
Nutmeg-Mace	Add ½ teaspoon mace and ½ teaspoon nutmeg to dry ingredients.	■	■	
Orange	Fold 2 tablespoons grated orange peel into batter.	■	■	■
Toasted Coconut	Fold 1 to 1½ cups flaked coconut, toasted, into batter.	■	■	■

YARDSTICK FOR YIELDS

Size and kind	Servings
8-inch layer cake	10 to 14
9-inch layer cake	12 to 16
8- or 9-inch square cake	9
13x9x2-inch oblong cake	12 to 15
Angel, chiffon or sponge cake	12 to 16

ONLY THE BEST FOR THIS BOOK—AND YOU

From the hundreds of cake recipes developed every year in the Betty Crocker Kitchens, we have selected the very best basic cakes to include in this chapter. Some are made with cocoa and water, some with cocoa and buttermilk; others are made with sweet chocolate, still others with unsweetened chocolate. We've followed similar procedures with all possible variations for white and yellow cakes as well. Now, after all the testing and tasting, we think—and our home testers agree—that we have made the right choices. Try them and see. We're sure you'll like them, too.

Shortening-type Cakes

No time to bake a cake? Not true. Gone are the separate chores of creaming, sifting and beating, even for the classic layer cakes. Now you can beat everything together all at once—and you've used only one bowl!

True, our one-bowl method was developed with the electric mixer in mind—but you can also mix by hand, if you wish. First, stir the ingredients together to moisten and blend them; then beat 150 strokes for *every* minute of beating time (3 minutes—450 strokes).

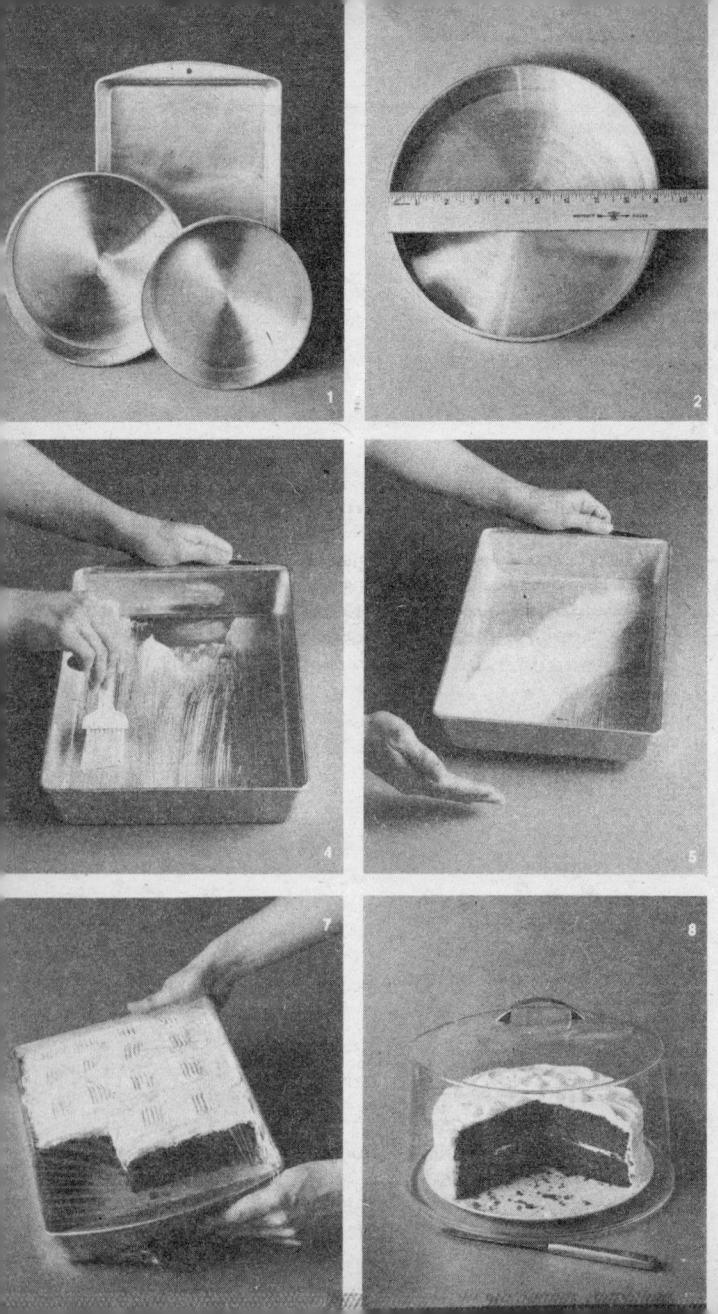

TIPS FOR CAKE BAKERS

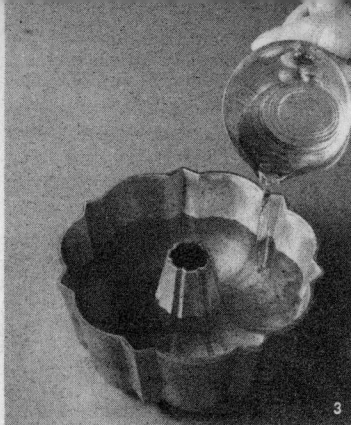

1. Use shiny metal pans. If using a heatproof glass pan, reduce oven temperature by 25°.

2. Be sure pan is correct size. To check size, measure across top of pan from inside edge to inside edge.

3. To determine amount of batter for odd-shaped pan, fill with measured water; use half that amount of batter.

4. Grease bottom and side of pans generously with shortening. (Do not use butter, margarine or oil).

5. To flour pans, tap and shake to cover completely. Invert pan and shake out excess flour.

6. Pans should be placed in middle of oven and at least 1 inch from edge. Do not let pans touch.

7. To store cake with creamy-type frosting, loosely cover with foil or plastic wrap; or use a cake safe.

8. To store cake with fluffy-type frosting, slip knife under cake safe so it will *not* be airtight.

9. Store cake with whipped cream frosting in the refrigerator. Cover with inverted bowl if desired.

These, too, are the cakes to transform into cupcakes and sheet cakes. (We recommend using 18.5-ounce packages of white, chocolate and yellow cake mixes as well as Silver White Cake, page 140, Cocoa Fudge Cake, page 136, Golden Layer Cake, page 145, and New Starlight Cake, page 146.

Here are some points to keep in mind when you make your next shortening-type cake.

■ To bake, place pans on middle rack at least 1 inch from the side of the oven. Be sure that pans do not touch each other.

■ To test for doneness, insert a wooden pick into the center of the cake. If it comes out clean, the cake is done.

■ For perfectly shaped cupcakes, bake in paper-lined muffin pans. Fill cups half-full; bake as directed in recipe or on package.

■ To bake a sheet cake, bake cake in a greased and floured jelly roll pan at 350° for 25 to 30 minutes. Cool in pan.

BEST CHOCOLATE CAKE

Truly best with its rich, chocolaty color and moist, fudgy flavor. Try one of the suggested frostings or just a dollop of sweetened whipped cream on each piece.

2 cups all-purpose flour* or cake flour	¾ cup buttermilk
2 cups sugar	½ cup shortening
1 teaspoon soda	2 eggs (⅓ to ½ cup)
1 teaspoon salt	1 teaspoon vanilla
½ teaspoon baking powder	4 ounces melted
¾ cup water	unsweetened chocolate (cool)

Heat oven to 350°. Grease and flour baking pan, 13x9x2 inches, or two 9-inch or three 8-inch round layer pans. Measure all ingredients into large mixer bowl. Blend ½ minute on low speed, scraping bowl constantly. Beat 3 minutes high speed, scraping bowl occasionally. Pour evenly into pan(s).

Bake oblong 40 to 45 minutes, layers 30 to 35 minutes or until wooden pick inserted in center comes out clean. Cool.

If desired, frost cake with Peanut Butter Broiled Topping (page 197). Chocolate-Spice Butter Frosting (page 188) or Satiny Beige Frosting (page 192).

*If using self-rising flour, omit soda, salt and baking powder.

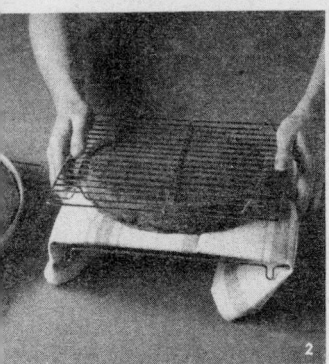

TIPS FOR SHORTENING-TYPE CAKES

1. Cool layers in pans on wire racks about 5 minutes. Cover another rack with a towel; place towel side down on top of layer and invert as a unit. Remove pan.

2. Place original rack on bottom of layer; turn over both racks (as a unit) so layer is right side up. Repeat with other layer(s). Allow layers to cool completely on racks.

3. To test for doneness, insert wooden pick near center of cake after minimum baking time. If pick comes out clean, the cake is done.

4. To cut cake, use a thin sharp knife or a serrated knife. Insert point of knife into center of cake and keep point down as you slice, drawing knife toward you.

VARIATIONS

■ *New Orleans Spice Cake:* Omit vanilla and add 1 teaspoon cloves before mixing.

■ *Valentine Heart Cake:* Bake cake in layers. In chilled bowl, whip 1½ cups chilled whipping cream, ¼ cup confectioners' sugar and ½ teaspoon almond extract until stiff. With decorators' tube or spoon, form thin rim of whipped cream around edge of bottom layer.

Fill center with half of 1 can (1 pound 5 ounces) cherry pie filling. Top with other layer. With tip of knife, outline large heart on top of cake. Frost side and top of cake remaining outside heart shape with whipped cream. Fill heart with remaining cherry filling. Chill.

BLACK MIDNIGHT CAKE

2¼ cups all-purpose flour* or cake flour	¼ teaspoon baking powder
1⅔ cups sugar	1¼ cups water
⅔ cup cocoa	¾ cup shortening
1¼ teaspoons soda	2 eggs (⅓ to ½ cup)
1 teaspoon salt	1 teaspoon vanilla

Heat oven to 350°. Grease and flour baking pan, 13x9x2 inches, or two 9-inch or three 8-inch round layer pans. Measure all ingredients into large mixer bowl. Blend ½ minute on low speed, scraping bowl constantly. Beat 3 minutes high speed, scraping bowl occasionally. Pour into pan(s).

Bake oblong about 45 minutes, layers 30 to 35 minutes or until wooden pick inserted in center comes out clean. Cool.

If desired, frost cake with White Mountain Frosting (page 191).

Do not use self-rising flour in this recipe.

COCOA FUDGE CAKE

2 cups cake flour or 1⅔ cups all-purpose flour*	1 teaspoon salt
	1½ cups buttermilk
1½ cups sugar	½ cup shortening
⅔ cup cocoa	2 eggs (⅓ to ½ cup)
1½ teaspoons soda	1 teaspoon vanilla

Heat oven to 350°. Grease and flour baking pan, 13x9x2 inches, or 2 round layer pans, 8 or 9x1½ inches.

If using self-rising flour, decrease soda to ¾ teaspoon and omit salt.

Measure all ingredients into large mixer bowl. Blend ½ minute on low speed, scraping bowl constantly. Beat 3 minutes high speed, scraping bowl occasionally. Pour into pan(s).

Bake oblong 35 to 40 minutes, layers 30 to 35 minutes or until wooden pick inserted in center comes out clean. Cool.

If desired, frost cake with Cocoa Butter Frosting (page 188) or Brown Sugar Meringue (page 197).

RED DEVILS FOOD CAKE

1¾ cups all-purpose flour* or cake flour	½ cup shortening
1 cup granulated sugar	2 eggs (⅓ to ½ cup)
½ cup brown sugar (packed)	2 ounces melted unsweetened chocolate (cool)
1½ teaspoons soda	
¾ teaspoon salt	1 teaspoon vanilla
1¼ cups buttermilk	½ teaspoon red food color

Heat oven to 350°. Grease and flour baking pan, 13x9x2 inches, or two 9-inch or three 8-inch round layer pans. Measure all ingredients into large mixer bowl. Blend ½ minute on low speed, scraping bowl constantly. Beat 3 minutes high speed, scraping bowl occasionally. Pour into pan(s).

Bake oblong about 40 minutes, layers 30 to 35 minutes or until wooden pick inserted in center comes out clean. Cool.

If desired, frost cake with Glossy Chocolate Frosting (page 188) or Cream Cheese Frosting (page 188).

*Do not use self-rising flour in this recipe.

CHOCOLATE BUTTERMALLOW CAKE

Bake Red Devils Food Cake (above) in oblong pan. Cool 10 minutes. Remove from pan and cool completely.

Spread Butterscotch Filling (page 138) over top of cake to within ½ inch of edge. Sprinkle ½ cup finely chopped nuts over filling. Frost sides and top of cake with Marshmallow Frosting (page 138). Melt ½ square unsweetened chocolate; dip back of spoon into chocolate and form attractive swirls on frosting.

BUTTERSCOTCH FILLING

½ cup light brown sugar
  (packed)
¼ cup cornstarch

¼ teaspoon salt
½ cup water
1 tablespoon butter

Stir together sugar, cornstarch and salt. Stir in water. Cook, stirring constantly, until mixture thickens and boils. Boil and stir 1 minute. Blend in butter. Cool.

MARSHMALLOW FROSTING

2 egg whites
1½ cups sugar
  ¼ teaspoon cream of tartar
  1 tablespoon light corn
   syrup

⅓ cup water
¾ cup marshmallow crème
  or ¼ pound marshmallows
  (about 16), quartered

Combine egg whites, sugar, cream of tartar, syrup and water in top of double boiler. Place over boiling water; beat with rotary beater until stiff peaks form, scraping pan occasionally. Remove from heat. Add marshmallow crème and continue beating until of spreading consistency.

CHOCOLATE BUTTERMALLOW LAYER CAKE

Bake Red Devils Food Cake (page 137) in 2 round layer pans, 9x1½ inches. Cool.

Spread Butterscotch Filling (above) over bottom layer. Sprinkle ½ cup finely chopped nuts over filling. Top with other layer and frost side and top of cake with Marshmallow Frosting (above). Melt ½ square unsweetened chocolate; dip back of spoon into chocolate and form swirls on top of cake.

GERMAN CHOCOLATE CAKE

This is the grass-roots recipe that swept the country to become a classic.

½ cup boiling water
1 bar (4 ounces) sweet
  cooking chocolate
1 cup butter or margarine,
  softened
2 cups sugar
4 egg yolks
1 teaspoon vanilla

2½ cups cake flour
1 teaspoon soda
½ teaspoon salt
1 cup buttermilk
4 egg whites, stiffly beaten
  Coconut Pecan Frosting
  (right)

Heat oven to 350°. Grease 3 round layer pans, 8 or 9x1½ inches, or 2 square pans, 8x8x2 or 9x9x2 inches. Line bottoms of pans with waxed paper. In small bowl, pour boiling water over chocolate, stirring until chocolate is melted; set aside to cool.

In large mixer bowl, cream butter and sugar until light and fluffy. Add egg yolks, one at a time, beating after each addition. On low speed, blend in chocolate and vanilla. Mix in flour, soda and salt alternately with buttermilk, beating after each addition until batter is smooth. Fold in egg whites. Divide batter among pans.

Bake 8-inch round layers 35 to 40 minutes, 9-inch round layers 30 to 35 minutes, 8-inch squares 45 to 50 minutes, 9-inch squares 40 to 45 minutes or until top springs back when touched lightly with finger. Cool. Fill layers and frost top of cake with Coconut-Pecan Frosting.

COCONUT-PECAN FROSTING

1 cup evaporated milk	1 teaspoon vanilla
1 cup sugar	1⅓ cups flaked coconut
3 egg yolks	1 cup chopped pecans
½ cup butter or margarine	

Combine evaporated milk, sugar, egg yolks, butter and vanilla in small saucepan. Cook and stir over medium heat until thick, about 12 minutes. Stir in coconut and pecans. Beat until thick enough to spread.

Makes 2½ cups.

BROWNIE FUDGE CAKE

Brownie mix makes a rich fudge cake—quick, delicious and just the right size.

1 package (15.5 ounces) fudge brownie mix	½ cup finely chopped nuts Quick Fudge Frosting (page 191)
½ cup water	
2 eggs	

Heat oven to 350°. Grease and flour square pan, 9x9x2 inches. Measure brownie mix (dry), half the water and the eggs into small mixer bowl. Blend ½ minute on low speed, scraping bowl constantly. Beat 1 minute medium speed, scraping bowl occasionally. Add remaining water; beat 1 minute longer. Fold in nuts. Pour into pan.

Bake about 30 minutes or until top springs back when touched lightly with finger. While warm, frost cake with Quick Fudge Frosting.

BROWNIE NUT CAKE

1¼ cups all-purpose flour* or cake flour	3 tablespoons shortening
1⅓ cups sugar	1 egg
1¼ teaspoons baking powder	½ teaspoon vanilla
½ teaspoon salt	3 ounces melted unsweetened chocolate (cool)
¼ teaspoon soda	
1 cup milk	⅔ cup finely chopped nuts

Heat oven to 350°. Grease and flour square pan, 8x8x2 or 9x9x2 inches. Measure all ingredients into large mixer bowl. Blend ½ minute on low speed, scraping bowl constantly. Beat 3 minutes high speed, scraping bowl occasionally. Pour into pan.

Bake 40 to 50 minutes or until wooden pick inserted in center comes out clean. Cool.

If desired, frost cake with ½ recipe Fudge Frosting (page 190) or ½ recipe Chocolate Cream Cheese Frosting (page 189).

*If using self-rising flour, omit baking powder and salt.

SILVER WHITE CAKE

2¼ cups cake flour or 2 cups all-purpose flour*	½ cup shortening
1½ cups sugar	1 cup milk
3½ teaspoons baking powder	1 teaspoon vanilla
1 teaspoon salt	4 egg whites (½ cup)

Heat oven to 350°. Grease and flour baking pan, 13x9x2 inches, or 2 round layer pans, 8 or 9x1½ inches. Measure flour, sugar, baking powder, salt, shortening, milk and vanilla into large mixer bowl. Blend ½ minute on low speed, scraping bowl constantly. Beat 2 minutes

*Do not use self-rising flour in this recipe.

high speed, scraping bowl occasionally. Add egg whites; beat 2 minutes high speed, scraping bowl occasionally. Pour into pan(s).

Bake oblong 35 to 40 minutes, layers 30 to 35 minutes or until wooden pick inserted in center comes out clean. Cool.

If desired, frost with White Mountain Frosting (page 191), Lemon Swirl (page 190) or Chocolate Butter Frosting (page 185).

Note: For cupcakes, pour batter into paper-lined muffin cups, filling each ½ full. Bake 20 minutes. 2 dozen cupcakes.

VARIATIONS

■ *Filbert Nut Cake:* Add 1 cup ground filberts or hazelnuts to ingredients in mixer bowl. Bake cake in layers. Fill layers and frost cake with Maple Frosting: In large

For a perfect Checkerboard Cake, place foil ring in the center of each pan; make sure the two batters are level.

mixer bowl, combine ⅔ cup soft butter, 2 egg whites, 2 tablespoons maple syrup and 4 cups (1 pound) confectioners' sugar. Beat until frosting is smooth and of spreading consistency.

■ *Lady Baltimore Cake:* Bake cake in layers. Prepare White Mountain Frosting (page 191). For Filling: Mix 1 cup of the frosting, ½ cup finely chopped walnuts, ⅓ cup cut-up raisins and ⅓ cup figs, cut into strips.

Fill layers with half the filling; spread remainder over top of cake. Frost side and top of cake.

■ *Lemon-filled White Cake:* Spread oblong cake or fill layers with Clear Lemon Filling (page 201) and frost with White Mountain Frosting (page 191). If desired, sprinkle frosted cake with about 1 cup flaked or shredded coconut.

■ *Pink Checkerboard Cake:* After greasing and flouring layer pans, make circle dividers for center of pans by folding two 13x6-inch pieces of aluminum foil lengthwise twice, forming 2 strips, each 13x1½ inches. Shape strips into 4-inch circles; fasten with paper clips. Place foil divider in center of each pan.

Divide batter in half. To one half, stir in ¼ teaspoon red food color. Fill center of one pan with pink batter and outer circle with white batter. Fill center of other pan with white batter and outer circle with pink. (Be sure batter in both circles is at same level.) Remove dividers. Bake. Fill and frost cake with Vanilla Butter Frosting (page 185); if desired, decorate cake with maraschino cherries.

PETITS FOURS

One package (18.5 ounces) white cake mix can also be used. Bake at 350° for 20 to 25 minutes.

Follow recipe for Silver White Cake (page 140) except —pour batter into greased and floured jelly roll pan, 15½x10½x1 inch. Bake 25 minutes. Cool. Cut cake into small squares, rounds, diamonds, hearts or other fancy shapes.

Glaze cake pieces by placing upside down, a few at a time, on wire rack over large bowl or baking dish. Pour Petits Fours Icing (page 144) over top so entire cake piece is covered at one time. (Glaze that drips off cakes into bowl can be reheated and used again.) Decorate tops

Cut cooled cake into various shapes with cookie cutters.

Pour glaze over cake pieces; a baking dish catches drips.

Delicate Petits Fours and tea for an afternoon party.

with silver dragées, candy flowers, Gumdrop Roses (page 183) or Decorators' Icing (page 189).

About thirty-five 2-inch squares.

Note: Petits Fours can also be glazed by placing each cake piece on a fork over icing (in double boiler) and spooning the glaze over each. With spatula or another fork, push cake off onto wire rack to set glaze.

PETITS FOURS ICING

9 cups sifted confectioners' sugar (about 2 pounds)
½ cup water
½ cup light corn syrup
1 teaspoon vanilla
½ teaspoon almond extract

Combine ingredients in top of double boiler and heat over boiling water just to lukewarm. (Do not overheat icing or it will become dull.) Remove from heat, leaving icing over hot water to keep it thin. If desired, tint parts of icing delicate pastel colors with food color. If necessary, add hot water, just a few drops at a time, until of spreading consistency.

VARIATION

■ *Apricot-glazed Petits Fours:* Before pouring icing over Petits Fours, glaze each cake piece with Apricot Glaze: Heat 1 jar (12 ounces) apricot preserves with 3 tablespoons water; strain.

Place Petit Four on fork; hold over saucepan and pour warm glaze over each. Place on wire rack; let stand about 1 hour or until set. Glaze with Petits Fours Icing as directed above.

BONNIE BUTTER CAKE

⅔ cup butter or margarine, softened
1¾ cups sugar
2 eggs (⅓ to ½ cup)
1½ teaspoons vanilla
3 cups cake flour or 2¾ cups all-purpose flour*
2½ teaspoons baking powder
1 teaspoon salt
1¼ cups milk
French Silk Frosting (page 189).

Heat oven to 350°. Grease and flour baking pan, 13x9x2 inches, or two 9-inch or three 8-inch round layer pans. In large mixer bowl, mix butter, sugar, eggs and vanilla until fluffy. Beat 5 minutes on high speed,

*If using self-rising flour, omit baking powder and salt.

scraping bowl occasionally. On low speed, mix in flour, baking powder and salt alternately with milk. Pour into pan(s).

Bake oblong 45 to 50 minutes, layers 30 to 35 minutes or until wooden pick inserted in center comes out clean. Cool.

Frost cake with French Silk Frosting or, if desired, with Lemon Swirl Frosting (page 190).

LOAF O' GOLD

2 cups all-purpose flour*	¼ cup shortening
1 cup sugar	¼ cup butter or margarine,
3 teaspoons baking powder	softened
1 teaspoon salt	2 eggs (⅓ to ½ cup)
¾ cup milk	1 teaspoon vanilla

Heat oven to 350°. Grease and flour loaf pan, 9x5x3 inches, or 2 loaf pans, 8½x4½x2½ inches, or 12-cup bundt pan. Measure all ingredients into large mixer bowl. Blend ½ minute on low speed, scraping bowl constantly. Beat 3 minutes high speed, scraping bowl occasionally. Pour into pan(s).

Bake 65 to 70 minutes or until wooden pick inserted in center comes out clean.

*If using self-rising flour, omit baking powder and salt.

VARIATIONS

■ *Marble Pound Cake:* Pour ½ cup of the batter into small bowl; stir in 1 ounce melted unsweetened chocolate (cool). Pour remaining batter into pan(s); spoon chocolate batter over top and swirl.

■ *Toasted Pecan Pound Cake:* Fold ¾ cup toasted finely chopped pecans into batter.

GOLDEN LAYER CAKE

2¼ cups cake flour	½ cup shortening
1½ cups sugar	1 cup milk
3 teaspoons baking powder	1½ teaspoons vanilla
1 teaspoon salt	2 eggs (⅓ to ½ cup)

Heat oven to 350°. Grease and flour baking pan, 13x9x2 inches, or 2 round layer pans, 8 or 9x1½ inches. Measure all ingredients into large mixer bowl. Blend

½ minute on low speed, scraping bowl constantly. Beat 3 minutes high speed, scraping bowl occasionally. Pour into pan(s).

Bake oblong 40 to 45 minutes, layers 30 to 35 minutes or until wooden pick inserted in center comes out clean. Cool.

If desired, frost cake with Maple-Nut Butter Frosting (page 185) or Fudge Frosting (page 190).

NEW STARLIGHT CAKE

A basic but versatile yellow cake.

2 cups all-purpose flour*	1 cup milk
1½ cups sugar	1 teaspoon vanilla
3½ teaspoons baking powder	3 eggs (½ to ⅔ cup)
1 teaspoon salt	
½ cup shortening (half butter or margarine, softened, if desired)	

Heat oven to 350°. Grease and flour baking pan, 13x9x2 inches, or 2 round layer pans, 8 or 9x1½ inches. Measure all ingredients into large mixer bowl. Blend ½ minute on low speed, scraping bowl constantly. Beat 3 minutes high speed, scraping bowl occasionally. Pour into pan(s).

Bake oblong 40 to 45 minutes, layer 30 to 35 minutes or until wooden pick inserted in center comes out clean. Cool.

If desired, frost cake with Easy Penuche Frosting (page 191) or with Butterscotch Broiled Topping (page 196).

*If using self-rising flour, omit baking powder and salt.

VARIATIONS

■ *Eggnog Cake:* Follow recipe for New Starlight or Golden Layer Cake except—add 1 teaspoon nutmeg and ¼ teaspoon ginger to ingredients in mixer bowl and substitute rum flavoring for vanilla.

Frost cake with Creamy Fluff Frosting: In small mixer bowl, chill 1 package (7.2 ounces) fluffy white frosting mix (dry), 1 teaspoon rum flavoring and 1½ cups whipping cream at least 1 hour. Blend on low speed;

beat on medium speed until soft peaks form. Because of whipped cream in frosting, cake must be kept refrigerated.

■ *Lord Baltimore Cake:* Bake New Starlight or Golden Layer Cake in layers. Prepare Pink Mountain Frosting (page 192). For Filling: Mix 1 cup of the frosting, ½ cup toasted flaked coconut or ¼ cup toasted dried macaroon crumbs, ¼ cup *each* toasted chopped pecans, toasted chopped blanched almonds and chopped maraschino cherries.

Fill layers with half the Filling; spread remainder over top. Frost side and top of cake with remaining frosting.

DINETTE CAKE

1½ cups cake flour or 1¼ cups all-purpose flour*	¾ cup milk
1 cup sugar	⅓ cup shortening
1½ teaspoons baking powder	1 egg
½ teaspoon salt	1 teaspoon vanilla

Heat oven to 350°. Grease and flour square pan, 8x8x2 or 9x9x2 inches. Measure all ingredients into large mixer bowl. Blend ½ minute on low speed, scraping bowl constantly. Beat 3 minutes high speed, scraping bowl occasionally. Pour into pan.

Bake 35 to 40 minutes or until wooden pick inserted in center comes out clean. Cool.

If desired, frost cake with ½ recipe Peppermint Cream Cheese Frosting (page 189) or ½ recipe Coconut Broiled Topping (page 197).

If using self-rising flour, omit baking powder and salt.

YELLOW WHIPPED CREAM CAKE

1½ cups chilled whipping cream	1½ cups sugar
3 eggs (½ to ⅔ cup)	2 teaspoons baking powder
1½ teaspoons vanilla	½ teaspoon salt
2¼ cups cake flour or 2 cups all-purpose flour*	

Heat oven to 350°. Grease and flour baking pan, 13x9x2 inches, or 2 round layer pans, 8 or 9x1½ inches. In chilled bowl, beat cream until stiff. Beat eggs until

If using self-rising flour, omit baking powder and salt.

thick and lemon colored. Fold eggs and vanilla into whipped cream. Stir together remaining ingredients; fold gently into cream-egg mixture until blended. Pour into pan(s).

Bake oblong about 45 minutes, layers 30 to 35 minutes or until wooden pick inserted in center comes out clean. Cool.

If desired, frost cake with Velvet Cream Frosting (page 193) or top with Cherry Topping (page 198).

BLACK FOREST CHERRY CAKE

With this torte-like cake, you'll think you're ready to compete with a Viennese pastry chef.

Bake Yellow Whipped Cream Cake (page 147) in layers. Prepare Cherry Filling (below).

In chilled bowl, beat 1½ cups chilled whipping cream and ¼ cup confectioners' sugar until very stiff.

To assemble cake, place one layer upside down on serving plate. With decorators' tube or spoon, form thin rim of the sweetened whipped cream around outer edge of layer. Fill center with Cherry Filling. Place other layer top side up on filling. Gently spread whipped cream on side and top of the cake.

Grate ⅓ bar sweet cooking chocolate. Gently press the chocolate by teaspoonsfuls onto side of the cake.

If desired, place whipped cream in decorators' tube with star tip. Pipe border of cream around edge of cake. Beginning from center of cake, outline individual portions in a spoke-fashion design. Place desired number of reserved dipped cherries in each outlined portion. Because of the whipped cream, cake must be kept refrigerated.

CHERRY FILLING

2 tablespoons cornstarch
2 tablespoons sugar
1 can (1 pound) pitted dark sweet cherries, drained (reserve syrup)

1 tablespoon brandy flavoring

Stir together cornstarch and sugar in small saucepan. Add enough water to reserved syrup to measure 1 cup; stir into sugar-cornstarch mixture. Cook, stirring constantly, until mixture thickens and boils. Boil and stir 1 minute. Cool to lukewarm.

Stir in brandy flavoring. Dip 36 cherries into thickened syrup; set cherries aside. Cut remaining cherries into quarters and stir into thickened syrup. Chill thoroughly.

VARIATION

■ *Cherry Torte Eleganté:* Double all ingredients in Cherry Filling but do not cut up the remaining sweet cherries.

CHOCOLATE WHIPPED CREAM CAKE

1⅔ cups chilled whipping cream	1 teaspoon almond extract
3 eggs (½ to ⅔ cup)	2½ cups cake flour or 2¼ cups all-purpose flour*
3 ounces melted unsweetened chocolate (cool)	1½ cups sugar
	2¼ teaspoons baking powder
	½ teaspoon salt

Heat oven to 350°. Grease and flour baking pan, 13x9x2 inches, or 2 round layer pans, 8 or 9x1½ inches. In chilled bowl, beat cream until stiff. Beat eggs until thick and lemon colored. Fold eggs, chocolate and almond extract into cream.

Stir together remaining ingredients; fold gently into cream-egg mixture until well blended and batter is uniformly brown. Pour into pan(s).

Bake oblong about 45 minutes, 8-inch layers 35 to 40 minutes, 9-inch layers 30 to 35 minutes or until wooden pick inserted in center comes out clean. Cool.

If desired, frost cake with Browned Butter Frosting (page 185) or top with Toffee Topping or Caramel Fluff (page 198).

*If using self-rising flour, omit baking powder and salt.

ALMOND TORTE

Bake Chocolate Whipped Cream Cake (above) in layers. Cool. Split to make 4 layers.

Prepare Almond Whipped Cream Filling (page 150). Fill layers and frost top of cake with filling, using ¼ of the filling (about ¾ cup) for each layer. Sprinkle chocolate shot in ring around top edge of cake. Decorate cake with blanched almonds. Because of the whipped cream, cake must be kept refrigerated.

ALMOND WHIPPED CREAM FILLING

2 cups chilled whipping cream

1½ teaspoons almond extract
½ cup confectioners' sugar

In chilled bowl, beat cream, almond extract and sugar until stiff.

BANANA-NUT CAKE

2¼ cups cake flour
1⅔ cups sugar
1¼ teaspoons baking powder
1¼ teaspoons soda
1 teaspoon salt
⅔ cup shortening

⅔ cup buttermilk
3 eggs (½ to ⅔ cup)
1¼ cups mashed ripe bananas
⅔ cup finely chopped nuts

Heat oven to 350°. Grease and flour baking pan, 13x9x2 inches, or two 9-inch or three 8-inch round layer pans. Measure all ingredients into large mixer bowl. Blend ½ minute on low speed, scraping bowl constantly. Beat 3 minutes high speed, scraping bowl occasionally. Pour into pan(s).

Bake oblong 45 to 50 minutes, layers 35 to 40 minutes or until wooden pick inserted in center comes out clean. Cool.

If desired, frost cake with Vanilla Butter Frosting (page 185) or Cream Cheese Frosting (page 189).

BUTTERMILK SPICE CAKE

Try with Butterscotch Broiled Topping, page 196.

2½ cups all-purpose flour* or cake flour
1 cup granulated sugar
¾ cup brown sugar (packed)
1 teaspoon baking powder
1 teaspoon soda
1 teaspoon salt

¾ teaspoon cinnamon
¾ teaspoon allspice
½ teaspoon cloves
½ teaspoon nutmeg
1⅓ cups buttermilk
½ cup shortening
3 eggs (½ to ⅔ cup)

Heat oven to 350°. Grease and flour baking pan, 13x9x2 inches, or 2 round layer pans, 8 or 9x1½ inches. Measure all ingredients into large mixer bowl. Blend ½ minute on low speed, scraping bowl constantly. Beat 3 minutes high speed, scraping bowl occasionally. Pour into pan(s).

*If using self-rising flour, omit baking powder, soda and salt.

Bake oblong 45 minutes, layers 40 to 45 minutes or until wooden pick inserted in center comes out clean. Cool.

CHOCOLATE CHIP CAKE

Tiny flecks of chocolate and a rich butterscotch filling team up to create a moist, flavorful cake.

2 cups all-purpose flour*	½ cup semisweet chocolate pieces, finely chopped
1 cup dark brown sugar (packed)	1½ teaspoons vanilla
½ cup granulated sugar	Butterscotch Filling (below)
3 teaspoons baking powder	¼ cup finely chopped walnuts
1 teaspoon salt	
½ teaspoon soda	Chocolate Chip Glaze (below)
½ cup shortening	
1¼ cups milk	
3 eggs (½ to ⅔ cup)	

Heat oven to 350°. Grease and flour 2 round layer pans, 8 or 9x1½ inches. Measure all ingredients except filling, walnuts and glaze into large mixer bowl. Blend ½ minute on low speed, scraping bowl constantly. Beat 3 minutes high speed, scraping bowl occasionally. Pour into pans.

Bake 40 to 45 minutes or until wooden pick inserted in center comes out clean. Cool. Fill layers with Butterscotch Filling, sprinkling nuts over filling. Spread Chocolate Chip Glaze over top of cake.

*If using self-rising flour, omit baking powder, salt and soda.

BUTTERSCOTCH FILLING

½ cup light brown sugar (packed)	¼ teaspoon salt
¼ cup cornstarch	½ cup water
	1 tablespoon butter

Stir together sugar, cornstarch and salt. Stir in water. Cook, stirring constantly, until mixture thickens and boils. Boil and stir 1 minute. Blend in butter. Cool.

CHOCOLATE CHIP GLAZE

½ cup semisweet chocolate pieces	2 tablespoons butter
	1 tablespoon light corn syrup

Heat all ingredients over low heat, stirring constantly, until chocolate is melted. Cool slightly.

WILLIAMSBURG ORANGE CAKE

This rich, mellow orange cake—laced with golden raisins and nuts and topped with tangy orange frosting—deserves a special occasion to show it off.

2¾ cups cake flour or 2½ cups all-purpose flour*	3 eggs (½ to ⅔ cup)
1½ cups sugar	1½ teaspoons vanilla
1½ teaspoons soda	1 cup golden raisins, cut up
¾ teaspoon salt	½ cup finely chopped nuts
1½ cups buttermilk	1 tablespoon grated orange peel
½ cup butter or margarine, softened	Williamsburg Butter Frosting (below)
¼ cup shortening	

Heat oven to 350°. Grease and flour baking pan, 13x9x2 inches, or two 9-inch or three 8-inch round layer pans. Measure all ingredients except frosting into large mixer bowl. Blend ½ minute on low speed, scraping bowl constantly. Beat 3 minutes high speed, scraping bowl occasionally. Pour into pan(s).

Bake oblong 45 to 50 minutes, layers 30 to 35 minutes or until wooden pick inserted in center comes out clean. Cool. Frost cake with Williamsburg Butter Frosting.

*If using self-rising flour, decrease soda to ½ teaspoon and omit salt.

WILLIAMSBURG BUTTER FROSTING

For oblong cake or two 9-inch layers:

⅓ cup soft butter or margarine	3 to 4 tablespoons orange-flavored liqueur or, if desired, orange juice
3 cups confectioners' sugar	2 teaspoons grated orange peel

For three 8-inch layers:

½ cup soft butter or margarine	4 to 5 tablespoons orange-flavored liqueur or, if desired, orange juice
4½ cups confectioners' sugar	1 tablespoon grated orange peel

Blend butter and sugar. Stir in liqueur and orange peel; beat until smooth.

OATMEAL SPICE CAKE

1½ cups all-purpose flour*
1 cup quick-cooking oats
1 cup brown sugar (packed)
½ cup granulated sugar
1½ teaspoons soda
1 teaspoon cinnamon
½ teaspoon salt
½ teaspoon nutmeg

½ cup shortening
1 cup water
2 eggs (½ to ⅔ cup)
2 tablespoons dark molasses
Coconut Topping or Pineapple-Coconut Topping (below)

Heat oven to 350°. Grease and flour baking pan, 13x9x2 inches. Measure all ingredients except topping into large mixer bowl. Blend ½ minute on low speed, scraping bowl constantly. Beat 3 minutes high speed, scraping bowl occasionally. Pour into pan.

Bake 35 to 40 minutes or until wooden pick inserted in center comes out clean. Cool slightly. Spread topping over cake.

Set oven control at broil and/or 550°. Place cake 3 inches from heat. Broil 2 to 3 minutes or until topping is golden brown.

*If using self-rising flour, omit soda and salt.

COCONUT TOPPING

¼ cup butter, melted
⅔ cup brown sugar (packed)

½ cup flaked coconut
½ cup chopped pecans
3 tablespoons light cream

Mix all ingredients thoroughly.

PINEAPPLE-COCONUT TOPPING

1 cup brown sugar (packed)
1 can (8¾ ounces) crushed pineapple, well drained

¼ cup soft butter or margarine
½ cup chopped nuts
½ cup flaked coconut

Mix all ingredients thoroughly.

QUICK DATE CAKE

1 package (14 ounces) date bar mix
½ cup hot water
2 eggs

1 teaspoon baking powder
½ cup finely chopped walnuts

Heat oven to 375°. Grease square pan, 8x8x2 inches. Combine date filling from date bar mix and hot water.

Blend in crumbly mix, eggs, baking powder and nuts. Spread in pan.

Bake about 30 minutes or until top springs back when touched lightly with finger.

Note: This recipe can be doubled and baked in greased baking pan, 13x9x2 inches.

APPLESAUCE CAKE

A moist, fluffy version of an old-fashioned favorite. Canned applesauce is the new-fashioned plus.

2½ cups all-purpose flour* or cake flour	½ teaspoon allspice
2 cups sugar	1½ cups canned applesauce
1½ teaspoons soda	½ cup water
1½ teaspoons salt	½ cup shortening
¼ teaspoon baking powder	2 eggs (⅓ to ½ cup)
¾ teaspoon cinnamon	1 cup raisins
½ teaspoon cloves	½ cup finely chopped walnuts

Heat oven to 350°. Grease and flour baking pan, 13x9x2 inches, or 2 round layer pans, 8 or 9x1½ inches. Measure all ingredients into large mixer bowl. Blend ½ minute on low speed, scraping bowl constantly. Beat 3 minutes high speed, scraping bowl occasionally. Pour into pan(s).

Bake oblong 60 to 65 minutes, layers 50 to 55 minutes or until wooden pick inserted in center comes out clean. Cool.

If desired, frost cake with Browned Butter Frosting (page 185) or Satiny Beige Frosting (page 192).

*Do not use self-rising flour in this recipe.

Cake Mix Cakes

Bake a cake mix and you have a delicious dessert. But bake a mix with added ingredients, or frost and fill the cake using extra-special recipes, and you have a custom-made dessert stamped with your own individuality.

TRIPLE FUDGE CAKE

1 package (4 ounces)
  chocolate pudding and pie
  filling
1 package (18.5 ounces)
  devils food cake mix

½ cup semisweet chocolate
  pieces
½ cup chopped nuts

Heat oven to 350°. Grease and flour baking pan, 13x9x2 inches. In large saucepan, cook chocolate pudding and pie filling as directed on package. Blend cake mix (dry) thoroughly into hot pudding, beating by hand or with mixer 1 to 2 minutes. Pour into pan. Sprinkle batter with chocolate pieces and nuts.

Bake 30 to 35 minutes or until wooden pick inserted in center comes out clean. Serve warm or cool and, if desired, with whipped cream.

CAROLINA LEMON POUND CAKE

Heat oven to 350°. Grease and flour tube pan, 10x4 inches, 12-cup bundt pan or 2-quart anodized aluminum mold. Prepare 1 package (18.5 ounces) lemon cake mix as directed on package except—use 2 tablespoons less water. If desired, add ½ cup finely chopped nuts. Pour into pan.

Bake 45 to 55 minutes or until wooden pick inserted in cake comes out clean. Cool 10 minutes; remove from pan. Dust with confectioners' sugar, glaze with Lemon Glaze (below) or serve with ice cream and fresh or frozen fruit.

LEMON GLAZE

Measure 1¾ cups lemon creamy-type frosting mix (dry) into small bowl; blend in 2 to 3 tablespoons hot water and 1 tablespoon light corn syrup. Beat until smooth. Add 1 to 2 teaspoons water if necessary.

MAPLE SYRUP CAKE

1 package (18.5 ounces)
  yellow cake mix
⅓ cup sugar

1 teaspoon cinnamon
1 cup maple-flavored syrup
½ cup chopped nuts

Bake cake in baking pan, 13x9x2 inches, as directed on package. Cool 5 minutes. Cut cake into large diamond shapes. Mix sugar and cinnamon; sprinkle over top of cake. Heat syrup slightly; pour over cake. Sprinkle with nuts. Let stand a few minutes. Serve warm or cool.

MOCHA-MARBLE CAKE

Bake 1 package (19 ounces) marble cake mix in 2 round layer pans, 8 or 9x1½ inches, or baking pan, 13x9x2 inches, as directed except—substitute cold coffee for the water or add 1 tablespoon instant coffee to the dry mix. Frost with Mocha-Chip Frosting (below).

MOCHA-CHIP FROSTING

Prepare 1 package (7.2 ounces) fluffy white frosting mix as directed except—substitute hot coffee for the boiling water or add 2 teaspoons instant coffee to the dry mix. After beating, fold in ½ cup semisweet chocolate pieces or ½ cup shaved semisweet or unsweetened chocolate if desired.

COUNTRY LOAF CAKE

Heat oven to 350° (325° for glass pans). Grease and flour 2 loaf pans, 9x5x3 inches. Prepare any flavor layer cake mix (about 18.5 ounces) as directed on package except—use 2 tablespoons less water. Pour into pans.

Bake 30 to 35 minutes or until wooden pick inserted in center comes out clean. Cool.

VARIATIONS

■ *Almond Loaf Cake:* Prepare white cake mix, adding ½ teaspoon almond extract to batter. Before baking, sprinkle ½ cup sliced almonds over batter in pans.

■ *Anise Loaf Cake:* Prepare white cake mix, adding 1 tablespoon crushed anise seed before adding the water.

■ *Glazed Nut Loaf:* Fold ⅓ cup finely chopped nuts into Country Loaf Cake batter. While cakes are warm, spread Creamy Glaze (page 195) over top, letting it drizzle down sides of cakes. Decorate tops with candied cherries and nuts.

LEMON-ORANGE CAKE

Orange juice concentrate is the surprise filling between the lemony layers.

1 package (18.5 ounces) lemon cake mix
1 can (6 ounces) frozen orange juice concentrate, thawed

2 tablespoons butter or margarine, softened
½ cup confectioners' sugar

Bake cake in 2 round layer pans, 8 or 9x1½ inches, as directed on package. Cool. Split to make 4 layers.

Reserve 1 tablespoon orange juice concentrate for glaze. Fill layers with remaining concentrate, using 3 tablespoons between each layer. Mix reserved 1 tablespoon concentrate, the butter and confectioners' sugar. Spread over top of cake. Chill thoroughly before serving.

TOASTED MARSHMALLOW CAKE

A small but rich cake with a luscious snow-capped topping. Plus an extra layer for snacking.

1 package (18.5 ounces) devils food cake mix
8 large marshmallows

⅓ cup brown sugar (packed)
⅓ cup chopped nuts

Heat oven to 350°. Prepare cake mix as directed on package except—pour half the batter (about 2½ cups) into greased and floured square pan, 9x9x2 inches. (Bake remaining batter in greased and floured round layer pan, 8 or 9x1½ inches, as directed on package; use as desired.)

Cut marshmallows in half crosswise and arrange in rows over batter in pan. Mix brown sugar and nuts; sprinkle over top. Bake 25 to 35 minutes. (If marshmallows become too brown, cover cake with aluminum foil.) Serve warm.

Note: For a larger cake, pour all the batter into greased and floured baking pan, 13x9x2 inches. Increase marshmallows to 12, brown sugar to ½ cup and chopped nuts to ½ cup. Bake 40 to 45 minutes.

HAZELNUT TORTE

1 package (18.5 ounces)
   yellow cake mix
1 cup finely chopped
   hazelnuts or filberts
1½ cups chilled whipping
   cream

⅓ cup confectioners' sugar
1 package (15.4 ounces)
   chocolate fudge frosting
   mix

Bake cake in 2 round layer pans, 8 or 9x1½ inches, as directed on package except—fold hazelnuts into batter. Cool. Split to make 4 layers.

In chilled bowl, beat cream and sugar until stiff. Fill layers. Prepare frosting as directed on package. Frost side and top of cake. If desired, garnish top with additional hazelnuts. Because of the whipped cream, refrigerate any leftover cake.

FESTIVE CRANBERRY CAKE

1 package (18.5 ounces)
   white cake mix
1½ cups chilled whipping
   cream

⅓ cup confectioners' sugar
1 jar (14 ounces) cranberry-
   orange relish

Bake cake in 2 round layer pans, 9x1½ inches, as directed on package. Cool thoroughly. Split to make 4 layers.

In chilled bowl, beat cream and sugar until stiff. Stack layers, spreading each with ¼ of the whipped cream, then topping cream with ¼ of the cranberry-orange relish and swirling it into whipped cream.

Chill cake 1 to 2 hours before serving. Because of the whipped cream, refrigerate any leftover cake.

12 to 16 servings.

VARIATIONS

■ *Cranberry-Pineapple Cake:* Do not split layers. Stir together 1 can (8¾ ounces) crushed pineapple and the cranberry-orange relish; drain.

Fill layers with ⅔ cup of the whipped cream covered with half the cranberry-pineapple mixture. Frost side and top of cake with remaining whipped cream and cover top of cake with remaining cranberry-pineapple mixture.

■ *Scandinavian Lingonberry Cake:* Substitute 1 jar (14 ounces) lingonberries for the cranberry-orange relish.

BANANA UPSIDE-DOWN CAKE

¼ cup butter or margarine
½ cup brown sugar (packed)
2 or 3 bananas
1 package (18.5 ounces)
 yellow or devils food
 cake mix

Sweetened whipped
cream

Heat oven to 350°. Melt butter over low heat in square pan, 8x8x2 or 9x9x2 inches, or round layer pan, 8 or 9x1½ inches. Sprinkle brown sugar over butter. Peel bananas; cut into ½-inch slices and arrange slices evenly over sugar mixture.

Prepare cake mix as directed on package except— pour half the batter (about 2½ cups) evenly over banana slices.

Bake 35 to 45 minutes or until wooden pick inserted in center comes out clean. Invert cake immediately onto plate; leave pan over cake a few minutes. Serve warm topped with sweetened whipped cream. (Bake remaining batter in greased and floured 8- or 9-inch round layer pan as directed on package. Use cake as desired.)

9 servings.

BERRY BASKET CAKE

A picture-pretty cake to honor the fresh berries in spring and summer.

1 package (18.5 ounces)
 yellow cake mix
3 egg whites
¼ teaspoon cream of tartar

6 tablespoons sugar
½ teaspoon vanilla
Sweetened fresh berries

Bake cake in 2 round layer pans, 9x1½ inches, as directed on package. Cool.

Heat oven to 400°. Place one layer on ungreased baking sheet. Beat egg whites and cream of tartar until foamy. Beat in sugar, 1 tablespoon at a time; continue beating until stiff and glossy. Do not underbeat. Beat in vanilla.

Pile mounds of the meringue around top edge of cake for basket effect. Bake 8 to 10 minutes or until light brown. Serve warm or cool with sweetened fresh berries heaped in center of cake. (Reserve other layer for future use.)

6 to 8 servings.

Foam-type Cakes

Chiffon, angel food and sponge cakes, with their lacy lightness and delicacy, are the spectaculars of the cake world. Comforting to waistline-watchers, too—no frosting, fewer calories.

All three depend on a foaming meringue for their lightness, but they differ in other ways.

Angel food cake has no leavening, no shortening and no yolks. Angel cakes may be baked in loaf pans as well as the usual tube pan.

Sponge cakes use both the whites *and* yolks of eggs. Sometimes leavening is called for, but shortening is never used. (Sponge cakes may also be used for rolled cakes, such as the jelly roll.)

Chiffon cakes combine the qualities of foam-type cakes and shortening-type cakes. While their lightness depends on the egg white meringue, they also use egg yolks, leavening and shortening. They are moist and keep well.

Some success tips to keep in mind:

■ Beat egg whites until stiff, straight peaks form. Separate the eggs as soon as they are removed from the refrigerator but let them come to room temperature before beating. Be sure the bowl and beater are dry, free of fat, oil or egg yolk.

■ Bake cake in tube pan on bottom rack in oven.

■ Do not open oven until minimum baking time has elapsed.

■ Cakes baked in a tube pan are done when cracks in top feel dry and no imprint remains when top is touched lightly. Foam-type cakes baked in oblong, layer or jelly roll pans are done when a wooden pick inserted in center comes out clean.

■ To remove *cooled* cake from tube pan, loosen first by moving spatula or table knife up and down against

TIPS FOR ANGEL FOOD AND CHIFFON CAKES

1. Egg whites must be beaten and stiff peaks form. Be sure egg whites are at room temperature.

2. To fold, cut down through center of beaten egg whites, along bottom and up side, rotate ¼ turn. Repeat.

3. Use a spatula to break down large air pockets and to seal batter against side of pan and tube.

4. To test angel food cake for doneness, touch cracks. They should feel dry and no imprint should remain.

5. Cool cake upside down in pan. Support tube on funnel or bottle so cake does not touch counter.

6. To cut cake, use a serrated knife and a light sawing motion. An electric knife also does a good job.

side of pan. Next, turn the pan over and hit one side against the counter. The cake will slip out. (If using a pan with a non-stick coating, follow manufacturer's directions.)

ORANGE CHIFFON CAKE

2¼ cups cake flour or 2 cups all-purpose flour*
1½ cups sugar
3 teaspoons baking powder
1 teaspoon salt
½ cup salad oil
5 egg yolks (with cake flour) or 7 egg yolks (with all-purpose flour)

¾ cup cold water
2 tablespoons grated orange peel
1 cup egg whites (7 or 8)
½ teaspoon cream of tartar
Orange (or Lemon) Butter Icing (below)

Heat oven to 325°. Stir together flour, sugar, baking powder and salt. Make a "well" and add in order: oil, egg yolks, water and orange peel. Stir until smooth.

Measure egg whites and cream of tartar into large mixer bowl. Beat until whites form very stiff peaks. Gradually pour egg yolk mixture over beaten whites, gently folding *just* until blended. Pour into ungreased tube pan, 10x4 inches.

Bake about 75 minutes or until top springs back when touched lightly with finger. Invert tube pan on funnel; let hang until cake is completely cool.

Frost cake with Orange (or Lemon) Butter Icing. If desired, arrange mandarin orange segments around base of cake; garnish top of cake with a flower of orange segments and a maraschino cherry.

*If using self-rising flour, omit baking powder and salt.

ORANGE (OR LEMON) BUTTER ICING

⅓ cup soft butter or margarine
3 cups confectioners' sugar
1½ tablespoons grated orange (or lemon) peel

About 3 tablespoons orange (or lemon) juice

Blend butter, sugar, orange or lemon peel and juice until smooth.

VARIATIONS

■ *Chocolate Chip Chiffon Cake:* Increase sugar to 1¾ cups, add 2 teaspoons vanilla and omit orange peel. Just before pouring batter into pan, gently fold in 3 squares (1 ounce each) sweet, semisweet or unsweetened chocolate, grated. Top cake with Almond Fluff (page 199) or spread with Chocolate Glaze (page 196).

■ *Lemon Chiffon Cake:* Omit orange peel; add 2 teaspoons grated lemon peel and 2 teaspoons vanilla.

■ *Maple Pecan Chiffon Cake:* Use ¾ cup granulated sugar and ¾ cup brown sugar (packed) for the sugar; add 2 teaspoons maple flavoring and omit orange peel. Just before pouring batter into pan, gently fold in 1 cup very finely chopped pecans. Spread cake with Butter-Rum Glaze (page 196) or Browned Butter Glaze (page 196).

■ *Spice Chiffon Cake:* Add 1 teaspoon cinnamon and ½ teaspoon *each* nutmeg, allspice and cloves to the dry ingredients; omit orange peel. Spread cake with Orange Glaze (page 196) or serve with Caramel Fluff (page 198).

TWO-EGG YELLOW CHIFFON CAKE

2 eggs, separated	1 teaspoon salt
1½ cups sugar	⅓ cup salad oil
2¼ cups cake flour	1 cup milk
3 teaspoons baking powder	1½ teaspoons vanilla

Heat oven to 350°. Grease and flour baking pan, 13x9x2 inches, or 2 round layer pans, 8 or 9x1½ inches. In small mixer bowl, beat egg whites until foamy. Beat in ½ cup of the sugar, 1 tablespoon at a time; continue beating until very stiff and glossy. Set meringue aside.

Measure remaining sugar, the flour, baking powder and salt into large mixer bowl. Add oil, half the milk and the vanilla; beat 1 minute on high speed, scraping bowl constantly. Add remaining milk and the egg yolks; beat 1 minute, scraping bowl occasionally. Fold in meringue. Pour into pan(s).

Bake oblong 40 to 45 minutes, layers 30 to 35 minutes or until wooden pick inserted in center comes out clean. Cool. If desired, frost cake with Pineapple Butter Frosting (page 185).

VARIATION

■ *Lemon Chiffon Cake:* Decrease vanilla to 1 teaspoon and add 1 teaspoon grated lemon peel.

ORANGE CAKE

Follow recipe for Two-Egg Yellow Chiffon Cake (above) except—omit milk and vanilla; add grated peel of 1 orange and juice of 1 orange plus enough milk to measure 1 cup liquid. Bake cake in 2 round layer pans, 8 or 9x1½ inches. Cool.

Split to make 4 layers. Fill layers with Orange Filling (below). In chilled bowl, beat 1 cup chilled whipping cream until stiff. Frost side and top of cake.

ORANGE FILLING

Prepare 1 package (3 ounces) vanilla pudding and pie filling as directed on package except—omit milk and add grated peel of 1 orange and juice of 1 orange plus enough water to measure 1 cup liquid. Cool. In chilled bowl, beat ½ cup chilled whipping cream until stiff. Fold in pudding.

TWO-EGG CHOCOLATE CHIFFON CAKE

2 eggs, separated	⅓ cup salad oil
1½ cups sugar	1 cup buttermilk or milk
1¾ cups cake flour	2 ounces melted
1 teaspoon salt	unsweetened chocolate
¾ teaspoon soda	(cool)

Heat oven to 350°. Grease and flour baking pan, 13x9x2 inches, or 2 round layer pans, 8 or 9x1½ inches. In small mixer bowl, beat egg whites until foamy. Beat in ½ cup of the sugar, 1 tablespoon at a time; continue beating until very stiff and glossy. Set meringue aside.

Measure remaining sugar, the flour, salt and soda into large mixer bowl. Add oil and half the buttermilk; beat 1 minute on high speed, scraping bowl. Add remaining buttermilk, the egg yolks and chocolate; beat

1 minute, scraping bowl occasionally. Fold in meringue. Pour into pan(s).

Bake oblong 40 to 45 minutes, layers 30 to 35 minutes or until wooden pick inserted in center comes out clean. Cool. If desired, frost cake with Cherry Butter Frosting (page 185).

VARIATION

■ *Chocolate Creole Chiffon Cake:* Omit buttermilk and substitute 1 tablespoon instant coffee dissolved in 1 cup boiling water and cooled.

BAVARIAN TORTE

Bake Two-Egg Chocolate Chiffon Cake (left) in 2 round layer pans, 8 or 9x1½ inches. Cool. Split to make 4 layers. Fill layers and frost top of torte with Crème Filling (below), sprinkling each layer with 1 to 2 tablespoons grated unsweetened chocolate. Refrigerate at least 8 hours.

CRÈME FILLING

1½ cups chilled whipping cream	⅔ cup brown sugar (packed)
1 package (8 ounces) cream cheese, softened	1 teaspoon vanilla
	⅛ teaspoon salt

In chilled bowl, beat cream until stiff. Blend cream cheese, sugar, vanilla and salt. Fold in cream.

ALMOND-PEACH ANGEL FOOD CAKE

1 package (15 or 16 ounces) angel food cake mix	1½ cups chilled whipping cream
Almond-Peach Filling (page 166)	¼ cup confectioners' sugar

Bake cake as directed on package. Prepare cake for filling (see Angel Food Waldorf, page 282).

Place cake on serving plate; fill cavity with Almond-Peach Filling. Replace top of cake. In chilled bowl, beat cream and sugar until stiff; frost cake. Garnish with reserved peach slices. Refrigerate at least 2 hours before serving.

ALMOND-PEACH FILLING

1 package (12 ounces)
  frozen sliced peaches,
  thawed
1 teaspoon lemon juice
  Boiling water
1 package (6 ounces)
  orange-flavored gelatin

½ cup toasted chopped
  almonds
½ teaspoon almond extract
6 drops red food color
6 drops yellow food color
1 cup chilled whipping
  cream

Drain peaches, reserving syrup. Reserve 6 peach slices; sprinkle with lemon juice and refrigerate.

Crush remaining peaches. Measure reserved syrup and add enough boiling water to measure 2 cups. Pour over gelatin in large bowl, stirring until gelatin is dissolved. Stir in crushed peaches, almonds, extract and food colors. Chill until very thick.

In chilled bowl, beat cream until stiff. Beat gelatin mixture at high speed until thick and fluffy or about double in volume. Fold in cream.

ANGEL FOOD CAKE

ANGEL FOOD SUPREME

1 cup cake flour
¾ cup plus 2 tablespoons
  sugar
12 egg whites (1½ cups)
1½ teaspoons cream of tartar

¼ teaspoon salt
¾ cup sugar
1½ teaspoons vanilla
½ teaspoon almond extract

ANGEL FOOD DELUXE

1 cup cake flour
1½ cups confectioners' sugar
12 egg whites (1½ cups)
1½ teaspoons cream of tartar

¼ teaspoon salt
1 cup granulated sugar
1½ teaspoons vanilla
½ teaspoon almond extract

Heat oven to 375°. Stir together flour and first amount of sugar; set aside.

In large mixer bowl, beat egg whites, cream of tartar and salt until foamy. Add second amount of sugar, 2 tablespoons at a time, beating on high speed until meringue holds stiff peaks. Gently fold in flavorings. Sprinkle flour-sugar mixture, ¼ cup at a time over meringue, folding in gently just until flour-sugar mixture disappears. Push batter into ungreased tube pan, 10x4 inches. Gently cut through batter.

Bake 30 to 35 minutes or until top springs back when touched lightly with finger. Invert tube pan on funnel; let hang until cake is completely cool.

If desired, top cake with Toffee Topping (page 198), Butter-Rum Glaze (page 196) or Cinnamon Whipped Cream (page 199).

VARIATIONS

■ *Cherry Angel Food Cake:* Before pushing Angel Food Supreme batter into pan, fold in ½ cup chopped maraschino cherries, well drained.

■ *Coconut Angel Food Cake:* Before pushing Angel Food Deluxe batter into pan, fold in 1 cup shredded coconut, ½ cup at a time.

IMPERIAL ANGEL

Bake Angel Food Cake (pages 166-167). Cool. Slice 1 quart strawberries. Prepare 1 envelope (2 ounces) dessert topping mix as directed on package. Fold in 2 teaspoons grated orange peel and 1 teaspoon almond extract. Fold strawberries into topping. Top slices of cake with strawberry topping.

12 servings.

Note: 1 package (16 ounces) frozen strawberry halves, thawed, can be substituted for the fresh strawberries.

DAFFODIL CAKE

1 cup cake flour	¾ cup sugar
¾ cup plus 2 tablespoons sugar	6 egg yolks
12 egg whites (1½ cups)	1½ teaspoons vanilla
1½ teaspoons cream of tartar	½ teaspoon almond extract
¼ teaspoon salt	Lemon Glaze or Creamy Glaze (page 168)

Heat oven to 375°. Stir together flour and ¾ cup plus 2 tablespoons sugar; set aside.

In large mixer bowl, beat egg whites, cream of tartar and salt until foamy. Add remaining ¾ cup sugar, 2 tablespoons at a time, beating on high speed until meringue holds stiff peaks. In small mixer bowl, beat egg yolks about 5 minutes or until very thick and lemon colored. Gently fold flavorings into meringue.

Sprinkle flour-sugar mixture, ¼ at a time, over meringue, folding in gently *just* until flour-sugar mixture disappears. Pour half the batter into another bowl; gently fold in egg yolks. Spoon yellow and white batters alternately into ungreased tube pan, 10x4 inches. Gently cut through batters to swirl.

Bake on bottom shelf of oven about 40 minutes or until top springs back when touched lightly with finger. Invert pan on funnel; let hang until cake is completely cool. Spread cake with one of the glazes.

LEMON GLAZE

1 cup confectioners' sugar
½ teaspoon grated lemon peel
1 teaspoon lemon juice
About 2 tablespoons milk
1 drop yellow food color

Mix all ingredients until smooth.

CREAMY GLAZE

Mix 1½ cups confectioners' sugar, 2 tablespoons soft butter, ½ teaspoon almond extract and 1 to 2 tablespoons hot water until smooth.

FLUFFY SPONGE CAKE

6 egg yolks (about ½ cup)
1½ cups sugar
1½ cups all-purpose flour* or cake flour
1 teaspoon baking powder
½ teaspoon salt
⅓ cup cold water
2 teaspoons vanilla
1 teaspoon lemon extract
1 teaspoon grated lemon peel, if desired
6 egg whites (¾ cup)
½ teaspoon cream of tartar

Heat oven to 325°. In small mixer bowl, beat egg yolks until very thick and lemon colored, about 5 minutes. Pour yolks into large mixer bowl; gradually beat in sugar. On low speed, mix in flour, baking powder and

*If using self-rising flour, omit baking powder and salt.

salt alternately with water, flavorings and lemon peel.

In another large mixer bowl, beat egg whites and cream of tartar until stiff. Gradually fold egg yolk mixture into egg whites. Pour into ungreased tube pan, 10x4 inches.

Bake 60 to 65 minutes. Invert pan on funnel; let hang until cake is completely cool. If desired, spoon sweetened fresh fruit or thawed frozen fruit over slices of cake; top with sweetened whipped cream or dairy sour cream.

JELLY ROLL

3 eggs (½ to ⅔ cup)	1 teaspoon baking powder
1 cup granulated sugar	¼ teaspoon salt
⅓ cup water	About ⅔ cup jelly or jam
1 teaspoon vanilla	Confectioners' sugar
1 cup cake flour or ¾ cup all-purpose flour*	

Heat oven to 375°. Line jelly roll pan, 15½x10½x1 inch, with aluminum foil or waxed paper; grease. In small mixer bowl, beat eggs about 5 minutes or until very thick and lemon colored. Pour eggs into large mixer bowl; gradually beat in granulated sugar. On low speed, blend in water and vanilla. Gradually add flour, baking powder and salt, beating just until batter is smooth. Pour into pan, spreading batter to corners.

Bake 12 to 15 minutes or until wooden pick inserted in center comes out clean. Loosen cake from edges of pan; invert on towel sprinkled with confectioners' sugar. Carefully remove foil; trim off stiff edges if necessary.

While hot, roll cake and towel from narrow end. Cool on wire rack. Unroll cake; remove towel. Beat jelly slightly with fork to soften; spread over cake. Roll up; sprinkle with confectioners' sugar.

10 servings.

If using self-rising flour, omit baking powder and salt.

VARIATIONS

■ *Lemon Cake Roll:* Omit jelly. Spread unrolled cake with cooled Clear Lemon Filling (page 201). Roll up; sprinkle with confectioners' sugar. Chill at least 1 hour. Serve with sweetened whipped cream. 10 servings.

■ *Strawberry-filled Roll:* Omit jelly. About 1 hour before serving, beat ½ cup chilled whipping cream and 2 tablespoons confectioners' sugar in chilled bowl until stiff. Spread on unrolled cake. Arrange 2 cups sliced fresh strawberries over whipped cream. Roll up; sprinkle with confectioners' sugar. Chill. Serve with sweetened whipped cream. 8 to 10 servings.

CHOCOLATE ROLL

1 cup cake flour or ¾ cup all-purpose flour*	1 cup granulated sugar
¼ cup cocoa	⅓ cup water
1 teaspoon baking powder	1 teaspoon vanilla
¼ teaspoon salt	1 cup whipping cream, sweetened and whipped
3 eggs (½ to ⅔ cup)	Confectioners' sugar

Heat oven to 375°. Line jelly roll pan, 15½x10½x1 inch, with aluminum foil or waxed paper; grease. Stir together flour, cocoa, baking powder and salt; set aside.

In small mixer bowl, beat eggs about 5 minutes or until very thick and lemon colored. Pour eggs into large mixer bowl; gradually beat in granulated sugar. On low speed, blend in water and vanilla. Gradually add flour mixture, beating just until batter is smooth. Pour into pan, spreading batter to corners.

Bake 12 to 15 minutes or until wooden pick inserted in center comes out clean. Loosen cake from edges of pan; invert on towel sprinkled with confectioners' sugar. Carefully remove foil; trim off stiff edges if necessary.

While hot, roll cake and towel from narrow end. Cool on wire rack. Unroll cake; remove towel. Spread whipped cream over cake. Roll up; sprinkle with confectioners' sugar or, if desired, frost with Chocolate Glaze (page 196).

10 servings.

If using self-rising flour, omit baking powder and salt.

Be sure to roll cake from narrow end.

Fruitcakes

Time to start your fruitcakes? Make them 3 to 4 weeks in advance and let them mellow in their wraps. For a richer flavor, pour wine or brandy over the cake before wrapping, or wrap in wine-dampened cloths and place in a tightly covered container; store in a cool place. (Decorate and glaze after storing.) Always serve fruitcake thinly sliced; cut with a non-serrated or electric knife.

YELLOW FRUITCAKE

Rich with fruit and nuts—a fruitcake masterpiece.

3 cups all-purpose flour*
1½ cups sugar
1½ teaspoons baking powder
¾ teaspoon salt
¾ cup shortening
¾ cup butter or margarine, softened
⅔ cup orange juice
9 eggs (2¼ cups)
1 pound candied cherries, cut in half (about 2½ cups)
1 package (15 ounces) golden raisins (about 3 cups)

¾ pound candied pineapple, cut up (about 2 cups)
¼ pound candied citron, cut up (about ⅔ cup)
¼ pound candied orange peel, cut up (about ⅔ cup)
1 can (4 ounces) flaked coconut
½ pound blanched whole almonds (1½ cups)
½ pound pecan halves (about 2 cups)

Heat oven to 275°. Line 2 loaf pans, 9x5x3 inches, with aluminum foil; grease. Measure all ingredients except fruits and nuts into large mixer bowl. Blend ½ minute on low speed, scraping bowl constantly. Beat 3 minutes high speed, scraping bowl occasionally. Stir in fruits and nuts. Spread mixture evenly in pans.

Bake 2½ to 3 hours or until wooden pick inserted in center comes out clean. If necessary, cover with aluminum foil the last hour of baking to prevent excessive browning. Remove from pans; cool. Wrap in plastic wrap or aluminum foil; store in cool place.

*Do not use self-rising flour in this recipe.

Note: Do not use 8½ x4½ x2½ -inch loaf pans.

DELUXE OLD-FASHIONED FRUITCAKE

3 cups all-purpose flour*
1⅓ cups sugar
2 teaspoons salt
1 teaspoon baking powder
2 teaspoons cinnamon
1 teaspoon nutmeg
1 cup orange juice
1 cup salad oil
4 eggs (⅔ to 1 cup)
¼ cup dark molasses
1 package (15 ounces)
golden raisins (about
3 cups)

1 package (8 ounces) pitted
dates, halved (1½ cups)
⅓ pound whole red and
green candied cherries
(¾ cup)
⅓ pound red and green
candied pineapple, cut up
(about 1 cup)
½ pound whole Brazil nuts
(1⅔ cups)

Heat oven to 275°. Line 2 loaf pans, 9x5x3 or 8½x
4½x2½ inches, with aluminum foil; grease. Measure
all ingredients except fruits and nuts into large mixer
bowl. Blend ½ minute on low speed, scraping bowl constantly. Beat 3 minutes high speed, scraping bowl occasionally. Stir in fruits and nuts. Spread mixture evenly
in pans.

Bake 2½ to 3 hours or until wooden pick inserted in
center comes out clean. If necessary, cover with aluminum foil the last hour of baking to prevent excessive
browning. Remove from pans; cool. Wrap in plastic wrap
or aluminum foil; store in cool place.

*Do not use self-rising flour in this recipe.

JEWELED FRUITCAKE

1 package (8 ounces) dried
apricots (about 2 cups)
1 package (8 ounces) pitted
dates (1½ cups)
¾ pound whole Brazil nuts
(1½ cups)
1 cup drained red and
green maraschino
cherries

⅓ pound red and green
candied pineapple, cut up
(about 1 cup)
¾ cup all-purpose flour*
¾ cup sugar
½ teaspoon baking powder
½ teaspoon salt
3 eggs (½ to ⅔ cup)
1½ teaspoons vanilla

Heat oven to 300°. Line loaf pan, 9x5x3 or 8½x4½x
2½ inches, with aluminum foil; grease. Leaving apricots,

*If using self-rising flour, omit baking powder and salt.

dates, nuts and cherries whole, mix all ingredients thoroughly. Spread mixture evenly in pan.

Bake 1 hour 45 minutes or until wooden pick inserted in center comes out clean. If necessary, cover with aluminum foil the last 30 minutes of baking to prevent excessive browning. Remove from pan; cool. Wrap in plastic wrap or aluminum foil; store in cool place.

OLD-FASHIONED FRUITCAKE

Traditional but not-quite-so-rich version of fruitcake. Ideal for those who don't really love fruitcake but who feel it's a "must" for the holidays.

3 cups all-purpose flour*	¼ cup dark corn syrup
1⅓ cups sugar	2 cups raisins
2 teaspoons salt	1 package (8 ounces) pitted
1 teaspoon baking powder	dates, cut up (1½ cups)
2 teaspoons cinnamon	1 pound mixed candied
1 teaspoon nutmeg	fruits (2 cups)
1 cup orange juice	½ pound pecan halves
1 cup salad oil	(about 2 cups)
4 eggs (⅔ to 1 cup)	

Heat oven to 275°. Line 2 loaf pans, 9x5x3 or 8½ x 4½x2½ inches, with aluminum foil; grease. Measure all ingredients except fruits and nuts into large mixer bowl. Blend ½ minute on low speed, scraping bowl constantly. Beat 3 minutes high speed, scraping bowl occasionally. Stir in fruits and nuts. Spread mixture evenly in pans.

Bake 2½ to 3 hours or until wooden pick inserted in center comes out clean. If necessary, cover with aluminum foil the last hour of baking to prevent excessive browning. Remove from pans; cool. Wrap in plastic wrap or aluminum foil; store in cool place.

*Do not use self-rising flour in this recipe.

GLAZES FOR FRUITCAKES

To add a sheen of sweetness, pour a thin glaze over your favorite fruitcake before or after storing. Each of the following is enough for one fruitcake. Since most of our recipes give you two cakes, try a different glaze on each cake.

Apple Jelly Glaze: Heat ¼ cup apple or currant jelly over low heat until smooth, stirring occasionally.

Sweet Glaze: Heat 2 tablespoons light corn syrup and 1 tablespoon water just to rolling boil. Cool to luke-warm.

BAKING CHART FOR FRUITCAKES

Unless specified in the recipe, all fruitcakes can be baked in a variety of pans.

Pan Size	Oven Temperature	Baking Time
1-pound tall coffee can	275°	2 to 2½ hours
4x3-inch can (6-ounce walnut can)	275°	1 to 1½ hours
Miniature loaf pans. 4½ x2¾ x1¼ inches	275°	1 to 1½ hours
Muffin cups	275°	40 to 50 minutes
3¼ x2½-inch can (3½-ounce coconut can)	275°	50 to 60 minutes

Special Occasion Cakes

Delicious, easy-to-make cakes for red-letter days.
Use only these Cakes for Cutups:
Silver White Cake (page 140)
Black Midnight Cake (page 136)
Cocoa Fudge Cake (page 136)
Red Devils Food Cake (page 137)
New Starlight Cake (page 146)
White, yellow and chocolate cake mixes (plain mixes are best; butter cake mixes are too rich).

CAT CAKE

Bake one of the Cakes for Cutups (above) in 2 round layer pans, 8x1½ inches. Cool.

Use one layer for body; cut other layer as shown in

diagram. Arrange layer and pieces on large tray or aluminum foil-covered cardboard as shown in diagram. With canned chocolate frosting or Chocolate Butter Frosting (page 188), join all parts and frost sides and top of cake. Use gumdrops for eyes, mouth and nose, shoestring licorice for whiskers, lines on eyes and paws.

TIC TAC TOE CAKE

Heat oven to 350°. Grease and flour 2 square pans, 8x8x2 or 9x9x2 inches. Prepare 1 package (18.5 ounces) devils food cake mix as directed except—pour into pans and bake 8-inch 30 to 35 minutes or 9-inch layers 25 to 30 minutes. Cool.

Prepare 1 package (7.2 ounces) fluffy white frosting mix as directed except—tint with few drops green food color; after mixing, fold in ¼ teaspoon peppermint extract. Fill layers and frost cake. To decorate, use shoestring licorice and candies.

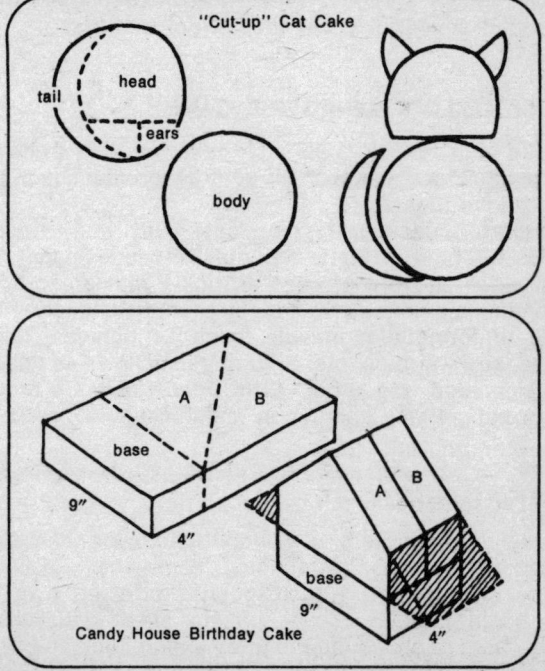

"Cut-up" Cat Cake

tail head ears body

base 9" 4"

base 9" 4"

Candy House Birthday Cake

CANDY HOUSE BIRTHDAY CAKE

Bake one of the Cakes for Cutups (page 175) in baking pan, 13x9x2 inches. Remove from pan; cool. Cut cake as shown in diagram on page 175.

Prepare 1 package (7.2 ounces) fluffy white frosting mix as directed or White Mountain Frosting (page 191). On tray or aluminum foil-covered cardboard, place "base" of cake, using 9-inch side for front. Place triangles together with long side down on base as shown in diagram. Trim corners and base so pieces fit together smoothly. Join all pieces with frosting. Frost entire house.

Beginning at lower end of roof, overlap pastel candy wafers for roof design. Place appropriate number of candles in chimney area. Form windows and doors with strips of shoestring licorice. Using strips of green spearmint leaf candies for leaves and stems and candy circles for flowers, press into frosting at base of house.

For grass, sprinkle green-tinted coconut around house. To serve cake, cut slices from roof first.

MARSHMALLOW MENAGERIE CAKE

Bake your favorite 13x9-inch cake. Remove from pan and cool. Place cake on large tray or aluminum foil-covered cardboard.

Prepare 1 package (7.2 ounces) fluffy white frosting mix as directed or White Mountain Frosting (page 191). Frost sides and top of cake. Sprinkle with green-tinted coconut. Join miniature and large marshmallows with picks to form little animals, such as bunnies, bears, turtles, giraffes, pigs, etc. Snip marshmallows as needed for tails, ears and other parts. Place animals around top of cake. Place candles in marshmallows.

BIRTHDAY BEAR CAKE

Bake your favorite 8- or 9-inch round layer cake. Cool.

Melt 1 package (6 ounces) semisweet chocolate pieces (1 cup) and 1 tablespoon shortening over hot (not boiling) water. Cover baking sheet with waxed paper. Spread chocolate mixture 1/8 inch thick on baking sheet. Chill until firm.

Prepare 1 package (7.2 ounces) fluffy white frosting mix as directed or White Mountain Frosting (page 191). If desired, tint with food color. Fill layers and frost side and top of cake.

With bear cookie cutter or paper pattern, cut out figures from chocolate mixture. Make figures the width of a wedge of cake so each slice will have a complete figure. Remove figures carefully from waxed paper; place figures at regular intervals on side of cake. Press birthday candles into gumdrops and place one on top of cake, just above each bear. Join bears and gumdrops with pieces of shoestring licorice.

UNCLE SAM'S HAT CAKE

Stars and stripes for 4th of July celebration. Use green-tinted frosting on the same cake shape for St. Patrick's Day.

Bake one of the Cakes for Cutups (page 174) in baking pan, 13x9x2 inches. Remove from pan; cool thoroughly.

Place cake upside down on large tray or aluminum foil-covered cardboard. Cut 1½-inch strip from end of cake. Cut strip into two 3-inch pieces; place pieces at sides of one end of cake to form band on hat.

Prepare 1 package (7.2 ounces) fluffy white frosting mix as directed or White Mountain Frosting (page 191). Frost sides and top of cake. Make 4 or 5 white stars on band by using paper star-shaped cutouts and sprinkling blue sugar around them; remove cutouts.

Make red and white stripes above band of cake, using 2 spatulas or cardboard strips as guides and sprinkling red sugar between them.

MUSICAL BIRTHDAY CAKE

Adult birthday cake suitable for any age—candies and candles form notes of popular birthday songs.

Bake your favorite 13x9-inch cake. Remove from pan; cool. Place cake upside down on large tray or aluminum foil-covered cardboard.

Prepare 1 package (15.4 ounces) creamy white frosting mix as directed or Vanilla Butter Frosting (page 185).

Tint frosting if desired. Frost sides and top of cake.

Prepare Chocolate Decorators Icing (page 185). With icing in decorators tube or in envelope cone, make a treble clef and staff (5 horizontal lines with 4 spaces between) on cake. Write "Happy Birthday to You" below the staff.

Press small gumdrops into oval shapes and place on lines to duplicate notes of song. Place birthday candles to right of gumdrop notes. If desired, additional candles can be placed around the edges of cake.

CHRISTMAS SNOW CAKE

Bake your favorite 8- or 9-inch round layer cake. Cool.

Prepare 1 package (7.2 ounces) fluffy white frosting mix as directed or White Mountain Frosting (page 191) except—after mixing, fold in ½ teaspoon almond extract. Frost cake. Sprinkle cake with flaked coconut.

Place piece of plain paper on back of cake pan and cut out circle the size of cake. Draw Christmas tree in center of paper; cut out tree. Place circle with tree pattern on cake. Sprinkle green-tinted coconut in the tree shape, carefully following pattern. Fill base of tree with shaved chocolate. Remove circle.

Roll red gumdrops on granulated sugar until flat. With small star cutter, cut star in each gumdrop. Insert small red candles in gumdrop stars and place on branches of tree. If desired, decorate tree with silver dragées.

CHRISTMAS TREE CAKE

Pour batter for one of the white or yellow Cakes for Cutups (page 174) into baking pan, 13x9x2 inches. Sprinkle batter with 2 tablespoons green sugar and 2 tablespoons multicolored nonpareils. Swirl through batter with spatula. Bake as directed. Remove from pan; cool.

Cover large tray or piece of cardboard with aluminum foil or foil wrapping paper. Cut cake as shown in diagram on page 179.

Prepare 1 package (7.2 ounces) fluffy white frosting mix as directed or White Mountain Frosting (page 191). Tint frosting green with 1 or 2 drops green food color. Arrange cake pieces A and B on tray to make tree shape (see diagram). Frost. Place piece C on top; frost sides and top, making strokes through frosting to resemble tree branches.

Sprinkle cake with green sugar. Insert 3 candy canes in end of the cake to make trunk. If desired, decorate with chocolate-coated candies.

FATHER'S DAY CAKE

Bake your favorite 13x9-inch cake. Remove from pan and cool.

Prepare 1 package (7.2 ounces) fluffy white frosting mix as directed or White Mountain Frosting (page 191). If desired, tint with food color. Frost sides and top of cake. Outline collar and tie with black shoestring licorice. Sprinkle tie with colored sugar and decorate with colored candies.

MOTHER'S DAY CAKE

Bake your favorite 13x9-inch cake. Remove from pan and cool.

Prepare 1 package (7.2 ounces) fluffy white frosting mix as directed or White Mountain Frosting (page 191); tint with red food color. Frost sides and top of cake. Decorate cake with pink candies to form collar, buttons and ruffled front.

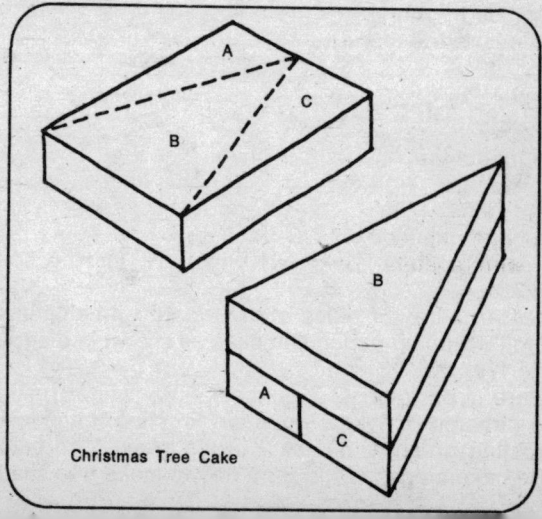

Christmas Tree Cake

FILLING AND FROSTING A TWO-LAYER CAKE

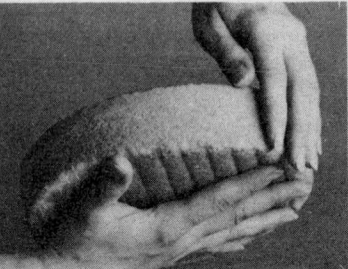

1. Before frosting cake, remove loose crumbs from side and edges of *cooked* layers. Support cake firmly with one hand and brush gently but thoroughly with the other.

2. Place one layer *upside down* on plate; spread about ½ cup of frosting to within ½ inch of edge. (Use a spatula with a flexible blade, a stiff blade may dig into cake).

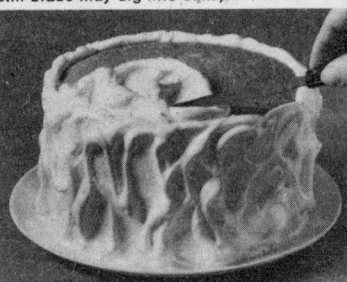

3. Place second layer *right side up* on filling. Coat side with thin layer of frosting, swirl more frosting on side, forming a ¼-inch ridge above top of cake.

4. Spread remaining frosting over top of cake, just meeting the built-up ridge around side. Make attractive swirls or leave top smooth for decoration.

FROSTING AN OBLONG CAKE

FROSTING CUPCAKES

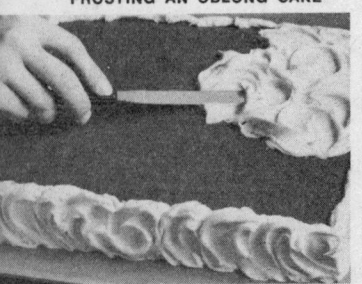

To frost sides as well as top, place cooked cake *right side up* on tray (fill sides with frosting to straighten). Or leave cake in the pan and frost only the top.

Twirl top of each cupcake *very lightly* in fluffy-type frosting—try White Mountain or Double Boiler (both on page 190) or a fluffy-type frosting mix.

FROSTING AN ANGEL FOOD OR CHIFFON CAKE

1. Invert cooled cake onto waxed paper. If frosting cake, brush loose crumbs off top and side; if glazing, brush crumbs off top only.

2. To split cake, measure even widths and mark with wooden picks; using picks as a guide, cut across cake with long sharp knife and a light sawing motion.

3. To frost, coat side of cake with thin layer of frosting to seal in crumbs, swirl more frosting on side, forming a slight ridge above top of cake. Then frost top.

4. To glaze, pour or spoon small amount of glaze at a time on top of cake and spread, allowing some to drizzle unevenly down side. (See page 195 for glazers).

QUICK FROSTING DESIGNS

Fork Weave: Draw lines of fork in parallel rows across length of cake; then draw across width of cake, changing the direction of each row. (Use a creamy-type frosting).

Spiral: Hold flexible spatula at center of layer cake; draw spatula very slowly toward you, rotating cake plate as you do so. (Use a creamy type frosting).

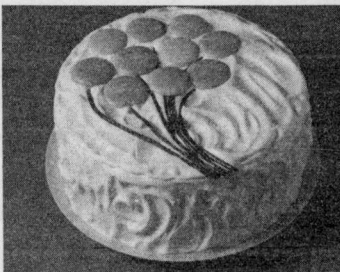

Cookie Cutter Cake: Frost cake with white frosting. Dip a cookie cutter into liquid food color; press into frosting, making an imprint on top of cake. Repeat around top of cake, dipping cutter into food color each time.

Balloon Cake: Frost cake with a white frosting or one that has been delicately tinted with food color. On top of cake, arrange paste mint-wafer "balloons." Use shoe-string licorice for the balloon strings.

Abstract Cupcakes: Frost cupcakes with white frosting. Divide more frosting into several parts; tint each part a different color. Fill a decorators' tube with frosting; make your own bright designs on top of cupcakes.

Carnival Cake: Frost cake with fluffy-type white frosting. Mark top into 8 wedges. Form foil into a V-shape the same size as each wedge. Place on cake; sprinkle confetti candy within foil over every other wedge.

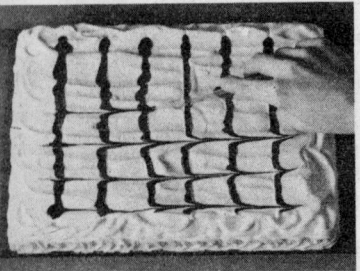

Shadow Design: Frost an oblong cake with white frosting. Melt 1 ounce unsweetened chocolate and ¼ teaspoon shortening. Using teaspoon, drizzle melted chocolate in parallel lines on top of cake. Immediately draw spatula or knife through lines.

Allegretti Design: Frost cake with a fluffy-type white frosting. Melt 1 ounce unsweetened chocolate and ¼ teaspoon shortening. Using teaspoon, drizzle the melted chocolate around top edge of cake, allowing it to run down the side unevenly.

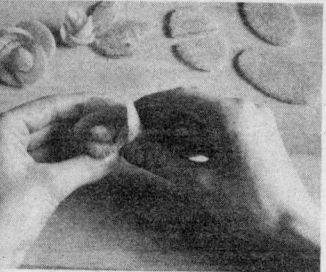

Gumdrop Roses: For each rose, foil 4 large gumdrops on well-sugared board into ⅛-inch ovals. Sprinkle sugar over gumdrops. Cut ovals in half. Roll one half-oval tightly to form center of rose. Place more half-ovals around center, overlapping slightly; press together at base. Trim base. Cut leaves from rolled green gumdrops.

Brazil Nut Flowers: Place about 10 shelled Brazil nuts in 1 cup boiling water. Remove pan from heat and let stand about 5 minutes. Remove one nut at a time and quickly slice lengthwise (with vegetable parer), cutting off paper-thin curls. Arrange curls around halved candied cherries.

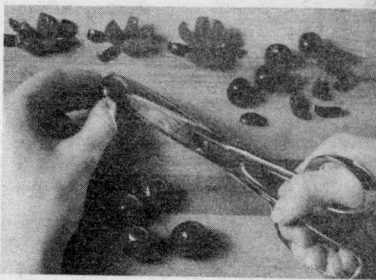

Chocolate Curls: With a vegetable parer or thin, sharp knife. Slice across block of sweet milk chocolate with long, thin strokes. Large-size milk chocolate candy bars can also be used.

Cherry Flowers: Snip well-drained red maraschino cherries into 6 sections, cutting about ¾ of the way through. Spread sections apart gently to resemble petals. Cut leaves from green maraschino cherries.

Citrus Decorations: Cut thin slices from an orange or a lemon. Using a small sharp knife or miniature cutter, cut a design of your choice around peel.

Frosted Grapes: Dip small clusters of green grapes into slightly beaten egg white, then dip into granulated sugar. Dry clusters on wire racks.

ANNIVERSARY CAKE

3 packages (18.5 ounces each) white cake mix

4 cans (16.5 ounces each) vanilla frosting

Bake 1 package cake mix in baking pan, 13x9x2 inches, as directed. Cool. Repeat for second cake. Prepare third cake mix as directed except—bake half the batter in greased and floured square pan, 9x9x2 inches, 25 to 30 minutes at 350°. Cool. With remaining batter, bake 15 to 18 cupcakes as directed on package. (Use as desired.)

Place one of the oblongs upside down on mirror, tray or large serving plate; frost top. Place second oblong on top; frost sides and top.

Cut square cake in half to make 2 rectangles, each 9x4½ inches. Place one on center of frosted oblong cake. Frost top; place other half on top; frost sides and top.

Decorate cake, using decorators' tube with Decorator's Icing (page 189) or 1 can (16.5 ounces) vanilla ready-to-spread frosting.

About 50 servings.

Cutting: Top tier—about 18 pieces (cut 2 slices lengthwise by 9 crosswise); bottom tier—about 48 pieces (cut 4 slices lengthwise by 12 crosswise).

Decorating tips: (Petal, leaf, star and writing tips can be used with decorator's tube.) *Fluted Edge Border*— Hold leaf tip on side at 45° angle; with even pressure, move tube along with series of slight up and down motions. *Shell Border*—Hold tube at 60° angle to cake surface. Begin squeezing. As shell builds up, raise tube about ¼ inch; ease off on pressure as you pull down. The shell comes down to a point by stopping all pressure at the end of the shell. If desired, outline shell border with writing tip.

Cooked & Uncooked Frostings

To frost or not to frost? A cake without frosting may, and does, have its merits—but ask your friends about the cakes they like best, and they'll describe the frosting.

VANILLA BUTTER FROSTING

⅓ cup soft butter or
   margarine
3 cups confectioners' sugar

1½ teaspoons vanilla
   About 2 tablespoons milk

Blend butter and sugar. Stir in vanilla and milk; beat until frosting is smooth and of spreading consistency.

Fills and frosts two 8- or 9-inch layers or frosts a 13x9-inch cake.

Note: To fill and frost three 8-inch layers, use ½ cup soft butter or margarine, 4½ cups confectioners' sugar, 2 teaspoons vanilla and about 3 tablespoons milk.

VARIATIONS

■ *Brown Butter Frosting:* Heat butter in saucepan over medium heat until a delicate brown.

■ *Cherry Butter Frosting:* Stir in 2 tablespoons drained chopped maraschino cherries and 2 drops red food color.

■ *Maple-Nut Butter Frosting:* Substitute ½ cup maple-flavored syrup for the vanilla and milk; stir in ¼ cup finely chopped nuts.

■ *Orange (or Lemon) Butter Frosting:* Omit vanilla and substitute orange (or lemon) juice for the milk; stir in 2 teaspoons grated orange (or ½ teaspoon grated lemon) peel.

■ *Peanut Butter Frosting :* Substitute peanut butter for the butter; increase milk to ¼ to ⅓ cup.

■ *Pineapple Butter Frosting:* Omit vanilla and milk; stir in ⅓ cup well-drained crushed pineapple.

CHOCOLATE DECORATORS' ICING

Melt 1 ounce unsweetened chocolate and 1 teaspoon butter or margarine over hot water. Remove from heat; blend in 1 cup sifted confectioners' sugar and 1 tablespoon hot water. Beat until smooth. If necessary, add hot water, a teaspoon at a time, until of desired consistency.

Note: A canned chocolate frosting can be substituted for the Chocolate Decorators' Icing.

Writing Tips: Use to make numbers, letters, borders, lattice work and delicate outlines.

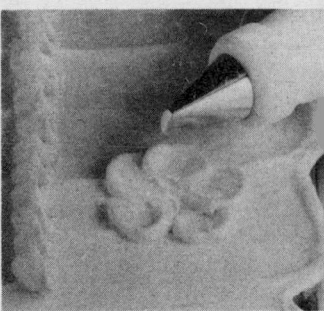

Petal Tip: Use to make petals for roses and other flowers; also for borders and ribbons.

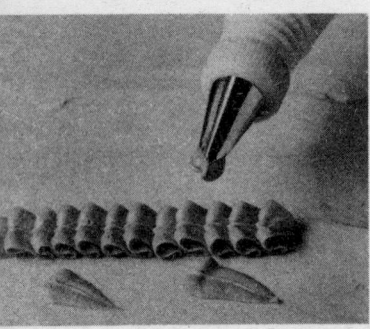

Leaf Tip: Use to make leaves and long delicate petals; also for elaborate borders and designs.

Experiment with a variety of tips in a single design or pattern to create the desired effect.

TO MAKE ROSES

Attach waxed paper to flower nail with frosting. With narrow end of petal tip up and turning nail slowly, press out frosting to form center.

To form first petal, make standing half-circle to one side of center. Add 2 more petals, forming triangle. Add more petals, overlapping.

Star Tips: Use to pipe small borders around cake, to make simple flowers, rosettes and fancy letters.

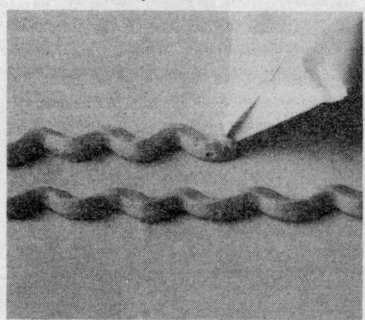

Envelope Cone: Place about 1/3 cup frosting in envelope, fold sides. Snip off corner to make tip.

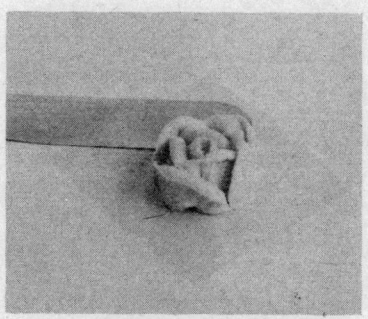

Remove waxed paper with rose from nail and place on countertop until set. Carefully lift rose from waxed paper with spatula and place on cake.

CHOCOLATE BUTTER FROSTING

Rich, creamy chocolate goodness.

⅓ cup soft butter or
   margarine
2 ounces melted
   unsweetened chocolate
   (cool)

2 cups confectioners' sugar
1½ teaspoons vanilla
   About 2 tablespoons milk

Mix thoroughly butter and cooled chocolate. Blend in sugar. Stir in vanilla and milk; beat until frosting is smooth and of spreading consistency.

Fills and frosts two 8- or 9-inch layers or frosts a 13x9-inch cake.

Note: To fill and frost three 8-inch layers, use ½ cup soft butter or margarine, 3 ounces melted unsweetened chocolate (cool), 3 cups confectioners' sugar, 2 teaspoons vanilla and about 3 tablespoons milk.

VARIATIONS

■ *Chocolate-Nut Butter Frosting:* Stir in ¼ cup finely chopped nuts.

■ *Chocolate-Spice Butter Frosting:* Blend in ½ teaspoon cinnamon and ¼ teaspoon nutmeg with the sugar.

■ *Cocoa Butter Frosting:* Substitute ⅓ cup cocoa for the chocolate.

■ *Mocha Butter Frosting:* Blend in 1½ teaspoons powdered instant coffee with the sugar.

GLOSSY CHOCOLATE FROSTING

The perfect companion for Red Devils Food Cake.

3 tablespoons shortening
3 ounces unsweetened
   chocolate
2 cups confectioners' sugar

¼ teaspoon salt
⅓ cup milk
1 teaspoon vanilla

Melt shortening and chocolate in saucepan over low heat. Stir in remaining ingredients; beat until smooth. Place pan of frosting in bowl of ice and water; continue beating until of spreading consistency. If desired, stir in ½ cup of finely chopped nuts.

Fills and frosts two 8- or 9-inch layers or frosts a 13x9-inch cake.

CREAM CHEESE FROSTING

1 package (3 ounces)
   cream cheese, softened
1 tablespoon milk

1 teaspoon vanilla
Dash salt
2½ cups confectioners' sugar

Blend cheese, milk, vanilla and salt. Gradually add sugar, beating until frosting is smooth and of spreading consistency. If necessary, stir in additional milk, 1 teaspoon at a time.

Fills and frosts two 8- or 9-inch layers or frosts a 13x9-inch cake.

VARIATIONS

■ *Chocolate Cream Cheese Frosting:* Before adding sugar, stir in 2 ounces melted unsweetened chocolate (cool).

■ *Coffee Cream Cheese Frosting:* Blend in 1 tablespoon powdered instant coffee with the cheese.

■ *Peppermint Cream Cheese Frosting:* Stir in 3 drops red food color and 2 tablespoons crushed peppermint candy. If desired sprinkle top of frosted cake with crushed peppermint candy.

DECORATORS' ICING

Mix 2 cups confectioners' sugar and 1 tablespoon water. Add more water, 1 teaspoon at a time, until icing is of the consistency that can be used easily in a decorators' tube and yet hold its shape.

¾ cup.

FRENCH SILK FROSTING

2⅔ cups confectioners' sugar
 ⅔ cup soft butter
  2 ounces melted
    unsweetened chocolate
    (cool)

¾ teaspoon vanilla
2 tablespoons milk

In small mixer bowl, blend sugar, butter, chocolate and vanilla on low speed. Gradually add milk; beat until smooth and fluffy.

Enough frosting for two 9-inch layer or three 8-inch layer cakes.

LEMON SWIRL

The mellow tang of cream cheese coupled with the freshness of lemon adds up to a frosting that's "not too sweet."

1 package (3 ounces)
  cream cheese, softened
½ cup soft butter or
  margarine
4 cups confectioners' sugar

1 teaspoon vanilla
2 to 3 teaspoons grated
  lemon peel
  About 3 tablespoons
  lemon juice

Beat all ingredients until frosting is fluffy and of spreading consistency. If necessary, stir in additional lemon juice, 1 teaspoon at a time.

Fills and frosts two 8- or 9-inch layers or frosts a 13x9-inch cake.

FUDGE FROSTING

This is the easy way to make fudge frosting. No thermometer or "soft-ball" test needed! Instead you beat the frosting as it cools in iced water.

½ cup shortening
2 cups sugar
3 ounces unsweetened
  chocolate

⅔ cup milk
½ teaspoon salt
2 teaspoons vanilla

Mix all ingredients except vanilla in 2½-quart saucepan. Heat to rolling boil, stirring occasionally. Boil 1 minute without stirring. Place pan of frosting in bowl of ice and water. Beat frosting until smooth and of spreading consistency. Stir in vanilla.

Fills and frosts two 8- or 9-inch layers or frosts a 13x9-inch cake.

DOUBLE BOILER (7-MINUTE) FROSTING

2 egg whites (¼ cup)
1½ cups sugar
¼ teaspoon cream of tartar
  or 1 tablespoon light
  corn syrup

⅓ cup water
1 teaspoon vanilla

Combine egg whites, sugar, cream of tartar and water in top of double boiler. Beat on high speed 1 minute with electric mixer. Place over boiling water (water should not touch bottom of pan); beat on high speed 7 minutes. Remove pan from boiling water; add vanilla. Beat 2 minutes longer on high speed.

Fills and frosts two 8- or 9-inch layers or frosts a 13x9-inch cake.

QUICK FUDGE FROSTING

½ cup granulated sugar
2 tablespoons cocoa
2 tablespoons butter or
  margarine
¼ cup milk
1 tablespoon light
  corn syrup

Dash salt
½ to ¾ cup confectioners'
  sugar
½ teaspoon vanilla

Mix sugar and cocoa in saucepan. Add butter, milk, corn syrup and salt; heat to boiling, stirring frequently. Boil vigorously 3 minutes, stirring occasionally. Cool. Beat in confectioners' sugar and vanilla.

Frosts an 8- or 9-inch square cake.

EASY PENUCHE FROSTING

½ cup butter or margarine
1 cup brown sugar (packed)

¼ cup milk
2 cups confectioners' sugar

Melt butter in saucepan. Stir in brown sugar. Heat to boiling, stirring constantly. Boil and stir over low heat 2 minutes. Stir in milk; heat to boiling. Remove from heat and cool to lukewarm.

Gradually stir in confectioners' sugar. Place pan of frosting in bowl of ice and water; beat until of spreading consistency. If frosting becomes too stiff, heat slightly, stirring constantly.

Fills and frosts two 8- or 9-inch layers or frosts a 13x9-inch cake.

WHITE MOUNTAIN FROSTING

½ cup sugar
¼ cup light corn syrup
2 tablespoons water

2 egg whites (¼ cup)
1 teaspoon vanilla

Combine sugar, corn syrup and water in small saucepan. Cover; heat to rolling boil over medium heat. Remove cover and boil rapidly, without stirring, to 242° on candy thermometer (or until small amount of mixture dropped into very cold water forms a firm ball).

As mixture boils, beat egg whites until stiff peaks form. Pour hot syrup very slowly in a thin stream into the beaten egg whites, beating constantly on medium speed. Beat on high speed until stiff peaks form; add vanilla during last minute of beating.

Fills and frosts two 8- or 9-inch layers or frosts a 13x9-inch cake.

VARIATIONS

■ *Cocoa Frosting:* Sift ¼ cup cocoa over frosting and gently fold in until blended.

■ *Lemon Frosting:* Substitute 1 tablespoon lemon juice for the vanilla and add ¼ teaspoon grated lemon peel and 10 drops yellow food color during last minute of beating.

■ *Pink Mountain Frosting:* Substitute maraschino cherry juice for the water.

■ *Satiny Beige Frosting:* Substitute brown sugar (packed) for the granulated sugar and decrease vanilla to ½ teaspoon.

Mix-quick Frostings

Don't overlook packaged frosting mixes—and the good frostings that come in cans. Not just when you're in a hurry but because they spread smoothly, look great and taste good!

Form overlapping petals with tip of flexible spatula. (See page 194.)

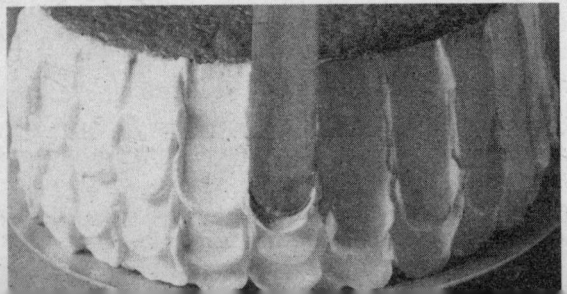

GOURMET FROSTING

Sour cream adds the extra-special flavor to a favorite frosting mix.

Use 1 package (15.4 or 14.3 ounces) creamy white, chocolate fudge, dark chocolate fudge or lemon frosting mix.

Combine ⅔ cup dairy sour cream and the frosting mix (dry) in small mixer bowl. Cover; chill at least 2 hours.

Blend ¼ cup butter or margarine; softened, into frosting mixture; beat on low speed 1 minute. *Do not overbeat*—overbeating thins frosting. Fill and frost cake. Chill frosted cake before serving; refrigerate any leftover cake.

Fills and frosts two 8- or 9-inch layers or frosts a 13x9-inch cake.

VELVET CREAM FROSTING

For this elegant frosting treatment, you will need two 9-inch cake layers. Split to make 4 layers.

Use 1 package (15.4 or 14.3 ounces) creamy white, chocolate fudge, dark chocolate fudge or lemon frosting mix.

Combine 1½ cups whipping cream, 1 teaspoon vanilla and *2 cups* of the frosting mix (dry) in small mixer bowl. Cover; chill 1 hour. Reserve remaining frosting mix.

Blend chilled frosting mix and cream; beat on medium speed until stiff. Spread between cake layers.

For glaze, beat reserved frosting mix (dry), 2 to 3 tablespoons hot water and 1 tablespoon light corn syrup until smooth. If necessary, add 1 to teaspoons more water until glaze is of proper consistency.

Frost top of cake with glaze, allowing some to drizzle down side. If desired, sprinkle top of cake with chopped nuts. Chill before serving; refrigerate any leftover cake.

FLUFFY CHEESE FROSTING

Frosting mix plus cream-cheese—for the easiest and creamiest of cake toppers.

Use 1 package (15.4 or 14.3 ounces) creamy white, chocolate fudge or lemon frosting mix.

In small mixer bowl, beat 1 package (8 ounces) cream cheese, softened, and 1 tablespoon milk until smooth and creamy. Beat in frosting mix (dry) until smooth and fluffy. If necessary, add 1 teaspoon milk to make frosting proper consistency.

Fills and frosts two 8- or 9-inch layers of a 13x9-inch cake.

PETAL FROSTING

Combine 1 package (7.2 ounces) fluffy white frosting mix (dry) and 1½ cups whipping cream in small mixer bowl. Cover; chill 1 hour.

Blend chilled frosting mix and cream; beat until stiff. If desired, tint with food color.

To frost, scoop about 1 teaspoon frosting on tip of small flexible spatula. Beginning at base of cake, form small petal by pressing spatula with frosting against side of cake. Repeat to form petals in rows around cake, overlapping petals slightly. Make larger petals on top of cake. Chill; refrigerate any leftover cake.

EASY VARIATIONS WITH MIXES

Follow the package directions, then. . . .

WITH CREAMY WHITE

(Use a 15.4-ounce package.)

■ *Banana-Nut:* Omit water; before blending, add ⅓ cup mashed banana and ½ teaspoon lemon juice. Sprinkle finely chopped nuts over cake.

■ *Lemon, Lime or Orange:* Substitute fruit juice for the water.

■ *Peppermint:* After beating, stir in ½ teaspoon peppermint extract and 3 to 4 drops green food color.

■ *Spice:* Before blending, add ½ teaspoon cinnamon, ¼ teaspoon nutmeg and 2 teaspoons cloves.

■ *Strawberry:* Substitute crushed fresh or thawed frozen berries for the water.

WITH CHOCOLATE FUGE

(Use a 15.4-ounce package.)

■ *Mocha:* Before blending, add 2 teaspoons powdered instant coffee.

■ *Peppermint Fudge:* After beating, stir in ¼ to ½ teaspoon peppermint extract.

■ *Rocky Road:* After beating, fold in ½ cup miniature marshmallows and ½ cup finely chopped peanuts.

WITH FLUFFY WHITE

(Use a 7.2-ounce package.)

■ *Cherry-Nut:* After beating, fold in ⅓ cup well-drained chopped maraschino cherries and ½ cup finely chopped nuts.

■ *Chocolate Chip:* After beating, fold in ½ cup semi-sweet chocolate pieces.

■ *Mocha:* Before blending, add 2 teaspoons powdered instant coffee.

■ *Orange-Coconut:* After beating, fold in 1 tablespoon grated orange peel and ½ cup flaked coconut.

■ *Peppermint:* After beating, stir in ¼ teaspoon peppermint extract.

Glazes

Looking for a change of pace? Don't forget glazes— for glamour and for ease. Be a traditionalist: Pick any one of these and spoon it over your favorite angel food or chiffon cake—letting it run down the sides, of course. Be a decorator: Use a glaze to trim that special holiday bread. Be a change-of-pacer: Use one as a surprise frosting for plain refrigerator cookies. We bet you forgot how many ways you can use glazes!

CHOCOLATE GLAZE

Melt 2 ounces unsweetened chocolate and 3 table-spoons butter or margarine over low heat. Remove from heat; stir in 1 cup confectioners' sugar and ¾ teaspoon vanilla. Mix in about 2 tablespoons hot water, 1 teaspoon at a time, until glaze is of proper consistency.

CREAMY GLAZE

⅓ cup butter or margarine
2 cups confectioners' sugar
1½ teaspoons vanilla

2 to 4 tablespoons hot water

Melt butter in saucepan. Blend in sugar and vanilla. Stir in water, 1 tablespoon at a time, until glaze is of proper consistency.

Glazes a 10-inch chiffon or angel food cake.

VARIATIONS

■ *Browned Butter Glaze:* Heat butter in saucepan over medium heat until it becomes a delicate brown color.

■ *Butter-Rum Glaze:* Substitute 2 tablespons white rum or, if desired, 1½ teaspoons rum flavoring for the vanilla; stir in hot water, 1 teaspoon at a time, until glaze is of proper consistency.

■ *Chocolate Glaze:* Stir in 2 ounces melted unsweetened chocolate (cool) with the sugar.

■ *Orange or Lemon Glaze:* Add ½ teaspoon grated orange or lemon peel to melted butter and substitute orange or lemon juice for the vanilla and water.

Broiled Toppings

Searching for a special topping? Try a broiled one! Spread one of these over a simple cake (warm from the oven) and slip it under the broiler for a few minutes. You're set!

BUTTERSCOTCH BROILED TOPPING

¼ cup soft butter or margarine
⅔ cup brown sugar (packed)

1 cup finely chopped nuts
2 tablespoons milk

Mix thoroughly butter, brown sugar and nuts. Stir in milk. Spread mixture evenly over warm 13x9-inch cake.

Set oven control at broil and/or 550°. Place cake 5 inches from heat; broil about 3 minutes or until topping bubbles and browns slightly. (Watch carefully—mixture burns easily.)

Frosts a 13x9-inch cake.

VARIATIONS

■ *Coconut Broiled Topping:* Decrease nuts to ½ cup; add 1 cup flaked coconut with the nuts and increase milk to 3 tablespoons.

■ *Crunchy Broiled Topping:* Decrease nuts to ½ cup; add ½ cup whole wheat flakes cereal with the nuts and increase milk to 3 tablespoons.

BROWN SUGAR MERINGUE

2 egg whites (¼ cup)	1 tablespoon lemon juice
1 cup brown sugar (packed)	½ cup finely chopped nuts

Just before cake is removed from oven, beat egg whites until foamy. Gradually beat sugar and lemon juice into egg whites, beating until stiff. Carefully spread on *hot* 13x9-inch cake. Sprinkle with nuts. Bake in 400° oven 8 to 10 minutes or until brown.

Frosts a 13x9-inch cake.

PEANUT BUTTER BROILED TOPPING

¼ cup soft butter or margarine	¼ cup peanut butter
⅔ cup brown sugar (packed)	1 cup peanuts, finely chopped
3 tablespoons milk	

Mix thoroughly butter, sugar, milk and peanut butter; stir in peanuts. Spread mixture evenly on warm 13x9-inch cake. Set oven control at broil and/or 550°. Place cake 5 inches from heat; broil about 3 minutes or until topping bubbles and browns slightly. (Watch carefully—mixture burns easily.)

Frosts a 13x9-inch cake.

Whipped Toppings

When a glamorous dessert is indicated but the cook's schedule is crowded, try one of these whipped cream toppings on a mix-made cake.

CHERRY TOPPING

Chill 1 can (1 pound 5 ounces) cherry pie filling. In chilled bowl, beat ¾ cup chilled whipping cream, ½ teaspoon almond extract and 3 tablespoons confectioners' sugar until stiff. Fold in pie filling. Serve on squares of yellow or white cake.

8 servings.

HONEY-GINGER FLUFF

In chilled bowl, beat 2 cups chilled whipping cream until stiff, gradually adding ¼ cup honey and ½ teaspoon ginger.

Serve on squares of spice or yellow cake or use to frost a 10-inch angel food cake. Chill 1 to 2 hours before serving; refrigerate any leftover cake or fluff.

8 servings.

TOFFEE TOPPING

Chill 6 bars (¾ ounce each) chocolate-covered toffee candy; crush bars. In chilled bowl, beat 2 cups chilled whipping cream and ½ cup confectioners' sugar until stiff. Fold in crushed candy.

Serve on slices of angel food cake or use to frost a 10-inch angel food cake. Chill 1 to 2 hours before serving; refrigerate any leftover cake or topping.

8 servings.

CARAMEL FLUFF

In chilled bowl, beat 2 cups chilled whipping cream, ¾ cup brown sugar (packed) and 1 teaspoon vanilla until stiff.

Serve on squares of spice or chocolate cake or use to frost a 10-inch angel food cake. Sprinkle with shaved chocolate. Chill 1 to 2 hours before serving; refrigerate any leftover cake or fluff.

8 servings.

MINT FLUFF

In chilled bowl, beat 2 cups chilled whipping cream until stiff. Gently fold in ⅓ cup green crème de menthe.*

Serve on slices of angel food cake. If desired, garnish each serving with a sprig of mint and a maraschino cherry.

8 servings.

*Or, if desired, omit crème de menthe; before beating, add ½ teaspoon mint extract, 10 drops green food color and ¼ cup sugar to the whipping cream.

ALMOND FLUFF

In chilled bowl, beat 2 cups chilled whipping cream until stiff. Gently fold in ½ cup white crème de cacao.*

Serve on slices of angel food cake. Garnish each serving with ½ teaspoon toasted diced almonds.

8 servings.

*Or, if desired, omit crème de cacao; while beating cream, gradually add ½ cup instant sweetened chocolate drink (dry).

WHIPPED CREAM TOPPINGS

For 1 cup whipped cream: In chilled bowl, beat ½ cup chilled whipping cream and 1 tablespoon granulated or confectioners' sugar until stiff.

For 1½ cups whipped cream: In chilled bowl, beat ¾ cup chilled whipping cream and 2 tablespoons granulated or confectioners' sugar until stiff.

For 2⅓ cups whipped cream: In chilled bowl, beat 1 cup chilled whipping cream and 3 tablespoons granulated or confectioners' sugar until stiff.

Flavored Whipped Creams: For 1 cup whipping cream, add one of the following during the last minute of beating:

½ teaspoon cinnamon	½ teaspoon almond extract
½ teaspoon nutmeg	½ teaspoon peppermint
1 teaspoon vanilla	extract
½ teaspoon rum flavoring	¼ teaspoon maple flavoring
1 teaspoon grated orange peel	¼ teaspoon ginger
1 teaspoon grated lemon peel	

Fillings

Pick a cake. Pick a frosting. And then—here's the extra—pick a filling! Now you have a dessert! A cake to serve as something special—all by itself. Remember this next time you have company coming for dessert and coffee.

STREAMLINED CREAM FILLING

Look! We've devoloped a brand-new, one-step cooking method for this favorite filling.

⅓ cup sugar
2 tablespoons cornstarch
⅛ teaspoon salt

1½ cups milk
2 egg yolks, slightly beaten
2 teaspoons vanilla

Mix thoroughly sugar, cornstarch and salt in medium saucepan. Stir milk into egg yolks; gradually stir egg mixture into dry ingredients. Cook over medium heat, stirring constantly, until mixture thickens and boils. Boil and stir 1 minute. Remove from heat; stir in vanilla. Cool.
Fills an 8- or 9-inch two-layer cake.

VARIATIONS

■ *Almond Cream Filling:* Decrease vanilla to ½ teaspoon; stir in 1 teaspoon almond extract and ½ cup toasted slivered blanched almonds.

■ *Chocolate Cream Filling:* Increase sugar to ⅔ cup; add 1 square (1 ounce) unsweetened chocolate after stirring in egg mixture or stir in 1 envelope (1 ounce) premelted unsweetened chocolate with the vanilla.

BUTTER-NUT FILLING

½ cup sugar
1 tablespoon flour
¼ cup orange juice
½ cup butter or margarine

¼ cup chopped dates or
  raisins
2 egg yolks, slightly beaten
½ cup finely chopped nuts

Combine sugar, flour, orange juice, butter and dates in saucepan. Cook over low heat, stirring constantly, until mixture thickens and boils. Boil and stir 1 minute. Remove from heat.

Gradually stir at least half the hot mixture into egg yolks. Stir into remaining hot mixture in saucepan. Heat to boiling; stir in nuts. Cool.

Fills an 8- or 9-inch two-layer cake.

CLEAR LEMON FILLING

Wonderfully tart and delicious.

¾ cup sugar
3 tablespoons cornstarch
¼ teaspoon salt
¾ cup water
1 teaspoon grated lemon
   peel

1 tablespoon butter or
   margarine
⅓ cup lemon juice

Mix sugar, cornstarch and salt in saucepan. Gradually stir in water. Cook, stirring constantly, until mixture thickens and boils. Boil and stir 1 minute.

Remove from heat; add lemon peel and butter. Gradually stir in lemon juice and, if desired, 4 drops yellow food color. Cool thoroughly. If filling is too soft, refrigerate until set.

Fills an 8- or 9-inch two-layer cake.

Cookies

And always cookies in the cookie jar! Is there a
happier symbol of a friendly house? Cookies for
children to share with their friends. Cookies for
the family watching TV. Cookies for an afternoon
tea. Cookies for a hike, cookies for a picnic,
cookies to comfort a boy who's had a bump,
cookies with a glass of milk. Cookies "just
because."

Tips for Cookie Makers

Know your cookie types: Cookies are classified by the
way they're formed—drop, bar, molded, rolled, pressed,
refrigerated. (Read about each type on the following
pages.) The basic ingredients may be the same for all
these, but the proportions vary—to produce either a
"soft" or a "stiff" dough. Once you've tried the basic
cookies, you'll want to experiment with different spices
or flavorings or decorations.

Follow the recipe. Read through the recipe, and be
sure you understand it. Then heat the oven. Assemble
the ingredients (putting them all on a tray provides a
built-in double check that nothing will be omitted). Collect the utensils. Measure the ingredients. Clear the
deck for action.

Use a good baking sheet. For evenly browned cookies, choose shiny, bright baking sheets at least 2 inches
narrower and shorter than the oven. (Do not grease
unless called for in the recipe.) Always place dough
on a cool baking sheet; dough spreads on a hot one.
It saves time to work with 3 or 4 baking sheets—you can
fill and bake at the same time.

The "test" cookie. Bake one cookie—just one. If it
spreads more than desired, add 1 to 2 tablespoons of
flour to the dough. If the cookie is too dry, add 1 to 2
tablespoons of cream or milk. Keep in mind that liquid
proportions are affected by egg size and by the dryness

of flour. Flour stored in humid conditions will absorb less liquid in a dough than if stored in a dry place.

Rolling and shaping. When rolling dough, use a pastry cloth and a stockinet-covered rolling pin. These will make the rolling easier and help prevent the dough from sticking to the board. When shaping dough for molded, drop or refrigerator cookies, try to make each cookie the same size and thickness to assure uniform baking.

Baking. Placement counts. For delicately browned cookies, place one rack at a time in the center of the oven. A minute can make a real difference in the finished cookies. Look at the cookies at the end of the minimum baking time. Be careful not to overbake. Unless the recipe states otherwise, remove cookies from baking sheet immediately. Use a wide spatula to lift them onto wire racks. (Cookies continue to bake as long as they stay on the hot sheet.)

Storing. Crisp, thin cookies should be stored in a container with a loose-fitting cover. If they soften, recrisp by placing in 300° oven for 3 to 5 minutes. Soft cookies should be stored in a tightly covered container. A piece of bread or apple placed in the container helps keep the cookies soft if you change it frequently.

Freezing. Both cookie dough and baked cookies can be frozen and stored from 9 to 12 months. Arrange baked cookies in a sturdy box lined with plastic wrap or aluminum foil; separate each layer of cookies with more wrap or foil; seal foil. Close box, label and freeze. Thaw cookies by allowing them to stand at room temperature for about 10 minutes.

Package dough for drop cookies in an airtight container, aluminum foil or plastic wrap. Thaw until just soft enough to spoon onto baking sheet. Shape dough for refrigerator cookies in rolls; wrap in aluminum foil or plastic wrap and freeze. Thaw just enough to slice.

Drop Cookies

Drop cookies are everybody's friends—easy to bake, easy to eat, easy to pop in the cookie jar. Some may contain treats such as chocolate pieces, gumdrops or chopped nuts.

Drop cookies are aptly named. They are made by simply dropping the dough by spoonfuls onto a baking sheet. Keep them about 2 inches apart unless the recipe states otherwise.

Well-baked drop cookies are slightly mounded and fairly uniform in shape, with a delicately browned exterior. If your cookies are irregular in size or shape, the dough was improperly dropped. If the edges are dark and crusty, the cookies were overbaked or the baking sheet was too large for the oven. Overbaking also results in a dry, hard cookie; underbaking, on the other hand, produces a doughy cookie. When excessive spreading occurs, one or more of the following reasons may have been the cause: 1) the dough was too warm; 2) the baking sheet was too hot; 3) the oven temperature was incorrect.

CHOCOLATE DROP COOKIES

½ cup butter or margarine, softened
1 cup sugar
1 egg
2 ounces melted unsweetened chocolate (cool)
⅓ cup buttermilk
1 teaspoon vanilla

1¾ cups all-purpose flour*
½ teaspoon soda
½ teaspoon salt
1 cup chopped nuts, if desired
Chocolate Icing or Browned Butter Icing (below and right)

Mix thoroughly butter, sugar, egg, chocolate, buttermilk and vanilla. Stir in flour, soda, salt and nuts. Cover; chill 1 hour.

Heat oven to 400°. Drop dough by rounded teaspoonfuls 2 inches apart onto ungreased baking sheet. Bake 8 to 10 minutes or until almost no imprint remains when touched with finger.

Immediately remove from baking sheet; cool. Frost with Chocolate Icing.

4½ dozen cookies.

*If using self-rising flour, omit soda and salt. If using quick-mixing flour, increase buttermilk to ½ cup.

CHOCOLATE ICING

Melt 2 ounces unsweetened chocolate and 2 tablespoons butter or margarine over low heat. Remove from heat; blend in 3 tablespoons water and about 2 cups confectioners' sugar.

BROWNED BUTTER ICING

Heat ¼ cup butter or margarine over low heat until golden brown. Remove from heat; blend in 2 cups confectioners' sugar, 1 teaspoon vanilla and about 2 tablespoons light cream.

VARIATIONS

■ *Chocolate-Cherry Drops:* Omit nuts and stir in 2 cups cut-up candied or maraschino cherries. Use Chocolate Icing.

■ *Cocoa Drop Cookies:* Increase butter to ⅔ cup; omit chocolate and stir in ½ cup cocoa.

■ *Double Chocolate Drops:* Stir in 1 package (6 ounces) semisweet chocolate pieces.

CHOCOLATE CHIP COOKIES

⅔ cup shortening
⅔ cup butter or margarine, softened
1 cup granulated sugar
1 cup brown sugar (packed)
2 eggs
2 teaspoons vanilla

3 cups all-purpose flour*
1 teaspoon soda
1 teaspoon salt
1 cup chopped nuts
2 packages (6 ounces each) semisweet chocolate pieces

Heat oven to 375°. Mix thoroughly shortening, butter, sugars, eggs and vanilla. Stir in remaining ingredients. (For a softer, rounder cookie, add ½ cup flour.)

Drop dough by rounded teaspoonfuls 2 inches apart onto ungreased baking sheet. Bake 8 to 10 minutes or until light brown. Cool slightly before removing from baking sheet.

About 7 dozen cookies.

*If using self-rising flour, omit soda and salt.

VARIATION

■ *Salted Peanut Cookies:* Substitute 2 cups salted peanuts for the chocolate pieces and nuts. Before baking, flatten each cookie with bottom of glass that has been greased and dipped in sugar.

RANGER COOKIES

½ cup shortening
½ cup granulated sugar
½ cup brown sugar (packed)
1 egg
½ teaspoon vanilla
1 cup all-purpose flour*
½ teaspoon soda

¼ teaspoon baking powder
¼ teaspoon salt
1 cup quick-cooking oats
1 cup fortified whole wheat
  flakes cereal
½ cup shredded coconut

Heat oven to 375°. Mix thoroughly shortening, granulated sugar, brown sugar, egg and vanilla. Stir in remaining ingredients.

Drop dough by rounded teaspoonfuls 2 inches apart onto ungreased baking sheet. Bake 10 minutes. Immediately remove from baking sheet.

3 dozen cookies.

*If using self-rising flour, omit soda, baking powder and salt. If using quick-mixing flour, mix 2 tablespoons milk into shortening mixture.

JUBILEE JUMBLES

2¾ cups all-purpose flour*
1½ cups brown sugar
  (packed)
1 teaspoon salt
½ teaspoon soda
1 cup dairy sour cream
½ cup shortening

2 eggs
1 teaspoon vanilla
1 cup chopped nuts, if
  desired
Browned Butter Glaze
(below)

Mix thoroughly all ingredients except glaze. If dough is soft, cover and chill.

Heat oven to 375°. Drop dough by level tablespoonfuls 2 inches apart onto ungreased baking sheet. Bake 10 minutes or until almost no imprint remains when touched with finger.

Immediately remove from baking sheet; cool. Spread with Browned Butter Glaze.

4½ to 5 dozen cookies.

*If using self-rising flour, omit salt and soda.

BROWNED BUTTER GLAZE

Heat ⅓ cup butter or margarine over low heat until golden brown. Remove from heat; blend in 2 cups confectioners' sugar and 1½ teaspoons vanilla. Stir in 2 to 4 tablespoons hot water until of spreading consistency.

■ *Applesauce Jumbles:* Omit sour cream and stir in ¾ cup applesauce, 1 cup raisins, 1 teaspoon cinnamon and ¼ teaspoon cloves.

■ *Coconut Jumbles:* Omit nuts and stir in 1 cup shredded coconut.

■ *Fruit Jumbles:* Omit nuts and stir in 2 cups candied cherries, cut into halves, 2 cups cut-up dates and 1½ cups chopped pecans. Drop dough by rounded teaspoonfuls onto ungreased baking sheet. Before baking, place a pecan half on top of each cookie. Omit glaze. About 7 dozen cookies.

■ *Gumdrop Jumbles:* Omit nuts and stir in 4 cups cut-up gumdrops. Drop dough by tablespoonfuls onto greased and floured baking sheet; bake. Omit glaze. About 6 dozen cookies.

OATMEAL COOKIES

¾ cup shortening	1 teaspoon salt
1 cup brown sugar (packed)	1 teaspoon cinnamon
½ cup granulated sugar	½ teaspoon soda
1 egg	½ teaspoon cloves
¼ cup water	1 cup raisins
1 teaspoon vanilla	1 cup chopped nuts
1 cup all-purpose flour*	3 cups quick-cooking oats

. Heat oven to 350°. Mix thoroughly shortening, sugars, egg, water and vanilla. Stir in remaining ingredients.

Drop dough by rounded teaspoonfuls 1 inch apart onto greased baking sheet. Bake 12 to 15 minutes or until almost no imprint remains when touched with finger. Immediately remove from baking sheet. Store in tightly covered container.

About 5 dozen cookies.

*If using self-rising flour, omit salt and soda.

■ *Banana Oatmeal Cookies:* Omit water, increase soda to 1 teaspoon and stir 1 cup mashed banana (2 to 3 medium) into shortening mixture.

Be sure to drop dough by rounded teaspoonfuls.

BROWN SUGAR DROPS

1 cup shortening	½ cup buttermilk or water
2 cups brown sugar (packed)	3½ cups all-purpose flour*
2 eggs	1 teaspoon each soda and salt

Mix thoroughly shortening, sugar, eggs and buttermilk. Blend in flour, soda and salt. Cover; chill 1 hour.

Heat oven to 400°. Drop dough by rounded teaspoonfuls about 2 inches apart onto greased baking sheet. Bake 8 to 10 minutes or until almost no imprint remains when touched with finger. Immediately remove from baking sheet.

About 6 dozen cookies.

*If using self-rising flour, omit salt and soda.

GINGER CREAMS

Puffy, cake-like ginger gems.

⅓ cup shortening	½ teaspoon salt
½ cup sugar	½ teaspoon soda
1 egg	½ teaspoon nutmeg
½ cup molasses	½ teaspoon cloves
½ cup water	½ teaspoon cinnamon
2 cups all-purpose flour*	½ recipe Vanilla Butter Frosting (page 185)
1 teaspoon ginger	

Mix thoroughly shortening, sugar, egg, molasses and water. Blend in remaining ingredients except frosting. Cover; chill 1 hour.

*If using self-rising flour, omit salt and soda.

Heat oven to 400°. Drop dough by teaspoonfuls 2 inches apart onto ungreased baking sheet. Bake 8 minutes or until almost no imprint remains when touched with finger.

Immediately remove from baking sheet; cool. Frost with Vanilla Butter Frosting.

About 4 dozen cookies.

CREAM CHEESE COOKIES

Cake-mix cookies—light and luscious. They're so easy and quick, you'll bake them often.

¼ cup butter or margarine, softened	¼ teaspoon vanilla
1 package (8 ounces) cream cheese, softened	1 package (18.5 ounces) yellow or devils food cake mix
1 egg	

Cream butter and cheese. Blend in egg and vanilla. Add cake mix (dry), ⅓ at a time, mixing well after each addition. (If mixer is used, add last third of cake mix by hand.) Cover; chill 30 minutes.

Heat oven to 375°. Drop by scant teaspoonfuls onto ungreased baking sheet. Bake 8 to 10 minutes or until light brown. Cool slightly before removing from baking sheet.

6 to 8 dozen cookies.

Bar Cookies

These rich, moist cookies are always a special treat—as dessert, at a kaffeeklatsch or just for snacking. Dust them with confectioners' sugar, ice them or serve them plain. They'll disappear fast. And they're the easiest kind of cookie to make.

Here are some simple tips to follow:

■ Use a spatula to spread dough in pan. Spread evenly for an even texture.

■ For best results, your pan should be the size specified in the recipe. If it is smaller than recommended, the dough will be thick and will probably require longer baking. If it is larger, the dough will be thin and you will have to reduce baking time in order to prevent dryness.

■ Follow the tests for doneness carefully. Overbaked bar cookies are hard and dry.

■ Cut into bars or squares when slightly cool; bars will crumble if cut while they are too warm.

BROWNIES

The traditional fudgy brownies—favorites with just about everyone.

4 ounces unsweetened chocolate	1 teaspoon vanilla
⅔ cup shortening	1¼ cups all-purpose flour*
2 cups sugar	1 teaspoon baking powder
4 eggs	1 teaspoon salt
	1 cup chopped nuts

Heat oven to 350°. Grease baking pan, 13x9x2 inches. Melt chocolate and shortening in large saucepan over low heat. Remove from heat. Mix in sugar, eggs and vanilla. Stir in remaining ingredients. Spread in pan.

Bake 30 minutes or until brownies start to pull away from sides of pan. Do not overbake. Cool slightly. Cut into bars, about 2x1½ inches. If desired, spread with Glossy Chocolate Frosting (page 188) before cutting.

32 cookies.

*If using self-rising flour, omit baking powder and salt.

TOFFEE BARS

1 cup butter or margarine, softened	2 cups all-purpose flour*
1 cup brown sugar (packed)	¼ teaspoon salt
1 egg yolk	1 bar (3.5 ounces) milk chocolate candy
1 teaspoon vanilla	½ cup chopped nuts

Heat oven to 350°. Grease baking pan, 13x9x2 inches. Mix thoroughly butter, sugar, egg yolk and vanilla. Blend in flour and salt. Press evenly in bottom of pan.

Bake 25 to 30 minutes or until very light brown. (Crust

*If using self-rising flour, omit salt.

will be soft.) Remove from oven; immediately place separated pieces of chocolate candy on crust. As soon as chocolate is soft, spread evenly. Sprinkle with nuts. While warm, cut into bars, about 2x1½ inches.

32 cookies.

MONTEGO BAY BARS

1½ cups cut-up dates
2 tablespoons granulated sugar
¾ cup water
½ square (½ ounce) unsweetened chocolate
⅓ cup butter or margarine, softened
½ cup brown sugar (packed)
¾ cup all-purpose flour*
½ teaspoon salt
¼ teaspoon soda
¾ cup quick-cooking oats
⅓ cup finely chopped nuts

Heat oven to 400°. Grease square pan, 8x8x2 or 9x9x2 inches. Cook dates, granulated sugar, water and chocolate over low heat, stirring constantly, about 10 minutes or until mixture thickens; cool.

Cream butter and brown sugar. Mix in remaining ingredients. Press half the mixture evenly in bottom of pan. Spread with date mixture; top with remaining crumble mixture, pressing lightly. Bake 25 to 30 minutes or until golden brown. Cool; cut into bars, about 2x1½ inches.

2 dozen cookies.

*If using self-rising flour, omit salt and soda. If using quick-mixing flour, stir in 2 teaspoons milk.

DATE BARS

Date Filling (page 212)
½ cup butter or margarine, softened
¼ cup shortening
1 cup brown sugar (packed)
1¾ cups all-purpose flour*
1 teaspoon salt
½ teaspoon soda
1½ cups quick-cooking oats

Prepare Date Filling; cool. Heat oven to 400°. Grease baking pan, 13x9x2 inches. Cream butter, shortening and sugar. Mix in remaining ingredients. Press half the mixture evenly in bottom of pan. Spread with filling. Top with remaining crumble mixture, pressing lightly.

*If using self-rising flour, omit salt and soda. If using quick-mixing flour, stir in 3 to 4 teaspoons milk.

Bake 25 to 30 minutes or until light brown. While warm, cut into bars, about 2x1½ inches.

3 dozen cookies.

DATE FILLING

Mix 3 cups cut-up dates (1 pound), ¼ cup sugar and 1½ cups water in saucepan. Cook over low heat, stirring constantly, about 10 minutes or until thickened.

VARIATION

■ *Jam Bars:* Omit Date Filling and substitute 1 cup of your favorite jam.

PECAN FINGERS

¾ cup shortening (half butter or margarine, softened)	2 tablespoons flour
	½ teaspoon baking powder
	½ teaspoon salt
¾ cup confectioners' sugar	½ teaspoon vanilla
1½ cups all-purpose flour*	1 cup chopped pecans
2 eggs	
1 cup brown sugar (packed)	

Heat oven to 350°. Cream shortening and confectioners' sugar. Blend in 1½ cups flour. Press evenly in bottom of ungreased baking pan, 13x9x2 inches. Bake 12 to 15 minutes.

Mix remaining ingredients; spread over hot baked layer and bake 20 minutes longer. Cool; cut into bars, about 3x1 inch. 32 cookies.

*Self-rising flour can be used in this recipe.

VARIATION

■ *Coconut Chews:* Substitute ½ cup chopped walnuts and ½ cup flaked coconut for the pecans. While warm, spread with Orange-Lemon Icing: Mix 1½ cups confectioners' sugar, 2 tablespoons butter or margarine, melted, 3 tablespoons orange juice and 1 teaspoon lemon juice until smooth and of spreading consistency.

LEMON SQUARES

1 cup all-purpose flour*	1 cup granulated sugar
½ cup butter or margarine, softened	½ teaspoon baking powder
¼ cup confectioners' sugar	¼ teaspoon salt
2 eggs	2 tablespoons lemon juice

Heat oven to 350°. Mix thoroughly flour, butter and confectioners' sugar. Press in ungreased square pan, 8x8x2 inches, building up a ½-inch edge. Bake 20 minutes.

Beat remaining ingredients about 3 minutes or until light and fluffy. Pour over hot crust. Bake about 25 minutes longer or just until no imprint remains when touched lightly in center. Cool; cut into squares.

25 cookies.

*If using self-rising flour, omit baking powder and salt.

FILBERT BARS

¼ cup butter or margarine, softened	½ cup softened currant or raspberry jelly
¼ cup confectioners' sugar	Meringue-Filbert Topping (below)
1 egg yolk	
½ cup all-purpose flour*	

Heat oven to 350°. Mix thoroughly butter, sugar and egg yolk. Blend in flour. Press in bottom of ungreased square pan, 8x8x2 or 9x9x2 inches.

Bake 10 minutes. Spread with jelly, then with topping. Bake 20 minutes longer or until topping is golden brown. Cool slightly. Cut into bars, about 2x1 inch. If topping sticks to knife, dip knife into hot water occasionally.

32 cookies.

*Do not use self-rising flour in this recipe.

MERINGUE-FILBERT TOPPING

1 egg white	¼ cup sugar
¼ teaspoon cinnamon	½ cup finely chopped filberts

Beat egg white until foamy. Add cinnamon. Beat in sugar, 1 tablespoon at a time; continue beating until stiff and glossy. Fold in filberts.

COCONUT TOFFEE BARS

¼ cup butter or margarine,
    softened
¼ cup shortening
½ cup brown sugar
    (packed)

1 cup all-purpose flour*
    Almond-Coconut Topping
    or Coconut-Lemon
    Topping (below)

Heat oven to 350°. Cream butter, shortening and sugar. Blend in flour. Press evenly in bottom of ungreased baking pan, 13x9x2 inches.

Bake 10 minutes. Spread with topping. Bake 25 minutes longer or until topping is golden brown. Cool slightly. Cut into bars, about 3x1 inch.

    32 cookies.

*If using self-rising flour, omit baking powder and salt in Almond-Coconut Topping.

ALMOND-COCONUT TOPPING

2 eggs
1 cup brown sugar
    (packed)
1 teaspoon vanilla
2 tablespoons flour

1 teaspoon baking powder
½ teaspoon salt
1 cup shredded coconut
1 cup chopped almonds

Beat eggs; add remaining ingredients and mix.

COCONUT-LEMON TOPPING

2 eggs
1 cup brown sugar
    (packed)
1 teaspoon grated lemon
    peel

2 tablespoons lemon juice
½ teaspoon salt
1 cup shredded coconut
1 cup cut-up raisins
1 cup chopped walnuts

Beat eggs; add remaining ingredients and mix.

COOKIES IN QUANTITY Maybe it's holiday time, maybe just another time when you're celebrating. Either way, most everyone loves homemade cookies, and the following are real large-batch favorites: Chocolate Chips (page 205), Snickerdoodles (page 221) and Chocolate Refrigerator Cookies (page 217). You can even double some recipes, like Peanut Butter (page 222) and Oatmeal (page 207).

Refrigerator Cookies

Chill-and-bake cookies—always ready when you want them. They may be round, square, rectangular or oval; frosted or plain, pinwheels, checkerboards or ribbons; nut-trimmed, candy-trimmed or fruit-trimmed. And don't forget that young cook in your family—she'd love to help with these!

Here are helps and hints to guarantee perfect cookies every time:

■ Shape dough firmly with hands into a long, smooth roll of the diameter specified in the recipe. The dough should be just firm enough to hold its shape.

■ If desired, add flavor as well as trimming by rolling in *finely* chopped nuts, colored sugar or chocolate shot. (Coarsely chopped nuts will cause the dough to crumble when you slice it.)

■ Wrap rolled dough in waxed paper, plastic wrap or lightweight aluminum foil, twisting ends.

■ Chill in refrigerator until firm enough to slice easily. (This cookie dough can be made up ahead of time and stored in the freezer.)

■ When ready to bake, slice to desired thickness, using a thin, sharp knife. (You may have to let the dough warm up for a minute.) Keep the slices even so baked cookies will be uniform.

■ Watch baking time closely. Finished cookies should be lightly browned.

For even baking make each roll of refrigerator cookie dough the length and diameter specified in the recipe.

VANILLA REFRIGERATOR COOKIES

Looking for versatility? This ever-dependable favorite has many different faces.

1 cup butter or margarine, softened	1½ teaspoons vanilla
1 cup sugar	3 cups all-purpose flour*
2 eggs	1 teaspoon salt
	½ cup finely chopped nuts

Mix thoroughly butter, sugar, eggs and vanilla. Stir in flour, salt and nuts. Divide dough into 3 equal parts; shape each part into roll, 1½ inches in diameter and about 7 inches long. Wrap; chill at least 4 hours.

Heat oven to 400°. Cut rolls into ⅛-inch slices. Place 1 inch apart on ungreased baking sheet. Bake 8 to 10 minutes or until light brown. Immediately remove from baking sheet.

About 7 dozen cookies.

*If using self-rising flour, omit salt.

VARIATIONS

■ *Butterscotch Slices:* Substitute 1 cup brown sugar (packed) for the sugar.

■ *Cinnamon Cookie Slices:* Substitute ½ cup granulated sugar and ½ cup brown sugar (packed) for sugar and 3 teaspoons cinnamon for vanilla.

■ *Cookie Tarts:* Omit nuts. Before baking, spoon 1 teaspoon jelly or preserves on half the slices; top with remaining slices. Seal edges. Cut slits in top so filling shows. About 3½ dozen cookies.

■ *Orange-Almond Refrigerator Cookies:* Mix in 1 tablespoon grated orange peel with the butter and ½ cup finely chopped blanched almonds with the flour.

■ *Peanut Butter Cookies:* Decrease butter to ½ cup and add ½ cup crunchy peanut butter; substitute 1 cup dark brown sugar (packed) for the sugar. Omit nuts.

■ *Shamrocks:* Color dough with green food color. Divide dough into 4 parts. Shape each part into roll, 1 inch in diameter and 10 inches long. Wrap and chill. Cut into ⅛-inch slices. Place 3 slices with sides touching on ungreased baking sheet; press together. Cut stems from another slice. Bake about 7 minutes. About 6 dozen cookies.

BUTTER-RICH COOKIES

1 cup butter or margarine, softened
1 cup confectioners' sugar
1 teaspoon flavoring (vanilla, almond, wintergreen or rose)

2½ cups all-purpose flour*
¼ teaspoon salt
1 cup finely chopped pecans

Mix thoroughly butter, sugar and flavoring. Blend in flour and salt. (If dough is dry, add 3 to 4 teaspoons milk.) Shape dough into roll, about 2 inches in diameter. Roll in pecans. Wrap; chill at least 4 hours.

Heat oven to 400°. Cut roll into ⅛-inch slices. Place 1 inch apart on ungreased baking sheet. Bake 8 to 10 minutes or until light brown. Immediately remove from baking sheet. About 6 dozen cookies.

*Do not use self-rising flour in this recipe.

Cut chilled dough for Pinwheel Cookies into ⅛-inch slices.

For Ribbon Bar Cookies, press and even strips of dough.

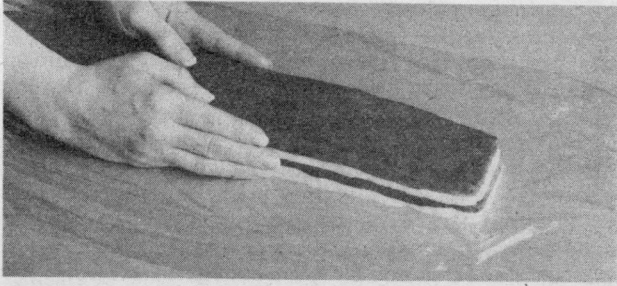

CHOCOLATE REFRIGERATOR COOKIES

1¼ cups butter or margarine, softened	½ cup cocoa
1½ cups confectioners' sugar	¼ teaspoon salt
1 egg	1½ cups finely chopped pecans
3 cups all-purpose flour* or cake flour	Fudge Frosting

Mix butter, sugar and egg. Stir in flour, cocoa and salt. Cover; chill 1 hour. Divide dough in half; shape each half into roll, 1½ inches in diameter. Roll in nuts. Wrap; chill 8 hours.

Heat oven to 400°. Cut rolls into ⅛-inch slices. (If dough crumbles while cutting, let warm slightly.) Place 1 inch apart on ungreased baking sheet. Bake about 8 minutes. Immediately remove from baking sheet; cool. Frost with Fudge Frosting.

About 8 dozen cookies.

*Do not use self-rising flour in this recipe.

FUDGE FROSTING

¼ cup shortening	¼ teaspoon salt
⅓ cup milk	1 teaspoon vanilla
1 cup sugar	
2 ounces melted unsweetened chocolate	

Heat all ingredients except vanilla to rolling boil, stirring occasionally. Boil 1 minute without stirring. Place pan in bowl of ice and water; beat until frosting is thick and cold. Stir in vanilla.

VARIATIONS

■ *Pinwheels:* Omit ½ cup cocoa. After dough is mixed, divide in half. Stir ¼ cup cocoa into 1 half. Chill 1 hour. On lightly floured cloth-covered board, roll plain dough into rectangle, 16x9 inches. Roll chocolate dough same size; place on top. Roll dough ³⁄₁₆ inch thick. Roll up tightly. Wrap, chill, slice and bake as above. Do not frost.

■ *Ribbon Bar Cookies:* Omit ½ cup cocoa. After dough is mixed, divide in half. Stir ¼ cup cocoa into 1 half. Chill 1 hour. On very lightly floured board, shape each part into 2 strips, each 2½ inches wide and 16 inches long. Layer strips, alternating colors. Press together. Wrap, chill, slice and bake as directed above. Do not frost.

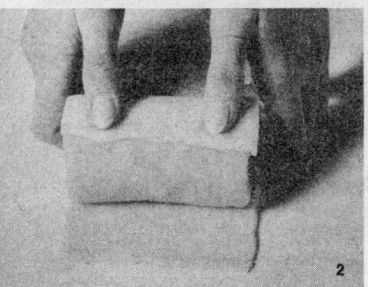

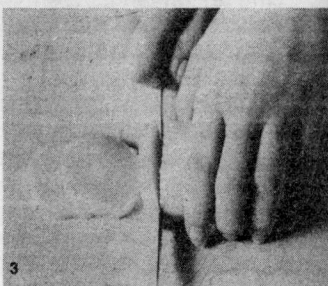

1. Tint and flavor 3 portions of dough; shape into rolls.

2. Wrap rectangle of plain dough around each tinted roll.

3. Cut chilled rolls into ⅛-inch slices.

4. Citrus cookies—what could be prettier for a spring tea.

FRUIT-SLICE COOKIES

1 cup butter or margarine, softened	1½ teaspoons grated lemon peel
1 cup granulated sugar	1½ teaspoons grated lime peel
2 eggs	
1½ teaspoons vanilla	1½ teaspoons grated orange peel
3 cups all-purpose flour*	
1 teaspoon salt	Colored sugars (yellow, green and orange)
Food colors (yellow, green and red)	

Mix thoroughly butter, granulated sugar, eggs and vanilla. Blend in flour and salt. Divide dough into 4 equal parts.

To one part, work in few drops yellow food color and the lemon peel. To another part, work in few drops green food color and the lime peel. To another part, work in few drops each red and yellow food color and the orange peel. (Leave remaining part plain.) Cover; chill 1 hour.

Shape each colored dough into roll, 2 inches in diameter and 4 inches long. Divide plain dough into 3 equal parts. Roll each part into rectangle, 6x4 inches. Wrap 1 rectangle around each roll of colored dough; press together firmly. Roll in matching colored sugar. Wrap; chill at least 4 hours.

Heat oven to 400°. Cut rolls into ⅛-inch slices. Place on ungreased baking sheet; cut each slice in half. Bake 6 to 8 minutes or just until set. Immediately remove from baking sheet.

About 10 dozen cookies.

*Do not use self-rising flour in this recipe.

Molded Cookies

Following are a few helpful hints:

■ Richer, softer doughs must be chilled before shaping. Work with small amounts, keeping the rest of the dough refrigerated.

■ To mold cookies, roll dough to desired shape between palms of hands. Be sure surface is smooth; this ensures even browning and texture. If the recipe tells you to flatten the cookie, use the bottom of a glass dipped in flour or press down with fork or thumb.

■ When molding fancy shapes such as crescents, candy canes, wreaths, bells and so on, take time to mold carefully so that the cookies will be uniform in size and shape.

GINGERSNAPS

A pungent gingersnap—crispy on the edges but soft in the center.

¾ cup shortening
1 cup brown sugar
(packed)
1 egg
¼ cup molasses
2¼ cups all-purpose flour*

2 teaspoons soda
1 teaspoon cinnamon
1 teaspoon ginger
½ teaspoon cloves
¼ teaspoon salt
Granulated sugar

Mix thoroughly shortening, brown sugar, egg and molasses. Blend in remaining ingredients except granulated sugar. Cover; chill 1 hour.

Heat oven to 375°. Shape dough by rounded teaspoonfuls into balls. Dip tops in granulated sugar. Place balls sugared side up 3 inches apart on lightly greased baking sheet. Bake 10 to 12 minutes or just until set. Immediately remove from baking sheet.

4 dozen cookies.

*If using self-rising flour, decrease soda to 1 teaspoon and omit salt.

SNICKERDOODLES

½ cup butter or margarine,
softened
½ cup shortening
1½ cups sugar
2 eggs
2¾ cups all-purpose flour*

2 teaspoons cream of tartar
1 teaspoon soda
¼ teaspoon salt
2 tablespoons sugar
2 teaspoons cinnamon

Heat oven to 400°. Mix thoroughly butter, shortening, 1½ cups sugar and the eggs. Blend in flour, cream of tartar, soda and salt. Shape dough by rounded teaspoonfuls into balls.

Mix 2 tablespoons sugar and the cinnamon; roll balls in mixture. Place 2 inches apart on ungreased baking sheet. Bake 8 to 10 minutes or until set. Immediately remove from baking sheet.

About 6 dozen cookies.

*If using self-rising flour, omit cream of tartar, soda and salt.

THUMBPRINT COOKIES

¼ cup butter or margarine,
   softened
¼ cup shortening
¼ cup brown sugar
   (packed)
 1 egg, separated
½ teaspoon vanilla

1 cup all-purpose flour*
¼ teaspoon salt
¾ cup finely chopped nuts
   Jelly or tinted
   Confectioners' Sugar Icing
   (page 224)

Heat oven to 350°. Mix thoroughly butter, shortening, sugar, egg yolk and vanilla. Work in flour and salt until dough holds together. Shape dough by teaspoonfuls into 1-inch balls.

Beat egg white slightly. Dip each ball into egg white; roll in nuts. Place 1 inch apart on ungreased baking sheet; press thumb deeply into center of each. Bake about 10 minutes or until light brown. Immediately remove from baking sheet; cool. Fill thumbprints with jelly.

About 3 dozen cookies.

*If using self-rising flour, omit salt.

PEANUT BUTTER COOKIES

An old favorite—and some new twists.

½ cup shortening (half
   butter or margarine,
   softened)
½ cup peanut butter
½ cup granulated sugar
½ cup brown sugar
   (packed)

1 egg
1¼ cups all-purpose flour*
¾ teaspoon soda
½ teaspoon baking powder
¼ teaspoon salt

Mix thoroughly shortening, peanut butter, granulated sugar, brown sugar and egg. Blend in flour, soda, baking powder and salt. Cover and chill.

Heat oven to 375°. Shape dough into 1-inch balls. Place 3 inches apart on lightly greased baking sheet. With fork dipped in flour, flatten in crisscross pattern to 2 inches. Bake 10 to 12 minutes or until set but not hard.

About 3 dozen cookies.

*If using self-rising flour, omit soda, baking powder and salt

VARIATIONS

■ *Invisible Mint Cookies:* Mold 1 level tablespoon around chocolate mint wafer; seal well. Sprinkle tops with finely chopped peanuts or chocolate shot. Place on lightly greased baking sheet. Bake 10 to 12 minutes or until set but not hard. About 3 dozen cookies.

■ *Peanut Butter and Jelly Cookies:* Shape dough into 1-inch balls. Roll in ½ cup finely chopped peanuts. Place about 3 inches apart on lightly greased baking sheet; press thumb deeply into center of each ball. Bake 10 to 12 minutes or until set but not hard. Spoon small amount of jelly or jam into each thumbprint. About 3½ dozen cookies.

■ *Yo-Yo Cookies:* Shape dough into ¾-inch balls. Place about 2 inches apart on lightly greased baking sheet. Do not flatten. Bake about 10 minutes or until set but not hard. When cool, put cookies together in pairs with jelly or jam. About 4½ dozen cookies.

JAM STICKS

King-size "all-day" cookies that are fun to make.

1 cup butter or margarine, softened	2½ cups all-purpose flour*
	1 teaspoon soda
1½ cups confectioners' sugar	1 teaspoon cream of tartar
1 egg	½ cup jam
1 teaspoon vanilla	Confectioners' Sugar
½ teaspoon almond extract	Icing (page 224)

Mix thoroughly butter, sugar, egg and flavorings. Blend in flour, soda and cream of tartar. If dough is too soft to handle, cover and chill about 1 hour.

Heat oven to 375°. Divide dough into 12 equal parts; on lightly greased baking sheet, shape each part into rectangle, 8x1½ inches. With wooden spoon handle, make a furrow lengthwise down center of each rectangle. Spread 1 teaspoon jam in furrow. Bake about 10 minutes. Cool on baking sheet 2 minutes. If desired, cut warm cookies diagonally into 1-inch slices. Remove to wire racks. When cool, drizzle with Confectioners' Sugar Icing.

12 cookies.

*If using self-rising flour, omit soda and cream of tartar.

CONFECTIONERS' SUGAR ICING

Mix 2 cups confectioners' sugar and 2 tablespoons plus 1 teaspoon milk until smooth.

GALAXY COOKIES

As varied as the stars. So easy, so delicious are these cookies that look like bonbons. And there's a surprise in each.

½ cup butter or margarine, softened	⅛ teaspoon salt
¾ cup confectioners' sugar	Dates, nuts, semisweet chocolate pieces and candied or maraschino cherries
1 tablespoon vanilla	
Food color, if desired	
1½ cups all-purpose flour*	Icing (below)

Heat oven to 350°. Mix thoroughly butter, sugar, vanilla and few drops food color. Work in flour and salt until dough holds together. (If dough is dry, mix in 1 to 2 tablespoons light cream.)

Mold dough by tablespoonfuls around date, nut, cherry or a few chocolate pieces. Place cookies about 1 inch apart on ungreased baking sheet. Bake 12 to 15 minutes or until set but not brown.

Cool; dip tops of cookies into Icing. If desired, decorate with coconut, nuts, colored sugar, candies, chocolate pieces or chocolate shot.

Makes 20 to 25 cookies.

*Do not use self-rising flour in this recipe.

ICING

Mix 1 cup confectioners' sugar, 2½ tablespoons light cream or 1½ tablespoons milk and 1 teaspoon vanilla until smooth. If desired, stir in few drops food color.

For a chocolate icing, increase light cream to 3 tablespoons or milk to 2 tablespoons and stir in 1 ounce melted unsweetened chocolate (cool).

VARIATIONS

■ *Brown Sugar Galaxy Cookies:* Substitute ½ cup brown sugar (packed) for the confectioners' sugar and omit food color.

■ *Chocolate Galaxy Cookies:* Omit food color and stir 1 ounce melted unsweetened chocolate (cool) into butter mixture.

RUSSIAN TEACAKES

Also called Mexican Wedding Cakes.

1 cup butter or margarine, softened	2¼ cups all-purpose flour*
½ cup confectioners' sugar	¼ teaspoon salt
1 teaspoon vanilla	¾ cup finely chopped nuts

Heat oven to 400°. Mix thoroughly butter, sugar and vanilla. Work in flour, salt and nuts until dough holds together. Shape dough into 1-inch balls. Place on ungreased baking sheet.

Bake 10 to 12 minutes or until set but not brown. While warm, roll in confectioners' sugar. Cool. Roll in sugar again.

About 4 dozen cookies.

*Do not use self-rising flour in this recipe.

VARIATION

■ *Ambrosia Balls:* Omit nuts; add 1 cup finely cut coconut and 1 tablespoon grated orange peel with the flour.

COCONUT-ORANGE TARTLETS

1 cup all-purpose flour*	1 egg
¼ cup sugar	Coconut-Orange Filling
½ teaspoon salt	(below)
½ cup butter or margarine	

Measure flour, sugar and salt into bowl. Cut in butter thoroughly. Beat egg slightly; pour into flour mixture. Mix until flour is moistened. Gather into a ball. Wrap; chill 4 hours or until firm.

Heat oven to 375°. Press about 1 teaspoon dough ⅛ inch thick on bottom and side of each ungreased 2x½-inch tartlet pan. Fill each tart with 1 teaspoon Coconut-Orange Filling. Place on baking sheet. Bake 12 minutes or until filling is golden brown. Remove pans to wire rack; cool slightly. Gently tap tartlets from pans.

3½ dozen cookies.

*Do not use self-rising flour in this recipe.

COCONUT-ORANGE FILLING

Mix 1 egg, slightly beaten, 1 can (4 ounces) flaked coconut, ⅔ cup sugar and ½ teaspoon grated orange or lemon peel.

LEMON SNOWDROPS

Refreshing lemon filling between buttery, lemon-flavored rounds.

1 cup butter or margarine,
  softened
½ cup confectioners' sugar
1 teaspoon lemon extract

2 cups all-purpose flour*
¼ teaspoon salt
Lemon Butter Filling (below)

Mix thoroughly butter, confectioners' sugar and lemon extract. Blend in flour and salt. If dough is soft, cover and chill.

Heat oven to 400°. Shape dough by *level* teaspoonfuls into balls. Place 1 inch apart on ungreased baking sheet; flatten slightly. Bake 8 to 10 minutes.

Immediately remove from baking sheet; cool. Put cookies together in pairs with Lemon Butter Filling. Roll in confectioners' sugar.

About 4 dozen cookies.

*If using self-rising flour, omit salt. If using quick-mixing flour, stir in 1 tablespoon milk.

LEMON BUTTER FILLING

½ cup sugar
2 tablespoons cornstarch
  Dash salt
½ cup water
2 tablespoons butter or
  margarine

2 teaspoons grated lemon
  peel
3 tablespoons lemon juice
3 drops yellow food color

Mix sugar, cornstarch and salt in saucepan. Stir in water gradually. Cook, stirring constantly, until mixture thickens and boils. Boil and stir 1 minute. Remove from heat. Stir in butter and lemon peel. Stir in lemon juice and food color. Cool thoroughly.

MAILING COOKIES Wrap separately or back-to-back in pairs in plastic wrap or bags, aluminum foil or waxed paper. Pack in covered coffee or shortening cans or in a sturdy box. Then place in packing box padded with crumpled or shredded paper. (Don't use popcorn as a filler.) Try these good travelers: Chocolate Chips (page 205), Jubilee Jumbles (page 206), Traditional Sugar Cookies (page 228). Russian Teacakes (page 225).

Rolled Cookies

Crisp and thin or soft and thick, what fun you and the youngsters can have making these cookies! Cut them to suit your fancy and the occasion—usher in the holidays and seasons with witches and jack-o'-lanterns, turkeys and pumpkins, Christmas trees and Santas, bunnies, flowers and Easter eggs. You can "paint" cookies, too (see Paintbrush Cookies on page 229). Give a zoo party or a doll party for your son or daugher's next birthday. Make animals or dolls and "paint" each guest's name on a cookie; use it for a place card.

If you can't find cutters for the shape you want, make them. Cut the desired pattern from heavy cardboard; grease. Lay pattern greased side down on rolled dough and cut around it with a sharp knife dipped in flour.

Here are a few tips to follow:

■ To prevent dough from sticking, rub flour into stockinet on rolling pin and lightly into pastry cloth.

■ If you're handling chilled dough, roll only part of it at a time; keep the remainder chilled.

■ Roll lightly and evenly to ensure cookies that bake evenly. (The thinner you roll, the crisper the cookies.)

■ Dip cookie cutter in flour; shake off excess. Then cut dough. (Cut cookies close together.)

■ To maintain shape, lift cookies to baking sheet with a spatula.

Cut rolled cookies close together; lift with spatula.

SCOTCH SHORTBREAD

¾ cup butter or margarine,
   softened

¼ cup sugar
2 cups all-purpose flour*

Heat oven to 350°. Cream butter and sugar. Work in flour. If dough is crumbly, mix in 1 to 2 tablespoons soft butter.

Roll dough ½ to ⅓ inch thick on lightly floured cloth-covered board. Cut into small shapes (leaves, ovals, squares, triangles). Place ½ inch apart on ungreased baking sheet. Bake about 20 minutes or until set. Immediately remove from baking sheet.

About 2 dozen 1½x1-inch cookies.

*Do not use self-rising flour in this recipe. If using quick-mixing flour, add 2 tablespoons milk.

TRADITIONAL SUGAR COOKIES

¾ cup shortening (part
   butter or margarine,
   softened)
1 cup sugar
2 eggs

1 teaspoon vanilla or ½
   teaspoon lemon extract
2½ cups all-purpose flour*
1 teaspoon baking powder
1 teaspoon salt

Mix thoroughly shortening, sugar, eggs and flavoring. Blend in flour, baking powder and salt. Cover; chill at least 1 hour.

Heat oven to 400°. Roll dough ⅛ inch thick on lightly floured cloth-covered board. Cut into desired shapes. Place on ungreased baking sheet. Bake 6 to 8 minutes or until very light brown.

About 4 dozen 3-inch cookies.

*If using self-rising flour, omit baking powder and salt.

VARIATIONS

■ *Filled Sugar Cookies:* Before baking, put cookies together in pairs with 1 teaspoon of a favorite fruit filling or a chocolate mint wafer. Press edges together with tines of fork. About 2 dozen cookies.

■ *Quick-frosted Sugar Cookies:* While cookies are warm, place 1 chocolate mint patty on each; when soft, spread almost to edge of cookie.

DELUXE SUGAR COOKIES

1 cup butter or margarine, softened	½ teaspoon almond extract
1½ cups confectioners' sugar	2½ cups all-purpose flour*
1 egg	1 teaspoon soda
1 teaspoon vanilla	1 teaspoon cream of tartar
	Granulated sugar

Mix thoroughly butter, confectioners' sugar, egg, vanilla and almond extract. Blend in flour, soda and cream of tartar. Cover; chill 2 to 3 hours.

Heat oven to 375°. Divide dough in half. Roll each half ³⁄₁₆ inch thick on lightly floured cloth-covered board. Cut into desired shapes; sprinkle with granulated sugar. Place on lightly greased baking sheet. Bake 7 to 8 minutes or until light brown on edge.

About 5 dozen 2- to 2½-inch cookies.

*If using self-rising flour, omit soda and cream of tartar.

VARIATION

■ *Paintbrush Cookies:* Do not sprinkle cookies with sugar; before baking, paint designs on cookies with small paintbrushes and Cookie Paint: Divide small amounts of evaporated milk (or mixture of 1 egg yolk and ¼ teaspoon water) among several cups. Color each with a different food color. If "paint" thickens, add few drops water.

BUTTER COOKIES

Small, crunchy, nut-flavored cookies.

1 cup butter or margarine, softened	½ cup sugar
2 cups all-purpose flour*	1 cup finely chopped walnuts

Heat oven to 350°. Mix thoroughly all ingredients. Roll dough ¼ inch thick on lightly floured cloth-covered board. Cut into 1½-inch circles. Place on ungreased baking sheet.

Bake 10 to 12 minutes. If desired, sprinkle with confectioners' sugar or put cookies together in pairs with raspberry jam.

About 8 dozen cookies.

*Do not use self-rising flour in this recipe.

CREAM WAFERS

Wonderful for a special tea or light dessert.

1 cup soft butter	Granulated sugar
⅓ cup whipping cream	Creamy Filling (below)
2 cups all-purpose flour*	

Mix thoroughly butter, cream and flour. Cover and chill.

Heat oven to 375°. Roll about ⅓ of dough at a time ⅛ inch thick on floured cloth-covered board (keep remaining dough refrigerated until ready to roll). Cut into 1½-inch circles.

Transfer rounds with spatula to piece of waxed paper that is heavily covered with granulated sugar; turn each round so that both sides are coated with sugar. Place on ungreased baking sheet. Prick rounds with fork about 4 times.

Bake 7 to 9 minutes or just until set but not brown; cool. Put cookies together in pairs with Creamy Filling.

About 5 dozen cookies.

*Do not use self-rising flour in this recipe.

CREAMY FILLING

Cream ¼ cup soft butter or margarine, ¾ cup confectioners' sugar and 1 teaspoon vanilla until smooth and fluffy. Tint with few drops food color. (Add few drops water if necessary for proper spreading consistency.)

FILLED TURNOVERS

Tender little turnovers with flavorful fillings . . . they're great fun to eat.

½ cup shortening	¼ teaspoon soda
1 cup sugar	Orange, Cherry,
2 eggs	Pineapple, Date, Fig,
1 teaspoon vanilla	Raisin, or Prune Filling
2½ cups all-purpose flour*	(pages 231 and 232)
½ teaspoon salt	Milk or light cream

Mix thoroughly shortening, sugar, eggs and vanilla. Blend in flour, salt and soda. Cover; chill 1 hour. Prepare filling.

*If using self-rising flour, omit salt and soda. If using quick-mixing flour, mix 1 tablespoon milk into shortening mixture.

Heat oven to 400°. Roll dough $\frac{1}{16}$ inch thick on lightly floured cloth-covered board. Cut into 3-inch circles or squares. Spoon 1 teaspoon filling on half of each circle. Fold dough over filling; press edges together.

Place 1 inch apart on ungreased baking sheet. Brush with milk; sprinkle with sugar. Bake 8 to 10 minutes or until very light brown. Immediately remove from baking sheet.

About 4½ dozen cookies.

ORANGE FILLING

1 cup sugar	2 tablespoons grated orange peel
¼ cup cornstarch	
½ teaspoon salt	2 tablespoons butter or margarine
1½ cups orange juice	

Mix sugar, cornstarch and salt in medium saucepan. Gradually stir orange juice into the sugar mixture. Cook over medium heat, stirring constantly, until mixture thickens and boils. Boil and stir 2 minutes. Stir in orange peel and butter. Cool thoroughly.

CHERRY FILLING

¾ cup sugar	18 maraschino cherries, chopped
3 tablespoons cornstarch	
¾ cup orange juice	1½ tablespoons butter or margarine
½ cup maraschino cherry syrup	

Mix sugar and cornstarch in saucepan. Gradually stir in orange juice. Stir in cherry syrup, cherries and butter. Cook, stirring constantly, until mixture thickens and boils. Boil and stir 1 minute. Cool thoroughly.

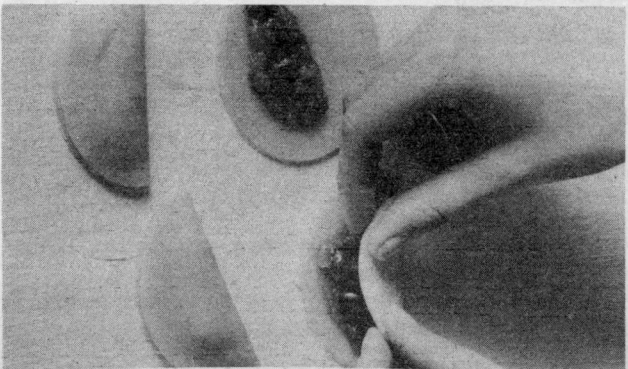

PINNEAPPLE FILLING

⅔ cup sugar	2 tablespoons lemon juice
3 tablespoons flour	1 tablespoon butter or
1 can (13½ ounces) crushed	margarine
pinneapple, well drained	Dash nutmeg
(reserve ½ cup syrup)	

Mix sugar and flour in saucepan. Stir in crushed pineapple, reserved pineapple syrup, the lemon juice, butter and nutmeg. Cook, stirring constantly, until mixture thickens, about 5 minutes. Cool thoroughly.

DATE, FIG, RAISIN OR PRUNE FILLING

2 cups figs, raisins or pitted	¾ cup sugar
dates, finely chopped, or	¾ cup water
2 cups mashed cooked	½ cup chopped nuts, if
prunes	desired

Combine all ingredients in saucepan. Cook, stirring constantly, until mixture thickens. Cool thoroughly.

Pressed Cookies

These tender, crisp cookies come in a wide assortment of sizes and shapes. And they are so professional-looking that your friends won't believe you made them yourself.

Follow the directions that come with your cookie press, but keep these tips in mind:

About the Dough

■ Use shortening, butter or margarine at room temperature. (The consistency affects the action of the other ingredients.) Cream the shortening-sugar mixture until it's light and fluffy. But don't overcream!

■ Test the dough for consistency before adding all the flour. To do this, put a small amount in the cookie press and squeeze out. The dough should be soft and pliable but not crumbly.

■ Chill dough only when specified in the recipe; otherwise, use at room temperature.

■ If dough seems too stiff, add the yolk of 1 egg. If dough it too soft, add 1 to 2 tablespoons flour.

About Pressing

■ Be sure your baking sheet is cool. Hold press so that it rests on sheet, unless using the star or the bar plate.

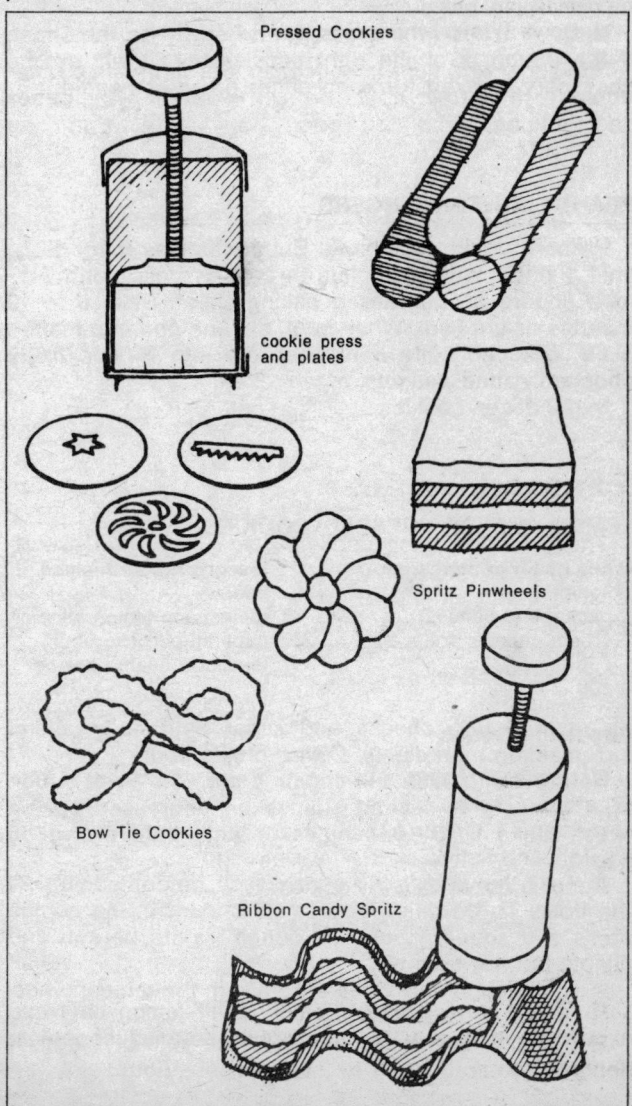

Pressed Cookies

cookie press and plates

Spritz Pinwheels

Bow Tie Cookies

Ribbon Candy Spritz

■ Do not raise press from the cookie sheet before enough dough has been turned out to form the cookie *on* the sheet. For some cookies, it may be necessary to wait a moment to allow the dough to adhere to sheet before lifting press.

■ Do not force the press down heavily on the sheet. If the dough is of the right consistency, it will not be necessary to exert force on either press or handle.

PEANUT BUTTER FINGERS

Prepare dough for Peanut Butter Cookies (page 222); chill 1 hour. With star plate in cookie press, form 2½-inch fingers on ungreased baking sheet. Bake 8 to 10 minutes or until set. When cool, dip one end into melted plain milk chocolate bars, then dip into ¾ cup finely chopped salted peanuts.

8 to 9 dozen cookies.

LEMON-CHEESE PRESSED COOKIES

1 cup butter or margarine, softened	1 teaspoon grated lemon peel
1 package (3 ounces) cream cheese, softened	1 tablespoon lemon juice
1 cup sugar	2½ cups all-purpose flour*
1 egg	1 teaspoon baking powder

Cream butter, cheese and sugar until fluffy. Blend in remaining ingredients. Cover; chill 1 hour.

Heat oven to 375°. Fill cookie press with ¼ of dough at a time; form desired shapes on ungreased baking sheet. Bake 8 to 10 minutes or until light brown on edges.

About 5 dozen 2-inch cookies.

*If using self-rising flour, omit baking powder.

VARIATION

■ *Chocolate Pressed Cookies:* Omit lemon peel and juice; stir in 2 ounces melted unsweetened chocolate (cool).

ORANGE CRISPS

½ cup shortening	1 tablespoon orange juice
½ cup butter or margarine, softened	1 egg
½ cup granulated sugar	2½ cups all-purpose flour*
½ cup brown sugar (packed)	¼ teaspoon soda
1 to 2 teaspoons grated orange peel	¼ teaspoon salt

Heat oven to 375°. Cream shortening, butter and sugars. Blend in remaining ingredients. Fill cookie press with ¼ of dough at a time; form desired shapes on ungreased baking sheet. Bake 10 to 12 minutes or until light brown on edges.

6 dozen 2-inch cookies.

*If using self-rising flour, omit soda and salt.

VARIATION

■ *Lemon Crisps:* Substitute 1 to 2 teaspoons grated lemon peel and 1 tablespoon lemon juice for the orange peel and juice.

SPRITZ

1 cup butter or margarine, softened	½ teaspoon salt
½ cup sugar	1 egg
2¼ cups all-purpose flour*	1 teaspoon almond extract or vanilla

Heat oven to 400°. Cream butter and sugar. Blend in remaining ingredients. Fill cookie press with ¼ of dough at a time; form desired shapes on ungreased baking sheet. Bake 6 to 9 minutes or until set but not brown.

About 5 dozen cookies.

*Do not use self-rising flour in this recipe.

VARIATIONS

■ *Bow Tie Cookies:* Blend 2 ounces melted unsweetened chocolate (cool) into butter-sugar mixture. With star plate in cookie press, form 2½-inch bow ties on ungreased baking sheet. Place cinnamon candy in center. Bake 9 to 10 minutes. About 3 dozen cookies.

■ *Chocolate Spritz:* Blend 2 ounces melted unsweetened chocolate (cool) into butter-sugar mixture.

■ *Christmas Decorated Spritz:* Before baking, top cookies with currants, raisins, candies, nuts, slices of candied fruits or candied fruit peels arranged in colorful and attractive patterns. Or after baking, decorate with colored sugars, nonpareils, red cinnamon candies and finely chopped nuts. Use a drop of corn syrup or egg white to hold decorations on baked cookies.

■ *Ribbon Candy Spritz:* Divide dough in half; tint each half a different color. Divide each color in half; pat each into rectangle, about 10x2½ inches. Stack rectangles, alternating colors; cut in half. Form ribbon candy molds by making strips, 3 inches wide, with 4 thicknesses of aluminum foil. Form molds by folding strips up over middle finger and pinching at sides. Place on baking sheet. With bar plate in cookie press, press half the dough at a time onto aluminum foil. Bake 6 to 9 minutes. Cool on foil.

■ *Spritz Pinwheels:* Divide dough into 3 equal parts. Color one part red and another part yellow; color the third part orange by mixing few drops each red and yellow food color. Shape ⅓ of each color into long roll; place side by side in cookie press. With pinwheel plate in cookie press, form cookies on ungreased baking sheet. Repeat with remaining dough. Bake 8 to 10 minutes. About 4½ dozen cookies.

Christmas Cookies

Christmas wouldn't be Christmas without the excitement that comes from making the traditional cookies. Everyone in the family finds an excuse to be in the kitchen. And, for once, no one has to urge the youngsters to lend a hand. Even the 4-year-old can help by pushing nuts and candied fruits into the dough or sprinkling colored sugars on top.

These cookies also make especially attractive Christmas gifts. Arranged on a pretty tray or on a plate and wrapped for hand-delivery, or boxed carefully and wrapped in gay Christmas paper, they are sure to get a warm welcome. Be sure to look through the other sections in this chapter for more cookies of holiday cheer.

BERLINERKRANZER

Little wreath cookies made every holiday season in Norway.

¾ cup butter or margarine,
  softened
¾ cup shortening
1 cup sugar
2 teaspoons grated orange
  peel

2 eggs
4 cups all-purpose flour*
1 egg white
2 tablespoons sugar
Red candied cherries
Green candied citron

Heat oven to 400°. Mix thoroughly butter, shortening, 1 cup sugar, the orange peel and eggs. Blend in flour.

Shape dough by rounded teaspoonfuls into ropes, each 6 inches long and ¼ inch in diameter. Form each rope into circle, bringing one end over and through in a single knot. Let ½ inch extend at each end. Place on ungreased baking sheet.

Beat egg white until foamy; add 2 tablespoons sugar, 1 tablespoon at a time, while beating. Brush tops of cookies with sweetened egg white. Press bits of red candied cherries on center of knot for holly berries; add little leaves of green citron. Bake 10 to 12 minutes or until set but not brown. Immediately remove from baking sheet.

About 6 dozen cookies.

*Self-rising flour can be used in this recipe.

ROSETTES

Fried light sweets—closely akin to timbales.

1 egg
½ cup all-purpose flour*
1 tablespoon sugar
½ teaspoon salt

½ cup milk
1 tablespoon salad oil
Confectioners' sugar

Heat fat or oil (3 to 4 inches) to 400° in small saucepan. Beat egg slightly; add remaining ingredients and beat until smooth. Strain batter.

Heat rosette iron in hot fat. Tap excess fat from iron. Dip iron into batter until ⅔ covered. Fry until golden brown. Remove from fat, inverting iron to drain fat. Gently push rosette from iron and invert on paper towels. Stir batter each time before dipping the heated iron. Sprinkle cookies with confectioners' sugar.

18 cookies.

*If using self-rising flour, omit salt.

Dip the hot rosette iron into batter until ⅔ covered.

After removing rosette from fat, invert iron to drain.

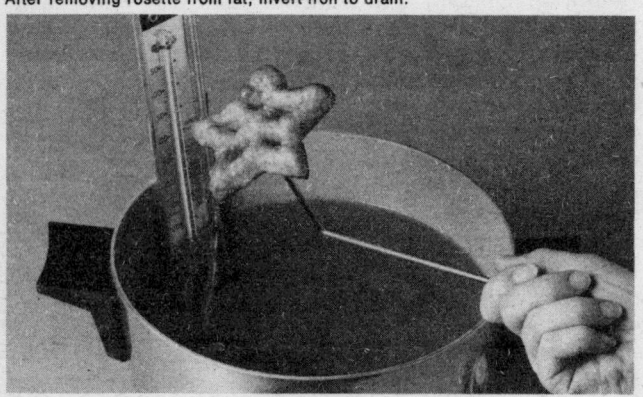

STAINED-GLASS COOKIES

Prepare dough for Deluxe Sugar Cookies (page 229); divide in half. Color portions of 1 half with about 5 food colors. Heat oven to 375°. Roll plain half of dough ⅛ inch thick on lightly floured cloth-covered board. Cut with decorative cookie cutters. Place on lightly greased baking sheet.

Roll colored doughs; cut out different shapes to match and fit on top of each plain cookie shape. If you wish to hang the cookies on your Christmas tree, place a small piece of a paper drinking straw through the top of each cookie before baking. Bake 7 to 8 minutes or until golden brown on edge.

About 2 dozen cookies.

SPRINGERLE

2 eggs
1 cup sugar

2¼ cups all-purpose flour*
Anise seed

Beat eggs and sugar about 5 minutes or until thick and lemon colored. Mix in flour. If dough is dry, stir 3 tablespoons milk, 1 tablespoon at a time, into mixture. Cover; chill at least 2 hours.

Roll dough ⅛ inch thick on lightly floured cloth-covered board. Press well-floured springerle form over dough to emboss designs. Cut out cookies and place on lightly floured board sprinkled with anise seed; let dry at least 10 hours.

Heat oven to 325°. Place cookies ½ inch apart on ungreased baking sheet. Bake 12 to 15 minutes or until light brown. Immediately remove from baking sheet.

About 8 dozen cookies.

*Do not use self-rising flour in this recipe.

CANDY CANE COOKIES

½ cup butter or margarine, softened
½ cup shortening
1 cup confectioners' sugar
1 egg
1½ teaspoons almond extract
1 teaspoon vanilla

2½ cups all-purpose flour*
1 teaspoon salt
½ teaspoon red food color
½ cup crushed peppermint candy
½ cup granulated sugar

Heat oven to 375°. Mix thoroughly butter, shortening, confectioners' sugar, egg and flavorings. Blend in flour

*If using self-rising flour, omit salt. If using quick-mixing flour, stir 2 tablespoons milk into butter mixture.

Press ropes together lightly; twist to form candy canes.

and salt. Divide dough in half; blend food color into one half.

Shape 1 teaspoon dough from each half into 4-inch rope. For smooth, even ropes, roll them back and forth on lightly floured board. Place ropes side by side; press together lightly and twist. Complete cookies one at a time. Place on ungreased baking sheet. Curve top down to form handle of cane.

Bake about 9 minutes or until set and very light brown. Mix candy and granulated sugar. Immediately sprinkle cookies with candy mixture; remove from baking sheet.

About 4 dozen cookies.

SANDBAKELSER

¾ cup butter or margarine, softened
¾ cup sugar
1 egg white
1¾ cups all-purpose flour*

⅓ cup blanched almonds, finely chopped
4 unblanched almonds, finely chopped

Mix thoroughly butter, sugar and egg white. Stir in remaining ingredients. Cover; chill 2 hours.

Heat oven to 350°. Press dough about ⅛ inch thick on bottom and side of each ungreased *sandbakelse* mold. Place on baking sheet. Bake 12 to 15 minutes. Cool. Tap molds to loosen cookies.

About 3 dozen cookies.

*Self-rising flour can be used in this recipe. If using quick-mixing flour, stir in 2 tablespoons milk.

PEPPERNUTS

½ cup shortening
¾ cup brown sugar (packed)
1 egg
½ cup molasses
3 drops anise oil
1 tablespoon hot water

3⅓ cups all-purpose flour*
½ teaspoon soda
½ teaspoon cinnamon
½ teaspoon cloves
¼ teaspoon salt
⅛ teaspoon white pepper

Heat oven to 350°. Mix thoroughly shortening, sugar,

*If using self-rising flour, omit soda and salt. If using quick-mixing flour, stir in 2 tablespoons milk.

egg, molasses, anise oil and water. Blend in remaining ingredients. Knead dough until of right consistency for molding.

Shape dough by level teaspoonfuls into balls. Place 1 inch apart on ungreased baking sheet. Bake about 12 minutes or until golden brown on bottom. Store in airtight container. For softer cookies, store with a slice of apple.

About 8 dozen cookies.

GINGERBREAD BOYS

½ cup shortening
½ cup sugar
½ cup dark molasses
¼ cup water
2½ cups all-purpose flour*
¾ teaspoon salt
½ teaspoon soda
¾ teaspoon ginger
¼ teaspoon nutmeg

⅛ teaspoon allspice
Raisins
Candied cherries or red gumdrops
Citron
String licorice
Decorators' Icing (page 189)

Cream shortening and sugar. Blend in molasses, water, flour, salt, soda, ginger, nutmeg and allspice. Cover; chill 2 to 3 hours.

Heat oven to 375°. Roll dough ¼ inch thick on lightly floured cloth-covered board. Cut with gingerbread boy cutter; place on ungreased baking sheet.

Press raisins into dough for eyes, nose and buttons. Use bits of candied cherries and strips of citron and string licorice for other trims. Bake 10 to 12 minutes. Immediately remove from baking sheet. Cool. Trim with Decorators' Icing.

About fifteen 4-inch cookies.

Note: For crisper cookies, roll dough ⅛ inch thick. Bake 8 minutes. About 2 dozen cookies.

*If using self-rising flour, omit salt and soda. If using quick-mixing flour, add 3 tablespoons milk.

LEBKUCHEN

Traditional honey cakes from the Black Forest.

½ cup honey
½ cup molasses
¾ cup brown sugar (packed)
1 egg
1 teaspoon grated lemon peel
1 tablespoon lemon juice

2¾ cups all-purpose flour*
1 teaspoon each cinnamon, cloves, allspice and nutmeg
½ teaspoon soda
⅓ cup cut-up citron
⅓ cup chopped nuts
Glazing Icing (below)

Mix honey and molasses in large saucepan; heat to boiling. Cool thoroughly. Stir in sugar, egg, lemon peel and juice. Mix in remaining ingredients except icing. Cover; chill at least 8 hours.

Heat oven to 400°. Roll small amount of dough at a time ¼ inch thick on lightly floured cloth-covered board. (Keep remaining dough refrigerated.)

Cut dough into rectangles, each 2½ x 1½ inches. Place 1 inch apart on greased baking sheet. Bake 10 to 12 minutes or until no imprint remains when touched lightly with finger. Brush icing lightly over cookies. Immediately remove from baking sheet; cool. Store in airtight container with slice of apple or orange.

About 5 dozen cookies.

*Do not use self-rising flour in this recipe.

GLAZING ICING

Mix 1 cup sugar and ½ cup water in small saucepan. Cook over medium heat to 230° on candy thermometer (or just until small amount of mixture spins a 2-inch thread). Remove from heat; stir in ¼ cup confectioners' sugar. If icing becomes sugary, reheat slightly, adding a little water.

VARIATION

■ *Nürnberger:* Omit molasses; increase honey to 1 cup and decrease cloves to ¼ teaspoon, allspice and nutmeg to ½ teaspoon. Cut dough into 2-inch circles. Round up each circle a bit toward center; place blanched almond halves around edge. Place small round of citron or candied cherry in center of each; bake as directed.

CHRISTMAS TREE COOKIES

Prepare dough for Vanilla Refrigerator Cookies (page 216) except—omit nuts; divide dough in half and chill 30 minutes.

Mold dough into 3 rolls, each 14 inches long, using 1 half for the largest roll, ⅔ of other half for medium roll and the remainder for smallest roll. Roll each in green sugar until evenly coated. Chill about 4 hours or until firm enough to slice.

Heat oven to 400°. Cut rolls into ¼-inch slices. Place 1 inch apart on ungreased baking sheet. Bake 8 to 10 minutes or until light brown on edges. Cool. Stack 3 rounds (large, medium, small) together with Icing (below) to form tree. Top with red cinnamon candy dipped in Icing.

About 4½ dozen cookies.

ICING

Mix 1 cup confectioners' sugar, ½ teaspoon vanilla and enough light cream to make spreading consistency.

KRUMKAKE

A tender, lacy, crispy cookie from Sweden.

4 eggs	1 teaspoon vanilla
1 cup sugar	¾ cup all-purpose flour*
½ cup butter or margarine, melted	2 teaspoons cornstarch
5 tablespoons whipping cream	

Heat ungreased krumkake iron over small electric or gas 6-inch surface unit on medium-high heat. Beat all ingredients until smooth.

Test iron with few drops of water; if they "skitter" around, iron is correct temperature. Drop ½ tablespoon batter on iron; close gently. Bake about 15 seconds on each side or until light golden brown. Keep iron over heat at all times. Remove with knife; immediately roll around wooden roller. (An old-fashioned clothespin works well.)

About 6 dozen cookies.

*Self-rising flour can be used in this recipe.

FATTIGMANDS BAKKELSER

10 egg yolks
⅓ cup confectioners' sugar
½ cup whipping cream
1 tablespoon cognac or other brandy
1 teaspoon ground cardamom
½ teaspoon grated lemon peel
2 to 2½ cups all-purpose flour*

In large mixer bowl, beat egg yolks and sugar about 10 minutes or until very thick and lemon colored. Stir in cream, cognac, cardamom and lemon peel. Mix in enough flour to make a stiff dough. Cover; chill at least 3 hours.

Heat fat or oil (2 inches) to 375°. Divide dough in half. Roll each half very thin, ⅛ to 1/16 inch thick, on well-floured board. Cut dough into 4x2-inch diamonds. Make 1-inch horizontal slit in center of each; draw a long point of diamond through slit and curl back in opposite direction.

Fry in hot fat about 15 seconds on each side or until light brown. Drain. Store in airtight container. Before serving, sprinkle with confectioners' sugar.

About 4 dozen cookies.

*Self-rising flour can be used in this recipe.

Draw one of long points of diamond through slit; curl back.

Sprinkle Fattigmands Bakkelser with confectioners' sugar.

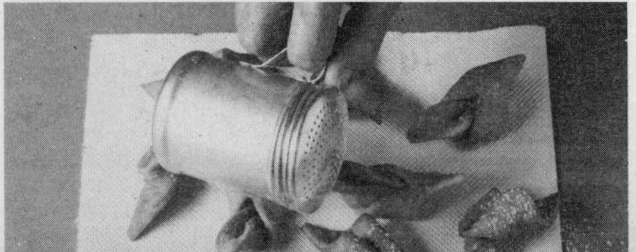

MARZIPAN COOKIES

Adapted from the attractive, unique marzipan candy.

1 cup butter or margarine, softened
½ cup sugar
2½ cups all-purpose flour*

½ to 1 teaspoon almond extract
Food color

Cream butter and sugar. Stir in flour and almond extract until mixture looks like meal. Divide into 3 equal parts. Color and make some of the shapes as directed below. Place cookies on ungreased baking sheet; chill ½ hour. Heat oven to 300°. Bake 30 minutes or until set but not brown.

About 4 dozen cookies.

*Do not use self-rising flour in this recipe.

RED DOUGH

Mix red food color into 1 part of dough.

Apples: Shape dough into small balls. Insert small piece of stick cinnamon in top of each for stem end and whole clove in bottom for blossom end. For Red Blush, dilute red food color with water and brush over balls. (Apples can also be made with Green Dough, below.)

Strawberries: Shape dough into small balls; form each into heart shape. For texture, prick with blunt end of wooden pick. Roll each in red sugar. Place piece of green-colored wooden pick or green dough into top of each for stem.

YELLOW DOUGH

Mix yellow food color into 1 part of dough.

Bananas: Shape dough into 3-inch rolls, tapering ends. Flatten tops slightly to make planes of banana and curve each slightly. Paint on characteristic markings with mixture of red, yellow and blue food color diluted with water.

Pears: Shape dough into small balls, then into cone shapes, rounding narrow end of each. Insert piece of stick cinnamon in narrow end for stem. Brush Red Blush (see Apples, above) on cheeks.

ORANGE DOUGH

Mix red and yellow food color into 1 part of dough.

Apricots: Shape dough into small balls. Make crease down 1 side of each with wooden pick. Insert whole clove in each for stem end. Brush with Red Blush (see Apples, page 245).

Oranges: Shape dough into small balls. Insert whole clove in each for blossom end. For peel texture, prick balls with end of wooden pick.

GREEN DOUGH

Mix green food color into 1 part of dough.

Green Peas: Form dough into 1½- to 2-inch flat rounds. Divide teaspoonfuls of dough into 3 or 4 parts; shape each into small ball. Place 3 or 4 balls in a row on each round; bring dough up and around small balls, pinching edges together.

MORAVIAN GINGER COOKIES

⅓ cup molasses	¼ teaspoon each cinnamon,
¼ cup shortening	ginger and cloves
2 tablespoons brown sugar	Dash each nutmeg and
1¼ cups all-purpose flour*	allspice
½ teaspoon salt	Easy Creamy Icing
¼ teaspoon soda	(page 247)
¼ teaspoon baking powder	

Mix thoroughly molasses, shortening and sugar. Blend in remaining ingredients except icing. Cover; chill at least 4 hours.

Heat oven to 375°. Roll dough ⅛ inch thick or, if desired, paper-thin on lightly floured cloth-covered board. Cut into desired shapes. Place ½ inch apart on ungreased baking sheet. Bake 8 minutes or until set.

Immediately remove from baking sheet; cool. Frost with Easy Creamy Icing. About 3 dozen 2-inch cookies (about 5 dozen if rolled paper-thin).

*If using self-rising flour, omit salt, soda and baking powder.

EASY CREAMY ICING

Mix 1 cup confectioners' sugar, ¼ teaspoon salt, ½ teaspoon vanilla and about 1½ tablespoons light cream until smooth and of spreading consistency. Tint with food color if desired.

PENNSYLVANIA DUTCH LIGHT GINGER COOKIES

The Pennsylvania Dutch cut these traditional cookies into many different shapes—stars, angels, hearts, trees and flowers.

1 cup butter or margarine, softened	1½ to 2 teaspoons ginger
1 cup confectioners' sugar	¾ teaspoon soda
1 tablespoon vinegar	¼ teaspoon salt
	2¼ cups all-purpose flour*

Heat oven to 400°. Mix thoroughly butter, sugar and vinegar. Blend in remaining ingredients. (If dough is too dry to handle easily, work in milk or cream, 1 teaspoon at a time.)

Roll dough ⅛ inch thick on lightly floured cloth-covered board. Cut into desired shapes. Place on ungreased baking sheet. Bake 6 to 8 minutes or until light brown. Cool slightly; carefully remove from baking sheet. If desired, decorate with Icing (below).

About 4 dozen 3-inch cookies.

Do not use self-rising flour in this recipe.

ICING

Mix 2 cups confectioners' sugar, ½ teaspoon vanilla and about 2 tablespoons light cream until smooth and of desired consistency. Icing can be tinted with food color and piped on with a decorators' tube.

Candies

Sweets to the sweet—sweets for the sweet—
and sweets to sweeten up the gloomiest day.
For there's nothing like a good old-fashioned
candy-making session to bring joy into your
kitchen and your heart. And there isn't a
grandmother or grandfather, an aunt or uncle,
who wouldn't treasure a candy gift the children
made themselves. Here you'll find practical
recipes, a few old favorites, a few new friends.
And a lot of ideas you can turn to good
advantage when you're looking for things to
send to children at school or to friends
far away.

Tips for Candy Makers

It isn't hard to make candy. It just takes a little care—a little sticking to the rules. And here are a few that will ensure your success:

■ Use the recommended size and type of cooking pan. A larger or smaller pan than the recipe specifies can affect the cooking time and the quality of the candy.

■ Never double a recipe. Increasing the amount of liquid and sugar is bound to increase the cooking time. If a larger amount of candy is desired, simply make another batch or two.

■ Use a good, dependable candy thermometer; it is inexpensive and a good investment for anyone who enjoys making candy. To get an accurate reading, be sure the thermometer is standing upright in the cooking mixture and that the bulb is not resting on the bottom of the pan. Read the thermometer at eye level and watch the temperature closely. Once it has reached 200°, it soars very quickly.

■ Test candy carefully. If you do not have a thermometer, use the cold-water test. Remove candy from heat and drop a small amount of the mixture from a clean spoon into a cupful of very cold water. (See chart below.) Be careful—small candy-makers have been known to eat so much in testing that there's not much left for the rest of the family.

■ Both humidity and altitude affect candy. If it is rainy, cook candy to a degree or so higher than the recipe states. Consult an altitude table to determine the boiling point in your area. You may want to test the temperature of boiling water before you start to cook the candy. If the water boils at 210° instead of the norm of 212°, then you should use 2 degrees less when you cook your candy.

HOW TO TEST CANDY

Stages	Cold Water Tests	Temperatures
Soft Ball	Can be picked up but flattens.	234° to 240° F.
Firm Ball	Holds its shape until pressed.	242° to 248° F.
Hard Ball	Holds its shape but is pliable.	250° to 268° F.
Soft Crack	Candy separates into hard but not brittle threads.	270° to 290° F.
Hard Crack	Candy separates into hard and brittle threads.	300° to 310° F.

All-time Favorites

Remember those rainy days when mother supervised the fudge making or taffy pulling? Or holiday time, when everyone pitched in to fill the bonbon dishes? Well, as you see, we think these warm traditions are still going on.

OLD-FASHIONED CHOCOLATE FUDGE

2 cups sugar
⅔ cup milk
2 ounces unsweetened chocolate or ⅓ cup cocoa
2 tablespoons corn syrup
¼ teaspoon salt

2 tablespoons butter or margarine
1 teaspoon vanilla
½ cup coarsely chopped nuts, if desired

Butter loaf pan, 9x5x3 inches. Combine sugar, milk, chocolate, corn syrup and salt in 2-quart saucepan. Cook over medium heat, stirring constantly, until chocolate is melted and sugar is dissolved. Cook, stirring occasionally, to 234° on candy thermometer (or until small amount of mixture dropped into very cold water forms a soft ball which flattens when removed from water).

Remove from heat; add butter. Cool mixture to 120° without stirring. (Bottom of pan will be lukewarm.) Add vanilla; beat vigorously and continuously 5 to 10 minutes with wooden spoon, until candy is thick and no longer glossy. (Mixture will hold its shape when dropped from spoon.) Quickly stir in nuts. Spread mixture evenly in buttered pan. Cool until firm. Cut into squares.

1 pound (thirty-two 1-inch squares).

VARIATIONS

■ *Penuche:* Substitute 1 cup brown sugar (packed) for 1 cup of the granulated sugar and omit chocolate.

■ *Pecan Roll:* Do not butter pan; substitute 1 cup brown sugar (packed) for 1 cup of the granulated sugar and omit chocolate. Shape candy into 12-inch roll and roll in ½ cup finely chopped pecans. Wrap; chill until firm. Cut roll into ¼-inch slices. 18 candies.

ROCKY ROAD CANDY

A melt-in-your-mouth combination of chocolate, peanuts and marshmallows.

1 package (6 ounces) semisweet chocolate pieces
1 square (1 ounce) unsweetened chocolate
1 tablespoon butter
2 eggs
1¼ cups confectioners' sugar
½ teaspoon salt
1 teaspoon vanilla
2 cups salted peanuts
2 cups miniature marshmallows

Melt chocolate pieces, chocolate and butter in large saucepan over low heat, stirring until smooth. Remove from heat.

Beat eggs until foamy. Mix in sugar, salt and vanilla. Blend in chocolate mixture. Stir in peanuts and marshmallows. Drop by teaspoonfuls onto waxed paper. Chill 2 hours or until firm. Store in refrigerator; remove just before serving.

About 4 dozen candies.

SOUTHERN PRALINES

Sugary wafers with the punch of pecans. These cookie-size sweets make a good lunchbox treat.

1 cup granulated sugar
1 cup brown sugar (packed)
½ cup light cream (20%)
¼ teaspoon salt

2 tablespoons butter or margarine
1 cup pecan halves

Lightly butter a sheet of aluminum foil. Combine sugars, cream and salt in large saucepan. Cook over medium heat, stirring constantly, to 228° on candy thermometer (or until mixture spins a thread about 2 inches long when dropped from a spoon).

Stir in butter and pecans. Continue cooking, stirring constantly, to 236° (or until small amount of mixture dropped into very cold water forms a soft ball which flattens when removed from water). Remove from heat; cool 5 minutes.

Beat mixture with wooden spoon until slightly thickened and candy just coats nuts but does not lose its gloss. Drop candy by large spoonfuls onto buttered foil.

About 1½ dozen candies.

PEANUT BRITTLE

The key to "brittleness" is "thinness." To ensure this quality, be sure to spread the candy mixture carefully and thinly.

1½ teaspoons soda
1 teaspoon water
1 teaspoon vanilla
1½ cups sugar
1 cup water

1 cup light corn syrup
3 tablespoons butter or margarine
1 pound shelled unroasted peanuts

Butter 2 baking sheets, each 15½x12 inches; keep warm. Combine soda, 1 teaspoon water and the vanilla; set aside.

Combine sugar, 1 cup water and the corn syrup in large saucepan. Cook over medium heat, stirring occasionally, to 240° on candy thermometer (or until small amount of syrup dropped into very cold water forms a soft ball which flattens when removed from water).

Stir in butter and peanuts. Cook, stirring constantly,

to 300° (or until small amount of mixture dropped into very cold water separates into threads which are hard and brittle). Watch carefully so mixture does not burn.

Immediately remove from heat; stir in soda mixture thoroughly. Pour half the candy mixture onto each warm baking sheet and quickly spread evenly about ¼ inch thick. Cool; break candy into pieces.

2 pounds.

SALT WATER TAFFY

Through legend comes the story of a candymaker from the shores of New Jersey. One day, when his supply of fresh water ran out, he tried a batch of taffy with the nearby salt water. Success!

1 cup sugar	2 tablespoons butter or
¾ cup light corn syrup	margarine
⅔ cup water	1 teaspoon salt
1 tablespoon cornstarch	2 teaspoons vanilla

Butter square pan, 8x8x2 inches. In 2-quart saucepan, combine sugar, corn syrup, water, cornstarch, butter and salt. Cook over medium heat, stirring constantly, to 256° on candy thermometer (or until small amount of mixture dropped into very cold water forms a hard ball). Remove from heat; stir in vanilla. Pour into pan.

When just cool enough to handle, pull taffy until satiny, light in color and stiff. If taffy becomes sticky, butter hands lightly. Pull into long strips, ½ inch wide. With scissors, cut strips into 1-inch pieces. Wrap pieces individually in plastic wrap or waxed paper. (Candy must be wrapped to hold its shape.)

About 1 pound.

Spread Peanut Brittle thinly on a warm baking sheet.

FONDANT-STUFFED DATES

4½ cups confectioners' sugar
⅔ cup sweetened condensed milk (not evaporated)
1 teaspoon vanilla
1 teaspoon almond extract
4 dozen pitted dates

Blend sugar, milk and flavorings. Knead fondant until smooth and creamy. Cover with damp cloth; refrigerate 24 hours.

Fill each date with fondant; roll in granulated or confectioners' sugar.

4 dozen candies.

VARIATION

■ *Easy Bonbons:* Blend in few drops food color to tint fondant. Refrigerate and shape into balls or patties.

DIVINITY

2⅔ cups sugar
⅔ cup light corn syrup
½ cup water*
2 egg whites
1 teaspoon vanilla
⅔ cup broken nuts

Stir sugar, corn syrup and water over low heat until sugar is dissolved. Cook, without stirring, to 260° on candy thermometer (or until small amount of mixture dropped into very cold water forms a hard ball).

In mixer bowl, beat egg whites until stiff peaks form. Continue beating while pouring hot syrup in a thin stream into egg whites. Add vanilla; beat until mixture holds its shape and becomes slightly dull. (Mixture may become too stiff for mixer.) Fold in nuts. Drop mixture from tip of buttered spoon onto waxed paper.

About 4 dozen candies.

Use 1 tablespoon less water on humid days.

BUTTER CRUNCH

1 cup butter
1 cup sugar
2 tablespoons water
1 tablespoon light corn syrup
¾ cup finely chopped nuts
1 package (6 ounces) semisweet chocolate pieces

Butter baking sheet. Melt butter in 2-quart saucepan over low heat. Add sugar; heat to boiling, stirring constantly. Stir in water and corn syrup. Cook over medium heat, stirring constantly, to 290° on candy thermometer (or until small amount of mixture dropped into very cold water separates into threads which are hard but not brittle).

Remove from heat; stir in nuts. Pour candy mixture onto baking sheet and spread about ¼ inch thick. As crunch cools, loosen from baking sheet 2 or 3 times with spatula.

Melt chocolate pieces over hot water. Spread half the chocolate over cooled crunch. (Keep remaining chocolate warm over hot water.) When firm, turn crunch and spread with chocolate. When firm, break into pieces. Store in tightly covered container in cool place.

About 1 pound.

TOFFEE

Crunchy toffee candy with a chocolate topping. Make it your own specialty.

1 cup pecans, chopped
¾ cup brown sugar (packed)
½ cup butter or margarine

½ package (6-ounce size) semisweet chocolate pieces (½ cup)

Butter square pan, 9x9x2 inches. Spread pecans in pan. Heat sugar and butter to boiling, stirring constantly. Boil over medium heat, stirring constantly, 7 minutes. Immediately spread mixture evenly over nuts in pan.

Sprinkle chocolate pieces over hot mixture; place baking sheet over pan so contained heat will melt chocolate. Spread melted chocolate over candy. While hot, cut into 1½-inch squares. Chill until firm.

3 dozen candies.

LOLLIPOPS

18 lollipop sticks
¼ cup butter or margarine
½ cup light corn syrup

¾ cup sugar
Few drops food color

Lightly butter baking sheet, 15½x12 inches. Arrange lollipop sticks on baking sheet. Combine butter, corn syrup and sugar in heavy 1-quart saucepan. Heat to boiling over medium-high heat, stirring occasionally. Reduce heat to medium. Continue cooking, stirring frequently, to 270° on candy thermometer (or until a few drops of syrup dropped into very cold water separate into threads which are hard but not brittle). Stir in food color.

Drop mixture by tablespoonfuls over end of each lollipop stick. If desired, while lollipops are hot, press on candy decorations. To decorate when cooled, brush underside of candy decorations with corn syrup and press onto lollipops. Cool lollipops thoroughly before removing from baking sheet.

Eighteen 2-inch lollipops.

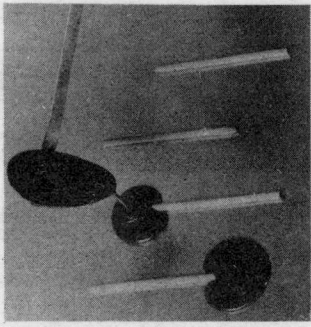

Cook to 270° on candy thermometer.

Pour mixture over end of each stick.

CREAM CARAMELS

½ cup finely chopped nuts
2 cups sugar
¾ cup light corn syrup

½ cup butter
2 cups light cream (20%)

Butter square pan, 8x8x2 inches. Spread nuts in pan. Combine sugar, corn syrup, butter and half the cream in large saucepan. Heat to boiling over medium heat, stirring constantly. Stir in remaining cream.

Cook over medium heat, stirring occasionally, to 245° on candy thermometer (or until small amount of mixture dropped into very cold water forms a firm ball).

Immediately spread mixture evenly over nuts in a pan. Cool. Cut into 1-inch squares.

About 5 dozen candies.

CARAMEL POPCORN BALLS

8 cups popper corn (about ½ cup unpopped)
¾ cup granulated sugar
¾ cup brown sugar (packed)
½ cup light corn syrup

½ cup water
1 teaspoon white vinegar
¼ teaspoon salt
¾ cup butter or margarine

Measure popped corn into large bowl. Combine sugars, corn syrup, water, vinegar and salt in 2-quart saucepan. Heat to boiling over medium-high heat, stirring frequently. Cook, stirring constantly, to 260° on candy thermometer (or until small amount of mixture dropped into very cold water forms a hard ball).

Reduce heat to low; stir in butter until melted. Pour syrup in thin stream over corn in bowl, stirring until corn is well coated. Cool slightly.

Butter hands; shape mixture into 3-inch balls and place on waxed paper.

16 balls.

VARIATION

■ *Nutty Caramel Corn:* Butter baking sheet, 15½x12 inches; mix 1 cup pecan halves and ½ cup blanched almonds with popped corn in bowl. Prepare syrup and pour over nuts and popped corn; stir until coated. Spread mixture on baking sheet. Cool; break into pieces. 1¾ pounds.

CARAMEL APPLES

Chocolate-lovers unite! Use chocolate caramel candies in the coating.

Wash 4 or 5 medium apples and dry thoroughly. Remove stem and blossom end of each.

In top of double boiler over hot water, heat 1 package (14 ounces) caramel candies, ½ teaspoon salt and 2 tablespoons water, stirring frequently, until caramels are melted and mixture is smooth.

Keeping sauce over hot water, place each apple in hot caramel sauce; spoon sauce over apple until it is completely coated. Insert wooden skewer in stem end; remove from sauce and place on waxed paper. Chill until caramel coating is firm.

SPICY SUGARED NUTS

1 tablespoon egg white	¼ cup sugar
2 cups pecans or walnuts	1 tablespoon cinnamon

Heat oven to 300°. Place nuts in small bowl; pour egg white over nuts and stir until nuts are coated and sticky.

Mix sugar and cinnamon; sprinkle over nuts, stirring until sugar mixture completely coats nuts. Spread on ungreased baking sheet. Bake 30 minutes.

About 2 cups.

To shape Popcorn Balls easily, butter hands thoroughly.

CANDIED ORANGE PEEL

Good to eat, true. But this sweet does double-duty as a decorative design—on your favorite white-frosted cake, for instance.

With sharp knife, score peel of 2 large oranges into quarters. Remove peel gently with fingers. Heat orange peel and 6 cups of water to boiling. Simmer 30 minutes; drain. Repeat process, cooking peel in another 6 cups water. With spoon, gently scrape off remaining white membrane from peel. Cut peel lengthwise into ¼-inch strips.

Heat 2 cups sugar and 1 cup water to boiling, stirring until sugar is dissolved. Add peel; simmer 45 minutes, stirring frequently. Turn mixture into strainer; drain thoroughly. Roll peel in 1½ cups sugar; spread on waxed paper to dry.

Quick-to-fix Sweets

A perfect variety for your youngsters—and perfect for you, too. All of these sweets are so easy and speedy-to-make that they're done before anyone has time to get bored. So when the Brownies want to make candy— to sell or eat—start them off with these.

You won't need to do any special shopping either; you'll find most of the ingredients are already on your shelves—like breakfast cereals and frosting mixes, marshmallows and nuts, coconut and chocolate chips.

NO-COOK DIVINITY

A perfect divinity—the easy way.

1 package (7.2 ounces) fluffy white frosting mix	½ cup boiling water
⅓ cup light corn syrup	1 package (1 pound) confectioners' sugar
1 teaspoon vanilla	1 cup chopped nuts

Combine frosting mix (dry), corn syrup, vanilla and boiling water in small mixer bowl. Beat on highest speed until stiff peaks form, about 5 minutes. Transfer to large mixer bowl; on low speed or by hand, gradually blend in confectioners' sugar. Stir in nuts.

Drop mixture by teaspoonfuls onto waxed paper. When outside of candy feels firm, turn over and allow to dry at least 12 hours. Store candy in airtight container.

5 to 6 dozen candies.

VARIATIONS

■ *Candied Cherry Delights:* Substitute 1 teaspoon almond extract for the vanilla and 1 cup chopped candied cherries for the nuts. If desired, tint with few drops red food color.

■ *Peppy Mints:* Substitute ½ teaspoon peppermint extract for the vanilla and 1 cup crushed peppermint candy for the nuts. If desired, tint with few drops green food color.

■ *Spanish Crunch:* Substitute dark corn syrup for the light corn syrup and salted shelled Spanish peanuts for the chopped nuts.

OPERA FUDGE

No-fail vanilla fudge—and with frosting mix!

3 tablespoons butter or margarine	1 package (15.4 ounces) creamy white frosting mix
3 tablespoons milk	½ cup chopped nuts

Butter loaf pan, 9x5x3 inches. In top of double boiler, melt butter in milk. Stir in frosting mix (dry) until smooth. Heat over rapidly boiling water 5 minutes, stirring occasionally. Stir in nuts.

Spread mixture evenly in buttered pan. Cool until firm. Cut into squares.

1 pound (thirty-two 1-inch squares).

VARIATION

■ *Cherry Opera Fudge:* Stir in ½ cup candied cherry halves with the nuts.

CRUNCHY MOCHA DROPS

Instant coffee adds the mocha flavor.

3 tablespoons butter or
  margarine
3 tablespoons milk
1 package (15.4 ounces)
  creamy white frosting mix

1 to 2 tablespoons instant
  coffee
1½ cups toasted flaked
  coconut

In top of double boiler, melt butter in milk. Stir in frosting mix (dry) and instant coffee until smooth. Heat over rapidly boiling water 5 minutes, stirring occasionally. Stir in coconut.

Keeping mixture over hot water, drop by teaspoonfuls onto waxed paper. Cool until firm.

4 to 5 dozen candies.

TOASTING COCONUT?

It's a snap! Just spread the flaked coconut in a shallow pan and pop it into a 350° oven for about 15 minutes or until it becomes a golden brown. Be sure to stir the coconut frequently for even browning.

Toasted coconut comes in handy for many candy recipes —and it's a delightful garnish for a simple fruit salad or for your favorite cake. Keep it stored in a tightly covered jar.

CORN PUFFS TOFFEE

In large skillet, heat 1 cup sugar and 1 cup butter to boiling, stirring constantly. Boil over medium heat, stirring constantly, about 10 minutes or until mixture caramelizes (becomes light brown and thickened). Remove from heat; stir in 2½ cups corn puffs cereal until well coated.

Turn onto ungreased baking sheet; spread mixture ¼ inch thick. Cool; break into pieces.

CHEWY-O'S

1 package (about 4 ounces)
  chocolate, butterscotch or
  vanilla pudding and pie
  filling (cooked type)

½ cup light corn syrup
⅓ cup peanut butter
4 cups O-shaped puffed oat
  cereal

Butter square pan, 9x9x2 inches. Blend pudding mix (dry) and corn syrup in large saucepan. Heat to boiling over medium heat, stirring constantly. Boil and stir 1 minute. Remove from heat; blend in peanut butter. Add cereal; stir until thoroughly coated.

Turn into pan; spread mixture evenly with buttered back of spoon. Cool about 30 minutes or until firm. Cut into 1¼ x ¾-inch pieces.

About 6 dozen candies.

TING-A-LINGS

In top of double boiler, melt 2 packages (6 ounces each) semisweet chocolate pieces or 12 ounces milk chocolate over hot water. Gradually add to 4 cups whole wheat flakes cereal, stirring gently until flakes are well coated. Drop mixture by tablespoonfuls onto waxed paper. Chill about 2 hours or until firm.

3½ dozen candies.

VARIATION

■ *Almond Ting-A-Lings:* Fold in ⅓ cup chopped toasted almonds with the cereal.

OVEN CARAMEL CORN

3¾ quarts (15 cups)
  popped corn
1 cup brown sugar (packed)
½ cup butter or margarine

¼ cup light corn syrup
½ teaspoon salt
½ teaspoon soda

Heat oven to 200°. Divide popped corn between 2 ungreased baking pans, 13x9x2 inches. Heat sugar, butter, corn syrup and salt, stirring occasionally, until bubbly around edges. Continue cooking over medium heat 5 minutes.

Remove from heat; stir in soda until foamy. Pour on popped corn; stir until corn is coated. Bake 1 hour, stirring every 15 minutes.

CHOCOLATE-COCONUT DROPS

2 squares (1 ounce each) ½ pound flaked coconut
   unsweetened chocolate (about 2 cups)
1 can (15 ounces) ½ cup chopped walnuts
   sweetened condensed
   milk (not evaporated)

Heat oven to 350°. Melt chocolate in saucepan over low heat; remove from heat and stir in milk, coconut and walnuts.

Drop mixture by teaspoonfuls onto ungreased baking sheet. Place in oven; turn off heat. Leave in oven about 15 minutes or until candy has glazed appearance. While warm, remove from baking sheet.

About 4 dozen candies.

CANDY TRIFLES

Here's an unusual combination. Planned to give plenty of crunch—and flavor options, too.

2 packages (6 ounces each) 1 cup Spanish peanuts
   semisweet chocolate, 1 to 2 cups chow mein
   butterscotch or caramel noodles
   pieces

In top of double boiler over hot water, melt chocolate pieces. Stir in nuts and noodles until well coated. Drop mixture by teaspoonfuls onto waxed paper. Chill until firm.

About 3 dozen candies.

PEANUT CLUSTERS

1 cup sugar   ½ teaspoon vanilla
¼ cup butter or margarine 1 cup oats
⅓ cup evaporated milk ½ cup Spanish peanuts
¼ cup crunchy peanut butter

In large saucepan, heat sugar, butter and milk to boiling, stirring constantly. Cook 3 minutes, stirring frequently. Remove from heat; mix in peanut butter and vanilla. Stir in oats and nuts.

Drop mixture by scant tablespoonfuls onto waxed paper. (If mixture becomes too stiff, stir in 1 or 2 drops milk.) Let stand until firm.

About 2½ dozen candies.

PEANUT BUTTER CREAMS

Here's a candy that's not cooked! Great for the children to make.

1 egg	1 tablespoon butter or
2 cups confectioners' sugar	margarine, softened
⅛ teaspoon salt	¾ cup finely chopped salted
½ teaspoon vanilla	peanuts
⅓ cup peanut butter	

Beat egg slightly in small mixer bowl. Beat in 1 cup of the sugar, the salt, vanilla, peanut butter and butter. Stir in remaining sugar. If necessary, add more confectioners' sugar to make firm enough to handle.

Shape mixture into 1-inch balls; roll balls in peanuts. Refrigerate.

3 dozen candies.

CHOCOLATE CLUSTERS

An easy-do chocolate-marshmallow-coconut confection. For kids of all ages.

1 package (6 ounces)	16 large marshmallows
semisweet chocolate	½ teaspoon vanilla
pieces	1 cup flaked coconut
⅓ cup butter or margarine	2 cups oats

Melt chocolate pieces, butter and marshmallows in large saucepan over low heat, stirring until smooth. Remove from heat; mix in vanilla, coconut and oats thoroughly. Drop mixture by teaspoonfuls onto waxed paper. Chill until firm.

About 3½ dozen candies.

APRICOT BALLS

A fruit and coconut cookie-candy that stores well. It's perfect for the holidays—just mix, shape, roll and chill.

1 package (8 ounces) dried apricots, ground or finely cut up

2½ cups flaked coconut

¾ cup sweetened condensed milk (not evaporated)

⅔ cup finely chopped nuts

Mix apricots, coconut and milk. Shape into 1-inch balls; roll each in nuts. Let stand 2 hours or until firm.

About 4 dozen candies.

VARIATIONS

■ *Apricot-Nut Balls:* Mix ⅔ cup nuts into fruit mixture and roll balls in confectioners' sugar.

■ *Lemon-Apricot Balls:* Mix 2 tablespoons lemon juice in with the apricots.

Desserts

Dessert! It's the high point of the meal. It's your chance to go dramatic, to be a little daring, to show you've been around. It's your big opportunity, even on a family night, to put a little extra-special love into your meal plan. And what an array awaits you—from crisps and cobblers to soufflés and crêpes. No time for a special dessert? No excuses now! Just glance through this chapter for those recipes we've keyed as "Quick 'n Easy" just for you. Choose one for tonight!

Fruit Desserts

Count on fruit to help hold the calorie line. And how delicious it is in desserts. It won't be hard for you to win high praises with these!

MAUI SUPREME

Fresh pineapple cubes mixed with minted whipped cream and served in pineapple shells.

½ cup mint-flavored apple jelly
¼ cup water
1 large pineapple, chilled
1 cup chilled whipping cream

Chopped macadamia nuts or toasted slivered blanched almonds

Heat jelly and water over low heat until smooth, stirring occasionally. Chill until thick and syrupy.

Cut pineapple in half lengthwise (through the green top). Then cut each in half again making 4 pieces, each with part of green top. Remove fruit from pineapple by cutting along curved edges with grapefruit knife. Cut fruit into cubes, removing any eyes and fibrous core. Drain pineapple shells cut side down.

In chilled bowl, beat cream until stiff. Gradually beat in syrup mixture. Carefully stir in cubed pineapple. Fill pineapple shells with fruit mixture; sprinkle with nuts.

4 servings.

GRAPES AND PINEAPPLE IN SOUR CREAM

Sour cream and brown sugar give a touch of elegance to these favorite fruits. And since all the preparation is done well ahead of time, this dessert is ideal dinner-party fare.

2 cups fresh seedless green
    grapes or 1 can (1 pound)
    seedless green grapes,
    drained

1 can (13½ ounces)
    pineapple tidbits, drained
¼ cup brown sugar (packed)
⅓ cup dairy sour cream

Combine grapes and pineapple. Reserving 1 tablespoon of the brown sugar, blend remaining sugar and the sour cream. Toss with fruits and chill.

Just before serving, sprinkle with reserved brown sugar.

4 servings.

VARIATIONS

■ *Strawberries in Sour Cream:* Substitute 3 cups fresh strawberry halves (about 1 pint) for the grapes and pineapple.

■ *Strawberries to Dip:* Wash 1 pint fresh strawberries; do not hull. Chill. To serve, divide berries among dessert dishes. Pass bowls of sour cream and brown sugar. Guests spoon some of each onto dessert plates and dip berries first into sour cream, then into sugar.

FIESTA FRUIT PLATTER

This colorful fruit arrangement is the perfect dessert for a summer patio party or buffet dinner.

Prepare Raspberry Sauce (page 267). Beat 1 package (3 ounces) cream cheese, softened, and 1 to 2 tablespoons milk until smooth. Cover and refrigerate.

Pile melon balls in center of large serving plate. Alternate clusters of fresh dark sweet cherries (with stems) and small bunches of fresh seedless green grapes around melon balls. Border with sliced fresh peaches.* Cut peeled bananas in half lengthwise, then crosswise; arrange spoke-fashion over peach slices. Garnish with fresh strawberries and mint leaves. Serve with Raspberry Sauce and cream cheese mixture.

*Dip peach and banana slices into lemon juice to prevent darkening.

RASPBERRY SAUCE

Stir together 2 cups fresh raspberries and ½ cup sugar; let stand 2 hours. (Or use one 10-ounce package frozen sweetened raspberries, thawed.) Rub through sieve.
¾ cup.

STRAWBERRIES ROMANOFF

Spoon into sherbet dishes and top each serving with a large strawberry—a lovely dessert.

1 quart fresh strawberries
½ cup confectioners' sugar
1 cup chilled whipping cream

¼ cup orange-flavored liqueur or, if desired, orange juice

Sprinkle strawberries with sugar; stir gently. Cover; chill 2 hours. Just before serving, beat cream in chilled bowl until stiff. Gradually stir in liqueur. Fold in strawberries.
6 servings.

Quick 'n Easy
HONEY BEE AMBROSIA

4 medium oranges
1 medium banana
½ cup orange juice

¼ cup honey
2 tablespoons lemon juice
¼ cup flaked coconut

Pare oranges; cut crosswise into thin slices and place in serving bowl. Peel bananas; cut thin slices into bowl with oranges. Toss fruits.

Blend orange juice, honey and lemon juice; pour over fruits. Sprinkle with coconut.
4 to 6 servings.

CAPTIVATING CANTALOUPE

2 medium cantaloupes
1 package (8 ounces) cream cheese, softened
1 can (1 pound 1 ounce) pitted dark sweet cherries, drained (reserve syrup)

1 teaspoon grated lemon peel
¼ cup toasted slivered blanched almonds

Cut thin slice from one end of each cantaloupe so they will stand upright. Slice other end of each cantaloupe until seeds are exposed. Scoop out seeds. Place each cantaloupe upright in bowl; freeze 3 hours or until cavity is slightly icy.

In small mixer bowl, beat cream cheese until smooth. Add 2 tablespoons of the reserved cherry syrup and the lemon peel; beat until fluffy. Stir in cherries and almonds; fill each cantaloupe.

Return to freezer *just* until filling is hardened, about 3 hours. Just before serving, cut each cantaloupe cross-wise into 4 slices.

8 servings.

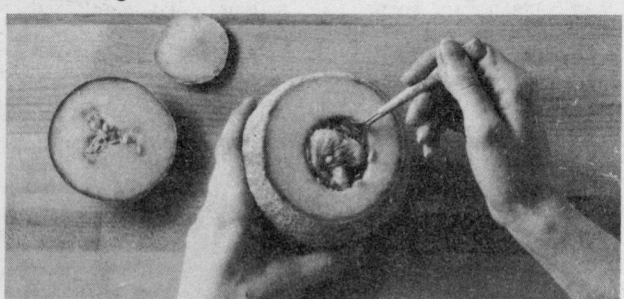

Scoop out seeds and membrane from cantaloupe.

Cut each frozen cantaloupe crosswise into 4 even slices.

COMPANY FRUIT COMPOTE

1 can (1 pound 6 ounces) pineapple pie filling
¼ teaspoon almond extract
1 can (1 pound) unpeeled apricot halves, drained (reserve syrup)
1 unpared medium apple, cut into bite-size pieces

1 medium banana, cut into thin slices
1 cup chilled whipping cream
¼ cup toasted slivered blanched almonds

Stir together pie filling, almond extract and ⅔ cup of the reserved apricot syrup. Fold in apricots, apple and banana. (The apple and banana should be well coated with pineapple mixture to prevent darkening.) Cover; chill 2 hours.

Just before serving, beat cream in chilled bowl until stiff; spoon onto fruit mixture and sprinkle with almonds.

6 to 8 servings.

PEARS AU CHOCOLAT

For each serving, put 2 well-drained canned pear halves together with 1 tablespoon canned chocolate frosting in cavity. (Remaining frosting can be covered and stored in refrigerator.) Stand pear upright in dessert dish; chill.

Just before serving, melt 1 tablespoon chocolate frosting per serving in custard cup placed in boiling water. Pour over pear.

RIVIERA PEACHES

8 fresh* or canned peach halves

⅓ cup red raspberry jelly
1 pint vanilla ice cream

Place 2 peach halves in each dessert dish. Melt jelly over low heat; pour over peaches. Chill several hours. Just before serving, top with scoops of ice cream.

4 servings.

*Dip fresh peach halves into lemon juice to prevent darkening.

VARIATION

■ *Peaches Deluxe:* Substitute canned brandied peaches; stir 1 tablespoon of the peach syrup into melted jelly and substitute pistachio ice cream for the vanilla.

Quick 'n Easy
CHOCOLATE FONDUE

Guests of all ages will enjoy this unusual dessert—but it's a special favorite of teenagers.

12 ounces milk chocolate, semisweet chocolate pieces or sweet cooking chocolate
¾ cup light cream (20%)

1 to 2 tablespoons kirsch, orange-flavored liqueur or brandy or, if desired, 2 teaspoons instant coffee
Dippers (below)

In heavy saucepan, melt chocolate and cream over low heat, stirring until smooth. Remove from heat; stir in liqueur. Pour into fondue pot or chafing dish to keep warm.

Guests select choice of Dippers and place on dessert plates; then, with fork, dip one by one into chocolate mixture.

6 to 8 servings.

DIPPERS

Apple wedges
Cubes of angel food cake
Strips of pound cake
Sliced bananas
Mandarin orange segments
Maraschino cherries
Marshmallows
Pineapple chunks
Fresh strawberries

Quick 'n Easy
PEACHES FLAMBÉ

¼ cup apricot jam
3 tablespoons sugar
½ cup water
4 large fresh peaches, peeled and sliced, or 1 can (1 pound 13 ounces) sliced peaches, drained

1 teaspoon lemon juice
¼ cup brandy
1 quart vanilla ice cream

Combine jam, sugar and water in medium saucepan or chafing dish; simmer over low heat about 5 minutes or until syrupy. Add peaches and continue cooking over low heat about 3 minutes or until almost tender. If using canned peaches, cook only long enough to heat through. Stir in lemon juice.

Heat brandy; pour over peaches and ignite. Stir well before serving. Spoon peaches and syrup over each serving of vanilla ice cream. If desired, garnish with sweetened whipped cream and toasted slivered almonds.

4 to 6 servings.

CHERRIES JUBILEE

You can finish this impressive dessert right at the table. Assemble the ingredients and utensils on a tray and use a chafing dish for the cooking.

1 can (1 pound) pitted dark sweet cherries, drained (reserve ¼ cup syrup)*
¼ cup rum
¾ cup currant jelly
1 teaspoon grated orange peel
¼ cup brandy
Vanilla ice cream

Combine reserved syrup and the rum; pour over cherries and chill 4 hours.

At serving time, melt jelly in chafing dish or saucepan over low heat. Stir in cherry mixture and orange peel. Cook, stirring constantly, until mixture simmers. Heat brandy in saucepan; slowly pour over cherries and ignite. Serve hot over ice cream.

8 to 10 servings.

*You can substitute 2 cups pitted fresh dark sweet cherries for the canned cherries and their syrup. Pour rum over the pitted fresh cherries.

BAKED APPLES

Choose baking apples such as Rome Beauty, Starr, Jersey Red, Winesap Northern Spy, Golden Delicious or Greening.

Heat oven to 375°. Core apples; remove 1-inch strip of skin around middle of each apple or pare upper half of each to prevent skin from splitting.

Place apples upright in baking dish. Fill center of each apple with 1 to 2 tablespoons granulated or brown sugar, 1 teaspoon butter or margarine and ⅛ teaspoon cinnamon. Pour water (¼ inch deep) into baking dish.

Bake about 30 to 40 minutes or until apples are tender when pierced with fork. (Time will vary with size and variety of apple.) If desired, spoon syrup in pan over apples several times during baking.

VARIATION

■ *Red Cinnamon Baked Apples:* Omit butter and cinnamon and place 1 tablespoon plus 1 teaspoon red cinnamon candies in center of each apple. Spoon syrup in pan over apples several times during baking.

APPLESAUCE

4 medium cooking apples, pared, quartered and cored
1 cup water

½ cup brown sugar (packed)
¼ teaspoon cinnamon
⅛ teaspoon nutmeg

Heat apples and water over medium heat to boiling. Reduce heat; simmer, stirring occasionally, 5 to 10 minutes or until tender. Stir in brown sugar, cinnamon and nutmeg; heat to boiling.
About 4 cups.

RHUBARB

A good basic recipe—pretty and tart.

Cut enough rhubarb into 1-inch pieces to measure 4 cups. Heat ¾ to 1 cup sugar and ½ cup water to boiling, stirring occasionally. Add rhubarb; simmer about 10 minutes or until rhubarb is tender and slightly transparent. If desired, stir in few drops red food color.
5 servings.

Quick 'n Easy
BROILED GRAPEFRUIT

Cut grapefruit in half; remove seeds. Cut around edge and sections to loosen; remove center. Sprinkle each half with 1 tablespoon brown sugar.
Set oven control at broil and/or 550°. Broil grapefruit 4 to 6 inches from heat 5 to 10 minutes or until juice bubbles and edge of peel turns light brown. Serve hot.
2 servings.

BAKED BANANAS

Heat oven to 375°. Peel large firm bananas; cut lengthwise in half. Place halves cut side down in greased baking dish. Brush with lemon juice; sprinkle each half with ½ teaspoon grated lemon peel and ½ tablespoon brown sugar. Drizzle with ½ tablespoon butter, melted. Bake 20 minutes. Serve warm, plain or with ice cream.

VARIATION

■ *Puerto Rican Baked Bananas:* Sprinkle each half with ⅛ teaspoon rum flavoring in addition to the other ingredients.

BAKED FRESH FRUIT COMPOTE

1 jar (10 ounces) currant jelly	2 pears, pared, cut in half and cored
½ cup water	2 peaches, peeled and cut in half
4 plums, cut in half	

Heat oven to 350°. Heat jelly and water over low heat until smooth, stirring occasionally. Arrange fruits cut side down in baking dish, 11½x7½x1½ inches; pour hot syrup over fruits.

Bake about 25 minutes or until fruits are tender. During baking, spoon syrup over fruits occasionally to keep tops of fruits moist. Serve warm.

4 servings.

COOKED DRIED FRUIT

Prepare fruits such as apples, apricots, figs, peaches, pears and prunes as directed on package. Or soak in cold water until plump; simmer in same water in tightly covered saucepan 30 to 45 minutes or until tender. Sweeten to taste.

CHEESE FOR THE FRUIT TRAY Offer variety in texture and flavor. Try these combinations: Roquefort with Swiss or Fontina and Port du Salut; Gourmandise with Cream and Edam or Gouda; Camembert or Brie with Bel Paese and Liederkranz. Team with fresh fruit. (See pages 326 and 327 for more dessert cheeses.)

Crisps and Cobblers

Crispy! Crunchy! Fruity! Flavorful! Just reading about dumplings and crisps and cobblers is enough to make you hungry.

APPLE CRISP

4 cups sliced pared tart apples (about 4 medium)
⅔ to ¾ cup brown sugar (packed)
½ cup all-purpose flour
½ cup oats
¾ teaspoon cinnamon
¾ teaspoon nutmeg
⅓ cup butter or margarine, softened

Heat oven to 375°. Grease square pan, 8x8x2 inches. Place apple slices in pan. Mix remaining ingredients thoroughly. Sprinkle over apples.

Bake 30 minutes or until apples are tender and topping is golden brown. Serve warm and, if desired, with light cream or ice cream.

6 servings.

VARIATION

■ *Cherry Crisp:* Substitute 1 can (1 pound 5 ounces) cherry pie filling for the apples; use lesser amount of sugar.

RHUBARB CRISP

4 cups cut-up fresh rhubarb
½ teaspoon salt
1⅓ to 2 cups sugar (depending on tartness of rhubarb)
¾ cup all-purpose flour*
1 teaspoon cinnamon
⅓ cup butter or margarine
Light cream or sweetened whipped cream

Heat oven to 350°. Place rhubarb in ungreased baking dish, 10x6x1½ inches. Sprinkle with salt. Measure sugar, flour and cinnamon into bowl. Add butter and mix thoroughly until mixture is crumbly. Sprinkle evenly over rhubarb.

Bake 40 to 50 minutes or until topping is golden brown. Serve warm with light cream.

6 servings.

*If using self-rising flour, omit salt.

Quick 'n Easy
DATE-PEACH CRUMBLE

Heat oven to 375°. Prepare date filling and crumbly mix as directed on 1 package (14 ounces) date bar mix. Combine date filling and 1 can (1 pound 13 ounces) sliced peaches or pears, drained.

Press half the crumbly mix lightly into bottom of 1½-quart casserole. Cover with fruit mixture. Sprinkle with remaining crumbly mix.

Bake 30 to 35 minutes or until topping is golden brown. Serve warm with sweetened whipped cream or ice cream.

6 to 8 servings.

APPLE DUMPLINGS

Pastry for 9-inch
Two-crust Pie (page 501)
6 baking apples (each about
3 inches in diameter),
pared and cored

3 tablespoons raisins
3 tablespoons chopped nuts
2 cups brown sugar (packed)
1 cup water

Heat oven to 425°. Prepare pastry as directed except —roll ⅔ of dough into 14-inch square; cut into 4 squares. Roll remaining dough into rectangle, 14x7 inches; cut into 2 squares. Place apple on each square.

Mix raisins and nuts; fill center of each apple. Moisten corners of squares; bring 2 opposite corners of pastry up over apple and press together. Fold in sides of remaining corners (as if wrapping a package); bring corners up over apple and press together. Place dumplings in ungreased baking dish, 11½x7½x1½ inches.

Heat brown sugar and water to boiling; carefully pour around dumplings. Spooning syrup over dumplings 2 or 3 times during baking, bake about 40 minutes or until crust is golden and apples are tender. Serve warm or cool; if desired, top with sweetened whipped cream.

6 servings.

VARIATION

■ *Peach Dumplings:* Substitute 6 fresh peaches, peeled and halved, for the apples and ¼ cup cranberry relish for the raisins and nuts.

FRESH BLUEBERRY COBBLER

"Cobble up" means to put together in a hurry. Tender biscuit topping on your choice of fresh fruits makes an easy yet hearty dessert—a great favorite in New England.

½ cup sugar	1 tablespoon sugar
1 tablespoon cornstarch	1½ teaspoons baking powder
4 cups fresh blueberries	½ teaspoon salt
1 teaspoon lemon juice	3 tablespoons shortening
1 cup all-purpose flour*	½ cup milk

Heat oven to 400°. Blend ½ cup sugar and the cornstarch in medium saucepan. Stir in blueberries and lemon juice. Cook, stirring constantly, until mixture thickens and boils. Boil and stir 1 minute. Pour into ungreased 2-quart casserole. Keep fruit mixture hot in oven while preparing biscuit topping.

Measure flour, 1 tablespoon sugar, the baking powder and salt into bowl. Add shortening and milk. Cut through shortening 6 times; mix until dough forms a ball. Drop dough by 6 spoonfuls onto hot fruit.

Bake 25 to 30 minutes or until biscuit topping is golden brown. Serve warm and, if desired, with cream.

6 servings.

*If using self-rising flour, omit baking powder and salt.

VARIATIONS

■ *Fresh Cherry Cobbler:* Substitute 4 cups pitted fresh red tart cherries for the blueberries; increase sugar in fruit mixture to 1¼ cups, cornstarch to 3 tablespoons and substitute ¼ teaspoon almond extract for the lemon juice.

■ *Fresh Peach Cobbler:* Substitute 4 cups sliced fresh peaches (peeled) for the blueberries and add ¼ teaspoon cinnamon to the sugar-cornstarch mixture.

■ *Fresh Plum Cobbler:* Substitute 4 cups unpeeled sliced fresh plums for the blueberries; increase sugar in fruit mixture to ¾ cup, cornstarch to 3 tablespoons and add ½ teaspoon cinnamon to the sugar-cornstarch mixture.

Quick 'n Easy
CHERRY COBBLER

1 can (1 pound 5 ounces) cherry pie filling	½ teaspoon salt
½ teaspoon almond extract	3 tablespoons shortening
1 cup all-purpose flour*	½ cup milk
1 tablespoon sugar	2 tablespoons toasted slivered blanched almonds
1½ teaspoons baking powder	

Heat oven to 400°. Combine pie filling and almond extract in ungreased 1½-quart casserole. Place in oven 10 to 15 minutes or until hot and bubbly.

Measure flour, sugar, baking powder and salt into bowl. Add shortening and milk. Cut through shortening 6 times. Stir in almonds; mix until dough forms a ball. Drop dough by 6 spoonfuls onto hot pie filling. Bake 25 to 30 minutes or until biscuit topping is golden brown. Serve warm.

6 servings.

*If using self-rising flour, omit baking powder and salt.

VARIATIONS

■ *Blueberry Cobbler:* Substitute 1 can (1 pound 5 ounces) blueberry pie filling and ½ teaspoon grated orange peel for the cherry pie filling and almond extract; substitute ½ cup orange juice for the milk in biscuit topping and omit almonds.

■ *Peach Cobbler:* Omit cherry pie filling and almond extract; instead, combine 1 can (1 pound 13 ounces) sliced peaches (with syrup), ½ teaspoon cinnamon and 3 tablespoons cornstarch in saucepan. Cook, stirring constantly, until mixture thickens and boils. Boil and stir 1 minute. Pour into 1½-quart casserole. Omit almonds in topping.

■ *Pear Cobbler:* Omit cherry pie filling and almond extract; instead, combine 1 can (1 pound 13 ounces) pears, ¼ teaspoon nutmeg and 3 tablespoons cornstarch in saucepan. Cook, stirring constantly, until mixture thickens and boils. Boil and stir 1 minute. Pour into 1½-quart casserole. Mix ⅓ cup shredded Cheddar cheese with the flour in biscuit topping and omit almonds.

Shortcakes and Cake Desserts

When is a cake not a cake? When it's just a bit crustier and topped with fruit; when it's soft but sauced, layered with pudding, buried under whipped cream. Totally tempting! And if calories scare you, there's always a good-tasting low-calorie topping!

PEACH PRALINE SHORTCAKE

1½ cups all-purpose flour*	1 egg
3 teaspoons baking powder	¾ cup milk
½ teaspoon salt	4 cups sliced fresh
¼ teaspoon soda	peaches, sweetened
½ cup brown sugar (packed)	1 cup dairy sour cream
⅓ cup shortening	½ cup brown sugar (packed)
½ cup coarsely chopped pecans	

Heat oven to 375°. Grease round layer pan, 8x1½ inches. Measure flour, baking powder, salt and soda into bowl. Cut in ½ cup brown sugar and the shortening thoroughly until mixture looks like meal. Stir in pecans. Combine egg and milk; stir into flour mixture just until blended. Pat into pan.

Bake 20 to 25 minutes or until wooden pick inserted in center comes out clean. Split shortcake while warm. Fill and top with peaches. Blend sour cream and ½ cup brown sugar. Serve with shortcake.

6 to 8 servings.

*If using self-rising flour, omit baking powder and salt.

Quick 'n Easy
FRUIT SHORTCAKE

Use fruit pie filling. So quick and easy.

Bake Large Quick Shortcake (right). While warm, fill with about ⅔ of 1 can (1 pound 5 ounces) fruit pie filling. Spoon remaining pie filling over top. Garnish with sweetened whipped cream.

6 to 8 servings.

STRAWBERRY SHORTCAKE

1 quart fresh strawberries	⅓ cup shortening
1 cup sugar	1 cup milk
2 cups all-purpose flour*	Butter or margarine
2 tablespoons sugar	Light cream or sweetened
3 teaspoons baking powder	whipped cream
1 teaspoon salt	

Slice strawberries; sprinkle with 1 cup sugar and let stand 1 hour.

Heat oven to 450°. Grease round layer pan, 8x1½ inches. Measure flour, 2 tablespoons sugar, the baking powder and salt into bowl. Cut in shortening thoroughly until mixture looks like meal. Stir in milk just until blended. Pat into pan.

Bake 15 to 20 minutes or until golden brown. Split shortcake while warm. Spread with butter; fill and top with berries. Serve warm with cream.

8 servings.

*If using self-rising flour, omit baking powder and salt.

QUICK SHORTCAKES

INDIVIDUAL

Bake Fruit Shortcake as directed on package of buttermilk baking mix.

SQUARES

Prepare Fruit Shortcake dough as directed on package of buttermilk baking mix except—pat dough into rectangle, 9x6 inches, on ungreased baking sheet. Cut dough into 3-inch squares. Bake 10 to 15 minutes. Split squares while warm.

6 servings.

LARGE

Prepare Fruit Shortcake dough as directed on package of buttermilk baking mix except—pat half the dough into ungreased round layer pan, 8x1½ inches; dot with butter or margarine. Pat remaining dough into 8-inch circle and place on top. Bake 15 to 20 minutes.

COTTAGE PUDDING

About 1 hour before serving, prepare 9-inch Dinette Cake (page 147) and Butter Sauce (below), Cherry Topping (page 309) or Old-Fashioned Lemon Sauce (page 318). Serve cake warm, topped with warm sauce.

9 servings.

BUTTER SAUCE

Combine ½ cup butter, 1 cup sugar and ¾ cup light cream (20%) in saucepan. Cook over low heat, stirring constantly, until smooth.

GINGERBREAD

2¼ cups all-purpose flour*	1 egg
or cake flour	1 teaspoon soda
⅓ cup sugar	1 teaspoon ginger
1 cup dark molasses	1 teaspoon cinnamon
¾ cup hot water	¾ teaspoon salt
½ cup shortening	

Heat oven to 325°. Grease and flour square pan, 9x9x2 inches. Measure all ingredients into large mixer bowl. Blend ½ minute on low speed, scraping bowl constantly. Beat 3 minutes medium speed, scraping bowl occasionally. Pour into pan.

Bake 50 minutes or until wooden pick inserted in center comes out clean. Serve warm and, if desired, with whipped cream or applesauce.

9 servings.

*Do not use self-rising flour in this recipe.

VARIATION

■ *Haddon Hall Gingerbread:* Bake Gingerbread. Beat 1 package (8 ounces) cream cheese, softened, and ¼ cup milk until fluffy. Prepare Old-fashioned Lemon Sauce (page 318).

Cut Gingerbread into 12 pieces. Split each piece to make 2 layers. Fill layers with about ½ tablespoon of the cream cheese mixture. Top pieces with remaining cheese mixture. Serve with warm lemon sauce. 12 servings.

PINEAPPLE UPSIDE-DOWN CAKE

¼ cup butter or margarine
½ cup brown sugar (packed)
1 can (8½ ounces) sliced
   pineapple, drained

7 maraschino cherries
6 pecan halves
Dinette Cake batter
(page 147)

Heat oven to 350°. Melt butter over low heat in round layer pan, 9x1½ inches. Sprinkle brown sugar evenly over butter. Place pineapple slice in center of pan. Cut remaining slices in half; arrange halves cut sides out around pineapple ring in pan. Place cherries in pineapple slices; arrange pecans around center ring.

Prepare Dinette Cake batter. Pour evenly over fruit in pan.

Bake 35 to 45 minutes or until wooden pick inserted in center comes out clean. Invert onto plate. Leave pan over cake a few minutes. Serve warm and, if desired, with whipped cream.

9 servings.

MOCHA BROWNIE TORTE

An attractive rich chocolate dessert—easy to make.

1 package (15.5 ounces)
   fudge brownie mix
¼ cup water
2 eggs
½ cup finely chopped nuts
1½ cups chilled whipping
   cream

⅓ cup brown sugar (packed)
1 tablespoon powdered
   instant coffee
Shaved chocolate

Heat oven to 350°. Grease and flour 2 round layer pans, 9x1½ inches. Blend brownie mix (dry), water and eggs. Stir in nuts. Spread in pans.

Bake 20 minutes. Cool 5 minutes in pans; remove from pans and place layers on wire racks to cool thoroughly.

In chilled bowl, beat cream until it begins to thicken. Gradually add sugar and coffee; continue beating until stiff. Fill layers with 1 cup of the whipped cream mixture. Frost with remaining whipped cream mixture. Sprinkle with chocolate. Chill at least 1 hour.

10 to 12 servings.

NUT CRACKER SWEET TORTE

6 eggs, separated	1 cup fine graham cracker
½ cup sugar	crumbs (about 12
2 tablespoons salad oil	crackers)
1 tablespoon rum flavoring	1 square (1 ounce)
½ cup sugar	unsweetened chocolate,
¼ cup all-purpose flour	grated
1¼ teaspoons baking powder	1 cup finely chopped nuts
1 teaspoon cinnamon	Rum-flavored Whipped
½ teaspoon cloves	Cream (below)

Heat oven to 350°. Line the bottoms of 2 round layer pans, 8 or 9x1½ inches, with aluminum foil. In large mixer bowl, beat egg whites until foamy. Beat in ½ cup sugar, 1 tablespoon at a time; continue beating until stiff and glossy.

In small mixer bowl, blend egg yolks, oil and rum flavoring on low speed. Add ½ cup sugar, the flour, baking powder, cinnamon and cloves; beat 1 minute medium speed. Fold egg yolk mixture into whites. Fold in graham cracker crumbs, grated chocolate and chopped nuts. Pour batter into pans.

Bake 30 to 35 minutes or until top springs back when touched lightly. Immediately invert pans, resting rims on edges of 2 inverted pans. Cool completely.

Loosen edges of layers with knife; hit pan sharply on table. Remove foil from layers. Split cakes to make 4 layers.

Fill layers and frost top of torte with Rum-flavored Whipped Cream. If desired, garnish with additional grated chocolate or chocolate curls. Chill at least 7 hours. (Torte mellows and becomes moist.)

12 servings.

RUM-FLAVORED WHIPPED CREAM

In chilled bowl, beat 2 cups chilled whipping cream, ½ cup confectioners' sugar and 2 teaspoons rum flavoring until stiff.

ANGEL FOOD WALDORF

Bake 1 package (15 or 16 ounces) white angel food cake mix as directed. Place cake upside down; slice off entire top of cake about 1 inch down and set aside. Make cuts down into cake 1 inch from outer edge and 1 inch from edge of hole, leaving substantial "walls"

With a spoon, carefully remove cake within the "wall."

Angel Food Waldorf—ideal for a dessert-and-coffee party.

on each side. With a curved knife or spoon, remove cake within cuts, being careful to leave a base of cake 1 inch thick. Place cake on serving plate.

In chilled bowl, beat 3 cups chilled whipping cream, 1½ cups confectioners' sugar, ¾ cup cocoa and ¼ teaspoon salt until stiff. Fold ⅓ cup toasted slivered almonds into half the whipped cream mixture; spoon into cake cavity. Press mixture firmly into cavity to avoid "holes" in cut slices. Replace top of cake and press gently.

Frost cake with remaining whipped cream mixture. Sprinkle with ⅓ cup toasted slivered almonds. Chill at least 4 hours or until set.

12 to 16 servings.

CHOCOLATE CAKE AND ICE-CREAM ROLL

Prepare Chocolate Roll (page 170) except—do not fill with whipped cream. Just before unrolling cake to remove towel, soften 1 pint vanilla ice cream slightly. Stir in 1½ teaspoons instant coffee. (Coffee ice cream can be substituted.) Spread ice cream on cake. Roll up; wrap in plastic wrap. Freeze several hours or until firm.

Prepare Chocolate Rum Sauce (page 284). Drizzle some sauce over roll; serve remaining sauce.

10 servings.

CHOCOLATE RUM SAUCE

In top of double boiler, combine 1 package (14.3 ounces) dark chocolate fudge frosting mix (dry), 3 tablespoons butter or margarine and 2 tablespoons light corn syrup. Gradually stir in ½ cup milk. Heat over rapidly boiling water 5 minutes, stirring occasionally. Remove from heat; stir in 2 tablespoons dark rum.* Cool to room temperature before serving. Refrigerate any leftover sauce in covered container.

2 cups.

*If desired, omit dark rum and increase milk to ⅔ cup.

BOSTON CREAM PIE

Bake Dinette Cake (page 147) in round layer pan, 9x1½ inches. Cool. Split cake to make 2 thin layers. Fill layers with Cream Filling (below).

Spread top with Chocolate Glaze (page 196). Refrigerate any remaining cake.

8 to 10 servings.

CREAM FILLING

⅓ cup sugar	1½ cups milk
2 tablespoons cornstarch	2 egg yolks, slightly beaten
⅛ teaspoon salt	2 teaspoons vanilla

Blend sugar, cornstarch and salt in medium saucepan. Combine milk and egg yolks; gradually stir into sugar mixture. Cook over medium heat, stirring constantly, until mixture thickens and boils. Boil and stir 1 minute. Remove from heat; stir in vanilla. Cool to room temperature.

BLITZ TORTE

4 eggs, separated	¼ teaspoon salt
½ cup confectioners' sugar	½ cup sliced unblanched
½ cup granulated sugar	almonds
½ cup shortening	2 tablespoons granulated
¾ cup confectioners' sugar	sugar
3 tablespoons milk	Streamlined Cream Filling
1 cup all-purpose flour*	(page 200)
1 teaspoon baking powder	

Heat oven to 325°. Grease and flour 2 round layer pans, 8x1½ inches. Beat egg whites until foamy. Beat

*If using self-rising flour, omit baking powder and salt.

in ½ cup each granulated sugar and confectioners' sugar, 1 tablespoon at a time; continue beating until stiff and glossy. Set meringue aside.

Measure shortening, ¾ cup confectioners' sugar, the egg yolks and milk into large mixer bowl. Blend ½ minute on low speed, scraping bowl constantly. Add flour, baking powder and salt; beat 1 minute medium speed, scraping bowl occasionally. Spread in pans. Spread half the meringue on batter in each pan. Sprinkle each with half the almonds, then with 1 tablespoon granulated sugar. Bake 35 to 40 minutes or until meringue is set. Cool.

Prepare Streamlined Cream Filling. With spatulas, carefully remove layers from pans. Place 1 layer meringue side up on serving plate. Spread with filling. Top with other layer, meringue side up. Chill at least 1 hour.

12 servings.

Cheesecakes

Cheesecake may be made in advance, and kept in the refrigerator for several days. Slip the cheesecake, still in its pan, into a plastic bag; tie tightly and store. If there's any left over—which seems unlikely—do the same thing. Put the remaining pieces on a saucer or pie pan and slip into the plastic bag.

LEMON CHEESECAKE

1½ cups graham cracker crumbs (about 20 crackers)
3 tablespoons sugar
¼ cup butter or margarine, melted
1 package (6.5 ounces) lemon fluff frosting mix

1 package (8 ounces) cream cheese, softened
1½ cups dairy sour cream
1 package (10 ounces) frozen strawberries, thawed

Heat oven to 300°. Mix thoroughly graham cracker crumbs, sugar and butter. Reserve ⅓ cup crumb mixture. Press remaining mixture evenly in bottom of square pan, 9x9x2 inches.

Prepare frosting mix as directed on package. Blend cream cheese and sour cream in large mixer bowl. Gradually beat in frosting. Pour cream cheese mixture over crumb mixture. Sprinkle with reserved crumbs.

Bake 45 minutes. Cool slightly and chill. Serve with strawberries.

9 servings.

VARIATION

■ *Sour Cream Cheesecake:* Substitute 1 package (7.2 ounces) fluffy white frosting mix for the lemon frosting mix and your favorite frozen fruit or canned pie filling for the strawberries.

COMPANY CHEESECAKE

Delicate, creamy filling baked in a springform pan.

1¼ cups graham cracker crumbs (about 16 crackers)	1 cup sugar
	2 teaspoons grated lemon peel
2 tablespoons sugar	¼ teaspoon vanilla
3 tablespoons butter or margarine, melted	3 eggs
2 packages (8 ounces each) plus 1 package (3 ounces) cream cheese, softened	1 cup dairy sour cream, Cherry Glaze or Strawberry Glaze (right)

Heat oven to 350°. Stir together graham cracker crumbs and 2 tablespoons sugar. Mix in butter thoroughly. Press mixture evenly in bottom of 9-inch springform pan. Bake 10 minutes. Cool.

Reduce oven temperature to 300°. Beat cream cheese in large mixer bowl. Gradually add 1 cup sugar, beating until fluffy. Add lemon peel and vanilla. Beat in eggs, one at a time. Pour over crumb mixture.

Bake 1 hour or until center is firm. Cool to room temperature. Spread with sour cream or glaze. Chill at least 3 hours. Loosen edge of cheesecake with knife before removing side of pan.

12 servings.

CHERRY GLAZE

Drain 1 can (1 pound) pitted red tart cherries, reserving liquid. Add enough water to cherry liquid to measure 1 cup. Mix ½ cup sugar and 2 tablespoons cornstarch in small saucepan. Stir in the 1 cup liquid. Cook, stirring constantly, until mixture thickens and boils. Boil and stir 1 minute. Remove from heat; stir in cherries and 4 drops red food color. Cool thoroughly.

STRAWBERRY GLAZE

Mash enough fresh strawberries to measure 1 cup. Blend 1 cup sugar and 3 tablespoons cornstarch in small saucepan. Stir in ⅓ cup water and the strawberries. Cook, stirring constantly, until mixture thickens and boils. Boil and stir 1 minute. Cool thoroughly.

Custards and Puddings

In Europe you'll find soft custard served with *everything*—fresh fruit, stewed fruit, even cake. Enrich your culinary repertoire with perfect custards and puddings like these.

CREAMY STIRRED CUSTARD

3 eggs, slightly beaten	2½ cups milk
⅓ cup sugar	1 teaspoon vanilla
Dash salt	

Blend eggs, sugar and salt in top of double boiler. Gradually stir in milk. Place enough hot water in bottom

Place pan with custard cups on oven rack; then add water.

of double boiler so that top part does not touch water. Cook over medium heat, stirring constantly, about 20 minutes or until mixture just coats a silver spoon. (Water in double boiler should not boil.)

Remove top of double boiler from heat; stir vanilla into custard. Place top of double boiler in cold water until custard is cool. (If custard should curdle, beat vigorously, with rotary beater until smooth.) Cover; chill 2 to 3 hours.

6 servings.

VARIATION

■ *Floating Island:* Substitute 2 whole eggs plus 2 egg yolks for the 3 eggs; reserve whites. Chill custard thoroughly, about 3 hours.

Heat oven to 350°. Butter six 5-ounce custard cups; sprinkle with sugar to coat. Beat reserved egg whites and ⅛ teaspoon cream of tartar until foamy. Beat in ¼ cup sugar, 1 tablespoon at a time; continue beating until stiff and glossy. Stir in ¼ teaspoon vanilla. Spoon meringue into cups, pressing mixture gently into cups to remove air pockets. Place cups in baking pan, 13x 9x2 inches; pour in very hot water (1 inch deep).

Bake 20 to 25 minutes or until light brown. Remove cups from water; unmold into dessert dishes. Cool slightly and chill. Just before serving, spoon custard around meringue. 6 servings.

BEST BAKED CUSTARD

For a little extra sparkle, top custard with raspberries or blueberries.

3 eggs, slightly beaten	1 teaspoon vanilla
⅓ cup sugar	2½ cups milk, scalded
Dash salt	Nutmeg

Heat oven to 350°. Blend eggs, sugar, salt and vanilla. Gradually stir in milk. Pour into six 6-ounce custard cups. Sprinkle with nutmeg. Place cups in baking pan, 13x 9x2 inches; pour very hot water into pan to within ½ inch of tops of cups.

Bake about 45 minutes or until knife inserted halfway

between center and edge comes out clean. Remove cups from water. Serve custard warm or chilled.

6 servings.

■ *Caramel Custard:* Before preparing custard, heat ½ cup sugar in small heavy skillet over low heat, stirring constantly, until sugar melts and is golden brown. Divide syrup among custard cups; tilt and rotate each cup to coat the bottom. Allow syrup to harden in cups about 10 minutes.

Pour custard mixture over syrup. Bake. Invert custard cups to unmold and serve warm or let cool to room temperature, or chill and unmold at serving time. Caramel syrup will run down side of custard forming a sauce.

VANILLA CREAM PUDDING

A simplified method for cooking cream pudding.

⅓ cup sugar	2 egg yolks, slightly beaten
2 tablespoons cornstarch	2 tablespoons butter or
⅛ teaspoon salt	margarine, softened*
2 cups milk	2 teaspoons vanilla

Blend sugar, cornstarch and salt in 2-quart saucepan. Combine milk and egg yolks; gradually stir into sugar mixture. Cook over medium heat, stirring constantly, until mixture thickens and boils. Boil and stir 1 minute. Remove from heat; stir in butter and vanilla. Pour into dessert dishes. Cool slightly and chill.

4 servings.

*Do not use soft-type margarine in this recipe.

VARIATIONS

■ *Butterscotch Pudding:* Substitute ⅔ cup brown sugar (packed) for the granulated sugar and decrease vanilla to 1 teaspoon.

■ *Chocolate Pudding:* Increase sugar to ½ cup and stir ⅓ cup cocoa into sugar-cornstarch mixture. Omit butter.

MOCK CRÈME BRÛLÉE

The original Crème Brûlée was spooned over fruit in dessert dishes.

1 package (about 3 ounces)
vanilla pudding and pie
filling

½ cup chilled whipping
cream
½ cup brown sugar (packed)

Cook pudding and pie filling as directed on package. Press plastic wrap on top of pudding; cool to room temperature. Stir pudding once or twice.

In chilled bowl, beat cream until stiff. Fold into pudding. Pour into ungreased 9-inch pie pan. Sprinkle brown sugar evenly on pudding.

Set oven control at broil and/or 550°. Broil pudding about 5 inches from heat about 1 minute or until sugar melts and begins to caramelize. Chill at least 2 hours. Carefully spoon pudding into dessert dishes.

6 to 8 servings.

POT DE CRÈME AU CHOCOLAT

A smooth chocolate custard cream from France. So rich that very small portions are served.

1 bar (4 ounces) sweet
cooking chocolate
2 tablespoons sugar

¾ cup light cream (20%)
2 egg yolks, slightly beaten
½ teaspoon vanilla

Heat chocolate, sugar and cream over medium heat, stirring constantly, until chocolate is melted and mixture is smooth. Gradually beat into egg yolks. Stir in vanilla.

Pour into demitasse cups or other small dessert dishes. Chill. If desired, garnish with whipped cream.

4 to 6 servings.

VARIATION

■ *Pot de Crème Mousse:* Decrease sugar to 1 tablespoon and the cream to ½ cup. Beat 2 egg whites until foamy. Beat in ¼ cup sugar, 1 tablespoon at a time; continue beating until stiff and glossy. Fold into chocolate mixture. 6 to 8 servings.

TAPIOCA CREAM

2 egg yolks, slightly beaten
2 cups milk
2 tablespoons sugar
2 tablespoons quick-cooking tapioca
¼ teaspoon salt
1 teaspoon vanilla
2 egg whites
¼ cup sugar
Light cream or whipped cream

Combine egg yolks, milk, 2 tablespoons sugar, the tapioca and salt in saucepan. Cook over low heat, stirring constantly, until mixture boils. Cool slightly and chill. Stir in vanilla.

Beat egg whites until foamy. Beat in ¼ cup sugar, 1 tablespoon at a time; continue beating until stiff and glossy. Fold into tapioca mixture.

If desired, fresh or drained canned fruit can be folded into pudding or pudding can be poured over fruit in dessert dishes. Serve with light cream.

6 servings.

AMBROSIA TAPIOCA

½ cup sugar
¼ cup quick-cooking tapioca
Dash salt
2½ cups orange juice
1 cup orange sections
¼ cup chopped dates
¼ cup flaked coconut

Combine sugar, tapioca, salt and orange juice in medium saucepan. Let stand 5 minutes. Cook over medium heat, stirring constantly, until mixture boils.

Cool slightly. Stir in orange sections and dates. Chill at least 1 hour. Just before serving, spoon tapioca into dessert dishes and sprinkle with flaked coconut.

6 servings.

VANILLA DELUXE PUDDING

Beat 1 cup dairy sour cream and 1 cup milk with rotary beater until smooth. Add 1 package (about 3½ ounces) vanilla instant pudding; beat until smooth and slightly thickened. Pour into dessert dishes. Chill 15 to 20 minutes or until set.

4 servings.

RICE PUDDING

A hearty pudding that calls for instant rice.

½ cup water
½ cup uncooked instant rice
3 eggs, slightly beaten
½ cup sugar
2 teaspoons vanilla

¼ teaspoon salt
2½ cups milk, scalded
½ cup raisins, if desired
Cinnamon

Heat oven to 350°. Heat water to boiling. Remove from heat; stir in rice. Cover and let stand about 5 minutes.

Blend eggs, sugar, vanilla and salt. Gradually stir in milk. Mix in rice and raisins. Pour into ungreased 1½-quart casserole; sprinkle rice mixture with cinnamon. Place casserole in square pan 9x9x2 inches; pour very hot water (1¼ inches deep) into pan.

Bake about 70 minutes or until knife inserted halfway between center and edge comes out clean. Remove casserole from water. Serve pudding warm or cool. If desired, serve with Cinnamon-Blueberry Sauce (page 318) or Cherry Topping (page 309).

6 to 8 servings.

BAKED RICE PUDDING

½ cup uncooked regular
rice
1 cup water
½ cup sugar
1 tablespoon cornstarch
Dash salt

2 eggs, separated
2½ cups milk
1 tablespoon lemon juice
½ cup raisins
¼ cup sugar

Stir together rice and water in saucepan. Heat to boiling, stirring once or twice. Reduce heat; cover and simmer 14 minutes without removing cover or stirring. All water should be absorbed.

Heat oven to 350°. Blend ½ cup sugar, the cornstarch and salt. Beat egg yolks slightly. Add yolks and milk to sugar-cornstarch mixture; beat with rotary beater. Stir in rice, lemon juice and raisins. Pour into ungreased 1½-quart casserole. Place casserole in pan of very hot water (1 inch deep). Bake about 1½ hours, stirring occasionally, or until pudding is creamy and most of liquid is absorbed. Remove casserole from oven but not from pan of hot water.

Increase oven temperature to 400°. Beat egg whites until foamy. Beat in ¼ cup sugar, 1 tablespoon at a time; continue beating until stiff and glossy. Spread on pudding. Bake 8 to 10 minutes or until meringue is golden brown. Serve warm.

6 to 8 servings.

Note: If desired, omit meringue. Just before serving, sprinkle pudding with cinnamon or nutmeg.

GLORIFIED RICE

1 cup cooked rice, cooled	2 tablespoons drained
⅓ cup sugar	chopped maraschino
1 can (13½ ounces)	cherries
crushed pineapple,	1 cup chilled whipping
drained	cream, whipped
½ teaspoon vanilla	
⅓ cup miniature	
marshmallows	

Mix rice, sugar, pineapple and vanilla. Stir in marshmallows and cherries. Fold in whipped cream.

6 to 8 servings.

Quick 'n Easy
CHOCOLATE DELUXE PUDDING

A creamy rich dessert—quick to make for unexpected guests.

In large mixer bowl, blend 1 package (4½ ounces) chocolate instant pudding and 1 cup milk on low speed. Add 2 cups chilled whipping cream; beat about 2 minutes medium speed or until soft peaks form. Pour into dessert dishes. Chill at least 15 to 20 minutes. Garnish with whipped cream or chocolate curls.

6 to 8 servings.

Note: If desired, dessert topping mix can be substituted for the whipping cream: Beat 2 cups cold milk and 1 envelope (about 2 ounces) dessert topping mix about 2 minutes or until mixture begins to thicken. Gradually blend in 1 package (4½ ounces) chocolate instant pudding; continue beating about 3 minutes or until soft peaks form.

BAKED PRUNE WHIP

A lovely light dessert.

1 cup cut-up cooked prunes
3 egg whites
⅓ cup sugar
¼ teaspoon salt
1 tablespoon lemon juice

¼ cup chopped pecans
Sweetened whipped cream
or Creamy Stirred Custard
(page 287)

Heat oven to 350°. Beat prunes, egg whites, sugar and salt until stiff. Fold in lemon juice and pecans. Pour into ungreased 1½-quart casserole. Place casserole in pan of very hot water (1 inch deep).

Bake 30 to 35 minutes or until puffed and thin film has formed on top. Serve warm with whipped cream.

4 to 6 servings.

DELUXE BREAD PUDDING

A departure from the usual method. Toasted bread slices are spread with butter, brown sugar and cinnamon, topped with custard mixture, then baked.

4 slices bread
2 tablespoons butter or
margarine
⅓ cup brown sugar (packed)
½ teaspoon cinnamon
⅓ cup raisins

3 eggs, slightly beaten
⅓ cup granulated sugar
1 teaspoon vanilla
Dash salt
2½ cups milk, scalded

Heat oven to 350°. Butter 1½-quart casserole. Toast bread slices lightly. Spread with butter; sprinkle with brown sugar and then cinnamon. Put 2 toast slices together, making 2 sandwiches. Remove crusts; cut each sandwich into 4 rectangles. Arrange rectangles in single layer in casserole; sprinkle with raisins.

Blend eggs, granulated sugar, vanilla and salt. Gradually stir in milk; pour over toast rectangles. Place casserole in pan of very hot water (1 inch deep). Bake 65 to 70 minutes or until knife inserted halfway between center and edge comes out clean. Remove casserole from water. Serve pudding warm or cool.

6 to 8 servings.

INDIAN PUDDING

3 cups milk
⅔ cup dark molasses
⅔ cup yellow cornmeal
⅓ cup sugar
1 teaspoon salt

¾ teaspoon cinnamon
¾ teaspoon nutmeg
¼ cup butter or margarine
1 cup milk

Heat oven to 300°. Grease 2-quart casserole. Heat 3 cups milk and the molasses. Mix cornmeal, sugar, salt, cinnamon and nutmeg. Gradually stir into hot milk mixture. Add butter. Cook over low heat, stirring constantly, about 10 minutes or until thickened. Pour into casserole. Pour 1 cup milk over pudding; do not stir. Bake 3 hours. If desired, serve with cream, ice cream or whipped cream.

8 servings.

LEMON PUDDING CAKE

2 eggs, separated
1 teaspoon grated lemon
  peel
¼ cup lemon juice

⅔ cup milk
1 cup sugar
¼ cup all-purpose flour*
¼ teaspoon salt

Heat oven to 350°. Beat egg whites until stiff peaks form; set aside. Beat egg yolks. Blend in lemon peel, juice and milk. Add sugar, flour and salt; beat until smooth. Fold into whites. Pour into ungreased 1-quart casserole. Place casserole in pan of very hot water (1 inch deep).

Bake 45 to 50 minutes. Serve warm or cool and, if desired, with whipped cream.

6 servings.

*If using self-rising flour, omit salt.

HOT FUDGE PUDDING CAKE

1 cup all-purpose-flour*
¾ cup granulated sugar
2 tablespoons cocoa
2 tablespoons baking powder
¼ teaspoon salt
½ cup milk

2 tablespoons shortening,
  melted
1 cup finely chopped nuts
1 cup brown sugar (packed)
¼ cup cocoa
1¾ cups hot water

Heat oven to 350°. Measure flour, granulated sugar,

*If using self-rising flour, omit baking powder and salt.

2 tablespoons cocoa, the baking powder and salt into bowl. Blend in milk and shortening; stir in nuts. Pour into ungreased square pan, 9x2x2 inches. Stir together brown sugar and ¼ cup cocoa; sprinkle over batter. Pour *hot* water over batter.

Bake 45 minutes. While warm, spoon cake into dessert dishes and spoon sauce over each serving. If, desired, serve with sweetened whipped cream or ice cream.

9 servings.

DELUXE ENGLISH TRIFLE

An elegant spoon-up finish for any dinner.

Buttermilk baking mix
½ cup raspberry jam
⅓ cup sherry
1 package (about 3 ounces) vanilla pudding and pie filling
⅓ cup toasted slivered almonds
¾ cup chilled whipping cream
3 tablespoons confectioners' sugar
Chopped candied cherries

Bake Velvet Crumb Cake in square pan, 8x8x2 inches, as directed on package of baking mix. Cool. Carefully split cake to make 2 layers. Fill with raspberry jam. Cut into 9 or 12 pieces. Arrange pieces in baking dish, 11½ x 7½ x 1½ inches. Sprinkle with wine.

Cook pudding and pie filling as directed on package except—increase milk to 2½ cups. Cool to room temperature. Pour pudding over cake; sprinkle with almonds.

In chilled bowl, beat cream and confectioners' sugar until stiff; spread on cake in baking dish. Chill at least 4 hours. Garnish with cherries; cut into servings.

9 to 12 servings.

DATE CRÈME CRUNCH PARFAIT

Heat oven to 400°. Mix thoroughly ¼ cup butter or margarine and the crumbly mix from 1 package (14 ounces) date bar mix. Spread in baking pan, 13x9x2 inches.

Bake 10 to 12 minutes or until golden brown. Remove from oven; crumble. Cool.

Cook 1 package (about 3 ounces) vanilla pudding and pie filling as directed on package. Stir in 1 teaspoon vanilla; cool slightly. Stir ⅓ cup hot water into date filling.

Beginning and ending with crumbled mixture, alternate layers of crumbled mixture, date filling and pudding in parfait glasses or dessert dishes. Chill. If desired, top with sweetened whipped cream.

4 to 6 servings.

Quick 'n Easy
DATE PUDDING

After your family has enjoyed this wonderfully rich, chewy date pudding, they'll ask for it often.

3 eggs	2½ cups chopped dates
1 cup sugar	1 cup finely chopped nuts
¼ cup all-purpose flour*	Sweetened whipped
1 teaspoon baking powder	cream
¼ teaspoon salt	

Heat oven to 350°. Grease square pan, 9x9x2 inches. Beat eggs until light and fluffy. Gradually add sugar, beating until very thick. Mix in flour, baking powder and salt. Stir in dates and nuts. Pour into pan.

Bake 30 minutes. Serve warm with whipped cream.

9 to 12 servings.

If using self-rising flour, decrease baking powder to ½ teaspoon.

STEAMED DATE PUDDING

½ cup hot water	½ teaspoon mace
1 package (14 ounces)	½ teaspoon cinnamon
date bar mix	¼ teaspoon nutmeg
2 eggs	Hard Sauce (page 299)
½ cup finely chopped nuts	

Grease well a 3-cup oven-proof glass bowl. Stir together water and date filling. Mix in crumbly mix, eggs, nuts, mace, cinnamon and nutmeg. Pour into bowl. Cover with aluminum foil.

Place rack in saucepan and pour boiling water into pan up to level of rack. Place bowl or pudding on rack. Cover saucepan. Keep water boiling over low heat to steam pudding 2 hours. (If it is necessary to add water during steaming, lift lid and quickly add boiling water.)

Remove foil and let pudding stand about 5 minutes before removing from bowl. Cut into wedges; serve warm with Hard Sauce.

8 servings.

ENGLISH PLUM PUDDING

Our best plum pudding. To reheat, wrap pudding in aluminum foil and heat in 350° oven, 1 hour.

1 cup all-purpose flour*
1 teaspoon soda
1 teaspoon salt
1 teaspoon cinnamon
¾ teaspoon mace
¼ teaspoon nutmeg
1½ cups cut-up raisins (½ pound)
2 cups currants (½ pound)
¾ cup finely cut-up citron (¼ pound)
⅓ cup each cut-up candied orange and candied lemon peel
½ cup finely chopped walnuts
1½ cups soft bread crumbs
2 cups ground suet (½ pound)
1 cup brown sugar (packed)
3 eggs, beaten
⅓ cup currant jelly
¼ cup fruit juice
Hard Sauce (right)

Grease well 2-quart ring mold or turk's head mold. Measure flour, soda, salt, cinnamon, mace and nutmeg into large bowl. Stir in fruits, nuts and bread crumbs. Mix suet, brown sugar, eggs, jelly and fruit juice. Stir into flour-fruit mixture. Pour into mold. Cover mold with aluminum foil.

Place rack in Dutch oven and pour boiling water into pan up to level of rack. Place filled mold on rack. Cover Dutch oven. Keep water boiling over low heat to steam pudding 4 hours or until wooden pick inserted in center comes out clean. (If it is necessary to add water during steaming, lift lid and quickly add boiling water.) Unmold; cut into slices and serve with Hard Sauce.

16 servings.

*If using self-rising flour, decrease soda to ½ teaspoon.

Note: For a good old-fashioned flaming pudding, pour heated brandy on unmolded pudding and light with a match.

HARD SAUCE

½ cup butter or margarine, softened

1 cup confectioners' sugar
2 teaspoons vanilla

Mix thoroughly all ingredients. If desired, for a fluffier sauce, beat 1 egg white until stiff peaks form; blend into sauce. Chill at least 1 hour.

Crêpes and Soufflés

What do you do about crêpes, soufflés and blintzes? Write them off as the "things other people cook"? Not if you can read. These recipes have been so well tested, you just can't fail!

CRÊPES

1½ cups all-purpose flour*
1 tablespoon sugar
½ teaspoon baking powder
½ teaspoon salt
2 cups milk

2 eggs
½ teaspoon vanilla
2 tablespoons butter or margarine, melted

Measure flour, sugar, baking powder and salt into bowl. Stir in remaining ingredients. Beat with rotary beater until smooth.

For each crêpe, lightly butter 8-inch skillet; heat over medium heat until butter is bubbly. Pour scant ¼ cup of the batter into skillet; immediately rotate pan until batter covers bottom. Cook until light brown; turn and brown on other side.

If desired, while warm spread applesauce, sweetened strawberries, currant jelly or raspberry jam thinly on crêpes; roll up. Sprinkle with sugar.

12 crêpes.

*If using self-rising flour, omit baking powder and salt.

Note: A larger skillet can be used if necessary.

CRÊPES SUZETTE

Crêpes (page 299)
⅔ cup butter or margarine
¾ teaspoon grated orange peel

⅔ cup orange juice
¼ cup sugar
⅓ cup brandy
⅓ cup orange liqueur

Prepare Crêpes. When removing from griddle, stack so first baked side is down. Cool, keeping crêpes covered to prevent them from drying out.

In 10-inch skillet, heat butter, orange peel and juice and sugar to boiling, stirring occasionally. Boil and stir 1 minute. Reduce heat and simmer.

In small saucepan, heat brandy and orange liqueur, but do not boil. To assemble Crêpes Suzette, fold crêpes into fourths; place in hot orange sauce and turn once. Arrange crêpes around edge of skillet. Pour warm brandy mixture into center of skillet and ignite. Spoon flaming sauce over crêpes. Place 2 crêpes on each dessert plate; spoon sauce over.

6 servings.

CHERRY BLINTZES

Crêpes (page 299)
1 cup dry cottage cheese
½ cup dairy sour cream
1 to 2 tablespoons sugar
½ teaspoon grated lemon peel

1 teaspoon vanilla
¼ cup butter or margarine
1 cup dairy sour cream
1 can (1 pound 5 ounces) cherry pie filling

Prepare Crêpes except—brown only on one side. Cool, keeping crêpes covered to prevent them from drying out.

Blend cottage cheese, ½ cup sour cream, the sugar, lemon peel and vanilla. Place about 1½ tablespoons of the cheese mixture in center of browned side of each crêpe. Fold sides of crêpe up over filling, overlapping edges; roll up.

In skillet, melt butter over medium heat until bubbly. Place blintzes, seam side down, in skillet. Cook until golden brown, turning once. Top each with rounded tablespoon of sour cream and about 3 tablespoons of the pie filling.

12 servings.

CHOCOLATE SOUFFLÉ

Even those who shy away from cheese or vegetable soufflés are sure to enjoy this delicious dessert version.

½ cup sugar
2 tablespoons cornstarch
1 cup milk
2 squares (1 ounce each) unsweetened chocolate*
3 egg yolks

2 tablespoons butter or margarine, softened
1 teaspoon vanilla
4 egg whites
½ teaspoon salt
¼ teaspoon cream of tartar

Blend sugar and cornstarch in small saucepan. Gradually stir in milk; add chocolate. Cook over medium heat, stirring constantly, until chocolate is melted and mixture thickens and boils. Boil and stir 1 minute. Remove from heat.

In small mixer bowl, beat egg yolks until very thick and lemon colored. Gradually beat in chocolate mixture. Stir in butter and vanilla. Cool to room temperature.

Heat oven to 350°. Butter and sugar a 6-cup soufflé dish. Make 4-inch band of triple thickness aluminum foil 2 inches longer than circumference of dish; butter one side and sprinkle with sugar. Extend depth of dish by securing foil band, buttered side in, around top of dish. (A buttered and sugared 2-quart casserole can be used instead of soufflé dish and foil band.)

In large mixer bowl, beat egg whites, salt and cream of tartar just until stiff peaks form. Stir about ¼ of egg whites into chocolate mixture. Gently fold in remaining whites. Carefully pour into dish.

Bake 50 minutes or until knife inserted halfway between center and edge comes out clean. *Serve immediately.* Carefully remove foil band and divide soufflé into sections with 2 forks. If desired, serve with sweetened whipped cream, Creamy Stirred Custard (page 287) or Hard Sauce (page 299).

6 servings.

*Do not use premelted chocolate.

Note: Do not be alarmed if cracks appear on the top; they are characteristic of this recipe.

RASPBERRY CROWN ROYAL

A spectacular finale for a gourmet meal. Well worth the extra time and effort.

2 envelopes unflavored gelatin	Dash salt
3 tablespoons granulated sugar	¼ cup granulated sugar
3 packages (10 ounces each) frozen raspberries, partially thawed and broken apart	1 teaspoon unflavored gelatin
	3 tablespoons water
	3 cups chilled whipping cream
1 tablespoon lemon juice	1 tablespoon confectioners' sugar
5 egg whites	

Extend depth of 7½-cup soufflé dish by securing 4-inch band of double thickness aluminum foil around top. In saucepan, blend 2 envelopes gelatin and 3 tablespoons granulated sugar. Stir in raspberries and lemon juice. If desired, reserve few whole berries for garnish. Heat, stirring constantly, until gelatin is dissolved and mixture boils. Chill until mixture mounds slightly when dropped from spoon.

Beat egg whites and salt until foamy. Gradually beat in ¼ cup granulated sugar, 1 tablespoon at a time; continue beating until stiff and glossy.

Sprinkle the 1 teaspoon gelatin in the water to soften; place over boiling water to dissolve. In chilled bowl, beat cream, confectioners' sugar and dissolved gelatin until soft peaks form.

Reserve 1 cup whipped cream mixture; cover and refrigerate. Fold egg whites and half the remaining whipped cream mixture into raspberry mixture; spoon into soufflé dish just until even with rim of dish.

Ending with the remaining raspberry mixture, alternate thin layers of other half of the whipped cream mixture and raspberry mixture. Chill at least 8 hours.

Just before serving, run edge of knife around inside of foil band and remove band. Place reserved whipped cream in decorators' tube; decorate top of soufflé. If desired, garnish with reserved raspberries. Serve each person both the raspberry and cream portions of soufflé.

10 to 12 servings.

Pastry Desserts

Today you don't have to be a master chef to create flaky, tender puff paste. Modern know-how and easy-to-follow directions have put this art well within the ability of everyone.

STREAMLINED PUFF PASTRY DOUGH

Here's our new, simplified version of puff pastry—so easy that even beginners can do it.

1 cup butter   ½ cup dairy sour cream
1½ cups all-purpose flour*

Cut butter into flour until completely mixed. Stir in sour cream until thoroughly blended. Divide dough in half; wrap each and chill at least 8 hours.

Heat oven to 350°. Roll pastry on well-floured cloth-covered board as directed in the recipes below and on pages 304–305. Chill scraps before rerolling.

*Self-rising flour can be used in this recipe. Baking time may be shorter.

JAM TARTLETS

Roll each of the pastry ⅟₁₆ inch thick; cut into 2-inch shapes. Cut small hole in center of half the shapes. Brush with mixture of 3 tablespoons sugar and 1 tablespoon water; place on top of plain shapes. Fill hole with about ½ teaspoon jam. Bake on ungreased baking sheet about 20 minutes. About 3½ dozen tartlets.

FLAKY PASTRY FANS

Roll each half of the pastry into rectangle, 16x8 inches, on sugared cloth-covered board. Fold ends to meet in middle, forming a square. Sprinkle with sugar. Fold in folded edges to meet in center and pinch these edges together to make center seam. Fold in half to form a square (as if closing a book). Flatten lightly; fold in half again in the same direction. (See Parmesan Fans, page 19.) Cutting parallel to folded edge, cut dough into ¼-inch slices. Place on ungreased baking sheet, fanning out each slice. Sprinkle with sugar. Bake 20 to 25 minutes. About 2 dozen fans.

NAPOLEONS

Roll half the pastry into rectangle, 12x10 inches. Cut into 15 rectangles, each 4x2 inches. Brush with mixture of 3 tablespoons sugar and 1 tablespoon water. Bake on ungreased baking sheet 15 to 18 minutes or until light brown. Repeat with second half of the pastry. Cool.

Mix 1 cup confectioners' sugar and 1 tablespoon milk; spread on 10 of the rectangles. Drizzle 1 ounce melted semisweet chocolate on frosted rectangles. Prepare 1 package (4½ ounces) chocolate instant pudding as directed on package except—substitute ½ cup dairy sour cream for ½ cup of the milk. Put 3 rectangles together with 1 tablespoon pudding between each. Top layer should be frosted. 10 napoleons.

CREAM-FILLED LEAVES

Roll each half the pastry ⅟₁₆ inch thick; cut with 3½-inch fluted leaf cutter. Brush with mixture of 3 tablespoons sugar and 1 tablespoon water. Bake on ungreased baking sheet 15 to 20 minutes. Cool.

Top one leaf with Rum-flavored Whipped Cream: In chilled bowl, beat 1 cup chilled whipping cream, ¼ cup confectioners' sugar and ½ teaspoon rum flavoring until stiff. Place another leaf on top. Decorate with dot of whipped cream and maraschino cherries or chocolate curls. 12 leaves.

FRUITED CHEESE TARTLETS

Roll half the pastry ⅟₁₆ inch thick; cut into rounds with plain or scalloped cutter. In ⅔ of rounds, cut out 1-inch circles. Place plain rounds on ungreased baking sheet. Brush with mixture of 3 tablespoons sugar and 1 tablespoon water. Top each with a round with center removed; brush with glaze and top with another round with center removed (3 layers—1 plain, 2 with centers removed). Roll second half of the pastry in same manner. Bake about 25 minutes or until light brown. Cool.

Soften 2 packages (3 ounces each) cream cheese in bowl; beat in 1 cup dairy sour cream, 1 tablespoon sugar and about ¼ teaspoon pumpkin pie spice. Spoon into shells; top each with fresh fruit dipped in sugar or dot with jam.

About 3 dozen tartlets.

CREAM PUFFS

Easier mixing—eggs are added all at one time instead of one by one. Cream puffs are surprisingly easy to make—and they can be done well in advance.

1 cup water	Vanilla Cream Pudding
½ cup butter or margarine	(page 289) or sweetened
1 cup all-purpose flour	whipped cream
4 eggs	Confectioners' sugar

Heat oven to 400°. Heat water and butter to rolling boil. Stir in flour. Stir vigorously over low heat about 1 minute or until mixture forms a ball. Remove from heat. Beat in eggs, all at one time; continue beating until smooth. Drop dough by scant ¼ cupfulls 3 inches apart onto ungreased baking sheet.

Bake 35 to 40 minutes or until puffed and golden. Cool away from draft. Cut off tops. Pull out any filaments of soft dough. Carefully fill puffs with Vanilla Cream Pudding. Replace tops; dust with confectioners' sugar. Refrigerate until serving time.

12 cream puffs.

VARIATIONS

■ *Chocolate Eclairs:* Shape dough by ¼ cupfuls into "fingers," 4½ inches long and 1½ inches wide. Bake. When cool, fill with Vanilla Cream Pudding (page 289).

Frost with Chocolate Icing: Melt 1 ounce unsweetened chocolate and 1 teaspoon butter over low heat. Remove from heat; stir in 1 cup confectioners' sugar and about 2 tablespoons hot water. Beat until smooth. Refrigerate eclairs until serving time.

12 eclairs.

■ *Petits Choux (Midget Puffs):* Drop dough by slightly rounded teaspoonfuls onto ungreased baking sheet. Bake 25 to 30 minutes.

About 5 dozen puffs.

■ *Quick Cream Puffs:* Fill Cream Puffs with your favorite flavor ice cream or fruit pie filling or with Pudding Cream Filling: In small mixer bowl, blend 1 package (about 3½ ounces) vanilla instant pudding and 1 cup milk on low speed. Add 2 cups chilled whipping cream; beat about 2 minutes medium speed or until soft peaks form.

12 cream puffs.

SUNDAE BUBBLE CROWN

Bake Petits Choux (page 305). Prepare Chocolate Fudge Sauce (below); cool to room temperature. When ready to assemble crown, soften 2 quarts vanilla ice cream. In 10-inch tube pan with removable bottom, place a layer of cream puffs. Spread with 1 quart of the ice cream. Repeat layers of puffs, ice cream and puffs. Drizzle ½ cup sauce over top. Freeze 8 hours or until firm.

Remove from freezer about 15 minutes before serving. To remove crown from pan, loosen around edge with spatula and push bottom up and out of pan. With two broad spatulas, lift crown from bottom of pan and place on serving plate. Cut into slices and serve with remaining fudge sauce.

16 servings.

CHOCOLATE FUDGE SAUCE

In top of double boiler, combine 1 package (15.4 ounces) chocolate fudge frosting mix (dry), 2 tablespoons light corn syrup and 3 tablespoons butter or margarine. Slowly stir in ⅔ cup milk. Heat over boiling water 5 minutes, stirring occasionally.

DREAM PUFF SUNDAES

Petits Choux (page 305)　　　½ cup confectioners' sugar
1 quart vanilla ice cream　　　Chocolate Sauce
2 cups chilled whipping　　　(page 307)
　　cream

Bake Petits Choux. Cool slowly away from draft. Cut off tops with sharp knife. Scoop out any filaments of soft dough; fill each generously with ice cream. Place in freezer; place half the puffs in 4-quart bowl. Spoon half the whipped cream over puffs; fold gently to combine puffs and cream. Repeat with remaining puffs and cream. Pour into 3-quart bowl. Drizzle Chocolate Sauce over top; swirl to give marbled effect.

12 to 14 servings.

CHOCOLATE SAUCE

In top of double boiler, heat ½ cup light cream (20%) and 1½ bars (4 ounces each) sweet cooking chocolate over boiling water until chocolate melts. Beat until smooth; cool.

Meringue Desserts

Make your own meringues! What do you do with those extra egg whites you put in the refrigerator? Make meringues, of course. Crackly, angel-white meringues to fill with ice cream or fruit or custard. Meringue tortes to serve at a party. They take a while to bake—but the results are well worth the time.

MERINGUE SHELL

To make meringues of special shapes, draw outline on brown paper, spoon meringue into outline.

Heat oven to 275°. Cover baking sheet with heavy brown paper. Beat 3 egg whites (⅓ to ½ cup) and ¼

Use back of spoon to shape individual Meringue Shells.

teaspoon cream of tartar until foamy. Beat in ¾ cup sugar, 1 tablespoon at a time; continue beating until stiff and glossy. Do not underbeat. On brown paper, shape meringue into 9-inch circle, building up side.

Bake 1½ hours. Turn off oven; leave meringue in oven with door closed 1 hour. Remove from oven; finish cooling meringue away from draft. Fill with ice cream and top with fresh berries, cut-up fruit, chocolate or butterscotch sauce.

8 to 10 servings.

VARIATION

■ *Individual Meringue Shells:* Drop meringue by ⅓ cupfuls onto brown paper. Shape mounds into circles, building up sides. Bake 1 hour. Turn off oven; leave meringues in oven with door closed 1½ hours. Remove from oven; finish cooling meringues away from draft.

8 to 10 shells.

LEMON SCHAUM TORTE

Meringue Shell (page 307)
¾ cup sugar
3 tablespoons cornstarch
¼ teaspoon salt
¾ cup water
3 egg yolks, slightly beaten
1 tablespoon butter or margarine
1 teaspoon grated lemon peel
⅓ cup lemon juice
1 cup chilled whipping cream

Bake Meringue Shell. Mix sugar, cornstarch and salt in medium saucepan. Stir in water gradually. Cook over medium heat, stirring constantly, until mixture thickens and boils. Boil and stir 1 minute. Stir at least half the hot mixture gradually into egg yolks. Blend into hot mixture in pan. Boil and stir 1 minute.

Remove from heat; stir in butter, lemon peel and lemon juice. Cool to room temperature. Spoon into shell. Chill at least 12 hours. In chilled bowl, beat cream until stiff; spread on filling.

8 to 10 servings.

CHOCOLATE MERINGUE TORTE

Meringue Shell (page 307)
⅔ cup granulated sugar
2 tablespoons cornstarch
⅛ teaspoon salt
3 egg yolks, slightly beaten
1½ cups milk

2 ounces unsweetened chocolate
1 teaspoon vanilla
1 cup chilled whipping cream
¼ cup confectioners' sugar

Bake Meringue Shell. Blend granulated sugar, cornstarch and salt in medium saucepan. Combine egg yolks and milk; gradually stir into sugar mixture. Add chocolate. Cook over medium heat, stirring constantly, until chocolate melts and mixture thickens and boils. Boil and stir 1 minute. Remove from heat; stir in vanilla. Cool to room temperature; chill 1 hour. Spoon into shell. Chill at least 12 hours.

In chilled bowl, beat cream and confectioners' sugar until stiff; spread on filling.

8 to 10 servings.

CHERRY BERRIES ON A CLOUD

Meringue Shell (page 307)
1 package (3 ounces) cream cheese, softened
½ cup sugar
½ teaspoon vanilla
1 cup chilled whipping cream or 1 envelope (about 2 ounces) dessert topping mix

1 cup miniature marshmallows
Cherry Topping (below)

Bake Meringue Shell. Blend cream cheese, sugar and vanilla. in chilled bowl, beat cream until stiff. (If using dessert topping mix, prepare as directed on package.)

Gently fold whipped cream and the marshmallows into cream cheese mixture. Pile into shell. Cover; chill at least 12 hours. Just before serving, top with Cherry Topping; cut into wedges.

6 to 8 servings.

CHERRY TOPPING

Stir together 1 can (1 pound 5 ounces) cherry-pie filling and 1 teaspoon lemon juice.

Refrigerated and Frozen Desserts

A dessert that's ready and waiting—what a boon to a working wife or an impromptu hostess! And what a temptation to a refrigerator raider! Smooth and appealing, these delicious delights disappear faster than fast. But happily their ease of preparation encourages the cook to make them often.

STRAWBERRY BAVARIAN CREAM

Light and colorful—always a favorite with children and adults. A delightful do-ahead dessert.

1 package (10 ounces) frozen sliced strawberries, thawed
1 cup boiling water
1 package (3 ounces) strawberry-flavored gelatin

1 cup chilled whipping cream or 1 envelope (about 2 ounces) dessert topping mix

Drain strawberries, reserving syrup. Pour boiling water over gelatin in bowl, stirring until gelatin is dissolved. Add enough cold water to reserved syrup to measure 1 cup; stir into dissolved gelatin. Chill until almost set.

In chilled bowl, beat cream until stiff. (If using dessert topping mix, prepare as directed on package.) Beat gelatin until foamy. Fold gelatin and strawberries into whipped cream.

Pour into 1-quart mold or into individual molds. Chill until firm. Unmold; if desired, serve with sweetened whipped cream or Creamy Stirred Custard (page 287) and garnish with strawberries or other fruits.

6 to 8 sevings.

VARIATIONS

■ *Pineapple Bavarian Cream:* Substitute 1 can (8½ ounces) crushed pineapple, drained, for the strawberries and 1 package (3 ounces) lemon-flavored gelatin for the strawberry-flavored gelatin.

■ *Raspberry Bavarian Cream:* Substitute 1 package

(10 ounces) frozen raspberries for the strawberries and 1 package (3 ounces) raspberry-flavored gelatin for the strawberry-flavored gelatin.

CHOCOLATE PEPPERMINT DREAM

1½ cups chocolate wafer crumbs (about 25 wafers)
3 tablespoons butter or margarine, melted
24 large marshmallows or 2¼ cups miniature marshmallows
½ cup milk
1 teaspoon vanilla

⅛ teaspoon salt
6 drops peppermint extract
6 drops red food color
1 cup chilled whipping cream or 1 envelope (about 2 ounces) dessert topping mix
2 tablespoons crushed peppermint candy

Mix wafer crumbs and butter thoroughly. Press mixture evenly in bottom of square pan, 8x8x2 inches.

Heat marshmallows and milk over medium heat, stirring constantly, until marshmallows are melted. Remove from heat; stir in vanilla, salt, peppermint extract and food color. Chill until thickened.

In chilled bowl, beat cream until stiff. (If using dessert topping mix, prepare as directed on package.) Blend in marshmallow mixture. Pour over crumb crust. Cover; chill at least 12 hours. Just before serving, sprinkle with candy.

9 servings.

PINEAPPLE REFRIGERATOR DESSERT

A delicious treat for the whole family—each forkful calls for another. And don't overlook the apricot and banana variations.

1¼ cups graham cracker crumbs (about 16 crackers)
2 tablespoons granulated sugar
¼ cup butter or margarine, melted
½ cup butter or margarine, softened
1 cup confectioners' sugar
1 egg

1 cup chilled whipping cream or 1 envelope (about 2 ounces) dessert topping mix
1 can (1 pound 4½ ounces) crushed pineapple, well drained
Sweetened whipped cream
Maraschino cherries

Mix thoroughly graham cracker crumbs, granulated

sugar and melted butter. Press half the crumb mixture evenly in bottom of square pan, 8x8x2 inches.

In small mixer bowl, beat ½ cup butter, the confectioners' sugar and egg until mixture is light and fluffy. Spread carefully and evenly over crumbs in pan.

In chilled bowl, beat cream until stiff. (If using dessert topping mix, prepare as directed on package.) Fold in crushed pineapple. Spread over butter mixture. Sprinkle with remaining graham cracker crumbs. Cover; chill at least 12 hours. Cut into squares; serve with whipped cream and maraschino cherries.

9 servings.

VARIATIONS

■ *Apricot Refrigerator Dessert.* Omit pineapple. Simmer 1 cup cut-up dried apricots (4 ounces) and 1 cup water, stirring occasionally, about 20 minutes or until apricots are tender and water is absorbed. Chop apricots until mushy; mix in ¼ cup sugar. Cool. Spread apricot mixture over butter mixture in pan. In chilled bowl, beat cream until stiff; spread on apricot layer.

■ *Banana Refrigerator Dessert:* Omit pineapple and spread on butter layer a mixture of ½ cup finely chopped nuts, 1 banana, mashed, and ¼ cup maraschino cherries, quartered and drained. In chilled bowl, beat cream until stiff; spread on fruit-nut layer.

CHOCOLATE DELIGHT

Delicious way to use leftover angel food cake

½ large angel food cake
1 package (6 ounces) semisweet chocolate pieces
4 eggs
1 cup chilled whipping cream or 1 envelope (about 2 ounces) dessert topping mix

1 teaspoon vanilla
¾ cup chopped nuts

Tear cake into small pieces. Place half the cake pieces in baking dish, 13½x9x2 inches.

In top of double boiler over hot water, melt chocolate pieces. Cool. Beat eggs until thick and lemon colored. Stir in chocolate.

In chilled bowl, beat cream until stiff. (If using dessert topping mix, prepare as directed on package.) Fold in chocolate mixture, vanilla and nuts. Pour half the chocolate mixture over cake pieces in baking dish. Cover with remaining cake pieces; pour remaining chocolate mixture over top. Cover; chill at least 12 hours. If desired, serve with whipped cream.

10 to 12 servings.

FROSTED MINT

Such a refreshing combination of flavors.

1 envelope unflavored gelatin
1 can (1 pound 4¼ ounces) crushed pineapple, drained (reserve ½ cup syrup)
⅓ cup mint-flavored apple jelly
3 drops green food color
1 cup chilled whipping cream*

In small saucepan, sprinkle gelatin on reserved syrup to soften; stir over low heat until gelatin is dissolved. Stir in jelly and food color. Cook over medium heat, stirring constantly, until jelly is melted. Stir in pineapple. Chill, stirring occasionally, until mixture mounds slightly when dropped from spoon.

In chilled bowl, beat cream until stiff. Fold in gelatin mixture. Pour into square pan. 8x8x2 inches, or into parfait glasses. Chill until firm.

6 to 8 servings.

*Do not substitute dessert topping mix for the whipped cream.

CRANBERRY ICE

1 pound cranberries
2 cups water
2 cups sugar
¼ cup lemon juice
1 teaspoon grated orange peel
2 cups cold water

Cook cranberries in 2 cups water about 10 minutes or until skins break. Rub berries through sieve to make smooth pulp. Stir in sugar, juice and peel. Stir in 2 cups cold water. Pour into baking dish, 8x8x2 inches. Freeze until firm, stirring 2 or 3 times to keep smooth. Let stand at room temperature 10 minutes before serving.

About 1 quart.

LEMON SHIVER

2 eggs
½ cup sugar
¼ cup light corn syrup
1 teaspoon grated lemon peel
Juice of 1 lemon (about 2 tablespoons)
Juice of 1 orange (about ⅓ cup)
1 cup light cream (20%)
½ cup milk

Beat eggs until silghtly thick and lemon colored. Mix in sugar and corn syrup. Beat in peel, lemon and orange juices, cream and milk. Pour into baking dish, 8x8x2 inches; freeze until mushy. Pour into bowl; beat with rotary beater. Return mixture to baking dish; freeze until firm.

1 quart.

FROZEN STRAWBERRY DESSERT

1 package (10 ounces) frozen sliced strawberries, thawed
1 cup sugar
1 egg white
¼ cup lemon juice
1 cup chilled whipping cream
Sweetened whipped cream

Beat strawberries (with syrup), sugar, egg white and lemon juice 5 minutes or until slightly thickened. In chilled bowl, beat cream until stiff; fold in strawberry mixture. Pour into baking dish, 8x8x2 inches. Cover and freeze until firm. Top with whipped cream.

6 to 8 servings.

BEST BAKED ALASKA

1 package (18.5 ounces) devils food cake mix
1 quart brick chocolate chip ice cream
4 egg whites
½ teaspoon cream of tartar
⅔ cup dark brown sugar (packed)

Heat oven to 350° Bake cake mix in 1 round layer pan. 9x1½ inches, and 1 square pan, 9x9x2 inches. Bake round layer 30 to 35 minutes* and square layer 25 to 30 minutes.

*Freeze rounded layer for other use.

Cover baking sheet with aluminum foil. Place cooled square cake on baking sheet. Place ice cream on cake. Leaving 1-inch edge, trim cake around ice cream. Freeze cake and ice cream.

Heat oven to 500°. Beat egg whites and cream of tartar until foamy. Beat in brown sugar, 1 tablespoon at a time; continue beating until stiff and glossy. Completely cover cake and ice cream with meringue, sealing it to foil on sheet. (If desired, it can be frozen up to 24 hours at this point.)

Bake on lowest rack in oven 3 to 5 minutes or until meringue is light brown. Trim foil to edge of meringue; transfer cake to serving plate. Cut into 6 slices; cut each slice in half. Serve immediately.

12 servings.

ORANGE MALLOW

32 large marshmallows or 3 cups miniature marshmallows
1 teaspoon grated orange peel
⅔ cup orange juice
1 cup chilled whipping cream or 1 envelope (about 2 ounces) dessert topping mix

Stir together marshmallows, orange peel and juice in saucepan. Cook over medium heat, stirring constantly, until marshmallows are melted. Chill until thickened.

In chilled bowl, beat cream until stiff. (If using dessert topping mix, prepare as directed on package.) Blend in marshmallow mixture. Pour into square pan, 8x8x2 inches. Freeze about 4 hours or until firm.

9 servings.

FRENCH VANILLA ICE CREAM

½ cup sugar
¼ teaspoon salt
1 cup milk
3 egg yolks, beaten
1 tablespoon vanilla
2 cups chilled whipping cream

For crank-type freezer: Mix sugar, salt, milk and egg yolks in saucepan. Cook over medium heat, stirring constantly, just until bubbles appear around edge of mixture in pan. Cool to room temperature. Stir in vanilla and cream.

Pour into freezer can; put dasher in place. Cover can and adjust crank. Place can in freezer tub. Fill freezer tub ⅓ full of ice; add remaining ice alternately with layers of rock salt (6 parts ice to 1 part rock salt). Turn crank until it turns with difficulty. Draw off water. Remove lid; take out dasher. Pack mixture down. Replace lid. Repack in ice and rock salt. Let ripen several hours.

For refrigerator: Mix sugar, salt, milk and egg yolks in saucepan. Cook over medium heat, stirring constantly, just until bubbles appear around edge of mixture in pan. Cool to room temperature. Stir in vanilla.

Pour into refrigerator tray. Freeze until mushy and partially frozen, ½ to 1 hour. In chilled bowl, beat cream until soft peaks form. Spoon partially frozen mixture into another chilled bowl; beat until smooth. Fold in whipped cream. Pour into 2 refrigerator trays; freeze 3 hours or until firm, stirring often during first hours. Cover with waxed paper to prevent crystals from forming.

1 quart.

VARIATIONS

■ *Chocolate Ice Cream:* Decrease vanilla to 1 teaspoon and increase sugar to 1 cup. Stir 2 squares (1 ounce each) unsweetened chocolate, melted,* into hot mixture in saucepan.

*Do not use premelted chocolate.

■ *Fresh Peach Ice Cream:* Decrease vanilla to 1 teaspoon. Mash 4 or 5 peeled ripe peaches to measure 2 cups. Mix ½ cup sugar with peaches. After adding cream, stir in peach mixture.

■ *Fresh Strawberry Ice Cream:* Decrease vanilla to 1 teaspoon. Mash 1 pint fresh strawberries with ½ cup sugar. After adding cream, stir in berries. If desired, add few drops red food color.

■ *Frozen Custard Ice Cream:* Decrease salt to ⅛ teaspoon and whipping cream to 1 cup.

■ *Frozen Strawberry Ice Cream:* Decrease vanilla to 1 teaspoon. Thaw 1 package (16 ounces) frozen strawberry halves. After adding cream, stir in strawberries. If desired, add few drops red food color.

■ *Nut Brittle Ice Cream:* After adding cream, stir in 1 cup crushed almond, pecan or peanut brittle.

■ *Pistachio Ice Cream:* After adding cream, stir in ½ cup chopped pistachio nuts or almonds and ½ teaspoon *each* almond extract and green food color.

■ *Wintergreen or Peppermint Ice Cream:* Decrease vanilla to 1 teaspoon. After adding cream, stir in ½ cup crushed wintergreen or peppermint candy. If desired, add few drops green or red food color.

Dessert Sauces

The right sauce used the right way can turn an ordinary dessert into a dazzling delight. Use sauce as a topping, use it as a layering but, above all, use it with imagination.

FUDGE SAUCE

1 can (14½ ounces) evaporated milk
2 cups sugar
4 ounces unsweetened chocolate

¼ cup butter or margarine
1 teaspoon vanilla
½ teaspoon salt

Heat milk and sugar to rolling boil, stirring constantly. Boil and stir 1 minute. Add chocolate, stirring until melted. Beat over heat until smooth. (If sauce has slightly curdled appearance, beat vigorously until creamy smooth.) Remove from heat; blend in butter, vanilla and salt.

3 cups.

BUTTERSCOTCH SAUCE

1½ cups brown sugar (packed)
½ cup light corn syrup
¼ cup butter or margarine

½ cup whipping cream
1 teaspoon vanilla

Heat brown sugar, syrup and butter over low heat to boiling, stirring constantly. Remove from heat; stir in cream and vanilla. Stir just before serving.

About 1 cup.

HONEY-APRICOT SAUCE

Mix thoroughly ½ cup honey and ½ cup apricot brandy. Spoon over ice cream and, if desired, sprinkle with uncooked ground coffee.

About 1 cup.

CINNAMON-BLUEBERRY SAUCE

2 tablespoons sugar
1 teaspoon cornstarch
1 cup frozen blueberries
2 tablespoons water
1 tablespoon lemon juice
¼ teaspoon cinnamon

Blend sugar and cornstarch in saucepan. Stir in remaining ingredients. Cook, stirring constantly, until mixture boils. Reduce heat; simmer 5 minutes, stirring occasionally. Serve warm.

About ⅔ cup.

PRALINE SAUCE

¼ cup butter or margarine
½ cup confectioners' sugar
2 tablespoons maple syrup
¼ cup water
1 teaspoon rum or, if desired, ½ teaspoon rum flavoring
½ cup finely chopped nuts

Heat butter over medium heat until golden brown. Cool. Gradually add sugar, mixing until smooth. Stir in syrup and water.

Heat to boiling; boil and stir 1 minute. Cool slightly. (The sauce thickens as it cools.) Stir in rum and nuts.

About 1 cup.

OLD-FASHIONED LEMON SAUCE

1 cup sugar
½ cup butter or margarine
¼ cup water
1 egg, well beaten
¾ teaspoon grated lemon peel
3 tablespoons lemon juice

Combine all ingredients in medium saucepan. Heat to boiling over medium heat, stirring constantly. Serve warm.

1⅓ cups.

Eggs and Cheese

*Partners in protein—eggs and cheese! For good
lunch and supper dishes any time, you can
always turn to eggs and cheese—alone or in
combination. And here's a collection of happy
choices—soufflés, omelets, fondues, quiche, a
Welsh rabbit—the foods everyone at every age
thinks well of. And for breakfast, or any time—
every kind of egg imaginable.*

Some Egg Facts

Size: Eggs are most often available as extra-large,
large and medium. Most of the recipes in this book were
tested with large eggs. When it is essential to the recipe's success, the amounts are also given in liquid measure.

Grade: Federal standards grade eggs as AA, A, B and
C grades. AA and A are best for poaching, frying and
eating in the shell. The yolks are firm, round and high.
The thick white is large in amount and stands high around
the yolk; the thin white is small in amount. Grade B eggs
are more economical but have the same nutritive value
as AA and A, they are good for use in other cooking.

Color: Brown eggs or white, deep yellow yolks or
pale yellow ones—the flavor, nutritive value and cooking performance are the same. The shell color is the
result of pigment; the yolk color, of feed.

Storage: Eggs should be refrigerated at 45 to 55°
with the large end up. Cold eggs are more easily separated; egg whites at room temperature beat up faster
to a larger volume.

Cooking temperature: With the exception of French-type omelets (which are cooked quickly), eggs should be prepared over low heat.

Beating egg whites: Be sure both bowl and beater are spotlessly clean and dry—also that there is no yolk in the white. Egg whites will not beat up properly if either bowl or beater is even slightly moist or greasy or if there is the tiniest speck of yolk in the white. A properly beaten white should more than triple its volume.

Folding in egg whites: The lightness of soufflé or sponge cake depends on the airiness of the batter after the beaten egg whites have been added. For best results, take ¼ of the beaten egg whites and *stir* into batter. (This lightens the batter base.) Using a rubber scraper, pile rest of egg whites on top of batter; then follow procedure for folding. Cut down through the mixture, then slide the spatula across the bottom and up the side of the bowl.

Combining egg yolks with a hot mixture: Add a little of hot mixture to beaten yolks, stirring continuously. Then stir blended egg mixture into remaining hot mixture; continue stirring until smooth.

Storing leftover yolks and whites: Place egg yolks in tight-lidded jar, cover with water and store in refrigerator. They will keep 2 to 3 days. Egg whites can be stored for 1 week to 10 days in a tightly covered jar in refrigerator or they can be frozen. (Try freezing each white in a plastic ice cube container; remove to plastic bag for storage.) Two tablespoons of defrosted liquid egg white is equivalent to one fresh egg white.

Using leftover egg yolks and whites: Use yolks to enrich and thicken cream sauces and for Hollandaise or mayonnaise; whites may be used for meringues or saved for an angel food cake.

Equivalents

4 to 6 whole eggs
8 to 10 egg whites ⎬ = 1 cup
12 to 14 egg yolks

Basic Eggs

Let's face it—most people are pretty fussy when it comes to the way they like their eggs. So it behooves a good cook to know how to make an egg behave in six very basic ways. And here they are, with helpful hints.

SOFT-COOKED EGGS

For a change of pace, sprinkle with dry bread crumbs and dot with butter.

Cold Water Method: Place eggs in saucepan; add enough cold water to come at least 1 inch above eggs. Heat rapidly to boiling. Remove from heat; cover. Let stand 1 to 3 minutes, depending on desired doneness. Immediately cool eggs in cold water several seconds to prevent further cooking. Cut eggs in half; scoop egg from shell.

Boiling Water Method: Place eggs in bowl of warm water to prevent shells from cracking. Fill saucepan with enough water to come at least 1 inch above eggs; heat to boiling. With spoon, transfer eggs from warm water to boiling water. Remove from heat; cover. Let stand 6 to 8 minutes, depending on desired doneness. Immediately cool eggs in cold water several seconds to prevent further cooking. Cut in half; scoop egg from shell.

HARD-COOKED EGGS

Cold Water Method: Place eggs in saucepan; add enough cold water to come at least 1 inch above eggs. Heat rapidly to boiling. Remove from heat; cover. Let stand 22 to 24 minutes. Immediately cool eggs in cold water to prevent further cooking. Tap egg to crackle shell. Roll egg between hands to loosen shell, then peel. Hold egg under running cold water to help ease off shell.

Boiling Water Method: Place eggs in bowl of warm water to prevent shells from cracking. Fill saucepan with enough water to come at least 1 inch above eggs; heat to boiling. With spoon, transfer eggs from warm water to boiling water. Reduce heat to below simmering; cook 20 minutes. Immediately cool eggs in cold water to prevent further cooking. Tap egg to crackle shell. Roll egg between hands to loosen shell, then peel. Hold egg under running cold water to help ease off shell.

DEVILED EGGS

6 hard-cooked eggs
½ teaspoon salt
½ teaspoon dry mustard
¼ teaspoon pepper

3 tablespoons salad dressing, vinegar or light cream (20%)

Cut peeled eggs lengthwise in half. Slip out yolks; mash with fork. Mix in seasonings and salad dressing. Fill whites with egg yolk mixture, heaping it up highly.
6 servings.

VARIATIONS

■ *Catsup-flavored Deviled Eggs:* Decrease salt to ¼ teaspoon, omit salad dressing and mix 5 tablespoons catsup into egg yolk mixture.

■ *Deviled Eggs with Olives:* Decrease salt to ¼ teaspoon, omit dry mustard and mix ¼ cup finely minced ripe olives and ⅛ teaspoon curry powder into egg yolk mixture.

■ *Zesty Deviled Eggs:* Decrease salt to ¼ teaspoon and mix one of the following into egg yolk mixture:

2 slices bacon, crispy fried and finely crumbled
½ cup finely shredded process American cheese

2 tablespoons snipped parsley
1 teaspoon horseradish

When storing Deviled Eggs in plastic wrap, be sure to twist ends and tuck under to ensure an airtight seal.

POACHED EGGS

In saucepan or skillet, heat water (1½ to 2 inches) to boiling; reduce to simmer. Break each egg into a measuring cup or saucer; slip eggs one at a time into water, holding cup or saucer close to water's surface.

Cook 3 to 5 minutes or until of desired doneness. Lift eggs from water with slotted spatula. Season with salt and pepper.

VARIATIONS

■ *Eggs Poached in Milk:* Substitute milk for the water. When serving, pour hot milk over eggs on hot toast.

■ *Eggs Poached in Bouillon:* Add 2 chicken or beef bouillon cubes to the water before boiling.

■ *Eggs Poached in Egg Poacher:* Into poacher, pour water to just below bottom of egg cups; heat water to boiling. Butter metal egg cups. Break eggs into greased cups. Set egg cups in frame over boiling water. Cover; steam 3 to 5 minutes or until of desired doneness.

FRIED EGGS

Sunny-side up or once over lightly, fried eggs are favorites with the menfolk.

In heavy skillet, heat butter or bacon drippings to ⅛-inch depth just until hot enough to sizzle drop of water. Break each egg into a measuring cup or saucer; carefully slip eggs one at a time into skillet. Immediately reduce heat to low.

Cook slowly, spooning butter over eggs until whites are set and a film forms over yolks (sunny-side up). Or turn eggs over gently when whites are set and cook until of desired doneness. Season with salt and pepper.

VARIATION

■ *Poached-fried Eggs:* Heat just enough butter or bacon drippings to grease skillet. Cook eggs over low heat until edges turn white. Add ½ teaspoon water for 1 egg, decreasing proportion slightly for each additional egg. Cover skillet tightly. Cook until of desired doneness.

SCRAMBLED EGGS

Eggs that double as a supper dish.

For each serving, break 2 eggs into bowl with 2 tablespoons milk or cream, ¼ teaspoon salt and dash pepper. Mix with fork, stirring thoroughly for a uniform yellow, or mixing just slightly if streaks of white and yellow are preferred.

Heat ½ tablespoon butter or margarine in skillet over medium heat until just hot enough to sizzle a drop of water. Pour egg mixture into skillet.

As mixture begins to set at bottom and side, gently lift cooked portions with spatula so that thin, uncooked portion can flow to bottom. Avoid constant stirring. Cook until eggs are thickened throughout but still moist, about 3 to 5 minutes.

VARIATIONS

■ *Scrambled Eggs in Double Boiler:* Cook egg mixture in top of double boiler over simmering, not boiling, water. Stir occasionally until thick and creamy.

■ *Party Scrambled Eggs:* For each serving, stir one of the following into egg mixture in bowl:

2 tablespoons shredded Cheddar, Monterey (Jack) or Swiss cheese

2 tablespoons chopped mushrooms

2 tablespoons snipped chives

2 tablespoons snipped parsley

2 tablespoons crispy fried and crumbled bacon*

2 tablespoons finely shredded dried beef*

2 tablespoons chopped cooked ham*

*Omit salt.

BAKED SHIRRED EGGS

Heat oven to 325°. For each serving, break an egg carefully into buttered 5- or 6-ounce baking dish. Season with salt and pepper. If desired, top each with 1 tablespoon milk or light cream, dot with soft butter or sprinkle with 1 tablespoon shredded Cheddar cheese.

Bake eggs uncovered 15 to 18 minutes, depending on desired doneness and depth of baking dish. Whites should be set, but yolks soft. Serve in baking dish.

POACHED EGGS

1. Hold cup close to water's surface; slip egg into water.

2. Lift eggs carefully from skillet with slotted spatula.

SCRAMBLED EGGS

BAKED (SHIRRED) EGGS.

Bake until whites are set and yolks are soft.

Lift set portion; uncooked mixture will flow to bottom.

FRIED EGGS

1. Spoon butter over eggs, forming a film over yolk.

2. Or, when edges turn white, spoon water into skillet.

 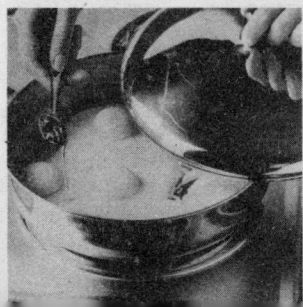

SOFT CHEESES

1. **Brie** (bree): French origin. Edible crust. Mild to pungent. As an appetizer, for dessert.

2. **Camembert** (kam'-em-bear): French origin. Edible crust. Pungent. Appetizer, dessert.

3. **Club:** Canadian origin. Often flavored. As an appetizer, in sandwiches, for dessert.

4. **Cottage:** Large or small curds, dry or creamed. Salad, snack, cooking.

5. **Cream:** U.S. origin. Very mild. Chill slightly. In salads, as a snack, for dessert.

6. **Gourmandise:** French origin. Cherry brandy flavor. As an appetizer, for dessert.

7. **Liederkranz:** U.S. origin. Edible crust. Pungent. As an appetizer, for dessert.

8. **Ricotta** (rih-kah'-tuh): Italian origin. Mild. Curd or dry. For cooking, for dessert.

SEMISOFT CHEESES

1. **Bel Paese** (bel-pah-ay'-ze): Italian origin. Mild. As an appetizer, for dessert.

2. **Brick:** U.S. origin. Mild to sharp flavor; firm to soft. As a snack, in sandwiches.

3. **Monterey (Jack):** California origin. Mild. Appetizer, cooking, sandwich.

4. **Mozzarella, Scamorze:** Italian origin. Mild. For cooking, as a snack.

5. **Muenster** (mun'-ster): German origin. Mild to sharp. Appetizer, sandwich.

6. **Port du Salut** (por-du-sal-lu): French origin. Mild to robust. Appetizer, dessert.

7. **Roquefort** (rok'-for): French origin. Sharp, salty. Appetizer, salad, dessert.

8. **Samsoe:** Danish origin. Mild, softer than Swiss, small "eyes." Sandwich, Snack.

FIRM TO HARD CHEESES

1. **Blue:** Probable French origin. Tangy, sharp. Appetizer, salad, dessert.

2. **Cheddar:** English origin. Mild to very sharp. As a snack, for cooking, for dessert.

3. **Cheshire:** English origin. Crumbly texture. As a snack, for cooking (Welsh rabbit).

4. **Edam, Gouda:** Dutch origin. Inedible casing. Mild. As an appetizer, for dessert.

5. **Fontina** (fahn-tee'nah): Italian origin. Mellow; scattered "eyes." Appetizer, dessert.

6. **Gjetöst** (yate'-ohst): Norwegian origin. "Carameled" flavor. Sandwich, snack.

7. **Gorgonzola:** Italian origin. Piquant flavor; crumbly. In salads, for dessert.

8. **Gruyère** (gree-air'): Swiss origin. Nutty, sharper than Swiss. Cooking dessert.

9. **Kashkaval** (kotch-kah-vaih'): Yugoslavian origin. Salty. Appetizer, snack, dessert.

10. **Noekkelöst** (nok'-kel-ohst): Norwegian origin. Mild, seeded. Sandwiches, snack.

11. **Provolone** (pro-vo-lo'-nee): Italian origin. Smoked; mild to sharp. Cooking, snack.

12. **Swiss:** Mild, nutty, sweet flavor. Appetizer, sandwich, cooking, dessert.

VERY HARD CHEESES

1. **Parmesan:** Italian origin. Inedible casing. Sharp. Usually grated for cooking.

2. **Romano:** Italian origin. Piquant. Granular. Usually grated, also as a snack.

3. **Sap Sago** (sap-say'-go): Flavored with clover. Swiss origin. Usually grated.

4. **Sbrinz:** Swiss origin. Medium to sharp. Often grated, also as a snack.

Egg and Cheese Main Dishes

Alone or as partners, eggs and cheese make sturdy standbys. They come to the rescue for all kinds of meatless meals: quick, economical, even elegant. In a matter of minutes, they can be transformed into fluffy soufflés, tender omelets, fondue, quiche Lorraine and Welsh rabbit.

CREAMED HAM AND EGGS

3 tablespoons butter or margarine	⅛ teaspoon pepper
3 tablespoons flour	2¼ cups milk
½ teaspoon dry mustard	1 cup diced cooked ham
¼ teaspoon salt	4 hard-cooked eggs, quartered

Melt butter in saucepan over low heat. Blend in flour and seasonings. Cook over low heat, stirring until mixture is smooth and bubbly. Remove from heat. Stir in milk. Heat to boiling, stirring constantly. Boil and stir 1 minute. Gently stir in ham and eggs; heat through.

6 servings.

VARIATIONS

■ *Creamed Eggs:* Omit dry mustard and ham and increase eggs to six.

■ *Creamed Eggs with Salmon or Tuna:* Omit dry mustard and ham; gently stir 1 can (7¾ ounces) salmon, drained and flaked, or 1 can (6½ ounces) tuna, drained and flaked, into white sauce with the eggs.

■ *Eggs à la Goldenrod:* Prepare Creamed Eggs except—reserve three of the egg yolks; press through sieve onto each serving.

■ *Garnished Creamed Eggs:* Sprinkle servings with one of the following:

4 slices bacon, crisply fried and crumbled	2 tablespoons chopped ripe olives
2 tablespoons shredded process cheese	

EGGS ON CORNED BEEF HASH

1 can (15 ounces) corned beef hash	6 eggs Salt and pepper

Heat oven to 350°. In each of six ungreased 5- or 6-ounce baking dishes, press about ¼ cup hash against bottom and side. Break 1 egg into each dish. Season with salt and pepper. If desired, sprinkle each with 1 tablespoon shredded Cheddar cheese. Bake uncovered 20 to 25 minutes.

6 servings.

EGGS FLORENTINE CASSEROLE

2 packages (10 ounces each) frozen chopped spinach
2 tablespoons minced onion
2 tablespoons lemon juice
½ cup shredded Cheddar cheese
4 hard-cooked eggs, sliced
3 tablespoons butter or margarine

3 tablespoons flour
½ teaspoon salt
½ teaspoon dry mustard
¼ teaspoon pepper
2¼ cups milk
½ cup dry bread crumbs
1 tablespoon butter or margarine, melted

Heat oven to 400°. Cook spinach as directed on package; drain. Stir in onion and lemon juice. Spread spinach in ungreased baking dish, 8x8x2 inches. Sprinkle with cheese; top with egg slices.

Melt 3 tablespoons butter in saucepan over low heat. Blend in flour and seasonings. Cook over low heat, stirring until mixture is smooth and bubbly. Remove from heat. Stir in milk. Heat to boiling, stirring constantly. Boil and stir 1 minute. Pour over eggs.

Toss bread crumbs in melted butter; sprinkle over sauce. Bake uncovered 20 minutes.

4 to 6 servings.

EGGS CONTINENTAL

¼ cup dry bread crumbs
1 tablespoon butter or margarine, melted
4 hard-cooked eggs, sliced
3 slices bacon, diced
1 cup dairy sour cream
1 tablespoon milk

1 tablespoon instant minced onion
½ teaspoon salt
¼ teaspoon paprika
⅛ teaspoon pepper
½ cup shredded Cheddar cheese

Heat oven to 350°. Toss bread crumbs in butter; divide among 4 buttered 10-ounce baking dishes. Layer egg slices over crumbs.

Fry bacon until crisp; drain. Stir together bacon, sour cream, milk, onion and seasonings; spoon over eggs. Top with cheese. Bake uncovered 10 to 15 minutes or until cheese is melted.

4 servings.

EGGS BENEDICT

Prepare Blender Hollandaise Sauce (page 572); hold sauce over warm water. Split 3 English muffins; toast and butter each half. Fry 6 thin slices cooked ham in butter until light brown. Prepare 6 poached eggs (page 323). Place 1 ham slice on cut side of each muffin; top with a poached egg. Spoon warm sauce over eggs.

6 servings.

DEVILED EGGS WITH CHEESE-SHRIMP SAUCE

9 hard-cooked eggs
3 tablespoons mayonnaise
1 tablespoon chopped sweet pickle
2 teaspoons vinegar
½ teaspoon dry mustard
Dash Worcestershire sauce
Dash pepper
1 can (4 ounces) mushroom stems and pieces, drained

1 can (4½ ounces) shrimp, rinsed and drained
¾ cup milk
1 can (10¾ ounces) condensed Cheddar cheese soup
4 cups hot cooked rice (page 345)

Cut peeled eggs in half lengthwise. Slip out yolks; mash with fork. Mix in mayonnaise, pickle, vinegar, mustard, Worcestershire sauce and pepper. Fill egg whites with the egg yolk mixture, heaping it up lightly.

Heat oven to 350°. Heat mushrooms, shrimp, milk and soup just to boiling, stirring occasionally. Spread rice in ungreased baking dish, 11½ x 7½ x 1½ inches.

Arrange eggs in 3 rows on rice; pour soup mixture over eggs and rice. Bake uncovered 15 minutes. If desired, garnish with snipped parsley.

6 to 8 servings.

The Deviled Eggs fit perfectly if you use the correct pan.

EGG FOO YONG

2 tablespoons salad oil
3 eggs
1 cup bean sprouts, drained
½ cup chopped cooked pork

2 tablespoons chopped onion
1 tablespoon soy sauce
Sauce (below)

Heat oil in large skillet. Beat eggs until thick and lemon colored; stir in bean sprouts, pork, onion and 1 tablespoon soy sauce.

Pour ¼ cup mixture at a time into skillet; with broad spatula, push cooked egg up over meat to form a patty. When patties are set, turn to brown other side. Serve hot with Sauce.

5 servings.

SAUCE

1 teaspoon cornstarch
1 teaspoon sugar
1 teaspoon vinegar

2½ tablespoons soy sauce
½ cup water

Combine all ingredients in small saucepan. Cook, stirring constantly, until mixture thickens and boils. Boil and stir 1 minute.

CHEESE SOUFFLÉ

A light and airy soufflé. Everyone goes for the classic cheese version—perhaps that's because they've never tried anything else. On page 332 we offer you an elegant shrimp vacation, and on page 697 you'll find soufflés featuring spinach and broccoli.

¼ cup butter or margarine
¼ cup all-purpose flour
½ teaspoon salt
¼ teaspoon dry mustard
Dash cayenne red pepper

1 cup milk
1 cup shredded Cheddar cheese (about 4 ounces)
3 eggs, separated
¼ teaspoon cream of tartar

Heat oven to 350°. Butter 4-cup soufflé dish or 1-quart casserole. Make a 4-inch band of triple thickness aluminum foil 2 inches longer than circumference of dish; butter one side. Extend depth of dish by securing foil band, buttered side in, around top of dish.

Melt butter in saucepan over low heat. Blend in flour and seasonings. Cook over low heat, stirring until mixture is smooth and bubbly. Remove from heat.

Stir in milk. Heat to boiling, stirring constantly. Boil

and stir 1 minute. Stir in cheese until melted. Remove from heat.

Beat egg whites and cream of tartar until stiff but not dry; set aside. Beat egg yolks until very thick and lemon colored; stir into cheese mixture. Stir about ¼ of the egg whites into cheese mixture. Gently fold mixture into remaining egg whites.

Carefully pour into soufflé dish. Bake 50 to 60 minutes or until knife inserted halfway between edge and center comes out clean. *Serve immediately.* Carefully remove foil band and divide soufflé into sections with 2 forks.

4 servings.

VARIATION

■ *Shrimp Soufflé:* Omit mustard, cayenne red pepper and cheese; add 1 can (4½ ounces) shrimp, rinsed and drained, and 1 teaspoon tarragon leaves to sauce mixture before adding the beaten egg yolks.

SUPER VEGETABLE SOUFFLÉ

A tasty luncheon soufflé, made easy with a condensed soup base.

1 can (10¾ ounces) condensed cream of vegetable soup (undiluted)	¼ teaspoon dry mustard
	¼ teaspoon dill weed
	6 eggs, separated
1 cup shredded Cheddar cheese (about 4 ounces)	¼ teaspoon cream of tartar

Heat oven to 350°. Butter 8-cup soufflé dish or 2-quart casserole. Make a 4-inch band of triple thickness aluminum foil 2 inches longer than circumference of dish; butter one side. Extend depth of dish by securing foil band, buttered side in, around top of dish.

Combine soup, cheese and seasonings in small saucepan; heat slowly until cheese is melted. Remove from heat.

In large mixer bowl, beat egg whites and cream of tartar until stiff but not dry; set aside. In small mixer bowl, beat egg yolks until very thick and lemon colored; stir into cheese mixture. Stir about ¼ of egg whites into cheese mixture. Gently fold mixture into remaining egg whites.

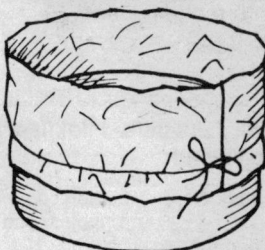

Add extra height to a soufflé dish or casserole by tying a buttered 4-inch band of triple thickness aluminum foil around the rim of dish.

Carefully pour into soufflé dish. Bake 50 to 60 minutes or until knife inserted halfway between edge and center comes out clean. *Serve immediately*. Carefully remove foil band and divide soufflé into sections with 2 forks.

6 servings.

FRENCH OMELET

The French classic—smooth on the outside, creamy inside. Make it one of your specialities for brunch, lunch or dinner.

Mix 3 eggs with fork until whites and yolks are just blended. In 8-inch skillet or omelet pan, heat about 1 tablespoon butter or margarine over medium-high heat. As butter melts, tilt skillet in all directions to coat side thoroughly. When butter *just* begins to brown, skillet is hot enough to use.

Quickly pour eggs all at once into skillet. With left hand, start sliding skillet back and forth rapidly over heat. At the same time, stir quickly with fork to spread eggs continuously over bottom of skillet as they thicken. Let stand over heat a few seconds to lightly brown bottom of omelet; do not overcook. (Omelet will continue to cook after folding.)

Tilt skillet; run fork under edge of omelet, then jerk skillet sharply to loosen eggs from bottom of skillet. With fork, fold portion of omelet nearest you just to center. (Allow for portion of omelet to slide up side of skillet.)

Grasp skillet handle with hand; turn omelet onto warm plate, flipping folded portion of omelet over so far side is on bottom. If necessary, tuck sides of omelet under.

Season with salt and pepper. If desired, brush omelet with a little butter to make it shine.

1 or 2 servings.

VARIATIONS

■ *Filled Omelet:* Just before folding omelet, sprinkle with one of the following:

3 slices bacon, crisply fried and crumbled	2 tablespoons preserves
	1 tablespoon snipped chives
¼ cup shredded Cheddar cheese	

■ *Herb Omelet:* Just before folding omelet, sprinkle with basil, chevil, thyme or marjoram leaves and 1 tablespoon each snipped chives and parsley.

■ *Western Omelet:* Stir ¼ cup finely minced cooked ham, 2 tablespoons chopped onion and 2 tablespoons chopped green pepper into egg mixture before pouring into skillet.

PUFFY OMELET

A soufflé-like omelet. Try it with cheese sauce or mushroom sauce.

4 eggs, separated	⅛ teaspoon pepper
¼ cup water	1 tablespoon butter or
¼ cup teaspoon salt	margarine

In small mixer bowl, beat egg whites with water and salt until stiff but not dry. In another mixer bowl, beat egg yolks with pepper until very thick and lemon colored. Fold into egg whites.

Heat oven to 325°. Heat butter in 10-inch skillet with oven-proof handle until just hot enough to sizzle a drop of water. Pour omelet mixture into skillet; level surface gently. Reduce heat. Cook slowly until puffy and light brown on bottom, about 5 minutes. (Lift omelet at edge to judge color.)

Place in oven; bake 12 to 15 minutes or until knife inserted in center comes out clean.

Tip skillet and loosen omelet by slipping pancake turner or spatula under; fold omelet in half, being careful not to break it. Slip onto heated platter. Serve immediately.

2 or 3 servings.

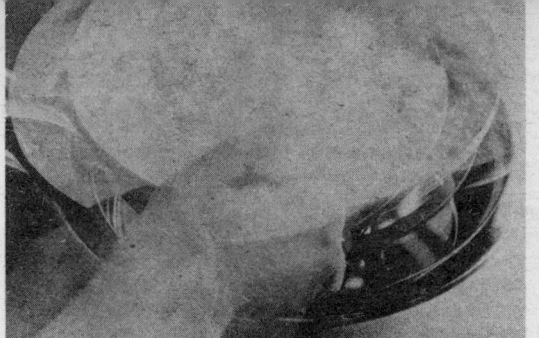

Stir quickly, sliding skillet back and forth over heat.

Tilt skillet; fold omelet edge nearest you just to center.

Turn onto plate; far side flips over onto unfolded portion.

PUFFY OMELET WITH MUSHROOM-SHRIMP SAUCE

Served with a hearty, easy-to-make sauce, this omelet will sate even a ravenous appetite.

Puffy Omelet (page 334)
½ cup milk
1 can (10½ ounces) condensed cream of mushroom soup
¼ cup minced celery

1 teaspoon minced onion
1 tablespoon lemon juice
3 drops red pepper sauce
1 can (4½ ounces) shrimp, rinsed and drained

Prepare Puffy Omelet. While omelet bakes, stir milk gradually into soup in saucepan. Heat over medium heat, stirring constantly, until sauce is bubbly.

Stir in celery, onion, lemon juice and red pepper sauce. Fold in shrimp; heat through. Keep sauce warm over low heat.

When omelet is baked, pour half the sauce over omelet in skillet. Fold omelet and remove to heated platter; pour remaining sauce over top. If desired, sprinkle with paprika.

2 or 3 servings.

OMELET CAHUENGA

Puffy Omelet (above)
1 small ripe avocado
¾ cup dairy sour cream
½ teaspoon salt

⅛ teaspoon dill weed
1 large tomato, peeled, diced and drained

Prepare Puffy Omelet. While omelet bakes, peel and dice avocado. Just before serving, heat sour cream, salt and dill weed. Gently stir in tomato; heat 1 minute. Carefully mix in avocado.

When omelet is baked, pour half the sauce over omelet in skillet. Fold omelet and remove to heated platter; pour remaining sauce over top. If desired, garnish omelet with crisply fried slices of bacon.

2 or 3 servings.

SPANISH OMELET

A basic French Omelet filled and topped with a zingy tomato sauce.

- 1 tablespoon minced green pepper
- 1 tablespoon minced onion
- 2 teaspoons butter or margarine
- 1 can (8 ounces) tomato sauce
- 2 teaspoons sugar
- 1 teaspoon Worcestershire sauce
- Dash cayenne red pepper
- 2 French Omelets (page 333)

In medium skillet, cook and stir green pepper and onion in butter over low heat until onion is tender. Stir in tomato sauce, sugar and seasonings. Simmer 10 minutes or until sauce is thickened; keep warm over low heat.

Prepare French Omelets (one at a time) as directed except—just before folding, spoon ¼ of tomato sauce mixture onto each omelet. Spoon remaining sauce over tops.

2 to 4 servings.

SCRAMBLED EGGS IN CREAM PUFF BOWL

- ½ cup water
- ¼ cup butter or margarine
- ½ cup all-purpose flour*
- ⅛ teaspoon salt
- 2 eggs
- 9 eggs
- 1 cup cottage cheese with chives
- ¼ teaspoon salt
- 3 tablespoons butter or margarine

Heat oven to 400°. Grease 9-inch glass pie pan. Heat water and ¼ cup butter to a rolling boil. Stir in flour and ⅛ teaspoon salt. Stir vigorously over low heat until mix-

*Self-rising flour can be used in this recipe.

Gently pile scrambled eggs into bowl; serve immediately.

ture leaves side of pan and forms a ball, about 1 minute.

Remove from heat; cool slightly, about 10 minutes. Add 2 eggs (all at once), beating until smooth and glossy. Spread batter evenly in pie pan (have batter touching side of pan but do not spread it up the side). Bake 45 to 50 minutes.

During the last 15 minutes bowl bakes, prepare scrambled eggs: Beat 9 eggs thoroughly; stir in cottage cheese and ¼ teaspoon salt. Heat butter in large skillet over medium heat until just hot enough to sizzle drop of water. Pour egg mixture into skillet.

As mixture begins to set at bottom and side, gently lift cooked portions with spatula so that thin, uncooked portion can flow to bottom. Avoid constant stirring. Cook until eggs are thickened throughout but still moist. Mound eggs into cream puff bowl. Cut bowl into wedges.

6 servings.

WELSH RABBIT

The story goes that long ago in Wales the peasants, not allowed to hunt on the estates of noblemen, served melted cheese as a substitute for rabbit, popular prize of the hunt. It became a famous dish of Ye Olde Cheshire Cheese, meeting place of England's illustrious penmen.

¼ cup butter or margarine	1 cup milk
¼ cup all-purpose flour	½ cup beer*
½ teaspoon salt	2 cups shredded Cheddar
¼ teaspoon pepper	cheese (about 8 ounces)
¼ teaspoon dry mustard	4 to 6 slices toast
¼ teaspoon Worcestershire sauce	

Melt butter in medium saucepan over low heat. Blend in flour and seasonings. Cook over low heat, stirring until mixture is smooth and bubbly. Remove from heat. Stir in milk. Heat to boiling, stirring constantly. Boil and stir 1 minute.

Gradually add beer to sauce mixture. Stir in cheese; heat over low heat, stirring constantly, until cheese is melted. Serve over toast. If desired, garnish with paprika.

4 to 6 servings (about ½ cup sauce per serving).

*If desired, omit beer and stir 1½ cups milk into the flour mixture.

TUNA-CHEESE BAKE

1 package (8 ounces)
  macaroni and Cheddar
  dinner
1 can (6½ ounces) tuna,
  drained
1 can (3 ounces) sliced
  mushrooms, drained

2 teaspoons chopped
  pimiento
⅓ cup dairy sour cream
¼ cup broken cashews

Prepare macaroni and Cheddar as directed on package for saucepan method. Stir in tuna, mushrooms and pimiento; heat through. Stir in sour cream. Sprinkle each serving with cashews. If desired, garnish with parsley or strips of green pepper.

4 servings.

CHEESE FONDUE

1 clove garlic, halved
2 cups dry white wine
2 tablespoons flour
1 pound Swiss cheese,*
  shredded (about 4 cups)

3 tablespoons kirsch
  Salt and pepper to taste
  French bread, cut into 1-
  inch cubes

Rub cut clove of garlic on bottom and side of earthenware fondue dish or heavy skillet. Add wine; heat over low heat until bubbles rise to surface (wine must not boil).

Sprinkle flour over cheese; toss until cheese is coated. Keeping fondue dish over low heat, add cheese, about ½ cup at a time, stirring with wooden spoon after each addition until cheese is melted. (Each addition of cheese must be completely melted before adding more.)

Stir in kirsch and seasonings. If desired, stir in nutmeg to taste. Place fondue dish over low heat at table.

Use long-handled forks to spear bread cubes, then dip and swirl in fondue with a stirring motion. (Fondue must be stirred continuously to prevent it from separating.) If fondue becomes too thick, add a little heated wine.

4 servings.

*The Swiss cheese should be natural (not process) and aged at least 6 months.

EXPERIMENT WITH CHEESE

There are literally hundreds of cheeses, and once you become familiar with some of the better-known varieties the fun has just begun. You'll want to learn how to substitute one cheese for another. For instance, try Cheshire instead of Cheddar cheese in Welsh Rabbit, experiment with Monterey Jack and Ricotta in Lasagne and use Roquefort or Gorgonzola in recipes that call for Blue cheese.

Just one word of caution. Don't become too adventuresome—it's best to substitute cheese of the same texture. See pages 326 and 327 for more information on cheese and its many uses.

OVEN CHEESE FONDUE

10 slices white bread
6 eggs
3 cups milk
2 tablespoons snipped parsley
1 teaspoon dry mustard
1 teaspoon salt
2 cups shredded process sharp American cheese (about 8 ounces)
3 tablespoons finely chopped onion

Heat oven to 325°. Remove crusts from bread; cut bread into cubes. Beat eggs, milk and seasonings. Stir in bread cubes, cheese and onion.

Pour mixture into ungreased baking dish, 11½ x 7½ x 1½ inches. Bake uncovered 1 hour or until center is set. 8 servings.

VARIATION

■ *Oven Shrimp Fondue:* Stir in 2 cups cleaned cooked or canned shrimp.

PUFFY CHEESE BAKE

A dish with stick-to-the-ribs warmth.

4 slices bread, buttered
2 eggs
1 cup light cream (20%)
2 tablespoons butter or margarine, melted
½ teaspoon salt
½ teaspoon dry mustard
¼ teaspoon paprika
Dash cayenne red pepper
1½ cups shredded process American cheese (about 6 ounces)

Heat oven to 350°. Butter baking dish, 8x8x2 inches. Cut each slice of bread diagonally into 4 triangles.

Line bottom and sides of baking dish with bread triangles. (For a crown effect, place 8 triangles upright against sides of dish. Arrange remaining triangles on bottom of dish.)

Beat eggs slightly; add remaining ingredients and mix well. Pour mixture into baking dish. Bake uncovered 30 to 40 minutes.

4 servings.

TUNA-MACARONI CASSEROLE

1 package (8 ounces) macaroni and Cheddar dinner	¼ cup sliced pitted ripe olives
1 can (6½ ounces) tuna, drained	¼ cup butter or margarine, melted
¼ cup chopped green pepper	¼ teaspoon garlic powder
	1 cup croutons

Prepare macaroni and Cheddar as directed on package for oven method except—use 2¼ cups water. Stir in tuna, green pepper and olives. Cover; bake 20 minutes.

Blend butter and garlic powder; stir in croutons. Stir casserole and sprinkle croutons over top. Bake uncovered 5 minutes longer.

4 servings.

CHEDDAR CHEESE PIE

9-inch Baked Pie Shell (page 501)	½ teaspoon salt
3 cups shredded sharp natural Cheddar cheese (about ¾ pound)	½ teaspoon dry mustard
	½ teaspoon Worcestershire sauce
1 teaspoon instant minced onion	3 eggs
	6 medium tomatoes, peeled
	Salt and pepper

Bake pie shell. Heat oven to 325°. Heat cheese, onion, salt, mustard and Worcestershire sauce over low heat, stirring until cheese is melted. Remove from heat.

In large bowl, beat eggs until foamy; gradually add cheese mixture and continue beating until smooth. Pour into baked pie shell. Bake 25 minutes or until filling is *just* set. Remove pie from oven.

Cut tomatoes into thin slices. Overlap slices around edge of pie to form a wreath; sprinkle with salt and pepper. Bake 15 minutes longer.

6 to 8 servings.

OLD-FASHIONED MACARONI AND CHEESE

6 to 7 ounces elbow
   macaroni (about 2 cups)
2 tablespoons grated onion
1 teaspoon salt
¼ teaspoon pepper
3 cups shredded process
   sharp American cheese
   (about ¾ pound)

2 cups Thin White Sauce
   (page 566)
1 tablespoon butter or
   margarine

Heat oven to 375°. Cook macaroni as directed on page 352. Place half the macaroni in ungreased 2-quart casserole. Sprinkle with half the onion, salt, pepper and cheese; repeat. Pour white sauce over casserole. Dot with butter. Cover; bake 30 minutes. Uncover; bake 15 minutes longer.

6 to 8 servings.

QUICHE LORRAINE

Serve as a first course or as the main dish.

Pastry for 9-inch One-
   crust Pie (page 501)
12 slices bacon (about ½
   pound), crisply fried and
   crumbled
1 cup shredded natural
   Swiss cheese (about 4
   ounces)

⅓ cup minced onion
4 eggs
2 cups whipping cream or
   light cream (20%)
¾ teaspoon salt
¼ teaspoon sugar
⅛ teaspoon cayenne red
   pepper

Heat oven to 425°. Prepare pastry. Sprinkle bacon, cheese and onion in pastry-lined pie pan. Beat eggs slightly; beat in remaining ingredients. Pour cream mixture into pie pan. Bake 15 minutes.

Reduce oven temperature to 300° and bake 30 minutes longer or until knife inserted 1 inch from edge comes out clean. Let stand 10 minutes before cutting. Serve in wedges.

6 main-dish servings (8 appetizer servings).

Rice, Pasta
and Cereals

Rice is nice! As a dinner vegetable, a friendly base for foods you cream, a pudding for dessert. And rice is the mainstay food for million of people on the face of the earth. Pasta is popular —and you don't have to be Italian to enjoy it in more than one of its many forms. Try the recipes based on cornmeal, too—these are hearty peasant foods, beloved the whole world over. And as for cereals? What would we do without them!

Rice

Mounded and fluffy, each grain whole, separate and tender—that's how rice should and could be if you prepare it properly. Resist the extra stir or just one peek; and when stirring or fluffing, always use a fork to avoid crushing the grains. Avoid overcooking; it produces a mush. Don't buy just one kind of rice—enjoy them all!

Regular Rice: The hull and bran have been removed by polishing. Short grain rice is less expensive than long grain; it is used for casseroles, puddings and creamy desserts. Long grain rice is a better all-purpose rice and cooks fluffier, flakier and drier; it is used for curries, Chinese dishes and as a vegetable.

Processed (Converted) Rice: This type contains the vitamins found in the husk of brown rice but is polished like white rice. It can be substituted for regular rice, but the cooking time is longer.

Precooked (Instant) Rice: Commercially cooked, rinsed and dried. It is good as part of a main dish—and quick to fix at any time.

Brown Rice: A vitamin-rich whole grain, with only the outer hull removed. It has a nutty flavor and is used as a side dish.

Wild Rice: Long-grained and dark greenish-brown in color. (And not really rice but the seed of an aquatic grass.) Expensive, it is often sold combined with brown rice.

RICE TIPS

■ *To Reheat Cooked Rice:* Heat cooked rice in top of double boiler over hot water, about 10 minutes or until rice is hot and fluffy. Or place rice in heavy pan with tightly fitted cover. Sprinkle water over rice, using about 2 tablespoons water to 1 cup rice. Cover; heat over low heat 5 to 8 minutes or until hot and fluffy.

■ *To Refrigerate Cooked Rice:* Place rice in bowl and cover tightly or wrap completely to prevent drying out. Keeps 4 to 5 days.

■ *To Freeze Cooked Rice:* Store rice in covered freezer container or wrap completely. Keeps up to 6 months.

AT-A-GLANCE RICE YIELDS

Yield	Rice	Water	Salt
For about 1 cup cooked rice:			
Regular white rice	⅓ cup	⅔ cup	¼ teaspoon
Processed rice	¼ cup	⅔ cup	¼ teaspoon
Precooked (instant) rice	½ cup	½ cup	¼ teaspoon
For about 1½ cups cooked rice:			
Regular white rice	½ cup	1 cup	½ teaspoon
Processed rice	⅓ cup	1 cup	¼ teaspoon
Precooked (instant) rice	¾ cup	¾ cup	¼ teaspoon
For about 2 cups cooked rice:			
Regular white rice	⅔ cup	1⅓ cups	½ teaspoon
Processed rice	½ cup	1¼ cups	½ teaspoon
Precooked (instant) rice	1 cup	1 cup	½ teaspoon
For about 3 cups cooked rice:			
Regular white rice	1 cup	2 cups	1 teaspoon
Processed rice	¾ cup	2 cups	1 teaspoon
Precooked (instant) rice	1½ cups	1½ cups	1 teaspoon
Wild rice	1 cup	2½ cups	1 teaspoon
For about 4 cups cooked rice:			
Regular white rice	1⅓ cups	2⅔ cups	1 teaspoon
Processed rice	1 cup	2½ cups	1 teaspoon
Precooked (instant) rice	2 cups	2 cups	1 teaspoon
Brown rice	1 cup	2½ cups	1 teaspoon

TO COOK RICE

Refer to the chart on page 344 for just the right amount of rice.

Regular Rice: Heat rice, water and salt to boiling, stirring once or twice. Reduce heat to simmer; cover pan tightly and cook 14 minutes. (Do not lift cover or stir.) Remove pan of cooked rice from heat. Fluff rice lightly with fork; cover and let steam 5 to 10 minutes.

Processed, Instant and Precooked Rice: Follow package directions.

Brown Rice: Follow directions for Regular Rice (above) except—increase cooking time to 30 to 40 minutes.

Wild Rice: Wash wild rice by placing in wire strainer; run cold water through it, lifting rice with fingers to clean thoroughly. Heat rice, water and salt to boiling, stirring once or twice. Reduce heat to simmer; cover pan tightly and cook 40 to 50 minutes or until tender. After cooking rice 30 minutes, check to see that rice is not sticking to pan. If necessary, add ¼ cup water.

OVEN-STEAMED RICE

The ideal plan for preparing crowd-size amounts of rice. And whenever you're entertaining, what better way to keep the top of the range clear for sauces and skillet dishes?

2 cups boiling water   1 teaspoon salt
1 cup uncooked regular rice

Heat oven to 350°. Mix all ingredients thoroughly in ungreased 1- or 1½-quart casserole or in baking dish, 10x6x1½ or 11½x7½x1½ inches.

Cover tightly. Bake 25 to 30 minutes or until liquid is absorbed and rice is tender.

For large quantities, double or triple all ingredients and bake in 3-quart casserole or in baking dish, 13½x9x2 inches.

3 to 4 cups cooked rice; 4 to 6 servings.

Note: To vary the flavor, substitute chicken or beef bouillon for the water and add spices such as chervil, curry, dill weed, onion, orange peel, parsley or saffron.

RICE FLAVOR-ADDERS

COOK-INS

A simple way to change the flavor and color of a plain rice is to vary the cooking liquid. Try any one of the following substitutions:

■ Chicken or beef broth or bouillon for all of the water.
■ Chicken consommé diluted as directed on can for all of the water.
■ Apple juice for half of the water.
■ Orange juice for half of the water.
■ Pineapple juice for half of the water.
■ Tomato juice for half of the water.

STIR-INS

For color, flavor or just for a change.

Prepare 3 cups hot cooked rice (page 345); stir in one of the following—

■ *Almond:* ½ cup slivered almonds browned in 2 tablespoons butter.
■ *Bacon:* 4 slices bacon, diced, crisply fried and drained.
■ *Browned Butter:* ¼ cup butter heated until light brown.
■ *Carrot:* ½ cup shredded carrot and 2 tablespoons butter, melted.
■ *Lemon:* 2 teaspoons lemon juice and 2 tablespoons butter, melted.
■ *Marmalade:* ¼ cup marmalade and 2 tablespoons butter, melted.
■ *Mushroom:* 1 can (3 or 4 ounces) sliced mushrooms or mushroom stems and pieces, drained, heated in 2 tablespoons butter.
■ *Olive:* ½ cup chopped ripe or pimiento-stuffed olives or 10 pitted ripe or pimiento-stuffed olives, sliced.
■ *Onion:* 2 tablespoons minced onion cooked and stirred in 2 tablespoons butter until tender.
■ *Parsley:* 2 tablespoons snipped parsley.

FIESTA RICE

1 medium onion, finely
  chopped (about ½ cup)
¼ cup chopped green pepper
3 tablespoons butter or
  margarine
1 can (1 pound) stewed
  tomatoes

1 tablespoon salt
⅛ teaspoon pepper
3 cups cooked rice (page
  345)

In large skillet, cook and stir onion and green pepper in butter until onion is tender. Stir in tomatoes, salt, pepper and rice. Simmer uncovered over low heat, about 15 minutes, until flavors are blended and mixture is hot.

6 servings (about ½ cup each).

INDIAN PILAF

Serve with crusty broiled chicken.

¼ cup butter or margarine
1 medium onion, chopped
  (about ½ cup)
1½ cups uncooked regular
  rice
½ teaspoon salt
½ teaspoon allspice

½ teaspoon turmeric
¼ teaspoon curry powder
⅛ teaspoon pepper
3½ cups chicken broth*
¼ cup blanched slivered
  almonds

Heat oven to 350°. Melt butter in skillet. Add onion and rice; cook and stir until rice is yellow and onion is tender. Stir in next 5 seasonings. Pour into ungreased 2-quart casserole.

Heat chicken broth to boiling; stir into rice mixture. Cover tightly; bake 30 to 40 minutes or until liquid is absorbed and rice is tender. Stir in almonds.

8 servings (½ cup each).

*Chicken broth can be made by dissolving 4 chicken bouillon cubes in 3½ cups boiling water, or use canned chicken broth.

RICE RING

Prepare 4 cups rice (page 345). Lightly press into well-buttered 4-cup ring mold. Keep hot until serving time. Invert warm serving plate over mold; turn over. Remove ring mold.

8 servings.

CURRIED RICE

- 1 tablespoon minced onion
- 2 tablespoons butter or margarine
- ½ to 1 teaspoon curry powder
- ¼ teaspoon salt
- ¼ teaspoon pepper
- 3 cups hot cooked rice (page 345)
- ¼ cup toasted slivered almonds*
- ¼ cup chopped pimiento-stuffed or pitted ripe olives

In small skillet, cook and stir onion in butter until onion is tender. Stir in curry powder, salt and pepper. Mix into hot rice. Sprinkle almonds and olives over rice.

6 servings (about ½ cup each).

*To toast almonds, place on baking sheet; toast in 350° oven 10 minutes.

FRIED RICE

- ¼ cup chopped onion
- 2 tablespoons chopped green pepper
- 2 tablespoons salad oil
- 2 cups cooked rice (page 345)
- 1 can (5 ounces) water chestnuts, drained and thinly sliced
- 1 can (3 ounces) sliced mushrooms, drained
- 2 tablespoons soy sauce
- 3 eggs, beaten

In large skillet, cook and stir onion and green pepper in oil until onion is tender. Stir in rice, water chestnuts, mushrooms and soy sauce. Cook over low heat 10 minutes, stirring frequently. Stir in beaten eggs; cook and stir 2 to 3 minutes longer.

4 or 5 servings (about ½ cup each).

SAVORY RICE BLEND

- ¼ cup uncooked wild rice
- 3 tablespoons butter or margarine
- 1 small onion, chopped
- ½ cup chopped celery
- 2½ cups chicken broth*
- 1 tablespoon parsley flakes
- ½ teaspoon salt
- ½ teaspoon bottled brown bouquet sauce
- ¼ teaspoon sage
- ¼ teaspoon basil
- 1 can (4 ounces) mushroom stems and pieces, drained
- ¼ cup uncooked regular rice
- 1 cup dairy sour cream, if desired

*Chicken broth can be made by dissolving 3 chicken bouillon cubes in 2½ cups boiling water, or use canned chicken broth.

Heat oven to 350°. Wash and drain wild rice. Melt butter in small skillet. Add onion, celery and wild rice; cook and stir until onion is tender. Pour into ungreased 1½-quart casserole. Heat chicken broth to boiling; pour over wild rice mixture. Stir in parsley flakes, salt, brown bouquet sauce, sage, basil and mushrooms. Cover tightly; bake 45 minutes.

Remove from oven; stir in regular rice. Cover; bake 40 to 45 minutes longer or until all liquid is absorbed and rice is tender. Stir in sour cream.

7 servings (about ½ cup each).

WILD RICE WITH MUSHROOMS AND ALMONDS

1 cup uncooked wild rice
¼ cup butter or margarine
½ cup slivered almonds
2 tablespoons snipped chives or chopped green onions

1 can (8 ounces) mushroom stems and pieces, drained
3 cups chicken broth*

Wash and drain wild rice. Melt butter in large skillet. Add rice, almonds, chives and mushrooms; cook and stir until almonds are golden brown, about 20 minutes.

Heat oven to 325°. Pour rice mixture into ungreased 1½-quart casserole. Heat chicken broth to boiling; stir into rice mixture. Cover tightly; bake about 1½ hours or until all liquid is absorbed and rice is tender and fluffy.

6 to 8 servings.

*Chicken broth can be made by dissolving 3 chicken bouillon cubes in 3 cups boiling water, or use canned chicken broth.

BULGUR PILAF

A sweet, nutty flavored pilaf served instead of rice.

2 tablespoons minced onion
2 tablespoons chopped green pepper
2 tablespoons butter or margarine
2 cups chicken broth*

1 cup bulgur wheat
1 can (3 ounce) sliced mushrooms, drained
½ teaspoon salt
Dash pepper

In medium skillet, cook and stir onion and green pep-

*Chicken broth can be made by dissolving 2 chicken bouillon cubes in 2 cups boiling water, or use canned chicken broth.

per in butter until onion is tender. Stir in remaining ingredients. Cover; heat to boiling. Reduce heat; simmer 15 minutes.

4 servings.

Note: Bulgur wheat, sometimes called parboiled wheat, is whole wheat that has been cooked, dried, partially debranned and cracked into coarse fragments. It resembles whole wheat in nutritive properties and is used as an alternate for rice in many recipes. This ancient all-wheat food originated in the Near East.

INTERNATIONAL CULINARY COUSINS

The Italians often cook their rice—risotto—in much the same fashion as the Indians do pilaf (see above). They both start by sautéeing rice and onions in butter. The skillet remains on top of the stove for risotto, however. The boiling chicken or beef broth is added at intervals as the rice absorbs it.

Pasta

This wheat-flour dough, for which we thank Southern Italy, comes in myriad sizes and shapes. Tubular, fine-stringed or flat; shells or bows; ruffled, curly-edged or scalloped. Equally varied are the sauces that top it. Some pastas can be layered with meat and cheese or stuffed with fresh cheese, then sauced and baked. (Try Italian Spaghetti and Lasagne on pages 496–497.)

Pasta Yields

1 package (6 or 7 ounces) macaroni (2 cups) = 4 cups cooked; 4 to 6 servings

1 package (7 or 8 ounces) spaghetti = 4 cups cooked; 4 to 6 servings

8 ounces egg noodles (4 to 5 cups) = 4 to 5 cups cooked 4 to 6 servings

TO COOK MACARONI, SPAGHETTI AND NOODLES

Traditional Method: Add 1 tablespoon salt to 3 quarts rapidly boiling water in deep kettle. Add 7 or 8 ounces macaroni, spaghetti or noodles into water gradually so that water continues to boil. (If spaghetti strands are left whole, place one end in water; as they soften, gradually coil them into kettle until submerged.)

Boil uncovered, stirring occasionally, just until tender* (7 to 10 minutes or as directed on package). Test by cutting several strands with fork against side of kettle. Drain quickly in colander or sieve. If macaroni product is to be used in a salad, rinse in cold water.

Easy Method: Drop 7 or 8 ounces macaroni, spaghetti or noodles into 6 cups rapidly boiling salted water (4 teaspoons salt). Heat to rapid boiling. Cook, stirring constantly, 3 minutes.* Cover tightly. Remove from heat and let stand 10 minutes. Drain. If macaroni product is to be used in a salad, rinse in cold water.

4 to 6 servings.

*For thicker macaroni products, such as lasagne, kluski noodles, etc., follow manufacturer's directions.

Note: Toss cooked and drained macaroni, spaghetti or noodles with 3 tablespoons butter; this will keep pieces separated.

HOMEMADE EGG NOODLES

2 cups all-purpose flour*   2 teaspoons salt
3 egg yolks   ¼ to ½ cup water
1 egg

Measure flour into bowl; make a well in center and add egg yolks, whole egg and salt. With hands, thoroughly mix egg into flour. Add water, 1 tablespoon at a time, mixing thoroughly after each addition. (Add only enough water to form dough into a ball.)

Turn dough onto well-floured cloth-covered board; knead until smooth and elastic, about 10 minutes. Cover; let rest 10 minutes.

Divide dough into 4 equal parts. Roll dough, 1 part at a time, into paper-thin rectangle, keeping remaining

*If using self-rising flour, omit salt.

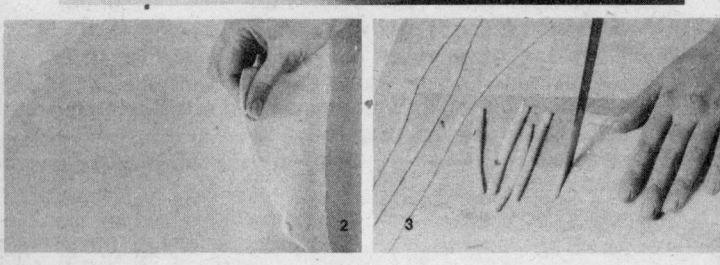

1. Measure flour into mixing bowl. Make a well in center and add egg yolks, whole egg and salt.

2. Carefully roll paper-thin rectangle of dough around rolling pin; do not stretch.

3. Use a sharp knife to cut dough into strips. Cut a few at a time, then shake out.

4. Cook noodles until tender. Drain quickly but thoroughly in a colander or sieve.

dough covered. Roll rectangle around rolling pin; slip out rolling pin.

Cut dough crosswise into ⅛-inch strips for narrow noodles and ¼-inch strips for wide noodles. Shake out strips and place on towel to dry, about 2 hours.

When dry, break dry strips into smaller pieces. Cook in 3 quarts boiling salted water (1 tablespoon salt) 12 to 15 minutes or until tender. Drain thoroughly.

About 6 cups (10 ounces).

NOODLE STIR-INS

Last-minute additions to add color, flavor and variety.

Cook 8 ounces noodles as directed on page 352; stir one of the following into the drained noodles—

■ *Almonds:* ¼ cup slivered almonds browned in 2 tablespoons butter.

■ *Browned Buttered Crumbs:* ½ cup dry bread crumbs browned in 2 tablespoons butter.

■ *Herbs:* ½ teaspoon *each* thyme leaves, basil leaves, snipped parsley and snipped chives or minced onion stirred into 2 tablespoons butter, melted.

■ *Onion and Green Pepper:* ¼ cup chopped green pepper and 2 tablespoons chopped onion cooked and stirred in 2 tablespoons butter until onion is tender.

■ *Parmesan Cheese:* Stir in 2 tablespoons butter, then fold in ¼ cup grated Parmesan cheese.

■ *Poppy Seed:* 2 teaspoons poppy seed and 1 tablespoon butter.

EGG NOODLE RING

Heat oven to 375°. Butter 6-cup ring mold. Cook 8 ounces wide egg noodles as directed on page 352. Return drained noodles to kettle; stir in 2 to 3 tablespoons butter.

Press noodles into ring mold. Place ring mold in pan of hot water (1 inch deep). Bake 20 minutes. Invert warm serving plate over mold; turn over. Remove ring mold.

5 or 6 servings.

NOODLES ALFREDO

8 ounces wide egg noodles
½ cup butter or margarine
½ cup light cream (20%)
1 cup grated Parmesan
   cheese
1 tablespoon parsley flakes
¼ teaspoon salt
Dash pepper

Cook noodles as directed on page 352. While noodles cook, heat butter and cream in small saucepan over low heat until butter is melted. Stir in cheese, parsley flakes, salt and pepper; keep warm over low heat.

Return drained noodles to kettle. Pour sauce over noodles, stirring gently until noodles are well coated.

5 to 6 servings.

NOODLES ROMANOFF

8 ounces wide egg noodles
2 cups dairy sour cream
¼ cup grated Parmesan
   cheese
1 tablespoon snipped chives
1 teaspoon salt
⅛ teaspoon pepper
1 large clove garlic, crushed
2 tablespoons butter or
   margarine
¼ cup grated Parmesan
   cheese

Cook noodles as directed on page 352. While noodles cook, stir together sour cream, ¼ cup cheese, the chives, salt, pepper and garlic.

Return drained noodles to kettle and stir in butter. Fold in sour cream mixture. Arrange on warm platter; sprinkle with ¼ cup cheese.

6 to 8 servings.

PARTY NOODLES ROMANOFF

Prepare 1 package (5.5 ounces) noodles Romanoff as directed on package except—stir in one of the following:

1 tablespoon snipped chives
1 teaspoon poppy seed
1 tablespoon chopped green
   onion
½ cup cottage cheese and
   1 tablespoon snipped
   chives
½ cup shredded Parmesan
   cheese

Garnish with paprika or snipped parsley.
4 servings.

Cornmeal

Used in stuffings, breads and puddings, or served as mush, cornmeal is a traditional favorite. In the broad Po River Valley of Central and Northern Italy, where corn is a staple food, gravied mush is served as Polenta. Gnocchi, another Italian cornmeal specialty, can also be made with potatoes.

FRIED CORNMEAL MUSH

Do some of the preparation the night before and get a warm start on a wintry day—the easy way.

1 cup cornmeal
1 cup cold water
3 cups boiling water
1 teaspoon salt
2 tablespoons butter or margarine
Flour
Syrup or jelly

Grease loaf pan, 9x5x3 or 8½x4½x2 inches. Mix cornmeal and cold water in saucepan. Stir in boiling water and salt. Cook, stirring constantly until mixture thickens and boils. Cover; cook over low heat 10 minutes. Spoon into pan. Cover; chill at least 12 hours.

Invert pan to unmold cornmeal mush. Cut loaf into ½-inch slices. Melt butter in large skillet. Coat slices with flour; brown on each side in skillet. Serve hot with syrup and, if desired, with bacon, ham or sausage.

9 servings.

GNOCCHI

A traditional Northern Italian dish. Serve it as a first course or as a side dish.

2½ cups milk
1 cup white cornmeal
1 tablespoon butter or margarine
2 eggs, well beaten
¼ teaspoon salt
2 tablespoons butter or margarine
¼ to ½ cup grated Parmesan cheese

Butter square pan, 8x8x2 inches. Heat milk to scalding in medium saucepan. Reduce heat; stirring constantly, sprinkle cornmeal slowly into hot milk. Cook, stirring constantly, about 5 minutes or until thick (spoon will stand upright in the gnocchi). Remove from heat;

1. The cornmeal mixture for Gnocchi is very stiff.

2. Golden brown Gnocchi—prepared in a baking dish.

mix in 1 tablespoon butter, the eggs and salt. Beat until smooth. Spread in pan; cool and refrigerate 2 to 3 hours.

Just before serving, heat oven to 425°. Cut cornmeal mixture into sixteen 1½-inch circles. (Use cookie cutter or rim of small glass.) Place 4 circles in each individual casserole; dot with 2 tablespoons butter and sprinkle with cheese. Bake 10 or 12 minutes or until heated through.

Set oven control at broil and/or 550°. Place casseroles in broiler so tops are 2 to 3 inches from heat. Broil about 2 minutes or until golden brown.

4 servings.

Note: If individual casseroles are not available, bake circles in baking dish or ovenproof skillet.

Cereals

Start the most important meal of the day with cereal. Mix and match them, hot and cold. Slice fruit on your favorites. Ever try salt on cereal? Or add a little butter?

CEREAL FUNNY FACES

Start with a bowl of favorite dry cereal.

Frosty the Snowman: Dampen 3 large marshmallows and stack (they'll stick together). The top marshmallow is the face. Use pieces of raisins for the eyes, a red cinnamon candy for the mouth and a pitted prune for the hat. Stand snowman upright on cereal.

Minnie Mouse: Place pear half cut side down on cereal. Make face at narrow end: raisin eyes, a red cinnamon candy or cherry-piece mouth and almond slices for ears. Use a miniature marshmallow for the tail.

Skipperdee Turtle: Place 4 walnut halves on cereal. They form the legs. Drop heaping spoonful of any flavor canned frosting onto nuts. Use a shelled whole walnut or 2 halves for the turtle's head.

Trixy the Rabbit: Use a large marshmallow for the head, another cut in half for the ears. Pinch ends to make points and flatten centers of ears. Tint ears and eyes with red food color. Make small slits in cheek area for whiskers of almond slices or slivers. Use pieces of cherry for mouth. Put ears on cereal first, then put head in place.

Man from Mars: Place pear half cut side down on cereal. At narrow end, place 2 long slivers of apple for antennas. Use almond slivers or slices for eyes, an apple wedge for the mouth and a pitted prune for the beard.

Circus Carousel: Place a scoop of any flavor ice cream or marshmallow crème on cereal. Press animal crackers into ice cream.

FRUITED HOT CEREALS

Prepare your favorite hot cereal as directed on package except—when heating water to boiling, add one of the following for each serving:

4 or 5 dried apricot halves, cut up

3 or 4 dates, cut up

4 or 5 prunes, cut up

2 tablespoons raisins

DRY CEREAL SEASONINGS

What a way to start the day!

Enhance each serving of ready-to-eat cereal with one of the following:
- Flavored Milk (page 45)
- Softened ice cream
- 1 teaspoon flavored gelatin
- 1 to 2 teaspoons instant cocoa
- ¼ cup miniature marshmallows
- ¼ cup raisins

FLAVORED HOT CEREALS

These quick stir-ins help to make an everyday hot cereal more interesting.

Prepare hot cereal as directed on package except—for each serving, stir in one of the following:

■ 2 tablespoons applesauce; top with 1 tablespoon brown sugar

■ 1 tablespoon instant cocoa

■ 1 teaspoon flavored gelatin

■ 1 to 2 tablespoons jam, jelly or marmalade

■ 1 to 2 tablespoons maple syrup, light molasses or honey

■ ¼ cup miniature marshmallows or marshmallow crème

■ 2 tablespoons mandarin orange segments; top with 1 tablespoon brown sugar

Meats

Meat—your meals and your food budget revolve around it. Feel stymied trying to provide interesting meals that are budget conscious? Take heart—the pages that follow are chock-full of the kind of information dear to a thrifty cook's heart. And get to know your meat retailer. Ask him questions. If he recommends a cut you've never had—or never even heard of—don't be afraid to try it. You may have a new family favorite on your hands!

How Much Should You Buy?

To some extent, the amount of meat to buy depends on the appetites of your family. Other factors to consider are the time needed for preparation, the amount of storage space you have available, and how much bone there is in the cut. In most instances, the recipe will help you judge the amount of meat you need. But should you come across some special cut on sale and decide to take advantage of it, these general guidelines will be helpful:

Boneless meat (ground meat, tenderloin slices)	¼ to ⅓ pound per serving
Boneless roasts (beef, veal, pork, lamb)	⅓ to ½ pound per serving
Small bone in (pork loin, rib roasts, ham)	½ pound per serving
Medium bone in (pot-roasts, country-style ribs)	½ to ¾ pound per serving
Large bone in (shanks, spareribs, back ribs, short ribs)	¾ to 1 pound per serving

Grades of Meat and What They Mean

The round stamp bearing the abbreviated words "U.S. Inspected and Passed" is your guarantee that the meat on which the stamp appears is wholesome and that the plant in which the meat was processed has met the federal standards of cleanliness. The stamp need not be trimmed from the meat; the marking fluid used is a harmless vegetable coloring.

The U.S. Department of Agriculture grades of meat quality are found in a shield-shaped stamp. In descending order, these grades are: *USDA Prime, Choice, Good, Standard, Commercial* and *Utility*. Many meat packers use special brand names to denote quality.

Most meats carried by retail stores are *Choice*. (*Prime* is usually available only in special restaurants. Grades below *Good* are usually used by the packers in combination meats and are not sold in retail stores.) As you shop for meat, look for flecks of fat within the lean; this is "marbling." It increases juiciness, flavor and tenderness. Ribs and loins of high-quality beef, lamb and mutton are usually aged. Aging develops additional tenderness and characteristic flavor. You can ask your retailer to give you aged beef.

How to Store Meat

Meat will begin to lose flavor and spoil if you don't store it quickly and properly right after you buy it. Fresh meats, to be at their best, should be used within 2 to 3 days; ground meat and variety meats within 24 hours. If it is to be used within 1 or 2 days, fresh prepackaged meat may be stored in its original wrapper; if the meat is to be kept for a longer period, loosen the ends of the wrapper or store as described below. Fresh meat which is not prepackaged should be stored unwrapped or wrapped loosely in waxed paper, plastic wrap or aluminum foil. This allows the air to partially dry the surface of the meat and thus retard the growth of bacteria. Meat should never be washed. Cured and smoked meats, sausages and ready-to-serve meats may be stored in their original wrappings.

Cooked meats and the liquid in which meats have been cooked should be cooled quickly, then covered and stored in refrigerator. Cooling can be hastened by placing the pan in cold water.

How to Freeze Meat

Just about all meats freeze well and maintain their

quality if wrapped properly, frozen quickly and kept at a temperature of 0° or below. (Don't use the ice cube compartment of your refrigerator as a substitute for a freezer for more than a week.) And keep in mind that the condition of the meat at defrosting will be the same as it was at freezing. Therefore, if you do plan to freeze meat, do so as soon as possible after marketing.

Before wrapping, prepare the meat for final use by trimming off excess fat and, to conserve freezer space, remove bones where you can. Do not salt. Choose freezer wrapping carefully and follow directions for its use: follow freezer directions for freezing. Wrap the meat tightly, then label and date before placing in freezer.

For top quality, most frozen meats should be used within 3 months; beef corned briskets, while smoked hams and pork sausage should be used within 2 weeks. Do not freeze smoked arm picnics, canned hams or other canned meats.

For defrosting, place wrapped meat in refrigerator or let stand at room temperature just until defrosted and then place in refrigerator.

How to Cook Meat

Cooked by the wrong method, the tenderest cut of meat can become very leathery; cooked by the right method, the toughest cut becomes tender. Know your cooking methods and the method recommended for the cut you plan to use.

There are two types of heat—dry (without liquid) and moist (with steam or liquid). And there are six basic methods for cooking meat: roasting, broiling, panbroiling, frying, braising and cooking in liquid. The correct method for each cut of meat depends upon its tenderness, its size and its thickness. If you study the cooking recommendations on the meat charts and the general cooking methods below, you should be able to cook any cut of meat without a recipe.

Roasting is recommended for large, tender cuts of beef, veal, pork and lamb. Consult the Roasting Chart for each type of meat to determine time, temperature and degree of doneness. Place meat fat side up on a rack in a shallow roasting pan. Do not cover. Do not add water. Just a word about searing. The old idea of searing meat to keep in the juices has been discarded. It is, however, sometimes done to develop aroma and flavor in the outside slices or to produce drippings of a rich brown color.

Broiling is recommended for tender steaks, chops, sliced ham or bacon or ground meat. (Steaks and chops should be a least ¾ inch thick; ham slices at least ½ inch thick.) Place meat on rack 2 to 5 inches from source of heat. Broil until top side is brown, then turn and cook to desired degree of doneness.

Panbroiling is suitable for thin cuts (no more than 1 inch thick) of the same type recommended for broiling. Use a heavy pan or griddle; it is not necessary to preheat the pan. For very lean cuts, brush pan with a small amount of shortening, if desired; otherwise, do not add fat and do not add water. Cook meat slowly until browned on both sides, turning occasionally and pouring off fat as it accumulates.

Panfrying is suitable for thin, tender pieces of meat which have been made tender by scoring, cubing or grinding. Unless pan is coated with a non-stick substance, add a small amount of fat to the pan or allow fat to accumulate as meat cooks. Brown meat on both sides over medium heat; turn occasionally until done. Do not cover.

Braising is recommended for less tender cuts of meat and for certain tender cuts, particularly pork. Place meat in heavy pan and brown slowly on all sides. Pour off drippings, season and add a small amount of liquid, if necessary. (More tender cuts may not need liquid.) Cover tightly and simmer either on top of range or in 300 to 325° oven until meat is tender.

Cooking in liquid is used for large, less tender cuts and stew meat. Brown meat on all sides, if desired. Cover meat with liquid as directed and season. Cover kettle and simmer until meat is tender. Do not boil.

Note: We are indebted to Reba Staggs of the National Live Stock and Meat Board for their materials and her assistance in the preparation of the recipes and information on meats.

Beef

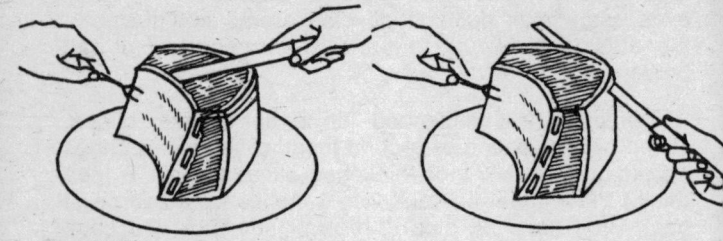

RIB ROAST

1. Place roast with large side down on platter. If necessary, remove wedge-shaped slice from large end so roast will stand firmly. To carve, insert fork below first rib. Slice from the outside of roast toward the rib side.

2. After making several slices, cut along inner side of rib bone with knife. As each slice is released, slide knife under it and lift to plate.

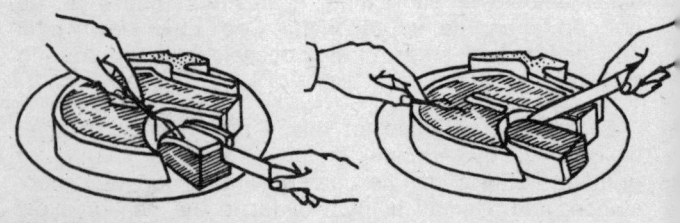

BLADE POT-ROAST

1. With fork in meat, cut between the muscles and around the bones (bones are easily removed). Remove one solid section of pot-roast at a time.

2. Turn section so that meat grain runs parallel to platter. Carve across the grain of meat; slices should be about ¼ inch thick.

PORTERHOUSE STEAK

1. Place steak on platter with bone to carver's right as shown. Insert fork in steak; cut around bone as closely as possible. Set bone aside. Holding meat with fork, carve 1-inch wide slices across the full width of steak. For thick steaks, slice on the diagonal instead. (See Corned Brisket instructions at right.)

CORNED BRISKET

1. Place corned brisket on platter as shown. Carve across the 2 or 3 "faces" of brisket as shown. Make slices in rotation so that the "faces" will remain equal to each other in size. Cut *thin* slices at a slight angle, always across the grain.

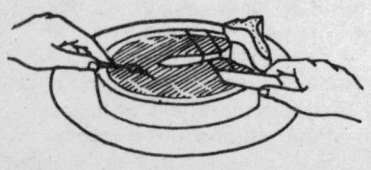

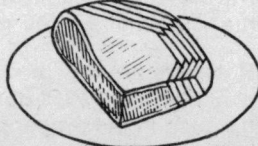

Pork

 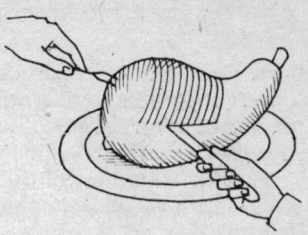

WHOLE HAM

1. Place ham on platter with fat side up and shank facing right. Cut a few slices from the thin side (thin side will face carver if ham is a left leg and away from him if ham is a right leg). Turn ham so it rests on cut side. Make slices down to bone.
2. Run knife horizontally along bone to release slices.

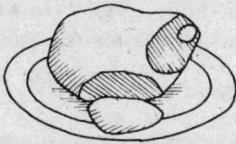 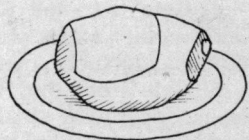

PICNIC SHOULDER

1. Cut off a lengthwise slice from shoulder. Turn meat so that it rests on this cut surface.
2. Make vertical cuts as shown; turn knife and cut horizontally along bone to remove boneless piece for carving. For additional servings, remove remaining meat from arm bone and carve.

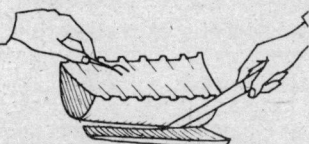 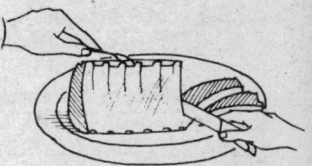

LOIN ROAST

1. After cooking, remove backbone from ribs to facilitate carving. Place roast on platter with rib side toward carver.
2. With fork firmly inserted in roast, cut slices on each side of rib bones. (Every other slice will contain a bone).

Lamb
LEG OF LAMB

1. Place roast on platter with shank bone to carver's right. Cut a few lengthwise slices from thin side. Turn leg over so that it rests on cut side. Make vertical slices down to the leg bone.
2. Cut horizontally along bone to release slices.

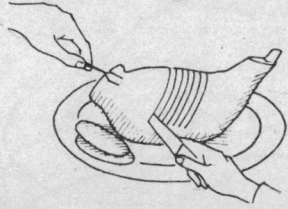 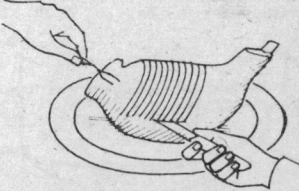

Beef

1. Cuts from the Chuck Boneless chuck eye roast,*
chuck short ribs, blade pot-roast or steak, arm pot-roast
or steak, boneless shoulder pot-roast or steak, cross rib
pot-roast (braise, cook in liquid).

2. Cuts from the Rib Rib roast, rib steak, boneless rib
steak, rib eye or Delmonico roast or steak (roast, broil,
panfry).

3. Cuts from the Short Loin T-bone steak, porterhouse
steak, top loin steak, boneless top loin steak, tenderloin
or filet mignon steak or roast (roast, broil, panfry).

4. Cuts from the Sirloin Pin bone sirloin steak, flat
bone sirloin steak, wedge bone sirloin steak, boneless
sirloin steak (broil, panfry).

5. Cuts from the Round Rolled rump roast,* round
steak, top round steak,* bottom round steak or roast,*
eye of round, heel of round, cubed steak* (braise, cook in
liquid).

6. Cuts from the Tip Tip roast or steak,* tip kabobs*
(braise).

7. Cuts from the Flank Flank steak,* flank steak roll*
(braise, cook in liquid).

8. Cuts from the Short Plate Short ribs, skirt steak roll*
(braise, cook in liquid).

9. Cuts from the Brisket Fresh brisket, corned brisket
(braise, cook in liquid).

10. Cuts from the Foreshank Shank cross cuts (braise,
cook in liquid).

Ground beef and stew beef come from the flank, short
plate, foreshank, chuck or round.

*Some cuts from very high quality beef may be roasted, broiled or panfried
instead of braised.

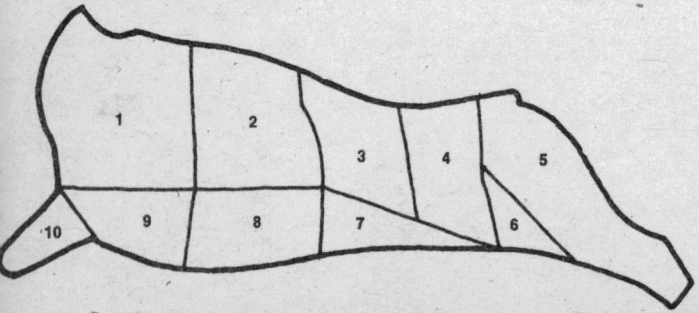

BEEF CUTS YOU SHOULD KNOW

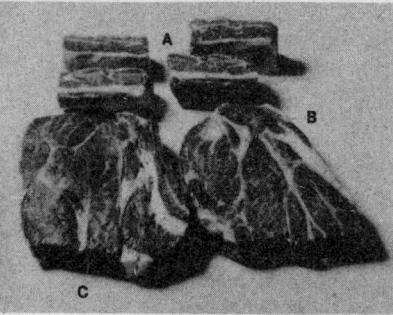

A. Chuck short ribs **B.** Blade steak
C. Cross rib pot-roast

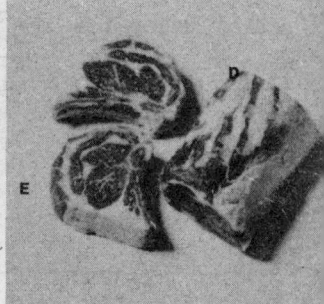

D. Rib eye (Delmonico) roast
E. Rib steaks

F. Porterhouse steak **G.** T-bone steak
H. Top loin steak

I. Tip roast
J. Wedge bone sirloin steak

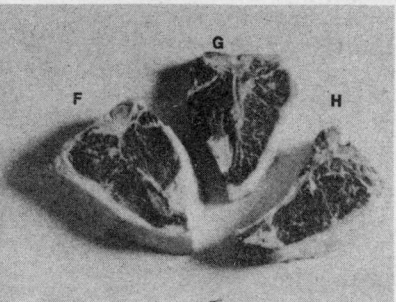

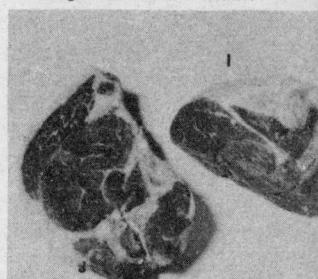

K. Rolled rump roast **L.** Top round
steak
M. Eye of round **N:** Bottom round
steak

O. Short ribs (short plate) **P.** Stew
beef **Q.** Cubed steak

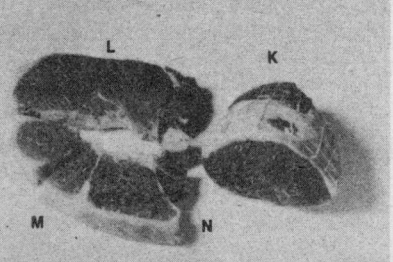

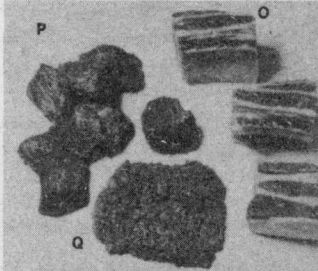

HOW TO ROAST BEEF

Select roast from those listed in chart on pages 370–371. Allow about ½ pound per person—less for boneless roasts, more for roasts with a bone. If desired, season with salt and pepper before, during or after roasting (salt only goes into meat ¼ to ½ inch).

Place meat fat side up on rack in open shallow roasting pan. The rack keeps the meat out of the drippings. (With a rib roast, the ribs form a natural rack.) It is not necessary to baste.

Insert meat thermometer so tip is in center of thickest part of meat and does not touch bone or rest in fat. Do not add water. Do not cover.

Roast meat in 325° oven. (It is not necessary to preheat oven.) Roast to desired degree of doneness (see Timetable), using thermometer reading as *final* guide.

Roasts are easier to carve if allowed to set 15 to 20 minutes after removing from oven. Since meat continues to cook after removal from oven, if roast is to "set," it should be removed from oven when thermometer registers 5 to 10° lower than the desired doneness.

Note: For assistance in carving a rib roast, see page 364.

YORKSHIRE PUDDING WITH ROAST BEEF

Thirty minutes before rib or boneless rib roast is done, prepare Yorkshire Pudding (below). Heat square pan, 9x9x2 inches, in oven. Remove roast from oven; spoon off drippings and add melted shortening, if needed, to measure ½ cup.

Increase oven temperature to 425°. Return roast to oven. Place hot drippings in heated square pan; pour in Yorkshire Pudding batter. Bake 10 minutes. Remove roast; continue baking pudding 25 to 30 minutes longer. Cut pudding into squares; serve with roast.

6 to 9 servings.

YORKSHIRE PUDDING

1 cup all-purpose flour*	1 cup milk
½ teaspoon salt	2 eggs

Mix all ingredients with hand beater just until smooth.

Do not use self-rising flour in this recipe.

SPIT-BARBECUED ROASTS

Select a 5-pound boneless roast (beef, veal, pork or lamb). Insert spit rod lengthwise through center of roast; secure with holding forks. Check balance by rotating spit in palms of hands. Insert meat thermometer in center of thickest part of meat, making sure it does not touch fat or spit.

Arrange medium-hot coals at back of firebox; place foil drip pan under spit area. Cook roast on rotisserie as directed in the timetable below, using thermometer reading as the final guide to desired doneness. Add coals when necessary to maintain even heat. If desired, baste during last part of cooking period with one of the barbecue sauces on page 582.

Roast will be easier to carve if allowed to "set" 20 minutes in a warm place. Remove meat from rotisserie and take out spit rod when thermometer registers 5 to 10° below desired doneness. The meat will continue to cook while "setting."

8 to 10 servings.

TIMETABLE FOR SPIT-BARBECUED ROASTS

Cut	Cooking Time (Minutes per pound)	Thermometer Reading
Boneless Beef Rib	about 25	140° (rare)
	about 35	160° (medium)
	about 40	170° (well)
Rolled Leg of Lamb	about 40	175 to 180°
Boneless Pork Loin	about 45	170°
Boneless Veal Shoulder	about 40	170°

BEEF TENDERLOIN WITH BEARNAISE SAUCE

Brush 4-pound beef tenderloin with melted butter or margarine. Place on rack in open shallow roasting pan. Insert meat thermometer so tip is in center of thickest part of meat.

Roast tenderloin in 425° oven 45 to 60 minutes or until thermometer registers 140°. Serve with Béarnaise Sauce (page 572).

10 to 12 servings.

TIMETABLE FOR ROASTING BEEF
(Oven Temperature 325°)

Cut	Approximate Weight	Meat Thermometer Reading
Rib	6 to 8 pounds	140° (rare) 160° (medium) 170° (well)
	4 to 6 pounds	140° (rare) 160° (medium) 170° (well)
Boneless Rib	5 to 7 pounds	140° (rare) 160° (medium) 170° (well)
Rib Eye (Delmonico)*	4 to 6 pounds	140° (rare) 160° (medium) 170° (well)
Rolled Rump (high quality)	4 to 6 pounds	150 to 170°
Tip (high quality)	3½ to 4 pounds	140 to 170°
Tenderloin (whole)**	4 to 6 pounds	140° (rare)
Tenderloin (half)**	2 to 3 pounds	140° (rare)

*Roast at 350°   **Roast at 425°

CHARCOAL-GRILLED STEAK

Select 1- to 2-inch-thick steaks. For each person, allow 1 pound of any steak with a bone, such as sirloin, porterhouse, top loin or T-bone; allow ½ pound of boneless cuts, such as tenderloin.

Trim excess fat from edge of steak; slash remaining fat at 2-inch intervals to prevent curling. Place steak on grill 4 inches from hot coals; cook as directed in the Timetable.

Season steak with salt and pepper after turning and after removing from grill. Test for doneness by making a knife slit alongside bone.

TIMETABLE FOR GRILLING EACH SIDE

	1 inch thick	2 inches thick
Rare	4 to 5 minutes	12 to 13 minutes
Medium	7 to 8 minutes	15 to 17 minutes
Well	10 to 11 minutes	22 to 25 minutes

Approximate Cooking Time (Minutes per Pound)
23 to 25
27 to 30
32 to 35
26 to 32
34 to 38
40 to 42
32
38
48
18 to 20
20 to 22
22 to 24
25 to 30
35 to 40

Total	45 to 60 minutes
Time	45 to 50 minutes

Note: Less tender cuts of beef, such as boneless shoulder steaks, slices of chuck eye roast, whole bottom or top round steaks, slices of eye of round roast or tip steaks, can be used for charcoal grilling. These cuts should be from high-quality beef; if not, they should be marinated or treated with a commercial meat tenderizer (used as directed by the manufacturer).

HOW TO BROIL BEEF

Diagonally slash outer edge of fat on steak at 1-inch intervals to prevent curling (do not cut into lean). Set oven control at broil and/or 550°. Place meat on rack in broiler pan; place broiler pan so tops of ¾- to 1-inch steaks are 2 to 3 inches from heat, 1- to 2-inch steaks are 3 to 5 inches from heat. Broil until brown. The meat should be about half done (see Timetable on page 372).

If desired, season brown side with salt and pepper. (Always season *after* browning as salt tends to draw moisture to surface and delay browning.) Turn meat; broil until brown. If desired, serve with your choice of the toppings on page 372.

TIMETABLE FOR BROILING BEEF STEAKS

Cut	Approximate Total Cooking Time	
	Rare	Medium
Chuck Eye Steak (high quality)		
1 inch	24 minutes	30 minutes
1½ inches	40 minutes	45 minutes
Rib or Rib Eye Steak		
1 inch	15 minutes	20 minutes
1½ inches	25 minutes	30 minutes
2 inches	35 minutes	45 minutes
Top Loin Steak		
1 inch	15 minutes	20 minutes
1½ inches	25 minutes	30 minutes
2 inches	35 minutes	45 minutes
Sirloin Steak		
1 inch	20 minutes	25 minutes
1½ inches	30 minutes	35 minutes
Porterhouse Steak		
1 inch	20 minutes	25 minutes
1½ inches	30 minutes	35 minutes
T-bone Steak		
1 inch	20 minutes	25 minutes
1½ inches	30 minutes	35 minutes
Tenderloin (Filet Mignon) (4 to 8 ounces)	10 to 15 minutes	15 to 20 minutes
Ground Beef Patties (1 inch)	15 minutes	25 minutes

STEAK TOPPINGS

Spread a zesty topping on steaks just as soon as they're removed from the broiler or grill. Each of the following combinations serves four.

Blue Cheese: Blend 2 ounces blue cheese and ½ teaspoon Worcestershire sauce.

Mushroom-Onion: Melt 2 tablespoons butter or margarine in skillet. Add 1 cup thinly sliced onion, ½ cup sliced fresh mushrooms, ½ teaspoon salt and 2 cloves garlic, crushed; cook and stir until onion is tender.

Mustard Butter: Mix 2 tablespoons prepared mustard, 1 tablespoon snipped parsley, ¼ teaspoon onion salt and ¼ cup soft butter or margarine.

Sesame Butter: Beat ¼ cup soft butter or margarine, 1 teaspoon Worcestershire sauce and ½ teaspoon garlic salt. Stir in 1 tablespoon toasted sesame seed.

LONDON BROIL

Flank steak, a less tender beef cut, is not usually broiled—but if done very rare and cut across the grain, it's delicious.

1 tablespoon butter or margarine	1 teaspoon lemon juice
2 medium onions, thinly sliced	2 cloves garlic, crushed
¼ teaspoon salt	½ teaspoon salt
2 tablespoons salad oil	¼ teaspoon pepper
	2-pound high-quality flank steak, scored*

Melt butter in skillet. Add onions and ¼ teaspoon salt; cook and stir until onions are tender. Keep warm over low heat.

Stir together salad oil, lemon juice, garlic, ½ teaspoon salt and the pepper; brush on top side of meat. Set oven control at broil and/or 550°. Broil meat 2 to 3 inches from heat about 5 minutes or until brown. Turn meat; brush with oil mixture and broil 5 minutes longer.

Cut meat across grain at a slanted angle into thin slices; serve with onions.

6 to 8 servings.

*Cut lightly in a crisscross pattern—usually done by your meat retailer.

STEAK DIANE

Tender pieces of beef tenderloin topped with a specially seasoned butter sauce.

½ cup thinly sliced fresh mushrooms	¼ cup butter or margarine
2 tablespoons minced onion	2 tablespoons snipped parsley
1 clove garlic, crushed	2 tablespoons butter or margarine
⅛ teaspoon salt	1-pound beef tenderloin,* cut into 8 slices
1 teaspoon lemon juice	
1 teaspoon Worcestershire sauce	

Cook and stir mushrooms, onion, garlic, salt, lemon juice and Worcestershire sauce in ¼ cup butter until mushrooms are tender. Stir in parsley; keep sauce warm.

Melt 2 tablespoons butter in skillet; turning once, cook tenderloin slices over medium-high heat to medium doneness, about 3 to 4 minutes on each side. Serve with mushroom-butter sauce.

4 servings.

*A rib eye (Delmonico) steak can be used in this recipe.

MINUTE STEAKS

4 beef cubed steaks
½ cup all-purpose flour
¼ cup shortening

½ teaspoon salt
¼ teaspoon pepper

Coat steaks with flour. Melt shortening in skillet; cook steaks over medium-high heat until brown and crispy, about 4 minutes on each side.

Season steaks with salt and pepper. If desired, top each steak with butter or margarine.

4 servings.

VARIATION

■ *Steaks Stroganoff:* In large skillet, cook and stir 1 medium onion, thinly sliced, in 1 tablespoon butter until tender. Remove onion and set aside.

In same skillet, cook steaks as directed except—omit salt and pepper. Place steaks on warm platter.

Pour fat from skillet. Stir together onion, ½ cup dairy sour cream and ½ teaspoon salt in skillet; heat through. Serve over steaks.

SWISS STEAK

Round steak simmered in a zesty sauce. This colorful, old-fashioned recipe is sure to be a family favorite.

¼ cup all-purpose flour
½ teaspoon salt
¼ teaspoon pepper
  2-pound beef round steak,
    1 inch thick
2 tablespoons shortening

1 can (8 ounces) tomatoes
½ cup minced onion
¼ cup minced green pepper
½ teaspoon salt
⅛ teaspoon pepper

Stir together flour, salt and pepper. Sprinkle one side of meat with half the flour mixture; pound in. Turn meat and pound in remaining flour mixture. Cut meat into 6 serving pieces.

Melt shortening in large skillet; brown meat over medium heat, about 15 minutes. Cover tightly; simmer 1 hour. Add small amount of water if necessary.

Mix remaining ingredients; pour over meat. Cover tightly; simmer 30 minutes or until tender.

6 servings.

BEEF TIP EN BROCHETTE

2 pounds high-quality beef
   tip, cut into 1¼-inch cubes
1 can (10½ ounces)
   condensed beef
   consommé
⅓ cup sherry or, if desired,
   apple juice

2 tablespoons soy sauce
2 cloves garlic, crushed
¼ teaspoon onion powder
1 tablespoon plus 1
   teaspoon cornstarch

Place meat in ungreased baking dish, 13½x9x2 inches. Heat remaining ingredients except cornstarch to boiling. Reduce heat; simmer uncovered 5 minutes. Cool. Pour consommé mixture over meat. Cover tightly; refrigerate at least 3 hours, turning meat occasionally.

Thread 4 or 5 cubes of meat on each of 6 to 8 skewers. In small saucepan, slowly stir consommé mixture into cornstarch. Cook, stirring constantly, until mixture thickens and boils. Boil and stir 1 minute. Brush sauce on meat.

Set oven control at broil and/or 550°. Broil meat 4 inches from heat 7 minutes. Turn skewers; brush meat with sauce and broil 7 minutes longer.

Place skewers on hot platter; spoon remaining sauce over meat. If desired, serve with parsley rice.

6 to 8 servings.

ROUND STEAK WITH RICH GRAVY

3-pound beef round steak,
   1 inch thick
⅓ cup all-purpose flour
3 tablespoons shortening
1 envelope (about 1½
   ounces) dry onion soup
   mix

½ cup water
1 can (10½ ounces)
   condensed cream of
   mushroom soup

Sprinkle one side of meat with half the flour; pound in. Turn meat and pound in remaining flour. Cut meat into 6 to 8 serving pieces.

Melt shortening in large skillet; brown meat in shortening over medium heat, about 15 minutes. Sprinkle onion soup mix over meat. Mix water and soup; pour over meat. Cover tightly; simmer 1½ to 2 hours or until tender.

Place meat on warm platter. Heat remaining gravy mixture to boiling, stirring constantly; pour over meat.

6 to 8 servings.

FLANK STEAK FIXUP

2-pound flank steak, scored
1 clove garlic, halved
1 teaspoon salt
¼ teaspoon pepper
4 to 6 slices bacon
½ cup all-purpose flour
1 can (8 ounces) tomato
  sauce
½ teaspoon salt
⅛ teaspoon marjoram leaves
1 tablespoon snipped
  parsley
½ cup finely chopped onion

Rub steak with garlic; season with 1 teaspoon salt and the pepper. Cut meat crosswise into 4 to 6 serving pieces. In large skillet, partially cook bacon. Drain bacon; reserve drippings in skillet.

Place slice of bacon on each piece of meat; roll up and secure with wooden picks. Coat rolls with flour. Brown rolls in reserved bacon drippings over medium heat.

Stir together tomato sauce, ½ teaspoon salt, the marjoram leaves, parsley and onion; pour over meat. Cover tightly; simmer 45 to 60 minutes or until tender.

Place rolls on warm platter; remove wooden picks. Heat sauce to boiling, stirring constantly; pour over rolls.

4 to 6 servings.

POT-ROAST IN FOIL

4-pound beef chuck pot-
  roast* (arm, blade, chuck
  eye or cross rib)
1 envelope (about 1½
  ounces) dry onion soup
  mix
1 can (10½ ounces)
  condensed cream of
  mushroom soup

Place 30x18-inch piece of heavy-duty aluminum foil in baking pan, 13x9x2 inches; place meat on foil. Sprinkle soup mix over top of meat and spread with cream of mushroom soup. Fold foil over meat and seal securely. Cook in 300° oven 4 hours.

8 to 10 servings.

*A rolled rump, top round or bottom round roast can be used in this recipe.

Note: For assistance in carving a beef blade pot-roast, see page 365.

NEW ENGLAND POT-ROAST

¼ cup all-purpose flour
1 tablespoon plus 2 teaspoons salt
1¼ teaspoons pepper
4-pound beef chuck pot-roast* (arm, blade, chuck eye or cross rib)
2 tablespoons shortening
1 jar (5 ounces) horseradish, if desired

1 cup water
8 small potatoes, pared and halved
8 medium carrots, halved crosswise and lengthwise
8 small onions
½ teaspoon salt
Gravy (below)

Stir together flour, 1 tablespoon plus 2 teaspoons salt and the pepper; rub mixture on meat thoroughly. Melt shortening in large skillet or Dutch oven; brown meat over medium heat, about 15 minutes.

Reduce heat; spread horseradish on both sides of meat. Add water; cover tightly and simmer on top of range or in 325° oven 4 hours or until meat is tender.

About 1 hour before end of cooking time, add vegetables and ½ teaspoon salt. Place meat and vegetables on warm platter; keep warm while making gravy. Serve gravy with meat and vegetables.

6 to 8 servings.

*A rolled rump, top round or bottom round roast can be used in this recipe.

Note: For assistance in carving a beef blade pot-roast, see page 365.

GRAVY

Pour drippings (fat and juices) into a bowl, leaving brown particles in pan. Let fat rise to top of drippings; skim off fat, reserving ¼ cup. Place reserved fat in pan. Blend in ¼ cup all-purpose flour. Cook over low heat, stirring until mixture is smooth and bubbly. Remove from heat.

Measure meat juice; add water to measure 2 cups liquid and stir into flour mixture. Heat to boiling, stirring constantly. Boil and stir 1 minute. Season with salt and pepper.

About 2 cups.

LEFTOVER BEEF? Cooked beef puts on a new face and gains new favor when used in any of these recipes: Chef's Salad, Chopped Beef Sandwich Filling, Croquettes, Quick Meat Pie, Quickie Beef Stew, Shepherd's Pie, Skillet Hash.

SPICED GERMAN POT-ROAST

2 tablespoons shortening	1 teaspoon salt
4-pound beef chuck pot-roast* (arm, blade, chuck eye or cross rib)	½ teaspoon pepper
	1 cup water
	Spicy Gravy (below)

Melt shortening in large skillet or Dutch oven; brown meat over medium heat, about 15 minutes. Season meat with salt and pepper.

Reduce heat; add water to skillet and cover tightly. Simmer on top of range or in 325° oven 3 hours or until tender. Place meat on warm platter; keep warm while making gravy. Serve gravy with meat.

6 to 8 servings.

*A rolled rump, top round or bottom round roast can be used in this recipe.

Note: For assistance in carving a beef blade pot-roast, see page 365.

SPICY GRAVY

Pour drippings (fat and juices) into a bowl, leaving brown particles in pan. Let fat rise to top of drippings; skim off fat, reserving ¼ cup. Place reserved fat in pan. Blend in ¼ cup all-purpose flour. Cook over low heat, stirring until mixture is smooth and bubbly. Remove from heat.

Measure meat juice; add water to measure 2 cups liquid and stir into flour mixture. Heat to boiling, stirring constantly. Boil and stir 1 minute.

Stir in 2 cloves garlic, crushed, 1½ teaspoons salt, ½ teaspoon pepper, ¼ teaspoon ginger, ¼ cup catsup and 2 tablespoons vinegar. Reduce heat; simmer 10 minutes, stirring occasionally.

About 2 cups.

QUICK SAUERBRATEN

4-pound beef rolled rump roast	2 bay leaves
1 package (⅘ ounce) instant meat marinade	1 teaspoon pickling spice
	¼ teaspoon pepper
⅔ cup white vinegar	2 tablespoons shortening
1 medium onion, sliced	2 tablespoons flour
	Gingersnap Gravy (below)

Place meat in deep skillet or Dutch oven. Mix marinade and vinegar; pour over meat. With sharp fork, pierce surface of meat; marinate 15 minutes, turning occasionally.

Add onion, bay leaves, pickling spice and pepper. Cover tightly; simmer on top of range or in 325° oven 3 hours. Remove meat.

Strain drippings and discard spices. Measure drippings and add water to measure 2½ cups liquid. Melt shortening in skillet. Blend in flour. Cook over low heat, stirring until mixture is smooth and bubbly. Remove from heat. Gradually stir in liquid. Heat to boiling, stirring constantly. Boil and stir 1 minute.

Add meat; cover and simmer 30 minutes or until tender, turning meat once. Place meat on warm platter; keep warm while preparing Gingersnap Gravy. Serve gravy with meat.

10 to 12 servings.

GINGERSNAP GRAVY

Stir ⅓ cup crushed gingersnaps and 1 teaspoon sugar into gravy in pan. Heat to boiling, stirring constantly. Boil and stir 1 minute.

About 2 cups.

VARIATION

■ *Sauerbraten Dinner:* Simmer meat 3½ hours. Remove and keep warm. (This is the only cooking period for meat.) Omit shortening and flour; stir 12 gingersnaps, crushed, and 2 teaspoons sugar into the 2½ cups liquid (strained drippings plus water) and return to skillet or Dutch oven. Add 2- to 3-pound red cabbage, cut into 10 to 12 wedges; cover and heat to boiling. Prepare Dumplings (page 67); drop dough onto wedges. Cook uncovered 10 minutes; cover and cook 10 minutes longer.

OLIVE SURPRISE ROAST

4-pound beef rolled rump roast
1 jar (4½ ounces) pimiento-stuffed small olives, drained
1 large onion, sliced

1 can (10¾ ounces) condensed tomato soup
3 tablespoons shortening
1 soup can hot water
Tomato Gravy (below)

With point of knife, make about 5 deep crisscross gashes in a circle as far in as the middle on each end of roast. Open gashes; push about 5 olives into each. Melt shortening in Dutch oven; brown meat over medium heat, 15 minutes.

Place onion slices on meat. Mix soup and water; pour over meat. Cover tightly; simmer on top of range or in 325° oven 2½ hours or until tender. Place meat on warm platter; keep warm while making Tomato Gravy. Serve with gravy.

8 servings.

TOMATO GRAVY

Measure hot meat broth; if necessary, add water to measure 3 cups liquid. Heat liquid to boiling. In tightly covered jar, shake ¾ cup cold water and ⅓ cup all-purpose flour; stir into hot liquid. Heat to boiling, stirring constantly. Boil and stir 1 minute. Season with salt and pepper.

MUSTARD SHORT RIBS

4 pounds beef short ribs, cut into pieces	1 tablespoon sugar
⅓ cup prepared mustard	1 teaspoon salt
2 tablespoons lemon juice	½ teaspoon pepper
2 cloves garlic, crushed	4 medium onions, sliced
	¼ cup shortening

Place meat in shallow glass dish. Mix mustard, lemon juice, garlic, sugar, salt and pepper; spread on meat. Top with onions. Cover tightly; refrigerate 24 hours, turning meat occasionally.

Brown ribs in shortening over medium heat; pour off drippings. Add onions and pour marinade over meat. Cover tightly; cook in 350° oven 2 hours.

4 servings.

BEEF BRISKET BAR-B-Q

4- to 5-pound well-trimmed beef fresh brisket	1 tablespoon Worcestershire sauce
1½ teaspoons salt	1½ teaspoons liquid smoke
½ cup catsup	1 bay leaf, crumbled
¼ cup vinegar	¼ teaspoon pepper
½ cup finely chopped onion	

Rub meat with salt. Place in ungreased baking dish, 13½x9x2 inches. Stir together remaining ingredients; pour over meat. Cover tightly; bake in 325° oven 3 hours or until tender.

10 to 12 servings.

Note: To carve meat, cut thin diagonal slices across the grain at a slanting angle from 2 or 3 "faces" of meat (see page 364).

CORNED BEEF AND CABBAGE

Leftover corned beef won't go to waste. Try it in a delicious Reuben Sandwich (page 658).

5-pound well-trimmed beef
  corned brisket
2 cloves garlic, crushed
1 medium onion, quartered

1 medium head green
  cabbage, cut into 8
  wedges

Place meat in large kettle; cover with cold water. Add garlic and onion; heat to boiling. Reduce heat; cover tightly and simmer 3½ hours or until tender. Place meat on warm platter; keep warm. Skim fat from liquid. Add cabbage; simmer uncovered 15 minutes.

10 to 12 servings.

Note: To carve meat, cut thin diagonal slices across the grain at a slanting angle from 2 or 3 "faces" of meat (see page 364).

VARIATION

■ *New England Boiled Dinner:* About 20 minutes before meat is tender, skim fat from liquid. Add 10 small onions, 10 medium carrots, 6 potatoes, pared and halved or quartered, and, if desired, 3 turnips, cubed. Cover; simmer 20 minutes. Remove meat. Add cabbage; simmer uncovered 15 minutes or until vegetables are tender.

FONDUE BOURGUIGNONNE

Several hours before serving, trim fat from 2 pounds beef tenderloin* and cut meat into bite-size pieces (1-inch cubes). Cover meat and refrigerate. Prepare any or all of the dipping sauces on page 382.

About 15 minutes before serving, mound pieces of meat on bed of greens. Pour salad oil into metal fondue pot to depth of 1 to 1½ inches. (If desired, butter or margarine can be used for ¼ of oil.) Transfer oil to saucepan and heat until bread cube browns in 1 minute.

Carefully pour hot oil into fondue pot; place pot on stand and ignite denatured alcohol burner or canned cooking fuel.

Use long-handled fork to spear cube of meat, dip into hot oil and cook until meat is crusty on the outside, juicy and rare inside. Since the long fork will be very hot by

*Boneless beef sirloin can be used in this recipe.

this time, meat should be dipped in sauce and eaten with a second fork.

4 to 6 servings.

ANCHOVY BUTTER SAUCE

Drain 1 can (2 ounces) anchovy fillets. Mix thoroughly ½ cup soft butter or margarine, the anchovy fillets and ⅛ teaspoon pepper. Refrigerate. Bring to room temperature before serving.

¾ cup.

GARLIC BUTTER SAUCE

Beat ½ cup soft butter or margarine until fluffy. Stir in 1 tablespoon snipped parsley and 1 clove garlic, crushed. Refrigerate. Bring to room temperature before serving.

½ cup.

BLUE CHEESE SAUCE

½ cup dairy sour cream	¼ teaspoon salt
¼ cup crumbled blue cheese	
1 teaspoon Worcestershire sauce	

Mix all ingredients thoroughly. Refrigerate until serving time.

¾ cup.

HOT 'N SPICY SAUCE

1 cup chili sauce	1 clove garlic, crushed
1 medium onion, chopped (about ½ cup)	1 teaspoon brown sugar
3 tablespoons lemon juice	½ teaspoon red pepper sauce
2 tablespoons salad oil	¼ teaspoon dry mustard
2 tablespoons vinegar	¼ teaspoon salt

Mix all ingredients in small saucepan. Heat to boiling; reduce heat and simmer 5 minutes. Serve warm or cool.

1¼ cups.

HORSERADISH SAUCE

1 cup dairy sour cream	⅛ teaspoon salt
2 tablespoons horseradish	⅛ teaspoon pepper
½ teaspoon lemon juice	
¼ teaspoon Worcestershire sauce	

Mix all ingredients thoroughly; refrigerate until serving time.

1 cup.

Pork

1. Cuts from the Boston Shoulder Blade Boston roast, boneless blade Boston roast (braise, roast); smoked shoulder roll (roast, cook in liquid); blade steak (braise, panfry).

2. Cuts from the Loin Boneless top loin roast, blade loin roast, center loin roast, sirloin roast (roast); tenderloin (roast, braise, panfry); back ribs, country-style ribs (roast, braise, cook in liquid); Canadian-style bacon (roast, boil, panfry); rib chop, loin chop, sirloin chop, top loin chop, blade chop, butterfly chop, sirloin cutlet (braise, broil, panfry); smoked loin chop (broil, panfry).

3. Cuts from the Leg (Ham) Smoked ham—shank or rump (butt) portion (roast, cook in liquid); boneless leg or fresh ham; boneless smoked ham, canned ham (roast); center smoked ham slice (broil, panfry).

4. Cuts from the Spareribs-Bacon (Side Pork) Salt pork (broil, panfry, cook in liquid, bake); spareribs (roast, braise, cook in liquid); sliced bacon, slab bacon (broil, panfry, bake).

5. Cuts from the Picnic Shoulder Fresh hock, smoked hock (braise, cook in liquid); neckbones (cook in liquid); fresh arm picnic (roast); smoked arm picnic (roast, cook in liquid); arm roast (roast); arm steak (braise, panfry).

6. Cuts from the Jowl Smoked jowl (cook in liquid, broil, panfry).

7. Cuts from the Forefoot and Hindfoot Pig's feet (cook in liquid; braise).

Pork cubes, cubed steak, ground pork and sausage may come from several sections.

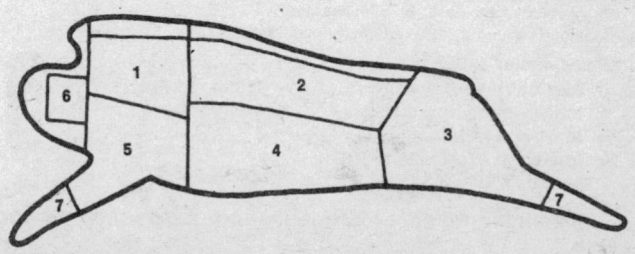

HOW TO ROAST FRESH PORK

Select roast from those listed in chart on pages 386–387. Allow about ½ pound per person—less for boneless roasts, more for roasts with a bone. If desired, season with salt and pepper before, during or after roasting (salt only goes into the meat ¼ to ½ inch).

Place meat fat side up on rack in open shallow roasting pan. The rack keeps the meat out of the drippings. (In some roasts, the ribs form a natural rack.) It is not necessary to baste.

Insert meat thermometer so tip is in center of thickest part of meat and does not touch bone or rest in fat. Do not add water. Do not cover.

Roast meat in 325° oven. (It is not necessary to preheat oven.) Roast to desired degree of doneness (see Timetable), using thermometer reading as *final* guide. Roasts are easier to carve if allowed to set 15 to 20 minutes after removing from oven. Since meat continues to cook after removal from oven, if roast is to "set," it should be removed from oven when thermometer registers 5° lower than the desired doneness.

Note: For assistance in carving a pork loin roast, see page 265.

PORK CUTS YOU SHOULD KNOW

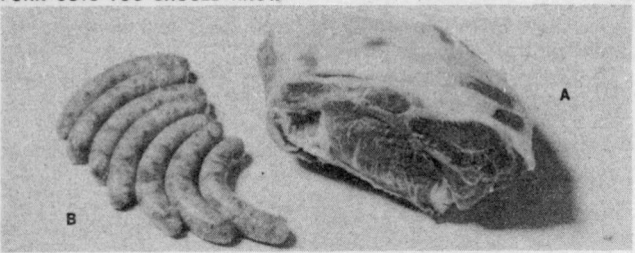

A. Blade Boston roast   B. Link sausage
I. Sliced bacon   J. Smoked arm picnic   K. Spareribs   L. Fresh hocks

GLAZES FOR ROAST FRESH PORK

Instead of using any other seasoning, during the last hour of roasting, brush meat every 15 minutes with your choice of the following glazes (enough for a 4-pound roast). Serve any remaining glaze as a sauce.

Currant Glaze: Heat 1 jar (10 ounces) currant jelly, ¼ cup prepared mustard and ½ teaspoon onion salt over low heat, stirring constantly, until jelly is melted. Boil and stir 3 minutes.

About ¾ cup.

Orange Glaze: Heat 1 can (6 ounces) frozen orange juice concentrate, ½ cup honey and ½ teaspoon ginger to boiling, stirring constantly. Boil and stir 3 minutes.

About 1¼ cups.

SEASONINGS FOR ROAST FRESH PORK

Before roasting, rub meat with your choice of these seasonings (enough for a 4-pound roast).

Herb Salt: Cut 1 clove garlic in half; rub meat with garlic. Mix 1 teaspoon sage, 1 teaspoon marjoram leaves and 1 teaspoon salt.

Mustard Rub: Mix 1 tablespoon prepared mustard, 1 tablespoon lemon juice, ½ teaspoon salt, ½ teaspoon onion powder and ¼ teaspoon pepper.

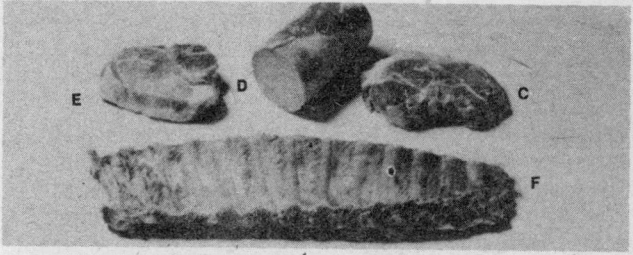

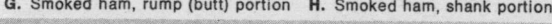

C. Sirloin chop **D.** Canadian-style bacon **E.** Loin chop **F.** Back ribs
G. Smoked ham, rump (butt) portion **H.** Smoked ham, shank portion

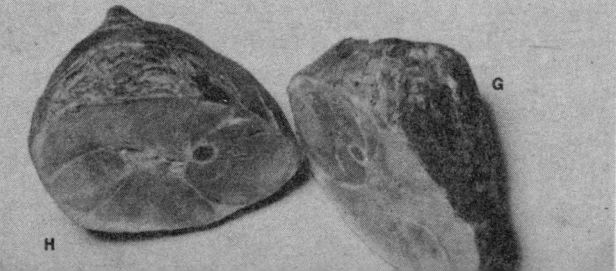

TIMETABLE FOR ROASTING FRESH PORK
(Oven Temperature 325°)

Cut	Approximate Weight	Meat Thermometer Reading
Loin		
Center	3 to 5 pounds	170°
Half	5 to 7 pounds	170°
Blade or Sirloin	3 to 4 pounds	170°
Boneless Top (double)	3 to 5 pounds	170°
Boneless Top	2 to 4 pounds	170°
Arm Picnic	5 to 8 pounds	170°
Boston Shoulder		
Boneless Blade Boston	3 to 5 pounds	170°
Blade Boston	4 to 6 pounds	170°
Leg (fresh ham)		
Whole (bone in)	12 to 14 pounds	170°
Boneless	10 to 14 pounds	170°
Half (bone in)	5 to 8 pounds	170°
Tenderloin	½ to 1 pound	
Spareribs, Back Ribs, Country-style Ribs*		

*All three are always cooked until well done.

GLAZED RIBS

4 pounds spareribs*
1 can (15 ounces) tomato sauce
1 envelope (7 ounce) onion salad dressing mix
¼ cup vinegar
¼ cup light molasses
2 tablespoons salad oil
1 teaspoon dry mustard
1 cup water

Place spareribs meaty side up in open shallow roasting pan. Heat remaining ingredients to boiling, stirring constantly. Boil and stir 3 minutes. Pour sauce over meat. Roast in 350° oven 1½ hours or until done, basting 4 or 5 times.

4 servings.

*Pork back ribs or country-style ribs can be used in this recipe.

VARIATION

■ *Saucy Glazed Ribs:* Omit water and do not pour sauce on meat before roasting. Roast ribs 1 hour; pour half the sauce on meat and roast 15 minutes. Pour remaining sauce on meat and continue roasting 15 minutes or until done.

Approximate Cooking Time (Minutes per Pound)	
	30 to 35
	35 to 40
	40 to 45
	35 to 45
	30 to 35
	30 to 35
	35 to 40
	40 to 45
	22 to 26
	24 to 28
	35 to 40
Total	¾ to 1 hour
Time	1½ to 2½ hours

CHARCOAL-GRILLED SPARERIBS

Place 4 pounds spareribs in large pan; add enough water to cover. Cover; heat to boiling. Reduce heat and simmer 20 minutes. Remove spareribs from water; drain.

Place spareribs bone side down on grill 3 inches from medium coals; cook 20 minutes. Turn and cook about 30 minutes longer or until done (no pink in center), turning and basting frequently with 1 cup New Orleans Tomato Sauce (page 582). Serve with the remaining hot sauce.

4 servings.

CHARCOAL-GRILLED PORK CHOPS

Trim excess fat from four 1- to 1½-inch-thick pork chops. Place chops on grill 4 inches from medium coals; cook 60 to 70 minutes, turning every 15 minutes, or until meat is done (no pink in center). If desired, brush chops during last half of cooking time with Sauce O' Gold (page 582).

4 servings.

HOW TO BROIL FRESH PORK

Diagonally slash outer edge of fat on chops or steaks at 1-inch intervals to prevent curling (do not cut into lean). Set oven control at broil and/or 550°. Place meat on rack in broiler pan; place broiler pan so top of meat is 3 to 5 inches from heat. Broil until light brown.

The meat should be about half done by this time (see Timetable). If desired, season brown side with salt and pepper. (Always season *after* browning as salt tends to draw moisture to surface and delay browning.) Turn meat; broil until brown.

TIMETABLE FOR BROILING FRESH PORK

Cut	Approximate Total Cooking Time
Chops (¾ to 1 inch)	20 to 25 minutes
Blade Steaks (½ to ¾ inch)	20 to 22 minutes
Patties (1 inch)	20 to 25 minutes
Kabobs (1½ x 1½ x ¾ inch)	22 to 25 minutes

TENDERLOIN PATTIES WITH CHUTNEY PEACHES

¼ cup shortening
6 pork tenderloin patties
⅓ cup water
½ teaspoon salt
⅓ cup drained chopped chutney

1 can (1 pound 13 ounces) cling peach halves,* drained

Melt shortening in large skillet; brown patties over medium heat. Drain off fat. Reduce heat; add water.

Season patties with salt and top with 2 tablespoons of the chutney. Cover tightly; simmer 30 minutes or until done.

Fill peach halves with remaining chutney; serve with meat.

6 servings.

*Or, if desired, use 1 jar (1 pound 13 ounces) spiced peach halves.

Note: If desired, warm peach halves (last 5 minutes of cooking) before filling with chutney.

CRANBERRY-ORANGE PORK STEAKS

2 tablespoons shortening
4 pork blade steaks, ¾ inch thick
1 teaspoon salt
1 package (10 ounces) frozen cranberry-orange relish, thawed

2 tablespoons orange juice
¼ teaspoon nutmeg
4 thin orange slices

Melt shortening in large skillet; brown steaks. Season both sides of steaks with salt. Stir together relish, orange juice and nutmeg; spread on steaks.

Cover tightly; simmer 1 hour or until tender. Serve each steak with twisted orange slice.

4 servings.

CORN-STUFFED PORK CHOPS

1 can (7 ounces) vacuum-packed whole kernel corn with peppers
1 cup soft bread cubes
¼ cup finely chopped onion
1 teaspoon salt

½ teaspoon sage
6 pork rib chops, 1 inch thick (with pockets cut into chops from bone side)
2 tablespoons shortening

Mix corn (with liquid), bread cubes, onion, salt and sage. Stuff pork chop pockets with corn mixture.

Melt shortening in large skillet; brown chops, about 15 minutes. Reduce heat; cover tightly and simmer 1 hour or until done.

6 servings.

CURRIED PORK CHOPS AND APRICOTS

2 tablespoons shortening
6 pork loin or rib chops, 1 inch thick
1 can (1 pound 1 ounce) apricot halves, drained
1 medium onion, finely chopped (about ½ cup)

¼ cup butter or margarine
¼ cup all-purpose flour
1 teaspoon salt
1 teaspoon curry powder
2 cups milk
1 can (6 ounces) sliced mushrooms, drained

Melt shortening in skillet; brown chops over medium heat. Place in ungreased baking dish, 13½x9x2 inches; arrange apricot halves cut side down on meat.

In medium skillet, cook and stir onion in butter until onion is tender. Stir in flour, salt and curry powder. Cook over low heat, stirring until mixture is bubbly. Remove from heat. Stir in milk gradually. Heat to boiling, stirring constantly. Boil and stir 1 minute. Stir in mushrooms; pour over chops.

Cover tightly; bake in 350° oven 45 minutes or until meat is done. Uncover; bake 15 minutes longer.

6 servings.

BAKED HAM

Select ham or other cut from those listed in chart on pages 392–393. Allow about ½ pound per person—less for boneless roasts, more for a roast with a bone. Place ham fat side up on rack in open shallow roasting pan. The rack keeps the meat out of the drippings. It is not necessary to baste.

Insert meat thermometer so tip is in center of thickest part of meat and does not touch bone or rest in fat. Do not add water. Do not cover.

Roast meat in 325° oven. (It is not necessary to preheat oven.) Roast to desired degree of doneness (see Timetable), using thermometer reading as *final* guide.

Ham is easier to carve if allowed to set 15 to 20 minutes after removing from oven. Since meat continues to cook after removal from oven, if ham is to "set," it should be removed when thermometer registers 5° lower than desired doneness.

If desired, serve with Cherry Sauce (page 574), Hot Cranberry Sauce (page 574), Mustard Sauce (page 575) or Raisin Sauce (page 575).

Note: For assistance in carving a whole ham or an arm picnic, see page 265.

GLAZES FOR BAKED HAM

For a glazed ham, remove ham 30 minutes before it is done. Pour drippings from pan. Remove any skin from ham. Score fat surface of ham lightly, cutting uniform diamond shapes. If desired, insert whole clove in each. Pat or brush on your choice of the following glazes (enough for 4-pound ham); continue baking 30 minutes.

Brown Sugar Glaze: Mix 1 cup brown sugar (packed), ½ teaspoon dry mustard and 1 tablespoon vinegar. About ¾ cup.

Apricot Glaze: Mix ½ cup brown sugar (packed), 1 tablespoon cornstarch, ½ teaspoon ginger and ¼ teaspoon salt in small saucepan. Stir in 1 can (12 ounces) apricot nectar and 1 tablespoon lemon juice. Cook over medium heat, stirring constantly, until mixture thickens and boils. Boil and stir 1 minute. About 1½ cups.

Pineapple Glaze: Mix 1 cup brown sugar (packed), 1 tablespoon cornstarch and ¼ teaspoon salt in small saucepan. Stir in 1 can (8½ ounces) crushed pineapple (with syrup), 2 tablespoons lemon juice and 1 tablespoon prepared mustard. Cook over medium heat, stirring constantly, until mixture thickens and boils. Boil and stir 1 minute. 1¾ cups.

Pockets cut from bone side hold stuffing securely.

Corn-stuffed Pork Chops

TIMETABLE FOR ROASTING SMOKED PORK
(Oven Temperature 325°)

Cut	Approximate Weight	Meat Thermometer Reading
Ham (cook before eating)		
Whole	10 to 14 pounds	160°
Half	5 to 7 pounds	160°
Shank Portion	3 to 4 pounds	160°
Rump (Butt) Portion	3 to 4 pounds	160°
Ham (fully cooked)		
Whole	10 to 15 pounds	140°
Half	5 to 7 pounds	140°
Loin	3 to 5 pounds	160°
Arm Picnic (cook before eating)	5 to 8 pounds	170°
Arm Picnic (fully cooked)	5 to 8 pounds	140°
Shoulder Roll	2 to 3 pounds	170°
Canadian-style Bacon	2 to 4 pounds	160°
Ham Loaf	2 pounds	160°
Ham Patties	1 inch thick	

SMOKED HAM SLICE

In general, use slices 1 inch thick. Diagonally slash outer edge of fat at 1-inch intervals to prevent curling. Then proceed with your favorite method of cooking.

To Bake: Place slice in ungreased baking dish. If desired, spread with ½ recipe Brown Sugar Glaze (page 389). Bake in 325° oven 30 minutes.

To Panfry: It is best to use ½-inch-thick ham slice. Rub skillet with small piece of fat cut from slice. Cook over medium heat about 3 minutes or until light brown. Turn; cook 3 minutes longer.

To Broil: Set oven control at broil and/or 550°. Place ham slice on rack in broiler pan; place broiler pan so top of ham slice is 3 inches from heat. Broil about 10 minutes or until light brown. Turn ham slice; broil about 6 minutes longer. If desired, during last 2 minutes of broiling, brush with 3 tablespoons jelly, slightly beaten.

CHARCOAL-GRILLED SUGARED HAM

2 fully cooked center-cut smoked ham slices, 1 inch thick (about 3½ pounds)

1 cup brown sugar (packed)
⅓ cup horseradish
¼ cup lemon juice

Approximate Cooking Time (Minutes per Pound)
18 to 20
22 to 25
35 to 40
35 to 40
15 to 18
18 to 24
25 to 30
30 to 35
25 to 30
35 to 40
35 to 40

Total	1½ hours
Time	¾ to 1 hour

Score each side of ham ¼ inch deep in diamond pattern. Combine remaining ingredients in small saucepan; heat to boiling; stirring constantly.

Place ham slices in grill 3 inches from medium coals; cook 15 minutes on each side, basting frequently with brown sugar mixture.

6 to 8 servings.

BARBECUED HAM SLICE

1 package (0.6 ounce) Italian salad dressing mix
¼ cup catsup
1 tablespoon salad oil
1 tablespoon vinegar
1 fully cooked smoked ham slice, 1 inch thick

Blend dressing mix, catsup, oil and vinegar; set aside. Set oven control at broil and/or 550°. Diagonally slash outer edge of fat at 1-inch intervals to prevent curling. Broil 3 inches from heat 10 minutes or until light brown. Brush with catsup mixture during last minute of broiling.

Turn ham slice; broil about 6 minutes longer, brushing with catsup mixture during last minute.

4 servings.

SMOKED PORK HOCKS WITH SAUERKRAUT

4 smoked pork hocks (about 4 pounds)	2 cans (1 pound each) sauerkraut, drained
4 cups water	½ teaspoon celery seed
1 onion, sliced	1 apple, cut into eighths
½ teaspoon marjoram leaves	

Place meat, water, onion and marjoram leaves in large kettle or Dutch oven. Heat to boiling. Reduce heat; cover tightly and simmer 1½ hours.

Drain liquid from kettle, reserving 1 cup. Add reserved liquid, sauerkraut and celery seed to meat in kettle. Cover; simmer 15 minutes. Add apple; simmer 15 minutes longer.

4 servings.

LEFTOVER HAM? Cooked ham is the perfect plus in any of these recipes: Eggs Benedict, Ham-Cheese-Potato Casserole, Barbecued Limas and Ham, Creamed Ham and Eggs, Ham Pancakes, Continental Cheese Ring with Ham, Stormy Day Bean Soup.

Lamb

1. **Cuts from the Neck** Neck slices (braise).

2. **Cuts from the Shoulder** Cushion shoulder roast, boneless shoulder roast, square shoulder roast (roast); arm chop, blade chop, boneless blade or Saratoga chop (broil, panfry).

3. **Cuts from the Rib** Rib roast, crown roast (roast); rib chop, Frenched rib chop (broil, panfry).

4. **Cuts from the Loin** Loin roast, boneless double loin roast (roast); boneless double loin chop, loin chop (broil, panfry).

5. **Cuts from the Sirloin-Leg** Sirloin roast, boneless sirloin roast, sirloin half of leg, shank half of leg, American leg, French-style leg, center leg, rolled leg, combination leg (roast); leg chop (steak), sirloin chop (broil, panfry).

6. Cuts from the Breast Breast, rolled breast, stuffed breast (roast, braise); riblets (braise); spareribs (braise, roast); stuffed chop (broil, panfry).

7. Cuts from the Shanks Foreshank, hindshank (braise, cook in liquid). Lamb cubes, cubed steak and ground lamb may come from any section.

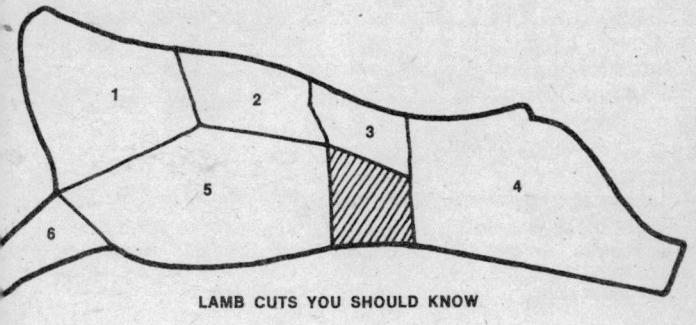

LAMB CUTS YOU SHOULD KNOW

uare shoulder roast

B. Neck slice
C. Boneless blade (Saratoga) chop

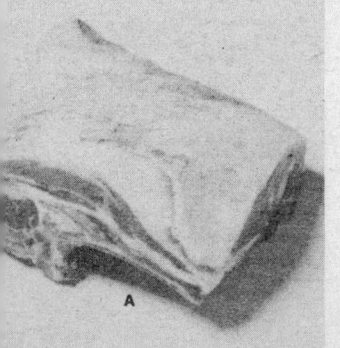

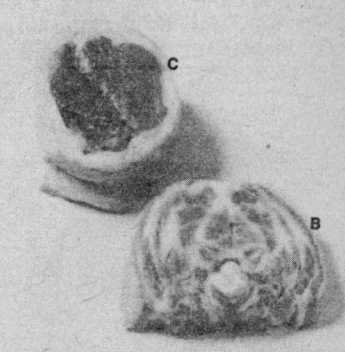

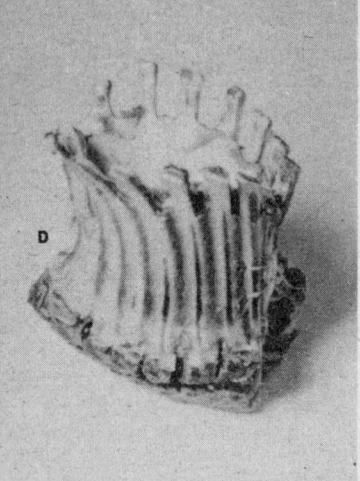

D. Crown roast

E. Loin chops

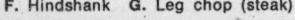

F. Hindshank G. Leg chop (steak)   H. Foreshank I. Boneless riblets J. Ri

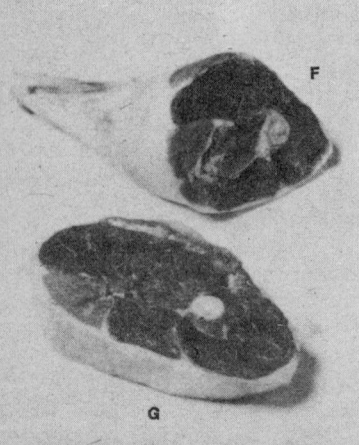

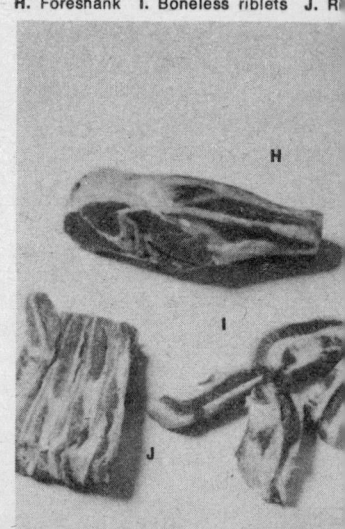

HOW TO ROAST LAMB

Select roast from those listed in chart below. Do not remove "fell" (the paperlike covering). Roasts keep their shape better, cook in less time and are juicier when the "fell" is left on.

If desired, season meat with salt and pepper before, during or after roasting (salt only goes into the roast ¼ to ½ inch). For a quick seasoning, 4 or 5 scattered small slits can be cut in meat with tip of sharp knife and slivers of garlic inserted—but be sure to remove garlic before serving.

Place meat fat side up on rack in open shallow roasting pan. The rack keeps the meat out of the drippings. (With a rib roast, the ribs form a natural rack.) It is not necessary to baste; with the fat on top, the meat does its own basting.

Insert meat thermometer so tip is in center of thickest part of meat and does not touch bone or rest in fat. Do not add water. Do not cover.

Roast meat in 325° oven. (It is not necessary to preheat oven.) Roast to desired degree of doneness (see Timetable), using thermometer reading as *final* guide.

Roasts are easier to carve if allowed to set 15 to 20 minutes after removing from oven. Since meat continues to cook after removal from oven, if roast is to "set," it should be removed from oven when thermometer registers 5 to 10° lower than the desired doneness.

Note: For assistance in carving a roast leg of lamb, see page 265.

TIMETABLE FOR ROASTING LAMB
(Oven Temperature 325°)

Cut	Approximate Weight	Meat Thermometer Reading	Approximate Cooking Time (Minutes per Pound)
Shoulder			
Square	4 to 6 pounds	175 to 180°	30 to 35
Boneless	3 to 5 pounds	175 to 180°	40 to 45
Cushion	3 to 5 pounds	175 to 180°	30 to 35
Crown Roast	4 to 6 pounds	175 to 180°	40 to 45
Rib*	1½ to 3 pounds	170 to 180°	35 to 45
Leg	5 to 8 pounds	175 to 180°	30 to 35
Rolled Leg	3 to 5 pounds	175 to 180°	35 to 40

*Roast at 375°.

SEASONINGS FOR ROAST LAMB

Before roasting, rub meat with your choice of these seasonings (enough for a 4-pound roast).

Curried Onion Salt: Mix 2 teaspoons curry powder, 1½ teaspoons instant minced onion, ½ teaspoon salt and ¼ teaspoon pepper.

Dill-Rosemary Salt: Mix 2 teaspoons dill weed, 1 teaspoon salt, ½ teaspoon rosemary leaves and ¼ teaspoon pepper.

Herbed Salt: Mix 2 teaspoons ground cumin, ½ teaspoon basil leaves, ¼ teaspoon salt and ¼ teaspoon chili powder.

GLAZES FOR ROAST LAMB

Instead of using any other seasoning or inserting garlic in meat, during the last hour of roasting, brush meat every 15 minutes with your choice of the following glazes (enough for a 4-pound roast). Serve any remaining glaze as a sauce.

Apricot Glaze: Heat ¼ cup mint-flavored apple jelly until melted. Stir in 2 jars (4¾ ounces) strained apricots (baby food). About 1 cup.

Minted Glaze: Heat 1 jar (10 ounces) mint-flavored apple jelly, 2 cloves garlic, crushed, and 1 tablespoon water, stirring constantly, until jelly is melted. About ¾ cup.

Oriental Glaze: Mix 2 tablespoons brown sugar, 2 teaspoons cornstarch and ½ teaspoon basil leaves in small saucepan. Stir in ¼ cup soy sauce and ¼ cup sherry or, if desired, apple juice. Cook, stirring constantly, until mixture thickens and boils. Boil and stir 1 minute. About ½ cup.

STUFFED CROWN ROAST

Season meat with salt and pepper. Place meat bone ends up in open shallow roasting pan; wrap bone ends with aluminum foil to prevent excessive browning. To hold shape, place a small ovenproof cup or bowl in crown.

Insert meat thermometer so tip is in center of thickest part of meat and does not rest on fat or bone. Do not add water. Do not cover. Roast in 325° oven to desired degree of doneness (see Timetable, page 397) or until thermometer registers 175°.

An hour before meat is done, remove bowl or cup from center of crown; fill crown with stuffing. (Use about 2 cups stuffing for 4-pound lamb crown.) Cover just the stuffing with aluminum foil during first 30 minutes of roasting. When done, remove foil from bone ends and, if desired, replace with paper frills. To carve, cut between ribs.

HOW TO BROIL LAMB CHOPS

Choose loin, rib or shoulder lamb chops, allowing 1 or 2 chops for each person. Remove "fell" (the paperlike covering) if it is on chops. Diagonally slash outer edge of fat on meat at 1-inch intervals to prevent curling. Set oven control at broil and/or 550°. Place chops on rack in broiler pan; place broiler pan so tops of ¾- to 1-inch chops are 2 to 3 inches from heat, 1- to 2-inch chops are 3 to 5 inches from heat. Broil until brown.

The chops should be about half done by this time (see Timetable). If desired, season brown side with salt and pepper. (Always season after browning as salt tends to draw moisture to surface and delay browning.) Turn chops; broil until brown.

TIMETABLE FOR BROILING LAMB CHOPS

Thickness	Approximate Total Cooking Time*
1 inch	12 minutes
1½ inches	18 minutes
2 inches	22 minutes

*Time given is for medium doneness; lamb chops are not usually served rare.

CHARCOAL-GRILLED LAMB CHOPS

Choose loin, rib or shoulder lamb chops, allowing 1 or 2 chops for each person. Trim excess fat from chops. Place meat on grill 4 inches from medium coals. Cook as directed in the Timetable. Test for doneness by making knife slit alongside bone; meat should be juicy and slightly pink.

TIMETABLE FOR GRILLING
EACH SIDE

Thickness	Minutes per Side
¾ inch	10 to 12
1 inch	14 to 16
1½ inches	16 to 18
2 inches	20 to 22

PARTY LAMB CHOPS

8 lamb rib or loin chops or
    4 lamb sirloin chops, 1 inch
    thick

4 slices process Swiss
    cheese
    Thin onion slices

Set oven control at broil and/or 550°. Broil chops
3 inches from heat until brown, about 7 minutes. Cut
cheese to fit chops; set aside.

Turn chops; broil 5 to 7 minutes longer. Place onion
and trimmed cheese slice on each chop and broil 2 minutes or until cheese begins to melt.

4 servings.

SUNSHINE LAMB CHOPS

The golden glaze adds just a hint of mustard.

½ cup honey
½ cup prepared mustard
⅛ teaspoon onion salt
⅛ teaspoon pepper

8 lamb rib or loin chops or
    4 lamb sirloin chops, 1
    inch thick

Heat honey, mustard, onion salt and pepper, stirring
occasionally; keep warm over low heat.

Set oven control at broil and/or 550°. Broil chops
3 inches from heat 7 minutes; brush with honey mixture.
Turn chops; broil 5 minutes longer, brushing again with
honey mixture. Serve remaining glaze with chops.

4 servings.

LAMB KABOBS

1½ pounds lamb boneless
    shoulder,* cut into 1½-
    inch cubes
1 bottle (8 ounces) French
    dressing with garlic

1 large green pepper
1 large onion
1 pint cherry tomatoes
    Salad oil

Place meat in shallow glass dish; pour dressing over
meat. Cover tightly; refrigerate at least 4 hours, turning
meat occasionally.

Cut pepper and onion into 1-inch pieces. Prick cherry
tomatoes with tip of knife. On each of 8 metal skewers
(8 inches long), alternate tomatoes and pieces of meat,
pepper and onion, leaving a small space between each.
Brush with salad oil.

*Rolled lamb leg can be used in this recipe.

Set oven control at broil and/or 550°. Broil kabobs 3 inches from heat about 20 minutes, turning and brushing with marinade every 5 minutes to brown evenly.

4 servings.

LAMB CHOPS HAWAIIAN

4 lamb shoulder chops (arm or blade), 1 inch thick
1 can (13½ ounces) pineapple chunks, drained (reserve syrup)
¼ cup soy sauce
¼ cup vinegar
½ teaspoon dry mustard
1 tablespoon shortening
¼ cup brown sugar (packed)
1 teaspoon cornstarch

Place chops in shallow glass dish. Stir together reserved pineapple syrup, soy sauce, vinegar and mustard; pour over chops. Cover tightly; refrigerate at least 4 hours, turning chops occasionally.

Drain chops, reserving marinade. Melt shortening in large skillet; brown chops over medium heat. Add ¼ cup reserved marinade to chops in skillet. Cover tightly; cook over low heat 30 to 45 minutes or until tender.

Mix sugar and cornstarch in small saucepan; stir in remaining reserved marinade. Heat to boiling, stirring constantly; reduce heat and simmer 5 minutes. Add pineapple chunks and heat through. Serve pineapple sauce with chops.

4 servings.

GOURMET LAMB ROAST

6-pound lamb boneless shoulder
2 cans (10½ ounces each) condensed beef broth (bouillon)
2 tablespoons mixed pickling spices
1½ teaspoons poultry seasoning
1 teaspoon salt
2 tablespoons grated lemon peel
3 tablespoons lemon juice
¼ cup shortening
Lemon-Spice Gravy (below)

Place meat in deep glass bowl. Heat beef broth, pickling spices, poultry seasoning, salt, lemon peel and juice just to boiling; pour over meat and refrigerate until marinade is cool. Turn meat. Cover tightly; refrigerate 24 hours, turning meat several times.

Remove meat from marinade. Brown meat in shortening over medium heat, about 15 minutes. Drain off fat. Strain marinade; pour 1 cup over meat, reserving the remaining marinade.

Cover tightly; place in 325° oven and bake 2½ to 3 hours or until done. Place meat on warm platter; keep warm while preparing Lemon-Spice Gravy. Serve gravy with meat.

12 servings.

LEMON-SPICE GRAVY

Pour drippings (fat and juices) into a bowl, leaving brown particles in pan. Let fat rise to top of drippings; skim off fat, reserving ¼ cup. Place reserved fat in pan. Blend in ¼ cup plus 2 tablespoons all-purpose flour. Cook over low heat, stirring until mixture is smooth and bubbly. Remove from heat.

Measure remaining marinade; add water to measure 3 cups liquid and stir into flour mixture. Heat to boiling, stirring constantly. Boil and stir 1 minute.

ITALIAN LAMB SHANKS

Here's your chance to try a "new" cut of meat.

4 lamb shanks (about ¾ pound each)	¼ cup all-purpose flour
	1 tablespoon parsley flakes
1 bottle (8 ounces) Italian salad dressing	½ teaspoon salt
	¼ teaspoon onion salt
½ cup grated Parmesan cheese	⅓ cup shortening

Place meat in shallow glass dish; pour salad dressing over meat. Cover tightly; refrigerate at least 5 hours, turning meat occasionally. Drain meat, reserving marinade.

Mix Parmesan cheese, flour, parsley flakes, salt and onion salt. Coat meat with cheese mixture, reserving remaining cheese mixture. Melt shortening in Dutch oven or large skillet; brown shanks over medium heat, turning occasionally.

Reduce heat; sprinkle remaining cheese mixture over shanks. Add reserved marinade; cover tightly. Simmer, turning occasionally, 2½ hours or until tender. Serve additional grated Parmesan cheese with the lamb shanks.

4 servings.

■ *Chicken Italian:* Substitute 3- to 4-pound broiler-fryer chicken, cut up, for the lamb shanks; reduce cooking time to 1 hour. 4 or 5 servings.

LEFTOVER LAMB? Leftovers become praise-winning planned-overs when used in any of these recipes: Lamb Curry, Swedish Lamb with Dill Sauce, Shepherd's Pie.

BAR-B-Q LAMB RIBLETS

4 pounds lamb riblets	¼ cup vinegar
1 can (15 ounces) tomato sauce	¼ cup light molasses
	2 tablespoons salad oil
1 envelope (0.7 ounce) onion salad dressing mix	1 teaspoon dry mustard
	1 cup water

Place riblets meaty side up in open shallow roasting pan. Heat remaining ingredients to boiling, stirring constantly. Boil and stir 3 minutes. Pour sauce over meat. Roast in 350° oven 1½ hours or until done, basting 4 or 5 times.

4 servings.

Veal

1. Cuts from the Shoulder Arm roast, blade roast, boneless shoulder roast (roast, braise); arm steak, blade steak (braise, panfry).

2. Cuts from the Rib Rib roast, crown roast (roast); rib chop, boneless rib chop (braise, panfry).

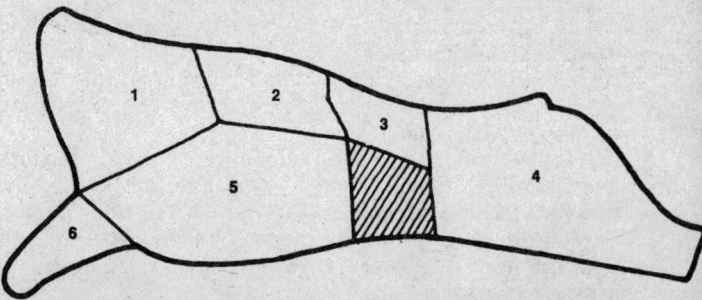

3. Cuts from the Loin Loin roast (roast, braise); loin chop, kidney chop, top loin chop (braise, panfry).

4. Cuts from the Sirloin-Round (Leg) Sirloin roast, boneless sirloin roast (roast); rump roast, boneless rump roast, round roast (roast, braise); sirloin chop, round steak, cutlet (braise, panfry).

5. Cuts from the Breast Breast, stuffed breast (roast, braise); riblets, boneless riblets (braise, cook in liquid); stuffed chop (braise, panfry).

6. Cuts from the Shank Shank, shank cross cut (braise, cook in liquid). Ground veal, patties, mock chicken legs and city chicken may come from any section.

VEAL CUTS YOU SHOULD KNOW

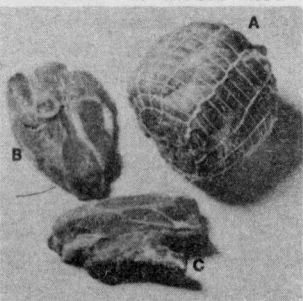

A. Boneless shoulder roast **B.** Arm steak **C.** Blade steak

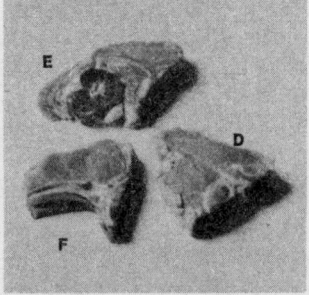

D. Loin chop **E.** Kidney chop **F.** Rib chop

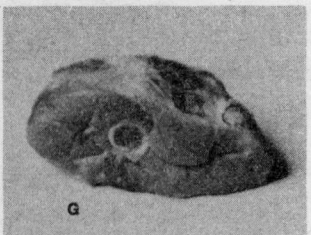

G. Rump roast

H. Round roast

I. Cutlets

J. Riblets **K.** City chicken **L.** Mock chicken legs

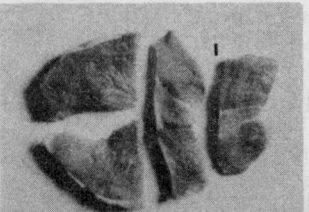

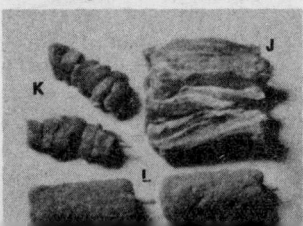

HOW TO ROAST VEAL

Select roast from those listed in chart below. Allow about ½ pound per person—less for boneless roasts, more for roasts with a bone. If desired, season with salt and pepper before, during or after roasting (salt only goes into the roast ¼ to ½ inch).

Place meat fat side up on rack in open shallow roasting pan. The rack keeps the meat out of the drippings. (With a rib roast, the ribs form a natural rack.) If roast has little or no fat, place 2 or 3 slices bacon or salt pork on top. Insert meat thermometer so tip is in center of thickest part of meat and does not touch bone or rest in fat. Do not add water. Do not cover.

Roast meat in 325° oven. (It is not necessary to pre-heat oven.) Roast to desired degree of doneness (see Timetable), using thermometer reading as *final* guide.

Roasts are easier to carve if allowed to set 15 to 20 minutes after removing from oven. Since meat continues to cook after removal from oven, if roast is to "set," it should be removed from oven when thermometer registers 5 to 10° lower than the desired doneness.

TIMETABLE FOR ROASTING VEAL
(Oven Temperature 325°)

Cut	Approximate Weight (Pounds)	Meat Thermometer Reading	Approximate Cooking Time (Minutes per Pound)
Round or Sirloin	5 to 8	170°	25 to 35
Loin	4 to 6	170°	30 to 35
Rib	3 to 5	170°	35 to 40
Boneless Rump	3 to 5	170°	40 to 45
Boneless Shoulder	4 to 6	170°	40 to 45

LIME BASTE FOR ROAST VEAL

½ cup butter or margarine, melted
1 tablespoon grated lime peel
¼ cup lime juice
1 teaspoon marjoram
½ teaspoon thyme

Stir together all ingredients. Baste veal roast occasionally with mixture.

About ¾ cup.

BARBECUED VEAL ROAST

4-pound veal boneless rump or sirloin roast*	1 teaspoon celery seed
2 teaspoons salt	1 teaspoon dry mustard
½ teaspoon pepper	¼ teaspoon onion salt
¾ cup catsup	2 tablespoons vinegar
½ cup water	2 teaspoons Worcestershire
1 tablespoon brown sugar	sauce

Rub surface of roast with mixture of salt and pepper. Place roast on rack in open shallow roasting pan. Insert meat thermometer so tip is in center of thickest part of meat. Do not add water. Do not cover. Roast in 325° oven 2 hours.

In small saucepan, gently simmer remaining ingredients 15 minutes. Pour half the sauce mixture over roast; continue roasting about 1 hour, brushing meat occasionally with remaining sauce mixture. Meat thermometer should register 170°.

6 to 8 servings.

*A veal boneless shoulder roast can be used in this recipe.

VEAL CORDON BLEU

A European classic of veal, ham and Swiss cheese.

4 veal cutlets (about 4 ounces each) or 1-pound veal round steak, ½ inch thick	½ teaspoon salt
	¼ teaspoon pepper
	¼ teaspoon allspice
	1 egg, slightly beaten
4 thin slices boiled or cooked ham	½ cup dry bread crumbs
	3 tablespoons shortening
4 thin slices Swiss cheese	2 tablespoons water
2 tablespoons flour	

If using veal round steak, cut into 4 serving pieces. Pound meat until ¼ inch thick. Place a slice of ham and cheese on each piece of meat. Roll up carefully, beginning at narrow end; secure rolls with wooden picks.

Mix flour, salt, pepper and allspice; coat rolls with flour mixture. Dip rolls into egg, then roll in bread crumbs. Melt shortening in large skillet; brown rolls, about 5 minutes. Reduce heat and add water. Cover; simmer 45 minutes or until tender. Remove cover last 2 to 3 minutes to crisp rolls slightly.

4 servings.

Note: A smooth wooden mallet or the edge of a plate can be used to pound veal.

WIENER SCHNITZEL

4 veal cutlets (about 4 ounces each) or 1-pound veal round steak, ½ inch thick
½ cup all-purpose flour*
1 teaspoon salt
½ teaspoon paprika
¼ teaspoon pepper
1 egg
2 tablespoons water
1 cup dry bread crumbs
¼ cup shortening
1 lemon, cut into wedges

If using veal round steak, cut into 4 pieces. Mix flour, salt, paprika and pepper. Coat meat with flour mixture; pound until ¼ inch thick. Beat egg and water until blended. Dip meat into egg mixture, then coat with bread crumbs.

Melt shortening in large skillet; brown meat quickly. Reduce heat; cover and cook about 45 minutes or until tender. Serve with lemon wedges.

4 servings.

*If using self-rising flour, decrease salt to ½ teaspoon.

VEAL MUSTARD

4 veal rib, loin or sirloin chops, ¾ inch thick
1 teaspoon salt
½ teaspoon pepper
3 tablespoons prepared mustard
½ cup diced bacon
¾ cup light cream
2 tablespoons drained capers

Heat oven to 350°. Season chops with salt and pepper; spread both sides with mustard. Place in ungreased square pan, 9x9x2 inches. Sprinkle bacon on and around chops. Bake 1 hour 15 minutes. Place chops on warm platter; keep warm.

Drain all but 1 tablespoon fat from pan, leaving bacon and mustard in pan. Stir in cream and capers. Heat to boiling, stirring constantly. Reduce heat; simmer 10 minutes or until sauce is consistency of thin white sauce. Pour sauce over chops.

4 servings.

VEAL SCALOPPINE

6 veal cutlets (4 ounces each)
Salt and pepper
½ cup all-purpose flour*
2 tablespoons butter
2 tablespoons salad oil

1 can (3 ounces) sliced mushrooms
½ cup sweet Marsala or golden sherry
½ cup beef broth
2 tablespoons butter

Pound meat until ¼ inch thick. Season with salt and pepper; coat with flour. Melt 2 tablespoons butter with oil in large skillet; brown cutlets, 3 to 4 minutes on each side. Remove meat.

Pour all but 1 tablespoon fat from skillet. Add mushrooms, wine and ¼ cup of the broth to fat in skillet. Heat to boiling; boil 1 to 2 minutes, scraping bottom of skillet with spoon or spatula to remove brown particles. Return meat to skillet; heat to boiling. Cover; reduce heat and simmer about 30 minutes. Baste meat twice with liquid. Place meat on warm platter. Add remaining broth to skillet; heat to boiling. Boil and stir until liquid is of syrup consistency. Stir in 2 tablespoons butter until melted; pour sauce over meat.

6 servings.

*If using self-rising flour, use only ½ teaspoon salt.

VEAL BIRDS WITH SAUSAGE STUFFING

4 veal cutlets (4 ounces each)
1 cup packaged herb-seasoned stuffing
½ pound pork sausage, browned

¼ cup finely chopped celery
3 tablespoons shortening
1 can (10½ ounces) condensed cream of mushroom soup
¼ cup milk

Pound meat until ¼ inch thick. Prepare stuffing as directed on package; stir in drained sausage and the celery. Press about ½ cup stuffing on each piece of meat to ½ inch of edge. Roll up, beginning at narrow end; secure with wooden picks.

Melt shortening in medium skillet; brown rolls. Remove rolls; pour fat from skillet. Add soup and milk to skillet; heat through, stirring constantly. Add rolls and cover; simmer 45 minutes or until tender. To serve, pour gravy over meat.

4 servings.

VEAL SMITANE

1 medium onion, minced (about ½ cup)
2 tablespoons butter or margarine
1 tablespoon shortening
4 veal shoulder steaks (arm or blade), ½ inch thick
1 can (4 ounces) mushroom stems and pieces, drained
1 chicken bouillon cube
⅔ cup boiling water
½ teaspoon each salt and dill weed
¼ teaspoon pepper
1 teaspoon paprika
2 strips lemon peel (each 1 inch)
¾ cup dairy sour cream

In large skillet, cook and stir onion in butter until tender. Remove onion; set aside. Melt shortening in same skillet; cook steaks over medium heat, turning once, until golden brown. Sprinkle mushrooms and onion over meat. Dissolve bouillon cube in water; stir in salt, dill weed, pepper, paprika and lemon peel and add to meat. Cover; simmer 30 to 40 minutes or until tender. Place steaks on warm platter; keep warm.

Stir sour cream slowly into skillet; cook and stir over medium heat until sauce is consistency of thin white sauce. Pour sauce over steaks.

4 servings.

VEAL DAUBE

5-pound veal shoulder roast* (arm or blade)
1 clove garlic, halved
¼ cup all-purpose flour
1 teaspoon salt
½ teaspoon thyme
½ teaspoon sage
¼ teaspoon allspice
⅛ teaspoon pepper
2 bay leaves, crushed
⅓ cup shortening
4 carrots, sliced
2 celery stalks, diced
1 medium onion, finely chopped (about ½ cup)
1 cup water
Gravy (page 410)

Rub meat with garlic. Stir together flour, salt, thyme, sage, allspice, pepper and bay leaves; rub into meat.

Brown meat in shortening over medium heat, about 15 minutes. Remove meat from pan. Add carrots, celery and onion; cook and stir just until onion is tender. Spread vegetables in pan; place meat on top and add water.

Cover pan tightly; place in 325° oven and bake about 2½ hours or until meat is tender. Place meat and vegetables on warm platter; keep warm while preparing gravy. Serve gravy with meat and vegetables.

10 servings.

*A veal round roast can be used in this recipe.

GRAVY

Pour drippings (fat and juices) into a bowl, leaving brown particles in pan. Let fat rise to top of drippings; skim off fat, reserving ¼ cup. Place reserved fat in pan. Blend in ¼ cup all-purpose flour. Cook over low heat, stirring until mixture is smooth and bubbly. Remove from heat.

Measure meat juice; add water to measure 2 cups liquid and stir into flour mixture. Heat to boiling, stirring constantly. Boil and stir 1 minute. Season with salt and pepper.

2 cups.

HAMBURGERS

2 pounds ground beef
2 tablespoons instant minced onion
1 teaspoon salt
½ teaspoon pepper

Mix thoroughly all ingredients. Shape mixture into 6 patties, each about 3 inches in diameter and 1 inch thick.

To Broil: Set oven control at broil and/or 550°. Broil 3 inches from heat 3 to 4 minutes on each side for rare, 5 to 7 minutes for medium.

To Panfry: Fry in 1 to 2 teaspoons shortening over medium heat, turning frequently, about 10 minutes.

To Oven-bake: Place on rack in pan; bake in 350° oven 20 to 25 minutes for rare, 30 minutes for medium.

To Charcoal-grill: Add ½ cup water to ground beef mixture; shape into 10 patties. Place on grill 4 to 6 inches from hot coals. Cook about 12 minutes or until done, turning once.

6 servings.

VARIATIONS

■ *Horseradish Burgers:* Before mixing ingredients, add 2 tablespoons horseradish.

■ *Mustard and Pickle Burgers:* Before mixing ingredients, add 1 tablespoon dry mustard and ¼ cup drained pickle relish.

■ *Sesame Burgers:* Toast ¼ cup sesame seed 10 to 15 minutes in 350° oven until golden; add to ingredients before mixing.

TOPPINGS FOR HAMBURGERS

Caper Butter: Mix ⅓ cup soft butter or margarine, 3 tablespoons drained capers and 1 teaspoon parsley flakes.

Mushroom and Onion: In small skillet, cook and stir 1 cup thinly sliced onion in 1 tablespoon melted butter or margarine until onion is tender. Stir in 1 can (6 ounces) sliced mushrooms, drained, 1 teaspoon salt and ¼ teaspoon pepper; heat through. Serve warm.

Tomato-Chili: Mix 3 slices bacon, crisply fried and crumbled, 3 tablespoons chili sauce and 3 drops red pepper sauce.

HAM LOAF SUPERB

1 pound ground ham	¾ cup milk
½ pound ground veal	Dash pepper
½ pound ground lean pork	2 teaspoons prepared
2 eggs, beaten	mustard
¾ cup soft bread crumbs	¼ cup brown sugar (packed)

Mix thoroughly ham, veal, pork, eggs, bread crumbs, milk and pepper. Spread in ungreased loaf pan, 9x5x3 inches.

Stir together mustard and sugar; spread over loaf. Bake in 350° oven 1½ hours.

6 servings.

MEAT LOAF

1 pound ground beef	1 egg, beaten
¼ pound ground lean pork	¼ cup minced onion
¼ pound ground veal	1¼ teaspoons salt
1 cup dry bread crumbs or cubes and 1¼ cups milk or 3 medium slices white bread, torn into pieces, and 1 cup milk	¼ teaspoon each pepper, celery salt, garlic salt, dry mustard and sage
	1 tablespoon Worcestershire sauce

Mix all ingredients thoroughly. Spread in ungreased loaf pan, 9x5x3 inches. Bake in 350° oven 1½ hours.

6-servings.

VARIATIONS

■ *Barbecued Meat Loaf:* Spread ½ cup barbecue sauce over Meat Loaf or Beef Loaf just before baking.

■ *Beef Loaf:* Increase ground beef to 1½ pounds; omit ground pork, ground veal, celery salt, garlic salt, dry mustard and sage and add 1 tablespoon horseradish and 1 tablespoon catsup.

■ *Turned-out Meat Loaf:* Line loaf pan, 9x5x3 inches, with waxed paper; pat meat mixture for Meat Loaf or Beef Loaf firmly into pan. Unmold loaf in ungreased baking dish, 10x6x1½ inches; bake 1 hour 15 minutes.

SPANISH MEAT LOAF

1½ pounds ground beef	⅓ cup oats
1 can (8 ounces) tomato sauce	1 egg
	1 teaspoon salt
8 pimiento-stuffed large olives, sliced	¼ teaspoon pepper
1 medium onion, chopped (about ½ cup)	

Mix thoroughly beef, ⅓ cup of the sauce and the remaining ingredients. Spread in ungreased loaf pan, 9x5x3 inches. Spread remaining tomato sauce over loaf. Bake in 350° oven 1¼ hours.

6 servings.

WAIKIKI MEATBALLS

Tasty all-beef meatballs in a sweet-sour sauce.

1½ pounds ground beef	2 tablespoons cornstarch
⅔ cup cracker crumbs	½ cup brown sugar (packed)
⅓ cup minced onion	1 can (13½ ounces) pineapple tidbits, drained (reserve syrup)
1 egg	
1½ teaspoons salt	
¼ teaspoon ginger	⅓ cup vinegar
¼ cup milk	1 tablespoon soy sauce
1 tablespoon shortening	⅓ cup chopped green pepper

Mix thoroughly beef, crumbs, onion, egg, salt, ginger and milk. Shape mixture by rounded tablespoonfuls into balls. Melt shortening in large skillet; brown and cook meatballs. Remove meatballs; keep warm. Pour fat from skillet.

Mix cornstarch and sugar. Stir in reserved pineapple syrup, vinegar and soy sauce until smooth. Pour into skillet; cook over medium heat, stirring constantly, until mixture thickens and boils. Boil and stir 1 minute. Add meatballs, pineapple tidbits and green pepper; heat through.

6 servings.

SWEDISH MEATBALLS

1 pound ground beef	1 egg
½ pound ground lean pork	½ cup milk
½ cup minced onion	¼ cup salad oil
¾ cup dry bread crumbs	¼ cup all-purpose flour
1 tablespoon snipped parsley	1 teaspoon paprika
	½ teaspoon salt
2 teaspoons salt	⅛ teaspoon pepper
⅛ teaspoon pepper	2 cups water
1 teaspoon Worcestershire sauce	¾ cup dairy sour cream

Mix thoroughly beef, pork, onion, bread crumbs, parsley, 2 teaspoons salt, ⅛ teaspoon pepper, the Worcestershire sauce, egg and milk. Refrigerate 2 hours.

Shape mixture by rounded tablespoonfuls into balls. In large skillet, slowly brown and cook meatballs in oil. Remove meatballs and keep warm.

Blend flour, paprika, ½ teaspoon salt and ⅛ teaspoon pepper into oil in skillet. Cook over low heat, stirring until mixture is smooth and bubbly. Remove from heat; stir in water. Heat to boiling, stirring constantly. Boil and stir 1 minute. Reduce heat and gradually stir in sour cream, mixing until smooth. Add meatballs; heat through.

6 to 8 servings.

FRANKFURTERS AND SMOKED SAUSAGE

Frankfurters or other cooked smoked sausage links do not require cooking, they need only be heated.

To Simmer: Drop frankfurters into boiling water. Cover tightly; let simmer until heated through, about 5 to 10 minutes, depending on size of sausages.

To Panbroil: Melt small amount of shortening (1 to 2 tablespoons) in skillet; brown frankfurters, turning with tongs. Do not pierce with a fork.

To Broil: If desired, brush frankfurters with butter, margarine or other shortening. Set oven control at broil and/or 550°. Broil frankfurters about 3 inches from heat, turning with tongs to brown evenly.

To Charcoal-grill: Place frankfurters on grill 4 inches from medium coals. Cook 12 to 15 minutes or until heated through, turning frequently. If desired, while cooking, brush franks liberally with a mixture of 1 part horseradish and 2 parts brown sugar.

BATTER FRANKS

A heaven-sent treat for the youngsters. The all-American hot dog served like a lollipop.

1 pound frankfurters	2 tablespoons cornmeal
1 cup all-purpose flour*	3 tablespoons shortening
1½ teaspoons baking powder	1 egg, beaten
½ teaspoon salt	¾ cup milk

Wipe frankfurters dry. Heat fat or salad oil (3 to 4 inches) to 365° in deep fat fryer or heavy kettle. Measure flour, baking powder, salt and cornmeal into bowl. Cut in shortening thoroughly. Stir in egg and milk.

Dip frankfurters into batter, allowing excess batter to drip into bowl. Fry in deep fat, turning once, until brown, about 6 minutes. Drain. If desired, insert wooden skewer in end of each frankfurter.

5 servings (2 franks each).

*If using self-rising flour, omit baking powder and salt.

CHEESE BOATS

Split 1 pound frankfurters lengthwise, not cutting completely through. Place a strip of sharp process cheese, 2½ x 1½ x ¼ inch, in cut of each frankfurter. Wrap each with slice of bacon; secure with wooden picks.

Place cut side down on rack in broiler pan. Set oven control at broil and/or 550°. Broil 5 inches from heat about 15 minutes, turning when bacon is crisp.

5 servings (2 franks each).

CREOLE WIENERS

New way of serving "hot dogs"—barbecue good.

8 slices bacon, diced	¾ teaspoon salt
3 cups minced onion	⅛ teaspoon pepper
1 can (16 ounces) tomatoes	1 pound frankfurters

In large skillet, fry bacon and onion until bacon is crisp and onion is tender. Drain all but 2 tablespoons bacon drippings from skillet. Stir in tomatoes, salt and pepper. Heat to boiling; reduce heat and simmer 15 minutes, stirring occasionally. Add frankfurters; cover and simmer 15 minutes.

5 or 6 servings.

SAUSAGE (Uncooked Smoked or Fresh)

Brown 'n serve sausages are real quickies. They're fully cooked and need only be heated.

To Panfry: Place sausage links or patties in *cold* skillet. Add 2 to 4 tablespoons water; cover tightly and cook slowly 5 to 8 minutes, depending on size or thickness of sausages. Uncover; cook until well done, turning to brown evenly.

To Bake: Heat oven to 400°. Arrange sausages in single layer in ungreased shallow baking pan. Bake 20 to 30 minutes or until well done, turning sausages to brown evenly. Spoon off drippings as they accumulate.

SASSY SAUSAGES

1 cup water
⅓ cup red cinnamon candies
   Red food color
3 red tart apples, cored and
   cut into ½-inch rings

1 pound pork sausage links
3 tablespoons water

In skillet, heat 1 cup water, the cinnamon candies and few drops red food color until candies are melted. Place apple rings in syrup; cook slowly, turning occasionally, about 20 minutes or until tender.

Place links in another skillet; add 3 tablespoons water. Cover tightly; cook slowly 8 minutes. Uncover; cook, turning sausages until well browned. To serve, insert hot sausage link in center of each apple slice.

5 or 6 servings.

POLYNESIAN HAM LOAF

1 can (12 ounces) pork
   luncheon meat
2 teaspoons prepared
   mustard

4 slices pineapple
2 tablespoons brown sugar

Cut luncheon meat into 8 sections, cutting only a little more than halfway through loaf. Place in ungreased small baking dish. Spoon ½ teaspoon mustard *between* each 2 sections and insert ½ slice pineapple. Sprinkle sugar over loaf. Bake in 375° oven 20 minutes. To serve, cut through every other section.

4 servings.

COLD MEAT PLATTER DELUXE

Use your own choice of cold meats for this spread.

¼ pound liver sausage, cut
  into ¼-inch slices
6 slices cooked salami
  (about 3 ounces)
6 slices large bologna (about
  3 ounces)
6 slices pickle and olive loaf
  (about 4 ounces)
6 slices Swiss cheese (about
  5 ounces)
6 wedges Edam cheese
  (about 6 ounces)

Green onions, washed and
  trimmed
Pimiento-stuffed small
  olives
1 medium cucumber,
  washed, scored with fork
  and cut into ¼-inch slices
Sweet pickles
Spiced crab apples

Arrange ingredients on large serving plate.
6 servings.

BACON

To Panfry: Place slices of bacon in *cold* skillet. Cook
over low heat 8 to 10 minutes, turning to brown bacon
evenly on both sides.

To Bake: Place separated slices of bacon on rack in
broiler pan. Bake bacon in 400° oven 10 minutes or until
brown. Do not turn.

To Broil: Place separated slices of bacon on rack in
broiler pan; place broiler pan so top of bacon is 3 inches
from heat. Set oven control at broil and/or 550°. Broil
bacon until brown, about 2 minutes. Turn slices; broil
1 minute longer.

CANADIAN-STYLE BACON

To Panfry: Place ⅛-inch slices Canadian-style bacon
in *cold* skillet. Cook over low heat 8 to 10 minutes, turning to brown evenly on both sides.

To Bake: If necessary, remove casing from 2-pound
piece Canadian-style bacon. Place bacon fat side up on
rack in open shallow roasting pan. Insert meat thermometer so tip is in center of bacon. Bake uncovered in 325°
oven 1 to 1¼ hours or until thermometer registers 160°.

To Broil: Place ¼-inch slices Canadian-style bacon on
rack in broiler pan. Set oven control at broil and/or
550°. Broil bacon 2 to 3 inches from heat until brown,
about 3 minutes. Turn bacon slices; broil 3 minutes
longer.

CANADIAN-STYLE BACON ROAST WITH PINEAPPLE

2-pound piece
  Canadian-style bacon
1 can (1 pound 4½ ounces)
  crushed pineapple

¼ cup honey
1 teaspoon ginger
¼ cup water

If necessary, remove casing from bacon; place bacon fat side up in ungreased baking dish, 8x8x2 inches.

Stir together pineapple (with syrup), honey, ginger and water; pour over bacon. Insert meat thermometer so tip is in center of bacon.

Roast uncovered in 325° oven 1 to 1¼ hours or until thermometer registers 160°. Baste bacon occasionally with pineapple mixture during roasting. Place bacon on platter; spoon pineapple mixture over meat. Cut into ¼-inch slices.

6 to 8 servings.

KIDNEYS

Wash kidneys; remove membrane, hard parts and white veins before cooking. Pat kidneys dry. If desired, cut kidneys into slices or pieces. Lamb kidneys are smaller and are usually split or left whole. Beef kidney is less tender than other kidneys and should be cooked in liquid or braised.

SAUTEED LAMB OR VEAL KIDNEYS

1 pound lamb or veal
  kidneys
1 clove garlic, halved
⅓ cup chopped onion

¼ cup butter or margarine
1 teaspoon salt
¼ teaspoon pepper
½ teaspoon paprika

Wash kidneys; remove membrane, hard parts and white veins. Pat dry; split lamb kidneys or cut veal kidneys into pieces. Rub large skillet with garlic. Cook and stir onion in butter until tender.

Add kidneys; cook and stir over medium heat 20 to 25 minutes or until inside is no longer pink. Place kidneys in serving dish; season with salt, pepper and paprika. If desired, garnish with parsley and lemon slices.

4 servings.

LIVER

Beef and pork liver are frequently braised or fried and are sometimes ground for loaves and patties. Baby beef, veal (calf) and lamb liver are usually panfried, broiled or panbroiled. Before cooking, peel or trim any membrane from liver.

To Panfry: Have liver sliced ½ to ¾ inch thick. Coat with flour. Melt ¼ cup shortening in skillet; fry liver over medium-high heat until brown, 2 to 3 minutes on each side. Season to taste.

To Broil: Have veal (calf) or lamb liver sliced ½ to ¾ inch thick. Dip into melted bacon drippings, butter or margarine. Set oven control at broil and/or 550°. Broil 3 to 5 inches from heat just long enough for meat to change color and become light brown, about 3 minutes on each side.

To Braise: Have beef or pork liver sliced ½ to ¾ inch thick. Coat liver with flour and brown in small amount of fat. Add ¼ cup liquid; cover tightly and cook on top of range or in 350° oven 20 to 30 minutes. For a large piece, increase liquid to ½ cup; cook about 30 minutes per pound.

DILLED LIVER AND ONION

½ cup all-purpose flour*	¼ cup shortening
2 teaspoons salt	½ cup minced onion
¼ teaspoon pepper	½ teaspoon dill weed
1 pound sliced beef or pork liver	

Stir together flour, salt and pepper. Coat liver with flour mixture. Melt shortening in large skillet; brown liver over medium heat. Reduce heat; sprinkle liver with onion and dill. Cover tightly; simmer 20 minutes.

4 servings.

If using self-rising flour, decrease salt to 1½ teaspoons.

LIVER AND ONIONS

Have 1 pound liver sliced ½ to ¾ inch thick. In large skillet, cook and stir 2 cups thinly sliced onion in 3 tablespoons butter until tender. Remove from skillet; keep warm. Panfry liver as directed above. Add onions last minute of cooking.

4 servings.

LIVER AND BACON

Have 1 pound liver sliced ½ to ¾ inch thick. In large skillet, fry 8 slices bacon until crisp. Remove and drain; keep warm. Coat liver slices in ½ cup all-purpose flour. Fry in hot bacon drippings over medium-high heat until brown, about 2 to 3 minutes on each side. Season with salt and pepper. Serve with bacon.

4 servings.

SWEETBREADS

Sweetbreads are soft in consistency, tender and delicately flavored. They should be precooked immediately to keep them white and firm, then they can be broiled, fried, braised, creamed or served in a sauce.

To Precook: Wash 1 pound sweetbreads. Heat 2 quarts water, 2 teaspoons salt and 2 tablespoons lemon juice to boiling. Add sweetbreads and heat to boiling. Reduce heat; cover and simmer 20 minutes. Drain; plunge sweetbreads into cold water. With sharp knife, remove membrane and veins and cut sweetbreads into pieces.

CREAMED SWEETBREADS

1 pound sweetbreads	1 cup milk
3 tablespoons butter or margarine	½ cup shredded sharp process cheese
3 tablespoons flour	1 tablespoon lemon juice
¼ teaspoon salt	1 can (3 ounces) sliced mushrooms, drained
¼ teaspoon dry mustard	Parsley
⅛ teaspoon pepper	

Precook sweetbreads. Melt butter in large saucepan over low heat. Blend in flour, salt, mustard and pepper. Cook over low heat, stirring until mixture is smooth and bubbly. Remove from heat. Stir in milk. Heat to boiling, stirring constantly. Boil and stir 1 minute.

Add cheese and lemon juice, stirring until cheese is melted. Stir in sweetbreads and mushrooms; heat through. Garnish with parsley.

4 servings.

TONGUE

Tongue can be purchased fresh, pickled, corned, smoked or canned. Tongue is a less tender variety meat and requires long slow cooking in liquid. To cook, cover tongue with water. When cooking fresh tongue, add 1 teaspoon salt for each quart of water. Cover tightly; simmer beef tongue 3 to 4 hours, veal or calf tongue 2 to 3 hours or until tender. Drain; plunge tongue into cold water.

Peel skin from tongue, cut away roots, bones and cartilage. Hot tongue is delicious served with buttered chopped spinach or Harvard beets.

If tongue is served cold, reserve cooking liquid. After removing skin, roots, bones and cartilage, allow tongue to cool in reserved liquid. Serve sliced cold tongue with a horseradish sauce.

GLAZED BEEF TONGUE

3- to 3½-pound beef tongue
1 can (8¾ ounces) crushed pineapple, drained
¼ cup brown sugar (packed)
1 teaspoon grated orange peel

Cook tongue as directed above. Place in ungreased baking dish, 11½ x 7½ x 1½ inches. Mix pineapple, brown sugar and orange peel; spread over tongue. Cover; cook in 350° oven 30 minutes.

6 to 8 servings.

TRIPE

Tripe can be purchased fresh, pickled or canned. It has a very delicate flavor and is one of the less tender variety meats, requiring long, slow cooking in liquid.

Tripe is partially cooked when it is purchased; however, precooking in water is preliminary to all ways of serving. Precook covered with salted water (1 teaspoon salt for each quart of water). Cook beef tripe 1 to 1½ hours or until tender.

Tripe can also be purchased fully cooked. Cooked tripe can be served as follows: .

■ Topped with well-seasoned tomato sauce.

■ Brushed with melted butter or margarine and broiled until light brown, 10 to 15 minutes for beef tripe.

■ Creamed.

HEART

Heart is flavorful, but one of the less tender of all the variety meats. Braising and cooking in liquid are the preferred methods of cooking.

To cook in liquid, cover heart with water; add 1 teaspoon salt for each quart of water. Cover tightly and cook slowly until tender. For beef heart, cook 3 to 4 hours; for veal, pork or lamb heart, cook 2½ to 3 hours.

STUFFED BEEF HEART

3-pound beef heart
2 cups dry bread cubes
¼ cup chopped celery
1 tablespoon instant minced onion
1 tablespoon butter or margarine, melted
½ teaspoon salt
¼ teaspoon marjoram leaves
¼ teaspoon thyme leaves
⅛ teaspoon pepper
2 tablespoons shortening
1 can (10½ ounces) condensed beef consommé
¼ cup water

Cut heart lengthwise down one side. Remove excess fat and large blood vessels. Wash heart thoroughly; pat dry. Stir together bread cubes, celery, onion, butter, salt, marjoram leaves, thyme leaves and pepper. Place mixture in heart, fastening opening with skewers, then lacing shut with string.

Melt shortening in Dutch oven; brown heart. Reduce heat; add consommé and water. Cover tightly; simmer on top of range or in 325° oven 3 hours or until tender. To serve, slice heart on the diagonal.

6 to 8 servings.

BRAINS

Brains are soft in consistency, very tender and have a delicate flavor. They should be cooked immediately. Precooking makes them firm; then they can be broiled, fried, braised, creamed or served in a sauce.

To Precook: Wash 1 pound brains. Heat 1 quart water, 1 teaspoon salt and 1 tablespoon lemon juice to boiling. Add brains; heat to boiling. Reduce heat; cover tightly and simmer 20 minutes. Drain; plunge brains into cold water. With sharp knife, remove membrane.

Precooked brains can be served in the following ways:

■ Broken into small pieces and scrambled with eggs.
■ Reheated in a rich cream or well-seasoned tomato sauce.
■ Dipped into slightly beaten egg, then into crumbs and fried in small amount of shortening or in deep fat until a delicate golden brown.
■ In croquettes. ·
■ In salads.

BROILED BRAINS

Precook 1 pound brains. Place brains on rack in broiler pan. Stir together ¼ cup butter or margarine, melted, and 1 clove garlic, crushed; brush brains with half the butter.

Set oven control at broil and/or 550°. Broil brains 3 inches from heat 5 minutes. Turn brains; brush with remaining butter and broil 5 minutes longer. If desired, garnish with parsley.

4 servings.

Fish and Seafood

On the East Coast, on the West Coast, on the shores of lakes—fish takes its place as an all-time favorite food. Great restaurants attest to its popularity and great cooks are famous for their gentle ways with the fruits of the sea. Here we have rounded up a very special collection of recipes from both Coasts—and from lands across the sea. Protein-plenty. Penny-wise. Pound-thoughtful (your pounds). Now— no matter what part of the country you live in —thanks to frozen fish and canned and frozen shellfish, these recipes could become your own specialties.

If you have ever gone on a fishing trip equipped with frying pan or dined at a restaurant where you net the fish that is served to you just minutes later, then you know the first law of fish cooking: The best fish is the freshest fish.

How to Select Fresh Fish

The eyes should be bright, clear, full and bulging; the gills, reddish-pink; the scales, bright in color with a sheen. Fresh fish does not have a "fishy" odor and the flesh is firm and elastic; it will spring back when pressed.

Amount to Buy

How much fish you buy, fresh or frozen, will depend upon what form you select.

Whole fish is just as it comes from the water. You will need 1 pound per serving.

Drawn fish is whole but eviscerated. Allow 1 pound per serving.

Dressed or pan-dressed fish are eviscerated and

scaled. They usually have head, tail and fins removed. The smaller fish (less than 1 pound) are called pan-dressed. Allow ½ pound dressed fish per serving.

Steaks are taken from large dressed fish; they are cross-section slices cut about ¾ inch thick. Allow ½ pound per serving.

Fillets, the sides of the fish, are cut lengthwise away from the backbone. They are practically boneless, with little or no waste. Butterfly fillets are double fillets held together by skin. Allow ⅓ to ½ pound per serving.

Sticks are uniform cuts from frozen blocks of fish fillets. They are coated with batter, breaded, partially cooked, packaged and frozen. Allow ⅓ to ½ pound per serving.

Buying Shellfish

Shellfish are available in canned or frozen forms. Some are smoked and some are breaded. If you live in an area where fresh shellfish are plentiful, you will have no trouble buying some forms alive. The amount to buy varies considerably; consult your recipe or your dealer.

Methods of Cooking Fish and Shellfish

Whatever the method, the most important point to remember when cooking fish is: Don't overcook. Fish does not need cooking to tenderize it, as the Japanese or Latin Americans can testify. Fish may be steamed, poached, fried, boiled, broiled, baked or planked (literally cooked on a wooden plank). The last three methods are usually best for fat fish,* while lean fish remain firm and moist when steamed or poached. Exceptions may be made if lean fish are basted. Both fat and lean fish are suitable for frying. Shellfish are usually steamed, boiled, fried, broiled or baked.

*Fat fishes include butterfish, sea herring, mackerel, salmon, shad, Spanish mackerel, catfish, lake trout and whitefish. Most other fish are lean.

BAKED FISH

2 pounds fish fillets or steaks	1 teaspoon grated onion
Salt and pepper	¼ cup butter or margarine,
2 tablespoons lemon juice	melted

Heat oven to 350°. If fillets are large, cut into serving

pieces. Season with salt and pepper. Mix juice, onion and butter. Dip fish into butter mixture; place in greased square pan, 9x9x2 inches. Pour remaining butter mixture over fish. Bake uncovered 25 to 30 minutes or until fish flakes easily with fork. If desired, sprinkle with paprika.

About 6 servings.

BAKED STUFFED FISH

8- to 10-pound fish (salmon, cod, snapper or lake trout), cleaned
salt and pepper
Garden Vegetable Stuffing (below)

Salad oil
½ cup butter or margarine, melted
¼ cup lemon juice

Heat oven to 350°. Wash fish quickly in cold water and pat dry. Rub cavity with salt and pepper; stuff with Garden Vegetable Stuffing. Close opening with skewers and lace with string. (If you have extra stuffing, place in baking dish; cover and place in oven 20 minutes before serving.)

Brush fish with salad oil; place in open shallow roasting pan. Bake about 1½ hours or until fish flakes easily with fork, basting occasionally with mixture of butter and lemon juice during baking.

10 to 12 servings.

GARDEN VEGETABLE STUFFING

2 medium onions, chopped (about 1 cup)
¼ cup butter or margarine
2 cups dry bread cubes
1 cup coarsely shredded carrot
1 cup cut-up fresh mushrooms

½ cup snipped parsley
1½ tablespoons lemon juice
1 egg
1 clove garlic, minced
2 teaspoons salt
¼ teaspoon each marjoram and pepper

Cook and stir onion in butter until onion is tender. Lightly mix in remaining ingredients.

CREOLE FLOUNDER

2 pounds flounder or
  pollock fillets
1½ cups chopped tomatoes
  ½ cup chopped green
  pepper
  ⅓ cup lemon juice
  1 tablespoon salad oil

2 teaspoons salt
2 teaspoons instant
  minced onion
1 teaspoon basil leaves
¼ teaspoon coarsely
  ground black pepper
4 drops red pepper sauce

Heat oven to 500°. Place fish in greased baking dish,
13½x9x2 inches. Combine remaining ingredients; spoon
over fish.

Bake 5 to 8 minutes or until fish flakes easily with
fork. If desired, garnish with tomato wedges and green
pepper rings.

6 servings.

FILLET OF SOLE BONNE FEMME

1 pound sole or flounder
  fillets
2 tablespoons butter or
  margarine, melted
3 tablespoons lemon juice
¼ cup minced onion
½ pound mushrooms,
  washed, trimmed and
  sliced, or 1 can (6
  ounces) sliced mushrooms,
  drained

2 tablespoons butter or
  margarine
2 tablespoons flour
¼ teaspoon salt
⅛ teaspoon pepper
1 cup milk

Heat oven to 350°. Place fish in ungreased baking
dish, 11½x7½x1½ inches. Combine the melted butter,
lemon juice and onion; pour over fish. Turn fish to coat
both sides with butter mixture. Bake skin side up 20 to
30 minutes or until fish flakes easily with fork.

Cook and stir mushrooms in 2 tablespoons butter until
mushrooms are tender. Stir in flour, salt and pepper.
Cook over low heat, stirring until mixture is bubbly.
Remove from heat. Stir in milk. Heat to boiling, stirring
constantly. Boil and stir 1 minute. If desired, thin sauce
with juices from fish; pour over fish before serving.

3 or 4 servings.

BROILED FISH

2 pounds fish fillets or
   steaks, about 1 inch thick
1 teaspoon salt

⅛ teaspoon pepper
¼ cup butter or margarine,
   melted

Set oven control at broil and/or 550° Grease broiler
pan and place in oven to heat. If fillets are large, cut into
serving pieces. Season both sides of fish with salt and
pepper. If fish has not been skinned, place skin side up
in broiler pan; brush with butter.

Broil 2 to 3 inches from heat 5 to 8 minutes or until
light brown. Brush fish with butter; turn carefully and
brush again with butter. Broil 5 to 8 minutes longer or
until fish flakes easily with fork.

6 servings.

VARIATION

■ *Broiled Fish Italiano:* Omit salt, pepper and butter;
baste fish with ¼ cup Italian salad dressing during broiling.

PANFRIED FISH

2 pounds fish fillets, steaks
   or pan-dressed fish
1 teaspoon salt
⅛ teaspoon pepper
1 egg
1 tablespoon water

1 cup all-purpose flour,
   buttermilk baking mix,
   cornmeal or grated
   Parmesan cheese
   Shortening (part butter)

If fillets are large, cut into serving pieces. Season both
sides of fish with salt and pepper. Blend egg and water.
Dip fish into egg, then coat with flour.

Heat shortening (⅛ inch) in skillet. Turning fish carefully to brown both sides, cook in shortening over
medium heat about 10 minutes.

4 to 6 servings.

VARIATION

■ *Fish Almondine:* Just before serving, top fish with
Almond Butter: Brown ¼ cup butter or margarine in small
skillet; add ¼ cup toasted slivered blanched almonds,
¼ teaspoon salt and 2 teaspoons lemon juice.

OVEN-FRIED FILLETS

Special features: no basting, no turning, no careful watching. What could be easier?

2 pounds fish fillets or steaks ¼ cup butter or margarine,
1 tablespoon salt   melted
½ cup milk
1 cup dry bread crumbs

Heat oven to 500°. If fillets are large, cut into serving pieces. Stir salt into milk. Dip fish into milk, then coat with bread crumbs. Place in well-greased baking pan, 13x9x2 inches.

Pour melted butter over fish. Place pan on rack that is slightly above middle of oven; bake uncovered 10 to 12 minutes or until fish flakes easily with fork.

6 servings.

DEEP-FRIED FISH OR SHALLOW-FRIED FISH

Use several types of fish if you wish. Serve with Tartar Sauce (page 578) or with lemon halves (wrapped in cheesecloth).

2 pounds fish fillets, steaks   ⅛ teaspoon pepper
  or pan-dressed fish   2 eggs, slightly beaten
1 cup all-purpose flour*   1 cup dry bread crumbs
1 teaspoon salt

Heat fat or oil (3 to 4 inches) to 375° in deep fat fryer or kettle. If fillets are large, cut into serving pieces. Stir together flour, salt and pepper. Coat fish with flour mixture; dip into eggs, then coat with bread crumbs. Fry in deep fat about 4 minutes or until golden brown.

Or shallow-fry fish in hot shortening (1½ to 2 inches) in skillet about 4 minutes or until brown.

6 servings.

*If using self-rising flour, omit salt.

VARIATION

■ Batter-fried Fish: Prepare Thin Fritter Batter (page 68). Coat fillets with flour, then dip into batter to coat completely. Fry in deep fat about 3 minutes or until golden brown. Or fry in hot shortening (1½ to 2 inches) in large skillet about 4 minutes or until golden brown.

POACHED FISH

Try something new in the way of garnishing fish—strips of green or red pepper, slices or wedges of hard-cooked egg, sliced cold cooked beets, pickles, mint, perhaps even orange wedges.

1 medium onion, sliced	1 teaspoon salt
3 slices lemon	2 peppercorns
3 sprigs parsley	1 pound fish fillets
1 bay leaf	

In large skillet, heat to boiling 1½ inches water with onion, lemon slices, parsley, bay leaf, salt and peppercorns.

Arrange fish in single layer in skillet. Cover; simmer 4 to 6 minutes or until fish flakes easily with fork.

2 or 3 servings.

POMPANO EN PAPILLOTE

2 pompano fillets* (about ½ pound each)	Soft butter or margarine
New Orleans Mushroom Sauce (page 430)	¾ cup cleaned cooked shrimp (about 12 medium)

Cut fillets in half crosswise. Poach fish as directed (above) except—simmer only 3 minutes and reserve ½ cup fish stock.

Heat oven to 350°. Prepare New Orleans Mushroom Sauce. Cut 4 rectangles, each about 12x8 inches, of heavy-duty aluminum foil; brush top side of each with butter.

Spoon 3 tablespoons of New Orleans Mushroom Sauce on one half of each rectangle. Place a piece of fish on sauce; top with 3 shrimp and 1 tablespoon sauce. Fold other half of each foil rectangle over fish and fold edges together to seal.

Place foil packet on baking sheet; bake 20 minutes. To serve, cut slits in top of each packet and fold back foil.

4 servings.

*Fillets of trout, pike, halibut or haddock can be substituted for the pompano fillets.

NEW ORLEANS MUSHROOM SAUCE

½ cup reserved fish stock
1 chicken bouillon cube or
  1 teaspoon instant chicken
  bouillon
3 tablespoons butter or
  margarine
3 tablespoons flour

¼ teaspoon salt
⅛ teaspoon pepper
⅛ teaspoon celery salt
½ cup milk
1 can (3 ounces) sliced
  mushrooms, drained

Heat fish stock to boiling. Dissolve bouillon cube in stock; set aside. Melt butter in small saucepan. Blend in flour and seasonings. Cook over low heat, stirring until mixture is smooth and bubbly. Remove from heat.

Stir in milk and bouillon stock. Heat to boiling, stirring constantly. Boil and stir 1 minute. Stir in mushrooms; heat through.

POACHED FISH WITH CUCUMBER SAUCE

Poach fish as directed on page 429 except—use 3 pounds fish fillets and poach in two 12-inch skillets, doubling the seasonings. Serve with Cucumber Sauce (below).

CUCUMBER SAUCE

¼ cup shortening
2 tablespoons flour
2 cups milk
3 egg yolks, slightly beaten
1 medium cucumber, pared,
  seeded and diced

1 can (4½ ounces) shrimp,
  rinsed, drained and
  coarsely chopped (1 cup)
1 teaspoon salt
¼ teaspoon nutmeg
⅛ teaspoon pepper

Melt shortening in medium saucepan. Blend in flour. Cook over low heat, stirring until mixture is smooth and bubbly. Remove from heat. Stir in milk. Heat to boiling, stirring constantly. Boil and stir 1 minute. Remove from heat.

Stir at least half the hot mixture into egg yolks. Blend egg mixture into remaining hot mixture. Boil and stir 1 minute. Stir in remaining ingredients; heat through. Serve warm.

3 cups.

COOKED SHRIMP

1½ pounds fresh or frozen raw shrimp (in shells)	4 cups water
	2 tablespoons salt

Peel shrimp. (If shrimp is frozen, do not thaw; peel under running cold water.) Make a shallow cut lengthwise down back of each shrimp; wash out sand vein.

Heat water to boiling. Add salt and shrimp; cover and heat to boiling. Reduce heat and simmer 5 minutes. Drain. Remove any remaining particles of sand vein.

2 cups cleaned cooked shrimp (¾ pound).

Note: To cook shrimp before peeling, increase salt to ¼ cup. After cooking shrimp, drain and peel. Remove sand vein.

SHRIMP DE JONGHE

Shellfish-lovers' delight—bubbly casseroles filled with herb-flavored shrimp.

2 pounds cleaned cooked shrimp	Dash each nutmeg, mace and thyme
4 cloves garlic, sliced	2 teaspoons salt
1 cup butter or margarine	¼ teaspoon pepper
¼ teaspoon tarragon leaves	½ cup chicken broth*
¼ teaspoon snipped parsley	1 cup dry bread crumbs
½ teaspoon minced onion	Parsley

Heat oven to 400°. Divide shrimp among 8 ungreased individual casseroles (each about 5 inches in diameter). Cook and stir garlic in butter until butter browns. Remove from heat. Remove garlic pieces; add remaining ingredients except bread crumbs.

Toss ¼ cup of the garlic butter with bread crumbs. Pour remaining butter mixture over shrimp in casseroles and top with buttered crumbs. Bake uncovered 10 minutes. (Do not overbake shrimp as they tend to become tough.) Garnish with sprigs of parsley.

8 servings.

*Chicken broth can be made by dissolving 1 chicken bouillon cube in ½ cup boiling water, or use canned chicken broth.

BROILED LOBSTER TAILS WITH LEMON BUTTER SAUCE

2 quarts water
2 tablespoons salt
1 package (1 pound 8
   ounces) frozen South
   African rock lobster tails

⅓ cup butter or margarine,
   melted
Lemon Butter Sauce
   (below)

Heat water and salt to boiling in saucepan. Add lobster tails; cover tightly and heat to boiling. Reduce heat; simmer about 15 minutes. Drain.

With kitchen scissors, cut away thin undershell (covering meat of lobster tails). To prevent tails from curling, insert long metal skewer from meat side through tail to shell side, then back through shell and meat at opposite end. Place tails meat side up on broiler rack. Brush with butter.

Set oven control at broil and/or 550°. Broil tails meat side up 3 inches from heat 2 to 3 minutes. Remove skewers and serve with Lemon Butter Sauce in lemon cups.

3 or 4 servings.

LEMON BUTTER SAUCE

½ cup butter or margarine
1 tablespoon lemon juice
1 tablespoon snipped
   parsley

¼ teaspoon red pepper
   sauce

Heat all ingredients over low heat, stirring constantly, until butter is melted. Keep warm.

BOILED LOBSTER

Serve with lemon wedges and melted butter.

3 quarts water
3 tablespoons salt

2 live lobsters (about
   1 pound each)

Heat water and salt to boiling in large kettle. Plunge lobsters headfirst into water. Cover; heat to boiling. Reduce heat; simmer about 10 minutes. Drain. Place lobster on its back. With a sharp knife, cut lengthwise in half.

Remove the stomach, which is just back of the head, and the intestinal vein, which runs from the stomach to the tip of the tail. Do not discard the green liver and coral roe. Crack claws.

2 servings.

LOBSTER THERMIDOR

2 live lobsters (about
  1 pound each)
2 tablespoons chopped
  onion
1 can (3 ounces) sliced
  mushrooms, drained
2 tablespoons butter or
  margarine
2 tablespoons flour
¼ teaspoon salt
⅛ teaspoon each pepper
  and paprika

½ cup light cream (20%)
½ cup chicken broth*
½ teaspoon Worcestershire
  sauce
1 egg yolk, beaten
2 tablespoons sherry
3 tablespoons dry bread
  crumbs
1 tablespoon grated
  Parmesan cheese

Cook lobsters as directed for Boiled Lobster (at left) except—simmer only 5 minutes. Remove meat carefully (you should have about 2 cups); reserve shells. Separate meat into small pieces.

Heat oven to 450°. Cook and stir onion and mushrooms in butter until onion is tender. Stir in flour, salt, pepper and paprika. Cook over low heat, stirring until mixture is bubbly. Remove from heat. Stir in cream, chicken broth and Worcestershire sauce. Heat to boiling, stirring constantly. Boil and stir 1 minute. Remove from heat.

Stir at least half the hot mixture into egg yolk. Blend egg mixture into remaining hot mixture. Stir in wine and lobster meat; heat through.

Place shells in baking pan, 13x9x2 inches. Fill with lobster mixture. Mix bread crumbs and cheese; sprinkle over mixture. Bake 5 to 8 minutes.

4 servings.

*Chicken broth can be made by dissolving 1 chicken bouillon cube in ½ cup boiling water, or use canned chicken broth.

VARIATION

■ *Lobster Tails Thermidor:* Substitute 4 frozen lobster tails (5 to 6 ounces each) for the live lobsters; double amounts of other ingredients. After filling shells, place remaining lobster mixture in individual casserole and bake as directed.

Note: To cook frozen lobster tails, heat 2 quarts water and 2 tablespoons salt to boiling. Add lobster tails; cover and heat to boiling. Reduce heat; simmer 15 minutes. When cool, cut through membranes lengthwise. Remove membranes. Remove meat from shells; separate into small pieces.

SCALLOP KABOBS

1 pound scallops	½ teaspoon salt
1 can (4 ounces) button mushrooms, drained	Dash pepper
	12 bacon slices
2 tablespoons salad oil	1 can (13½ ounces)
2 tablespoons soy sauce	pineapple chunks, drained
2 tablespoons lemon juice	Green pepper chunks
2 tablespoons snipped parsley	Melted butter

If the large sea scallops are used, cut each into 3 or 4 pieces. Wash scallops; remove any shell particles. Place scallops and mushrooms in shallow glass dish. Combine oil, soy sauce, lemon juice, parsley, salt and pepper; pour over scallops and mushrooms. Cover; refrigerate 30 minutes, turning scallops and mushrooms once.

Partially fry bacon; drain and cut slices in half. On skewers, alternate scallops, mushrooms, bacon, pineapple and green pepper.

Set oven control at broil and/or 550°. Broil kabobs 3 inches from heat 5 to 8 minutes, turning once and basting with butter.

4 servings.

Note: To charcoal-grill kabobs, cook 4 inches from medium coals 6 to 8 minutes on each side.

COQUILLES ST. JACQUES

A la Parisienne—one of the most popular versions of the traditional baked scallop recipe. Delicate flavor and a touch of elegance that's sure to please discriminating men and women alike.

1 pound scallops
2 tablespoons minced onion
1 tablespoon butter or margarine
1 tablespoon lemon juice
¾ teaspoon salt
⅛ teaspoon marjoram leaves
Dash paprika
¾ cup dry white wine
¼ pound mushrooms, washed, trimmed and coarsely chopped (about 1½ cups)

⅓ cup butter or margarine
¼ cup all-purpose flour
1 cup whipping cream
2 teaspoons snipped parsley
1 tablespoon butter or margarine
⅓ cup dry bread crumbs

If the large sea scallops are used, cut each into 3 or 4 pieces. Wash scallops; remove any shell particles and drain.

In medium saucepan, cook and stir onion in 1 tablespoon butter until onion is tender. Add scallops, lemon juice, salt, marjoram leaves, paprika and wine; simmer uncovered 10 minutes. Add mushrooms; simmer 2 minutes longer. Drain liquid from scallop mixture; set aside.

Melt ⅓ cup butter in medium saucepan over low heat. Blend in flour. Cook over low heat, stirring until mixture is smooth and bubbly. Remove from heat. Stir in reserved liquid and the cream. Heat to boiling, stirring constantly. Boil and stir 1 minute. Stir in parsley.

Reserving about ½ cup sauce in saucepan, pour remainder over scallop and mushroom mixture; heat through, stirring frequently. Immediately spoon scallop mixture into 6 individual baking shells; spread each with about 1 tablespoon reserved sauce.

Melt 1 tablespoon butter in small skillet; add bread crumbs, stirring until brown. Place shells on baking sheet. Set oven control at broil and/or 550°; broil shells 5 inches from heat 5 to 8 minutes or until bubbly and brown. Sprinkle crumbs over shells.

6 servings.

FRENCH FRIED SEAFOOD

½ cup all-purpose flour*	Seafood (page 437)
1 teaspoon salt	2 eggs, slightly beaten
¼ teaspoon pepper	1 cup dry bread crumbs

Heat fat or oil (3 to 4 inches) to 375° in deep fat fryer or kettle. Stir together flour, salt and pepper. Coat seafood with flour mixture; dip into beaten eggs, then coat with bread crumbs. Fry in deep fat until golden brown (see Timetable). Serve with catsup or Cocktail Sauce (page 576).

3 or 4 servings.

*If using self-rising flour, decrease salt to ½ teaspoon.

TIMETABLE FOR FRENCH FRIED SEAFOOD

Seafood	Cooking Time
1 pound shrimp	2 to 3 minutes
12 ounces scallops	3 to 4 minutes
1 pint oysters	2 to 3 minutes
1 pint clams	2 to 3 minutes

VARIATIONS

■ *Panfried Oysters or Clams:* Fry oysters or clams in ⅛ inch melted butter or margarine over medium heat about 2 minutes on each side.

■ *Batter-fried Seafood:* Prepare Thin Fritter Batter (page 68). Coat seafood with 1 cup all-purpose flour; dip into batter. Fry in deep fat; turning once, until golden brown (see Timetable).

TIMETABLE FOR BATTER-FRIED SEAFOOD

Seafood	Cooking Time
1 pound shrimp	4 to 5 minutes
12 ounces scallops	3 to 4 minutes

BOILED HARD-SHELL CRABS

6 quarts water	24 live hard-shell blue crabs
⅓ cup salt	Cocktail Sauce (page 580)

Heat water and salt to boiling in large kettle. Drop crabs into kettle. Cover; heat to boiling. Reduce heat; simmer 15 minutes. Drain; serve crabs hot or cold with Cocktail Sauce.

6 servings.

To Remove Meat: With left hand, grasp body of crab with large claws to the right. Break off large claws. Pull off top shell with right hand. Cut or break off legs. Scrape off the gills; carefully remove digestive and other organs located in center part of body.

FRIED SOFT-SHELL CRABS

12 soft-shell blue crabs	¾ cup all-purpose flour*
2 eggs	¾ cup dry bread crumbs
¼ cup milk	Shortening
2 teaspoons salt	

Have your fish retailer dress the crabs for eating. Rinse in cold water; drain.

Beat eggs, milk and salt until blended. Stir together flour and crumbs. Dip crabs into egg mixture, then coat with flour mixture.

Heat shortening (⅛ inch) in large skillet. Turning crabs carefully, fry in shortening over medium heat 8 to 10 minutes or until brown. If desired, serve with lemon wedges.

6 servings.

*If using self-rising flour, decrease salt to 1¼ teaspoons.

Note: Soft-shell crabs can be deep-fat fried. Heat fat (3 to 4 inches) to 375° in deep-fat fryer or kettle. Place crabs in basket; fry in deep fat 3 to 4 minutes or until brown.

BOILED DUNGENESS CRABS

3 live Dungeness crabs   ½ cup salt
8 quarts boiling water   Melted butter

Have your fish retailer dress the crabs for eating. Wash body cavity. Heat water and salt to boiling. Drop crabs into kettle. Cover; heat to boiling. Reduce heat; simmer 15 minutes. Drain. Crack claws and legs. Serve hot with butter or, if desired, chill crabs and serve with mayonnaise.

6 servings.

STEAMED CLAMS

Wash 6 pounds shell clams ("steamers") thoroughly, discarding any broken-shell or open (dead) clams. Place in a steamer* with ½ cup boiling water; steam 5 to 10 minutes or until clams open. Serve hot in shells with melted butter and cups of broth.

6 servings.

*If a steamer is not available, add 1 inch water to kettle with clams. Cover tightly.

SCALLOPED OYSTERS

1 pint select or large oysters 1 teaspoon salt
½ to ¾ cup light cream (20%) 2 teaspoons celery seed
3 cups soft bread crumbs   ¼ teaspoon pepper
½ cup butter or margarine,
 melted

Heat oven to 375°. Grease baking dish, 11½x7½x1½ inches. Arrange oysters (with liquor) in baking dish. Pour about half the cream over oysters.

Combine bread crumbs, butter and seasonings; sprinkle over oysters. Pour remaining cream over ingredients (liquid should come about ¾ of the way up on oysters). If desired, sprinkle with paprika. Bake uncovered 30 to 40 minutes.

4 servings.

Poultry

*Chicken every Sunday ... turkey on
Thanksgiving ... wishing on a wishbone ...
squabbling for the drumstick. If one or more of
these isn't a part of your family tradition, you
must have grown up somewhere else. Both
chicken and turkey, hot or cold, are year-round
favorites, year-round budget-beaters, year-round
contributors to good cheer and good health.
Have them often!*

Which Chicken to Buy

The kind of chicken you select depends upon how you want to prepare it and how many you are planning to serve. Allow ½ to ¾ pound of poultry per serving. The name of the chicken indicates its age and approximate size. From the chickens available, choose the kind that meets your needs.

And thanks to a new law—the Wholesome Poultry Products Inspection Act of 1968—you can be sure that the poultry you buy has been processed under sanitary conditions and has met federal standards.

■ Rock Cornish hens, sometimes called game hens, are the smallest member of the chicken family. They weigh 1½ pounds or less. Generally, it's best to allow one bird per person. Cornish hens may be split and broiled, but are particularly delicious when stuffed and roasted.

■ Broiler-fryers are about 9 weeks old and weigh from 1½ to 3 pounds. They are all-purpose chickens, used for broiling, frying, roasting or even for stewing.

■ Roasters are about 12 weeks old and usually a little larger than broiler-fryers. They weigh from 2½ to 5 pounds. They are the best choice for roasting.

■ Capons, which have an abundance of white meat, usually weigh from 4½ to 7½ pounds. They are usually roasted.

■ Stewing chickens, or hens, are about 1½ years old and usually weigh from 2½ to 5 pounds. They provide a generous amount of meat and are thought to have more flavor than younger birds. They are also tougher than broiler-fryers and are therefore better suited for fricassees, stews and soups.

Storing Poultry

To store fresh poultry: Wrap *loosely* in transparent plastic wrap or foil and store in the coldest part of the refrigerator until ready to cook. Fresh poultry may be kept 1 to 2 days.

To freeze fresh poultry: Wash, pat dry and wrap *tightly* in foil. (Giblets separately.) Freeze until ready to use. Can be kept for 2 to 3 months.

To thaw frozen chicken: Place on refrigerator shelf in freezer wrap. Allow about 12 hours for thawing. If needed sooner, place chicken in wrap under running cold water for ½ to 1½ hours. See page 442 for directions for thawing frozen turkey.

To store leftover poultry: Refrigerate meat, dressing and gravy separately. Cooked meat may be kept 1 or 2 days. Mealsize portions may be frozen and held up to 1 month.

Carving Turkey or Chicken

Place legs to carver's right. Gently pulling leg away from body, cut through joint between leg and body. Remove leg. Cut between drumstick and thigh; slice off meat. Next, make a deep horizontal cut into breast just above wing. Insert fork in top of breast, and starting halfway up breast, carve thin slices down to the cut, working upward.

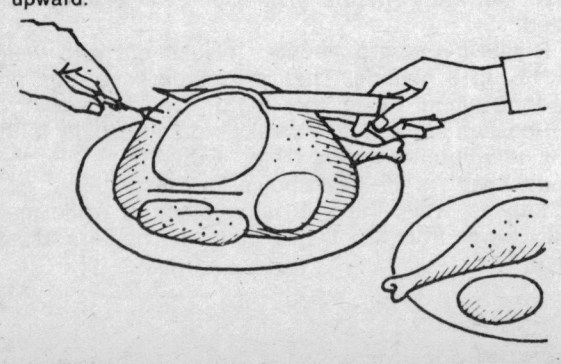

ROAST TURKEY

When buying turkeys under 12 pounds, allow ¾ to 1 pound per serving. For heavier birds, 12 pounds and over, allow ½ to ¾ pound per serving.

Wash turkey and pat dry. If desired, rub cavity lightly with salt. Do not salt cavity if turkey is to be stuffed.

Stuff turkey just before roasting—not ahead of time. (See Bread Stuffing, page 445.) Fill wishbone area with stuffing first. Fasten neck skin to back with skewer. Fold wings across back with tips touching. Fill body cavity lightly. (Do not pack—stuffing will expand while cooking.) Tuck drumsticks under band of skin at tail or tie together with heavy string, then tie to tail.

Heat oven to 325°. Place turkey breast side up on rack in open shallow roasting pan. Brush with shortening, oil or butter. Insert meat thermometer so tip is in thickest part of inside thigh muscle or thickest part of breast meat and does not touch bone. Do not add water. Do not cover.

Follow Timetable (page 442) for approximate total cooking time. Place a tent of aluminum foil *loosely* over turkey when it starts to turn golden. When ⅔ done, cut band of skin or string holding legs.

There is no substitute for a meat thermometer for determining the doneness of a turkey. Placed in the thigh muscle, it should register 185° when the turkey is done. If the bird is stuffed, the point of the thermometer can be placed in the center of the stuffing and will register 165° when done. If a thermometer is not used, test for doneness about 30 minutes before Timetable so indicates. Move drumstick up and down—if done, the joint should give readily or break. Or press drumstick meat between fingers; the meat should be very soft.

When turkey is done, remove from oven and allow to stand about 20 minutes for easiest carving. As soon as possible after serving, remove every bit of stuffing from turkey. Cool stuffing, meat and any gravy promptly; refrigerate separately. Use gravy or stuffing within 1 or 2 days; heat them thoroughly before serving. Serve cooked turkey meat within 2 or 3 days after roasting. If frozen, it can be kept up to 1 month.

TIMETABLE FOR ROASTING TURKEY

Ready-to-Cook Weight	Approximate Total Cooking Time	Internal Temperature
6 to 8 pounds	3 to 3½ hours	185°
8 to 12 pounds	3½ to 4½ hours	185°
12 to 16 pounds	4½ to 5½ hours	185°
16 to 20 pounds	5½ to 6½ hours	185°
20 to 24 pounds	6½ to 7 hours	185°

This timetable is based on chilled or completely thawed turkeys at a temperature of about 40° and placed in pre-heated ovens. Time will be slightly less for unstuffed turkeys. Differences in the shape and tenderness of individual turkeys can also necessitate increasing or decreasing the cooking time slightly. For best results, use a meat thermometer. For prestuffed turkeys, follow package directions carefully; do not use Timetable.

TURKEY THAWING DIRECTIONS

If You Cook It Immediately: Remove wrap. Place frozen turkey on rack in shallow pan. Cook 1 hour in 325° oven. Remove neck and giblets from body cavity and wishbone area. Immediately return to oven.

If You Cook It Later Today: Leave in wrap. Thaw in running water or water that is changed frequently (about ½ hour per pound). Cook or refrigerate immediately.

If You Cook It Tomorrow: Leave in wrap. Wrap frozen turkey in 2 or 3 layers of newspaper. Place on tray. Thaw at room temperature (about 1 hour per pound). Refrigerate or cook immediately.

If You Cook It Day After Tomorrow: Thaw wrapped turkey in refrigerator. (Turkey over 12 pounds may take up to 3 days.)

Be Sure You Don't:
Allow thawed bird to stand at room temperature.
Prepare stuffing or stuff bird until ready to cook.
Thaw commercially stuffed birds.

BONELESS TURKEY ROASTS OR ROLLS

Follow package directions. If directions are not available, follow directions for Roast Turkey except—if roast is not preseasoned, rub surface lightly with salt and pepper. Baste or brush roast with butter or pan drippings during roasting. Continue roasting until meat thermometer inserted in center of roast registers 170°.

TIMETABLE FOR BONELESS ROASTS OR ROLLS

Ready-to-Cook Weight	Approximate Total Cooking Time*	Internal Temperature
3 to 5 pounds	2½ to 3 hours	170°
5 to 7 pounds	3 to 3½ hours	170°
7 to 9 pounds	3½ to 4 hours	170°

*Allow approximately ½ hour additional time if cooking from the frozen state.

ROAST HALVES AND QUARTERS OF TURKEY

Prepare half and quarter turkeys according to the basic instructions for whole turkeys except—skewer skin to meat along cut edges to prevent shrinking from meat during roasting. Place skin side up on rack in open shallow roasting pan. Place meat thermometer in thickest part of inside thigh muscle or thickest part of breast. Be sure it does not touch bone.

TIMETABLE FOR ROAST HALVES AND QUARTERS

Ready-to-Cook Weight	Approximate Total Cooking Time	Internal Temperature
5 to 8 pounds	2½ to 3 hours	185°
8 to 10 pounds	3 to 3½ hours	185°
10 to 12 pounds	3½ to 4 hours	185°

BARBECUED TURKEY DRUMSTICKS

4 turkey drumsticks (about 1 pound each)
2 teaspoons salt
½ teaspoon pepper
½ cup water

¼ cup butter or margarine
½ cup catsup
⅓ cup brown sugar (packed)
1 teaspoon dry mustard
¼ teaspoon nutmeg

Arrange drumsticks in skillet. Season with salt and pepper; add water. Cover tightly; simmer, turning occasionally, 2 to 2½ hours. If all water evaporates, add small amounts at a time.

Heat oven to 425°. In oven, melt butter in baking pan, 13x9x2 inches. Place drumsticks in pan, turning each to coat with butter. Bake uncovered 15 minutes. Reduce heat to 350°. Mix catsup, brown sugar, mustard and nutmeg; pour over drumsticks. Bake uncovered 15 minutes longer.

4 servings.

COOKING TURKEY IN FOIL

This method of completely foil-wrapping the turkey produces a juicy, very well-cooked bird with a tendency for the skin and flesh to break.

Prepare turkey as directed for Roast Turkey (page 441). To wrap, place turkey breast side up in middle of large sheet of heavy-duty aluminum foil. (For larger birds, join two widths of foil.)

Brush with shortening, oil or butter. Place small pieces of aluminum foil over the ends of legs, tail and wing tips to prevent puncturing. Bring long ends of aluminum foil up over the breast of turkey and overlap 3 inches. Close open ends by folding up foil so drippings will not run into pan. Wrap loosely and do not seal airtight.

Heat oven to 450°. Place wrapped turkey, breast up, in open shallow roasting pan. Follow Timetable for approximate time. Open foil once or twice during cooking to judge doneness. When thigh joint and breast meat begin to soften, fold back foil completely to brown turkey and crisp skin. Insert meat thermometer at this time.

TIMETABLE FOR COOKING TURKEY IN FOIL

Ready-to-Cook Weight	Approximate Total Cooking Time	Internal Temperature
7 to 9 pounds	2¼ to 2½ hours	185°
10 to 13 pounds	2¾ to 3 hours	185°
14 to 17 pounds	3½ to 4 hours	185°
18 to 21 pounds	4½ to 5 hours	185°
22 to 24 pounds	5½ to 6 hours	185°

GLAZED TURKEY ROAST

4- to 5-pound frozen boneless turkey roast
1 can (7 ounces) jellied cranberry sauce
¼ cup corn syrup
1 teaspoon grated lemon peel
1 teaspoon lemon juice

Prepare turkey roast as directed on package. Heat cranberry sauce, corn syrup, lemon peel and lemon juice over low heat, stirring frequently.

Twenty minutes before roast is done, remove from

oven. Spoon off drippings. Pour cranberry glaze over turkey; roast uncovered 20 minutes, spooning glaze over turkey once. Place roast on warm platter; spoon glaze over top.

8 servings.

BREAD STUFFING

Allow ¾ cup stuffing for each pound of ready-to-cook chicken or turkey. A 1- to 1¼-pound Rock Cornish hen requires about 1 cup stuffing. Allow ¼ to ⅓ cup stuffing for each rib pork chop and about ½ cup per pound of dressed fish.

¾ cup minced onion	2 teaspoons salt
1½ cups chopped celery (stalks and leaves)	1½ teaspoons crushed sage leaves
1 cup butter or margarine	1 teaspoon thyme leaves
9 cups soft bread cubes	½ teaspoon pepper

In large skillet, cook and stir onion and celery in butter until onion is tender. Stir in about ⅓ of the bread cubes. Turn into deep bowl. Add remaining ingredients and toss. Stuff turkey just before roasting.

9 cups (enough for a 12-pound turkey).

VARIATIONS

■ *Apple-Raisin Stuffing:* Decrease bread cubes to 7 cups and increase salt to 1 tablespoon; add 3 cups finely chopped apples and ¾ cup raisins with the remaining ingredients.

■ *Corn Bread Stuffing:* Omit soft bread cubes and substitute corn bread cubes.

■ *Giblet Stuffing:* Simmer heart, gizzard and neck from chicken or turkey in seasoned water 1 to 2 hours or until tender. Add the liver the last 5 to 15 minutes of cooking. Drain giblets; chop and add with the remaining ingredients.

■ *Oyster Stuffing:* Decrease bread cubes to 8 cups and add 2 cans (8 ounces each) oysters, drained and chopped, with the remaining ingredients.

■ *Pecan Stuffing:* Decrease bread cubes to 8 cups and butter to ¾ cup; add 2 cups coarsely chopped pecans with the remaining ingredients.

■ *Sausage Stuffing:* Decrease bread cubes to 8 cups and omit salt. Add 1 pound bulk pork sausage, crumbled and browned, with the remaining ingredients. Substitute sausage fat for part of the butter.

■ *Stuffing Balls:* Shape stuffing (packed) by ½ cupfuls into balls; place in greased baking dish, 11½x7½x1½ inches. Cover; bake in 325° oven 30 minutes. Uncover; bake 15 minutes.

10 balls.

ROAST CHICKEN

Young chickens of any weight can be roasted, stuffed or unstuffed. A plump chicken, at least 2½ pounds, is particularly desirable. Allow about ¾ pound per serving.

Wash chicken and pat dry. If desired, rub cavity lightly with salt. Do not salt cavity if bird is to be stuffed.

Stuff chicken just before roasting—not ahead of time. (See Bread Stuffing, above.) Fill wishbone area with stuffing first. Fasten neck skin to back with skewer. Fold wings across back with tips touching. Fill body cavity lightly. (Do not pack—stuffing will expand while cooking.) Tie drumsticks to tail.

Heat oven (see Timetable). Brush chicken with melted butter or margarine. Place breast side up on rack in open shallow roasting pan. Do not add water. Do not cover. Follow Timetable for approximate total cooking time. Chicken is done when thickest parts are fork-tender and drumstick meat feels very soft when pressed between fingers.

TIMETABLE FOR ROASTING CHICKEN

Unless otherwise specified, times given are for unstuffed birds; stuffed chickens require about 15 minutes longer.

Ready-to-Cook Weight	Oven Temperature	Approximate Total Cooking Time
Broiler-Fryer		
1½ to 2 pounds	400°	¾ to 1 hour
2 to 2½ pounds	400°	1 to 1¼ hours
2½ to 3 pounds	375°	1¼ to 1¾ hours
3 to 4 pounds	375°	1¾ to 2¼ hours
Capon (stuffed)		
5 to 8 pounds	325°	2½ to 3½ hours

GIBLETS

Wash gizzard, heart, liver and neck. Cover all except liver with water; season with ½ teaspoon salt, 2 peppercorns, 2 cloves, a small bay leaf and a little onion. Heat to boiling; reduce heat and simmer 1 to 2 hours or until gizzard is fork-tender. Liver is very tender and can be fried, broiled or simmered in water, 5 to 10 minutes.

Giblet broth can be used in stuffing, gravy and recipes where chicken broth is specified. Cooked giblets can be cut up and added to gravy or stuffing. Refrigerate giblets and broth separately unless used immediately.

OVEN ROTISSERIE CHICKEN

Young chickens of any weight can be cooked on a rotisserie. (Two or more can be cooked at one time if length of spit rod permits.) It is not advisable to stuff a chicken for rotisserie cooking.

Wash chicken and pat dry. If desired, rub cavity lightly with salt. Fasten neck skin to back with skewer. Flatten wings over breast; tie with string to hold wings securely. Tie drumsticks securely to tail.

Insert spit rod through center of bird from tail end toward front. Secure with holding forks. Check balance by rotating spit in palms of hands. Place spit in rotisserie. Brush chicken with melted butter or margarine.

Follow manufacturer's directions for temperature setting and cook until thickest parts are fork-tender and drumstick meat feels very soft when pressed between fingers. (See Timetable on page 448.)

If desired, brush chicken with one of the barbecue sauces on pages 581–582 during last 15 to 25 minutes of cooking.

Trussing chickens for the rotisserie.

**TIMETABLE FOR
ROTISSERIE CHICKEN**

Ready-to-Cook Weight	Approximate Total Cooking Time
Broiler-Fryer	
1½ to 2 pounds	¾ to 1¼ hours
2 to 2½ pounds	1¼ to 1½ hours
2½ to 3 pounds	1½ to 1¾ hours

SPIT-BARBECUED CHICKEN

Outdoor cooking usually means hearty appetites. If you have a fairly long spit rod, we suggest you cook two broiler-fryers at the same time.

Prepare chicken and place on spit rod as directed for Oven Rotisserie Chicken (page 447).

Arrange medium-hot coals at back of firebox; place foil drip pan under spit area. Cook chicken on rotisserie 2½ hours or until drumstick is very soft to touch (with asbestos-gloved thumb). Brush chicken frequently during last 30 minutes of cooking with melted butter or a basting sauce (pages 581–582). Add coals to maintain even heat.

BAKED CHICKEN BREASTS SUPREME

2 tablespoons butter or margarine
2 tablespoons salad oil
6 large chicken breast halves (2½ to 3 pounds)
1 can (10½ ounces) condensed cream of chicken soup
½ cup light cream (20%)
½ cup dry sherry or, if desired, ½ cup apple juice plus 3 tablespoons sherry flavoring

1 teaspoon tarragon leaves
1 teaspoon Worcestershire sauce
¼ teaspoon chervil leaves
¼ teaspoon garlic powder
1 can (6 ounces) sliced mushrooms, drained

Heat oven to 350°. In oven, heat butter and oil in baking dish, 13½x9x2 inches, until butter is melted. Place chicken in baking dish, turning to coat with butter.

Arrange skin side up; bake uncovered 1 hour.

Heat soup, cream and wine, stirring occasionally. Stir in tarragon leaves, Worcestershire sauce, chervil leaves, garlic powder and mushrooms. Remove chicken from oven; drain fat from dish. Pour soup mixture over chicken. Cover tightly; cook 15 to 20 minutes longer or until fork-tender.

6 servings.

VARIATION

■ *Sherried Chicken with Fruit:* Omit tarragon leaves, Worcestershire sauce, chervil leaves and garlic powder; stir 1 can (13½ ounces) pineapple tidbits, drained, and ½ cup sliced seedless green grapes into soup mixture with the mushrooms.

FRIED CHICKEN

2½- to 3-pound broiler-fryer chicken, cut up	½ teaspoon paprika
½ cup all-purpose flour*	¼ teaspoon pepper
1 teaspoon salt	Salad oil

Wash chicken and pat dry. Mix flour, salt, paprika and pepper. Heat salad oil (¼ inch) in large skillet. Coat chicken with flour mixture.

Cook chicken in oil over medium heat 15 to 20 minutes or until light brown. Reduce heat; cover tightly and simmer 30 to 40 minutes or until thickest pieces are fork-tender. If skillet cannot be covered tightly, add 1 to 2 tablespoons water. Turn chicken once or twice to assure even cooking. Remove cover for last 5 minutes of cooking to crisp chicken.

4 servings.

*If using self-rising flour, decrease salt to ½ teaspoon.

VARIATIONS

■ *Maryland Fried Chicken:* Blend 2 eggs and 2 tablespoons water; after coating chicken with flour, dip pieces into egg mixture, then into 2 cups cracker crumbs or dry bread crumbs.

■ *Chicken Deluxe:* Substitute ¼ teaspoon ginger for the paprika; heat oven to 325° and after browning chicken, place skin side up in ungreased baking pan, 13x9x2 inches.

Mix ½ cup chicken broth, ¼ cup sherry or, if desired, apple juice and 1 clove garlic, crushed. Pour ¼ of broth mixture over chicken. Cover; bake 45 to 50 minutes or until thickest pieces are fork-tender. Baste chicken with remaining broth mixture during baking. Uncover last 5 minutes of baking to crisp chicken.

Note: Here's a quick and easy trick for coating chicken. Place the flour mixture in a paper or plastic bag. Add a few pieces of chicken to bag and shake until thoroughly coated; repeat until all pieces are coated.

BATTER-FRIED CHICKEN

2- to 3-pound broiler-fryer chicken, cut up
Thin Fritter Batter (page 68)

½ cup all-purpose flour*
1 teaspoon salt
1 teaspoon celery salt
½ teaspoon pepper

Wash chicken; place in kettle with enough water to cover. Heat to boiling. Reduce heat; cover and simmer 20 minutes. Remove chicken from broth; drain and pat dry.

Heat fat or oil (3 to 4 inches) to 360° in deep fat fryer or kettle. Prepare Thin Fritter Batter.

Mix flour, salt, celery salt and pepper; coat chicken pieces with flour mixture. Dip coated chicken into batter; fry in deep fat 5 to 7 minutes or until rich golden brown and fork-tender.

4 servings.

*If using self-rising flour, decrease salt to ½ teaspoon.

OVEN-FRIED CHICKEN

2½- to 3-pound broiler-fryer chicken, cut up
¼ cup shortening
¼ cup butter or margarine

½ cup all-purpose flour*
1 teaspoon salt
1 teaspoon paprika
¼ teaspoon pepper

Heat oven to 425°. Wash chicken and pat dry. In oven, melt shortening and butter in baking pan, 13x9x2 inches. Mix flour, salt, paprika and pepper. Coat chicken pieces thoroughly with flour mixture.

Place chicken skin side down in melted shortening.

*If using self-rising flour, decrease salt to ½ teaspoon.

Cook uncovered 30 minutes. Turn chicken; cook 30 minutes longer or until thickest pieces are fork-tender.
4 servings.

VARIATION

■ *Crusty Curried Chicken:* Omit flour mixture for coating chicken; substitute mixture of 1 cup buttermilk baking mix, 2 tablespoons curry powder, 1½ teaspoons salt and ¼ teaspoon pepper.

CHICKEN CACCIATORE

2½- to 3-pound broiler-fryer chicken, cut up	1 can (1 pound) tomatoes, drained
¼ cup shortening	1 can (8 ounces) tomato sauce
½ cup all-purpose flour	
2 cups thinly sliced onion rings	1 can (3 ounces) sliced mushrooms, drained
½ cup chopped green pepper	1 teaspoon salt
2 cloves garlic, crushed	¼ teaspoon oregano

Wash chicken and pat dry. Melt shortening in large skillet. Coat chicken pieces with flour. Cook chicken in shortening over medium heat 15 to 20 minutes or until light brown. Remove chicken; set aside.

Add onion rings, green pepper and garlic to skillet; cook and stir over medium heat until onion and pepper are tender. Stir in remaining ingredients. Add chicken to sauce. Cover tightly; simmer 30 to 40 minutes or until thickest pieces are fork-tender.
4 servings.

CHICKEN PAPRIKA

2½- to 3-pound broiler-fryer chicken, cut up	1 can (10½ ounces) tomato puree
½ cup all-purpose flour*	1 teaspoon paprika
1 teaspoon salt	2 teaspoons salt
1 teaspoon paprika	¼ teaspoon pepper
¼ teaspoon pepper	½ cup dairy sour cream
¼ cup shortening	
2 medium onions, finely chopped (about 1 cup)	

Wash chicken and pat dry. Mix flour, 1 teaspoon salt, 1 teaspoon paprika and ¼ teaspoon pepper. Melt short-

*If using self-rising flour, decrease the 1 teaspoon salt to ½ teaspoon.

ening in large skillet. Coat chicken with flour mixture. Cook chicken in shortening over medium heat 15 to 20 minutes or until light brown. Remove chicken; set aside.

Add onion to skillet; cook and stir until onion is tender. Stir in puree, 1 tablespoon paprika, 2 teaspoons salt and ¼ teaspoon pepper. Add chicken. Cover tightly; simmer 30 to 40 minutes or until thickest pieces are fork-tender. Remove chicken; keep warm. Stir sour cream into tomato mixture; heat just until warm. Pour over chicken.

4 servings.

BROILED CHICKEN

Young chickens, weighing 2½ pounds or less, can be broiled. They should be halved, quartered or cut into pieces.

Wash chicken and pat dry. For halves or quarters, turn wing tips onto back side. Set oven control at broil and/or 550°. Brush chicken with melted butter or margarine. Place chicken skin side down on rack in broiler pan; place broiler pan so top of chicken is 7 to 9 inches from heat. (If it is not possible to place the broiler pan this far from heat, reduce temperature to 450°.)

Broil chicken 30 minutes. Season brown side with salt and pepper. Turn chicken; if desired, brush with melted butter or margarine. Broil 20 to 30 minutes longer or until chicken is brown and crisp and thickest pieces are fork-tender.

CHARCOAL-GRILLED CHICKEN

Select a 2½- to 3-pound broiler-fryer chicken, cut into quarters. Place chicken quarters bone side down on grill 5 inches from medium coals; cook 20 to 30 minutes.

Turn chicken and cook 30 to 40 minutes longer, turning and brushing frequently with a basting sauce (pages 581–582). If desired, season browned chicken with salt and pepper.

4 servings.

STEWED CHICKEN

4- to 5-pound stewing chicken, cut up	1 carrot, sliced
1 sprig parsley	1 small onion, sliced
1 celery stalk with leaves, cut up	2 teaspoons salt
	½ teaspoon pepper

Wash chicken; remove any excess pieces of fat. Place chicken in kettle with giblets and neck and just enough water to cover. Add parsley, celery, carrot, onion, salt and pepper. Heat to boiling. Reduce heat; cover and simmer 2½ to 3½ hours or until thickest pieces are fork-tender. If not serving immediately, refrigerate and allow chicken to cool in broth.

When cool, remove meat from bones and skin in pieces as large as possible. Skim fat from broth. Refrigerate broth and chicken pieces separately in covered containers; use within several days. For longer storage, package chicken and broth together and freeze.

About 5 cups cubed cooked chicken and 5 to 6 cups broth.

Note: To stew a broiler-fryer chicken, select 3- to 4-pound broiler-fryer chicken and simmer about 45 minutes or until thickest pieces are tender.

About 3 to 4 cups cubed cooked chicken and 2 to 3½ cups broth.

Canned Chicken

1 can (5 ounces) boned chicken equals about ½ cup cubed chicken.

1 can (3 pounds 4 ounces) whole chicken equals 2½ cups cubed chicken.

SAVORY ROCK CORNISH HENS

A delicate, unusual raisin sauce as the finishing touch for roast hens. Good on a rice combination, too—part white and part wild.

4 Rock Cornish hens (1 to 1¼ pounds each)	⅔ cup raisins
	⅔ cup orange juice
Salt	¼ cup butter or margarine
Melted butter or margarine	¼ cup all-purpose flour
1 cup uncooked wild rice	1 teaspoon salt
1 can (13¾ ounces) chicken broth	¼ teaspoon paprika
	⅛ teaspoon pepper
½ teaspoon salt	2 cups milk

Thaw hens if frozen. Heat oven to 350°. Wash hens and pat dry. If desired, rub cavities lightly with salt. Place hens breast side up on rack in open shallow roasting pan; brush with melted butter. Do not add water. Do not cover. Roast 50 minutes, brushing hens 3 or 4 times with the melted butter.

While hens roast, wash rice thoroughly; drain. Into large saucepan, measure broth and enough water to measure 3 cups liquid. Add rice and ½ teaspoon salt. Heat to boiling, stirring once or twice. Reduce heat; cover tightly and simmer about 45 minutes or until all liquid is absorbed and rice is tender.

Increase oven temperature to 400°; roast hens 10 minutes longer or until brown. Combine raisins and orange juice in small saucepan; heat to boiling. Reduce heat and simmer 5 minutes; set aside.

Melt ¼ cup butter in small saucepan. Blend in flour, 1 teaspoon salt, the paprika and pepper. Cook over low heat, stirring until mixture is smooth and bubbly. Remove from heat; stir in milk. Heat to boiling, stirring constantly. Boil and stir 1 minute. Gradually stir in raisin-orange juice mixture.

Place hens on bed of hot wild rice; pour some of the raisin sauce over hens. Serve remaining sauce separately.

4 servings.

ORIENTAL ROCK CORNISH HENS

Party poultry. Elegant little hens with just the right tang of soy.

4 Rock Cornish hens (1 to 1¼ pounds each)
⅓ cup chopped onion
⅓ cup chopped celery
2 tablespoons butter or margarine
1 cup uncooked regular rice
1 can (13¾ ounces) chicken broth

1 can (8¾ ounces) crushed pineapple, drained
Melted butter or margarine
⅓ cup sugar
1 teaspoon cornstarch
⅓ cup soy sauce
⅛ teaspoon monosodium glutamate
¼ teaspoon ginger

Thaw hens if frozen. Heat oven to 350°. Wash hens and pat dry. In medium skillet, cook and stir onion and celery in 2 tablespoons butter until onion is tender. Stir in rice and chicken broth. Heat to boiling, stirring occasionally. Reduce heat; cover tightly and simmer over low heat about 20 minutes or until all liquid is absorbed. Stir in pineapple.

Stuff hens lightly with rice mixture; fasten openings with skewers and lace shut with string. Place hens breast side up on rack in open shallow roasting pan; brush with melted butter. Do not add water. Do not cover. Roast 1½ hours, brushing often with melted butter.

While hens roast, stir together sugar and cornstarch in small saucepan. Stir in soy sauce, monosodium glutamate and ginger. Cook over medium heat, stirring constantly, until mixture thickens and boils. Boil and stir 1 minute. Cool.

Brush hens with soy mixture. Roast 20 minutes longer, brushing hens again with soy mixture. Place on warm platter; pour remaining sauce over hens or serve separately.

4 servings.

VARIATION

■ *Chilled Cornish Hens:* Omit onion, celery, 2 tablespoons butter, the rice, broth and pineapple. Roast unstuffed hens 1 hour, basting with soy mixture twice during last 20 minutes of roasting. Cool hens and chill.

DUCKLING À L'ORANGE

1 ready-to-cook duckling (4 to 5 pounds)	¼ cup currant jelly
2 tablespoons minced onion	2 tablespoons shredded orange peel
¼ teaspoon tarragon leaves	2 tablespoons port or, if desired, cranberry cocktail
2 tablespoons butter or margarine	
½ cup orange juice	1 orange, pared and sectioned
⅛ teaspoon salt	1½ teaspoons cornstarch
⅛ teaspoon dry mustard	

Wash duckling and pat dry. Fasten neck skin to back with skewers. Lift wing tips up and over back for natural brace. Heat oven to 325°. Place duckling breast side up on rack in open shallow roasting pan.

Cook and stir onion and tarragon leaves in butter until onion is tender. Add orange juice, salt, mustard, currant jelly and orange peel. Heat over medium heat, stirring constantly, until jelly is melted. Reduce heat; stir in wine and orange sections.

Measure sauce; reserve half for glaze. Brush duckling with part of remaining orange sauce. Roast uncovered about 2½ hours, pricking skin with fork and brushing occasionally with remaining orange sauce. If duckling becomes too brown, place piece of aluminum foil lightly over breast. Duckling is done when drumstick meat feels very soft.

In small saucepan, stir reserved orange sauce slowly into cornstarch. Cook over medium heat, stirring constantly, until mixture thickens and boils. Boil and stir 1 minute. Just before serving, pour sauce over duckling.

4 servings.

ROAST WILD DUCK

2 wild mallard ducks	1 apple, cut into eighths
1 teaspoon salt	2 stalks celery, cut up
½ teaspoon pepper	½ cup butter or margarine, melted
¼ teaspoon rosemary leaves	
1 medium onion, cut into eighths	¼ teaspoon pepper
	¼ teaspoon rosemary leaves

Heat oven to 350°. Clean ducks; wash and pat dry. Stir together salt, ½ teaspoon pepper and ¼ teaspoon rosemary leaves; sprinkle in cavity and on outside of each duck.

Place half the onion, half the apple and half the celery in each cavity. Place ducks breast side down on rack in open shallow roasting pan. Roast 40 minutes. Combine butter, ¼ teaspoon pepper and ¼ teaspoon rosemary leaves; baste ducks frequently during roasting. Turn ducks and roast 50 minutes longer or until done. Ducks are done when juices are no longer pink when meat is pricked and meat is no longer pink when cut between leg and body. Remove ducks from pan; split in half lengthwise. Discard stuffing.

4 servings.

VARIATION

■ *Orange-braised Duck:* Omit basting mixture of butter, pepper and rosemary leaves. Place stuffed ducks breast side up on rack in roasting pan. Pour 1½ cups orange juice over ducks. Cover; bake 1½ hours or until done. Uncover; bake 20 minutes longer to brown. Split ducks and discard stuffing.

SERVING DUCKLING No slicing! Figure on half a fillet of breast plus a drumstick or thigh to each person. Or quarter or halve the duckling with poultry shears.

PHEASANT EN CRÈME

1 pheasant, quartered	¾ teaspoon salt
1 can (10½ ounces) condensed cream of chicken soup	⅓ cup chopped onion
	1 clove garlic, minced
	1 can (3 ounces) sliced mushrooms, drained
½ cup apple cider	Paprika
1 tablespoon plus 1 teaspoon Worcestershire sauce	

Heat oven to 350°. Place pheasant in ungreased baking dish, 9x9x2 inches. Mix soup, cider, Worcestershire sauce, salt, onion, garlic and mushrooms; pour over pheasant. Sprinkle generously with paprika.

Basting pheasant occasionally with sauce, bake uncovered 1½ to 2 hours or until fork-tender. After baking pheasant 1 hour, generously sprinkle again with paprika.

2 to 3 servings.

Note: For 2 pheasants, place pheasants in 13½x9x2-inch baking dish and double all ingredients.

4 to 6 servings.

VARIATION

■ *Chicken en Crème:* Substitute a broiler-fryer chicken (about 2 pounds) for the pheasant.

VENISON SAUERBRATEN

3- to 3½-pound venison chuck roast	2 teaspoons salt
2 onions, sliced	1½ cups red wine vinegar
2 bay leaves	1 cup boiling water
12 peppercorns	2 tablespoons shortening
12 juniper berries, if desired	12 gingersnaps, crushed
6 whole cloves	(about ¾ cup)
	2 teaspoons sugar

Place venison in earthenware bowl or glass baking dish with onions, bay leaves, peppercorns, cloves, berries, salt, vinegar and boiling water. Cover tightly; refrigerate at least 3 days, turning meat twice a day. Never pierce meat when turning.

Drain meat, reserving marinade. In heavy skillet, brown meat on all sides in shortening. Add marinade mixture. Cover tightly; simmer 3 to 3½ hours or until meat is tender. Remove meat and onions from skillet and keep warm.

Strain and measure liquid in skillet; add water, if needed, to measure 2½ cups liquid. Pour liquid into skillet; cover and simmer 10 minutes. Stir gingersnaps and sugar into liquid. Cover; simmer gently 3 minutes. Serve meat and onions on a platter; accompany with gingersnap gravy.

6 servings.

Main Dishes

*Meal-planning starts with the main dish. But it
doesn't have to be steak or chops—not when you
can choose from the great cuisines of the world.
Main dishes that are fun to make, easy to serve.
Obliging dishes that will stand and wait.
Surprising dishes that will make your party talked
about. For family suppers, for big buffets, there's
a wide world of good eating—right here.*

From casserole and skillet, from chafing dish and
broiler rack, here is a collection of satisfying main
courses for family or company. Most are actually meals-
in-one; others need but a side dish. What could be
better?

When time counts, use of our "Quick 'n Easy"
suggestions. (We've keyed them for easy spotting.)
Looking for something different in company fare? Try
Breast of Chicken on Rice, Classic Beef Stroganoff,
Pork Hawaiian or Veal Paprika with Noodles among
others. Add hot bread and a cool crisp salad, finish with
a spectacular dessert and coffee. If serving a crowd,
consult pages 499 to 504 for quantity recipes.

For best results in preparing casserole, here are a
couple of helpful hints:

Use a baking dish or casserole of the size and shape
specified in the recipe. If your dish is too large, the
moisture will evaporate; if too small, the food will bubble
over; if the dish is too deep, the food will be under-
cooked; if too shallow, it will be overcooked. It pays
to have a number of baking dishes in various sizes. In
addition to the practical considerations, they come in
so many beautiful colors and shapes that they add a
festive touch to any table.

If you prepare a main dish ahead of time, don't let it
stand at room temperature. Either refrigerate or freeze
it. And remember to allow additional time for heating
a chilled or frozen food. (See pages 741 and 749 for
specific instructions for freezing and thawing.)

Beef Main Dishes

Quick 'n Easy
HAMBURGER STROGANOFF

Company coming on short notice? Here's a recipe that belies its speed. Good on rice, too.

1 pound ground beef
1 medium onion, chopped (about ½ cup)
¼ cup butter or margarine
2 tablespoons flour
1 teaspoon salt
1 teaspoon garlic salt or 1 clove garlic, minced
¼ teaspoon pepper

1 can (8 ounces) mushroom stems and pieces, drained
1 can (10½ ounces) condensed cream of chicken soup
1 cup dairy sour cream
2 cups hot cooked noodles (page 352)
Snipped parsley

In large skillet, cook and stir ground beef and onion in butter until onion is tender. Stir in flour, salt, garlic salt, pepper and mushrooms; cook 5 minutes, stirring constantly. Remove from heat.

Stir in soup; simmer uncovered 10 minutes. Stir in sour cream; heat through. Serve over noodles. Sprinkle with snipped parsley.

4 to 6 servings.

Quick 'n Easy
TEXAS HASH

"Onion-lovers" delight in this unusual casserole.

1 pound ground beef
3 large onions (about 3½ inches in diameter), sliced
1 large green pepper, chopped
1 can (1 pound) tomatoes

½ cup uncooked regular rice
1 to 2 teaspoons chili powder
2 teaspoons salt
⅛ teaspoon pepper

Heat oven to 350°. In large skillet, cook and stir ground beef until light brown; drain off fat. Add onions and green pepper; cook and stir until onion is tender. Stir in tomatoes, rice, chili powder, salt and pepper; heat through.

Pour into ungreased 2-quart casserole. Cover; bake 1 hour.

4 to 6 servings.

Quick 'n Easy
GREEN BEANS WITH HAMBURGER

Soy sauce adds an Oriental punch.

1 pound ground beef
1 medium onion, thinly sliced
1 clove garlic, minced
1½ cups water
3 tablespoons soy sauce
1 tablespoon dark molasses
1 package (9 ounces) frozen cut green beans, broken apart

3 tablespoons cornstarch
¼ cup cold water
3 to 4 cups hot cooked rice (page 345)
French fried onion rings

Cook and stir ground beef and onion in large skillet until meat is brown and onion is tender. Stir in garlic, 1½ cups water, the soy sauce and molasses; heat to boiling. Add green beans and heat to boiling. Reduce heat; simmer uncovered 15 minutes.

Blend cornstarch and ¼ cup cold water; stir gradually into meat mixture. Cook, stirring constantly, until mixture thickens and boils. Boil and stir 1 minute. Serve over rice; garnish with onion rings. If desired, pass additional soy sauce.

4 servings.

FAMILY GOULASH

4 ounces fine noodles
1 pound ground beef
1 medium onion, chopped (about ½ cup)
2 cups sliced celery
½ cup catsup

1 jar (2½ ounces) sliced mushrooms
1 can (14½ ounces) tomatoes
2 teaspoons salt
¼ teaspoon pepper

Cook noodles as directed on page 352 except—use half the amounts of water and salt. While noodles cook, cook and stir ground beef and onion in large skillet until meat is brown and onion is tender. Drain off fat.

Stir in drained noodles, celery, catsup, mushrooms (with liquid), tomatoes, salt and pepper. Cover; simmer 30 to 45 minutes.

4 servings.

ITALIAN SPAGHETTI

2 pounds ground beef
1 medium onion, finely
  chopped (about ½ cup)
1 green pepper, finely
  chopped
2 cans (15 ounces each)
  tomato sauce
2 cans (12 ounces each)
  tomato paste
1 can (7½ ounces) pitted
  ripe olives, drained
  and sliced

2 envelopes (1½ ounces
  each) Italian-style
  spaghetti sauce mix
  with mushrooms
3 cups water
1 tablespoon sugar
1 teaspoon oregano leaves
2 cloves garlic, crushed
1 bay leaf, crumbled
16 ounces Italian-style
  spaghetti
  Grated Parmesan cheese

Cook and stir ground beef, onion and green pepper until meat is brown and onion is tender. Stir in remaining ingredients except spaghetti and cheese. Cover; simmer 1½ hours, stirring sauce occasionally.

Cook spaghetti as directed on page 352. Serve meat sauce over hot spaghetti; pass Parmesan cheese.

8 servings.

VARIATION

■ *Spaghetti with Meatballs:* Omit ground beef; stirring occasionally, cook remaining ingredients except spaghetti and Parmesan cheese for 1 hour. While sauce cooks, prepare Meatballs (below); add to sauce and cook 30 minutes longer.

MEATBALLS

1½ pounds ground beef
1 medium onion, chopped
  (about ½ cup)
¾ cup dry bread crumbs
1 tablespoon snipped
  parsley
1½ teaspoons salt

⅛ teaspoon pepper
1 teaspoon Worcestershire
  sauce
1 egg
½ cup milk
¼ cup salad oil

Mix all ingredients except salad oil. Shape by rounded tablespoonfuls into balls. In large skillet, cook meatballs in oil about 20 minutes.

LASAGNE

Like to entertain buffet style? Lasagne makes a perfect main dish. Partner it with a crisp salad like Zucchini Toss (page 590).

1 pound ground beef
6 ounces ground lean pork
¾ cup chopped onion
1 clove garlic, minced
1 can (1 pound) tomatoes
1 can (15 ounces) tomato sauce
2 tablespoons parsley flakes
2 tablespoons sugar
1 teaspoon salt
1 teaspoon basil leaves
3 cups (two 12-ounce cartons) creamed cottage cheese

½ cup grated Parmesan cheese
1 tablespoon parsley flakes
1½ teaspoons salt
1 teaspoon oregano leaves
1 package (8 ounces) lasagne noodles, cooked and well drained
¾ pound mozzarella cheese, shredded
½ cup grated Parmesan cheese

Cook and stir ground beef, ground pork, onion and garlic in large saucepan or Dutch oven until meat is brown and onion is tender. Drain off all fat.

Add tomatoes and break up with fork. Stir in tomato sauce, 2 tablespoons parsley flakes, the sugar, 1 teaspoon salt and the basil. Heat to boiling, stirring occasionally. Reduce heat; simmer uncovered 1 hour or until mixture is the consistency of spaghetti sauce.

Heat oven to 350°. Mix cottage cheese, ½ cup Parmesan cheese, 1 tablespoon parsley flakes, 1½ teaspoons salt and the oregano. Reserve ½ cup meat sauce for thin top layer.

In ungreased baking pan, 13x9x2 inches, layer ¼ each of the noodles, remaining meat sauce, the mozzarella cheese and cottage cheese mixture; repeat 3 times. Spread reserved meat sauce over top; sprinkle with ½ cup Parmesan cheese. (If desired, lasagne can be covered and refrigerated several hours at this point.)

Bake uncovered 45 minutes. (Allow an additional 10 to 15 minutes if lasagne has been refrigerated). For easier cutting, let stand 15 minutes after removing from oven.

12 servings (3-inch square per serving).

STUFFED GREEN PEPPERS

A pretty mold of Sunshine Salad (page 608) adds an interesting contrast in color and flavor.

6 large green peppers	⅛ teaspoon garlic salt
5 cups boiling salted water	1 cup cooked rice
1 pound ground beef	(page 345)
2 tablespoons chopped	1 can (15 ounces)
onion	tomato sauce
1 teaspoon salt	

Heat oven to 350°. Cut thin slice from stem end of each pepper. Remove all seeds and membranes. Wash inside and outside. Cook peppers in the boiling salted water 5 minutes; drain.

Cook and stir ground beef and onion in medium skillet until onion is tender. Drain off fat. Stir in salt, garlic salt, rice and 1 cup of the tomato sauce; heat through.

Lightly stuff each pepper with ½ cup meat mixture. Stand peppers upright in ungreased baking dish, 8x8x2 inches. Pour remaining tomato sauce over peppers. Cover; bake 45 minutes. Uncover; bake 15 minutes longer.

6 servings.

CHILI CON CARNE WITH TOMATOES

1 pound ground beef	2 teaspoons chili powder
2 medium onions, chopped	1 teaspoon salt
(about 1 cup)	⅛ teaspoon cayenne red
1 cup chopped green pepper	pepper
1 can (1 pound 12 ounces)	⅛ teaspoon paprika
tomatoes	1 can (15½ ounces) kidney
1 can (8 ounces) tomato	beans, drained
sauce	

Cook and stir ground beef, onion and green pepper in large skillet until meat is brown and onion is tender. Drain off fat. Stir in remaining ingredients except kidney beans.

Heat to boiling. Reduce heat; cover and simmer 2 hours, stirring occasionally. (Or cook uncovered about 45 minutes.) Stir in beans; heat.

4 or 5 servings (about 1 cup each).

STEAK SUPPER IN A FOIL PACKAGE

1½-pound chuck steak, 1 inch thick

1 can (10½ ounces) condensed cream of mushroom soup

1 envelope (about 1½ ounces) dry onion soup mix

3 medium carrots, quartered

2 stalks celery, cut into 2-inch pieces

3 medium potatoes, pared and quartered

2 tablespoons water

Heat oven to 450°. Place 24x18-inch piece of heavy-duty aluminum foil in baking pan; place meat on foil.

Stir together mushroom soup and onion soup mix; spread over meat. Top with vegetables; sprinkle water over vegetables. Fold foil over and seal securely. Cook 1½ hours or until tender.

4 servings.

Quick 'n Easy
PEPPER STEAK

1½ pounds sirloin steak, ½ inch thick

½ teaspoon salt

2 medium onions, chopped (about 1 cup)

1 cup beef broth*

3 tablespoons soy sauce

1 clove garlic, minced

2 green peppers, cut into 1-inch pieces

2 tablespoons cornstarch

¼ cup cold water

2 tomatoes, peeled and cut into eighths

3 to 4 cups hot cooked rice (page 345)

Trim fat and bone from meat; cut meat into 4 to 6 serving pieces. Grease large skillet lightly with fat from meat. Brown meat thoroughly on one side; turn and season with ¼ teaspoon salt. Brown other side of meat; turn and season with remaining ¼ teaspoon salt. Push meat to one section. Add onion; cook and stir until tender. Stir in broth, soy sauce and garlic. Cover; simmer 10 minutes or until meat is tender. Add green peppers. Cover; simmer 5 minutes.

Blend cornstarch and water; stir gradually into meat mixture. Cook, stirring constantly, until mixture thickens and boils. Boil and stir 1 minute. Add tomatoes; heat through. Serve over rice.

4 to 6 servings.

*Beef broth can be made by dissolving 1 beef bouillon cube in 1 cup boiling water, or use canned beef broth (bouillon).

SUKIYAKI

In Japan this is served with small bowls of slightly beaten egg in which to dip the hot meat and vegetables. If tofu (bean curd) is available, cut 3 cakes into 1-inch cubes and add with broth.

1 pound beef tenderloin or sirloin steak	2 large onions, thinly sliced
2 tablespoons salad oil	3 stalks celery, diagonally sliced
½ cup beef broth*	1 can (5 ounces) bamboo shoots, drained
2 tablespoons sugar	
⅓ cup soy sauce	3 cups washed and trimmed fresh spinach
½ pound mushrooms, washed, trimmed and thinly sliced	3 cups hot cooked rice (page 345)
1 bunch green onions (about 8 medium), cut into 1½-inch lengths	

Cut tenderloin across the grain into ¼-inch strips, about 2 inches long. In large skillet, brown meat in oil. Push meat to one section of skillet. Stir in beef broth, sugar and soy sauce.

Place mushrooms, green onions, onions, celery and bamboo shoots in separate sections of skillet. (Do not mix.) Cover; simmer 10 minutes. Add spinach; simmer 5 minutes longer. Serve over rice. If desired, pass additional soy sauce.

4 servings.

*Beef broth can be made by dissolving 1 beef bouillon cube in ½ cup boiling water, or use canned beef broth (bouillon).

CLASSIC BEEF STROGANOFF

1 pound beef tenderloin
   or sirloin steak, about
   ½ inch thick
2 tablespoons butter or
   margarine
½ pound mushrooms,
   washed, trimmed and
   sliced
1 medium onion, minced
   (about ½ cup)

1 can (10½ ounces)
   condensed beef broth
   (bouillon)
2 tablespoons catsup
1 small clove garlic, minced
1 teaspoon salt
3 tablespoons flour
1 cup dairy sour cream
3 to 4 cups hot cooked
   noodles (page 352)

Cut meat across the grain into ½-inch strips, about
1½ inches long. Melt butter in large skillet. Add mushrooms and onion; cook and stir until onion is tender, then remove from skillet. In same skillet, cook meat until light brown. Reserving ⅓ cup of the broth, stir in remaining broth, the catsup, garlic and salt. Cover; simmer 15 minutes.

· Blend reserved broth and flour; stir into meat mixture. Add mushrooms and onion. Heat to boiling, stirring constantly. Boil and stir 1 minute. Reduce heat. Stir in sour cream; heat. Serve over noodles.

4 servings.

BRAISED BEEF TIP OVER RICE

2 tablespoons shortening
2 pounds beef tip, cut into
   1-inch cubes
1 can (10½ ounces)
   condensed beef
   consommé
⅓ cup red Burgundy or, if
   desired, cranberry cocktail

2 tablespoons soy sauce
1 clove garlic, minced
¼ teaspoon onion salt
2 tablespoons cornstarch
¼ cup water
4 cups hot cooked rice
   (page 345) ·

Melt shortening in large skillet; brown meat on all sides. Stir in consommé, wine, soy sauce, garlic and onion salt. Heat to boiling. Reduce heat; cover and simmer 1 hour or until meat is tender.

Blend cornstarch and water; stir gradually into meat mixture. Cook, stirring constantly, until mixture thickens and boils. Boil and stir 1 minute. Serve over rice.

6 servings.

HUNGARIAN GOULASH

¼ cup shortening
2 pounds beef chuck or
round, cut into 1-inch
cubes
1 cup sliced onion
1 small clove garlic, minced
¾ cup catsup
2 tablespoons
Worcestershire sauce
1 tablespoon brown sugar

2 teaspoons salt
2 teaspoons paprika
½ teaspoon dry mustard
Dash cayenne red pepper
1½ cups water
2 tablespoons flour
¼ cup water
3 cups hot cooked noodles
(page 352)

Melt shortening in large skillet. Add beef, onion and garlic; cook and stir until meat is brown and onion is tender. Stir in catsup, Worcestershire sauce, sugar, salt, paprika, mustard, cayenne and 1½ cups water. Cover; simmer 2 to 2½ hours.

Blend flour and ¼ cup water; stir gradually into meat mixture. Heat to boiling, stirring constantly. Boil and stir 1 minute. Serve over noodles.

6 to 8 servings.

QUICK MEAT PIE

1 can (10¾ ounces)
condensed tomato soup
¾ cup water
2 tablespoons flour
1 teaspoon salt
¼ teaspoon rosemary leaves
⅛ teaspoon pepper
2 cloves garlic, crushed
2 cups cubed cooked beef
1 medium onion, chopped
(about ½ cup)

1 can (16 ounces) whole
potatoes, drained and
quartered
1 can (8 ounces) diced
carrots, drained
Pastry for One-crust Pie
(page 505)
½ cup shredded Cheddar
cheese

Heat oven to 425°. Blend soup, water, flour, salt, rosemary, pepper and garlic in large bowl; stir in beef, onion, potatoes and carrots. Pour into ungreased baking dish, 8x8x2 inches.

Prepare pastry as directed except—before adding liquid, stir in cheese. Roll pastry into 9-inch square; cut slits in pastry. Place on meat mixture; turn edges of pastry under and carefully press against sides of baking dish. Bake 20 minutes.

4 to 6 servings.

Quick 'n Easy
SKILLET HASH

2 cups chopped cooked beef	Dash each salt and pepper
2 cups chopped cooked potatoes	¼ cup shortening
⅔ cup chopped onion	⅔ cup water
2 tablespoons snipped parsley	

Combine beef, potatoes, onion, parsley, salt and pepper. Melt shortening in large skillet over medium heat. Spread meat mixture in skillet.

Brown hash 10 to 15 minutes, turning frequently with wide spatula. Stir in water. Reduce heat; cover and cook 10 minutes or until crisp.

4 servings.

VARIATION

■ *Corned Beef Hash:* Substitute 1 can (12 ounces) corned beef, chopped, for the cooked beef; add ¼ teaspoon garlic powder with the salt and omit water. Do not cover or cook hash after browning.

ALAMO TAMALE SUPPER

Olé! Accompany this zesty main dish with a salad of crisp greens. The dressing? Guacamole, of course. (The recipe is on page 5.) Serve a dessert of chocolate—a soufflé or pudding.

1 tablespoon shortening	1 teaspoon chili powder
1 medium onion, chopped (about ½ cup)	1 cup shredded sharp Cheddar cheese (about 4 ounces)
1 can (15 ounces) beef tamales in sauce	¼ cup sliced pitted ripe olives
1 can (8 ounces) whole kernel corn	
1 can (8 ounces) tomato sauce	

Heat oven to 350°. Melt shortening in medium skillet. Add onion; cook and stir until tender. Drain sauce from tamales; stir sauce, corn (with liquid), tomato sauce and chili powder into skillet. Simmer uncovered 5 minutes.

Pour into ungreased square pan, 9x9x2 inches. Stir in half the cheese. Remove papers from tamales; arrange tamales spoke-fashion in pan. Sprinkle olives and remaining cheese in center. Cover; bake 15 minutes.

4 servings.

Quick 'n Easy
DRIED BEEF CASSEROLE

1 cup uncooked elbow
macaroni (about 4 ounces)
1 can (10½ ounces)
condensed cream of
mushroom soup
½ cup milk
1 cup shredded Cheddar
cheese (about 4 ounces)

3 tablespoons finely
chopped onion
¼ pound dried beef,* cut
into bite-size pieces
2 hard-cooked eggs, sliced

Heat oven to 350°. Cook macaroni as directed on page 352 except—use only half the amounts of water and salt. Blend soup and milk. Stir in cheese, onion, drained macaroni and dried beef; fold in eggs.

Pour into ungreased 1½-quart casserole. Cover; bake 30 minutes or until heated through.

4 to 6 servings.

*If dried beef is too salty, pour boiling water over it and drain.

Pork Main Dishes

Pork shoulder, pork steaks, pork chops and ever-reliable ham can become your most useful main dish standbys. And talk about variety. Hearty appetites will really go for recipes like these.

BARBECUED LIMAS AND HAM

1½ cups dried large lima
beans
1 teaspoon salt
5 cups cold water
1 cup cubed cooked ham
1 medium onion, sliced

½ cup catsup
1 tablespoon
Worcestershire sauce
1 teaspoon salt
¼ teaspoon chili powder
Dash red pepper sauce

Heat beans, salt and water to boiling. Cover; simmer 1 hour. Drain, reserving ½ cup liquid. Heat oven to 350°. Layer beans, ham and onion in ungreased 2-quart bean pot or casserole. Stir together remaining ingredients and the reserved liquid; pour over beans. Cover; bake 1 hour or until beans are tender.

6 servings.

HAM-CHEESE-POTATO CASSEROLE

1 cup shredded sharp Cheddar cheese	1½ to 2 cups cubed cooked ham or canned pork luncheon meat
½ cup light cream (20%)	
2 cups diced cooked potatoes	2 tablespoons chopped pimiento

Heat oven to 350°. In medium saucepan, heat cheese and cream, stirring constantly, until cheese is melted and sauce is creamy. Remove from heat; stir in remaining ingredients. Pour into ungreased 1½-quart casserole. Cover; bake 45 minutes.

4 servings.

Quick 'n Easy
GOLDEN GATE CHOW MEIN

1 pound lean pork shoulder steak	3 tablespoons cornstarch
1 cup sliced celery	1 can (3 ounces) sliced mushrooms, drained (reserve ¼ cup liquid)
1 medium onion, chopped (about ½ cup)	
3 tablespoons soy sauce	1 can (1 pound) Chinese vegetables, drained
1 teaspoon monosodium glutamate	2 tablespoons brown gravy sauce (molasses type)
2 cups beef broth*	3 cups chow mein noodles

Trim excess fat from meat. Cut steak diagonally into very thin strips. Lightly grease large skillet with excess fat; brown meat on both sides. Stir in celery, onion, soy sauce, monosodium glutamate and broth. Cover; simmer 30 minutes.

Blend cornstarch and reserved mushroom liquid; gradually stir into meat mixture. Add mushrooms, Chinese vegetables and brown gravy sauce. Heat to boiling, stirring constantly. Boil and stir 1 minute. Serve over chow mein noodles.

4 servings.

Beef broth can be made by dissolving 2 beef bouillon cubes in 2 cups boiling water, or use canned beef broth (bouillon).

PORK AND SQUASH IN FOIL

For each serving:
1 pork chop, 1 inch thick
⅛ teaspoon salt
Dash pepper
½ acorn squash

1 tablespoon brown sugar
1 tablespoon honey
1 tablespoon butter or
margarine

Heat oven to 400°. Trim excess fat from pork chop. Place chop on 18x12-inch piece of heavy-duty aluminum foil. Season with salt and pepper.

Fill hollow of squash with brown sugar, honey and butter; place squash cut side up on chop. Wrap tightly in foil. Place on baking sheet. Bake about 1 hour or until squash and chop are tender.

PORK POT ORANGÉ

6 pork chops, 1 inch thick
1½ teaspoons salt
¼ teaspoon pepper
6 slices onion
⅓ cup brown sugar (packed)
½ cup water
1 teaspoon grated orange
peel
⅓ cup orange juice

2 tablespoons lemon juice
½ teaspoon salt
2 pounds sweet potatoes
or yams, pared and cut
into ½-inch slices
6 thin slices orange
1 tablespoon cornstarch
¼ cup cold water

Trim excess fat from chops; lightly grease large skillet with fat from one chop. Brown chops slowly on one side; turn and sprinkle with ¾ teaspoon salt and ⅛ teaspoon pepper. Brown other side of chops; turn and sprinkle with ¾ teaspoon salt and ⅛ teaspoon pepper.

Drain fat from skillet. Top each chop with an onion slice. Mix sugar, ½ cup water, the orange peel and juice, lemon juice and ½ teaspoon salt; pour over chops. Cover; simmer 30 minutes. Lift chops; add sweet potato slices to sauce. Replace chops; top each onion slice with orange slice. Cover; simmer 45 minutes or until potatoes are tender. Remove chops and potatoes.

Blend cornstarch and ¼ cup water; stir into sauce in skillet. Cook over medium heat, stirring constantly, until mixture thickens and boils. Boil and stir 1 minute. Pour over chops and sweet potatoes.

6 servings.

SWEET 'N SOUR PORK

Crunchy vegetables, tangy pineapple chunks, and pork combined in a flavorful sauce—a dish to tempt all.

3¾ pounds pork Boston
    shoulder, cut into 1-inch
    cubes
¾ cup all-purpose flour
1 tablespoon plus
    1 teaspoon ginger
½ cup salad oil
2 cans (13½ ounces each)
    pineapple chunks,
    drained (reserve syrup)
½ cup vinegar
½ cup soy sauce
1 tablespoon
    Worcestershire sauce

¾ cup sugar
1 tablespoon salt
¾ teaspoon pepper
2 small green peppers, cut
    into strips
1 can (1 pound) bean
    sprouts, drained
2 cans (5 ounces each)
    water chestnuts, drained
    and thinly sliced
2 tablespoons chili sauce
5 cups hot cooked rice
    (page 345)

Trim excess fat from pork. Mix half the flour and all the ginger. Coat pork thoroughly with flour mixture.

Heat oil in large heavy skillet or Dutch oven; brown pork on all sides, removing pieces as they brown.

Add water to reserved pineapple syrup to measure 1¾ cups liquid; gradually stir into remaining flour. Stir pineapple syrup mixture, vinegar, soy sauce and Worcestershire sauce into fat in skillet. Heat to boiling, stirring constantly. Boil and stir 1 minute. Stir in sugar, salt, pepper and meat. Reduce heat. Cover; simmer 1 hour or until meat is tender, stirring occasionally.

Add pineapple and green peppers; cook uncovered 10 minutes. Stir in bean sprouts, water chestnuts and chili sauce; cook 5 minutes longer. Serve over rice.

8 to 10 servings.

SCALLOPED POTATOES AND HAM

Follow recipe for Creamy Scalloped Potatoes or Scalloped Potatoes (both on page 713) except— place 1½ cups cubed cooked ham or ½ pound sliced cooked ham between layers of potatoes.

4 or 5 servings.

PORK HAWAIIAN

1 egg
2 tablespoons water
¼ cup all-purpose flour
¼ teaspoon salt
2 cups cubed cooked pork
3 tablespoons shortening
1 tablespoon cornstarch
1 can (13½ ounces)
   pineapple tidbits,
   drained (reserve syrup)

2 tablespoons vinegar
2 tablespoons soy sauce
1 medium green pepper,
   cut into strips
1 can (5 ounces) water
   chestnuts, drained and
   thinly sliced
1 can (3 ounces) sliced
   mushrooms, drained

Beat egg thoroughly in medium bowl. Add water, flour and salt; beat until smooth. Stir in meat, mixing until coated. Melt shortening in medium skillet. Add meat mixture; cook and stir until meat is brown. Remove from heat; keep warm.

Blend cornstarch, reserved pineapple syrup, the vinegar and soy sauce in saucepan. Cook over medium heat, stirring constantly, until mixture thickens and boils. Boil and stir 1 minute. Stir in pineapple, green pepper, water chestnuts and mushrooms. Cook and stir until green pepper is tender. Stir in meat; heat through.

6 servings.

HAM MEDITERRANEAN

7 or 8 ounces elbow
   macaroni (about 2 cups)
2 cups Medium White Sauce
   (page 566)
2 cups shredded process
   sharp American cheese
   (about 8 ounces)
2 cups cubed cooked ham
   or canned pork luncheon
   meat

1 can (3 ounces) sliced
   mushrooms, drained
2 teaspoons chopped
   pimiento
¼ cup broken cashews
   Snipped parsley

Cook macaroni as directed on page 352. While macaroni cooks, prepare Medium White Sauce. Stir cheese into hot sauce until melted.

Return drained macaroni to kettle. Stir in ham, mushrooms, pimiento and cheese sauce; heat through. To serve, sprinkle with cashews. Garnish with snipped parsley.

4 to 6 servings.

"HOT DOG" CASSEROLE

Instant mashed potato puffs

¼ cup sweet pickle relish, drained

2 tablespoons mayonnaise or salad dressing

1 tablespoon instant minced onion

2 teaspoons prepared mustard

4 to 6 frankfurters

Heat oven to 350°. Prepare potato puffs for 4 servings as directed on package. Stir in pickle relish, mayonnaise, onion and mustard. Spoon into ungreased 1-quart casserole.

Cut each frankfurter lengthwise in half, then cut crosswise in half. Insert frankfurter pieces upright around edge of mashed potatoes. Bake uncovered 25 to 30 minutes.

4 servings.

Quick 'n Easy
SPANISH RICE

6 slices bacon, diced

¼ cup chopped onion

¼ cup chopped green pepper

3 cups cooked rice (page 345)

1 can (1 pound) tomatoes

1½ teaspoons salt

⅛ teaspoon pepper

Fry bacon in large skillet until crisp; remove bacon and drain. Pour off all but 2 tablespoons drippings. Add onion and green pepper to drippings in skillet; cook and stir until onion is tender. Stir in bacon and remaining ingredients; cook uncovered over low heat about 15 minutes.

4 to 6 servings.

Note: To cook in oven, heat oven to 400°; pour mixture into greased 1½-quart casserole and bake uncovered 25 to 30 minutes.

VARIATIONS

■ *Spanish Rice with Sausage:* Omit bacon and substitute 7 to 8 pork sausage links, cut into ¾-inch pieces (2 cups); cook sausages until brown.

■ *Spanish Rice with Frankfurter:* Omit bacon and substitute 6 to 7 frankfurters, cut into ¾-inch pieces (2 cups);
cook and stir onion and green pepper in 2 tablespoons
butter or margarine.

Lamb Main Dishes

LAMB CURRY

¼ cup butter or margarine
1 medium onion, chopped
  (about ½ cup)
¼ cup chopped green pepper
¼ cup chopped celery
1 apple, pared and thinly
  sliced
1 teaspoon curry powder
¼ to ½ teaspoon salt

¼ cup all-purpose flour
2 cups chicken broth*
2 cups cubed cooked lamb
3 cups hot cooked rice
  (page 345)
¼ to ½ cup chopped
  peanuts, hard-cooked egg,
  or chutney

Melt butter in large saucepan. Add onion, green pepper, celery and apple slices; cook and stir gently until
onion is tender. Stir in curry powder, salt and flour. Cook
over low heat, stirring until mixture is hot. Remove from
heat. Gradually stir in broth. Heat to boiling, stirring
constantly. Boil and stir 1 minute. Stir in lamb; heat
through, stirring occasionally, about 10 minutes. Serve
over rice. Pass peanuts to sprinkle over top.

4 to 6 servings.

*Chicken broth can be made by dissolving 2 chicken bouillon cubes in 2 cups
boiling water, or use canned chicken broth.*

Quick 'n Easy
SHEPHERDS' PIE

Instant mashed potato
  puffs
2 tablespoons parsley flakes
2 cups cubed cooked lamb,
  beef or veal

¼ cup chopped onion
2 cups cooked vegetables
  (peas, carrots or corn)
2 cups gravy*

Heat oven to 350°. Prepare potato puffs for 8 servings

2 cans (10¾ ounces each) gravy can be used.

as directed on package except—stir in parsley flakes; set aside.

In ungreased 3-quart casserole, stir together remaining ingredients. Mound potatoes on meat mixture. Bake uncovered 30 minutes or until potatoes brown slightly.
6 servings.

BROILED LAMB DINNER

8 carrots, cut into 4-inch strips	1 teaspoon lemon juice
4 canned whole artichoke hearts	1 small loaf French bread
⅓ cup brown sugar (packed)	Soft butter or margarine
2 tablespoons soft butter or margarine	Rosemary leaves
1 teaspoon grated lemon peel	4 lamb loin chops, 1 inch thick
	Salt and pepper

Cook carrots in 1 inch boiling salted water until tender; drain. Place carrots and artichoke hearts in 9-inch round foil pan. Mix sugar, 2 tablespoons butter, the lemon peel and juice; spoon over vegetables. Cut bread into 1-inch slices; spread with butter and sprinkle with rosemary.

Diagonally slash outer edge of fat on meat at 1-inch intervals. Set oven control at broil and/or 550°. Broil chops 3 to 4 inches from heat 6 minutes. Season with salt and pepper; turn. Add pan to broiler rack; broil 6 minutes. During last 3 minutes, place bread buttered side up on rack.
4 servings.

SWEDISH LAMB WITH DILL SAUCE

2 tablespoons butter or margarine	¼ cup vinegar
2 tablespoons flour	1 to 2 tablespoons sugar
¼ teaspoon salt	1 teaspoon dill weed
Dash pepper	4 slices cooked lamb, ⅜ inch thick
¾ cup chicken broth*	2 hard-cooked eggs, sliced

Melt butter in medium skillet. Blend in flour, salt and pepper. Cook over low heat, stirring until mixture is

*Chicken broth can be made by dissolving 1 chicken bouillon cube in ¾ cup boiling water, or use canned chicken broth.

smooth and bubbly. Remove from heat. Stir in broth. Heat to boiling, stirring constantly. Boil and stir 1 minute.

Stir in vinegar, sugar and dill. Add lamb; spoon sauce over meat. Cook over low heat 5 minutes. Serve meat topped with egg slices and sauce.

4 servings.

Veal Main Dishes

Flavor hints of Hungary and the East—what more unusual ways of serving veal could you ask for? Added bonus: the unexpected crunch of nuts.

ORIENTAL VEAL CASSEROLE

1 pound veal shoulder,*
    cut into 1-inch cubes
    Flour
2 tablespoons shortening
1½ cups sliced celery
2 small onions, chopped
1 can (10½ ounces)
    condensed cream of
    chicken soup

1 can (10½ ounces)
    condensed cream of
    mushroom soup
1 soup can water
2 to 3 tablespoons soy
    sauce
½ cup uncooked regular
    rice

Heat oven to 325°. Coat meat with flour. Melt shortening in large skillet; cook meat until brown. Stir in remaining ingredients.

Pour into ungreased 3-quart casserole. Cover; bake 1½ hours. If desired, sprinkle with chopped cashews and serve with soy sauce.

5 or 6 servings.

*1 pound lean pork Boston shoulder, cut into 1-inch cubes, can be substituted for the veal.

VEAL PAPRIKA WITH NOODLES

2 pounds veal steak, ½ to
    ¾ inch thick
3 tablespoons shortening
1 tablespoon paprika
1 teaspoon salt

⅛ teaspoon pepper
⅛ teaspoon garlic salt
1 cup water
1 package (6 ounces)
    noodles almondine

Cut veal into serving pieces. Melt shortening in large skillet; cook meat until brown. Season with paprika, salt, pepper and garlic salt. Add water. Cover; simmer 1 hour or until veal is tender.

Prepare noodles almondine as directed on package for saucepan method except—reduce hot water to 1¼ cups. Arrange meat on noodles; reserve meat juice and serve separately as a sauce.

6 servings.

Combination Main Dishes

Here are perfect do-ahead croquettes and a potential quadruple-threat pizza—try four different toppings, each on half a circle, to please all tastes.

CROQUETTES

1 cup Thick White Sauce (page 566)	Salt and pepper
2 cups ground or finely chopped cooked meat (beef, veal, pork, ham or chicken)	1 egg
	2 tablespoons water
	¾ cup dry bread crumbs
	1 package (8 ounces) frozen peas in cream sauce
1 tablespoon minced onion	1 teaspoon minced onion
1 teaspoon snipped parsley	

Prepare Thick White Sauce. Stir in meat, 1 tablespoon minced onion and the parsley. Season with salt and pepper. Spread mixture in ungreased square pan, 8x8x2 inches. Cover; chill 2 to 3 hours.

Divide mixture into 12 equal parts; shape each into a ball. Beat egg and water until blended. Dip each ball into egg mixture, then roll in bread crumbs until completely coated. Cover croquettes; chill at least 2 hours.

Heat fat or oil (3 to 4 inches) to 365° in deep fat fryer or kettle. Fry croquettes in hot fat 1½ to 2 minutes or until light brown. (Handle croquettes carefully so crust is not punctured.) Drain. Keep croquettes warm in 350° oven until serving time.

Prepare peas as directed on package except—add minced onion before cooking. To serve, spoon hot peas in cream sauce over croquettes.

6 servings.

Note: Instead of peas in cream sauce, top croquettes with one of the sauces from our sauce chapter (pages

566 to 583). For instance ... for beef croquettes, Horse-radish Sauce or Mushroom Sauce; for pork croquettes, Dill Sauce or Hot Cranberry Sauce; for veal croquettes, Tomato Sauce; for ham croquettes, Mustard Sauce or Horseradish Sauce; for chicken croquettes, Allemande Sauce or Velouté Sauce.

STIR-N-ROLL PIZZA

2 cups all-purpose flour*	⅔ cup milk
2 teaspoons baking powder	¼ cup salad oil
1 teaspoon salt	2 tablespoons salad oil
	Pizza Toppings (below)

Heat oven to 425°. Measure flour, baking powder, salt, milk and ¼ cup salad oil into bowl. Stir vigorously until mixture leaves side of bowl. Gather dough together and press into ball. Knead dough in bowl 10 times to make smooth. Divide dough in half.

On lightly floured cloth-covered board, roll each half into 13-inch circle. Place on pizza pan or baking sheet. Turn up edge ½ inch and pinch or pleat. Brush circles with 2 tablespoons salad oil. Layer Pizza Toppings on circles in order listed. Bake 20 to 25 minutes. Cut into wedges to serve.

2 pizzas.

*If using self-rising flour, omit baking powder and salt.

PIZZA TOPPINGS

½ cup grated Parmesan cheese	½ teaspoon salt
1 can (8 ounces) tomato sauce	½ teaspoon oregano
1 tablespoon chopped onion	¼ teaspoon pepper
	½ pound shredded mozzarella cheese

VARIATIONS

■ *Anchovy Pizza:* Before adding mozzarella cheese, arrange 1 can (2 ounces) anchovies, drained, in spoke-fashion on circles.

■ *Ground Beef Pizza:* Before adding mozzarella cheese, sprinkle 1 pound ground beef, browned, on circles.

■ *Mushroom Pizza:* Before adding mozzarella cheese, sprinkle ½ cup sliced mushrooms, ¼ cup sliced pitted ripe olives and ¼ cup chopped green pepper on circles.

■ *Pepperoni Pizza:* Before adding mozarella cheese, sprinkle ½ cup thinly sliced pepperoni on circles.

■ *Sausage Pizza:* Before adding mozzarella cheese, sprinkle 2 cups cut-up brown'n serve sausages on circles.

Bean Main Dishes

Few main dishes are heartier than those based on the humble bean. And here are three favorites. Just add a salad and a bread. You're set!

Quick 'n Easy
SPEEDY BAKED BEANS

6 slices bacon, diced	⅓ cup chili sauce
2 medium onions, minced (about 1 cup)	1½ teaspoons prepared mustard
3 cans (1 pound 3 ounces each) baked beans with pork	

In large skillet, cook and stir bacon and onion until bacon is crisp. Stir in remaining ingredients. Heat until bubbly. Simmer uncovered, stirring occasionally, 15 to 20 minutes or until liquid is absorbed. (Or pour into ungreased 2-quart casserole; bake uncovered in 350° oven 45 minutes.)

8 servings.

BOSTON BAKED BEANS

1 pound dried navy or pea beans (about 2 cups)	¼ cup brown sugar (packed)
½ pound salt pork (without rind)	3 tablespoons molasses
	1 teaspoon salt
1 medium onion, sliced	¼ teaspoon dry mustard
	⅛ teaspoon pepper

Place beans in large saucepan and cover with water. Heat to boiling; boil 2 minutes. Remove from heat and let stand 1 hour. Add water, if necessary, to cover beans; simmer uncovered 50 minutes or until tender. (Do not boil or beans will burst.) Drain beans, reserving liquid.

Heat oven to 300°. Cut salt pork into several pieces; layer with beans and onion in ungreased 2-quart bean pot or casserole. Stir together remaining ingredients and 1 cup of the reserved liquid; pour over beans. Add enough of the remaining reserved liquid or water to almost cover beans. Cover; bake 3½ to 4 hours, removing cover for the last half of baking time. If beans look dry during baking, stir.

6 to 8 servings.

THREE-BEAN CASSEROLE

1 package (10 ounces) frozen lima beans

3 cans (about 1 pound 3 ounces each) baked beans (6 cups)

3 cans (about 15½ ounces each) kidney beans, drained (5 cups)

1 pound Italian link sausages or pork link sausages

½ pound cooked ham, cut into ½-inch cubes

1 medium onion, chopped (about ½ cup)

1 can (8 ounces) tomato sauce

½ cup catsup

¼ cup brown sugar (packed)

1 tablespoon salt

½ teaspoon pepper

½ teaspoon dry mustard

Heat oven to 400°. Cook lima beans as directed on package; drain. Turn into ungreased 4½-quart bean pot or casserole. Add baked beans and kidney beans.

In covered skillet, simmer sausages in small amount of water 5 minutes. Drain liquid from skillet and fry sausages until brown on all sides. (Do not prick sausages.) Cut each sausage into 2 or 3 pieces.

Add sausage pieces and ham to beans. Stir together remaining ingredients; pour over beans and gently mix. Bake uncovered 1 hour.

10 to 12 servings.

Poultry Main Dishes

The party Paella on page 483 is a spectacular that allows each guest to select his own favorite tidbits. The Spanish improvise on this dish, so why don't you? Additions might include meat, spicy sausages, small clams in the shell or green peppers. Other recipes are wonderful for *after* the holidays—perfect for leftovers.

PAELLA VALENCIANA

Exciting in flavor and appearance.

2½- to 3-pound broiler-fryer
 chicken, cut up
¼ cup olive oil
8 slices onion, ⅛ inch thick
4 medium tomatoes, cut up
1½ cups uncooked regular
 rice
3 cups chicken broth*
2 tablespoons paprika
2 tablespoons salt
½ teaspoon pepper
¼ teaspoon cayenne red
 pepper
⅛ teaspoon saffron

2 cups cleaned shrimp**
1 pound fish fillets
 (haddock or pike), cubed
1 can (5 ounces) lobster,
 drained and broken apart
1 package (10 ounces)
 frozen green peas, broken
 apart
1 can (15 ounces) artichoke
 hearts, drained
1 jar (4 ounces) sliced
 pimiento, drained

Wash chicken pieces and pat dry. In Dutch oven or heavy kettle, brown chicken in oil; remove chicken. Pour off fat.

Add onion and tomatoes; cook and stir 5 minutes or until onion is tender. Stir in rice, broth and next 5 seasonings. Add chicken. Cover tightly; simmer 20 minutes.

Gently stir in shrimp, fish, lobster and peas. Cover; simmer 15 minutes longer. Carefully stir in artichoke hearts and pimiento; heat through. If desired, garnish with parsley.

8 servings.

*Chicken broth can be made by dissolving 3 chicken bouillon cubes in 3 cups boiling water, or use canned chicken broth.

**From 1½ pounds fresh or frozen raw shrimp (in shells) or 2 packages (7 ounces each) frozen peeled shrimp.

CHICKEN FRICASSEE WITH DUMPLINGS

4½- to 5-pound stewing
 chicken, cut up
1 cup all-purpose flour
2 teaspoons salt
¼ teaspoon pepper
2 teaspoons paprika, if
 desired

Shortening or salad oil
1 cup water
3 tablespoons flour
Milk
Dumplings (page 484)

Wash chicken pieces and pat dry. Mix 1 cup flour, the salt, pepper and paprika. Coat chicken with flour mixture.

Heat thin layer of shortening in large skillet; brown chicken on all sides. Drain off fat; reserve.

To skillet, add water and, if desired, chopped onion, lemon juice or herbs, such as rosemary or thyme leaves. Cover tightly; cook chicken slowly 2½ to 3½ hours or until fork-tender, adding water if necessary. Remove chicken to warm platter; keep warm. Pour off liquid in skillet; reserve.

To make gravy, heat 3 tablespoons reserved fat in skillet. Blend in 3 tablespoons flour. Cook over low heat, stirring until mixture is smooth and bubbly. Remove from heat. Add enough milk to reserved liquid to measure 3 cups; pour into skillet. Heat to boiling, stirring constantly. Boil and stir 1 minute. Return chicken to gravy. Prepare dough for Dumplings; drop by spoonfuls onto hot chicken. Cook uncovered 10 minutes; cover and cook 20 minutes longer.

6 to 8 servings.

Note: To fricassee a broiler-fryer chicken, select 3- to 4-pound broiler-fryer chicken and cook slowly 45 minutes or until fork-tender.

DUMPLINGS

1½ cups all-purpose flour*	¾ teaspoon salt
2 teaspoons baking powder	3 tablespoons shortening
	¾ cup milk

Measure flour, baking powder and salt into bowl. (If desired, add 3 tablespoons snipped chives.) Cut in shortening thoroughly until mixture looks like meal. Stir in milk.

*If using self-rising flour, omit baking powder and salt.

BREAST OF CHICKEN ON RICE

1 can (10½ ounces) condensed cream of mushroom soup	1 envelope (about 1½ ounces) dry onion soup mix
1 soup can milk	2 chicken breasts, split in half
¾ cup uncooked regular rice	
1 can (4 ounces) mushroom stems and pieces	

Heat oven to 350°. Blend soup and milk; reserve ½

cup of the mixture. Stir together remaining soup mixture, the rice, mushrooms (with liquid) and half the onion soup mix. Pour into ungreased baking dish, 11½x7½x1½ inches.

Arrange chicken breasts on rice mixture. Pour remaining soup mixture over chicken and sprinkle with remaining onion soup mix. Cover; bake 1 hour. Uncover; bake 15 minutes longer.

4 servings.

Quick 'n Easy
CHICKEN CASSEROLE DELUXE

1 package (5.5 ounces) noodles Romanoff
1 can (10½ ounces) condensed cream of mushroom soup
2 cups cut-up cooked chicken or turkey
1 package (10 ounces) frozen chopped broccoli, thawed and drained
½ cup ripe olives, cut into wedges

Heat oven to 350°. Prepare noodles Romanoff as directed on package except—use ¾ cup milk. Stir in soup, chicken, broccoli and olives.

Pour into ungreased 2-quart casserole. Cover; bake 25 to 30 minutes or until broccoli is tender.

4 servings.

CHICKEN-RICE CASSEROLE

¼ cup chicken fat or butter
⅓ cup all-purpose flour
1½ teaspoons salt
⅛ teaspoon pepper
1 cup chicken broth*
1½ cups milk
1½ cups cooked white or wild rice (page 345)
2 cups cut-up cooked chicken or turkey
1 can (3 ounces) sliced mushrooms, drained
⅓ cup chopped green pepper
2 tablespoons chopped pimiento
¼ cup slivered almonds
Snipped parsley

Heat oven to 350°. Melt chicken fat in large saucepan over low heat. Blend in flour, salt and pepper. Cook over low heat, stirring until mixture is smooth and bubbly. Remove from heat. Stir in broth and milk. Heat to boiling, stirring constantly. Boil and stir 1 minute. Stir in remaining ingredients.

Pour into ungreased baking dish, 10x6x1½ inches, or 1½-quart casserole. Bake uncovered 40 to 45 minutes. Sprinkle with snipped parsley.

6 to 8 servings.

*Chicken broth can be made by dissolving 1 chicken bouillon cube in 1 cup boiling water, or use canned chicken broth.

CHICKEN TETRAZZINI

¼ cup butter or margarine
¼ cup all-purpose flour
½ teaspoon salt
¼ teaspoon pepper
1 cup chicken broth*
1 cup whipping cream
2 tablespoons sherry
1 package (7 ounces) spaghetti, cooked and drained (page 352)

2 cups cubed cooked chicken or turkey
1 can (3 ounces) sliced mushrooms, drained
½ cup grated Parmesan cheese

Heat oven to 350°. Melt butter in large saucepan over low heat. Blend in flour and seasonings. Cook over low heat, stirring until mixture is smooth and bubbly. Remove from heat. Stir in broth and cream. Heat to boiling, stirring constantly. Boil and stir 1 minute. Stir in wine, spaghetti, chicken and mushrooms.

Pour into ungreased 2-quart casserole. Sprinkle with cheese. Bake uncovered 30 minutes or until bubbly. To brown, place briefly under broiler.

6 servings.

*Chicken broth can be made by dissolving 1 chicken bouillon cube in 1 cup boiling water, or use canned chicken broth.

WHAT, NO LEFTOVERS? No leftover chicken or turkey for your favorite recipe? Turkey pieces are often available and can be stewed just like our Stewed Chicken (page 453). It's very nice for larger slices, too. Or, at any season of the year, ask your meat retailer to thaw a whole turkey and cut it up. Be sure to cook it right away, and do not refreeze before cooking. When refreezing, pack it in convenient family-size quantities. You'll be ready for any occasion!

CHICKEN POTLUCK PIE Last-minute guests and left-over chicken? Empty your refrigerator and emergency shelf as supplies and whim dictate. In the recipe below, you might substitute pitted black or pimiento-stuffed green olives, mushrooms, artichoke hearts, asparagus spears and an easy pie crust mix.

CHICKEN DINNER PIE

Pastry for 9-inch Two-crust Pie (page 501)
2 tablespoons butter or margarine
2 tablespoons flour
1 teaspoon salt
⅛ teaspoon pepper
⅛ teaspoon thyme
½ cup chicken broth*
½ cup light cream (20%)

2 cups cubed cooked chicken or turkey
1 can (1 pound) peas and carrots, drained, or 1 package (10 ounces) frozen peas and carrots, cooked and drained
1 can (8 ounces) small whole onions, drained

Heat oven to 425°. Prepare pastry as directed except —roll ⅔ of pastry for bottom crust; fit into 9-inch pie pan. Roll remainder into rectangle, about 10x6 inches. Cut rectangle into 12 strips, each ½ inch wide.

Melt butter in large saucepan over low heat. Blend in flour, salt, pepper and thyme. Cook over low heat, stirring until mixture is smooth and bubbly. Remove from heat. Stir in chicken broth and cream. Heat to boiling, stirring constantly. Boil and stir 1 minute. Stir in chicken and vegetables.

Pour into pastry-lined pie pan. Place 7 strips of pastry across filling; arrange remaining strips crisscross to make lattice top.

Trim; turn edge of bottom crust over strips. Seal and flute. Cover edge with 2- to 3-inch strip of aluminum foil to prevent excessive browning; remove foil last 15 minutes of baking. Bake 35 to 40 minutes or until golden brown.

6 servings.

*Chicken broth can be made by dissolving 1 chicken bouillon cube in ½ cup boiling water, or use canned chicken broth.

CHICKEN-MACARONI CASSEROLE

1½ cups uncooked elbow
    macaroni (about
    5 ounces)
1 cup shredded Cheddar
    cheese (about 4 ounces)
1½ cups diced cooked
    chicken or turkey
1 can (4 ounces) mushroom
    stems and pieces,
    drained

¼ cup chopped pimiento
1 can (10½ ounces)
    condensed cream of
    chicken soup
1 cup milk
½ teaspoon salt
½ teaspoon curry powder

Heat oven to 350°. Stir together all ingredients; pour into ungreased 1½-quart casserole. Cover; bake 1 hour.
4 to 6 servings.

CHICKEN-ALMOND CASSEROLE

4 cups cubed cooked
    chicken or turkey
1 can (4 ounces)
    mushrooms, drained
1 can (5 ounces) water
    chestnuts, drained and
    cut into slivers

⅔ cup blanched whole
    almonds
1 medium onion, minced
    (about ½ cup)
Chicken Sauce (below)
Paprika

Heat oven to 350°. Spread half the chicken in ungreased baking dish, 11½x7½x1½ inches, or 2-quart casserole. Top with mushrooms, water chestnuts, almonds and onion. Arrange remaining chicken on top.
Cover with Chicken Sauce. Sprinkle with paprika. Bake uncovered 45 minutes. If desired, serve with Cranberry-Orange Relish (page 562).
6 to 8 servings.

CHICKEN SAUCE

¼ cup chicken fat or butter
¼ cup all-purpose flour
½ teaspoon salt
¼ teaspoon pepper

1 cup chicken broth*
¾ cup milk
2 tablespoons sherry

*Chicken broth can be made by dissolving 1 chicken bouillon cube in 1 cup boiling water, or use canned chicken broth.

Melt chicken fat in medium saucepan over low heat. Blend in flour, salt and pepper. Cook over low heat, stirring until mixture is smooth and bubbly. Remove from heat. Stir in broth and milk. Heat to boiling, stirring constantly. Boil and stir 1 minute. Remove from heat; stir in wine.

About 2 cups.

CLASSIC TURKEY DIVAN

¼ cup butter or margarine
¼ cup all-purpose flour
1½ cups chicken broth*
2 tablespoons sherry
⅛ teaspoon nutmeg
½ cup whipping cream, whipped
½ cup grated Parmesan cheese
1½ pounds fresh broccoli, cooked and drained, or 2 packages (10 ounces each) frozen broccoli spears, cooked and drained

5 large slices cooked turkey or chicken breast meat (about ¾ pound)
½ cup grated Parmesan cheese

Melt butter in medium saucepan over low heat. Blend in flour. Cook over low heat, stirring until mixture is smooth and bubbly. Remove from heat. Stir in chicken broth. Heat to boiling, stirring constantly.

Boil and stir 1 minute. Remove from heat. Stir in wine and nutmeg; gently fold in whipped cream and ½ cup cheese.

Place hot broccoli in ungreased baking dish, 11½ x 7½ x 1½ inches; top with turkey slices. Pour sauce over meat. Sprinkle with ½ cup cheese.

Set oven control at broil and/or 550°. Broil 3 to 5 inches from heat until cheese is golden brown.

5 servings.

*Chicken broth can be made by dissolving 2 chicken bouillon cubes in 1½ cups boiling water, or use canned chicken broth.

CHICKEN OR TURKEY À LA KING

1 can (6 ounces) sliced
   mushrooms, drained
   (reserve ¼ cup liquid)
½ cup diced green pepper
½ cup butter or margarine
½ cup all-purpose flour*
1 teaspoon salt
¼ teaspoon pepper

2 cups light cream
1¾ cups chicken broth**
2 cups cubed cooked
   chicken or turkey
1 jar (4 ounces) pimiento,
   chopped
Toast Cups (page 81) or
   patty shells

In large skillet, cook and stir mushrooms and green pepper in butter 5 minutes. Blend in flour, salt and pepper. Cook over low heat, stirring until mixture is bubbly. Remove from heat. Stir in cream, broth and reserved mushroom liquid. Heat to boiling, stirring constantly. Boil and stir 1 minute. Stir in chicken and pimiento; heat through. Serve hot in Toast Cups.

   8 servings.

*If using self-rising flour, decrease salt to ½ teaspoon.

**Chicken broth can be made by dissolving 2 chicken bouillon cubes in 1¾ cups boiling water, or use 1 can (14 ounces) chicken broth.

CHICKEN CUSTARD CASSEROLE

3 cups soft bread crumbs
   (about 4 slices bread)
3 cups cut-up cooked
   chicken or turkey
1 cup chicken broth*
1 cup milk
1 can (4 ounces) mushroom
   stems and pieces, drained

2 eggs, beaten
¼ cup chopped pimiento
2 tablespoons chopped
   onion
1 teaspoon salt
⅛ teaspoon pepper

Heat oven to 350°. Mix all ingredients; pour into ungreased baking dish, 11½x7½x1½ inches. Place baking dish in pan of hot water (1 inch deep). Bake uncovered about 1 to 1¼ hours or until knife inserted 1 inch from edge comes out clean. Cut into squares; if desired, serve with Quick Mushroom Sauce (page 576).

   6 servings.

*Chicken broth can be made by dissolving 1 chicken bouillon cube in 1 cup boiling water, or use canned chicken broth.

Seafood Main Dishes

Fish favorites for everyone! Good trick: Tack the can-quick recipes on your "emergency" shelf—produce a masterpiece at a moment's notice!

BROILED SALMON DINNER

¼ cup lemon juice
2 teaspoons marjoram leaves
2 teaspoons onion salt
1 package (12 ounces) frozen hash brown potatoes
Melted butter or margarine

Seasoned salt
Pepper
4 salmon steaks, 1 inch thick
1 can (1 pound) peach halves, drained
Chopped chutney

Mix lemon juice, marjoram and onion salt; set aside. Grease broiler rack. Place frozen potatoes on rack; brush potatoes with melted butter and season lightly with seasoned salt and pepper.

Set oven control at broil and/or 550°. Broil potatoes 4 to 5 inches from heat 5 minutes. Brush potatoes again with melted butter. Place salmon on rack; baste with melted butter and half the lemon mixture. Broil 4 to 5 minutes. Turn salmon and potatoes; baste potatoes with melted butter and season with seasoned salt and pepper. Baste salmon with melted butter, remaining lemon mixture and season lightly with peper.

Place peach halves on broiler rack. Spoon 1 teaspoon chopped chutney into each peach half. Broil potatoes, fish and peaches 4 minutes or until fish flakes easily with fork and potatoes are golden brown.

4 servings.

Quick 'n Easy
SALMON AND NOODLES ROMANOFF

Heat oven to 350°. Prepare 1 package (5.5 ounces) noodles Romanoff as directed except—use ⅔ cup milk. Stir in 1 can (7¾ ounces) salmon, drained and flaked, ½ cup creamed cottage cheese and, if desired, 1 table-spoon snipped chives. Pour into ungreased 1-quart casserole. Cover; bake 15 to 20 minutes.

4 servings.

Quick 'n Easy
TUNA CHOW MEIN CASSEROLE

- 1 tablespoon butter or margarine
- 1 cup cut-up celery
- ¼ cup chopped onion
- 2 tablespoons chopped green pepper
- ½ can (5½-ounce size) chow mein noodles
- 1 can (6½ ounces) tuna (with liquid)

- 1 can (10½ ounces) condensed cream of mushroom soup
- ¼ cup milk
- ¼ cup water
- ⅛ teaspoon pepper
- ¾ cup salted cashew nuts

Heat oven to 350°. Melt butter in large skillet. Add celery, onion and green pepper; cook and stir until onion is tender. Reserving ¼ cup chow mein noodles, stir in remaining ingredients.

Pour mixture into ungreased 1½-quart casserole; sprinkle reserved chow mein noodles over top. Bake uncovered 30 minutes.

4 to 6 servings.

TUNA-NOODLE CASSEROLE

- 8 ounces noodles
- 2 cans (7 ounces each) tuna, well drained
- 1½ cups dairy sour cream (12 ounces)
- ¾ cup milk
- 1 can (3 ounces) sliced mushrooms, drained

- 1½ teaspoons salt
- ¼ teaspoon pepper
- ¼ cup dry bread crumbs
- ¼ cup grated Parmesan cheese
- 2 tablespoons butter or margarine, melted

Heat oven to 350°. Cook noodles as directed on page 352. Return drained noodles to kettle; stir in tuna, sour cream, milk, mushrooms, salt and pepper. Pour into ungreased 2-quart casserole.

Mix bread crumbs, cheese and butter; sprinkle over casserole. If desired, sprinkle paprika over bread crumb mixture. Bake uncovered 35 to 40 minutes or until bubbly.

6 to 8 servings.

LOBSTER EN CASSEROLE

¼ cup butter or margarine	½ bay leaf, crumbled
¾ cup thinly sliced carrots	2 cups milk
¾ cup finely chopped onion	2 cups diced cooked lobster
½ cup minced cooked ham	1 can (6 ounces) sliced
¼ cup all-purpose flour	mushrooms, drained
¼ teaspoon salt	1 cup shredded Gruyère or
¼ teaspoon pepper	brick cheese
¼ teaspoon basil	⅓ cup buttered bread crumbs
¼ teaspoon thyme	

Heat oven to 450°. Melt butter in large skillet. Add carrots, onion and ham; cook and stir until carrots are tender. Remove from heat. Stir in flour and seasonings. Cook over low heat, stirring until mixture is bubbly. Remove from heat. Stir in milk. Heat to boiling, stirring constantly. Boil and stir 1 minute. Stir in lobster and mushrooms.

Pour into ungreased 2-quart casserole. Sprinkle with ¾ cup of the cheese and top with crumbs. Sprinkle remaining cheese over top. Bake uncovered 5 minutes or until cheese is melted.

6 servings.

Quick 'n Easy
BAKED CRAB AND SHRIMP

1 medium green pepper, chopped	1 cup mayonnaise
1 medium onion, chopped (about ½ cup)	1 teaspoon Worcestershire sauce
1 cup chopped celery	½ teaspoon salt
1 can (6½ ounces) crabmeat,* drained and cartilage removed	⅛ teaspoon pepper
	1 cup dry bread crumbs
1 can (4½ ounces) shrimp,* rinsed and drained	2 teaspoons butter or margarine, melted

Heat oven to 350°. Mix all ingredients except bread crumbs and melted butter. Pour mixture into ungreased 1-quart casserole or 6 individual baking shells. Toss bread crumbs in melted butter; sprinkle over seafood mixture. Bake uncovered 30 minutes.

6 servings.

*1⅓ cups cooked crabmeat with cartilage removed, and 1 cup cleaned cooked shrimp can be substituted for the canned crabmeat and shrimp.

Quick 'n Easy
SHRIMP CREOLE

1 medium onion, minced (about ½ cup)	⅛ teaspoon cayenne red pepper
2 tablespoons butter or margarine	1 can (6 ounces) tomato paste
½ cup chopped green pepper	2 cups water
¼ cup diced celery	2 cups cleaned cooked shrimp*
1 bay leaf, crushed	3 cups hot cooked rice (page 345)
1 teaspoon snipped parsley	
1 teaspoon salt	

Cook and stir onion in butter until onion is tender. Stir in remaining ingredients except shrimp and rice. Cook over low heat, stirring occasionally, about 30 minutes. Stir in shrimp; heat through. Serve over rice.

6 servings.

From 1½ pounds fresh or frozen shrimp (in shells), 2 packages (7 ounces each) frozen peeled shrimp or 2 cans (4½ or 5 ounces each) shrimp.

AVERY ISLAND DEVILED SHRIMP

Deviled Shrimp Sauce (below)	½ cup dry bread crumbs
1 egg, slightly beaten	¼ cup butter or margarine
¼ teaspoon salt	2 cups hot cooked rice (page 345)
2 cups cleaned cooked shrimp*	

Prepare Deviled Shrimp Sauce. Mix egg and salt. Dip shrimp into egg mixture, then coat with bread crumbs.

Melt butter in medium skillet. Add shrimp and brown on both sides. Arrange shrimp on rice; pour sauce over shrimp.

4 servings.

From 1½ pounds fresh or frozen shrimp (in shells), 2 packages (7 ounces each) frozen peeled shrimp or 2 cans (4½ or 5 ounces each) shrimp.

DEVILED SHRIMP SAUCE

1 medium onion, chopped (about ½ cup)	2 tablespoons steak sauce
1 clove garlic, minced	1½ teaspoons dry mustard
2 tablespoons butter or margarine	½ teaspoon salt
1 can (10½ ounces) condensed chicken broth	¼ to ½ teaspoon red pepper sauce
½ cup water	1 to 2 tablespoons lemon juice

In medium saucepan, cook and stir onion and garlic in butter until onion is tender. Stir in chicken broth, water, steak sauce, mustard, salt and red pepper sauce.

Heat to boiling; simmer 15 minutes. Stir in lemon juice.

About 1½ cups.

SEAFOOD THERMIDOR

1 can (3 ounces) sliced
  mushrooms
1 tablespoon butter or
  margarine
2 cans (10¾ ounces each)
  condensed cream of
  shrimp soup
1 can (7½ ounces) crabmeat,
  drained and cartilage
  removed
2 cans (4½ ounces each)
  shrimp, rinsed and drained

1 can (5 ounces) lobster,
  drained
½ cup milk
¼ teaspoon dry mustard
¼ teaspoon paprika
  Dash cayenne red pepper
2 to 3 tablespoons sherry
  Toast points

Cook and stir mushrooms (with liquid) in butter until heated. Stir in remaining ingredients except wine and toast points. Heat to boiling, stirring constantly. Stir in wine. Serve over toast points.

6 servings.

Crowd-size Main Dishes

Big crowd coming? Be a kitchen general and plan ahead. Plan the things other people can do to help—they'll always ask. Plan what you'll do—the day before, the day of and just before the party. Plan right down to that last all-important look in your mirror. Then take pen in hand and make a checklist—and follow it!

Homemade bread (pages 90 to 101), rolls (pages 102 to 107) or doctored Bakery Breads (pages 85 to 89) are all to some degree do-aheaders. See page 620 for crowd-size salads and page 36 for coffee. The ideal dessert is the one that's made the day before. And there you are! Cool and calm—and ready.

LASAGNE

Layer upon layer of Italian pasta, meat sauce and cheeses. The ideal go-with salad: one of tossed greens. (See the chart on page 586.)

2 pound ground beef
¾ pound ground lean pork
3 medium onions, chopped (about 1½ cups)
2 cloves garlic, minced
2 cans (1 pound each) tomatoes
2 cans (15 ounces each) tomato sauce
¼ cup parsley flakes
¼ cup sugar
2 teaspoons salt
2 teaspoons basil leaves
6 cups (four 12-ounce cartons) creamed cottage cheese

1 cup grated Parmesan cheese
2 tablespoons parsley flakes
1 tablespoon salt
2 teaspoons oregano leaves
2 packages (8 ounces each) lasagne noodles, cooked and well drained
1½ pounds mozzarella cheese, shredded
1 cup grated Parmesan cheese

Cook and stir ground beef, ground pork, onion and garlic in Dutch oven or kettle until meat is brown and onion is tender. Drain off fat.

Add tomatoes and break up with fork. Stir in tomato sauce, ¼ cup parsley flakes, the sugar, 2 teaspoons salt and the basil. Heat to boiling, stirring occasionally. Reduce heat; simmer uncovered about 1 hour or until mixture is the consistency of spaghetti sauce.

Heat oven to 350°. Mix cottage cheese, 1 cup Parmesan cheese, 2 tablespoons parsley flakes, 1 tablespoon salt and the oregano leaves. Reserve 1 cup meat sauce for thin top layer.

In each of 2 ungreased baking pans, 13x9x2 inches, layer ¼ each of the noodles, remaining meat sauce, the mozzarella cheese and cottage cheese mixture; repeat. Spread reserved meat sauce over top; sprinkle each pan with ½ cup Parmesan cheese. (Lasagne can be refrigerated several hours at this point until time to bake.)

Bake uncovered 45 minutes. (Allow an additional 10 to 15 minutes if lasagne has been refrigerated.) For easier cutting, let stand 15 minutes after removing from oven.

24 servings (3-inch square per serving).

ITALIAN SPAGHETTI

6 medium onions, finely
  chopped (3 cups)
8 cloves garlic, minced
¼ cup olive oil
4 cans (1 pound each)
  tomatoes
4 cans (15 ounces each)
  tomato sauce
3 tablespoons parsley flakes
2 tablespoons sugar

1½ to 2 tablespoons salt
1 tablespoon plus 1
  teaspoon oregano
1 tablespoon plus 1
  teaspoon basil
4 pounds ground beef
1 package (2 pounds) long
  spaghetti
Grated Parmesan cheese

In large roasting pan or Dutch oven, cook and stir onion and garlic in oil until onion is tender. Stir in remaining ingredients except ground beef, spaghetti and cheese. Heat to boiling, stirring occasionally. Reduce heat; simmer uncovered 1 to 1½ hours. (Long cooking improves flavor.)

In large skillet, cook and stir ground beef until brown. Drain off fat. Stir meat into sauce mixture; simmer uncovered 20 to 30 minutes longer.

Cook spaghetti as directed on page 352. Serve meat-sauce mixture over hot spaghetti; pass Parmesan cheese.

24 servings (⅔ cup each).

HAMBURGER STROGANOFF

6 pounds ground beef
6 onions, chopped (about
  3 cups)
½ cup butter or margarine
¼ cup all-purpose flour
1 tablespoon plus 1
  teaspoon salt
4 cloves garlic, minced
1 teaspoon pepper
3 cans (8 ounces each)
  mushroom stems and
  pieces, drained

6 cans (10½ ounces each)
  condensed cream of
  chicken soup
6 cups dairy sour cream
24 ounces noodles, cooked
  and drained
1 cup snipped parsley

In Dutch oven or large roasting pan, cook and stir ground beef and onion in butter until meat is brown and onion is tender. Stir in flour, salt, garlic, pepper and mushrooms; cook 5 minutes, stirring constantly. Stir in soup; heat to boiling, stirring constantly. Reduce heat; simmer uncovered 10 minutes. Stir in sour cream; heat through. Serve over noodles and sprinkle with parsley.

24 servings (⅔ cup noodles and 1 cup meat mixture per serving).

CHUCK WAGON BEANS

½ pound bacon slices	3 tablespoons prepared mustard
3 pounds ground beef	
6 medium onions, finely chopped (about 3 cups)	1½ teaspoons salt
	½ teaspoon pepper
1 cup finely chopped celery	2 cans (1 pound 13 ounces each) molasses-style baked beans
⅔ cup beef broth*	
1½ cloves garlic, minced	
1½ cups catsup	

Heat oven to 375°. In Dutch oven or large roasting pan, fry bacon until crisp; remove and drain. Pour drippings from pan.

In same pan, cook and stir ground beef, onion and celery until meat is brown and onion is tender. Stir in broth and remaining ingredients. Cover; bake about 1 hour 15 minutes or until hot and bubbly. Crumble bacon; sprinkle over beans.

12 servings (1 cup each).

*Beef broth can be made by dissolving 1 beef bouillon cube in ⅔ cup boiling water, or use canned beef broth (bouillon).

CHILI CON CARNE

4 pounds ground beef	1 can (15 ounces) tomato sauce
8 medium onions, chopped (about 4 cups)	
	2 tablespoons sugar
4 cans (1 pound 12 ounces each) tomatoes	3 tablespoons chili powder
	1 tablespoon plus 1½ teaspoons salt
4 cans (15½ ounces each) kidney beans, drained (reserve liquid)	

Cook and stir ground beef and onion in Dutch oven or large roasting pan until meat is brown and onion is tender. Drain off fat.

Stir in tomatoes, reserved kidney bean liquid, the tomato sauce and seasonings. Heat to boling. Reduce heat; simmer uncovered 1 hour 15 minutes. Stir in beans. Simmer, stirring occasionally, about 15 minutes or until of desired consistency.

24 servings (1⅓ cups each).

SOUP AND SAUSAGE CASSEROLE

6 pounds pork sausage
4 cups chopped celery
4 medium onions, chopped (about 2 cups)
2 cups chopped green pepper
4 cups uncooked regular rice

6 envelopes (2 ounces each) dry chicken noodle soup mix
⅔ cup toasted slivered almonds
½ teaspoon saffron*
3 quarts boiling water
Snipped parsley

Heat oven to 350°. Shape sausage into 48 patties or, if sausage is in rolls, cut each roll into 8 slices. Brown sausage in large skillet over medium-low heat about 3 or 4 minutes on each side; remove and drain.

Pour fat from skillet, leaving just enough to coat bottom. Add celery, onion and green pepper; cook and stir until onion is tender.

In each of 4 ungreased baking pans, 13x9x2 inches, mix ¼ of the onion mixture (about 1½ cups), 1 cup rice, 1½ envelopes soup mix and ¼ of the almonds.

Dissolve saffron in boiling water; stir 3 cups into each pan. Arrange 12 sausage patties on mixture in each pan. Cover; bake about 45 minutes or until rice is tender and liquid is absorbed. Garnish with snipped parsley.

24 servings (2 sausage patties and 4½-inch square rice mixture per serving).

*If desired, omit saffron; add 10 drops yellow food color to each pan with the boiling water.

SCALLOPED POTATOES DINNER

4 cans (12 ounces each) pork luncheon meat, cubed, or 4½ cups cubed cooked ham
1½ cups chopped green pepper
3 medium onions, chopped (about 1½ cups)

6 cans (10½ ounces each) condensed cream of celery soup
5½ pounds potatoes, pared and thinly sliced (about 8⅔ cups)
½ cup toasted bread crumbs
2 teaspoons butter, melted

Heat oven to 350°. Stir together pork luncheon meat, green pepper, onion and soup. In each of 2 ungreased baking pans, 13x9x2 inches, spread ¼ of soup mixture;

top with half the potatoes and cover with ¼ of soup mixture.

Cover; bake about 1½ hours or until potatoes are fork-tender. Toss crumbs with melted butter. Remove covers from pans; sprinkle each top with half the crumbs. Bake 15 minutes longer.

16 servings.

ARROZ CON POLLO

6 broiler-fryer chickens (2½ to 3 pounds each), cut up	4 bay leaves, crumbled
¼ cup olive oil or salad oil	2 tablespoons snipped parsley
4 teaspoons salt	4 teaspoons salt
2 teaspoons garlic salt	4 cups uncooked regular rice
1½ teaspoons pepper	2 cans (7 ounces each) pimiento, drained and chopped
1½ teaspoons paprika	
½ teaspoon saffron*	1 package (24 ounces) frozen green peas
10 cups chicken broth**	
2 medium onions, chopped (about 2 cups)	

Heat oven to 350°. Wash chicken pieces and pat dry. Place chicken skin side up in 4 baking pans, 13x9x2 inches. Brush chicken with oil; season with 4 teaspoons salt, the garlic salt, pepper and paprika. Bake uncovered 30 minutes.

Dissolve saffron in chicken broth. Stir in onion, bay leaves, parsley and 4 teaspoons salt; heat to boiling. Remove chicken; drain fat from pans. Stir together 1 cup rice and about 2½ cups chicken broth mixture in each pan. Place chicken on rice mixture; cover pans tightly. Bake about 35 minutes or until rice is tender.

Cook peas as directed on package; drain. Stir in pimiento. Arrange chicken on warm platters. Stir peas and pimiento into rice; spoon around chicken.

24 servings (1 cup rice mixture per serving).

*If desired, omit saffron; add about 40 drops yellow food color to chicken broth.

**Chicken broth can be made by dissolving 10 chicken bouillon cubes in 2½ quarts boiling water, or use canned chicken broth.

Pies

*What's America's all-time favorite choice for
dessert? Most people agree—it's pie. And
heading the list is apple pie. Followed closely
by cherry pie and peach pie and lemon meringue
and a lot of others. So if you care about pleasing
—bake a pie. But make sure it's a perfect pie.
How? Simple. Spend a little time with this
chapter; pick up our sure-fire tips for flaky pastry.
Then try one of our recipes—family-tested and
guaranteed to satisfy. What more could you ask
of a dessert?*

STANDARD PASTRY

Tender, flaky pastry will encase every pie, if this basic recipe is
followed precisely. Or, if you prefer, substitute the Oil Pastry
(page 507).

8- OR 9-INCH ONE-CRUST PIE

1 cup all-purpose flour*	2 to 3 tablespoons cold
½ teaspoon salt	water
⅓ cup plus 1 tablespoon shortening or ⅓ cup lard	

10-INCH ONE-CRUST PIE

1⅓ cups all-purpose flour*	3 to 4 tablespoons cold
½ teaspoon salt	water
½ cup shortening or ¼ cup plus 3 tablespoons lard	

8- OR 9-INCH TWO-CRUST PIE

2 cups all-purpose flour*	4 to 5 tablespoons cold
1 teaspoon salt	water
⅔ cup plus 2 tablespoons shortening or ⅔ cup lard	

*If using self-rising flour, omit salt. Pie crusts made with self-rising flour
differ in flavor and texture from those made with plain flour.

10-INCH TWO-CRUST PIE

2⅔ cups all-purpose flour*	7 to 8 tablespoons cold
1 teaspoon salt	water
1 cup shortening or ¾ cup	
plus 2 tablespoons lard	

Measure flour and salt into bowl. Cut in shortening thoroughly. Sprinkle in water, 1 tablespoon at a time, mixing until all flour is moistened and dough almost cleans side of bowl (1 to 2 teaspoons water can be added if needed).

Gather dough into ball; shape into flattened round on lightly floured cloth-covered board. (For Two-crust Pie, divide dough in half and shape into 2 flattened rounds.) With floured stockinet-covered rolling pin, roll dough 2 inches larger than inverted pie pan. Fold pastry into quarters; unfold and ease into pan.

For One-crust Pie: Trim overhanging edge of pastry 1 inch from rim of pan. Fold and roll pastry under, even with pan; flute (see page 506). Fill and bake as directed in recipe.

For Baked Pie Shell: Prick bottom and side thoroughly with fork. Bake at 475° for 8 to 10 minutes.

For Two-crust Pie: Turn desired filling into pastry-lined pie pan. Trim overhanging edge of pastry ½ inch from rim of pan. Roll second round of dough. Fold into quarters; cut slits so steam can escape. Place over filling and unfold. Trim overhanging edge of pastry 1 inch from rim of pan. Fold and roll top edge under lower edge, pressing on rim to seal; flute (see page 506). Cover edge with 2- to 3-inch strip of aluminum foil to prevent excessive browning; remove foil last 15 minutes of baking. Bake as directed in recipe.

Note: If possible, hook fluted edge over edge of pie pan to prevent shrinking and help keep shape.

*If using self-rising flour, omit salt. Pie crusts made with self-rising flour differ in flavor and texture from those made with plain flour.

VARIATIONS FOR STANDARD PASTRY

■ *Electric Mixer Pastry:* Measure flour, salt and shortening into large mixer bowl; blend 1 minute on low speed, scraping bowl constantly. Add water; mix until all flour is moistened and dough begins to gather into beaters, about 10 seconds. If using quick-mixing flour, dough will begin to gather into beaters in about 1 minute. Scrape bowl constantly. Handle dough as directed for Standard Pastry.

■ *Flavored Pastry:* Stir one of the following into flour for Pastry for 8- or 9-inch One-crust Pie. Double the amount for an 8- or 9-inch Two-crust Pie.

1 teaspoon celery seed
½ cup shredded Cheddar cheese
1 teaspoon cinnamon
1½ teaspoons finely shredded lemon or orange peel

2 tablespoons finely chopped nuts
1 tablespoon toasted sesame seed

ABOUT FROZEN PIES

■ Freeze pie shells baked or unbaked.

■ Bake fruit pies before freezing.

■ To thaw baked pie shells, unwrap and let stand at room temperature. Or place in 350° oven about 6 minutes.

■ No need to thaw unbaked shells. Pop them in the oven in their frozen state.

■ Frozen baked shells will keep 4 months; unbaked shells, 2 months.

■ Do *not* freeze custard, cream or meringue pies. Custard and cream fillings separate; meringues toughen and shrink.

■ Bake pies in aluminum foil pie pans, if desired. Since these pans are shiny and reflect heat, place on baking sheet so bottom crust will brown evenly.

■ Freeze pies first, then wrap and store. Use heavyweight plastic wrap (seal with freezer tape), heavy-duty aluminum foil (seal with tight double-fold), plastic bags or other airtight containers. Label and date. Pies will keep 4 to 6 months.

■ Store frozen chiffon pies only 1 month.

■ To thaw chiffon pies, unwrap and let stand at room temperature 2 to 4 hours.

■ To heat baked pies, unwrap and let stand 30 minutes; heat in 350° oven just until warm. Place foil pans on baking sheet.

1. Add water, 1 tablespoon at a time, and toss with fork after each addition. Mix lightly.

2. After pastry is thoroughly mixed, press dough firmly together into a ball with hands. Handle dough just as you would a snowball.

4. If patching is necessary, cut piece of pastry to fit irregular edge or tear. Moisten edge of area to be patched and press piece firmly into place.

5. For best results, select heat-resistant glass pans for pie baking. Darkened pans and dull-finished aluminum pans are also good.

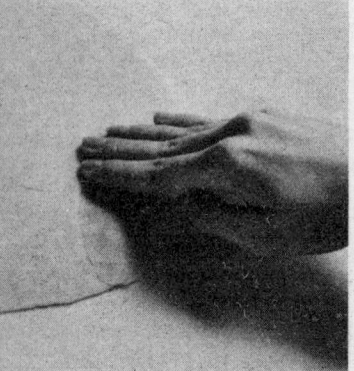

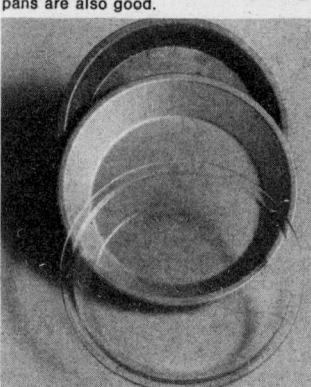

7. Leave 1-inch rim of top pastry beyond edge of pan. Fold and roll this rim under edge of bottom pastry.

8. While pinching the top and bottom edges together, form a stand-up rim on edge of pan to seal pastry and to make fluting easier.

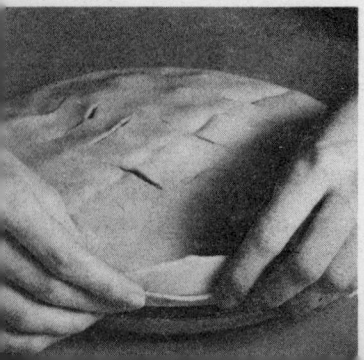

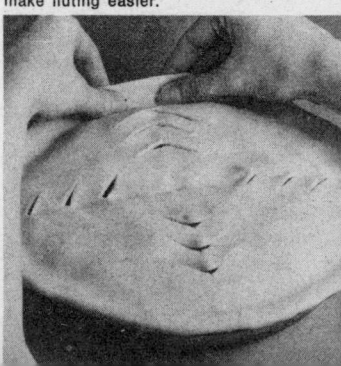

3. When rolling dough out, keep circular by periodically pushing edge in gently with cupped hands. Lift occasionally to prevent sticking.

6. Fold rolled-out pastry into quarters and carefully place in pie pan with point in center; unfold.

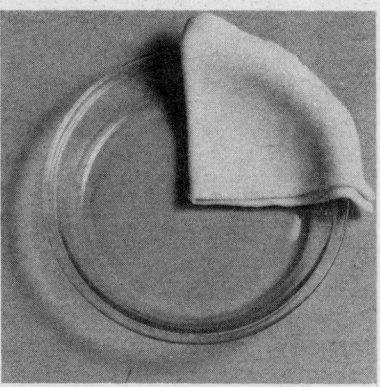

9. Crimp a 2- to 3-inch strip of aluminum foil over fluted edge to prevent overbrowning. Remove foil 15 minutes before end of baking time.

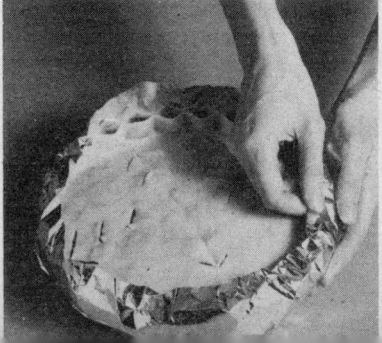

Fork: Flatten pastry evenly on rim of pie pan. Press firmly around edge with tines of fork. (Dip fork in flour from time to time to prevent sticking).

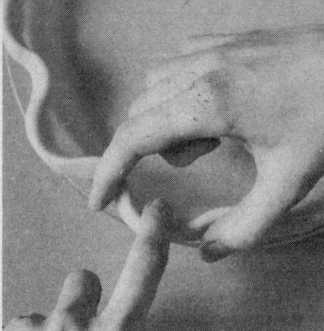

Ruffle: Place thumb and index finger about 1 inch apart on pastry rim. With other index finger, pull pastry between fingers and toward outside.

Cutouts: Trim pastry overhang even with pan. Moisten pastry cutouts and place on moistened rim, overlapping slightly. Press into place.

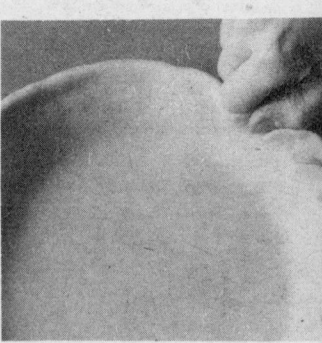

Rope: Place thumb on pastry rim at an angle. Pinch dough between index finger and thumb by pressing knuckle down into pastry and toward thumb.

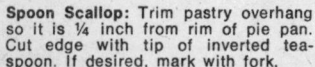
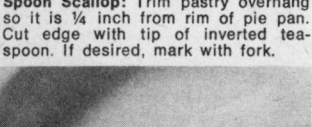

Spoon Scallop: Trim pastry overhang so it is ¼ inch from rim of pie pan. Cut edge with tip of inverted teaspoon. If desired, mark with fork.

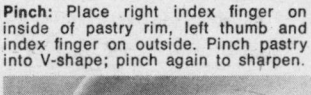

Pinch: Place right index finger on inside of pastry rim, left thumb and index finger on outside. Pinch pastry into V-shape; pinch again to sharpen.

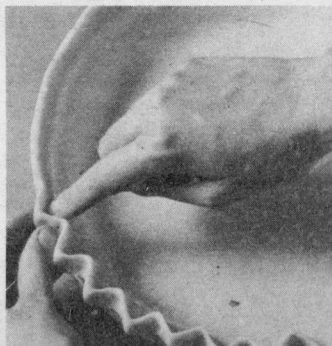

OIL PASTRY

8- OR 9-INCH ONE-CRUST PIE

1 cup plus 2 tablespoons
all-purpose flour*
½ teaspoon salt

⅓ cup salad oil
2 to 3 tablespoons cold
water

10-INCH ONE-CRUST PIE OR
8- OR 9-INCH TWO-CRUST PIE

1¾ cups all-purpose flour*
1 teaspoon salt
½ cup salad oil

3 to 4 tablespoons cold
water

10-INCH TWO-CRUST PIE

2⅔ cups all-purpose flour*
1½ teaspoons salt
¾ cup salad oil

4 to 5 tablespoons cold
water

Measure flour and salt into bowl. Add oil; mix until particles are size of small peas. Sprinkle in water, 1 tablespoon at a time, mixing until flour is moistened and dough almost cleans side of bowl. (If dough seems dry, 1 to 2 tablespoons oil can be added. Do not add water.) Gather dough together; press firmly into ball.

For One-crust Pie, shape dough into flattened round. (For Two-crust Pie, divide dough in half; place one half cut side down and flatten into round). Place flattened round between two 15-inch strips of waxed paper (for 9- or 10-inch pies, tape 2 pieces together to make wider strips).

Wipe table with damp cloth to prevent paper from slipping. Roll pastry 2 inches larger than inverted pie pan. Peel off top paper. Place pastry, paper side up, in pan. Peel off paper. Ease pastry loosely into pan.

Trim and complete as for Standard Pastry (page 501) except—Baked Pie Shell requires 12 to 15 minutes of baking at 475°.

For Two-crust Pie, roll top crust in same way as bottom crust. Cut slits after peeling off top paper; place over filling in pan. Trim and complete as directed on page 502.

*Do not use quick-mixing flour in this recipe. If using self-rising flour, omit the salt. Pie crusts made with self-rising flour will differ in flavor and texture from those made with plain flour.

BAKED TART SHELLS

Prepare pastry as directed for 8- or 9-inch One-crust Pie (page 501) except—roll dough into 13-inch circle, about ⅛ inch thick.

Cut circle into 4½-inch rounds; fit rounds over backs of muffin cups or small custard cups, making pleats so pastry will fit closely. (If using individual pie pans or tart pans, cut pastry rounds 1 inch larger than inverted pans; fit into pans.) Prick thoroughly with fork to prevent puffing.

Place on baking sheet. Bake at 475° for 8 to 10 minutes. Cool before removing from pans. Fill each tart with ⅓ to ½ cup of favorite filling.

Makes 8 tart shells.

JIFFY TARTS

Prepare Baked Tart Shells (above). Take your choice of the following fillings:

■ Spoon favorite canned fruit pie filling into shells. If desired, garnish with whipped cream.

■ Spoon favorite canned pudding into shells. Garnish if desired.

■ Fill each shell with a scoop of ice cream and top with favorite dessert sauce. If desired, garnish with chopped nuts, shaved chocolate or coconut.

■ Fill each shell with a scoop of ice cream and top with fresh or frozen (thawed) fruit. Berries and peaches are especially good.

■ Fill shells with sweetened fresh or well-drained canned fruit. Dot with jelly for color and flavor.

LATTICE TOP

Prepare pastry as directed for Two-crust Pie (page 501) except—leave 1-inch overhang on lower crust. After rolling circle for top crust, cut circle into strips, about ½ inch wide. Pastry wheel can be used for more decorative strips.

Place 5 to 7 strips (depending on size of pie) across filling in pie pan. Weave a cross-strip through center by first folding back every other strip going the other way.

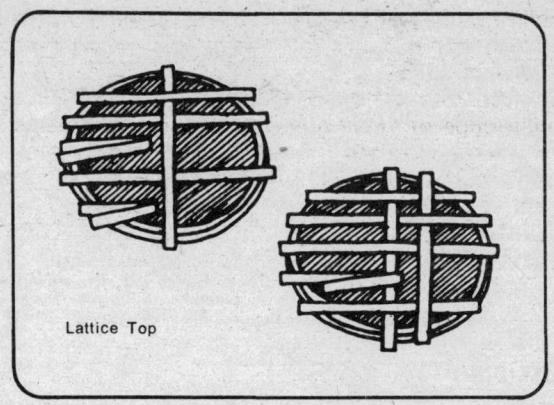

Lattice Top

Continue weaving until lattice is complete, folding back alternate strips each time cross-strip is added. (To save time, do not weave strips. Simply lay second half of strips across first strips.) Trim ends of strips.

Fold trimmed edge of lower crust over ends of strips, building up a high edge. (A juicy fruit pie is more likely to bubble over when topped by lattice than when the juices are held in by a top crust. Be sure to build up a high pastry edge.) Seal and flute.

Note: For a slightly different lattice design, weave the second half of strips diagonally across the first strips. Or, you can also twist each strip as it is placed on the filling.

MERINGUE PIE SHELL

Heat oven to 275°. Generously butter 9-inch pie pan. In small mixer bowl, beat 2 egg whites (¼ to ⅓ cup) and ¼ teaspoon cream of tartar until foamy. Beat in ½ cup sugar, 1 tablespoon at a time; continue beating until stiff and glossy. Do not underbeat. Pile into pie pan, pressing meringue up against side of pan.

Bake 45 minutes. Turn off oven; leave meringue in oven with door closed 45 minutes. Remove from oven; finish cooling away from draft.

CRUMB CRUSTS *For praiseworthy pies every time, pair a crunchy crumb*

Name	Crumbs	Sugar
Graham Cracker		
8-inch pie	1¼ cups (about 16 crackers)	2 tablespoons
9-inch pie	1½ cups (about 20 crackers)	3 tablespoons
10-inch pie	1¾ cups (about 24 crackers)	¼ cup
Cookie 9-inch pie (vanilla or chocolate wafers or gingersnaps)	1½ cups	

Heat oven to 350°. Mix crumbs, sugar and butter. If desired, reserve 2 to 3 tablespoons crumb mixture for topping.

FRUIT PIES

Fruit pies for all seasons—how lucky we are to have canned and frozen products! You'll find unusual stand-out seasonal pies, too.

APPLE PIE

8-INCH

Pastry for 8-inch Two-crust Pie (page 501)
½ cup sugar
3 tablespoons flour*
¼ teaspoon nutmeg
¼ teaspoon cinnamon

Dash salt
5 cups thinly sliced pared tart apples
1 tablespoon butter or margarine

9-INCH

Pastry for 9-inch Two-crust Pie (page 501)
¾ cup sugar
½ cup all-purpose flour*
½ teaspoon nutmeg
½ teaspoon cinnamon

Dash salt
6 cups thinly sliced pared tart apples
2 tablespoons butter or margarine

10-INCH

Pastry for 10-inch Two-crust Pie (page 502)
1 cup sugar
⅓ cup all-purpose flour*
1 teaspoon nutmeg
1 teaspoon cinnamon

Dash salt
8 cups thinly sliced pared tart apples
3 tablespoons butter or margarine

*If using self-rising flour, omit salt.

crust with a fluffy chiffon or velvety cream or ice-cream filling.

Butter or Margarine	Baking Temperature and Time
¼ cup, melted	350° 10 minutes
⅓ cup, melted	350° 10 minutes
½ cup, melted	350° 15 minutes
¼ cup, melted	350° 10 minutes

Press remaining mixture firmly and evenly against bottom and side of pie pan. Bake as directed in the chart above. Cool.

Heat oven to 425°. Prepare pastry. Stir together sugar, flour, nutmeg, cinnamon and salt; mix with apples. Turn into pastry-lined pie pan; dot with butter. Cover with top crust which has slits cut in it; seal and flute. Cover edge with 2- to 3-inch strip of aluminum foil to prevent excessive browning; remove foil last 15 minutes of baking.

Bake 40 to 50 minutes or until crust is brown and juice begins to bubble through slits in crust.

VARIATIONS

■ *Apple-Cheese Pie:* Follow recipe for 9-inch pie except—pour half the apple mixture into pastry-lined pie pan; cover with 5 slices (1 ounce each) process American cheese and top with remaining apples.

■ *Apple-Pecan Pie:* Follow recipe for 10-inch pie except—stir in ⅔ cup chopped pecans with the sugar. Increase baking time to 50 to 60 minutes; spread hot pie with Crunchy Pecan Glaze: In small saucepan, combine ¼ cup brown sugar (packed), ⅓ cup chopped pecans and 2 tablespoons light cream. Cook over low heat, stirring constantly, until of glaze consistency.

■ *Canned Apple Pie:* Follow recipe for 9-inch pie except—substitute 2 cans (1 pound 4 ounces each) apple slices, drained, for the fresh apples.

■ *Dutch Apple Pie:* Follow recipe for 9-inch pie except—make extra large slits in top crust; 5 minutes before pie is completely baked, pour ½ cup whipping cream through slits in top crust and bake 5 minutes. Best served warm.

■ *French Apple Pie:* Prepare pastry for 9-inch One-crust Pie (page 501); omit butter and top apple filling with Crumb Topping: Mix 1 cup of all-purpose flour,* ½ cup firm butter or margarine and ½ cup brown sugar (packed) until crumbly. Bake 50 minutes. Cover topping with aluminum foil last 10 minutes of baking if top browns too quickly. Best served warm.

*Do not use self-rising flour in this recipe.

■ *Green Apple Pie:* Follow recipe for 9-inch pie except—increase sugar to 1¼ cups and use green apples.

KNOW YOUR APPLES With apple pie on the Big Ten list of American favorites, you'll want to make a good one. A good apple pie starts with good apples. Tart, firm, juicy apples. Those rated excellent for pies are Cortland, Rhode Island Greening, McIntosh and Yellow Transparent. Those rated very good are Golden Delicious, Jersey Red, Jonathan, Lodi, Rome Beauty and Starr. Note: One pound equals 3 medium apples or 3 cups sliced apples.

CRAN-APPLE PIE

3 tablespoons cornstarch
2 tablespoons sugar
2 teaspoons grated orange peel
1 can (1 pound) whole cranberry sauce

1 can (1 pound 4 ounces) apples slices, drained
2 sticks or 1 packet pie crust mix
1 tablespoon butter or margarine

Heat oven to 425°. Mix cornstarch, sugar, orange peel and cranberry sauce in saucepan. Heat to boiling over medium heat, stirring constantly. Boil and stir 1 minute. Gently stir in apples; set aside.

Prepare pastry for 9-inch Two-crust Pie as directed on package. Spread cranberry mixture in pastry-lined pie pan; dot with butter. Cover with top crust which has slits cut in it; seal and flute. Cover edge with 2- to 3-inch strip of aluminum foil to prevent excessive browning; remove foil last 10 minutes of baking. Bake 40 minutes or until crust is brown.

DEEP DISH APPLE PIE

No apples? Substitute 3 cans (1 pound 4 ounces each) apple slices, drained, for the fresh apples; use half the amounts of sugar, flour, nutmeg, cinnamon and salt. Bake 45 minutes.

1½ cups sugar
½ cup all-purpose flour*
1 teaspoon nutmeg
1 teaspoon cinnamon
¼ teaspoon salt
12 cups thinly sliced pared apples (about 10 medium)

2 tablespoons butter or margarine
Pastry for 9-inch One-crust Pie (page 501)

Stir together sugar, flour, nutmeg, cinnamon and salt; mix with apples. Turn into ungreased square pan, 9x 9x2 inches; dot with butter.

Heat oven to 425°. Prepare pastry as directed except—roll into 10-inch square. Fold pastry in half; cut slits near center. Unfold over fruit in pan; fold edges under just inside edge of pan.

Bake 1 hour or until juice begins to bubble through slits in crust. Best served warm.

*If using self-rising flour, omit salt.

FRESH CRANBERRY-APPLE PIE

Pastry for 9-inch Two-crust Pie (page 501)
1¾ to 2 cups sugar
⅓ cup all-purpose flour
3 cups sliced pared tart apples (2 to 3 medium)

2 cups fresh or frozen cranberries
2 tablespoons butter or margarine

Heat oven to 425°. Prepare pastry. Stir together sugar and flour. In pastry-lined pie pan, alternate layers of apples, cranberries and sugar mixture, beginning and ending with apple layers; dot with butter.

Cover with top crust which has slits cut in it; seal and flute. Cover edge with 2- to 3-inch strip of aluminum foil to prevent excessive browning; remove foil last 15 minutes of baking. Bake 40 to 50 minutes or until crust is brown. Cool.

APPLE CRUMBLE PIZZA PIE

No pizza pan? Don't let that stop you. Roll dough into 13- to 14-inch circles; place on ungreased baking sheet and flute.

Pastry for 8- or 9-inch Two-crust Pie (page 501)	1 teaspoon cinnamon
6 to 7 tart apples	¼ teaspoon nutmeg
½ cup sugar	Crumble Topping (below)

Heat oven to 450°. Prepare pastry as directed except —roll 1 inch larger than 12- or 13-inch pizza pan. Ease into pizza pan; flute edge. Do not pare apples; cut into slices, about ½ inch thick (about 8 cups). Beginning at edge of crust and overlapping slices, cover crust with apples. Stir together sugar, cinnamon and nutmeg; sprinkle over apple slices. Top with Crumble Topping.

Bake 30 to 40 minutes or until edge is golden brown and apples are tender. Best served warm and, if desired, topped with cinnamon ice cream.

8 to 10 servings.

CRUMBLE TOPPING

Mix ¾ cup all-purpose flour,* ½ cup sugar and ½ cup firm butter or margarine until crumbly.

*Do not use self-rising flour in this recipe.

BLUEBERRY PIE

8-INCH

Pastry for 8-inch Two-crust Pie (page 501)	3 cups fresh blueberries
⅓ cup sugar	1 teaspoon lemon juice
¼ cup all-purpose flour	1 tablespoon butter or margarine
½ teaspoon cinnamon, if desired	

9-INCH

Pastry for 9-inch Two-crust Pie (page 501)	4 cups fresh blueberries
½ cup sugar	1 tablespoon lemon juice
⅓ cup all-purpose flour	2 tablespoons butter or margarine
½ teaspoon cinnamon, if desired	

10-INCH

Pastry for 10-inch
Two-crust Pie (page 502)
⅔ cup sugar
¼ cup plus 2 tablespoons
all-purpose flour
½ teaspoon cinnamon, if
desired

5 cups fresh blueberries
2 tablespoons lemon juice
3 tablespoons butter or
margarine

Heat oven to 425°. Prepare pastry. Stir together sugar, flour and cinnamon; mix with berries. Turn into pastry-lined pie pan; sprinkle with lemon juice and dot with butter.

Cover with top crust which has slits cut in it; seal and flute. Cover edge with 2- to 3-inch strip of aluminum foil to prevent excessive browning; remove foil last 15 minutes of baking.

Bake 8- and 9-inch pies 35 to 45 minutes, 10-inch pie 45 to 50 minutes or until crust is brown and juice begins to bubble through slits in crust.

VARIATIONS

■ *Canned Blueberry Pie:* Substitute drained canned blueberries for the fresh blueberries.

■ *Frozen Blueberry Pie:* Substitute unsweetened frozen blueberries, partially thawed, for the fresh blueberries. (One 12-ounce package frozen blueberries yields 2½ cups.)

GOOSEBERRY PIE

Pastry for 9-inch Two-crust
Pie (page 501)
1¾ cups sugar
½ cup all-purpose flour

4 cups fresh gooseberries
2 tablespoons butter or
margarine

Heat oven to 425°. Prepare pastry. Stir together sugar and flour. Turn half the berries into pastry-lined pie pan; sprinkle with half the sugar mixture. Repeat with remaining berries and sugar; dot with butter. Cover with top crust which has slits cut in it; seal and flute. Cover edge with 2- to 3-inch strip of aluminum foil to prevent excessive browning; remove foil for last 15 minutes of baking. Bake 35 to 45 minutes or until juice begins to bubble through slits in crust. Cool.

CHERRY PIE

8-INCH

Pastry for 8-inch Two-crust Pie (page 501)
1⅓ cups sugar
⅓ cup all-purpose flour
2 cans (1 pound each) pitted red tart cherries, drained
¼ teaspoon almond extract
2 tablespoons butter or margarine

9-INCH

Pastry for 9-inch Two-crust Pie (page 501)
1⅓ cups sugar
⅓ cup all-purpose flour
2 cans (1 pound each) pitted red tart cherries, drained
¼ teaspoon almond extract
2 tablespoons butter or margarine

10-INCH

Pastry for 10-inch Two-crust Pie (page 502)
1⅔ cups sugar
½ cup all-purpose flour
3 cans (1 pound each) pitted red tart cherries, drained
1 teaspoon almond extract
3 tablespoons butter or margarine

Heat oven to 425°. Prepare pastry. Stir together sugar and flour; mix with cherries. Turn into pastry-lined pie pan; sprinkle with almond extract and dot with butter. Cover with top crust which has slits cut in it; seal and flute. Cover edge with 2- to 3-inch strip of aluminum foil to prevent excessive browning; remove foil last 15 minutes of baking.

Bake 8- and 9-inch pies 35 to 45 minutes, 10-inch pie 40 to 50 minutes or until crust is brown and juice begins to bubble through slits in crust.

VARIATIONS

■ *Fresh Cherry Pie:* Follow recipe for 9-inch pie except—substitute 4 cups fresh red tart cherries, washed and pitted, for the canned cherries.

■ *Frozen Cherry Pie:* Follow recipe for 9-inch pie except—substitute 2 cans (1 pound 4 ounces each) frozen pitted red tart cherries, thawed and drained, for the canned cherries and decrease sugar to ½ cup.

ORANGE-GLAZED CHERRY PIE

Heat oven to 425°. Prepare Orange-flavored Pastry Variation for 8-inch Two-crust Pie (page 502). Turn 1 can (1 pound 5 ounces) cherry pie filling into pastry-lined pie pan. Cover with Lattice Top (page 509). Cover edge with 2- to 3-inch strip of aluminum foil to prevent excessive browning; remove foil last 15 minutes of baking. Bake 35 to 40 minutes. Spoon Orange Glaze (below) over warm pie; garnish with orange slice.

ORANGE GLAZE

Mix ½ cup confectioners' sugar, 2 teaspoons grated orange peel and 1 tablespoon orange juice.

GRAPE JAM PIE

Pastry for 9-inch Two-crust Pie (page 501)	¼ cup cornstarch
¼ cup water	1 jar (20 ounces) grape jam
¼ cup lemon juice	2 tablespoons butter or margarine

Heat oven to 425°. Prepare pastry. Blend water, lemon juice and cornstarch; stir in preserves. Turn into pastry-lined pie pan; dot with butter. Cover with top crust which has slits cut in it; seal and flute. Cover edge with 2- to 3-inch strip of aluminum foil to prevent excessive browning; remove foil last 15 minutes of baking. Bake 35 to 45 minutes or until crust is brown.

FRESH PEACH PIE

8-INCH

Pastry for 8-inch Two-crust Pie (page 501)	⅔ cup sugar
4 cups sliced fresh peaches (about 7 medium)	3 tablespoons flour
	¼ teaspoon cinnamon
1 teaspoon lemon juice	1 tablespoon butter or margarine

9-INCH

Pastry for 9-inch Two-crust Pie (page 501)	1 cup sugar
5 cups sliced fresh peaches (about 9 medium)	¼ cup all-purpose flour
	¼ teaspoon cinnamon
1 teaspoon lemon juice	2 tablespoons butter or margarine

10-INCH

Pastry for 10-inch
Two-crust Pie (page 502)
6 cups sliced fresh peaches
(about 11 medium)
1 teaspoon lemon juice

1¼ cups sugar
⅓ cup all-purpose flour
¼ teaspoon cinnamon
3 tablespoons butter or
margarine

Heat oven to 425°. Prepare pastry. Mix peaches and lemon juice. Stir together sugar, flour and cinnamon; mix with peaches. Turn into pastry-lined pie pan; dot with butter. Cover with top crust which has slits cut in it; seal and flute. Cover edge with 2- to 3-inch strip of aluminum foil to prevent excessive browning; remove foil last 15 minutes of baking.

Bake 8- and 9-inch pies 35 to 45 minutes, 10-inch pie 40 to 50 minutes or until crust is brown and juice begins to bubble through slits in crust.

VARIATION

■ *Canned Peach Pie:* Follow recipe for 9-inch pie except—substitute 2 cans (1 pound 13 ounces each) sliced peaches, drained, for the fresh peaches and decrease sugar to ½ cup.

PEACH MELBA PIE

Pastry for 9-inch Two-crust
Pie (page 501)
½ cup sugar
2 tablespoons cornstarch
3½ cups drained canned
sliced peaches (reserve
¼ cup syrup)
1 package (10 ounces)
frozen raspberries, thawed
and drained (reserve
syrup)

1 tablespoon butter or
margarine
Vanilla ice cream
Melba Sauce (page 519)

Heat oven to 425°. Prepare pastry. Stir together sugar and cornstarch in small saucepan. Stir in reserved peach syrup. Cook over medium heat, stirring constantly, until mixture thickens and boils. Boil and stir 1 minute. Mix hot syrup with peach slices. Place raspberries evenly in pastry-lined pie pan; cover with peach mixture and dot with butter.

Cover with top crust which has slits cut in it; seal and flute. Cover edge with 2- to 3-inch strip of aluminum foil to prevent excessive browning; remove foil last 15 minutes of baking.

Bake 40 to 45 minutes or until crust is brown. Serve with ice cream and Melba Sauce.

MELBA SAUCE

Mix 2 teaspoons cornstarch, ¼ cup currant jelly and ½ cup reserved raspberry syrup in small saucepan. Cook over medium heat, stirring constantly, until mixture thickens and boils. Boil and stir 1 minute. Cool.

PEACHES 'N CREAM PIE

Pastry for 9-inch One-crust Pie (page 501)
¾ cup sugar
3 tablespoons flour

5 fresh peaches, peeled and halved
¾ cup whipping cream
¼ teaspoon cinnamon

Heat oven to 450°. Prepare pastry. Stir together sugar and flour; spread half the mixture in pastry-lined pie pan. Place peach halves cut side down on sugar (overlap halves if necessary). Sprinkle remaining sugar mixture over peaches. Pour cream over peaches; sprinkle with cinnamon. Cover edge with 2- to 3-inch strip of aluminum foil to prevent excessive browning; remove foil last 15 minutes of baking.

Bake 10 minutes. Reduce oven temperature to 350°; bake 30 to 35 minutes longer. Cool.

FRESH PEAR PIE

Summer or winter pears can be used for this pie. Be sure to select firm and slightly underripe fruit for baking.

Pastry for 9-inch Two-crust Pie (page 501)
½ cup sugar
⅓ cup all-purpose flour
½ teaspoon mace, if desired

4 cups sliced pared fresh pears (about 7 medium)
1 tablespoon lemon juice
2 tablespoons butter or margarine

Heat oven to 425°. Prepare pastry. Stir together sugar, flour and mace; mix with pears. Turn into pastry-lined pie pan; sprinkle with lemon juice and dot with butter. Cover with top crust which has slits cut in it; seal and flute. Cover edge with 2- to 3-inch strip of aluminum foil to prevent excessive browning; remove foil last 15 minutes of baking.

Bake 40 to 50 minutes or until crust is brown and juice begins to bubble through slits in crust.

VARIATION

■ *Canned Pear Pie:* Decrease sugar to ⅓ cup and substitute 2 cans (1 pound each) sliced pears, drained, for the fresh pears.

FRESH PINEAPPLE PIE

2 medium pineapples
1 cup sugar
  Pastry for 9-inch Two-crust Pie (page 501)
1 cup sugar
½ cup all-purpose flour

½ teaspoon grated lemon peel
1 tablespoon lemon juice
2 tablespoons butter or margarine

Cut a thick slice from top and bottom of each pineapple. Cut remaining pineapple into 1-inch-thick slices; remove rind and core. Cut rings into ¼-inch pieces. Place in shallow dish; sprinkle with 1 cup sugar. Cover; refrigerate at least 5 hours.

Heat oven to 425°. Drain pineapple, reserving ½ cup syrup. Prepare pastry. Turn pineapple into pastry-lined pie pan. Stir together 1 cup sugar and the flour in small saucepan. Gradually stir in reserved syrup. Cook over medium heat, stirring constantly, until mixture thickens and boils. Boil and stir 1 minute. Remove from heat; stir in lemon peel and juice.

Pour syrup mixture over pineapple; dot with butter. Cover with top crust which has slits in it; seal and flute. Cover edge with 2- to 3-inch strip of aluminum foil to prevent excessive browning; remove foil last 15 minutes of baking.

Bake 35 to 45 minutes or until crust is brown and juice begins to bubble through slits in crust.

PLUM PIE

A rather tart but refreshing pie.

Pastry for 9-inch Two-crust
Pie (page 501)
½ cup sugar
⅓ cup all-purpose flour
½ teaspoon cinnamon

4 cups sliced fresh purple
plums
1 tablespoon lemon juice
2 tablespoons butter or
margarine

Heat oven to 425°. Prepare pastry. Stir together sugar, flour and cinnamon; mix with plums. Turn into pastry-lined pie pan; sprinkle with lemon juice and dot with butter. Cover with top crust which has slits cut in it; seal and flute. Cover edge with 2- to 3-inch strip of aluminum foil to prevent excessive browning; remove foil last 15 minutes of baking.

Bake 35 to 45 minutes or until crust is brown and juice begins to bubble through slits in crust.

RAISIN PIE

Called Funeral Pie by the Pennsylvania Dutch because it was served to mourners.

Pastry for 9-inch Two-crust
Pie (page 501)
2 cups raisins
2 cups water
½ cup sugar

2 tablespoons flour
½ cup finely chopped nuts
2 teaspoons grated lemon
peel
3 tablespoons lemon juice

Heat oven to 425°. Prepare pastry. Heat raisins and water to boiling; cook 5 minutes. Stir together sugar and flour; stir into raisin mixture. Cook over medium heat, stirring constantly, until mixture thickens and boils. Boil and stir 1 minute. Remove from heat. Stir in nuts, lemon peel and juice.

Pour hot filling into pastry-lined pie pan. Cover with top crust which has slits in it; seal and flute. Cover edge with 2- to 3-inch strip of aluminum foil to prevent excessive browning; remove foil last 15 minutes of baking.

Bake 30 to 40 minutes or until crust is brown and juice begins to bubble through slits in crust. Best served warm and, if desired, topped with a scoop of vanilla ice cream.

FRESH RHUBARB PIE

For the best pies, choose tender, pink rhubarb. Use the lesser amount of sugar for early rhubarb.

8-INCH

Pastry for 8-inch Two-crust Pie (page 501)
1 to 1¼ cups sugar
¼ cup all-purpose flour
¼ teaspoon grated orange peel, if desired

3 cups cut-up fresh rhubarb (½-inch pieces)
1 tablespoon butter or margarine

9-INCH

Pastry for 9-inch Two-crust Pie (page 501)
1⅓ to 1⅔ cups sugar
⅓ cup all-purpose flour
½ teaspoon grated orange peel, if desired

4 cups cut-up fresh rhubarb (½-inch pieces)
2 tablespoons butter or margarine

10-INCH

Pastry for 10-inch Two-crust Pie (page 502)
1¾ to 2 cups sugar
½ cup all-purpose flour
½ teaspoon grated orange peel, if desired

5 cups cut-up fresh rhubarb (½-inch pieces)
3 tablespoons butter or margarine

Heat oven to 425°. Prepare pastry. Stir together sugar, flour and orange peel. Turn half the rhubarb into pastry-lined pie pan; sprinkle with half the sugar mixture. Repeat with remaining rhubarb and sugar; dot with butter. Cover with top crust which has slits cut in it; seal and flute. Sprinkle with sugar. Cover edge with 2- to 3-inch strip of aluminum foil to prevent excessive browning; remove foil last 15 minutes of baking.

Bake 40 to 50 minutes or until crust is brown and juice begins to bubble through slits in crust.

VARIATION

■ *Rhubarb-Strawberry Pie:* Substitute sliced fresh strawberries for half the rhubarb and use the lesser amount of sugar.

OLD-FASHIONED MINCE PIE

8-INCH

Pastry for 8-inch Two-crust
Pie (page 501)
1 jar (18 ounces) prepared
mincemeat (2 cups)

1 cup diced pared tart
apples

9-INCH

Pastry for 9-inch Two-crust
Pie (page 501)
1 jar (28 ounces) prepared
mincemeat (3 cups)

1½ cups diced pared tart
apples

10-INCH

Pastry for 10-inch
Two-crust Pie (page 502)
2 jars (18 ounces each)
prepared mincemeat (4
cups)

2 cups diced pared tart
apples

Heat oven to 425°. Prepare pastry. Mix mincemeat
and apples. Turn into pastry-lined pie pan. Cover with
top crust which has slits cut in it; seal and flute. Cover
edge with 2- to 3-inch strip of aluminum foil to prevent
excessive browning; remove foil last 15 minutes of
baking.

Bake 8- and 9-inch pies 40 to 45 minutes and 10-inch
pie 60 to 65 minutes. Serve warm.

MINCE CREAM CHEESE PIE

Pastry for 9-inch One-crust
Pie (page 501)
1 jar (28 ounces) prepared
mincemeat (3 cups)

2 packages (3 ounces each)
cream cheese, softened
⅓ cup sugar
1 egg

Heat oven to 425°. Prepare pastry. Spread mincemeat in pastry-lined pie pan. Cover edge with 2- to 3-
inch strip of aluminum foil to prevent excessive browning. Bake 20 minutes.

In small mixer bowl, beat cream cheese, sugar and
egg until smooth. Remove pie from oven; remove foil.

Spread cream cheese mixture over mincemeat. Reduce oven temperature to 350°. Bake 20 to 25 minutes longer or until knife inserted in center of topping comes out clean.

MINCEMEAT-APPLE PIE

A jolly holiday pie layered with mincemeat and tart apple slices. For those with hearty appetites, serve à la mode.

Pastry for 9-inch One-crust Pie (page 501)	¼ cup water
¼ cup all-purpose flour	2 tablespoons red cinnamon candies
⅓ cup sugar	1 jar (18 ounces) prepared mincemeat (2 cups)
⅛ teaspoon salt	
1 tablespoon butter	3 tart apples

Heat oven to 425°. Prepare pastry. Sprinkle 2 tablespoons of the flour in pastry-lined pie pan. Mix remaining flour, the sugar, salt and butter until crumbly. Heat water and cinnamon candies, stirring until candies are dissolved; set aside. Spread mincemeat on pastry.

Pare apples and cut into quarters. Cut quarters into wedges, ½ inch thick at outer side. Cover mincemeat with 2 circles of overlapping apple wedges; sprinkle with sugar mixture. Spoon cinnamon syrup over top, moistening as much of sugar mixture as possible.

Cover edge of pastry with 2- to 3-inch strip of aluminum foil to prevent excessive browning; remove foil last 15 minutes of baking. Bake 40 to 50 minutes.

PEAR-MINCEMEAT PIE

Pastry for 9-inch Two-crust Pie (page 501)	6 canned large pear halves
1 jar (28 ounces) prepared mincemeat (3 cups)	6 maraschino cherries

Heat oven to 425°. Prepare pastry. Spread mincemeat in pastry-lined pie pan. Press pear halves into mincemeat with cut sides up and narrow ends toward center. Place a cherry in hollow of each pear half.

Cover with Lattice Top (page 509). Cover edge with 2- to 3-inch strip of aluminum foil to prevent excessive browning; remove foil last 15 minutes of baking. Bake 40 to 50 minutes or until crust is brown. Serve slightly warm.

SUMMER FRUIT PLATTER PIE

A rainbow of fresh fruit, featuring California's always-available strawberries.

Pastry for 8- or 9-inch
Two-crust Pie (page 501)
⅔ cup shredded sharp
natural Cheddar cheese
Clear Orange Sauce
(below)
1 pint fresh strawberries,
halved (reserve 7 whole
berries)

3 fresh peaches, peeled and
sliced
1½ cups seedless green
grapes
1 medium banana, cut into
⅛-inch slices
2 tablespoons sugar
Sweetened whipped
cream

Heat oven to 475°. Prepare pastry as directed except —before adding water, stir the shredded cheese into flour mixture; roll dough 1 inch larger than 14-inch pizza pan. (Pastry can be baked on baking sheet. Roll dough into 15-inch circle; place on ungreased baking sheet and flute.) Ease into pizza pan; flute edge. Prick bottom and side of pastry. Bake 8 to 10 minutes. Cool.

Prepare Clear Orange Sauce. Arrange strawberry halves around edge of pastry shell. Place peaches in a circle next to strawberries. Mound grapes in circle next to peaches; then arrange circle of overlapping banana slices. Place reserved whole berries in center. Sprinkle fruits with sugar. Spoon some of the orange sauce over fruits. Cut pie into wedges; serve with whipped cream and remaining sauce.

12 to 14 servings.

CLEAR ORANGE SAUCE

Stir together 1 cup sugar, ¼ teaspoon salt and 2 tablespoons cornstarch in small saucepan. Gradually stir in 1 cup orange juice, ¼ cup lemon juice and ¾ cup water. Cook over medium heat, stirring constantly, until mixture thickens and boils. Boil and stir 1 minute. Remove from heat. Stir in ½ teaspoon *each* grated orange and lemon peel. Cool.

VARIATION

■ *Winter Fruit Platter Pie:* Substitute 1 can (1 pound 13 ounces) sliced peaches, drained, and 1 can (15¾ ounces) pineapple spears, drained, for the fresh peaches and green grapes.

Winter Fruit Platter Pie

FRUIT SALAD PIE

A colorful compote of fresh, frozen and canned fruits. A delightful winter pie that tastes like a summer fruit salad.

Pastry for 9-inch Two-crust
Pie (page 501)
1 medium banana
1 package (10 ounces)
frozen strawberries,
thawed and drained
(reserve syrup)
1 can (1 pound 4½ ounces)
pineapple chunks, drained
(reserve syrup)

1 tablespoon lemon juice
½ cup sugar
¼ cup quick-cooking tapioca
¼ teaspoon salt
2 tablespoons butter or
margarine
Strawberry Sour Cream
Topping (below)

Heat oven to 425°. Prepare pastry. Slice banana into bowl; add berries, pineapple chunks, lemon juice and ¼ cup of the reserved pineapple syrup. Stir together sugar, tapioca and salt; mix with fruits. Turn into pastry-lined pie pan; dot with butter. Cover with top crust which has slits cut in it; seal and flute. Cover edge with 2- to 3-inch strip of aluminum foil to prevent excessive browning; remove foil last 15 minutes of baking.

Bake 40 to 50 minutes or until crust is brown. Cool. Serve with Strawberry Sour Cream Topping.

STRAWBERRY SOUR CREAM TOPPING

Blend 2 tablespoons reserved strawberry syrup and 1 cup dairy sour cream.

Custard and Meringue Pies

CUSTARD PIE

8-INCH

Pastry for 8-inch One-crust Pie (page 501)
3 eggs
⅓ cup sugar
¼ teaspoon salt
¼ teaspoon nutmeg
1¾ cups milk
1 teaspoon vanilla

9-INCH

Pastry for 9-inch One-crust Pie (page 501)
4 eggs
⅔ cup sugar
½ teaspoon salt
¼ teaspoon nutmeg
2⅔ cups milk
1 teaspoon vanilla

10-INCH

Pastry for 10-inch One-crust Pie (page 501)
5 eggs
1 cup sugar
½ teaspoon salt
¼ teaspoon nutmeg
3 cups milk
1½ teaspoons vanilla

Heat oven to 450°. Prepare pastry. Beat eggs slightly with rotary beater; beat in remaining ingredients. Pour into pastry-lined pie pan. (To prevent spills, place pie pan on oven rack or on open oven door to fill.) Bake 20 minutes.

Reduce oven temperature to 350°. Bake 8-inch pie 10 minutes longer, 9-inch pie 15 to 20 minutes longer and 10-inch pie 30 minutes longer or until knife inserted halfway between center and edge comes out clean.

PECAN PIE

Pastry for 9-inch One-crust Pie (page 501)
3 eggs
⅔ cup sugar
½ teaspoon salt
⅓ cup butter or margarine, melted
1 cup dark or light corn syrup
1 cup pecan halves or broken pecans

Heat oven to 375°. Prepare pastry. Beat eggs, sugar, salt, butter and syrup with rotary beater. Stir in nuts. Pour into pastry-lined pie pan. Bake 40 to 50 minutes or until filling is set.

SPICY WALNUT RAISIN PIE

Pastry for 9-inch One-crust
Pie (page 501)
3 eggs
⅔ cup sugar
½ teaspoon salt
½ teaspoon each cinnamon,
nutmeg and cloves

1 cup light or dark corn
syrup
⅓ cup butter or margarine,
melted
½ cup coarsely chopped
walnuts
½ cup raisins

Heat oven to 375°. Prepare pastry. Beat eggs, sugar, salt, cinnamon, nutmeg, cloves, syrup and butter thoroughly with rotary beater. Stir in walnuts and raisins. Pour into pastry-lined pie pan. Bake 40 to 50 minutes or until filling is set.

CHESS PIE

Pastry for 9-inch One-crust
Pie (page 501)
3 egg yolks
⅔ cup sugar
1 tablespoon flour

½ teaspoon salt
1⅓ cups whipping cream
1 teaspoon vanilla
1 cup cut-up dates
1 cup chopped walnuts

Heat oven to 350°. Prepare pastry. In small mixer bowl, beat egg yolks, sugar, flour and salt on medium speed until very thick and lemon colored. On low speed, blend in whipping cream and vanilla. Stir in dates and walnuts. Pour into pastry-lined pie pan. Bake 50 to 60 minutes or until top is golden.

OLD-FASHIONED PUMPKIN PIE

Here's the most traditional of all holiday pies, smooth and mildly spiced. Try the "cousin" to this favorite pie by substituting mashed cooked squash or sweet potatoes for the pumpkin.

8-INCH

Pastry for 8-inch One-crust
Pie (page 501)
1 egg
1¼ cups canned pumpkin
⅔ cup sugar
¼ teaspoon salt

¾ teaspoon cinnamon
¼ teaspoon ginger
⅛ teaspoon cloves
1¼ cups evaporated milk or
light cream

9-INCH

Pastry for 9-inch One-crust
Pie (page 501)
2 eggs
1 can (1 pound) pumpkin
(2 cups)
¾ cup sugar

½ teaspoon salt
1 teaspoon cinnamon
½ teaspoon ginger
¼ teaspoon cloves
1⅔ cups evaporated milk or
light cream

10-INCH

Pastry for 10-inch
One-crust Pie (page 501)
3 eggs
2¾ cups canned pumpkin
1 cup sugar
¾ teaspoon salt

½ teaspoon cinnamon
¾ teaspoon ginger
½ teaspoon cloves
2¼ cups evaporated milk or
light cream

Heat oven to 425°. Prepare pastry. Beat egg(s) slightly with rotary beater; beat in remaining ingredients. Pour into pastry-lined pie pan. (To prevent spills, place pie pan on oven rack or on open door when filling with pumpkin mixture.) Bake 15 minutes.

Reduce oven temperature to 350°. Bake 8-inch pie 35 minutes longer, 9-inch pie 45 minutes longer and 10-inch pie 55 minutes longer or until knife inserted in center comes out clean. Cool. If desired, serve with sweetened whipped cream.

CRUMB-TOPPED PUMPKIN PIE

2 sticks pie crust mix
1 can (1 pound) pumpkin
(2 cups)
1 can (15 ounces)
sweetened condensed milk
1 egg

½ teaspoon salt
¾ teaspoon cinnamon
½ teaspoon nutmeg
½ teaspoon ginger
Orange Crumble Topping
(page 530)

Heat oven to 375°. Prepare pastry for 9-inch One-crust Pie as directed on package. Beat pumpkin, milk, egg, salt, cinnamon, nutmeg and ginger with rotary beater. Pour into pastry-lined pie pan. Sprinkle with Orange Crumble Topping. Cover edge with 2- to 3-inch strip of aluminum foil to prevent excessive browning; remove foil last 15 minutes of baking.

Bake 50 to 55 minutes or until filling is set and pastry is brown.

ORANGE CRUMBLE TOPPING

Mix remaining pie crust stick, 2 teaspoons grated orange peel and ½ cup brown sugar (packed) until crumbly.

LEMON MERINGUE PIE

8-INCH

8-inch Baked Pie Shell
(page 501)
1 cup sugar
¼ cup cornstarch
1 cup water
2 egg yolks, slightly beaten
2 tablespoons butter or
margarine

1 teaspoon grated lemon
peel
⅓ cup lemon juice
2 drops yellow food color, if
desired
Meringue for 8-inch Pie
(page 532)

9-INCH

9-inch Baked Pie Shell
(page 501)
1½ cups sugar
⅓ cup plus 1 tablespoon
cornstarch
1½ cups water
3 egg yolks, slightly beaten
3 tablespoons butter or
margarine

2 teaspoons grated lemon
peel
½ cup lemon juice
2 drops yellow food color, if
desired
Meringue for 9-inch Pie
(page 532)

10-INCH

10-inch Baked Pie Shell
(page 501)
2 cups sugar
½ cup cornstarch
2 cups water
4 egg yolks, slightly beaten
¼ cup butter or margarine

2 teaspoons grated lemon
peel
⅔ cup lemon juice
2 drops yellow food color, if
desired
Meringue for 10-inch Pie
(page 532)

Bake pie shell. Heat oven to 400°. Mix sugar and corn-starch in medium saucepan. Gradually stir in water. Cook over medium heat, stirring constantly, until mixture thickens and boils. Boil and stir 1 minute. Gradually stir at least half the hot mixture into egg yolks. Blend into hot mixture in pan. Boil and stir 1 minute (2 minutes for 10-inch pie). Remove from heat; stir in but-

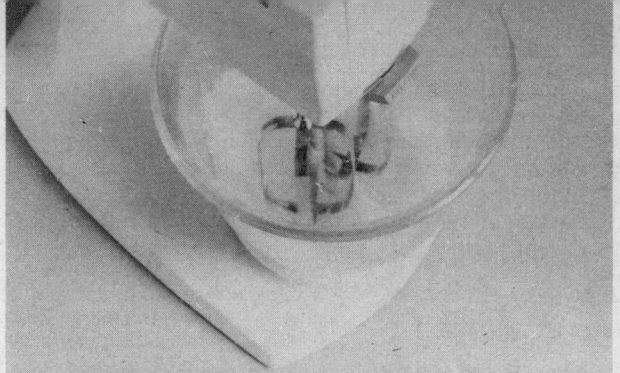

Beat egg whites and cream of tartar until foamy.

Continue beating until mixture stands in stiff peaks.

Spread meringue over filling; seal to edge of crust.

ter, lemon peel, lemon juice and food color. Pour into baked pie shell.

Heap meringue onto hot pie filling; spread over filling, carefully sealing meringue to edge of crust to prevent shrinking or weeping.

Bake about 10 minutes or until a delicate brown. Cool away from draft.

LIME MERINGUE PIE

9-inch Baked Pie Shell (page 501)
1½ cups sugar
⅓ cup cornstarch
3 egg yolks, slightly beaten
1½ cups water

2 teaspoons grated lime peel
¼ cup lime juice
2 drops green food color, if desired
Meringue for 9-inch Pie (below)

Bake pie shell. Heat oven to 400°. Stir together sugar and cornstarch in medium saucepan. Blend egg yolks and water; gradually stir into sugar mixture. Cook over medium heat, stirring constantly, until mixture thickens and boils. Boil and stir 1 minute. Remove from heat; stir in lime peel, lime juice and food color. Immediately pour into baked pie shell.

Heap meringue onto hot pie filling; spread over filling, carefully sealing meringue to edge of crust to prevent shrinking or weeping. Bake about 10 minutes or until a delicate brown. Cool away from draft.

MERINGUE FOR PIE

8-INCH PIE
2 egg whites
¼ teaspoon cream of tartar

¼ cup sugar
¼ teaspoon vanilla

9-INCH PIE
3 egg whites
¼ teaspoon cream of tartar

6 tablespoons sugar
½ teaspoon vanilla

10-INCH PIE
4 egg whites
¼ teaspoon cream of tartar

½ cup sugar
¾ teaspoon vanilla

Beat egg whites and cream of tartar until foamy. Beat

in sugar, 1 tablespoon at a time; continue beating until stiff and glossy. *Do not underbeat*. Beat in vanilla.

VARIATION

■ *Brown Sugar Meringue:* Substitute brown sugar (packed) for the granulated sugar.

ORANGE MERINGUE PIE

9-inch Baked Pie Shell (page 501)
1 cup sugar
3 tablespoons cornstarch
3 egg yolks, slightly beaten
1 cup orange juice
½ cup water

3 tablespoons butter or margarine
1 tablespoon lemon juice
1 tablespoon grated orange peel
Meringue for 9-inch Pie (left)

Bake pie shell. Heat oven to 400°. Stir together sugar and cornstarch in medium saucepan. Blend egg yolks, orange juice and water; gradually stir into sugar mixture. Cook over medium heat, stirring constantly, until mixture thickens and boils.

Boil and stir 1 minute. Remove from heat; stir in butter, lemon juice and orange peel. Immediately pour into baked pie shell.

Heap meringue onto hot pie filling; spread over filling, carefully sealing meringue to edge of crust to prevent shrinking or weeping. Bake about 10 minutes or until a delicate brown. Cool away from draft.

SOUR CREAM RAISIN MERINGUE PIE

9-inch Baked Pie Shell (page 501)
1½ tablespoons cornstarch
1 cup plus 2 tablespoons sugar
¼ teaspoon salt
¾ teaspoon nutmeg

1½ cups dairy sour cream
3 egg yolks, slightly beaten
1½ cups raisins
1 tablespoon lemon juice
Brown Sugar Meringue for 9-inch Pie (above)

Bake pie shell. Heat oven to 400°. Blend cornstarch, sugar, salt and nutmeg in saucepan. Blend in sour cream. Stir in egg yolks, raisins and lemon juice. Cook over medium heat, stirring constantly, until mixture thickens and boils. Boil and stir 1 minute. Immediately pour into baked pie shell.

Heap meringue onto hot pie filling; spread over filling, carefully sealing meringue to edge of crust to prevent shrinking or weeping. Bake about 10 minutes or until light brown. Cool away from draft.

Cream and Refrigerated Pies

CHOCOLATE PIE DELUXE

9-inch Graham Cracker Crust (page 510)
16 large marshmallows or 1½ cups miniature marshmallows
½ cup milk

3 bars (3.5 ounces each) milk chocolate
1 cup chilled whipping cream or 1 envelope (about 2 ounces) dessert topping mix

Prepare crust. Heat marshmallows, milk and chocolate over medium heat, stirring constantly, just until marshmallows and chocolate melt and blend. Chill until thickened.

In chilled bowl, beat cream until stiff. (If using dessert topping mix, prepare as directed on package.) Stir marshmallow mixture to blend; fold into whipped cream. Pour into crust. Chill at least 3 hours or until set. If desired, garnish with toasted slivered almonds.

GRASSHOPPER PIE

Chocolate Cookie Crust (page 510)
32 large marshmallows or 3 cups miniature marshmallows
½ cup milk
¼ cup green crème de menthe

3 tablespoons while crème de cacao
1½ cups chilled whipping cream
Few drops green food color, if desired

Prepare crust. Heat marshmallows and milk over medium heat, stirring constantly, just until marshmallows melt. Chill until thickened; blend in liqueurs.

In chilled bowl, beat cream until stiff. Fold marshmallow mixture into whipped cream; fold in food color. Pour into crust. If desired, sprinkle with grated semisweet chocolate. Chill at least 3 hours or until set.

VANILLA CREAM PIE

8-INCH

8-inch Baked Pie Shell (page 501)
½ cup sugar
3 tablespoons cornstarch
¼ teaspoon salt

2 cups milk
3 egg yolks, slightly beaten
1 tablespoon butter or margarine, softened
1 tablespoon vanilla

9-INCH

9-inch Baked Pie Shell (page 501)
⅔ cup sugar
¼ cup cornstarch
½ teaspoon salt
3 cups milk

4 egg yolks, slightly beaten
2 tablespoons butter or margarine, softened
1 tablespoon plus 1 teaspoon vanilla

10-INCH

10-inch Baked Pie Shell (page 501)
¾ cup sugar
¼ cup plus 2 tablespoons cornstarch
1 teaspoon salt

4 cups milk
5 egg yolks, slightly beaten
3 tablespoons butter or margarine, softened
1 tablespoon plus 2 teaspoons vanilla

Bake pie shell, Stir together sugar, cornstarch and salt in saucepan. Blend milk and egg yolks; gradually stir into sugar mixture. Cook over medium heat, stirring constantly, until mixture thickens and boils. Boil and stir 1 minute. Remove from heat; blend in butter and vanilla. Immediately pour into baked pie shell; press plastic wrap onto filling. Chill pie thoroughly, at least 2 hours. If desired, serve pie with sweetened whipped cream.

VARIATIONS

■ *Chocolate Cream Pie:* Follow recipe for 9-inch pie except—increase sugar to 1½ cups and cornstarch to ⅓ cup. Omit butter and stir in 2 ounces melted unsweetened chocolate with the vanilla.

■ *Coconut Cream Pie:* Follow recipe for 9-inch pie except—decrease vanilla to 2 teaspoons and stir in ¾ cup flaked coconut. Sprinkle ¼ cup flaked coconut over whipped cream on pie.

BANANA CREAM PIE

9-inch Baked Pie Shell (page 501)
⅔ cup sugar
¼ cup cornstarch
½ teaspoon salt
3 cups milk
4 egg yolks, slightly beaten

2 tablespoons butter or margarine, softened
1 tablespoon plus 1 teaspoon vanilla
2 large bananas
Sweetened whipped cream

Bake pie shell. Stir together sugar, cornstarch and salt in saucepan. Blend milk and egg yolks; gradually stir into sugar mixture. Cook over medium heat, stirring constantly, until mixture thickens and boils. Boil and stir 1 minute. Remove from heat; blend in butter and vanilla. Press plastic wrap onto filling in saucepan and cool to room temperature.

Peel and slice bananas; arrange layer of banana slices ½ inch deep in baked pie shell. Pour in cooled filling. Chill pie thoroughly, at least 2 hours. Just before serving, top pie with sweetened whipped cream.

VANILLA SOUR CREAM PIE

8-inch Graham Cracker Crust (page 510)
1 cup dairy sour cream

1 cup milk
1 package (about 3½ ounces) vanilla instant pudding

Prepare crust. Beat sour cream and milk with hand beater until smooth. Blend in pudding (dry) until smooth and slightly thickened. Pour into crust. Chill at least 1 hour or until set. If desired, serve with sweetened whipped cream.

VARIATIONS

■ *Banana Sour Cream Pie:* Prepare 9-inch Graham Cracker Crust (pages 510–511). Slice 2 or 3 bananas;

arrange slices evenly over crust. Pour filling over bananas. At serving time, top with additional banana slices if desired.

■ *Cherry-Chocolate Pudding Pie:* Prepare 9-inch Graham Cracker Crust (pages 510–511). Drain 1 can (1 pound 5 ounces) cherry pie filling, reserving ½ cup syrup. Spoon cherries into crust; spread reserved syrup over cherries. Substitute 1 package (4½ ounces) chocolate instant pudding for the vanilla instant pudding. Pour filling over cherries in crust.

■ *Chocolate Sour Cream Pie:* Substitute 1 package (4½ ounces) chocolate instant pudding for the vanilla instant pudding.

■ *Deluxe Strawberry Glacé Cream Pie:* Prepare 9-inch Graham Cracker Crust (pages 510–511). Slice 1 pint fresh strawberries. Prepare Strawberry Glacé: Mix ½ cup of the strawberries and ¼ cup water in small saucepan; simmer about 3 minutes. Stir together ½ cup sugar and 1½ tablespoons cornstarch; stir in ¼ cup water. Mix into hot strawberry mixture. Cook over medium heat, stirring constantly, until mixture thickens and boils. Boil and stir 1 minute. Cool. Pour cream filling into crust. Arrange remaining berries over filling. Cover with Strawberry Glacé and chill about 2 hours or until firm.

■ *Fruit Cream Pie:* Top chilled pie with sliced strawberries or peaches or drained crushed pineapple, or spread with thin layer of cherry, strawberry or blueberry preserves.

PINEAPPLE MALLOW PIE

9-inch Graham Cracker Crust (page 510)
32 large marshmallows or 3 cups miniature marshmallows
1 can (1 pound 4½ ounces) crushed pineapple, drained (reserve ½ cup syrup)

1 teaspoon vanilla
¼ teaspoon salt
1 cup chilled whipping cream or 1 envelope (about 2 ounces) dessert topping mix

Prepare crust. Heat marshmallows and reserved pineapple syrup over medium heat, stirring constantly, just until marshmallows melt. Remove from heat; stir in vanilla and salt. Chill until thickened.

In chilled bowl, beat cream until stiff. (If using dessert topping mix, prepare as directed on package.) Stir marshmallow mixture to blend. Reserving ½ cup crushed pineapple, fold remaining pineapple and the marshmallow into whipped cream. Pour into crust; garnish with reserved pineapple. Chill at least 3 hours or until set.

PUDDING PIE COMBOS

Bake 9- or 10-inch Baked Pie Shell (page 501).

Combine 1 package (4½ ounces) chocolate instant pudding and 1 package (about 3½ ounces) lemon instant pudding in large bowl. Prepare as directed for pie except —double the amount of milk specified for 1 package. Pour into baked pie shell; chill until firm. Just before serving, garnish pie with whipped cream and, if desired, lemon slices.

Note: 1 package (about 4 ounces) butterscotch instant pudding can be substituted for the lemon instant pudding. Garnish pie with chocolate curls.

COCONUT PUDDING PIE

9-inch Baked Pie Shell (page 501)
1 envelope (about 2 ounces) dessert topping mix
1 can (18 ounces) vanilla pudding
1 can (3½ ounces) flaked coconut
1 tablespoon orange-flavored liqueur or, if desired, orange juice
½ cup raspberry jam

Bake pie shell. Prepare dessert topping mix as directed on package. Fold in pudding and 1 cup of the coconut. Pour into baked pie shell. Sprinkle with remaining coconut. Chill at least 2 hours or until set. Stir liqueur into jam; serve with pie as a topping.

STRAWBERRY MINUTE PIE

8-inch Baked Pie Shell (page 501)
1 cup boiling water
1 package (3 ounces) strawberry-flavored gelatin
1 package (16 ounces) frozen sliced strawberries

Bake pie shell. Pour boiling water over gelatin; stir to dissolve. Add frozen strawberries; stir to break berries apart. When mixture is partially set, pour into baked pie shell. Chill until set. If desired, serve with sweetened whipped cream.

VARIATION

■ *Raspberry Minute Pie:* Substitute 1 package (3 ounces) raspberry-flavored gelatin for the strawberry-flavored gelatin and 2 packages (10 ounces each) frozen raspberries for the strawberries.

STRAWBERRY GLACÉ PIE

9-inch Baked Pie Shell (page 501)
6 cups fresh strawberries (about 1½ quarts)
1 cup sugar
3 tablespoons cornstarch
½ cup water
1 package (3 ounces) cream cheese, softened

Bake pie shell. Mash enough berries to measure 1 cup. Stir together sugar and cornstarch. Gradually stir in water and crushed strawberries. Cook over medium heat, stirring constantly, until mixture thickens and boils. Boil and stir 1 minute. Cool.

Beat cream cheese until smooth; spread on bottom of baked pie shell. Fill shell with remaining berries; pour cooked berry mixture over top. Chill at least 3 hours or until set.

VARIATIONS

■ *Peach Glacé Pie:* Substitute 5 cups sliced fresh peaches (7 medium) for the strawberries. To prevent peaches from darkening, use an ascorbic acid mixture as directed on the package.

■ *Raspberry Glacé Pie:* Substitute 6 cups fresh raspberries for the strawberries.

SILHOUETTE PARFAIT PIE

Bake 9-inch Baked Pie Shell (page 501).

Heat oven to 325°. Prepare Meringue for 9-inch Pie (page 532) as directed except—increase sugar to ¾ cup and after beating in sugar, sift 3 tablespoons cocoa over meringue; fold in carefully. Spread mixture evenly in baked pie shell, sealing meringue to fluted edge of crust.

Bake 25 minutes. (Meringue will be soft.) Cool thoroughly. Just before serving, fill with 1 quart vanilla ice cream; top with Fudge Sauce (page 306). If desired, other ice cream and sauce combinations can be substituted.

VARIATION

■ *Christmas Peppermint Pie:* Substitute pink peppermint ice cream for the vanilla. Top with Fudge Sauce and crushed peppermint candy.

Chiffon Pies

How many chiffon pies do you know how to make? Just lemon? That's too bad. Too bad when you think how much your family and friends might enjoy a pumpkin chiffon or strawberry chiffon or chocolate chiffon or Nesselrode.

So stop thinking about chiffon pies as restaurant specialties. You can master them for your own menus—with these people-tested recipes. (All the tips to assure success are included in the directions.) And see how nicely they fit into a busy day.

STRAWBERRY CHIFFON PIE

9-inch Baked Pie Shell (page 501)
¼ cup sugar
1 envelope unflavored gelatin
1 package (10 ounces) frozen strawberry halves, thawed

3 egg whites
¼ teaspoon cream of tartar
⅓ cup sugar
½ cup chilled whipping cream

Bake pie shell. Stir together ¼ cup sugar and the gelatin in saucepan; stir in strawberries. Cook over medium heat, stirring constantly, just until mixture boils. Place pan in bowl of ice and water or chill in refrigerator, stirring occasionally, until mixture mounds slightly when dropped from spoon.

Beat egg whites and cream of tartar until foamy. Beat in ⅓ cup sugar, 1 tablespoon at a time; continue beating until stiff and glossy. Do not underbeat. Fold strawberry mixture into meringue. In chilled bowl, beat cream until stiff; fold into strawberry meringue. Pile into baked pie shell. Chill at least 3 hours or until set.

CHOCOLATE CHIFFON PIE

9-inch Baked Pie Shell (page 501)
½ cup sugar
1 envelope unflavored gelatin
½ teaspoon salt
1⅓ cups water
2 ounces melted unsweetened chocolate (cool)

3 eggs, separated
1 teaspoon vanilla
¼ teaspoon cream of tartar
½ cup sugar
½ cup chilled whipping cream

Bake pie shell. Stir together ½ cup sugar, the gelatin and salt in small saucepan; stir in water and chocolate. Cook over medium heat, stirring constantly, until blended. Remove from heat. Beat egg yolks slightly; slowly stir in chocolate mixture. Return mixture to saucepan. Cook over medium heat, stirring constantly, just until mixture boils. Place pan in bowl of ice and water or chill in refrigerator, stirring occasionally, until mixture mounds slightly when dropped from spoon. Stir in vanilla.

Beat egg whites and cream of tartar until foamy. Beat in ½ cup sugar, 1 tablespoon at a time; continue beating until stiff and glossy. Do not underbeat. Fold chocolate mixture into meringue. In chilled bowl, beat cream until stiff; fold into chocolate mixture. Pile into baked pie shell. Chill at least 3 hours or until set. If desired, serve with sweetened whipped cream and sprinkle with chocolate curls.

PUMPKIN CHIFFON PIE

8-inch Baked Pie Shell
(page 501)
½ cup brown sugar (packed)
2 teaspoons unflavored
gelatin
¼ teaspoon each salt, ginger,
cinnamon and nutmeg

¾ cup canned pumpkin
2 eggs, separated
⅓ cup milk
¼ teaspoon cream of tartar
⅓ cup granulated sugar

Bake pie shell. In small saucepan, stir together brown sugar, gelatin, salt, ginger, cinnamon and nutmeg. Blend pumpkin, egg yolks and milk; stir into brown sugar mixture. Cook over medium heat, stirring constantly, just until mixture boils. Place pan in bowl of ice and water or chill in refrigerator, stirring occasionally, until mixture mounds slightly when dropped from spoon.

Beat egg whites and cream of tartar until foamy. Beat in granulated sugar, 1 tablespoon at a time; continue beating until stiff and glossy. Do not underbeat. Fold pumpkin mixture into meringue. Pile into baked pie shell. Chill at least 3 hours or until set. If desired, garnish with whipped cream.

BLACK BOTTOM PIE

A double dessert, rich and chocolatey on the bottom, light and rum-flavored on the top...sure to bring praise from your guests.

9-inch Baked Pie Shell
(page 501)
½ cup sugar
2 tablespoons cornstarch
½ teaspoon salt
2 cups milk
2 eggs, separated
2 teaspoons unflavored
gelatin

3 tablespoons cold water
2 tablespoons rum or 2
teaspoons rum flavoring
1 ounce melted
unsweetened chocolate
(cool)
¼ teaspoon cream of tartar
⅓ cup sugar

Bake pie shell. Stir together ½ cup sugar, the cornstarch and salt in saucepan. Blend milk and egg yolks; stir into sugar mixture. Cook over medium heat, stirring constantly, just until mixture boils. Reserve 1 cup of the custard mixture; set aside.

Soften gelatin in cold water; stir into remaining hot custard mixture. Stir in rum. Place in bowl of ice and water or chill in refrigerator, stirring occasionally, until mixture mounds slightly when dropped from spoon. Combine chocolate and the reserved custard mixture. Pour into baked pie shell.

Beat egg whites and cream of tartar until foamy. Beat in ⅓ cup sugar, 1 tablespoon at a time; continue beating until stiff and glossy. Do not underbeat. Fold remaining custard mixture into meringue. Spread on chocolate mixture. Chill at least 3 hours or until set. If desired, garnish with whipped cream; sprinkle with shaved chocolate.

LEMON CHIFFON PIE

8-INCH

8-inch Baked Pie Shell (page 501)
⅓ cup sugar
2 teaspoons unflavored gelatin
3 eggs, separated

½ cup water
¼ cup lemon juice
2 teaspoons grated lemon peel
¼ teaspoon cream of tartar
⅓ cup sugar

9-INCH

9-inch Baked Pie Shell (page 501)
½ cup sugar
1 envelope unflavored gelatin
4 eggs, separated

⅔ cup water
⅓ cup lemon juice
1 tablespoon grated lemon peel
½ teaspoon cream of tartar
½ cup sugar

10-INCH

10-inch Baked Pie Shell (page 501)
⅔ cup sugar
1 tablespoon plus 1 teaspoon unflavored gelatin
5 eggs, separated

¾ cup water
½ cup lemon juice
1 tablespoon plus 1 teaspoon grated lemon peel
½ teaspoon cream of tartar
½ cup sugar

Bake pie shell. Stir together sugar and gelatin in small saucepan. Blend egg yolks, water and lemon juice; stir into sugar mixture. Cook over medium heat, stirring constantly, just until mixture boils. Stir in peel. Place pan in bowl of ice and water or chill in refrigerator, stirring occasionally, until mixture mounds slightly when dropped from spoon.

Beat egg whites and cream of tartar until foamy. Beat in sugar, 1 tablespoon at a time; continue beating until stiff and glossy. Do not underbeat. Fold lemon mixture into meringue. Pile into baked pie shell. Chill at least 3 hours or until set.

GELATIN NEWS We've used chiffon pie shortcuts—especially for you. Most of these pies we simply mix the gelatin with sugar and then dissolve this combination in the liquid. They all cook together. No need to spend time and attention softening the gelatin in cold water first. Just mix and go. So who says chiffon pies are a bother?

NESSELRODE PIE

9-inch Baked Pie Shell (page 501)	1 cup milk
½ cup sugar	¼ teaspoon almond extract
1 envelope unflavored gelatin	¼ teaspoon cream of tartar
½ teaspoon salt	⅓ cup water
2 eggs, separated	½ cup chilled whipping cream
	1 jar (10 ounces) Nesselrode

Bake pie shell. Stir together ½ cup sugar, the gelatin and salt in saucepan. Blend egg yolks and milk; stir into sugar mixture. Cook over medium heat, stirring constantly, just until mixture boils. Place pan in bowl of ice and water or chill in refrigerator, stirring occasionally, until mixture mounds slightly when dropped from spoon. Stir in almond extract.

Beat egg whites and cream of tartar until foamy. Beat in ⅓ cup sugar, 1 tablespoon at a time; continue beating until stiff and glossy. Do not underbeat. Fold gelatin mixture into meringue.

In chilled bowl, beat cream until stiff. Fold whipped cream and Nesselrode into meringue mixture. Pile into baked pie shell. Chill at least 3 hours or until set.

EGGNOG PIE

9-inch Baked Pie Shell
(page 501)
½ cup sugar
1 envelope unflavored
gelatin
½ teaspoon salt
3 eggs, separated
1¼ cups milk

1 teaspoon light rum or ½
teaspoon rum flavoring
¼ teaspoon cream of tartar
½ cup sugar
½ cup chilled whipping
cream
Nutmeg

Bake pie shell. Stir together ½ cup sugar, the gelatin and salt in saucepan. Blend egg yolks and milk; stir into sugar mixture. Cook over medium heat, stirring constantly, just until mixture boils. Place pan in bowl of ice and water or chill in refrigerator, stirring occasionally, until mixture mounds slightly when dropped from spoon. Stir in rum.

Beat egg whites and cream of tartar until foamy. Beat in ½ cup sugar, 1 tablespoon at a time; continue beating until stiff and glossy. Do not underbeat. Fold gelatin mixture into meringue.

In chilled bowl, beat cream until stiff; fold into meringue mixture. Pile into baked pie shell. Sprinkle generously with nutmeg. Chill at least 3 hours or until set.

Preserves, Relishes and Garnishes

Betty's pickles! Aunt Alice's peach conserve! Mary's mint relish! Is there anything nicer than a gift you made yourself? Anything that gives you a deeper sense of satisfaction than a row of shining jars and glasses standing on your shelf? Pickles, jams, relishes, even garnishes—they all dress up your meals. So why not give your family your very best? It isn't all that hard!

Preserving

Because supermarket shelves are loaded with an abundance of excellent preserves and pickles, we've chosen only the unusual—and emphasized the quick to fix. If you're interested in information on traditional canning, write for: Home Canning of Fruits and Vegetables, U.S.D.A. Home and Garden Bulletin No. 8 (15 cents) or How to Make Jellies, Jams and Preserves at Home, U.S.D.A. Home and Garden Bulletin No. 56 (15 cents). (Send check or money order to the Superintendent of Documents, U.S. Government Printing Office, Washington, D.C. 20402.)

Types of Preserves

Jellies are the juice of fruits or berries boiled with sugar. (You'll note that all our recipes call for commercial pectin.)

Jams are made of whole crushed berries or fruits cooked with sugar to a soft consistency; they contain almost no free liquid.

Preserves are whole or sliced fruits preserved in a heavy sugar syrup.

Conserves are made from two or more fruits and usually contain raisins or nuts or both.

Fruit butters are fruit pulp cooked with sugar. They may be made from the pulp left after making jelly.

Pickles and relishes are whole, sliced or chopped fruits or vegetables preserved in a vinegar-sugar mixture or in brine.

Chutneys are relishes that are hot, spicy, sweet and sour all at once. They may be made of fruits or vegetables or both. Fresh or crystallized ginger is a common ingredient in chutneys.

Methods of Preserving

Jelly is preserved by the open-kettle method described on page 551. Most of the other preserves, including pickles and relishes, use a very similar method, described on page 555. However, when the fruit or vegetable is cold or only partially cooked, a water-bath process is used. It is also used in warm climates, where storage conditions are poor or when the sugar is reduced.

Storage

Store all preserves in a cool, dry, dark place.

Four Golden Rules for Success

■ To avoid spoilage, select only sound, firm-ripe, unbruised foods.

■ Make small batches and never double a recipe.

■ Jars used for open-kettle preserving must be sterilized; jars used in a water bath do not need sterilization.

■ Use only standard jars and lids intended for home preserving, and follow the manufacturer's instructions for sealing the jar. Label and date.

Water-bath Processing

For this process you will need a large kettle with a cover and a rack. The kettle should be deep enough so that the jars are covered by 1 to 2 inches of water. In addition, you will need a ladle with a lip; a jar lifter; and two large measuring cups, one for dry ingredients and one for liquids. Work quickly; prepare no more food than you can process at one time in the water bath. Hot jars will break with temperature changes; do not put on cold surfaces or leave in drafts.

To prepare jars and water bath: Just before cooking mixtures, examine tops and edges of standard jars to see that there are no nicks, cracks or sharp edges on sealing surfaces. Wash jars in hot soapy water. Rinse; cover with hot water. Let jars remain in hot water until ready to use. Prepare lids as directed by manufacturer. About 10 minutes before ready to use, fill water-bath kettle half full with hot water; heat. (The water should be hot but not boiling when jars are placed in kettle.) Invert jars on folded towel to drain.

To fill jars: Taking one hot jar at a time, pack in hot mixture to within ¼ inch of top. Wipe top and screw-threads of jar with damp cloth and seal immediately as directed by manufacturer. As each jar is sealed, place on rack in water bath, allowing enough space for water to circulate.

To process: When all jars are in kettle, add boiling water to cover them to depth of 1 to 2 inches. (Do not pour boiling water directly on jars.) Cover kettle. Heat water to boiling; reduce heat to hold water at a steady but gentle boil. Start counting processing time; process 10 minutes for the following recipes. Remove jars from kettle. If jars have been only partly sealed, follow manufacturer's instructions for completing seal.

To cool: Place jars upright a few inches apart on several thicknesses of cloth; keep out of draft. After about 12 hours, test for seal (metal caps or lids will be depressed in the center; lids with wire clamps and rubber seals will not leak when inverted). If the seal is incomplete, either bring the produce back to boiling and repack in sterilized jars with sterilized lids, or store in the refrigerator for *immediate* use. Store sealed jars in cool, dark place.

4-DAY WATERMELON PICKLES

Watermelon pieces stay light because oils of cinnamon and clove do not discolor as spices would.

6 cups water	4 cups sugar
9 cups cubed pared watermelon rind (¾-inch cubes)	1 cup white vinegar
	¼ teaspoon oil of cinnamon
	¼ teaspoon oil of cloves

First day: Heat water to boiling in large kettle. Add watermelon rind; simmer until tender when pierced with fork, 10 to 15 minutes. Drain rind thoroughly; place in glass bowl or crock. Combine remaining ingredients in saucepan; heat to boiling, stirring until sugar is dissolved. Pour hot syrup over rind. Cool. Cover; let stand overnight.

Second day: Drain rind, reserving syrup. Heat syrup to boiling; pour over rind. Cool. Cover; let stand overnight.

Third day: Repeat process as for second day.

Fourth day: Prepare jars and water bath as directed at left. Heat rind and syrup to boiling. If desired, add 1 to 2 drops red or green food color. Fill jars, process and cool and store as directed at left.

5 or 6 half-pints.

CHUNK PICKLES

24 cucumbers (each about 3 inches long)	2 cups vinegar
½ cup pickling salt	¼ cup mustard seed
8 cups water	1 tablespoon celery seed
2½ cups sugar	1 teaspoon curry powder

Wash unpared cucumbers; cut into 1-inch chunks. Dissolve salt in water; pour over cucumbers. Cover; let stand at room temperature 5 hours.

Prepare jars and water bath as directed at left. Drain cucumbers; rinse thoroughly and place in large kettle. Heat remaining ingredients to boiling, stirring until sugar is dissolved. Pour over cucumbers; heat to boiling. Fill jars, process and cool and store as directed at left.

5 or 6 half-pints.

HONEY-PEACH BUTTER

18 medium peaches, washed 2¼ cups sugar
   and peeled ¾ cup honey
¼ cup water

Chop peaches coarsely. Cook in water until soft; press through a sieve or food mill. Measure 6 cups pulp into large saucepan. Stir in sugar and honey; heat to boiling. Stirring frequently, boil gently 40 to 50 minutes or until mixture thickens.

While mixture cooks, prepare jars and water bath as directed on page 547. After mixture thickens, fill jars, process and cool and store as directed on page 547.

3 or 4 half-pints.

ROSY MINT RELISH

3 cups finely chopped
   unpared apples
2 cups finely chopped
   unpared pears
1 cup finely chopped onion
1 cup finely chopped green
   pepper
1 cup chopped golden
   raisins
1 cup chopped fresh mint
   leaves
½ cup finely chopped
   sweet red pepper
2½ cups sugar
1½ cups white vinegar
1 tablespoon salt

Prepare jars and water bath as directed on page 547. In large kettle, mix all ingredients; heat to boiling, stirring occasionally. Fill jars, process and cool and store as directed on page 547.

7 or 8 half-pints.

Try your food chopper for the relish ingredients.

Jellies

For jelly making you will need a large kettle with a broad, flat bottom. This will allow the sugar and juice mixture to boil more quickly and evenly and also prevent it from boiling over. You will also need a long-handled spoon for skimming the jelly, a pair of tongs for removing the glasses from the hot water and a can and a small pan for heating the paraffin. If you are using jelly jars instead of glasses, see page 555 for preparing, filling and sealing jars.

To prepare glasses: Wash glasses in hot soapy water; rinse well. Place in pan with folded cloth or rack on bottom. Cover glasses with hot, not boiling, water and heat to boiling. Boil gently 15 minutes; keep glasses in this hot water until ready for use. About 5 minutes before the end of jelly's cooking period, remove glasses from water and invert on folded towel out of draft to drain.

To fill glasses: Using a ladle, fill one hot, sterilized glass at a time to within ½ inch of top. Hold ladle close to top of glass to prevent air bubbles from forming.

To seal: Cover hot jelly immediately with a ⅛-inch layer of hot paraffin. To ensure a good seal, paraffin must touch side of glass and be even. Prick any bubbles that appear on paraffin as they may allow spoilage. When paraffin is hard, check seal. Cover glasses with metal or paper lids. Store in dark, dry place.

PORT WINE JELLY

A sparkling jewel-like jelly that's a gem of a meat accompaniment. Remember to "put up" extra glasses of this pretty jelly to give as gifts to friends and neighbors.

3 cups sugar
2 cups port

½ bottle (6-ounce size) liquid pectin

Prepare jelly glasses as directed above. In top of double boiler, stir together sugar and wine. Stirring constantly, heat over rapidly boiling water 3 minutes or until sugar is dissolved. Remove from heat; immediately stir in pectin. Fill glasses and seal and store as directed above.

4 or 5 eight-ounce glasses.

SPARKLING GRAPE JELLY

5 cups sugar
2 cans (6 ounces each)
   frozen grape juice
   concentrate, thawed
2 bottles (7 ounces each)
   lemon-lime carbonated
   beverage

¾ cup water
1 package (1¾ ounces) fruit
   pectin

Wash seven 8-ounce jelly glasses in hot soapy water. Rinse and invert on folded towel to drain. (Glasses should be hot and dry when filled with jelly.)

Stir together sugar and grape juice concentrate in

No paraffin is needed for Sparkling Grape Jelly. Fill glasses to ¼ inch of top. Cover with lid; refrigerate.

To seal Quick Jelly, and most jellies, pour layer of hot paraffin on top. Heat paraffin in can in pan of water.

large bowl. Add lemon-lime carbonated beverage and stir well. Heat water and pectin to boiling, stirring constantly; boil and stir 1 minute. Blend hot pectin liquid into grape juice mixture; stir 3 minutes.

Fill glasses as directed on page 551. Cover each glass with lid or aluminum foil. Let jelly stand at room temperature 24 hours. Place in refrigerator or, if jelly will not be used within 3 weeks, store in freezer.

6 or 7 eight-ounce glasses.

Note: To thaw frozen jelly, place in refrigerator several hours or let stand at room temperature.

QUICK JELLIES (ORANGE, TANGERINE OR GRAPE)

The flavor and color of fresh fruit—and from a can.

1 can (6 ounces) frozen orange, tangerine or grape juice concentrate, thawed	1 package (1¾ ounces) powdered fruit pectin 2 cups water 3¾ cups sugar

Prepare jelly glasses as directed on page 551. Stir juice, fruit pectin and water in saucepan until pectin is dissolved. Stirring constantly, cook over high heat about 2 minutes or until mixture comes to rolling boil. Add sugar; heat to rolling boil, stirring constantly. Remove from heat; immediately skim off foam. Fill glasses and seal and store as directed on page 555. (Or store covered in the refrigerator no longer than 2 months.)

4 eight-ounce glasses.

VARIATION

■ *Herb Jelly:* Wrap 2 tablespoons herbs tightly in cheesecloth (for orange juice, use marjoram leaves; for tangerine juice, use whole cloves; for grape juice, use tarragon leaves). Place in saucepan with 2 cups boiling water. Cover; let stand 10 minutes. To extract flavor, squeeze cheesecloth into water. Measure herb water and add enough water to measure 2 cups; substitute for the water in Quick Jellies recipe.

ORANGE-GRAPEFRUIT JELLY

A jelly recipe that knows no season because the fruit is a can of frozen orange-grapefruit concentrate. It tastes like an orange marmalade, looks like a golden jelly.

3¼ cups sugar
  1 cup water
  2 tablespoons whole allspice
  3 tablespoons lemon juice

½ bottle (6-ounce size) liquid pectin
1 can (6 ounces) frozen orange-grapefruit juice concentrate,* thawed

Prepare jelly glasses as directed on page 551. In large kettle, stir together sugar and water until sugar is dissolved. Tie allspice in double-thickness square of cheesecloth; place in sugar-water solution.

Heat to boiling, stirring constantly. Add lemon juice and boil 1 minute. Remove kettle from heat. Remove spice bag. Immediately stir in pectin and orange-grapefruit concentrate. Fill glasses and seal and store as directed on page 555.

3 or 4 eight-ounce glasses.

*½ cup (thawed) frozen orange juice concentrate and ¼ cup (thawed) frozen grapefruit juice concentrate can be substituted for the frozen orange-grapefruit concentrate.

QUICK PRESERVES (PEACH OR RASPBERRY)

With all the warm, rich goodness of the fresh fruit—to "put up" any time of the year.

2 packages (10 ounces each) frozen fruit (sliced peaches, raspberries, etc.), partially thawed

1 tablespoon lemon juice
2 tablespoons powdered fruit pectin
2 cups sugar

Prepare jelly glasses as directed on page 551. In covered saucepan, cook fruit and lemon juice over high heat 2 minutes. Stir in pectin; heat to rolling boil, stirring constantly. Boil and stir 1 minute. Add sugar; heat to rolling boil, stirring constantly. Boil and stir 1 minute.

Remove from heat; immediately skim off foam. Fill glasses and seal and store as directed on page 555. (Or store covered in the refrigerator no longer than 2 months.)

3 eight-ounce glasses.

Jams, Preserves, Conserves and Chutneys

To prepare jars: Examine tops and edges of standard jars to see that there are no nicks, cracks or sharp edges. Wash jars and lids in hot soapy water; rinse well. Place in pan with folded cloth or rack on bottom. Cover with hot, not boiling, water and heat to boiling. Boil gently 15 minutes; keep glasses in this water until ready for use. About 5 minutes before end of cooking period, remove sterilized jars from hot water and invert on folded clean towel to drain. Keep out of draft. The jars should be hot and dry when they're filled.

To fill jars: Using a ladle, fill one hot sterilized jar at a time to within ¼ inch of top; wipe top and screw-threads of jar with damp clean cloth and seal immediately as directed by manufacturer. Invert for a few seconds.

To cool and store: Place sealed jars upright a few inches apart on several thicknesses of cloth away from draft. When completely cool, test seal. Store in cool, dark place.

FRESH PEAR CHUTNEY

10 cups sliced pared pears (about 5 pounds)	3 cups vinegar
½ cup finely chopped green pepper	½ teaspoon salt
	½ teaspoon whole cloves
1½ cups raisins	½ teaspoon whole allspice
4 cups sugar	3 three-inch cinnamon sticks
1 cup cut-up crystallized ginger	

In large kettle, stir together pears, green pepper, raisins, sugar, ginger, vinegar and salt. Tie cloves, allspice and cinnamon sticks in double-thickness square of cheesecloth; place in kettle. Heat pear mixture to boiling, stirring frequently. Reduce heat. Stirring frequently, simmer 1½ to 2 hours or until chutney is dark and syrupy.

Thirty minutes before end of cooking period, prepare fruit jars as directed on page 555. Remove spice bag from chutney. Fill jars and cool and store as directed on page 555.

8 half-pints.

VARIATIONS

■ *Peach Chutney:* Substitute 10 cups sliced peeled peaches (about 5 pounds) for the pears.

■ *Plum Chutney:* Substitute 12 cups sliced unpeeled blue plums (about 5 pounds) for the pears.

PINEAPPLE CHUTNEY

2 cans (1 pound 4½ ounces each) crushed pineapple	4 cloves garlic, crushed
1 cup vinegar	¼ teaspoon cayenne red pepper
1 cup brown sugar (packed)	¼ teaspoon each cinnamon and cloves
2 cups raisins	⅓ cup chopped blanched almonds, if desired
1 tablespoon salt	
¼ cup cut-up crystallized ginger	

Prepare fruit jars as directed on page 555. In large kettle, stir together pineapple (with syrup) and remaining ingredients except almonds. Heat to boiling; reduce heat. Stirring frequently, cook over low heat 40 to 55 minutes or until chutney turns deep brown. Stir in almonds. Fill jars and cool and store as directed on page 555.

5 or 6 half-pints.

PINEAPPLE-RHUBARB JAM

1 pineapple	7 cups cut-up rhubarb
1 orange	7 cups sugar
1 lemon	

Remove top from pineapple. Cut pineapple into wedges and cut rind and eyes from wedges. Remove core. Cut unpeeled orange and lemon into quarters; discard seeds. Grind pineapple, orange and lemon in food chopper, using medium blade. Combine fruit and sugar. Cover; refrigerate at least 5 hours.

Prepare fruit jars as directed on page 555. Pour fruit mixture into large kettle; heat to boiling. Stirring frequently, boil gently over medium heat 25 minutes or until jam thickens. Fill jars and cool and store as directed on page 555.

8 half-pints.

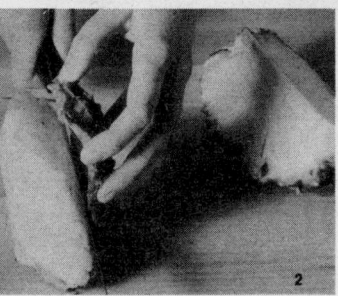

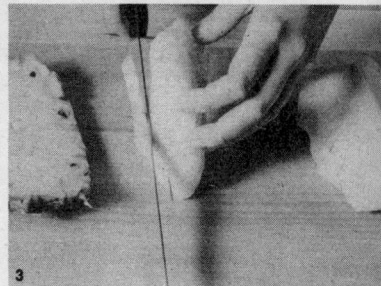

HOW TO CUT A PINEAPPLE

1. Twist out top; cut pineapple in half, then quarters.
2. Hold pineapple quarter securely; slice fruit from rind.
3. Cut off the pineapple core and remove any "eyes."
4. For chunks, slice quarter lengthwise, then crosswise.

PLUM CONSERVE

7 cups sliced unpeeled
  blue plums (about 3
  pounds)
4 cups sugar
3½ cups raisins
1 lemon, quartered and
  thinly sliced

1 orange, quartered and
  thinly sliced
1 cup coarsely chopped
  walnuts

Prepare fruit jars as directed above. In large kettle, stir together all ingredients except walnuts; heat to boiling. Stirring frequently, boil gently 20 to 25 minutes or until mixture thickens slightly. Stir in walnuts. Fill jars and cool and store as directed above. (Storage time for this conserve should not exceed 6 months.)

7 or 8 half-pints.

VARIATION

■ *Peach Conserve:* Substitute 7 cups sliced peeled peaches for the plums and add 2 tablespoons whole all-spice tied in cheesecloth to peach mixture before cooking. Remove spice bag at end of cooking period.

Quick-to-fix Relishes

Want an easy way to add new zest to yesterday's roast? Keep a few of these colorful and offbeat relishes around to liven up your meals.

PICKLED MUSHROOMS

1 envelope (0.63 ounce)
  Italian salad dressing mix
⅓ cup tarragon vinegar
2 tablespoons water
⅔ cup salad oil
1 tablespoon sugar
4 cloves garlic, crushed

6 drops red pepper sauce
1 medium onion, thinly
  sliced and separated into
  rings
2 cans (4 ounces each)
  button mushrooms,
  drained

Shake dressing mix, vinegar and water in tightly covered large jar. Add salad oil, sugar, garlic and red pepper sauce; cover and shake to mix. Add onion rings and mushrooms. Cover; refrigerate at least 8 hours. To serve, remove onion rings and mushrooms with slotted spoon.

2 cups.

FESTIVE CORN RELISH

Delicious with pork, veal, ham and chicken.

½ cup sugar
½ teaspoon salt
½ teaspoon celery seed
¼ teaspoon mustard seed
½ cup vinegar
¼ teaspoon red pepper sauce
1 can (12 ounces) whole kernel corn

2 tablespoons chopped green pepper
1 tablespoon instant minced onion
1 tablespoon chopped pimiento, if desired

Heat sugar, salt, celery seed, mustard seed, vinegar and red pepper sauce to boiling; boil 2 minutes. Remove from heat; stir in corn (with liquid) and remaining ingredients. Cool. Cover; refrigerate several days to blend flavors.

2 cups.

CARROT GARDEN RELISH

Garlic-pickled tiny carrots with rings of onion and bright green pepper.

2 cans (1 pound each) tiny whole carrots
2 medium green peppers, cut into thin rings
2 medium onions, thinly sliced and separated into rings
½ cup bottled garlic salad dressing

¼ cup sugar
¼ cup vinegar
¼ cup salad oil
1 teaspoon salt
½ teaspoon pepper
1 clove garlic, crushed

Combine carrots (with liquid), peppers and onion rings in covered container. Stir together remaining ingredients; pour over vegetables.

Cover; refrigerate at least 3 hours. Tip container occasionally to mix vegetables and dressing. To serve, remove vegetables with slotted spoon.

About 5 cups.

DILLED GREEN BEANS

Accompaniment for beef, pork and lamb.

1 can (1 pound) whole or cut green beans
1 medium onion, thinly sliced and separated into rings
¾ cup vinegar
½ cup salad oil
1 medium clove garlic, peeled and slivered

1 teaspoon sugar
1 teaspoon dill weed
½ teaspoon dry mustard
¼ teaspoon salt
¼ teaspoon cayenne red pepper

Drain beans, reserving liquid in measuring cup. Combine beans and onion rings. Add enough water to reserved bean liquid to measure 1 cup. Stir together liquid and remaining ingredients; pour over vegetables.

Cover; refrigerate at least 3 hours. Remove garlic slivers. To serve, remove vegetables with slotted spoon.

3 cups.

SUMMERTIME PICNIC RELISH

A nice accompaniment for sandwiches, hot dogs, hamburgers.

2 medium onions, finely chopped (about 1 cup)
1 cup finely chopped green pepper
2 tablespoons salad oil
4 medium tomatoes, peeled and chopped (about 3 cups)

2 tablespoons vinegar
1½ teaspoons salt
½ teaspoon sugar
¼ teaspoon dry mustard
⅛ teaspoon pepper

In large skillet, cook and stir onion and green pepper in oil over medium heat until onion is tender. Stir in remaining ingredients; heat to boiling. Cool. Cover; refrigerate several days.

3 cups.

GARLIC OLIVES

Especially good with roast beef.

1 can (8½ ounces) ripe
  olives, drained
1 jar (7 ounces) green olives,
  drained
½ cup vinegar

½ cup olive oil
½ cup salad oil
1 small onion, sliced
1 clove garlic, slivered

Split olives slightly; place in large jar with remaining ingredients. Cover tightly and shake. Refrigerate at least 2 hours. To serve, remove olives with slotted spoon.

3 cups.

PICKLED BEETS

Accompaniment for pork and veal.

2 cans (1 pound each)
  sliced beets
1½ cups sugar

¾ cup vinegar
2 three-inch cinnamon sticks

Drain beets, reserving liquid in small saucepan. Add sugar, vinegar and cinnamon sticks to reserved liquid. Heat to boiling, stirring constantly. Pour over beets; cool. Cover; refrigerate at least 8 hours. To serve, remove beets with slotted spoon.

About 3 cups.

GOURMET OLIVES AND TOMATOES

Accompaniment for roast beef and steak.

¾ cup salad oil
3 tablespoons vinegar
1 tablespoon lemon juice
3 cloves garlic, minced
10 peppercorns, crushed

1 can (1 pound) ripe olives,
  drained
1 carton (1 pint) cherry
  tomatoes

Shake oil, vinegar, lemon juice, garlic and peppercorns in tightly covered large jar. Add olives; cover and shake to coat olives evenly with liquid. Refrigerate at least 8 hours, tipping jar occasionally to distribute marinade.

About 5 hours before serving, wash tomatoes and

drain. Cut each in half; add to marinade in jar. To serve, remove vegetables with slotted spoon.

About 5 cups.

CRANBERRY SAUCE

Accompaniment for poultry and pork.

Wash 3 cups fresh cranberries; remove stems. Stir together 2 cups water and 2 cups sugar in saucepan. Heat to boiling; boil 5 minutes. Stir in cranberries. Heat to boiling; boil rapidly 5 minutes. Cool. Cover; refrigerate at least 8 hours.

4 cups.

CRANBERRY-ORANGE RELISH

Finely chop 4 cups cranberries and 1 large orange (peel and pulp) in food chopper. Stir in 2 cups sugar. Cover; refrigerate at least 3 hours.

3½ cups.

CRANBERRY-GINGER RELISH

Accompaniment for poultry, ham and veal.

1 can (1 pound) whole cranberry sauce	½ cup golden raisins
1 orange (pulp and peel), finely chopped	2 tablespoons finely chopped crystallized ginger

Stir together all ingredients. Cover; refrigerate at least 3 hours.

2 cups.

SPICED PEACHES

Accompaniment for ham, pork and chicken.

1 can (1 pound 13 ounces) peach halves, drained	3 three-inch cinnamon sticks
1½ cups honey	3 whole cloves
½ cup vinegar	

Place peach halves in 1-quart jar. Heat remaining ingredients to boiling; pour over peaches and cool. Cover; refrigerate at least 8 hours.

1 quart.

VARIATIONS

■ *Spiced Apricots:* Substitute 1 can (1 pound 14 ounces) apricot halves, drained, for the peach halves.

■ *Spiced Pears:* Substitute 1 can (1 pound 13 ounces) pear halves, drained, for the peach halves.

■ *Spiced Pineapple:* Substitute 1 can (1 pound 14 ounces) pineapple chunks, drained, for the peach halves.

MUSTARD-GLAZED FRUITS

¼ cup butter or margarine
½ cup brown sugar (packed)
3 tablespoons prepared mustard
1 can (1 pound) sliced peaches, drained
1 can (13½ ounces) pineapple chunks, drained
1 can (11 ounces) mandarin orange segments, drained
2 medium bananas, peeled and cut into 1-inch pieces
Nutmeg

Heat oven to 375°. Melt butter in medium saucepan; stir in sugar and mustard. Heat to boiling, stirring occasionally.

Remove from heat; stir in fruits. Pour into baking dish, 8x8x2 inches. Sprinkle lightly with nutmeg. Bake 20 minutes or until fruits are heated through. Serve warm.

4 cups.

Garnishes

Be sure to try these sprightly garnishes to zip up a sandwich, add color to potato salad or decorate an hors d'oeuvre tray. Circle a roast with fresh sprigs of watercress and Spiral Mushrooms broiled in butter. Turn a simple platter of sliced ham into a work of art by bordering it with Frosted Grapes.

And don't forget that many of the Quick-to-fix Relishes on pages 558 to 563 do double duty as colorful, tasty garnishes for main dishes.

CITRUS BLOSSOMS

Cut a thin slice from stem end of large lemon or lime. Holding cut end down, make slanted gashes in staggered fashion around side of fruit. Cut one short gash across top.

Thinly slice a smaller lemon or lime crosswise; cut slices in half. Using larger halved slices at the base of the flower and smaller ones at the top, insert peel side out in gashes.

LEMON OR LIME ROSES

Cut thin slice from stem end of lemon or lime. Starting just above cut end, cut around lemon in a continuous motion (without removing knife) to form a spiral of peel. Carefully curl the peel spiral to resemble a rose.

VEGETABLE DAISIES

Cut pared small turnip or rutabaga into thin slices; cut out circles with scalloped or round cutter. Make V-shaped notches around plain circles to form petals. Attach thin carrot shapes to center of each circle with wooden pick or dab of cream cheese.

SPIRAL MUSHROOMS

Remove stems and skin from large fresh mushrooms. On the rounded side of each cap, cut 5 curved slits from center to outer edge. Make a second set of cuts parallel to previous cuts; lift out small wedge of mushroom that remains between each cut.

PICKLE FANS

Use small sweet or dill pickles. Cut 4 lengthwise slits from one end of pickle almost to the other end. Spread gently to form an open fan.

FROSTED GRAPES

Dip small clusters of grapes into slightly beaten egg white, then into granulated or colored sugar. Dry on rack.

CARROT CURLS

Scrape carrots; with vegetable parer, cut lengthwise into paper-thin slices. Roll up and fasten with picks. Chill in bowl of ice and water. Remove picks before serving. If desired, draw sprig of parsley or watercress through each carrot curl, or place ripe olive in center.

CARROT STICKS

Scrape carrots; cut into narrow lengthwise strips. Chill in bowl of ice and water. If desired, dip ends of chilled carrot sticks into softened cream cheese; sprinkle with snipped parsley.

RADISH ROSES

Remove stem and root ends from large radishes. Cut thin petals around radishes; place in bowl of ice and water to open and crispen.

CELERY CURLS

Cut stalks of celery into short lengths. Slit both ends into narrow strips almost to center. To curl ends, chill in bowl of ice and water.

TOMATO BURSTS

Wash and remove stem from cherry tomato. Hollow out stem end slightly. Pipe about ½ teaspoon softened cream cheese into center. If desired, garnish cheese with a celery leaf or sprinkle with poppy seed or parsley flakes.

CHERRY TOMATO BLOSSOMS

Wash medium to large cherry tomato. Make 5 cuts at equal intervals into tomato, cutting from top almost to bottom. Cut five ⅛-inch slices of water chestnut.

Insert a water chestnut slice into each cut in tomato. Place tiny sprig of parsley in center of blossom. Arrange on parsley.

Sauces

The pride of a good cook—and the test of a good cook—is the smoothness, the subtle seasonings, the satisfying savor of her sauces and gravies. With these recipes even your most critical guest will be impressed!

WHITE SAUCE

THIN WHITE SAUCE

Like coffee cream—for vegetables and soup.

For each cup sauce:

1 tablespoon butter or margarine	¼ teaspoon salt
½ to 1 tablespoon flour*	⅛ teaspoon pepper
	1 cup milk

MEDIUM WHITE SAUCE

Like thick cream—for creamed and scalloped foods.

For each cup sauce:

2 tablespoons butter or margarine	¼ teaspoon salt
2 tablespoons flour	⅛ teaspoon pepper
	1 cup milk

THICK WHITE SAUCE

Like batter—for croquettes and soufflés.

For each cup sauce:

¼ cup butter or margarine	⅛ teaspoon pepper
¼ cup all purpose flour	1 cup milk
¼ teaspoon salt	

Melt butter in saucepan over low heat. Blend in flour, salt and pepper. Cook over low heat, stirring until mixture is smooth and bubbly. Remove from heat. Stir in milk. Heat to boiling, stirring constantly. Boil and stir 1 minute.

*Use smaller amount of flour with starchy vegetables (peas, potatoes), larger amount with non-starchy foods (cream of tomato soup).

1. Blend in flour until smooth.

2. Remove pan from heat; add milk.

3. Boil and stir White Sauce 1 minute.

VARIATIONS

■ *Cheese Sauce:* (For vegetables and rice, macaroni and egg dishes.) Prepare Medium White Sauce. Stir in ¼ teaspoon dry mustard and ½ cup shredded Cheddar cheese. Heat over low heat, stirring constantly, until cheese is melted and sauce is smooth.

■ *Cucumber Sauce:* (For salmon and other fish.) Prepare Medium White Sauce. Stir in ½ cup shredded or thinly sliced cucumber and dash cayenne red pepper; simmer 5 minutes, stirring occasionally.

■ *Curry Sauce:* (For chicken, lamb, shrimp and rice.) Follow recipe for Medium White Sauce except—stir in ½ teaspoon curry powder with the flour.

■ *Dill Sauce:* (For bland meat or fish.) Follow recipe for Medium White Sauce except—stir in 1 teaspoon minced fresh dill or ½ teaspoon dill weed and dash nutmeg wiht the flour.

■ *Egg Sauce:* (For salmon and other fish.) Prepare Medium White Sauce. Stir in 2 hard-cooked eggs, very finely chopped.

■ *Horseradish Sauce:* (For beef, lamb and ham.) Prepare Medium White Sauce. Stir in ⅓ cup horseradish and ¼ teaspoon dry mustard; heat through. Sprinkle with paprika before serving.

■ *Rich Cheese Sauce:* (For vegetables and rice, macaroni and egg dishes.) Prepare Medium White Sauce. Stir in 1 cup shredded Cheddar cheese, 1 teaspoon dry mustard, ½ teaspoon Worcestershire sauce and 1½ teaspoons cooking sherry. Heat over low heat, stirring constantly, until cheese is melted and sauce is smooth.

KETTLE GRAVY

For each cup gravy:

1 cup meat broth	2 tablespoons flour
¼ cup cold water	Salt and pepper

Place meat on warm platter; keep warm while preparing gravy. Skim excess fat from meat broth. (Store fat for future use in seasoning vegetables.) Measure broth; pour amount desired into pan.

Shake water and flour in covered jar. (For a smooth

mixture, it is important to put water in jar first, then the flour.) Stir flour mixture slowly into broth. Heat to boiling, stirring constantly. Boil and stir 1 minute. If desired, add few drops bottled brown bouquet sauce. Season with salt and pepper.

Note: The broth will have more flavor if meat is floured and browned slowly before simmering.

PAN GRAVY

For each cup gravy:

2 tablespoons drippings (fat and juices)
2 tablespoons flour

1 cup liquid* (meat juices, broth, water)
Salt and pepper

Place meat on warm platter; keep warm while preparing gravy. Pour drippings from pan into bowl, leaving brown particles in pan. Return 2 tablespoons drippings to pan. (Measure accurately as too little fat makes gravy lumpy.)

Blend in flour. (Measure accurately so gravy is not greasy.) Cook over low heat, stirring until mixture is smooth and bubbly. Remove from heat. Stir in liquid. Heat to boiling, stirring constantly. Boil and stir 1 minute. If desired, add few drops bottled brown bouquet sauce. Season with salt and pepper.

*Vegetable cooking water, consommé, tomato or vegetable juice can be used as part of gravy liquid.

VARIATIONS

■ *Creamy Gravy:* (For chicken, chops and veal.) Substitute milk for half the liquid.

■ *Mushroom Gravy:* (For beef, veal and chicken.) Before adding flour, cook and stir 1 cup washed, trimmed and sliced mushrooms in drippings until light brown. (Or one 2-ounce can mushroom stems and pieces can be used; drain and use mushroom liquid for part of the liquid in gravy.) Stir ½ teaspoon Worcestershire sauce into gravy.

■ *Thin Gravy:* Decrease drippings to 1 tablespoon and flour to 1 tablespoon.

PAN GRAVY

1. Measure the meat drippings exactly and return to pan.

2. Blend in exact amount of flour, scraping pan frequently.

3. Boil 1 minute, stirring constantly, until very smooth.

KETTLE GRAVY

1. Carefully skim the excess fat from the hot meat broth.

2. To ensure a smooth mixture, add the flour to the water.

3. Add flour-water slowly to broth, stirring constantly.

CLASSIC HOLLANDAISE SAUCE

2 egg yolks   ½ cup firm butter
3 tablespoons lemon juice

In small saucepan, stir egg yolks and lemon juice briskly with wooden spoon. Add half the butter; stir over very low heat until butter is melted.

Add remaining butter, stirring briskly until butter is melted and sauce thickens. (Be sure butter melts slowly as this gives eggs time to cook and thicken the sauce without curdling.) Serve hot or at room temperature.

1 cup.

Note: Leftover sauce can be stored covered in refrigerator for several days. Before serving, stir in small amount of hot water.

VARIATIONS

■ *Classic Béarnaise Sauce:* (For broiled meat and fish.) Stir in 1 tablespoon minced onion, 1 teaspoon tarragon leaves, ½ teaspoon chervil leaves and 2 tablespoons white wine or, if desired, 1 tablespoon white wine vinegar.

■ *Classic Mousseline Sauce:* (For fish, eggs, artichokes, broccoli, cauliflower and spinach.) Cool sauce to room temperature. Just before serving, beat ¼ cup chilled whipping cream in chilled bowl until stiff; fold into sauce. About 1½ cups.

BLENDER HOLLANDAISE SAUCE

3 egg yolks   2 drops red pepper sauce
1 tablespoon lemon juice   ½ cup butter, melted
½ teaspoon salt

In blender, mix all ingredients except butter. Slowly pour in butter while mixing on low speed. Refrigerate if not using immediately.

⅔ cup.

VARIATIONS

■ *Blender Béarnaise Sauce:* (For broiled meat and fish.) To sauce in blender, mix in 1 tablespoon minced onion, 1 teaspoon tarragon leaves, ½ teaspoon chervil leaves and 2 tablespoons white wine, or, if desired, 1 tablespoon white wine vinegar.

■ *Blender Mousseline Sauce:* (For fish, eggs, artichokes, broccoli, cauliflower and spinach.) Cool sauce to room temperature. Just before serving, beat ¼ cup chilled whipping cream in chilled bowl until stiff; fold into sauce. About 1¼ cups.

CREAMY HOLLANDAISE SAUCE

2 egg yolks
1 package (3 ounces) cream cheese, softened
2 tablespoons lemon juice
¼ teaspoon salt

In small saucepan, blend egg yolks, one at a time, into cream cheese, beating vigorously after each addition. Blend in lemon juice and salt. Cook over low heat, stirring vigorously, until sauce thickens.
⅔ cup.

VARIATIONS

■ *Creamy Béarnaise Sauce:* (For broiled meat and fish.) Stir in 1 tablespoon minced onion, 1 teaspoon tarragon leaves, ½ teaspoon chervil leaves and 2 tablespoons white wine or, if desired, 1 tablespoon white wine vinegar.

■ *Creamy Mousseline Sauce:* (For fish, eggs, artichokes, broccoli, cauliflower and spinach.) Cool sauce to room temperature. Just before serving, beat ¼ cup chilled whipping cream in chilled bowl until stiff; fold into sauce. About 1¼ cups.

BROWN SAUCE

2 tablespoons butter or margarine
1 thin slice onion
2 tablespoons flour
1 cup beef broth*
¼ teaspoon salt
⅛ teaspoon pepper

Heat butter in skillet over low heat until golden brown. Add onion; cook and stir until onion is tender. Discard onion.

Blend in flour. Cook over low heat, stirring until flour is deep brown. Remove from heat. Stir in broth. Heat to boiling, stirring constantly. Boil and stir 1 minute. Stir in salt and pepper.

1 cup.

Beef broth can be made by dissolving 1 beef bouillon cube in 1 cup boiling water, or use canned beef broth (bouillon).

VARIATIONS

■ *Bordelaise Sauce:* (For steaks, chops and hamburgers.) Substitute ½ cup red wine for ½ cup of the broth; stir in ½ teaspoon *each* snipped parsley, minced onion and crushed bay leaves and ¼ teaspoon thyme leaves with the broth and wine.

■ *Brown Devil Sauce:* (For steak.) Stir 1 teaspoon Worcestershire sauce, 1 teaspoon vinegar and 1 tablespoon snipped parsley into the sauce.

■ *Diable Sauce:* (For broiled chicken, roast or braised pork and pork chops.) Stir in 2 tablespoons chopped onion, 1 tablespoon snipped parsley, 1 tablespoon vinegar, ¼ teaspoon tarragon leaves, and ¼ teaspoon thyme leaves with the broth.

■ *Mushroom Sauce:* (For fish, meat and omelets.) Stir 1 cup washed, trimmed and sliced mushrooms or 1 can (3 ounces) sliced mushrooms, drained, into the melted butter. Brown slowly before adding flour. Stir in few drops Worcestershire sauce.

■ *Piquant Sauce:* (For tongue, beef, veal and fish.) Stir in ¼ cup white wine, 1 tablespoon *each* snipped parsley, chopped gherkins and minced onion and ½ teaspoon chervil leaves with the broth.

■ *Provençale Sauce:* (For meat, spaghetti, noodles and vegetables.) Gently stir 1 tomato, chopped, and 1 clove garlic, crushed, into the sauce.

CHERRY SAUCE

2 tablespoons cornstarch
½ cup sugar

1 can (1 pound) pitted red tart cherries

Blend cornstarch and sugar in saucepan. Stir in cherries (with liquid). Cook, stirring constantly, until mixture thickens and boils. Boil and stir 1 minute. If desired, stir in several drops red food color.

2 cups.

HOT CRANBERRY SAUCE

1 can (1 pound) whole cranberry sauce
1 teaspoon grated orange peel

½ teaspoon ginger
¼ teaspoon allspice

Combine all ingredients in saucepan. Heat, stirring

occasionally, until sauce is well blended. Serve warm.
About 1½ cups.

RAISIN SAUCE

3 tablespoons cornstarch	1 cup raisins
2 cups apple cider	
2 tablespoons butter or margarine	

Measure cornstarch into small saucepan. Gradually stir in apple cider. Add butter and raisins. Cook over medium heat, stirring constantly, until sauce thickens and boils. Boil and stir 1 minute. Serve warm.
About 2½ cups.

MUSTARD SAUCE

1 tablespoon butter or margarine	1 cup milk
1 tablespoon flour	3 tablespoons prepared mustard
½ teaspoon salt	1 tablespoon horseradish
¼ teaspoon pepper	

Melt butter in small saucepan over low heat. Blend in flour, salt and pepper. Cook over low heat, stirring constantly, until mixture is smooth and bubbly.

Remove from heat. Stir in milk. Heat to boiling, stirring constantly. Boil and stir 1 minute. Stir in mustard and horseradish; heat through. Serve warm.
About 1 cup.

GIBLET GRAVY

For chicken and turkey.

Cook gizzard, heart and neck of fowl in 4 cups salted water until tender, 1 to 2 hours. Add liver for the last 30 minutes. Remove meat from neck; finely chop giblets.

Follow recipe for Pan Gravy (page 569) except—substitute broth from giblets for the liquid. Stir giblets into gravy and heat through.

APRICOT-MINT SAUCE

For roast lamb.

2 jars (4¾ ounces each)
strained apricots (baby
food)

¼ cup mint-flavored apple
jelly
1 drop green food color

Mix thoroughly apricots, jelly and food color.
1 cup.

Note: If desired, use as a basting sauce. After lamb
roast has cooked 1 hour, baste with mixture of apricots
and jelly every 20 minutes during remaining cooking
period. Just before serving, stir food color into remaining
sauce.

TOMATO SAUCE

2 tablespoons chopped
onion
2 tablespoons chopped
green pepper
1 tablespoon butter or
margarine

1 can (8 ounces) tomato
sauce
¼ teaspoon salt
⅛ teaspoon pepper

Cook and stir onion and green pepper in butter until
onion is tender. Stir in tomato sauce. Season with salt
and pepper; heat through, stirring sauce occasionally.
1 cup.

TOMATO-MUSHROOM SAUCE

1 can (2 ounces) mushroom
stems and pieces,
drained, or ¼ pound
mushrooms, washed,
trimmed and sliced
1 tablespoon butter or
margarine

1 slice bacon, diced
1 tablespoon flour
1½ teaspoons sugar
⅛ teaspoon salt
1 cup tomato juice
2 tablespoons chopped
ripe olives

In medium skillet, cook and stir mushrooms in butter
until tender and brown; set aside. Fry bacon until crisp.
Stir in flour, sugar and salt. Cook over low heat, stirring
until mixture is bubbly. Remove from heat.

Stir in tomato juice. Heat to boiling, stirring constantly.
Boil and stir 1 minute. Stir in mushrooms and olives;
heat through.
1⅓ cups.

QUICK MUSHROOM SAUCE

1 can (3 ounces) sliced
   mushrooms, drained
   (reserve liquid)
2 tablespoons salad oil
2 tablespoons flour

1 beef bouillon cube or 1
   teaspoon instant beef
   bouillon
4 drops bottled brown
   bouquet sauce, if desired

In medium skillet, heat mushrooms in oil. Stir in flour. Cook over low heat, stirring until mixture is bubbly. Remove from heat.

Add enough water to reserved mushroom liquid to measure 1 cup; stir into mushroom mixture with bouillon cube. Heat to boiling, stirring constantly. Boil and stir 1 minute. Stir in brown bouquet sauce.

About 1⅓ cups.

EASY HORSERADISH SAUCE

For roast beef.

½ cup chilled whipping
   cream
3 tablespoons horseradish,
   well drained

½ teaspoon salt

In chilled bowl, beat whipping cream until stiff. Fold in horseradish and salt.

About 1 cup.

COCKTAIL SAUCE

For fish and seafood.

1 bottle (12 ounces) chili
   sauce
1 to 2 tablespoons
   horseradish
1 tablespoon lemon juice

½ teaspoon Worcestershire
   sauce
¼ teaspoon salt
   Dash pepper

Stir together all ingredients. Chill if desired.
About 1½ cups.

TARTAR SAUCE

1 cup mayonnaise
2 tablespoons finely
  chopped dill pickle
1 tablespoon snipped
  parsley

2 teaspoons chopped
  pimiento
1 teaspoon grated onion

Mix mayonnaise, pickle, parsley, pimiento and onion; refrigerate.
1 cup.

VELOUTE SAUCE

2 tablespoons butter or
  margarine
2 tablespoons flour
1 cup chicken,* veal or fish
  broth

¼ teaspoon salt
⅛ teaspoon pepper
⅛ teaspoon nutmeg

Melt butter in saucepan over low heat. Blend in flour. Cook over low heat, stirring until mixture is smooth and bubbly. Remove from heat. Stir in broth. Heat to boiling, stirring constantly. Boil and stir 1 minute. Stir in seasonings.
1 cup.

*Chicken broth can be made by dissolving 1 chicken bouillon cube in 1 cup boiling water, or use canned chicken broth.

VARIATIONS

■ *Almond Velouté Sauce:* (For leftover veal and chicken.) Just before serving, stir in ¼ cup toasted slivered almonds.

■ *Anchovy Velouté Sauce:* (For fish.) Stir 1½ teaspoons anchovy paste into butter-flour mixture and use fish broth; omit salt and stir in 1 tablespoon snipped parsley with the seasonings.

■ *Sauce Mornay:* (For meats, fish, eggs and vegetables.) Substitute ½ cup light cream (20%) for ½ cup of the broth. Stir in ⅛ teaspoon cayenne red pepper and ½ cup grated Parmesan or shredded Swiss cheese with the seasonings; heat through, stirring constantly, until cheese is melted.

■ *Hot Tartar Sauce:* (For fish and seafood.) After boiling and stirring sauce 1 minute, stir in ½ cup mayonnaise, 1 tablespoon *each* finely chopped sweet pickle, pimiento-stuffed olives, parsley and green pepper, 1 teaspoon minced onion and 1 teaspoon lemon juice. Heat through over low heat.

ENGLISH PARSLEY SAUCE

2 tablespoons flour	1 cup beef broth*
¼ teaspoon salt	2 tablespoons butter or
⅛ teaspoon pepper	margarine, melted
⅛ teaspoon nutmeg	¼ cup snipped parsley
2 egg yolks	

Mix flour, salt, pepper and nutmeg in small saucepan. Beat egg yolks and broth until blended; stir into flour mixture.

Heat to boiling, stirring constantly. Boil and stir 1 minute. Remove from heat; stir in butter and parsley.

1¼ cups.

Beef broth can be made by dissolving 1 beef bouillon cube in 1 cup boiling water, or use canned beef broth (bouillon).

VARIATION

■ *Normandy Sauce:* (For fish.) Substitute fish broth for the beef broth; omit parsley and stir in 1 tablespoon lemon juice and dash cayenne red pepper with the butter.

ALLEMANDE OR PARISIENNE SAUCE

2 tablespoons flour	2 tablespoons butter or
¼ teaspoon salt	margarine, melted
⅛ teaspoon pepper	2 tablespoons light cream
⅛ teaspoon nutmeg	(20%)
1 egg yolk	1 teaspoon lemon juice
1 cup chicken,* veal or fish broth	

Mix flour, salt, pepper and nutmeg in small saucepan. Beat egg yolk and broth until blended; stir into flour mixture.

Heat to boiling, stirring constantly. Boil and stir 1 minute. Remove from heat; stir in butter, cream and lemon juice.

1 cup.

Chicken broth can be made by dissolving 1 chicken bouillon cube in 1 cup boiling water, or use canned chicken broth.

QUICK VEGETABLE SAUCES

In chilled bowl, beat ½ cup chilled whipping cream.*
Fold in ½ cup mayonnaise and one of the following—

For asparagus, broccoli or Brussels sprouts: ¼ cup
capers.

For beets or carrots: 3 to 4 tablespoons horseradish.

For cauliflower: 2 tablespoons prepared mustard and
¼ teaspoon dill weed.

For corn or lima beans: ¼ cup chili sauce.

For green beans: ¼ cup well-drained pickle relish.

For green beans, peas or onions: ¼ cup toasted slivered almonds, salted pecans or cashews.

For tomatoes: ¼ cup well-drained finely chopped
cucumber.

½ cup dairy sour cream can be substituted for the whipping cream.

QUICK GLORIFIED BUTTERS

For vegetables and fish.

Melt ¼ cup butter or margarine and mix with one of the
following—

Almonds: 1 tablespoon chopped toasted almonds.

Capers: 1 tablespoon minced capers.

Celery Seed: 1 teaspoon celery seed.

Cheese: 2 tablespoons grated Parmesan cheese.

Chive-Parsley: 1 tablespoon snipped chives, 1 tablespoon snipped parsley and ½ teaspoon salt.

Curry: ¼ teaspoon curry powder.

Garlic: ¼ teaspoon garlic powder.

Horseradish: 1 tablespoon horseradish.

Lemon: 1 teaspoon grated lemon peel and 2 tablespoons lemon juice.

Lemon-Chive: 1 teaspoon grated lemon peel, 2 tablespoons lemon juice and 1 tablespoon snipped chives.

Mustard: ¼ teaspoon dry or prepared mustard, 1 teaspoon lemon juice, dash each sugar and salt.

Olive: 1 tablespoon finely chopped pitted ripe or
green olives and few drops lemon juice.

Poppy Seed: 1 teaspoon poppy seed, 2 tablespoons
lemon juice and dash cayenne red pepper.

BUTTER SAUCES

Drawn Butter: In small saucepan or skillet, heat butter or margarine over low heat until melted.

Browned Butter (Beurre Noisette): In small saucepan or skillet, heat butter or margarine until light brown.

Black Butter (Beurre Noir): In small saucepan or skillet, heat ⅓ cup butter or margarine until golden brown. Stir in 1 tablespoon vinegar or lemon juice; heat until bubbly. Add dash each salt and pepper. Serve immediately.

Maître d'Hôtel Butter: Blend 3 tablespoons soft butter or margarine, 1 tablespoon lemon juice, 1 tablespoon snipped parsley, ½ teaspoon salt and ⅛ teaspoon pepper.

FLAVOR PLUS

Put new fun in your cooking, indoors and out. Try the following sauces, for instance. They're great companions for the barbecue grill (see pages 749–753), but they can be just as exciting as brush-ons when you broil indoors.

They're not marinades, so they won't tenderize. What they will do, however, is add great flavor to meat, poultry or fish. But, remember if you're using them outdoors, baste sparingly—drippings can cause unwanted flare-ups.

RANCHO-RED SAUCE

Melt 1 jar (10 ounces) red currant jelly in small saucepan over low heat, stirring constantly. Blend in 2 tablespoons Worcestershire sauce. Baste meat during last 20 minutes of cooking period. Serve remaining sauce hot. 1 cup.

SAUCE O' GOLD

For lamb chops, pork chops and ham.

½ cup prepared mustard
½ cup honey
1 teaspoon salt

½ teaspoon rosemary leaves
¼ teaspoon pepper

Mix all ingredients. Baste meat during last half of cooking period. Just before serving, top meat with remaining sauce.

1 cup.

NEW ORLEANS TOMATO SAUCE

For basting spareribs, beef and lamb.

1 can (15 ounces) tomato sauce
1 envelope (7/10 ounce) onion salad dressing mix

¼ cup vinegar
¼ cup light molasses
2 tablespoons salad oil
1 teaspoon dry mustard

Combine all ingredients in small saucepan. Heat 3 minutes, stirring constantly. Baste meat during last half of cooking period.

2 cups.

LEMON SAUCE

For basting chicken and fish.

½ cup butter or margarine
½ clove garlic, crushed
2 teaspoons flour
⅓ cup water
3 tablespoons lemon juice
1½ teaspoons sugar

1 teaspoon salt
⅛ teaspoon pepper
⅛ teaspoon poultry seasoning
⅛ teaspoon red pepper sauce

Heat butter and garlic in small saucepan over low heat, stirring constantly, until butter is melted. Blend in flour. Cook over low heat, stirring until mixture is bubbly. Remove from heat. Stir in remaining ingredients. Heat to boiling, stirring constantly. Baste chicken or fish during cooking period.

1 cup.

Salads

Simple, classic salads! Slimming, health-brimming salads! Crisp, cool salads! Bright, sparkling salads! Taste-tempting salads! A salad can brighten a meal, enliven a meal, be a meal. Give equal attention to the dressing for your salad—and make your own. We have a special collection here. They're quick and easy, with unbeatable flavor. Every one is well worth the extra few minutes. You'll find your skill with a salad makes its own contribution to the quality of life in your house.

Green Salads

Know Your Greens: That's the beginning of a good salad. Not just lettuce, but leaves of crisp spinach, bright accents like dandelion, beet or mustard tops, watercress. The dark with the light, the crisp with the tender. Always buy crisp, fresh greens.

Handle Greens with Care: Just pull off the outer leaves of head lettuce. (And not too many if they're undamaged.) Wash greens only as you need them. Drain thoroughly and store in a plastic bag in the refrigerator.

Preparing to Serve: When ready to serve, select only the choice part of greens, discarding stems and cores. Tear greens; do not cut except when shredding or wedges are called for. Belgian endive may be stripped off as whole leaves or cut in slices which will come apart onion-fashion.

Make sure your greens are cold and dry. Vary your dressings, using the recipes on pages 586 and 622 to 629. Pour dressing over the salad at the last minute; use just enough to coat the leaves lightly. Toss gently but well.

Boston lettuce

Romaine

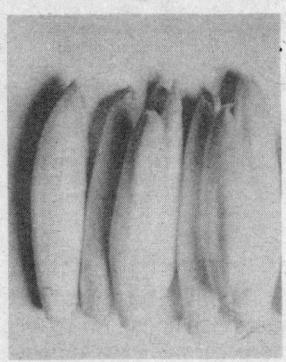

Belgian endive

Curly endive

Bronze lettuce

Escarole

TOSSED SALAD CHART
(for 6 to 8 servings)

Basic Greens	Add Salad Sparkers	
Choose one or more to total 12 cups	*Choose one or more to total 1½ cups.*	
Iceberg lettuce	Fresh vegetables:	Cooked vegetables:
Boston lettuce	Carrots, thinly	Artichoke hearts
Bibb lettuce	sliced	or bottoms,
Bronze lettuce	Cauliflowerets	plain or
Leaf lettuce	Cucumbers, sliced	marinated
Romaine	or diced	Dilled green beans
Escarole	Green peppers,	Green peas, beans
Spinach	diced or sliced	or sliced carrots,
Watercress	Mushrooms, sliced	marinated
Endive (French	Onions, sliced or	
or Belgian)	diced	Meat and fish:
Curly endive	Radishes, sliced	Ham, tongue, cold
	Tomatoes,	cuts, cut into
	quartered	julienne strips
	Zucchini, sliced	or cubes
		Shrimp, crabmeat
	Fruit:	or lobster, cut up
	Apples, cut into	
	wedges or sliced	Cheese:
	Avocados, sliced	Swiss or Cheddar
	Orange sections	cut into julienne
		strips or cubes

Arranging the Salad: Salads should be arranged attractively but simply. On some occasions, however, you might want a salad with more formal eye appeal. Try centering the bowl with a Tomato Flower (page 597) radiating avocado leaves. Circle the bowl with a hedge of watercress.

CAESAR SALAD

Make a show of this one! Arrange pre-measured ingredients on a tray and ask the man-of-the-house to toss the salad at the table.

1 clove garlic, halved
⅓ cup olive oil
8 anchovy fillets, cut up
1 teaspoon Worcestershire sauce
½ teaspoon salt
¼ teaspoon dry mustard
Freshly ground pepper

1 large or 2 small bunches romaine, washed and chilled
Coddled Egg (right)
1 lemon
Garlic Croutons (page 588)
⅓ cup grated Parmesan cheese

Toss with	Garnish with
Shake to mix.	Choose one or two to total ⅓ to ½ cup.
¼ cup salad oil, olive oil or combination	French fried onion rings
	Croutons
2 tablespoons cider, wine or tarragon vinegar	Bacon, crisply fried, crumbled
	Hard-cooked eggs, sliced
¾ teaspoon salt	Salted nuts
⅛ to ¼ teaspoon pepper	Blue cheese, crumbled
1 small clove garlic, crushed	

Just before serving, rub large salad bowl with cut clove of garlic. If desired, allow a few small pieces of garlic to remain in bowl. Add oil, anchovies, Worcestershire sauce, salt, mustard and pepper; mix thoroughly.

Into salad bowl, tear romaine into bite-size pieces (about 12 cups). Toss until leaves glisten. Break egg onto romaine; squeeze juice from lemon over romaine. Toss until leaves are well coated. Sprinkle croutons and cheese over salad; toss.

6 servings.

CODDLED EGG

Place cold egg in warm water. Heat to boiling enough water to completely cover egg. With a spoon, immerse egg into boiling water. Remove pan from heat. Cover and let stand 30 seconds. Immediately cool egg in cold water.

GARLIC CROUTONS

Heat oven to 400°. Trim crusts from 4 slices white bread. Generously butter both sides of bread slices; sprinkle with ¼ teaspoon garlic powder. Cut into ½-inch cubes; place in baking pan. Bake 10 to 15 minutes, stirring occasionally, until golden brown and crisp.

FLORENTINE SALAD

1½ pounds spinach	Dash pepper
1 clove garlic, slivered	3 hard-cooked eggs,
¾ cup salad oil	chopped
½ cup red wine vinegar	4 slices bacon, crisply fried
½ teaspoon salt	and crumbled

Wash spinach; remove stems and tear leaves into bite-size pieces. Dry; chill 2 hours. Let garlic stand in oil 1 hour; remove garlic.

Just before serving, mix oil, vinegar, salt and pepper in large salad bowl. Add spinach and toss with dressing until leaves are well coated. Sprinkle with chopped eggs and crumbled bacon; toss.

10 servings.

VARIATION

■ *Hot Florentine Salad:* Heat oil, vinegar, salt and pepper in small chafing dish or saucepan over low heat, stirring constantly. Toss hot dressing with spinach until leaves are well coated. Toss with chopped eggs and bacon. Serve immediately.

WILTED LETTUCE SALAD

Wilted lettuce won't wait. Serve immediately to enjoy its peak flavor.

2 bunches leaf lettuce, washed	⅓ cup chopped green onions
	¼ teaspoon salt
4 slices bacon, diced	⅛ teaspoon pepper
¼ cup vinegar	2 teaspoons sugar

Just before serving, shred lettuce with knife (about 4 cups). In large skillet, fry bacon until crisp. Add vinegar; heat through. Remove skillet from heat; add lettuce and onion. Season with salt, pepper and sugar; toss 1 to 2 minutes until lettuce is wilted.

4 servings.

■ *Dill Wilted Lettuce:* Stir ½ teaspoon dill weed and ½ teaspoon dry mustard into vinegar while heating.

Vegetable Salads

Vegetables—crunchy and raw or cooked just-to-crispness—how good they are in salads, and how rarely seen. It's a wonderful way to use leftovers, too. Try one for a deliciously light supper.

CREAMY SWISS SALAD

4 cups bite-size pieces salad greens, chilled
1 cup shredded Swiss cheese
¼ cup sliced pimiento-stuffed olives
2 hard-cooked eggs, chopped
½ cup mayonnaise or salad dressing
2 tablespoons light cream
1 teaspoon dry mustard
½ teaspoon salt
¼ teaspoon pepper

Combine salad greens, cheese, olives and eggs in large salad bowl. Blend mayonnaise, cream, mustard, salt and pepper; pour over greens and toss. If desired, garnish with tomato wedges.

6 to 8 servings.

BRUSSELS SPROUTS SALAD

2 packages (10 ounces each) frozen Brussels sprouts
¼ cup vinegar
¼ cup salad oil
1½ teaspoons chervil leaves
1 teaspoon salt
¼ teaspoon pepper
1 tomato
Snipped parsley

Cook Brussels sprouts as directed on package; drain. Shake vinegar, oil, chervil, salt and pepper in tightly covered jar. Pour dressing over hot Brussels sprouts, turning each until well coated. Cover; refrigerate at least 3 hours.

Just before serving, cut tomato into wedges; toss with Brussels sprouts. Sprinkle with parsley.

6 servings.

BACON-AND-EGG BEAN SALAD

2 cans (1 pound each) whole green beans, drained
1 medium onion, chopped (about ½ cup)
⅓ cup salad oil
¼ cup vinegar
½ teaspoon salt
¼ teaspoon pepper
4 hard-cooked eggs, chopped
¼ cup mayonnaise or salad dressing
1 teaspoon prepared mustard
2 teaspoons vinegar
¼ teaspoon salt
4 slices bacon, crisply fried and crumbled
Crisp lettuce

Combine beans, onion, oil, ¼ cup vinegar, ½ teaspoon salt and the pepper; toss. Cover and chill. Mix eggs, mayonnaise, mustard, 2 teaspoons vinegar and ¼ teaspoon salt. Cover and chill.

Just before serving, drain bean mixture thoroughly; toss with bacon. Serve on lettuce; top with a spoonful of egg-mayonnaise mixture. If desired, sprinkle with paprika.

6 servings.

ZUCCHINI TOSS

1 head lettuce, washed and chilled
1 small bunch romaine, washed and chilled
¼ cup olive oil or salad oil
2 medium zucchini, thinly sliced
1 cup sliced radishes
3 green onions, sliced
3 tablespoons crumbled blue cheese, if desired
2 tablespoons tarragon or wine vinegar
¾ teaspoon salt
1 small clove garlic, crushed
¼ teaspoon monosodium glutamate
Generous dash freshly ground pepper

Into large salad bowl, tear greens into bite-size pieces (about 10 cups). Toss with oil until leaves glisten. Add zucchini, radishes, onions and cheese. Combine vinegar, salt, garlic, monosodium glutamate and pepper; pour over salad mixture and toss.

6 to 8 servings.

MEDITERRANEAN SALAD BOWL

1 small eggplant (about 1 pound)
½ cup dairy sour cream
1 tablespoon lemon juice
1 tablespoon snipped parsley
½ teaspoon salt
½ teaspoon dill weed
¼ teaspoon coarsely ground pepper
1 small clove garlic, crushed
1 cup croutons
2 tablespoons butter, melted
4 cups bite-size pieces salad greens, chilled
Pitted ripe olives

Pare and cube eggplant; cook covered in 1 inch boiling salted water (½ teaspoon salt to 1 cup water) about 5 minutes or until just tender. Drain well; cover and chill.

Mix sour cream, lemon juice, parsley, salt, dill weed, pepper and garlic; cover and chill. Toss croutons in melted butter.

Just before serving, toss greens, eggplant, sour cream mixture and croutons. Garnish with olives.

5 to 6 servings.

THREE-BEAN SALAD

Marvelous make-ahead salad; so popular for picnics and barbecues.

1 can (1 pound) French-style green beans, drained
1 can (1 pound) wax beans, drained
1 can (1 pound) red kidney beans, drained
½ cup chopped green onions
¼ cup snipped parsley
1 bottle (8 ounces) Italian salad dressing
1 tablespoon sugar
2 cloves garlic, crushed
Crisp lettuce

Combine beans, onions and parsley in large bowl. Combine dressing, sugar and garlic; pour over bean mixture and toss. Cover; refrigerate at least 3 hours, stirring occasionally.

Just before serving, remove bean mixture with slotted spoon to lettuce-lined salad bowl.

5 or 6 servings.

VEGETABLE ANTIPASTO PLATTER

1 can (15 ounces) garbanzo beans
1 bottle (8 ounces) Italian salad dressing
4 Deviled Eggs (page 322)
1 can (8 ounces) pitted ripe olives, chilled
1 can (1 pound) tiny whole beets, chilled

1 can (11 ounces) hot green cherry peppers, chilled
2 jars (6 ounces each) marinated artichoke hearts, chilled
Celery sticks
1 can (2 ounces) anchovy fillets

Drain beans; place in glass or plastic jar. Pour salad dressing over beans. Cover; refrigerate at least 8 hours, stirring occasionally. Prepare Deviled Eggs; chill.

Just before serving, drain beans, olives, beets, peppers and artichoke hearts. Cut each beet in half. Arrange vegetables and eggs in separate sections on platter. Place anchovy fillets on eggs.

8 servings.

TOMATOES VINAIGRETTE

Marinate cooked vegetables (green beans, carrots, potatoes, Brussels sprouts) or raw cucumber slices in the same dressing for a surprise side dish.

8 to 12 thick tomato slices or peeled small tomatoes
1 cup olive oil or salad oil
⅓ cup wine vinegar
2 teaspoons oregano leaves
1 teaspoon salt

½ teaspoon pepper
½ teaspoon dry mustard
2 cloves garlic, crushed
Crisp lettuce
Minced green onion
Snipped parsley

If using small tomatoes, cut off stem ends. Arrange tomatoes in baking dish, 8x8x2 inches. In tightly covered jar, shake oil, vinegar, oregano, salt, pepper, mustard and garlic; pour over tomatoes. Cover; chill 2 to 3 hours, spooning dressing over tomatoes occasionally.

Just before serving, arrange tomatoes on lettuce. Sprinkle tomatoes with onion and parsley; drizzle some of the dressing over top.

6 to 8 servings.

VINAIGRETTE VEGETABLE PLATE

1 pound whole green beans or 2 bunches asparagus
1 cauliflower, separated into flowerets
1 jar (7 ounces) artichoke hearts, drained
¼ cup wine vinegar

2 tablespoons water
½ of 1 envelope (1⅞ ounces) Italian salad-dressing mix
½ of 1 envelope (1⅞ ounces) onion salad-dressing mix
⅔ cup salad oil

In separate saucepans, cook beans and cauliflower in 1 inch boiling salted water (½ teaspoon salt to 1 cup water) until just tender; drain. Arrange cooked vegetables and drained artichoke hearts in separate sections in shallow glass dish.

Shake vinegar, water and salad dressing mixes in tightly covered jar. Add oil; shake until mixed. Pour dressing over vegetables. Cover; refrigerate at least 2 hours, spooning dressing over vegetables occasionally. To serve, remove vegetables with slotted spoon.

4 servings.

COLESLAW

4 cups finely shredded or chopped cabbage (about ½ medium head)
¼ cup chopped onion
½ cup dairy sour cream

¼ cup mayonnaise or salad dressing
½ teaspoon seasoned salt
½ teaspoon dry mustard
Dash pepper

Combine cabbage and onion in large salad bowl. Blend remaining ingredients; pour over cabbage and toss. If desired, sprinkle with paprika.

6 to 8 servings.

VARIATIONS

■ *Apple 'n Cheese Slaw:* Omit onion, dry mustard and pepper. Combine 2 cups diced unpared tart apples and

½ cup crumbled blue cheese with the shredded cabbage.

■ *Herbed Slaw:* Omit mustard and pepper and add 1 teaspoon celery seed and ½ teaspoon chervil.

■ *Pineapple-Marshmallow Slaw:* Omit onion and add 1 can (13½ ounces) pineapple tidbits, drained, 1 cup miniature marshmallows and 1 tablespoon lemon juice.

■ *Red Cabbage Slaw:* Substitute 2 cups shredded red cabbage for half the cabbage.

VEGETABLE SALAD VARIETY

Combinations for taste, color—or just for a change. Serve on crisp salad greens, top with a tangy dressing (pages 622 to 629).

■ Cooked green peas, cooked French-style green beans, chopped green pepper, onion and celery; marinate in oil-and-vinegar dressing overnight and garnish with pimiento.

■ Shredded carrots and drained crushed pineapple or finely chopped celery; mix with raisins.

■ Sliced zucchini and cauliflowerets or thinly sliced radishes; toss with greens.

■ Tomato wedges, cucumber slices and cauliflowerets; marinate in French dressing and serve in lettuce cups.

■ Cooked baby lima beans, sliced mushrooms and sliced green onions; season with oregano.

■ Overlapping slices of tomato, unpared cucumber slices and onion rings or slices.

■ Shredded parsnips, chopped sweet onion, chopped celery and tiny pimiento-stuffed olives; toss with greens.

■ Small tomatoes stuffed with cottage cheese or cabbage salad; sprinkle with snipped chives, parsley or toasted almonds.

■ Mound of cottage cheese with diced green or red pepper, cucumber and onions.

■ Asparagus tips on thick tomato slices; sprinkle with shredded cheese.

■ Shredded carrots and diced celery; mix with raisins or nuts.

■ Chilled tomato halves; sprinkle with snipped parsley, chives or green onions.

■ Shredded carrots, chopped sweet onion, chopped celery, grated orange peel and orange sections.

OLD-FASHIONED CABBAGE SALAD

A crisp do-ahead slaw, dressed with oil and vinegar

1 teaspoon salt
¼ teaspoon pepper
½ teaspoon dry mustard
½ teaspoon celery seed
2 tablespoons sugar
¼ cup chopped green pepper
1 tablespoon chopped pimiento

1 teaspoon instant minced onion
3 tablespoons salad oil
⅓ cup white vinegar
4 cups finely shredded or chopped cabbage (about ½ medium head)

In large bowl, place all ingredients in order listed; mix well. Cover; refrigerate at least 3 hours. Just before serving, drain cabbage. If desired, garnish with watercress and sliced pimiento-stuffed olives.

6 servings.

DILLY CUCUMBER SALAD

8 cups thinly sliced pared cucumbers (about 4 medium)
1½ cups dairy sour cream
1 small clove garlic, crushed

2 tablespoons salad oil
2 teaspoons sugar
1 teaspoon salt
1 teaspoon white wine vinegar
½ teaspoon dill weed

Place cucumbers in large bowl. Mix remaining ingredients except dill weed; pour over cucumbers and mix gently. Sprinkle with dill weed. Cover; refrigerate at least 1 hour. Mix lightly before serving. If desired, sprinkle with snipped parsley.

8 to 10 servings.

COOK CUCUMBERS?

Why not? They're much like zucchini in flavor. Cut pared cucumbers into ¼-inch diagonal slices; cook covered in 1 inch boiling salted water about 5 minutes or until just tender. Drain. Stir in a dab of soft butter or margarine and season to taste with salt and pepper.

OLD-FASHIONED CUCUMBER SALAD

Make this in the morning to serve for dinner—or the night before a big picnic.

2 to 3 medium cucumbers	2 tablespoons sugar
1 tablespoon salt	¼ teaspoon pepper
¾ cup white vinegar	

Wash cucumbers. Pat dry and score with tines of fork. Cut cucumbers into transparent, paper-thin slices to measure 4 cups.

Place cucumber slices in deep bowl; sprinkle every few layers with salt. Cover cucumbers with a plate and weight them down with a heavy object (a can of fruit or coffee). Let stand at room temperature 2 hours.

Drain cucumbers thoroughly and press out remaining liquid. Stir together vinegar, sugar and pepper; pour over slices. Cover; refrigerate at least 4 hours. Drain cucumbers before serving.

4 to 6 servings.

POTATO SALAD

2 pounds potatoes (about 6 medium)	¼ cup Italian salad dressing
¼ cup finely chopped onion	½ cup mayonnaise or salad dressing
1 teaspoon salt	½ cup chopped celery
⅛ teaspoon pepper	2 hard-cooked eggs, cut up

Wash potatoes. Heat 1 inch salted water (½ teaspoon salt to 1 cup water) to boiling. Add unpared potatoes. Cover tightly; heat to boiling and cook 30 to 35 minutes or until tender. Drain; cool and peel. Cut potatoes into cubes; combine in bowl with onion. Sprinkle with salt and pepper; mix with Italian salad dressing. Cover; refrigerate at least 2 hours.

Just before serving, add mayonnaise; toss until potatoes are well coated. Stir in celery and eggs.

4 to 6 servings.

SHORTCUT POTATO SALAD IN TOMATO FLOWERS

1 package (5.5 ounces)
  scalloped potatoes
3 cups water
2 tablespoons salad oil
½ cup water
2 tablespoons white wine
  tarragon vinegar

¼ cup mayonnaise or salad
  dressing
1 teaspoon prepared
  mustard
½ cup chopped celery
2 hard-cooked eggs, cut up
  Tomato Flowers (below)

Empty potatoes into saucepan. Add 3 cups water; heat to boiling. Reduce heat and simmer about 15 minutes or until tender. Rinse potatoes with cold water; drain thoroughly. Place in bowl; cover and chill.

Blend seasoned sauce mix and oil in small saucepan; stir in ½ cup water and the vinegar. Heat to boiling over medium heat, stirring constantly. Cover and chill.

Just before serving, blend mayonnaise and mustard into sauce. Pour over potatoes with celery and eggs; stir gently. Spoon into Tomato Flowers.

4 servings.

TOMATO FLOWERS

Cut off stem ends of 4 chilled medium tomatoes. With cut side down, cut each tomato into sixths, cutting through to within 1 inch of bottom. Carefully spread out sections, forming a "flower." Sprinkle inside of each tomato with salt.

For tomato "flowers," cut crosswise, then diagonally.

HOT GERMAN POTATO SALAD

3 pounds potatoes (about 9 medium)
6 slices bacon
¼ cup chopped onion
2 tablespoons flour
2 tablespoons sugar

2 teaspoons salt
½ teaspoon celery seed
Dash pepper
¾ cup water
⅓ cup vinegar

Wash potatoes; pare thinly and remove eyes. Heat 1 inch salted water (½ teaspoon salt to 1 cup water) to boiling. Add potatoes. Cover tightly; heat to boiling and cook 30 to 35 minutes or until tender. Drain; set aside.

In large skillet, fry bacon until crisp; remove and drain. Cook and stir onion in bacon drippings until tender and golden brown. Stir in flour, sugar, salt, celery seed and pepper. Cook over low heat, stirring until bubbly. Remove from heat; stir in water and vinegar. Heat to boiling, stirring constantly. Boil and stir 1 minute.

Crumble bacon. Thinly slice potatoes. Carefully stir bacon and potatoes into hot mixture. Heat through, stirring lightly to coat potato slices.

5 or 6 servings.

Fruit Salads

What does a fruit salad bring to your table? Color! Texture! Sweetness! Juiciness! Summer into winter! A year-round parade of the riches of the orchards and gardens of the world.

Try one as a first course, California style; try one as dessert, with a thoughtful eye to the waistline. Try one!

PAPAYA SALAD

A papaya is a sweet subtropical fruit, sometimes known as melon-tree fruit.

Cut 2 large ripe papayas in half lengthwise; remove seeds. Pare and cut into slices; arrange on lettuce leaves. Serve with lime wedges or Limeade Dressing (page 629).

4 servings.

SPINACH-APPLE TOSS

1 pound spinach
2 tart red apples
8 slices bacon, crisply fried
  and crumbled

⅔ cup mayonnaise or salad
  dressing
⅓ cup frozen orange juice
  concentrate (thawed)

Wash spinach; remove stems and tear leaves into bite-size pieces; dry and chill. Just before serving, quarter, core and slice unpared apples into large salad bowl. Add spinach and bacon; toss. Mix mayonnaise and orange juice concentrate; serve separately to spoon over salad.
  8 servings.

WALDORF SALAD

2 cups diced unpared apple
  (about 2 medium)
1 cup diced celery
⅓ cup coarsely chopped
  nuts

½ cup mayonnaise or salad
  dressing

Combine apple, celery, nuts and mayonnaise; toss. If desired, mound salad in lettuce cups and garnish with maraschino cherries.
  4 to 6 servings.

SUMMER FRUIT BOWL

3 medium bananas
4 medium oranges, pared
  and sectioned (3 cups)
1 cup strawberries, halved

1 cup seedless green
  grapes, halved
Sour Cream-Honey
Dressing (below)

Peel bananas; slice into bowl. Cover completely with other fruit. Cover bowl and chill. Just before serving, pour dressing over fruit; toss until fruit is well coated.
  10 servings.

SOUR CREAM-HONEY DRESSING

Blend ½ cup dairy sour cream, 1 tablespoon honey and 1 tablespoon orange juice.

WINTER FRUIT BOWL

1 can (1 pound) pitted dark
   sweet cherries
1 can (13½ ounces)
   pineapple tidbits
1 can (11 ounces) mandarin
   orange segments

1 can (8¾ ounces) seedless
   green grapes
1 tart apple
   Sour Cream-Honey
   Dressing (page 599)

Have all fruit chilled. Just before serving, drain canned fruit thoroughly; place in large bowl. Cut unpared apple into quarters; core and cut into thin wedges; add to fruit in bowl. Pour dressing over fruit; toss until fruit is well coated.

7 or 8 servings.

ORANGE BOWL WITH CHEESE DRESSING

Blue Cheese-Lemon
   Dressing (below)
1 clove garlic, halved
1 head lettuce, washed and
   chilled
1 small bunch endive,
   romaine or chicory,
   washed and chilled

4 medium oranges
¼ teaspoon salt
   Freshly ground pepper

Prepare Blue Cheese-Lemon Dressing. Just before serving, rub large salad bowl with cut clove of garlic. Into bowl, tear salad greens into bite-size pieces (about 12 cups). Pare and section oranges (about 3 cups); add to greens. Season with salt and pepper; toss with dressing.

8 to 10 servings.

BLUE CHEESE-LEMON DRESSING

¼ cup crumbled blue cheese
¼ cup salad oil
¼ teaspoon grated lemon
   peel

1 tablespoon lemon juice
⅓ cup dairy sour cream
¼ teaspoon garlic salt
¼ teaspoon salt

Mash cheese with fork; blend in oil and beat until smooth. Mix in remaining ingredients thoroughly. Cover; refrigerate several hours to blend flavors. Bring dressing to room temperature before serving; mix with fork.

¾ cup.

SUNBURST FRUIT PLATE

Curried Cottage Cheese
  (below)
Three-fruit Dressing
  (below) or Lemonade
  Dressing (page 629)
Pineapple slices
Orange slices or sections
Clusters of grapes

Melon balls and slices
  (without rind)
Strawberries, washed and
  hulled
Banana
Orange and lime sherbet
Crisp lettuce cups

Prepare Curried Cottage Cheese and one of the dressings. Have all ingredients except banana chilled.

Just before serving, slice banana; dip slices into fruit juice or syrup to prevent darkening. Arrange fruit, Curried Cottage Cheese and scoops of sherbet on lettuce. Serve with Three-fruit or Lemonade Dressing.

4 servings.

CURRIED COTTAGE CHEESE

1½ cups (12-ounce carton)
  creamed cottage cheese
  (small curd)
¼ cup toasted slivered
  almonds

1 tablespoon mayonnaise
  or salad dressing
½ teaspoon curry powder

Mix all ingredients. Cover; refrigerate at least 1 hour to blend flavors.

THREE-FRUIT DRESSING

½ cup sugar
1½ tablespoons cornstarch
½ cup unsweetened
  pineapple juice

Grated peels of 1 small
  lemon and 1 small orange
2 tablespoons lemon juice
2 tablespoons orange juice

Mix sugar and cornstarch in small saucepan. Stir in pineapple juice. Cook, stirring constantly, until mixture thickens and boils.

Boil and stir 1 minute. Remove from heat. Stir in remaining ingredients; cool.

1¼ cups.

CHERRY-PINEAPPLE SALAD

1 medium pineapple
⅓ cup sugar
½ pound dark sweet cherries, pitted

Crisp salad greens
French dressing
Crumbled blue cheese

Remove rind from pineapple and cut into chunks (page 557). Place pineapple in shallow dish; sprinkle with sugar. Cover and chill.

Just before serving, drain pineapple. Arrange pineapple and cherries on greens. Drizzle dressing over fruit and sprinkle with blue cheese.

6 servings.

AVOCADO-CITRUS SALAD

1 ripe avocado
Lemon juice
Salt
1 orange or grapefruit
Watercress or parsley sprigs

Limeade or Lemonade
Dressing (page 629) or
Sweet French Dressing
(page 623)

Cut avocado in half crosswise; remove pit. Peel each half; cut into ¼-inch slices. Sprinkle slices with lemon juice and salt.

Pare and section orange or grapefruit. Arrange avocado slices and fruit sections; garnish with watercress. Serve with one of the dressings.

4 servings.

FRUIT SALAD FAVORITES

Color-packed combos. Serve on salad greens with a sweet fruit dressing (pages 622 to 629).

■ Cut-up orange sections or mandarin orange segments and diced apple or banana slices; garnish with coconut.

■ Pineapple spears and banana slices; roll in chopped peanuts.

■ Long slices of banana and cubes of jellied cranberry sauce.

■ Slices of pineapple topped with round slices of jellied cranberry sauce.

■ Fresh or canned pineapple spears, strawberries and halves of blue plums.

■ Cantaloupe balls, dark sweet cherries and green grapes.

■ Pineapple chunks, dark sweet cherries and pecans.

■ Orange and grapefruit sections and avocado slices or slices of unpared red apples; garnish with pomegranate seeds or sliced strawberries.

■ Apricot, peach or pear half or pineapple slice; top with tiny cream cheese balls rolled in chopped nuts (pistachios are especially attractive).

■ Sliced fresh pears and halved seeded Tokay grapes.

■ Halved green grapes or cherries in cavity of pear or peach halves.

■ Pear or peach halves; top with mayonnaise and shredded Cheddar cheese.

■ Fresh peach slices, green grapes and peanuts.

Molded Salads

Say it with food! There's never been a friendlier way to go to a covered-dish supper or to say hello to a new neighbor than to make and take your favorite molded salad. Nice thing about it—you can make it early in the morning or even the day before.

The mold can be plain or fancy, large or small; it can even be a substitute—an ice cube tray, a bowl, custard cups. Whatever you use, the rules for perfect molded salads stay the same:

■ Before you use a substitute or unmarked mold, be sure you know how much it holds. Fill mold with water, then measure by cupfuls.

■ Use recipe as is or double it. Don't try to adapt the recipe to your mold by using partial amounts.

■ Follow recipe directions for dissolving gelatin; flavored and unflavored gelatins are dissolved by different methods.

■ *Adding solids:* Allow gelatin mixture to thicken to the consistency of unbeaten egg white before adding solids—fruits, vegetables, nuts, etc. (Drain fruit well to avoid diluting gelatin.)

■ *To speed up thickening:* Place gelatin mixture in freezing compartment of refrigerator or in bowl of ice and water. Remove when mixture starts to thicken. (If gelatin becomes too set, soften over hot water.)

■ *Making patterns:* Arrange fruits or other solids in bottom of mold, then carefully add the thickened gelatin. Or, pour a layer of thickened gelatin into mold and arrange solids in desired pattern. Allow each layer to set before adding next layer; repeat until mold is full. Make a rainbow by layering colors of gelatin.

■ *Unmolding gelatin:* Dip mold in warm, not hot, water to depth of contents; loosen edge of salad with tip of paring knife. Place plate on top of mold and, holding tightly, invert plate *and* mold. Shake mold gently; remove carefully. Repeat process if necessary. Another method is to place plate on top of mold and, holding tightly, invert. Soak a kitchen towel in hot water, wring out; press around mold and into any depressions. Shake mold gently; remove. If mold does not slide off easily, reapply the hot, damp towel until it does.

TRIPLE-ORANGE AMBROSIAL SALAD

The flavor of the favorite citrus fruit in gelatin, sherbet and mandarin oranges. Light luscious.

2 cups boiling liquid (water or fruit syrup)
1 package (6 ounces) orange-flavored gelatin
1 pint orange sherbet
2 cans (11 ounces each) mandarin orange segments, drained
1 can (13½ ounces) pineapple chunks, drained
1 cup flaked coconut
1 cup miniature marshmallows
1 cup dairy sour cream or ½ cup whipping cream, whipped

Pour boiling liquid over gelatin in bowl, stirring until gelatin is dissolved. Add orange sherbet; stir until melted. Stir in 1 can of the mandarin orange segments (1 cup). Pour into 6-cup ring mold; chill until firm.

Combine remaining orange segments, the pineapple, coconut and marshmallows. Fold in sour cream. Chill at least 3 hours. Fill center of unmolded salad with fruit mixture.

10 to 12 servings.

CHERRY BLOSSOM MOLD

If using canned cherries, be sure to use the cherry syrup in the liquid. You'll get a richer color and a flavor-plus—and requests for seconds.

2 cups boiling liquid
  (water or fruit syrup)
1 package (6 ounces) cherry-
  flavored gelatin
2 cups dairy sour cream
2 cups pitted dark sweet
  cherries or 1 can (1 pound)
  dark sweet cherries,
  drained

⅓ cup slivered blanched
  almonds

Pour boiling liquid over gelatin in small mixer bowl, stirring until gelatin is dissolved. Cool. Add sour cream; beat until smooth. Chill until slightly thickened but not set.

Stir in cherries and almonds. Pour into 6-cup ring mold or into 10 individual molds. Chill until firm. If desired, garnish unmolded salad with additional cherries.
  10 servings.

FROZEN CRANBERRY-PINEAPPLE SALAD

1 can (1 pound 4½ ounces)
  crushed pineapple, well
  drained
1 can (1 pound) whole
  cranberry sauce

1 cup dairy sour cream
¼ cup coarsely chopped
  pecans

Mix thoroughly pineapple, cranberry sauce, sour cream and pecans. Pour into refrigerator tray. Freeze at least 3 hours or until firm.

Thirty minutes before serving, remove tray from freezer and place in refrigerator.
  6 to 8 servings.

LEMON-BLUE CHEESE ICE

Stir 1 pint lemon sherbet to soften. Mix in 2 to 3 tablespoons finely crumbled blue cheese. Place in refrigerator tray. Freeze several hours or until firm.

To serve, spoon onto bibb lettuce; garnish with marinated artichoke hearts.
  4 servings.

MOLDED CRANBERRY RELISH

1 cup boiling water
1 package (3 ounces) lemon-flavored gelatin
1 package (10 ounces) frozen cranberry-orange relish

1 can (8¾ ounces) crushed pineapple
1 tart apple, chopped
½ cup chopped celery
⅓ cup chopped nuts, if desired

Pour boiling water over gelatin in bowl, stirring until gelatin is dissolved. Add relish, pineapple (with syrup), apple, celery and nuts; stir until relish is thawed. Pour into 4-cup mold or into 6 to 8 individual molds. Chill until firm.

6 to 8 servings.

STRAWBERRY SNOWBALL SALAD

1 cup boiling water
1 package (3 ounces) strawberry-flavored gelatin
½ cup port, other sweet red wine or, if desired, cranberry cocktail

¼ cup cold water
1 package (3 ounces) cream cheese, softened
⅓ cup finely chopped nuts
1 tablespoon sugar
2 cups fresh strawberries

Pour boiling water over gelatin in bowl, stirring until gelatin is dissolved. Stir in wine and cold water. Chill until slightly thickened but not set.

Shape cream cheese into 18 balls; roll each in nuts. Sprinkle sugar over strawberries; mix gently. Pour ⅓ cup thickened gelatin into 6-cup ring mold.

Arrange cheese balls evenly in gelatin. Spoon in sweetened strawberries over the cheese balls and gelatin. Pour remaining thickened gelatin carefully over berries. Chill until firm. If desired, garnish with strawberries.

6 to 8 servings.

VARIATION

■ *Frozen Strawberry Salad Glacé:* Omit the cold water and substitute 1 package (1 pound) frozen strawberry halves for the fresh strawberries. Add frozen strawberries and wine to dissolved gelatin. Stir until gelatin begins to thicken.

CREAMY FROZEN FRUIT SALAD

- 1 package (8 ounces) Neufchâtel cheese, softened
- 1 cup dairy sour cream
- ¼ cup sugar
- ¼ teaspoon salt
- 1 can (1 pound 1 ounce) apricot halves, drained
- 1 can (8¾ ounces) crushed pineapple, drained
- 1 can (1 pound) pitted dark sweet cherries, drained
- 1 cup miniature marshmallows

In large mixer bowl, beat cheese until smooth. Add sour cream, sugar and salt; blend on low speed.

Cut apricots in half. Stir fruits and marshmallows into cheese mixture. Pour into 4½-cup mold or into 6 to 8 individual molds. Freeze at least 8 hours.

Ten to 15 minutes before serving, remove mold(s) from freezer and let stand at room temperature. If desired, garnish with stemmed dark sweet cherries.

6 to 8 servings.

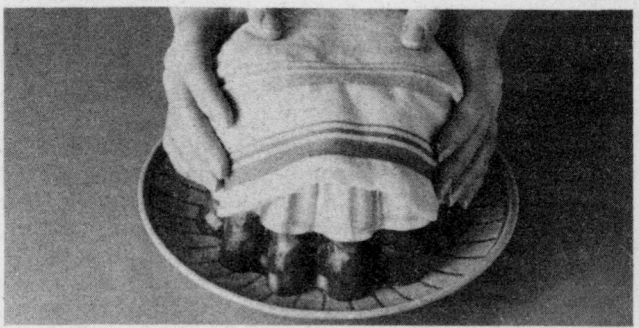

To unmold with hot damp towel, press into every crevice.

For easy unmolding, dip into hot water up to top of salad.

TANGY TOMATO ASPIC

Everyone's idea of a great molded salad. Be sure to try the variation for an elegant transformation.

1¼ cups boiling water
1 package (3 ounces) lemon-flavored gelatin
1 can (8 ounces) tomato sauce
1½ tablespoons vinegar
½ teaspoon salt
½ teaspoon onion juice
⅛ teaspoon red pepper sauce
Dash cloves
2 cups diced celery
Mayonnaise or salad dressing

Pour boiling water over gelatin in bowl, stirring until gelatin is dissolved. Stir in tomato sauce, vinegar and seasonings. Chill until slightly thickened but not set.

Stir in celery. Pour into 4-cup mold or into 6 individual molds. Chill until firm. If desired, garnish with ripe olives. Serve with mayonnaise or salad dressing.

6 servings.

VARIATION

■ *Gourmet Aspic:* Omit celery and double the amounts of aspic ingredients; chill aspic until slightly thickened.

Drain 1 can (14 ounces) cut asparagus spears and 1 can (7 ounces) artichoke hearts; arrange vegetables in 6-cup ring mold. Pour thickened aspic carefully over asparagus spears and artichoke hearts. Chill until firm. If desired, serve with Creamy Onion Dressing or Garlic Cheese Dressing (page 627). 10 servings.

SUNSHINE SALAD

1 cup boiling water
1 package (3 ounces) lemon-flavored gelatin
½ cup cold water
⅛ teaspoon salt
1 can (8¾ ounces) crushed pineapple
½ cup shredded carrots

Pour boiling water over gelatin in bowl, stirring until gelatin is dissolved. Stir in cold water, salt and pineapple (with syrup). Chill until slightly thickened but not set.

Stir in carrots. Pour into 4-cup ring mold or into 6 individual molds. Chill until firm.

6 servings.

PERFECTION SALAD

1 cup boiling water
1 package (3 ounces)
  lemon-flavored gelatin
2 tablespoons lemon juice
  or vinegar
1 teaspoon salt
1 cup cold water

1 cup finely diced celery
1 cup finely shredded
  cabbage
2 tablespoons finely
  chopped pimiento
⅓ cup chopped sweet
  pickles

Pour boiling water over gelatin in bowl, stirring until gelatin is dissolved. Stir in lemon juice, salt and cold water. Chill until slightly thickened but not set.

Stir in celery, cabbage, pimiento and sweet pickle. Pour into 6 to 8 individual molds. Chill until firm.

6 to 8 servings.

PATE SALAD LOAF

¼ cup cold water
½ cup tomato juice
1 envelope unflavored
  gelatin
¾ pound braunschweiger
1 cup tomato juice
½ cup mayonnaise or salad
  dressing
2 tablespoons lemon juice
2 teaspoons sugar
½ teaspoon salt
½ teaspoon dry mustard
⅛ teaspoon pepper
⅛ teaspoon cloves

¾ cup finely chopped celery
¼ cup chopped green pepper
¼ cup chopped pimiento-
  stuffed olives
¼ cup finely chopped green
  onions
  Crisp salad greens
1 package (10 ounces)
  frozen asparagus spears,
  cooked, drained and
  chilled
1 tomato, sliced
2 hard-cooked eggs, sliced

Combine water and ½ cup tomato juice; sprinkle gelatin on liquid to soften. Stir over low heat until gelatin is dissolved. Chill until slightly thickened.

Soften braunschweiger by mashing with spoon; stir into gelatin mixture along with remaining ingredients except salad greens, asparagus, tomato and eggs. Pour into loaf pan, 9x5x3 inches. Chill until firm. Unmold on greens; arrange asparagus and slices of tomato and eggs around loaf.

6 to 8 servings.

FRUITED CHICKEN MOLD

1¾ cups chicken broth*
1 package (3 ounces) lemon-flavored gelatin
¼ cup mayonnaise or salad dressing
¼ teaspoon salt
Dash pepper

1 cup diced cooked chicken
½ cup seedless green grapes
⅓ cup toasted slivered almonds

Oil 1-quart mold or 6 individual molds. Heat 1 cup of the chicken broth to boiling. Pour over gelatin in bowl, stirring until gelatin is dissolved. Add remaining chicken broth, the mayonnaise, salt and pepper; beat with rotary beater until blended. Place in freezer about 45 minutes or until firm around edge but soft in center.

Beat gelatin mixture until fluffy. Stir in chicken, grapes and almonds. Pour into mold(s). Chill in refrigerator until firm.

6 servings.

*Chicken broth can be made by dissolving 2 chicken bouillon cubes in 1¾ cups boiling water, or use canned chicken broth.

CONTINENTAL CHEESE RING WITH HAM

Salute vegetables—substitute cucumber slices and tomato wedges for the grapes.

1 envelope unflavored gelatin
¼ cup cold water
⅔ cup whipping cream
2 cups creamed cottage cheese
½ cup crumbled blue cheese
½ cup sliced pimiento-stuffed olives

¼ cup broken walnuts
¼ teaspoon salt
¼ teaspoon paprika
Crisp salad greens
Seedless green grapes
1 to 1½ pounds sliced cooked ham

Sprinkle gelatin on cold water to soften. Place over hot water to dissolve. Beat cream, adding gelatin as cream begins to thicken (cream will not become stiff). Stir in cheeses, olives, walnuts, salt and paprika. Pour into 4-cup ring mold. Chill until firm.

Unmold on greens; fill center with grapes. Arrange ham slices around ring; garnish with grapes.
6 servings.

First Course Salads

These delicious recipes only hint at the diversity of first course salads. Try small portions of Beef-and-Mushroom Salad (page 613) or Seafood Salad (page 617). The Summer Fruit Bowl (page 599) goes as well before the meal as with it.

ASPARAGUS WITH CURRIED MAYONNAISE

½ cup mayonnaise or salad
  dressing
¼ teaspoon curry powder

1 package (10 ounces)
  frozen asparagus spears
Pimiento strips

Stir together mayonnaise and curry powder. Cover; refrigerate about 3 hours to blend flavors. Cook asparagus as directed on package; drain and chill.

Place ¼ of asparagus on each plate. Top with curried mayonnaise; crisscross pimiento strips on mayonnaise.
4 servings.

CELERY VICTOR

1 bunch celery
1 can (10½ ounces)
  condensed beef broth
  (bouillon)

Italian salad dressing
Pimiento strips

Wash celery bunch; trim off root end but do not separate stalks. Remove coarse outer stalks and leaves, reserving leaves for garnish. Cut celery bunch crosswise once so bottom section is 5 inches long. (Refrigerate the top section for use at another time.) Cut bottom section into quarters; tie quarters with string.

Pour broth into skillet; add celery bundles. Cover; heat to boiling and cook about 15 minutes. Drain celery; place in shallow dish. Pour salad dressing over celery. Refrigerate 3 hours, turning bundles once or twice.

To serve, place a bundle cut side down on each plate; remove string. Garnish with pimiento strips and reserved celery leaves.

4 servings.

CELERY ROOT-GRAPE SALAD

1 cup water
1 teaspoon celery salt
¼ teaspoon pepper
1 tablespoon lemon juice
2 celery roots,* pared and cut into ½-inch squares (about 1 cup)
½ cup clear French dressing
1 can (13½ ounces) pineapple chunks, chilled

2 cups seedless green grapes or halved Tokay grapes, chilled
¼ cup toasted slivered almonds
½ cup mayonnaise or salad dressing
Romaine leaves or watercress

Heat water, celery salt, pepper and lemon juice to boiling. Add celery root; simmer 10 minutes. Drain celery root; place in shallow glass dish. Pour the clear French dressing over celery root. Cover and refrigerate at least 2 hours, stirring occasionally.

Just before serving, drain celery root and pineapple; combine with grapes and almonds. Add mayonnaise and toss. Serve on romaine leaves; if desired, garnish salad with small bunches of grapes.

6 to 8 servings.

*If celery root is not available, substitute 1 cup cut-up celery.

Main Dish Salads

Easy to make, easy to serve and a delight to the eye, a main course salad is the answer for every busy woman. Serve one to your bridge club or as Sunday supper for the family. Weight-conscious? Eat with a light heart and easy conscience. Want to try a "something different" picnic? Fill thermos bottles with icy beverages and steaming bouillon or coffee. Load your ice chest with plastic bags containing your pre-prepared salad ingredients and a jar of dressing; to this add assorted fruits and cheeses. Tuck in a long loaf of crusty sesame-seeded Italian bread and you're off for elegant *al fresco* eating—even if you go no farther than your own backyard.

BEEF-AND-MUSHROOM SALAD

1½-pound sirloin steak, 1½ inches thick
1 jar (4½ ounces) sliced mushrooms, drained
1 medium green pepper, sliced into thin rings
⅓ cup red wine vinegar
¼ cup salad oil
1 teaspoon salt
½ teaspoon onion salt
½ teaspoon Worcestershire sauce
¼ teaspoon pepper
¼ teaspoon tarragon leaves
2 cloves garlic, crushed
Crisp lettuce cups
Cherry tomatoes

Set oven control at broil and/or 550°. Place top of steak 3 to 4 inches from heat. Broil until medium, about 15 minutes per side; cool.

Cut steak into ⅜-inch strips. Arrange in baking dish, 13½x9x2 inches. Layer mushrooms over meat; top with pepper rings. Combine vinegar, oil and seasonings; pour over meat and vegetables. Cover; refrigerate at least 3 hours, spooning marinade over vegetables occasionally.

With a slotted spoon, remove vegetables to lettuce cups. Arrange strips of meat beside vegetables; garnish with tomatoes.

4 servings.

BACON-LETTUCE-TOMATO SALAD

Barbecue Salad Dressing (page 614)
1 head lettuce, washed and chilled
8 to 10 slices bacon, crisply fried
2 large tomatoes
2 cups cubed cooked chicken, chilled
1 hard-cooked egg, sliced

Prepare Barbecue Salad Dressing. Just before serving, tear lettuce into bite-size pieces (about 6 cups). Break bacon into large pieces. Cut each tomato into eighths.

Add bacon, tomatoes and chicken to lettuce; toss with dressing. Garnish with egg slices.

4 servings.

BARBECUE SALAD DRESSING

½ cup mayonnaise or salad
  dressing
¼ cup barbecue sauce
1 tablespoon instant minced
  onion

1 tablespoon lemon juice
½ teaspoon salt
¼ teaspoon pepper

Mix all ingredients; cover and chill.
About ¾ cup.

HAM 'N MANDARIN SALAD

1 clove garlic, halved
2 cups finely cubed cooked
  ham
1 cup thinly sliced celery
⅓ cup chopped green
  onions
½ cup chopped walnuts
1 can (11 ounces) mandarin
  orange segments, drained

¼ teaspoon pepper
⅓ cup mayonnaise or salad
  dressing
2 tablespoons light cream
1 tablespoon vinegar
  Watercress or chopped
  fresh mint

Rub salad bowl with cut clove of garlic. Combine ham, celery, onion, walnuts and orange segments in bowl; cover and chill.

Just before serving, blend pepper, mayonnaise, cream and vinegar; pour over ham mixture. Toss until ingredients are well coated. Garnish with watercress.

6 servings.

CHICKEN OR TURKEY SALAD

2 cups cubed cooked
  chicken or turkey
½ cup sliced celery
⅓ cup salad dressing or
  mayonnaise

½ teaspoon salt
½ teaspoon poultry
  seasoning
⅛ teaspoon onion salt
  Dash pepper

Combine chicken and celery in bowl. Mix salad dressing, salt, poultry seasoning, onion salt and pepper. Pour over chicken and celery; toss. Cover; chill 2 hours.

3 or 4 servings.

VARIATION

■ *Chicken "And" Salads:* To pep up flavor, just before serving fold in one of the following:

1 cup chilled fruit
(mandarin orange
segments, chopped
unpared apple, seedless
green grapes and/or
pineapple tidbits)

¼ cup chopped sweet pickle
4 slices bacon, crisply fried
and crumbled
⅓ cup chopped nuts

TUNA-MACARONI SALAD

1 package (6 or 7 ounces)
shell macaroni
1 cup cubed Cheddar
cheese
1 can (7 ounces) tuna,
drained
¾ cup sliced sweet pickles

⅓ cup minced onion
1 cup salad dressing or
mayonnaise
¾ teaspoon salt
¼ teaspoon pepper
2 cloves garlic, crushed

Cook macaroni as directed on page 352. Drain; rinse with cold water.

Combine macaroni, cheese, tuna, pickles and onion in large bowl. Stir together salad dressing, salt, pepper and garlic; pour over macaroni mixture and toss. Cover; chill at least 3 hours.

6 to 8 servings.

CHEF'S SALAD

1 head lettuce, washed and
chilled
1 small bunch romaine or
endive, washed and chilled
1 cup julienne strips cooked
meat (beef, ham, tongue)
1 cup julienne strips cooked
chicken or turkey
1 cup julienne strips Swiss
cheese
½ cup chopped green
onions

½ cup sliced celery
1 can (2 ounces) fillets of
anchovies, if desired
½ cup mayonnaise or salad
dressing
¼ cup French dressing
Ripe olives
2 hard-cooked eggs, sliced
2 tomatoes, cut into wedges

Into large salad bowl, tear lettuce and romaine into bite-size pieces (about 12 cups). Reserve few strips of meat and cheese. Toss remaining meat and cheese strips, the onion, celery and anchovies with the salad greens.

Blend mayonnaise and French dressing; pour over salad and toss. (If you prefer a clear dressing, use the traditional oil and vinegar.) Garnish with reserved meat and cheese strips, the olives, egg slices and tomato wedges.

4 servings.

HOT CHICKEN SALAD

- 2 cups cubed cooked chicken
- 2 cups thinly sliced celery
- 2 cups croutons
- 1 cup mayonnaise or salad dressing
- ½ cup chopped or slivered almonds, toasted
- 2 tablespoons lemon juice
- 2 teaspoons instant minced onion
- ½ teaspoon salt
- ½ cup shredded Cheddar or Swiss cheese

Heat oven to 450°. Mix all ingredients except 1 cup of the croutons and the cheese. Spoon into six 1-cup baking dishes. Sprinkle with remaining croutons and the cheese. Bake 10 to 15 minutes or until bubbly.

6 servings.

VARIATIONS

■ *Hot Tuna Salad:* Substitute 2 cans (6½ ounces each) tuna, drained, for the chicken.

■ *Hot Turkey Salad:* Substitute cubed cooked turkey for the chicken.

PALACE COURT SALAD

For each serving, arrange a mound of finely shredded lettuce on salad plate. Place a thick large tomato slice on lettuce. Arrange 1 large or 3 small artichoke heart(s) on tomato slice. Cover with chunks of cooked crabmeat, shrimp or chicken. Sieve hard-cooked egg around edge of lettuce. Serve with Russian dressing.

CRAB LOUIS

2 cans (7½ ounces each)
crabmeat or 2 packages
(6 ounces each) frozen
cooked crabmeat, thawed
Louis Dressing (below)
4 tomatoes, quartered

4 hard-cooked eggs,
quartered
Ripe or green olives
4 cups bite-size pieces salad
greens, chilled

Drain crabmeat and remove cartilage; chill. Prepare Louis Dressing. Arrange crabmeat, tomatoes, eggs and olives on greens. Pour Louis Dressing over salad.
4 servings.

LOUIS DRESSING

¾ cup chili sauce
½ cup mayonnaise or salad
dressing
1 teaspoon instant minced
onion

½ teaspoon sugar
¼ teaspoon Worcestershire
sauce
Salt to taste

Mix all ingredients. Cover and chill 30 minutes.
1¼ cups.

SEAFOOD SALAD

1 to 1¼ cups cooked shrimp,
crabmeat or lobster
1 cup thinly sliced celery
⅓ cup mayonnaise or salad
dressing

1 tablespoon minced green
onion
¼ teaspoon salt
Dash pepper

Combine seafood and celery in bowl. Mix mayonnaise, onion, salt and pepper. Pour over seafood and celery; toss. Cover; chill at least 2 hours.
3 or 4 servings.

HOW MUCH SHRIMP?

For every 1 cup cleaned cooked shrimp needed—

- prepare ¾ pound fresh or frozen raw shrimp (in shells, or . . .
- prepare 1 package (7 ounces) frozen peeled shrimp or . . .
- use 1 can (4½ or 5 ounces) shrimp.

RAINBOW SHRIMP SALAD

1 cup cleaned cooked shrimp	¼ cup minced onion
3 cups cooked rice	½ teaspoon salt
¼ cup sliced celery	¼ teaspoon pepper
¼ cup sliced pimiento-stuffed olives	3 tablespoons mayonnaise or salad dressing
¼ cup chopped green pepper	Crisp lettuce
¼ cup chopped pimiento	2 tomatoes, cut into wedges
	½ cup French dressing
	1 lemon, cut into wedges

Split each shrimp lengthwise. Combine shrimp, rice, celery, olives, green pepper, pimiento and onion in large bowl; cover and chill.

Just before serving, stir together salt, pepper and mayonnaise; toss with shrimp mixture. Spoon shrimp onto lettuce; garnish with tomato wedges and, if desired, with whole shrimp. Serve with French dressing and lemon wedges.

6 servings.

SALAD OF THE STATES

1 cup bite-size pieces lettuce	4 large pimiento-stuffed olives, sliced
1 cup bite-size pieces romaine	1 grapefruit, pared and sectioned
½ cup bite-size pieces watercress	1 ripe medium avocado
1½ cup cut-up cooked lobster, crabmeat, shrimp, chicken or turkey	¼ to ⅓ cup mayonnaise or salad dressing
½ cup chopped green onions (and tops)	Salt
	4 large tomatoes
	Crisp lettuce cups

Toss greens, lobster, onions, olives and grapefruit in large bowl; chill. Peel avocado and cut into cubes. Add avocado and mayonnaise to lobster mixture; toss. Season with salt.

Cut tomatoes into thin slices. Place 3 or 4 slices in each lettuce cup; top with lobster mixture.

4 to 6 servings.

CRAB-AVOCADO BAKED SALAD

1 can (7½ ounces) crabmeat or 1 package (6 ounces) frozen cooked crabmeat, thawed
⅓ cup chopped celery
3 hard-cooked eggs, chopped
2 tablespoons chopped pimiento
1 tablespoon chopped onion
½ teaspoon salt

½ cup mayonnaise or salad dressing
3 large or 4 small ripe avocados
Lemon juice
Salt
3 tablespoons dry bread crumbs
1 teaspoon melted butter
2 tablespoons slivered almonds

Heat oven to 400°. Drain crabmeat and remove cartilage. Mix crabmeat, celery, eggs, pimiento, onion, ½ teaspoon salt and the mayonnaise. Cut unpeeled avocados lengthwise in half; remove pit. Brush halves with lemon juice; sprinkle with salt. Fill avocado halves with crabmeat mixture.

Toss bread crumbs in melted butter; spoon over crabmeat. Place in shallow baking dish; bake uncovered 10 minutes. Sprinkle almonds over crumb topping; bake 5 minutes longer or until bubbly.

6 to 8 servings.

TUNA ON A SHOESTRING

A crunchy tuna salad with a surprise ingredient—crisp shoestring potatoes!

1 can (6½ ounces) tuna, drained
1 cup shredded carrots
1 cup diced celery
¼ cup minced onion
¾ to 1 cup salad dressing or mayonnaise

1 can (4 ounces) shoestring potatoes

Into large bowl, separate tuna into chunks. Add carrots, celery, onion and salad dressing; toss until tuna is well coated with dressing. Cover and chill.

Just before serving, fold in potatoes. If desired, garnish with parsley and carrot curls.

4 to 6 servings.

Crowd-size Salads

Planning a church supper, a Scout banquet or a progressive dinner? Match up these salads with our Crowd-size Main Dishes (pages 495 to 500). Here are some natural mates: Cranberry-Raspberry Mold with Scalloped Potato Dinner or Arroz con Pollo; Perfection Salad with Chuck Wagon Beans or Soup and Sausage Casserole; Easy-do Salade Provençal with Italian Spaghetti, Lasagne or Hamburger Stroganoff. The Tuna Buffet Salad is a main dish in itself—just add rolls and a dessert.

CRANBERRY-RASPBERRY MOLD

A hint of tartness in this creamy pink salad.

6 cups boiling water
3 packages (6 ounces each) raspberry-flavored gelatin
4 cups dairy sour cream
2 cans (1 pound each) whole cranberry sauce

Pour boiling water over gelatin in bowl, stirring until gelatin is dissolved. Chill until very thick but not set.

With rotary beater, beat in sour cream and cranberry sauce. Divide mixture between 2 baking pans, 13x9x2 inches. Chill until firm.

24 or 30 servings.

PERFECTION SALAD

4 cups boiling water
1 package (6 ounces) lemon-flavored gelatin
¼ cup lemon juice or vinegar
2 teaspoons salt
2 cups finely diced celery
2 cups finely shredded cabbage
¼ cup finely chopped pimiento
⅔ cup chopped sweet pickle

Pour boiling water over gelatin in bowl, stirring until gelatin is dissolved. Stir in lemon juice and salt; chill until very thick but not set.

Stir in celery, cabbage, pimiento and sweet pickle. Pour into baking pan, 13x9x2 inches. Chill.

12 or 15 servings.

TUNA BUFFET SALAD

8 cups uncooked elbow
macaroni (1 pound 8
ounces)
10 cans (9¼ ounces each)
tuna, drained and flaked
4 large cucumbers, pared
and diced (about 6 cups)
½ cup grated onion

2½ cups salad dressing or
mayonnaise
1 tablespoon salt
1½ teaspoons pepper
Lemon wedges
½ cup snipped parsley
Paprika

Cook macaroni as directed on page 352 except—use 3 times the amount of water and salt. Drain; rinse in cold water.

Combine macaroni, tuna, cucumber and onion in large bowl. Mix salad dressing, salt and pepper; pour over macaroni mixture and toss. Chill thoroughly. Serve with lemon wedges and garnish with parsley and paprika.

24 servings (1¼ cups each).

VARIATION

■ *Chicken or Turkey Buffet Salad:* Substitute 12 cups cut-up cooked chicken or turkey for the tuna and chilled cranberry sauce for the lemon wedges.

EASY-DO SALADE PROVENÇAL

A no-bowl way to a terrific salad. Remember this plastic-bag trick for crowd-size salads . . . when refrigerator space may really be a problem.

2 large heads lettuce,
washed
½ pound spinach, washed,
dried and stems removed
2 cans (3⅞ ounces each)
pitted ripe olives, drained

2 jars (6 ounces each)
marinated artichoke hearts
1 bottle (8 ounces) herb
dressing

Tear greens into bite-size pieces; divide between 2 large plastic bags. Chill.

Just before serving, add to each bag 1 can olives, 1 jar artichoke hearts (with liquid) and half the dressing. Close bags tightly; shake vigorously. Serve in large bowl.

12 servings.

Salad Dressings

The perfect salad deserves the perfect dressing—one that won't overpower it. And remember, too much will make the crispest greens limp.

A hearty steak can stand up to the he-man flavor of Blue Cheese Dressing (page 624); a cooling fruit salad with a sweet dressing will set off a hot curry. Experiment!

CLASSIC FRENCH DRESSING

For green salads.

¼ cup olive oil or salad oil
2 tablespoons tarragon or wine vinegar
¾ teaspoon salt
1 small clove garlic, crushed
¼ teaspoon monosodium glutamate
Generous dash freshly ground pepper

Toss salad greens (about 12 cups) with oil just until leaves glisten. Combine vinegar, salt, garlic, monosodium glutamate and pepper; toss with salad mixture.

About ⅓ cup.

FRENCH DRESSING

For green salads and vegetable salads.

1 cup olive oil, salad oil or combination
¼ cup vinegar
¼ cup lemon juice
1 teaspoon salt
½ teaspoon dry mustard
½ teaspoon paprika

Shake all ingredients well in tightly covered jar. Refrigerate. Shake again just before serving.

1½ cups.

VARIATIONS

■ *Blue Cheese Dressing:* Add ⅛ teaspoon Worcestershire sauce to ¼ cup crumbled blue or Roquefort cheese (about 1½ ounces); mash with fork. Blend in ½ cup French Dressing. ¾ cup.

■ *Garlic French Dressing:* Crush 1 clove garlic; mix in generous dash freshly ground pepper and ½ cup French Dressing. ½ cup.

■ *Sweet French Dressing:* (For fruit salads.) Stir 2 tablespoons confectioners' sugar into ½ cup French Dressing. ½ cup.

ITALIAN DRESSING

For green salads and vegetable salads.

1 cup salad oil	½ teaspoon dry mustard
¼ cup lemon juice	½ teaspoon onion salt
¼ cup white vinegar	½ teaspoon paprika
1 teaspoon salt	⅛ teaspoon thyme
1 teaspoon sugar	2 cloves garlic, crushed
½ teaspoon oregano leaves	

Shake all ingredients in tightly covered jar. Refrigerate at least 2 hours to blend flavors. Shake before serving.
1½ cups.

SEASONED SALAD OIL

In tightly covered jar, shake 1 cup salad oil and 2 cloves garlic, quartered, or 1 small onion, sliced. Let stand at least 4 days to blend flavors.
1 cup.

HERBED VINEGAR

In tightly covered jar, shake 1 cup white vinegar and one of the following:

¼ cup snipped fresh dill or ½ teaspoon dill weed	⅓ cup snipped fresh mint
¼ cup snipped chives	1 clove garlic, quartered

Refrigerate at least 4 days to blend flavors. Strain before using.
1 cup.

GREEN GODDESS DRESSING

For green salads—a glamour dressing.

1 clove garlic, crushed
3 tablespoons anchovy paste or finely chopped anchovy fillets
3 tablespoons finely snipped chives
1 tablespoon lemon juice
3 tablespoons tarragon wine vinegar

½ cup dairy sour cream
1 cup mayonnaise or salad dressing
⅓ cup finely snipped parsley
¼ teaspoon salt
⅛ teaspoon freshly ground pepper

Mix all ingredients. Cover and chill.
2 cups.

BLUE CHEESE DRESSING

For green salads and vegetable salads.

1 package (4 ounces) blue cheese, crumbled
1 package (3 ounces) cream cheese, softened

½ cup mayonnaise or salad dressing
⅓ cup light cream (20%)

Reserve ⅓ cup of the crumbled blue cheese. In small mixer bowl, blend remaining blue cheese and the cream cheese on low speed. Add mayonnaise and cream; beat on medium speed until creamy. Stir in reserved blue cheese. Cover; chill at least 3 hours to blend flavors.
About 1⅔ cups.

BOTTLED-QUICK SALAD DRESSING

Special touches to make bottled dressings your very own.

Blue Cheese-Garlic Dressing: (For green salads and vegetable salads.) Into 1 bottle (8 ounces) blue cheese dressing, add 2 cloves garlic, crushed. Cap tightly and shake thoroughly; refrigerate at least 3 hours to blend flavors. Shake before serving. 1 cup.

Confetti Dressing: (For green salads and vegetable salads.) In tightly covered jar, shake 1 bottle (8 ounces) oil-and-vinegar dressing, 1 tablespoon drained capers and 1 tablespoon finely chopped pimiento. Refrigerate at least 3 hours to blend flavors. Shake before serving. 1 cup.

Curried Onion Dressing: (For meat or seafood salads.) Into 1 bottle (8 ounces) creamy onion dressing, add ½ teaspoon curry powder. Cap tightly and shake thoroughly; refrigerate at least 3 hours to blend flavors. Shake before serving. 1 cup.

French Celery Seed Dressing: (For fruit salads.) Into 1 bottle (8 ounces) French dressing, add ½ teaspoon celery seed. Cap tightly and shake; refrigerate at least 3 hours to blend flavors. Shake before serving. 1 cup.

Fruited Blue Cheese Dressing: (For fruit salads.) In tightly covered jar, shake 1 bottle (8 ounces) blue cheese dressing, ¼ cup orange juice and 1 tablespoon lemon juice. Refrigerate at least 3 hours to blend flavors. Shake before serving. 1¼ cups.

Herbed Tomato Dressing: (For green salads and vegetable salads.) In tightly covered jar, shake 1 bottle (8 ounces) herb-and-garlic dressing and ½ cup tomato juice. Refrigerate at least 3 hours to blend flavors. Shake before serving. 1½ cups.

Moscow Dressing: (For vegetable or meat salads.) Mix 1 bottle (8 ounces) Russian dressing and ¼ cup dairy sour cream. Cover; refrigerate at least 3 hours to blend flavors. Stir gently before serving. 1¼ cups.

Parmesan Dressing: (For green salads and vegetable salads.) In tightly covered jar, shake 1 bottle (8 ounces) Italian-style dressing and 3 tablespoons grated Parmesan cheese. Refrigerate at least 3 hours to blend flavors. Shake before serving. 1 cup.

SALAD SECRET Hide the dressing! When you make a salad for a party, put your dressing in the bottom of the salad bowl. (Maybe it's the kind you can even mix there.) Then add the ingredients that taste best marinated— cucumbers, mushrooms, green onions, artichokes. Pile your salad greens right on top. Place the salad in the refrigerator until just before you're ready to serve. Place it on the buffet table—and toss it right there!

MAYONNAISE

The "can't-be-without" dressing. Makes an excellent base for Tartar Sauce (page 580).

1 egg yolk
1 teaspoon dry mustard
1 teaspoon sugar
¼ teaspoon salt

Dash cayenne red pepper
2 tablespoons lemon juice or vinegar
1 cup salad oil

In small mixer bowl, beat egg yolk, mustard, sugar, salt, pepper and 1 tablespoon of the lemon juice on medium speed until blended. Continue beating, adding salad oil *drop by drop.* As mixture thickens, increase rate of addition. Slowly stir in remaining lemon juice. Beat thoroughly. Chill.

About 1½ cups.

Note: Using a blender? You'll have to use a whole egg instead of just the egg yolk. Place ¼ cup of the oil, the whole egg and the remaining ingredients in blender. Mix on high speed 5 seconds and turn off. Beat on high speed, adding remaining salad oil *very slowly.* Turn off blender occasionally and clean sides with rubber scraper. Or follow the manufacturer's directions.

VARIATIONS

■ *Fruited Cream Dressing:* (For fruit salads.) Mix ½ cup Mayonnaise, 2 tablespoons orange juice, pinch salt and dash paprika. Fold in ¼ cup whipping cream, whipped. ¾ cup.

■ *Russian Dressing:* (For green salads and vegetable salads.) Mix ½ cup Mayonnaise, ¼ cup chili sauce and few drops onion juice. If desired, add 1 teaspoon lemon juice. ¾ cup.

■ *Thousand Island Dressing:* (For green salads and vegetable salads.) Mix ½ cup Mayonnaise, 1 tablespoon chili sauce, 1 tablespoon chopped pimiento-stuffed olives, 1 teaspoon snipped chives, 1 hard-cooked egg, chopped, ¼ teaspoon paprika, and salt and pepper to taste. If desired, thin with whipping cream. ¾ cup.

■ *Tomato-Cucumber Mayonnaise:* (For green salads and vegetable, meat or seafood salads.) Mix 1 cup Mayonnaise, ½ cup *each* drained diced tomato and cucumber, 1 teaspoon minced onion and dash salt. 1¾ cups.

MAYONNAISE-QUICK DRESSING

Be sure to try the variations at left, too.

Cranberry Dressing: (For fruit salads.) Mix 1 cup mayonnaise or salad dressing, ¼ cup cranberry cocktail and ½ teaspoon poppy seed. Cover; refrigerate at least 4 hours to blend flavors. About 1 cup.

Creamy Onion Dressing: (For green salads and vegetable, meat or seafood salads.) Mix 1 cup mayonnaise or salad dressing, ½ cup dairy sour cream and 2 tablespoons finely chopped green onion. Cover; refrigerate at least 4 hours to blend flavors. About 1¼ cups.

Parsley Cheese Dressing: (For vegetable, meat or seafood salads.) Mix 1 cup mayonnaise or salad dressing, ¼ cup pasteurized process sharp American cheese spread and 1 tablespoon snipped parsley. Cover; refrigerate at least 4 hours to blend flavors. About 1 cup.

COOKED SALAD DRESSING

¼ cup all-purpose flour	1½ cups milk
2 tablespoons sugar	⅓ cup vinegar
1 teaspoon salt	1 tablespoon butter or
1 teaspoon dry mustard	margarine
2 egg yolks	

Stir together flour, sugar, salt and mustard in medium saucepan. Beat egg yolks slightly; stir in milk. Stir egg-milk mixture slowly into the flour mixture.

Cook over medium heat, stirring constantly, until mixture thickens and boils. Boil and stir 1 minute. Remove from heat and stir in vinegar and butter. Cool thoroughly.

About 2 cups.

VARIATIONS

■ *Sour Cream Dressing:* Mix ½ cup cooled Cooked Salad Dressing, ½ cup dairy sour cream, 2 teaspoons snipped chives and generous dash coarsely ground black pepper. 1 cup.

■ *Whipped Cream Dressing:* In chilled bowl, beat ½ cup chilled whipping cream until stiff. Stir in ½ cup cooled Cooked Salad Dressing. About 1 cup.

FLUFFY FRUIT DRESSING

1 jar (7½ ounces)
   marshmallow crème
2 tablespoons orange juice

⅓ cup salad dressing
½ teaspoon vanilla

Blend marshmallow crème and orange juice with rotary beater. Stir in salad dressing and vanilla.
   About 1½ cups.

CARIBBEAN FRUIT SAUCE

2 egg yolks
   Dash salt
⅓ cup sugar
½ cup chilled whipping
   cream

2 tablespoons light rum or,
   if desired, 3 tablespoons
   orange juice and ¼
   teaspoon vanilla

In small mixer bowl, beat egg yolks with salt until very thick and lemon colored. Add sugar gradually and continue beating until mixture is thick.
   In chilled bowl, beat whipping cream until stiff. Fold egg yolk mixture into whipped cream. Fold in rum. Refrigerate any leftover sauce immediately.
   1¾ cups.

RUBY FRENCH DRESSING

1 cup salad oil
⅔ cup catsup
½ cup vinegar
½ cup sugar
2 tablespoons minced onion

1 tablespoon lemon juice
1 teaspoon salt
1 teaspoon pepper
1 teaspoon dry mustard
1 teaspoon paprika

Shake all ingredients well in tightly covered jar. Refrigerate at least 3 hours to blend flavors. Shake before serving.
   2⅔ cups.

LIMEADE OR LEMONADE DRESSING

⅓ cup frozen limeade or
   lemonade concentrate
   (thawed)
⅓ cup honey

⅓ cup salad oil
1 teaspoon celery or poppy
   seed

Blend all ingredients with rotary beater.
   1 cup.

MIX-QUICK SALAD DRESSINGS

Just a dash of a special something—and who would guess it started with a mix?

Creamy Garlic Dressing: (For meat or seafood salads.) Blend 1 envelope (0.7 ounce) garlic salad dressing mix with 1 cup dairy sour cream and 1 cup mayonnaise or salad dressing. Cover and refrigerate at least 3 hours to blend flavors. 2 cups.

Honey French Dressing: (For fruit salads.) Prepare 1 envelope (⅝ ounce) French salad dressing mix with apple cider vinegar as directed on envelope except— substitute honey for the water. Cover; refrigerate at least 3 hours to blend flavors. Shake before serving. 1 cup.

Roman Dressing: (For green salads and vegetable salads.) Prepare 1 enevlope (0.7 ounce) Parmesan salad dressing mix with white wine vinegar as directed on envelope. Add ½ teaspoon oregano leaves; shake again. Cover; refrigerate at least 3 hours to blend flavors. Shake before serving. 1 cup.

Soups and Stews

*What's the food that goes with just about
everything? Think a minute—and you might well
answer soup. Soup and sandwich. Soup and
salad. Sunday supper soup. Saturday lunch soup.
First-course soup. Main-course soup. New soups
from two soups. Great soups for a party. Cold
soup on a summer day. Hot soup on a stormy
night. "What can we have that's different?" "What
can we have that's quick but hearty?" Over and
over again, you know yourself, someone's sure
to say, "Let's just have soup!"*

Appetizer Soups

Piping hot or icy cold, a quick-to-make soup gets
dinner off to a great start. More and more hostesses
find that a mug of hot soup with a tray of crackers in
the living room is a friendly way to get the meal started.
Cold soups, too, can be served in chilled glasses or
punch cups. For a sit-down first course, improvise a
chiller: Mount a glass custard cup or other small cup
for the soup in a gaily-colored bowl filled with crushed
ice; if both your soup and dishes are white, add food
color to the ice trays before freezing.

CREAMED CELERY-CUCUMBER SOUP

1 can (10½ ounces) condensed cream of celery soup	2 tablespoons chopped green onion
1 soup can water	2 tablespoons chopped green pepper
¼ cup chopped pared cucumber	¼ cup dairy sour cream
	¼ teaspoon celery salt

Combine all ingredients; chill thoroughly.
6 servings (½ cup each).

VICHYSSOISE

French tradition made easy with instant potatoes.

1 small onion, grated
3 chicken bouillon cubes
or 3 teaspoons instant
chicken bouillon
1 cup water
¼ teaspoon salt

2 cups milk
1¼ cups instant mashed
potato puffs (dry)
1 cup light cream (20%)
Snipped chives or
watercress

Combine onion, bouillon cubes, water and salt in large saucepan. Heat to boiling. Reduce heat; cover and simmer about 10 minutes.

Remove from heat. Add ½ cup of the milk. Stir in potato puffs and whip with fork until fluffy. Gradually stir in remaining 1½ cups milk; heat just to boiling. Cover and chill thoroughly.

Just before serving, stir in cream, beating vigorously with fork until blended. Sprinkle each serving with snipped chives or watercress.

8 servings (½ cup each).

GAZPACHO

Zest up your dinner with this spicy starter of Spanish origin. Fill little bowls with the accompaniments and spoon them, to taste, onto the chilled soup. Or you might try serving it buffet style.

1½ cups tomato juice
1 beef bouillon cube or 1
teaspoon instant beef
bouillon
1 tomato, chopped
¼ cup chopped unpared
cucumber
2 tablespoons chopped
green pepper

2 tablespoons chopped
onion
2 tablespoons wine vinegar
1 tablespoon salad oil
½ teaspoon Worcestershire
sauce
3 drops red pepper sauce
Accompaniments

Heat tomato juice to boiling. Add bouillon cube; stir until dissolved. Stir in remaining ingredients except accompaniments; chill several hours.

Serve with accompaniments: herbed croutons and about ⅓ cup each chopped tomato, unpared cucumber, green pepper and onion.

5 servings (½ cup each).

JELLIED TOMATO MADRILÈNE

2 envelopes unflavored
  gelatin
1 can (18 ounces) tomato
  juice
3 chicken bouillon cubes or
  3 teaspoons instant
  chicken bouillon

2 cups boiling water
½ teaspoon grated onion
⅛ teaspoon salt
  Dash pepper
  Lemon wedges

Sprinkle gelatin on tomato juice to soften. Dissolve bouillon cubes in boiling water; add to gelatin mixture, stirring until gelatin is dissolved. Stir in onion, salt and pepper. Cool; chill until set. Break up with fork; garnish with lemon.

8 servings (½ cup each).

GUACAMOLE SOUP

2 ripe medium avocados
1½ cups water
1 cup milk
2 tablespoons lemon juice

2½ teaspoons seasoned salt
  Dash red pepper sauce
1 medium tomato, chopped

Cut avocados lengthwise into quarters. Remove pits and peel. Blend avocado, water and milk in blender until smooth. Add lemon juice, seasoned salt and red pepper sauce; mix thoroughly. Fold tomato into soup; chill thoroughly.

8 servings (½ cup each).

Note: No blender? Press avocado through sieve. Gradually beat in water, milk and lemon juice until smooth. Fold in seasonings and tomato.

BEEFY APPETIZER SOUP

1 can (10½ ounces)
  condensed beef broth
  (bouillon)
1 soup can water

1½ teaspoons horseradish
1 teaspoon lemon juice
¼ teaspoon dill weed

Combine all ingredients; heat through, stirring.
5 servings (½ cup each).

BEEF CONSOMMÉ

2 cans (10½ ounces each) condensed beef broth (bouillon)	¼ cup sliced carrot
	¼ cup sliced celery
	2 sprigs parsley
1 soup can water	1 small bay leaf
¼ cup sliced onion	⅛ teaspoon thyme leaves

Heat all ingredients to boiling. Reduce heat; cover and simmer 30 minutes. Strain.

8 servings (about ½ cup each).

VARIATION

■ *Chicken Consommé:* Substitute 2 cans (10½ ounces each) condensed chicken broth for the condensed beef broth (bouillon).

Lunch and Supper Soups

Go French for a day—with a bowl of steaming soup, a loaf of crispy bread, some cheese and fruit. It's a meal worth borrowing, beloved the world around.

With all the wide variety of canned soups, dried soups, frozen soups on supermarket shelves, there is still great creative satisfaction in making a great soup that's all your own. Try our Creamy Potato Soup (page 637) and run it through your blender with an extra ingredient or two and you can have cauliflower, broccoli, spinach, zucchini or carrot soup—as your fancy, and your left-overs, dictate.

Canned soups, of course, are a more immediate blessing. You can serve them as is, but by adding a can of this and a little of that, you may invent your own special soup.

CORN CHOWDER

Filling and flavorful—one of our favorites.

½ pound bacon, diced
1 medium onion, chopped
  (about ½ cup)
½ cup chopped celery (with
  tops)
2 tablespoons flour
4 cups milk
1 can (1 pound 1 ounce)
  cream-style corn

1 can (1 pound) tiny whole
  potatoes, diced
½ teaspoon salt
⅛ teaspoon pepper
  Snipped parsley
  Paprika

In large saucepan, fry bacon until crisp; remove and drain. Pour all but 3 tablespoons drippings from saucepan. Add onion and celery to drippings in pan; cook and stir until onion is tender.

Remove from heat; blend in flour. Cook over low heat, stirring until mixture is bubbly. Remove from heat. Stir in milk. Heat to boiling, stirring constantly. Boil and stir 1 minute.

Stir in corn, potatoes, salt and pepper; heat through. Stir in bacon. Sprinkle each serving with parsley and paprika.

6 servings (1 cup each).

CHICKEN NOODLE SOUP

2- to 3-pound broiler-fryer
  chicken*
  Salt
  Dash pepper
1½ cups fine noodles

1 tablespoon chopped
  onion
½ teaspoon salt
⅛ teaspoon pepper
1 bay leaf

Wash chicken but do not cut up. Cover chicken with water. Add ½ teaspoon salt per pound of chicken and the pepper. Heat to boiling. Reduce heat; cover and simmer 1½ hours or until chicken is tender.

Remove chicken from broth; remove meat from bones and cut into small pieces. Skim fat from broth. Measure broth into medium saucepan (you should have about 5 cups). Add chicken meat and remaining ingredients.

*If you prefer to use a stewing chicken, cut up and simmer 2½ to 3 hours.

Heat to boiling. Reduce heat and simmer until noodles are tender, 10 to 15 minutes. Remove bay leaf before serving.

6 to 8 servings (about 1 cup each).

FRENCH ONION SOUP

The classic French soup guarantees success—and so does its quick variation.

3 cups sliced onions (about 3 medium)
2 tablespoons butter
4 cups Beef Consommé (page 633)
1 teaspoon Worcestershire sauce
2 thin slices French bread, toasted
Grated Parmesan cheese

In covered large saucepan, cook onions in butter over low heat about 30 minutes, stirring occasionally. Add consommé and Worcestershire sauce; heat to boiling. Reduce heat; cover and simmer about 30 minutes.

Place ½ slice toasted bread in each of 4 soup bowls; pour hot soup over bread and sprinkle with Parmesan cheese.

4 servings (1 cup each).

VARIATION

■ *Quick French Onion Soup:* Substitute 2 cans (10½ ounces each) condensed beef broth (bouillon) and 1½ cups water for the Beef Consommé.

OLD-FASHIONED VEGETABLE SOUP

3 pounds beef shank cuts, cracked
1 quart water
1 bay leaf
5 peppercorns
1 cup sliced carrot
½ cup chopped celery
1 medium onion, chopped (about ½ cup)
1 can (1 pound) tomatoes
1 teaspoon salt
¼ teaspoon marjoram leaves
¼ teaspoon thyme leaves

Cover shanks with water; heat to boiling. Add bay leaf and peppercorns. Reduce heat; cover and simmer 1¾ hours or until meat on shanks is fork tender.

Remove shanks from stock; cut meat from shanks into ½-inch cubes. Let stock cool slightly. Skim fat from surface.

Strain stock into large saucepan. Add meat cubes and remaining ingredients. Heat to boiling. Cover; simmer 20 minutes or until carrots are tender.

8 servings (1 cup each).

SPLIT PEA SOUP

2 cups dried split peas (about 1 pound)
2 quarts water
1 ham bone*
1 cup minced celery

1 medium onion, finely chopped (about ½ cup)
1 sprig parsley
¼ teaspoon pepper

Heat peas and water to boiling; boil gently 2 minutes. Remove from heat; cover and let stand 1 hour.

Add remaining ingredients. Heat to boiling. Reduce heat and simmer 2½ to 3 hours or until peas are very soft.

Remove bone; trim meat from bone and add to soup. If desired, thin with milk or water. Season to taste.

6 servings (1 cup each).

*You can substitute ham shank or ham hocks for the ham bone.

STORMY DAY BEAN SOUP

1 pound dried navy beans
7 cups water
1 ham bone
2 cups cubed cooked smoked ham

¼ cup minced onion
½ teaspoon salt
1 bay leaf
Dash pepper

Rinse beans. Heat beans and water to boiling; boil gently 2 minutes. Remove from heat; cover and let stand 1 hour.

Add remaining ingredients. Heat to boiling. Reduce heat; cover and simmer about 1 hour and 15 minutes or until beans are soft. Skim off foam occasionally. (Add water if necessary.)

Remove bay leaf and ham bone. Trim meat from bone; add to soup. Season to taste.

7 servings (1 cup each).

CREAMY POTATO SOUP

2 tablespoons butter or margarine	¼ teaspoon celery salt
2 tablespoons finely chopped onion	⅛ teaspoon pepper
	3½ cups milk
1½ teaspoons salt	1⅓ cups instant mashed potato puffs (dry)

Heat butter, onion, salt, celery salt, pepper and milk to scalding. Stir in potato puffs; continue cooking until smooth, stirring constantly. (Soup should be consistency of heavy cream.) If desired, garnish each serving with paprika and parsley.

4 servings (1 cup each).

OYSTER STEW

¼ cup butter or margarine	½ cup light cream (20%)
1 pint fresh oysters	1 teaspoon salt
2 cups milk	Dash pepper

Melt butter in small saucepan. Add oysters (with liquor); cook and stir over low heat just until edges curl. Heat milk and cream in another saucepan. Stir in salt, pepper and oysters.

4 servings (1 cup each).

QUICK BORSCH

A double-quick version of the hearty Russian beet soup. And so versatile! Serve it hot or cold, as an appetizer or the star.

1 can (10½ ounces) condensed beef broth (bouillon)	1 cup shredded cabbage
	2 tablespoons minced onion
	1 teaspoon sugar
1 can (1 pound) shoestring beets	1 teaspoon lemon juice
	Dairy sour cream

Heat beef broth, beets (with liquid), cabbage, onion and sugar to boiling. Reduce heat; simmer gently 5 minutes. Stir in lemon juice and chill thoroughly. Top each serving with spoonful of sour cream.

3 or 4 servings (about 1 cup each).

CANNED SOUP COMBOS

■ 1 can (10½ ounces) condensed beef noodle soup, 1 can (10¾ ounces) condensed tomato soup, 1 soup can water and 1 soup can milk.

■ 1 can (10¾ ounces) condensed Cheddar cheese soup, 1 can (11¼ ounces) condensed split pea with ham soup, 1 soup can water and 1 soup can milk.

■ 1 can (10½ ounces) condensed chicken noodle soup, 1 can (10½ ounces) condensed onion soup and 2 soup cans water.

■ 1 can (10½ ounces) condensed chicken with rice soup, 1 can (10¾ ounces) condensed tomato soup, 1 soup can water and 1 soup can milk.

■ 1 can (10¾ ounces) condensed tomato soup, 1 can (10½ ounces) condensed chicken gumbo soup, 1 soup can water and 1 soup can milk.

■ 1 can (10¾ ounces) condensed tomato soup, 1 can (11¼ ounces) condensed split pea with ham soup, 1 soup can water and 1 soup can milk.

CHOWDER—TAKE YOUR STAND The battle waged over "authentic" chowder—that is, whether it's made with tomatoes or milk—is one that will never be resolved. The New Englander makes his chowder with salt pork, potatoes, onions, milk and fresh clams. Manhattanites claim that their tomato-rich version is more flavorful, less fattening. Where do you stand?

NEW ENGLAND CLAM CHOWDER

¼ cup diced bacon
¼ cup minced onion
1 can (10½ ounces) condensed cream of potato soup
¾ cup milk
2 cans (7 to 8 ounces each) minced clams
1 tablespoon lemon juice
⅛ teaspoon pepper

In large saucepan, cook and stir bacon and onion until bacon is crisp and onion is tender. Stir in soup and milk; heat through, stirring occasionally. Stir in clams (with liquor), lemon juice and pepper. Heat through.
4 servings (1 cup each).

MANHATTAN CLAM CHOWDER

¼ cup diced bacon
¼ cup minced onion
2 cans (7 to 8 ounces each)
    minced clams, drained
1 can (10½ ounces)
    condensed cream of
    potato soup

1 can (10¾ ounces)
    condensed tomato soup
1 soup can water
2 teaspoons snipped parsley
1 teaspoon salt
¼ teaspoon thyme leaves
⅛ teaspoon pepper

In large saucepan, cook and stir bacon and onion until bacon is crisp and onion is tender. Mix in remaining ingredients. Heat through, stirring occasionally.

    5 servings (1 cup each).

LOBSTER BISQUE

2 cans (11¼ ounces each)
    condensed green pea soup
2 cans (11 ounces each)
    condensed bisque of
    tomato soup
1 soup can milk
2 cups light cream (20%)
1 teaspoon salt

½ teaspoon pepper
1 teaspoon Worcestershire
    sauce
3 cans (5 ounces each)
    lobster meat, drained and
    broken apart
⅓ cup dry sherry*

Combine all ingredients except lobster meat and sherry in large saucepan. Beat with rotary beater; heat through. Stir in lobster meat and sherry; heat through.

    10 servings (1 cup each).

*If desired, omit sherry and add ⅓ cup milk.

SAVORY CREAM OF CHICKEN SOUP

1 can (10½ ounces)
    condensed cream of
    chicken soup
1 can (10½ ounces)
    condensed chicken with
    rice soup

½ cup milk
1 teaspoon tarragon leaves

Combine all ingredients; heat over low heat, stirring occasionally. If desired, garnish each serving with whipped cream and sprinkle with paprika.

    3 servings (1 cup each).

CALIFORNIA CREAM SOUP

A colorful salute to the West Coast.

1 can (10½ ounces)
  condensed cream of celery
  soup
1 can (10½ ounces)
  condensed cream of
  chicken soup
2 cups milk
⅔ cup light cream (20%)

¾ teaspoon salt
⅛ teaspoon pepper
1 ripe medium avocado,
  peeled and chopped
  (about ¾ cup)
¼ cup sliced pitted ripe
  olives
¼ cup chopped pimiento

Combine soups, milk, cream, salt and pepper; heat to simmering over low heat, stirring occasionally. Stir in avocado, olives and pimiento; heat through.
6 servings (1 cup each).

HEARTY TOMATO SOUP

1 medium onion, finely
  chopped (about ½ cup)
2 tablespoons butter or
  margarine
1 package (3 ounces) cream
  cheese, softened
2 cans (10¾ ounces each)
  condensed tomato soup

1 soup can milk
½ teaspoon paprika
½ teaspoon sweet basil
  leaves
⅛ teaspoon garlic powder

In medium saucepan, cook and stir onion in butter until onion is tender. Stir in cream cheese. Gradually stir in soup and milk; beat with rotary beater until smooth. Add seasonings. Heat, stirring frequently, but do not boil. If desired, garnish each serving with sieved egg yolk.
4 servings (1 cup each).

MUSHROOM-CORN SOUP

2 slices bacon
1 medium onion, chopped
  (about ½ cup)
1 can (8 ounces) cream-
  style corn

1 can (10½ ounces)
  condensed cream of
  mushroom soup
1 soup can milk

In saucepan, fry bacon until crisp; remove and drain. Add onion to bacon drippings in saucepan; cook and stir until onion is tender. Stir in corn, soup and milk; heat through, stirring occasionally. Crumble bacon; sprinkle over each serving.

3 servings (1 cup each).

Stews

France has long been known for its economical, lovingly cooked, flavorful stews. Once considered a dish for peasants, their excellence quickly elevated them to the realm of *haute cuisine*.

Nor is France alone in its love of stews. The Poles have their *bigos*, the Germans and Hungarians their goulashes, and so on. (You will find many of these potpourris in the Main Dishes chapter, pages 459 to 500.) But it is Americans who are true fans of all stews.

SKILLET LAMB STEW

1 tablespoon shortening	¼ teaspoon pepper
1½ pounds lamb shoulder, cut into 2-inch cubes	¼ teaspoon celery seed
2 merium onions, chopped (about 1 cup)	¼ teaspoon marjoram leaves
2 cups beef broth*	⅛ teaspoon thyme leaves
3 medium potatoes, pared and thinly sliced	1 package (10 ounces) frozen green peas, broken apart
½ teaspoon salt	

Melt shortening in large skillet; brown meat well. Drain off fat. Add onions; cook and stir until tender. Pour broth over meat and onions. Cover; simmer 2 hours.

Stir in potatoes and seasonings. Cover; simmer 30 minutes. Skim off excess fat. Stir in peas; cover and cook 10 minutes longer.

4 servings.

*Beef broth can be made by dissolving 2 beef bouillon cubes in 2 cups boiling water, or use canned beef broth (bouillon).

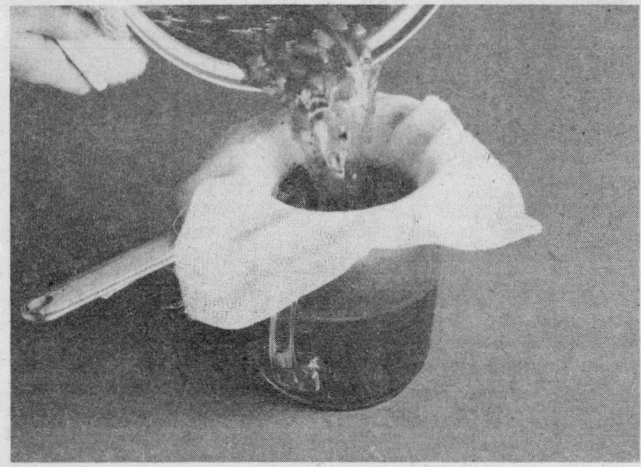

Strain Pot-au-Feu broth through cheesecloth-lined strainer.

POT-AU-FEU

To serve this French favorite authentically, offer the broth first, in large bowls; then bring out the meat-and-vegetable platter.

2 pounds beef fresh brisket, round or chuck roast	1 clove garlic, crushed
	1 sprig parsley
	1 turnip, quartered
½ pound marrow bone, cracked	4 carrots, halved lengthwise
2½ quarts cold water	4 leeks, trimmed to within 1 inch above white end and halved, or 1 medium onion, sliced
1 carrot, diced	
1 stalk celery, diced	
¼ cup chopped onion	
2 teaspoons salt	2 stalks celery, halved
5 peppercorns	1 onion, studded with 3 whole cloves
1 teaspoon thyme leaves	
1 bay leaf	

Place meat, bone and water in large kettle; add diced carrot and celery, chopped onion and next 6 seasonings. Heat to boiling. Reduce heat and simmer gently 3 hours, skimming off foam frequently. Add remaining ingredients. Cover; simmer 1 hour.

Arrange meat and vegetables on platter; keep warm. Strain broth through cheesecloth; season to taste. Serve broth separately in large soup bowls.

4 servings.

BEEF BOURGUIGNON

Dip slices of French bread right into the sauce.

2 tablespoons shortening	1 teaspoon salt
5 medium onions, sliced	¼ teaspoon marjoram
½ pound mushrooms, washed, trimmed and sliced	leaves
	¼ teaspoon thyme leaves
	⅛ teaspoon pepper
2 pounds beef boneless chuck, cut into 1-inch cubes	1½ tablespoons flour
	¾ cup beef broth*
	1½ cups red Burgundy

Melt shortening in large skillet. Add onions and mushrooms; cook and stir until onions are tender. Remove vegetables and drain. Brown meat in same skillet, adding shortening if necessary. Remove from heat.

Sprinkle next 4 seasonings over meat. Mix flour and broth; stir into skillet. Heat to boiling, stirring constantly. Boil and stir 1 minute. Stir in wine. Cover; simmer 1½ to 2 hours or until meat is tender. (The liquid should always just cover meat. If necessary, add more broth and wine—1 part broth to 2 parts wine.) Gently stir in onions and mushrooms; cook uncovered 15 minutes or until heated through.

6 servings.

*Beef broth can be made by dissolving 1 beef bouillon cube in ¾ cup boiling water, or use canned beef broth (bouillon).

QUICKIE BEEF STEW

1 can (1 pound) sliced carrots	¼ cup all-purpose flour
1 can (8 ounces) whole potatoes	1 envelope (about 1½ ounces) dry onion soup mix
1 can (8 ounces) cut green beans	3 cups cut-up cooked beef

Drain vegetables, reserving liquid. Combine flour and soup mix in large skillet. Add water to reserved liquid to measure 3 cups; stir into mixture in skillet. Heat to boiling, stirring constantly. Boil and stir 1 minute. Stir in vegetables and beef. Cover; cook over low heat about 10 minutes or until heated through.

4 servings (about 1½ cups each).

COQ AU VIN

3- to 3½-pound broiler-fryer
  chicken, cut up
½ cup all-purpose flour*
1 teaspoon salt
¼ teaspoon pepper
6 slices bacon
6 small onions
½ pound mushrooms,
  washed, trimmed and
  sliced

4 carrots, halved
1 cup chicken broth
1 cup red Burgundy
1 clove garlic, crushed
½ teaspoon salt
  Bouquet Garni (below)

Wash chicken and pat dry. Mix flour, salt and pepper.
Coat chicken with flour mixture. In large skillet, fry
bacon until crisp; remove and drain. Brown chicken in
hot bacon drippings.

Push chicken to one side; add onions and mushrooms
and cook and stir until onions are tender. Drain off fat.
Crumble bacon and stir in with remaining ingredients.

Cover; simmer about 1 hour or until chicken is tender.
Remove Bouquet Garni before serving. Skim off excess
fat. If desired, sprinkle chicken with snipped parsley.

4 servings.

*If using self-rising flour, decrease salt to ½ teaspoon.

BOUQUET GARNI

Tie ½ teaspoon thyme leaves, 1 bay leaf and 2 large
sprigs parsley in cheesecloth bag.

OLD-FASHIONED BEEF STEW

½ cup all-purpose flour
1 teaspoon salt
¼ teaspoon pepper
2 pounds beef stew meat,
  cut into 1-inch pieces
2 tablespoons shortening
6 cups hot water
3 pared medium potatoes,
  cut into 1-inch cubes
1 medium turnip, cut into
  1-inch cubes

4 carrots, cut into 1-inch
  slices
1 green pepper, cut into
  strips
1 cup sliced celery (1-inch
  pieces)
1 medium onion, diced
  (about ½ cup)
1 tablespoon salt
2 beef bouillon cubes
1 bay leaf

Mix flour, 1 teaspoon salt and the pepper. Coat meat

with flour mixture. Melt shortening in large skillet; brown meat thoroughly.

Add water; heat to boiling. Reduce heat; cover and simmer 2 hours. Stir in remaining ingredients. Simmer 30 minutes or until vegetables are tender.

If desired, thicken stew. In covered small jar, shake 1 cup cold water and 2 to 4 tablespoons flour until blended. Stir into stew; heat to boiling, stirring constantly. Boil and stir 1 minute.

6 servings.

VARIATIONS

■ *Oxtail Stew:* Substitute 4 pounds oxtails for the stew meat; increase first cooking period to 3½ hours.

■ *Chicken Stew:* Substitute 3- to 4-pound stewing chicken, cut up, for the stew meat and chicken bouillon cubes for the beef bouillon cubes. Increase first cooking period to 2½ hours; skim excess fat from broth before adding vegetables. If desired, serve with Dumplings (page 67).

Sandwiches

*An English earl invented it, so the story goes.
But it has remained for America to make the
sandwich a way of life. "Peanut butter 'n jelly,"
"burger, please," "ham on rye," "tuna," "ham
'n cheese," "BLT"—it's almost a national
language. But don't fall into a sandwich routine.
Next time you pack a lunch box or fix a quick
lunch, spring a surprise—a really different
sandwich!*

Sandwiches

There are three parts to a sandwich, as everybody knows. The bread. The spread. And the filling. Be sure to mix, match and vary each of them. The bread can be white or wheat or rye, a crusty roll, a "seedy" bun, nut or fruit bread in thin slices. The spread can be butter or margarine or mayonnaise with pleasant flavor variations. The fillings can be hot or cold, thick or thin, spicy or bland, crunchy or smooth, one layer or many.

When making sandwiches, firm bread is best. Spread each slice with softened butter or margarine to prevent the filling from soaking into the bread. Crisp lettuce leaves will also serve this purpose. Unless you plan to eat the sandwich right away, juicy filling companions such as cole slaw or tomatoes should be packed on the side.

Freezing Sandwiches

Save time! You may want to set up an assembly line and freeze a week's supply of sandwiches in advance (they will keep up to 3 weeks). Spread each slice of bread to the edges with softened butter or margarine. Fill and wrap each sandwich separately in freezing wrap. Label and freeze. Sliced meats, poultry and cheese, flaked tuna or salmon, cheese spreads and peanut butter all freeze well. Use fruit juice, dairy sour cream or applesauce to moisten slightly. Avoid jelly, mayonnaise or salad dressing, as they will make the sandwich soggy; hard-cooked egg whites, salad greens and fresh vegetables also do not freeze well. The sandwiches go wrapped from freezer to lunch box; they will defrost in 3 to 3½ hours, just in time for lunch. Do not refreeze. They may also be made the night before and stored in moisture-proof paper in the refrigerator.

SANDWICH BUTTERS

To spread on sandwiches for "extra-ordinary" flavor.

Chili-Oregano Butter: (Serve on beef sandwiches, hamburgers and hot dogs.) Mix ½ cup soft butter or margarine, 1 tablespoon chili sauce and ½ teaspoon oregano leaves.

Curry Butter: (Serve on lamb and ham sandwiches.) Mix ½ cup soft butter or margarine and 1 teaspoon curry powder.

Horseradish Butter: (Serve on tongue, roast beef and ham sandwiches.) Mix ½ cup soft butter or margarine and 1 tablespoon horseradish.

Lemon-Herb Butter: (Serve on seafood and beef sandwiches.) Mix ½ cup soft butter or margarine, 1 tablespoon lemon juice, 1 teaspoon parsley flakes and ½ teaspoon basil.

Parsley Butter: (Serve on roast lamb and beef sandwiches.) Mix ½ cup soft butter or margarine, 2 tablespoons snipped parsley and 2 teaspoons lemon juice.

Enough for 6 sandwiches.

NUT BREAD BUTTERS

Special, delicate flavors to set off nut breads.

Almond Butter: Mix ½ cup soft butter or margarine, 1 tablespoon finely chopped almonds and ½ teaspoon almond extract.

Date Butter: Mix ½ cup soft butter or margarine and ¼ cup finely chopped dates.

Orange Butter: Mix ½ cup soft butter or margarine, 1 tablespoon orange juice and 1 teaspoon grated orange peel.

Enough for 10 to 12 slices.

PACK-AND-CARRY SANDWICH CHART

Mix or match to add variety to pack-and-carry sandwiches.

Sandwich Breads and Rolls		Fillings
French	White	Sliced cooked beef, ham, lamb,
Italian	Whole wheat	pork, turkey or chicken
Onion	Biscuits	Tongue
Potato	Corn muffins	Assorted cold cuts
Pumpernickel	English muffins	Bacon
Raisin	Frankfurter buns	Canned luncheon meats
Rye	Hamburger buns	Cheese
Vienna	Hard rolls	Sliced hard-cooked eggs
		Jelly
		Peanut butter
		Softened cream cheese

Sandwich Fillings

If you are reaching for the spectacular, throw caution to the winds and empty your refrigerator as you fill sandwiches with sliced avocado or asparagus tips, chopped raw spinach or watercress in creamy mayonnaise, marinated cucumbers or wafer-thin slices of tomato and Bermuda onion. Let your taste buds be your guide.

EGG SALAD FILLING

6 hard-cooked eggs, chopped
½ cup finely chopped celery
1 tablespoon minced onion
⅓ cup mayonnaise or salad dressing
¼ teaspoon salt
Dash pepper

Stir together all ingredients until well mixed.
2 cups (enough for 6 sandwiches).

TUNA SALAD FILLING

1 can (7 ounces) tuna, drained
¼ cup finely chopped sweet pickle
½ cup mayonnaise or salad dressing
¼ teaspoon salt

Stir together all ingredients until well mixed.
1¼ cups (enough for 3 or 4 sandwiches).

Filling Companions

Sliced cucumber
Sliced green pepper
Sliced onion
Sliced radishes
Sliced tomato
Lettuce
Fresh spinach
Sliced Olives

VARIATION

■ *Tuna-Olive Filling:* Substitute ¼ cup sliced pimiento-stuffed olives or sliced pitted ripe olives for the sweet pickle.

CRABMEAT SALAD FILLING

1 can (7½ ounces) crabmeat, drained and cartilage removed
¼ cup dairy sour cream
¼ cup chopped celery
¼ teaspoon salt
½ teaspoon Worcestershire sauce

Stir together all ingredients until well mixed.
1¼ cups (enough for 3 or 4 sandwiches).

VARIATION

■ *Cheese-Crabmeat Salad Filling:* Add ½ cup shredded sharp Cheddar cheese and increase Worcestershire sauce to 1 teaspoon.

CHOPPED BEEF FILLING

1 cup chopped cooked beef
½ cup chopped celery
2 tablespoons minced onion
2 tablespoons sweet pickle relish, drained
1 tablespoon lemon juice
½ teaspoon salt
⅛ teaspoon pepper
⅓ cup salad dressing or mayonnaise

Stir together all ingredients until well mixed.
1½ cups (enough for 4 or 5 sandwiches).

CORNED BEEF-ONION FILLING

1 cup chopped cooked
   corned beef
½ cup mayonnaise or salad
   dressing

⅓ cup minced celery
1 tablespoon minced onion
2 tablespoons prepared
   mustard

Stir together all ingredients until well mixed.
1½ cups (enough for 4 or 5 sandwiches).

FRANK AND EGG FILLING

3 frankfurters, chopped (1
   cup)
1 hard-cooked egg, chopped
1 tablespoon finely chopped
   onion

⅓ cup chili sauce or catsup
¼ teaspoon salt
⅛ teaspoon pepper

Stir together all ingredients until well mixed.
1½ cups (enough for 4 or 5 sandwiches).

CHICKEN SALAD FILLING

1 cup chopped cooked
   chicken
½ cup chopped celery
1½ teaspoons lemon juice
¼ teaspoon salt

⅛ teaspoon pepper
¼ cup mayonnaise or salad
   dressing
1 hard-cooked egg, chopped

Stir together all ingredients until well mixed.
1½ cups (enough for 4 or 5 sandwiches).

VARIATION

■ *Chicken-Ham Salad Filling:* Add 1 cup chopped
cooked ham and increase mayonnaise to ½ cup.
2½ cups (enough for 7 or 8 sandwiches).

Lunchtime Sandwiches

Soup and sandwich, sandwich and a milk shake, sandwich and a piece of cake—Lunchtime, USA! And a very
good lunch it is. Expandable, too. Makes it easy to enrich your children's lives with the joy of bringing a *friend*
home for lunch.

CHILI DOGS

1 can (15 ounces) chili
  with beans
1 can (6 ounces) tomato
  paste
¼ cup chopped green pepper
¼ cup chopped onion
1 teaspoon prepared
  mustard

½ teaspoon salt
½ teaspoon chili powder
1 pound frankfurters (8 to
  10)
8 to 10 frankfurter buns,
  buttered

In saucepan, combine all ingredients except frankfurters and buns. Heat to boiling; reduce heat and simmer 10 minutes.

Drop frankfurters into boiling water; reduce heat. Cover; simmer 5 to 8 minutes.

Toast buns. Serve frankfurters in buns; top with chili mixture.

8 to 10 sandwiches.

HOT DOG TOASTIES

8 frankfurters
8 slices bread
  Soft butter or margarine
  Prepared mustard

8 slices process American
  cheese
¼ cup butter or margarine,
  melted

Drop frankfurters into boiling water; reduce heat. Cover; simmer 5 to 8 minutes.

Spread bread with soft butter and mustard. Place bread slices on ungreased baking sheet and top each with cheese slice.

Place frankfurters diagonally on cheese. Fold bread over to form triangle; secure with wooden picks. Brush with melted butter.

Set oven control at broil and/or 550°. Broil 3 to 4 inches from heat about 2 minutes or until golden brown.

8 sandwiches.

TACO HOT DOGS

⅓ cup chili sauce
1 teaspoon minced hot chili
  pepper or ¼ teaspoon red
  pepper sauce
5 frankfurters

5 frankfurter buns, buttered
⅔ cup shredded lettuce
⅓ cup shredded natural
  Cheddar cheese

Combine chili sauce and chili pepper. Drop frankfurters into boiling water; reduce heat. Cover; simmer 5 to 8 minutes.

Toast buns. Place frankfurters in buns. Spoon chili sauce mixture over frankfurters. Top with shredded lettuce and cheese.

5 sandwiches.

FRANKS WITH SAUERKRAUT

1 pound frankfurters (8 to 10)
1 can (1 pound) sauerkraut
8 to 10 frankfurter buns, buttered

Prepared mustard
Chopped onion

Drop frankfurters into boiling water; reduce heat. Cover; simmer 5 to 8 minutes.

Heat sauerkraut over low heat; drain. Serve frankfurters in buns; top with sauerkraut, mustard and chopped onion.

8 to 10 sandwiches.

INDIVIDUAL HOT SUB SANDWICHES

8 hard rolls
  Soft butter or margarine
8 slices salami or boiled ham
8 slices mozzarella cheese

8 slices cooked turkey or chicken
1 package (4 ounces) blue cheese, crumbled

Heat oven to 425°. Cut rolls horizontally into thirds. Spread *all* cut surfaces with butter. Place salami slice on bottom section of each roll and top with cheese slice. Add second section of roll and top with turkey slice and blue cheese. Top with third section of roll. Wrap each sandwich in aluminum foil; heat 15 to 20 minutes.

8 sandwiches.

HAMBURGERS

1 pound ground beef
1 tablespoon instant minced onion

½ teaspoon salt
¼ teaspoon pepper
4 hamburger buns, split

Mix ground beef, onion, salt and pepper. Shape mixture into four 4½-inch patties. Set oven control at broil and/or 550°. Broil hamburgers 3 inches from heat about 2 minutes per side for rare, 3 to 4 minutes per side for medium. Serve in buns. If desired, top burgers wtih a slice of tomato, onion or pickle.

4 sandwiches.

VARIATIONS

■ *Charcoal-grilled Hamburgers:* Add ¼ cup water to ground beef mixture. Shape into 5 patties. Place on grill 4 to 6 inches from hot coals. Cook, turning once, 12 minutes or until done.

■ *Panfried Hamburgers:* Turning frequently, fry patties in ½ teaspoon hot shortening over medium heat about 7 minutes.

■ *California Hamburgers:* Top each hamburger with lettuce, onion slice, tomato slice and about 1 teaspoon mayonnaise.

■ *Cheeseburgers:* About 1 minute before hamburgers are done, top each with cheese slice. Continue cooking until cheese melts.

DOUBLE DECKER BURGERS

Follow recipe for Hamburgers (page 652) except—before mixing ingredients, add 1 egg and ¼ cup dry bread crumbs. Shape mixture into 8 patties, about ½ inch thick.

Spread any of the fillings below on four of the patties.

FREEZER BURGERS

1 pound ground beef	½ cup finely crushed cracker
1 envelope (about 1½ ounces)	crumbs
dry onion soup mix	8 hamburger buns, split

Mix ground beef, onion soup mix and cracker crumbs. Shape mixture into eight 4½-inch patties. Wrap each patty in single thickness of aluminum foil; freeze. (Keep no longer than 3 months.) Wrap each bun in aluminum foil; freeze.

Heat frozen hamburgers and buns (in foil wrappings) in 425° oven 10 minutes.

8 sandwiches.

Top each with a remaining patty and seal edges firmly.
4 sandwiches.

MIX AND MATCH FILLINGS

Use one or more of the following: dill pickle slices,
pickle relish, prepared mustard, catsup, horseradish,
chopped onions, onion slices, tomato slices, Cheddar
cheese slices and shredded process American cheese.

SLOPPY JOES

1 pound ground beef
1 medium onion, chopped
(about ½ cup)
3 tablespoons catsup
3 tablespoons prepared
mustard

1 can (10½ ounces) con-
densed chicken gumbo
soup
6 hamburger buns, split and
toasted

In medium skillet, cook and stir ground beef and onion
until meat is brown and onion is tender. Stir in catsup,
mustard and soup. Simmer 15 minutes or until mixture
thickens slightly, stirring occasionally. Spoon over
bottom halves of buns; top with remaining halves.
6 sandwiches.

BEEF-EGG SCRAMBLE

¼ pound ground beef
¼ cup chopped onion
2 tablespoons chopped
green pepper
½ teaspoon salt

⅛ teaspoon pepper
3 eggs
1½ tablespoons water
4 hamburger buns, split and
toasted

Cook and stir ground beef, onion, green pepper, salt
and pepper until meat is brown and onion is tender.
Blend eggs and water; pour over meat mixture. Cook
over low heat just until eggs are set. Lift cooked portions
with spatula and turn to cook eggs evenly. Serve in
buns.
4 servings.

DEVILED PORK BUNS

8 thin slices cooked pork
¾ cup barbecue sauce
4 sesame hamburger buns,
split

Soft butter or margarine
4 slices onion
4 green pepper rings

Combine pork and barbecue sauce in saucepan. Sim-

mer uncovered 10 minutes, stirring occasionally. Spread
bun halves with butter or margarine; place cut side up
on broiler rack. Place onion slice and green pepper ring
on bottom half of each bun.

Set oven control at broil and/or 550°. Broil buns 4
to 5 inches from heat until golden.

Place 2 pork slices on each green pepper ring; spoon
remaining sauce over meat and top with other half of
bun.

4 sandwiches.

EASY DENVER SANDWICH

¼ cup minced onion	½ cup minced cooked ham
¼ cup minced green pepper	¼ teaspoon salt
2 tablespoons shortening (half butter or margarine)	⅛ teaspoon pepper
4 eggs	8 slices bread or toast, buttered

In 10-inch skillet, cook and stir onion and green pepper in hot shortening until onion is tender.

Beat eggs slightly; stir in ham, salt and pepper. Pour
egg mixture into skillet. Cook over low heat just until
set. Cut into 4 wedges and turn. Brown slightly. Serve
between bread slices.

4 sandwiches.

TUNA CHEESIES

1 can (6½ ounces) tuna, drained	8 slices bread or 4 English muffins, halved
¼ cup finely chopped onion	Butter or margarine
¼ cup chopped celery	8 slices tomato
2 tablespoons mayonnaise	8 slices process American cheese
¼ teaspoon salt	Mayonnaise
¼ teaspoon pepper	

Mix tuna, onion, celery, 2 tablespoons mayonnaise,
the salt and pepper. Set oven control at broil and/or
550°. Spread bread with butter and toast in broiler.

Spread tuna mixture on toast. Place tomato slice on
each and top with cheese slice trimmed to fit. Spread
mayonnaise over cheese.

Broil 5 inches from heat 3 to 5 minutes or until cheese
is melted and golden brown. Serve immediately. If desired, garnish with parsley or crisply fried bacon slices.

8 sandwiches.

CRABMEAT CHEESE BUNS

2 cups shredded process American cheese (about 8 ounces)	1 can (7½ ounces) crabmeat, drained and cartilage removed
⅓ cup butter or margarine	6 hamburger buns, split

Melt cheese and butter in medium saucepan over low heat. Remove from heat; stir in crabmeat. Place buns cut side up on broiler rack; spread each half with crabmeat mixture.

Set oven control at broil and/or 550°. Broil 4 to 5 inches from heat about 2 minutes or until golden brown and bubbly.

6 servings (2 halves each).

CURRIED CHICKEN SANDWICHES

1 cup chopped cooked chicken	½ cup mayonnaise or salad dressing
½ cup diced celery	¾ teaspoon curry powder
¼ cup diced onion	1 tablespoon lemon juice
½ cup chopped salted peanuts	8 slices toast, buttered

Mix thoroughly all ingredients except toast. Spread mixture on toast, being careful to bring it to edges. Set oven control at broil and/or 550°. Broil 3 inches from heat 3 minutes or until hot.

8 sandwiches.

Full-meal Sandwiches

Universal favorites for a light meal or a midnight supper, these sandwiches appeal to all tastes. Just for fun, spread out the makings and let each person create his own.

CLUB SANDWICHES

For those with hearty appetites, add slices of salami, cooked ham or hard-cooked eggs or green pepper rings.

18 slices white bread, toasted
    Mayonnaise or salad
    dressing
12 lettuce leaves
6 slices cooked chicken

18 slices tomato (about 3
    medium)
18 slices bacon, crisply fried
    Salt and pepper

Spread toast with mayonnaise (use butter or margarine, too, if desired). Place lettuce leaf and chicken slice on each of 6 toast slices. Cover with second slice toast. Top with lettuce leaf, 3 tomato slices and 3 bacon slices. Season with salt and pepper. Cover with third slice toast; secure with picks. To serve, cut each sandwich diagonally into halves or quarters.

6 sandwiches.

ITALIAN SUB SANDWICH

Sliced pimiento-stuffed olives garnish this sandwich.

1 loaf (1-pound) French
    bread
    Soft butter or margarine
4 or 5 crisp lettuce leaves
½ pound sliced salami
2 tomatoes, sliced
    Salt and pepper

4 ounces sliced Swiss
    cheese
½ pound sliced boiled ham
½ cucumber, thinly sliced
1 large onion, sliced
3 tablespoons prepared
    mustard

Cut bread in half horizontally. Spread bottom half with butter. Layer lettuce, salami and tomatoes on buttered bread; season with salt and pepper. Layer cheese, ham, cucumber and onion on top of tomatoes.

Spread top half of bread with mustard; place over lettuce. Secure loaf with picks or small skewers. To serve, cut into 6 sections.

6 servings.

VARIATION

■ *Zesty Sub:* Omit mustard. Stir together 1 tablespoon wine vinegar, 1 tablespoon olive oil and ¼ teaspoon garlic salt; dip lettuce leaves into mixture before using in sandwich.

HOT 'N ZIPPY SANDWICH LOAF

1 loaf (1 pound) unsliced white bread (about 8 inches long)	3 tablespoons prepared mustard
½ cup soft butter or margarine	1 tablespoon poppy seed
	1 tablespoon lemon juice
3 tablespoons instant minced onion	Dash cayenne red pepper
	12 slices Swiss cheese
	12 thin slices luncheon meat

Heat oven to 350°. Carefully trim crust from top of bread. At equal intervals make 6 diagonal cuts from top of loaf almost through to bottom. Place loaf on lightly greased baking sheet.

Mix butter, onion, mustard, poppy seed, lemon juice and cayenne pepper. Reserve about 3 tablespoons of the mixture. Spread remaining butter mixture into cuts.

Alternate 2 cheese slices and 2 meat slices in *each* cut, allowing each to stick out slightly at top and sides of bread. Spread reserved butter mixture over top and sides of loaf.

Bake 25 minutes; cover with foil during last 10 minutes of baking. To serve, slice completely through each diagonal cut, between meat slice and bread.

6 servings.

REUBEN SANDWICHES

For a change, butter both sides of the finished sandwich and try it grilled.

⅓ cup mayonnaise or salad dressing	½ pound sliced cooked corned beef
1 tablespoon chili sauce	1 can (1 pound) sauerkraut, drained
12 slices rye bread, buttered	
½ pound sliced Swiss cheese	

Mix mayonnaise and chili sauce; spread on 6 slices bread. Arrange cheese, corned beef and sauerkraut on spread slices; top with remaining bread slices.

6 sandwiches.

VARIATION

■ *Rachel Sandwiches:* Substitute 1½ cups coleslaw for the sauerkraut.

ANCHOVY OPEN-FACE SANDWICHES

Aspic, caviar, anchovy . . . and then some. Hearty—but with a strong touch of elegance. Serve two open-face sandwiches to each person.

12 slices dark pumpernickel bread
 Butter or margarine
1 can (12 ounces) tomato aspic, chilled
 Lettuce leaves

6 to 12 slices cooked tongue, chilled
6 to 12 slices Swiss cheese
1 jar (2 ounces) caviar
12 to 18 anchovy strips
 Bottled mustard sauce

Spread bread with butter. Remove aspic from can; cut into 6 slices. Place lettuce leaf on each of 6 slices bread; top with tongue, small leaf of lettuce and aspic slice.

Place cheese on remaining slices of bread; spoon caviar down center of cheese slices. Arrange twisted strips of anchovies on caviar. Pass mustard sauce.

 6 servings (2 halves each).

MOCK STROGANOFF BURGERS

A quick and casual approach to the chafing dish specialty. You'll find this sandwich as satisfying as any main dish.

1 pound ground beef
1 can (3 ounces) sliced mushrooms, drained
¼ cup chopped onion
¼ teaspoon garlic powder
2 tablespoons flour
1 teaspoon salt
¼ teaspoon pepper

⅛ to ¼ teaspoon nutmeg
1 cup dairy sour cream
1 can (1 pound) French-style green beans, drained (reserve ¼ cup liquid)
10 hamburger buns, split and toasted

Cook and stir ground beef, musrooms, onion and garlic powder until meat is brown and onion is tender. Sprinkle flour, salt, pepper and nutmeg over meat; cook over medium heat, stirring until mixture is heated through.

Stir in sour cream, green beans and reserved liquid. Cover and heat through, stirring occasionally. Serve in buns.

 10 sandwiches.

Party Sandwiches

These sandwiches look so pretty and so professional that you'll think they're hard to do. Actually, they're easy! Even easier if you use a spread that freezes well—such as Deviled Ham Spread or Creamy Cheese Spread. (See page 646 for freezing information.) Pack in a box in layers separated by waxed paper. Wrap; label; freeze. Rolled and ribbon sandwiches may be cut after defrosting, which takes about 1 or 2 hours.

OPEN-FACE SANDWICHES

Trim crusts from slices of bread; cut bread into desired shapes and spread with any of the spreads and fillings suggested below. (All of the recipes are on pages 664–666.)

Decorate with a garnish, such as sliced pimiento-stuffed or ripe olives, mushroom slices, anchovies, parsley, pimiento, radish slices, sweet pickle slices, shredded cheese or egg slices.

SPREADS FOR OPEN-FACE SANDWICHES

Avocado Spread
Cottage Cheese Spread
Creamy Cheese Spread
Deviled Ham Spread
Golden Cheese Spread
Ham Salad Filling
Olive-Nut Spread
Shrimp Salad Filling

PARTY SANDWICH LOAF

Here's one of the prettiest party loaves we've seen. When entertaining a crowd, use one white loaf and one whole wheat, alternating the slices.

Trim crust from 1 loaf unsliced sandwich bread. Cut loaf horizontally into 4 equal slices. Spread 3 slices with soft butter or margarine.

Place 1 slice on tray or platter. Spread evenly with Shrimp Salad Filling (page 665). Top with second slice and spread evenly with Olive-Nut Spread (page 665). Top with third slice and spread evenly with Deviled Ham Spread (page 666). Top with unbuttered bread slice.

Mix 2 packages (8 ounces each) cream cheese, softened, and ½ cup light cream. (A few drops food color can be added to tint mixture a delicate color.)

Frost top and sides of loaf with cream cheese mixture. Chill loaf about 30 minutes or until frosting has set. Wrap loaf in a damp cloth and chill at least 2½ hours.

12 to 14 slices.

PINWHEEL SANDWICHES

Trim crust from 1 loaf unsliced sandwich bread. Cut loaf horizontally into ¼-inch slices. Spread each slice with 2 tablespoons soft butter or margarine and ½ cup of one of the spreads suggested below. (All of the recipes are on pages 664–666.)

Cut each slice crosswise in half. Beginning at narrow end, roll up as for jelly roll. Secure with picks. Wrap and chill. Cut each roll into slices, about ½ inch thick.

6 sandwiches per roll.

SPREADS FOR PINWHEEL SANDWICHES

Creamy Cheese Spread
Deviled Ham Spread
Golden Cheese Spread

RIBBON SANDWICHES

Thin strips of bread with delicate fillings between—for your prettiest tea table. These little sandwiches may look difficult, but they're really quite easy to do. Best of all, you can make them well ahead of time.

Trim crust from 1 loaf white and 1 loaf whole wheat unsliced sandwich bread. Cut each loaf horizontally into 6 slices.

For each ribbon loaf, spread each of 2 slices white and 1 slice whole wheat bread with ½ cup of one of the spreads suggested below. (All of the recipes are on pages 664–666.) Assemble loaf, alternating white and

GENERAL PREPARATION TIPS

1. Trim loaf, completely removing all trace of crust.

OPEN-FACE SANDWICHES

For harmony, key garnish to the shape of the sandwich.

PARTY SANDWICH LOAF

Cover with a thin layer of frosting, then swirl on more.

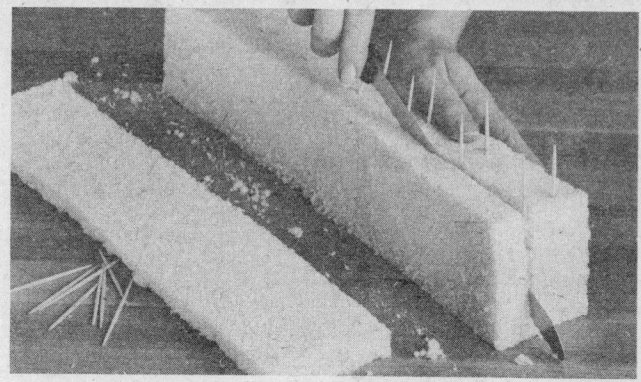

2. For a cutting guide, mark width of layers with picks.

PINWHEELS
These are excellent make-aheads—just slice and serve.

RIBBON SANDWICHES
For tea-size sandwiches, cut each slice in half.

whole wheat slices; top with unspread whole wheat slice. Wrap and chill.

Cut loaves into slices, about ½ inch thick; cut each slice in half.

3 loaves (about 10 dozen sandwiches).

SPREADS FOR RIBBON SANDWICHES

Cottage Cheese Spread
Creamy Cheese Spread
Deviled Ham Spread
Golden Cheese Spread

AVOCADO SPREAD

1 ripe avocado, peeled and pitted
1 teaspoon vinegar
2 teaspoons minced onion
½ teaspoon ascorbic acid mixture
¼ teaspoon salt

Mash avocado; mix in vinegar, onion, ascorbic acid mixture and salt thoroughly. To hold a short time, cover and refrigerate.

About ⅔ cup.

COTTAGE CHEESE SPREAD

1½ cups creamed cottage cheese (small curd)
⅓ cup dairy sour cream
2 tablespoons snipped parsley
1 tablespoon blue cheese salad dressing mix

Stir together all ingredients until well mixed.
About 2 cups.

CREAMY CHEESE SPREAD

2 packages (3 ounces each) cream cheese, softened
½ cup butter or margarine, softened
2 teaspoons paprika
1 teaspoon anchovy paste
1 teaspoon instant minced onion
1 teaspoon dry mustard

Stir together all ingredients until well mixed.
About 1 cup.

GOLDEN CHEESE SPREAD

2 cups shredded Cheddar
cheese
1 package (3 ounces) cream
cheese, softened
¼ cup mayonnaise or salad
dressing

½ teaspoon Worcestershire
sauce
⅛ teaspoon each onion salt,
garlic salt and celery salt

Stir together all ingredients until well mixed.
About 1½ cups.

HAM SALAD FILLING

2 cups ground or minced
cooked ham
½ cup mayonnaise or salad
dressing
½ cup chopped celery

2 tablespoons sweet pickle
relish, drained
1 tablespoon chopped onion
¼ teaspoon pepper

Stir together all ingredients until well mixed.
About 2 cups.

OLIVE-NUT SPREAD

1 package (3 ounces) cream
cheese, softened
½ cup finely chopped
walnuts

¼ cup chopped pimiento-
stuffed olives
2 tablespoons milk

Stir together all ingredients until well mixed.
About 1 cup.

SHRIMP SALAD FILLING

1 can (4½ ounces) broken
shrimp, rinsed and drained
1 hard-cooked egg, finely
chopped
2 tablespoons finely
chopped celery

1 tablespoon lemon juice
⅛ teaspoon salt
Dash pepper
3 tablespoons mayonnaise

Stir together all ingredients until well mixed.
About 1 cup.

DEVILED HAM SPREAD

1 can (4½ ounces) deviled
  ham
¼ cup dairy sour cream
2 tablespoons sweet pickle
  relish, drained

1 tablespoon grated onion
  Dash red pepper sauce

Stir together all ingredients until well mixed.
About 1 cup.

Vegetables

*Eat your spinach! Eat your carrots! Eat your lima
beans! How many of us are haunted by memories
of the vegetables we had to eat? Not today! Not
when you can have your favorites all year long.
And with candied carrots, bacon-flavored beans,
quick toppings, seasoned sauces—you can hardly
wait to zip up to the vegetable corner of your
dinner plate. Here are good ways to start.*

CANNED VEGETABLES

Drain vegetable liquid into saucepan. Heat to boiling;
boil until liquid is reduced to half. Add vegetable; heat
through.

Heat vegetables such as tomatoes, squash or cream-
style corn in saucepan. Season to taste.

Can Size	Number of Servings
8 ounces	2
16 ounces	3 or 4
1 pound 13 ounces	5 to 7

FROZEN VEGETABLES

Prepare frozen vegetables as directed on package.
Read carefully; directions vary from brand to brand.

Note: To use part of package, saw or cut frozen block
of vegetable. Also consider the frozen vegetables packaged in large-size bags which are easily separated into
exact amounts.

VEGETABLE CHEER Does your family shun vegetables? Here are a few double quick fix-ups: Sprinkle
broken or chopped nuts over each portion (maybe cashews, almonds, macadamias, Spanish peanuts); crumble
bacon bits over a green vegetable; grate a bit of cheese
onto each hot serving; add instant onion or lemon juice
to spark the flavor.

DILL CROUTON TOPPING

½ cup croutons
1 tablespoon butter or
  margarine, melted

¼ teaspoon dill weed
⅛ teaspoon salt

Stir together all ingredients. Sprinkle over hot cooked vegetables.

Makes ½ cup.

CRUMB TOPPING FOR VEGETABLES

½ cup dry bread crumbs
1 tablespoon butter or
  margarine, melted

⅛ teaspoon salt

Stir together all ingredients. Sprinkle over hot cooked vegetables or creamed vegetables.

Makes ½ cup.

VARIATION

■ *Nutmeg Crumb Topping:* Stir in ⅛ teaspoon nutmeg.

CEREAL TOPPING FOR VEGETABLES

Enhance vegetables with a buttery, crisp topping. A delightful disguise for warmed-overs.

½ cup crushed O-shaped
  puffed oat cereal or whole
  wheat flakes cereal

1 tablespoon butter or
  margarine, melted
⅛ teaspoon salt

Stir together all ingredients. Sprinkle over hot cooked vegetables or creamed vegetables.

Makes ½ cup.

VARIATIONS

■ *Marjoram Cereal Topping:* Stir in ⅛ teaspoon marjoram leaves.

■ *Oregano Cereal Topping:* Stir in ¼ teaspoon oregano leaves and ⅛ teaspoon basil leaves.

■ *Sage Cereal Topping:* Stir in ¼ teaspoon sage and ⅛ teaspoon dry mustard.

CREAMED VEGETABLES

Stretch your vegetables with a sauce. Use one vegetable or try a mixture of two or three. Remember this trick when you have to set that extra place on short notice.

1 tablespoon butter or margarine	⅛ teaspoon pepper
1 tablespoon flour	1 cup milk
¼ teaspoon salt	2 cups cooked vegetable(s)

Melt butter in medium saucepan over low heat. Blend in flour and seasonings. Cook over low heat, stirring until mixture is smooth and bubbly. Remove from heat. Stir in milk. Heat to boiling, stirring constantly. Boil and stir 1 minute. Stir vegetable(s) into sauce; heat through.
4 to 6 servings.

VARIATIONS

■ *Au Gratin Vegetables:* Heat oven to 325°. Add 1 teaspoon dry mustard to flour mixture and stir 1 cup shredded process American cheese into hot cream sauce. Cook, stirring constantly, until cheese is melted. Pour vegetable mixture into ungreased 1-quart casserole; sprinkle with ½ cup Cereal or Crumb Topping (left). Bake uncovered 15 minutes or until heated through.

■ *Scalloped Vegetables:* Heat oven to 325° and pour vegetable mixture into ungreased 1-quart casserole; sprinkle with ½ cup Cereal or Crumb Topping (left). Bake uncovered 15 minutes or until heated through.

■ *Vegetables in Cheese Sauce:* Add 1 teaspoon dry mustard to flour mixture and stir 1 cup shredded process American cheese (about 4 ounces) into hot cream sauce. Cook, stirring constantly, until cheese is melted.

QUICK VEGETABLES AU GRATIN

Literally, "au gratin" is French for "with crumbs." It usually means the addition of cheese to scalloped vegetables.

Heat oven to 325°. Stir together 1 can (10¾ ounces) condensed Cheddar cheese soup, ½ teaspoon Worcestershire sauce and ½ teaspoon dry mustard. Gently stir into 2 cups cooked vegetable(s).

Pour mixture into ungreased 1-quart casserole. Sprinkle with ½ cup Cereal or Crumb Topping (page 668). Bake uncovered 15 to 20 minutes or until heated through.

4 to 6 servings.

VEGETABLE COMBOS

Cook vegetables separately and then serve them mixed together for added mealtime variety. Try the following.

- Cauliflower and green peas.
- Onions and green peas.
- Carrot slices and green lima beans.
- Mushrooms and green peas.
- Diced carrots in nest of French-style green beans.
- Tomatoes and zucchini.
- Green lima beans in acorn squash halves.
- Acorn squash rings with green peas.
- Carrots and celery.
- Celery and mushrooms.
- Okra and tomatoes.
- Carrots and green peas.
- Brussels sprouts and celery.
- Stuffed tomatoes and buttered green peas.
- Summer squash, tomatoes and onions.
- Green lima beans and corn.
- Green cabbage and red cabbage.
- Brussels sprouts and carrot slices.
- Corn and green peas.

ARTICHOKES—FRENCH (GLOBE)

Amount for 4 servings: 4 (1 per serving).
Season available: September to May.
When shopping: Look for plump, heavy globes, compact scales (leaves); brown spots, indicating frost, are acceptable.

TO COOK ARTICHOKES

Allow 1 artichoke for each serving. Remove any discolored leaves and the small leaves at base of artichoke; trim stem even with base of artichoke. Cutting straight across, slice 1 inch off top; discard top. Snip off points of the remaining leaves with scissors. Rinse artichoke under cold water.

To prevent leaves from spreading during cooking, tie string around artichoke and from top to bottom to hold leaves in place. Invert cleaned artichoke in bowl containing 1 tablespoon lemon juice for each quart of water. (This prevents edges from discoloring.)

Artichokes should be cooked in large kettle. For 4 medium artichokes, heat 6 quarts water, ¼ cup salad oil, 2 tablespoons lemon juice, 1 clove garlic, quartered, and 1 teaspoon salt to boiling. Add artichokes; heat to boiling. Reduce heat; simmer uncovered 30 to 40 minutes, rotating occasionally, or until leaves pull out easily and bottom is tender when pierced with a knife. Remove artichokes carefully from water (use tongs or two large spoons), place upside down to drain.

TO SERVE AS A CHILLED FIRST COURSE

Cool artichokes; cover and refrigerate at least 4 hours. Remove string. Cut out choke if desired. (Choke is the fuzzy growth covering artichoke heart.) Open each artichoke like a flower to reach the interior. Pull out tender center cone of leaves; scrape off exposed choke with spoon. Replace cone of leaves if desired.

Place each artichoke in center of a luncheon plate or special artichoke plate. Accompany with a small cup of Hollandaise Sauce (page 572) or one of the Glorified Butters (page 581). If choke has been removed, the cavity can be filled with the sauce.

TO SERVE AS A HOT FIRST COURSE

Remove string but do not remove choke. Place artichoke upright on plate. Accompany with a small cup of Hollandaise Sauce (page 572) or Glorified Butters (page 581).

TO EAT ARTICHOKES

Pluck leaves one at a time. Dip base of leaf into a sauce or lemon butter. Turn leaf meaty side down and draw between teeth, scraping off meaty portion. Discard leaf on plate.

When all outer leaves have been removed, a center cone of small light-colored leaves covering the fuzzy center choke will be exposed (unless, of course, the choke has been removed before serving).

Pull or cut off cone of leaves. Slice off fuzzy choke with knife and fork; discard. Cut the remaining "heart," the prize section, into bite-size pieces; dip into sauce.

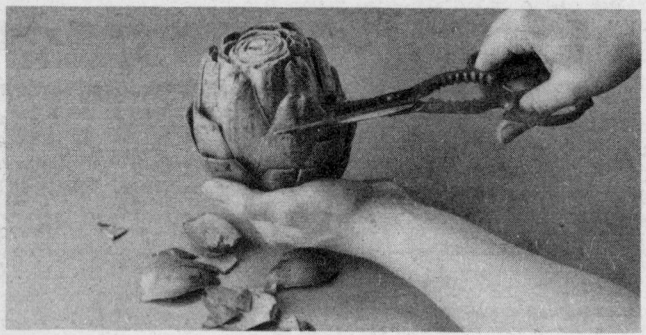

Slice 1 inch off top of artichoke; snip off leaf points.

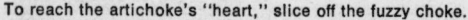

To reach the artichoke's "heart," slice off the fuzzy choke.

ARTICHOKES—JERUSALEM

Amount for 4 servings: 1½ pounds.
Season available: November through January.
When shopping: Look for firm, mold-free tubers.
Ways to serve: Buttered, with salt and pepper. . . . Varied with lemon juice and snipped parsley. . . . Creamed, French fried or baked.

TO PREPARE

Pare thinly. Leave whole, slice or dice.

TO COOK

Heat 1 inch salted water (½ teaspoon salt to 1 cup water) to boiling. Add artichokes. Cover and heat to boiling. Cook 15 to 35 minutes.

ASPARAGUS

Amount for 4 servings: 1½ pounds.
Season available: February through June.
When shopping: Look for smooth, round, tender green spears with closed tips.
Ways to serve: Buttered, with salt and pepper. . . . Varied with dash of lemon juice or mace or sprinkled with buttered crumbs. . . . Topped with Hollandaise Sauce (page 572) or medium White Sauce (page 566) to which diced hard-cooked eggs have been added. . . . Seasoned with allspice, dill weed, marjoram or savory.

TO PREPARE

Break off tough ends as far down as stalks snap easily. Wash asparagus thoroughly. Remove scales if sandy or tough. (If necessary, remove sand particles with a vegetable brush.) For spears, tie whole stalks in bundles with string or hold together with band of aluminum foil. Or, if desired, cut each stalk into 1-inch pieces.

TO COOK

Spears: In deep narrow pan or coffeepot, heat 1 inch salted water (½ teaspoon salt to 1 cup water) to boiling. Place asparagus upright in pan. Heat to boiling; cook uncovered 5 minutes. Cover and cook 7 to 10 minutes longer or until stalk ends are crisp-tender. Drain.

French (Globe) Artichokes,
Jerusalem Artichokes

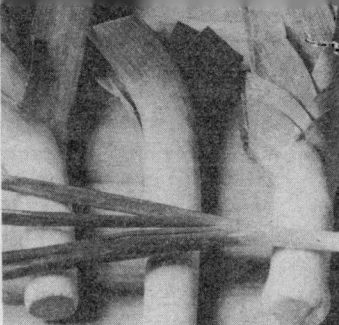

Leeks, Green Onion

Chinese Pea Pods, Mushrooms

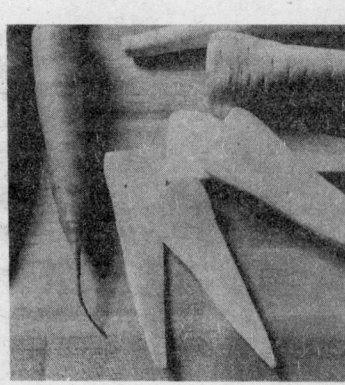

Carrots, Parsnips

Summer and Winter Squashes

Broccoli, Rutabaga, Turnips

Pieces: Cook lower stalk pieces uncovered in 1 inch boiling salted water (½ teaspoon salt to 1 cup water) 5 to 7 minutes. Add tips; cover and cook 5 to 8 minutes longer. Drain.

ASPARAGUS WITH SUNSHINE SAUCE

1½ pounds fresh asparagus*
¼ cup sauterne or other dry white wine**
1 tablespoon instant minced onion
1 tablespoon lemon juice
¾ cup mayonnaise
2 hard-cooked eggs, chopped

If using fresh asparagus, prepare and cook asparagus spears as directed on page 673.

In small saucepan, pour wine over onion. Stir in lemon juice and mayonnaise; heat just to boiling. Gently stir in eggs. Serve hot over spears.

4 to 6 servings.

*Or, use 2 packages (10 ounces each) frozen asparagus spears, cooked and drained, or 2 cans (15 ounces each) asparagus spears, heated and drained.

**Or, if desired, omit sauterne; add 2 tablespoons apple juice and increase lemon juice to 2 tablespoons.

SKILLET ASPARAGUS

Prepare 1 pound fresh asparagus spears as directed on page 673 except—do not tie stalks in bundles. Fill 10-inch skillet ½ full with water; add 1 teaspoon salt. Heat water to boiling; add asparagus. Heat to boiling. Cover, cook 8 to 12 minutes or until stalk ends are crisp-tender.*

Drain; return asparagus to skillet to dry and dot with 2 tablespoons soft butter or margarine.

3 or 4 servings.

*Or, use 1 package (10 ounces) frozen asparagus spears and cook 6 to 8 minutes.

ORIENTAL ASPARAGUS

Prepare 2 pounds fresh asparagus spears as directed on page 673 except—cut each stalk *on the diagonal* into 1-inch pieces.

In large skillet, heat ⅓ cup butter or margarine and

⅓ cup water to boiling. Add asparagus, ½ teaspoon salt and ⅛ teaspoon pepper. Cover; cook over high heat 5 to 8 minutes or until asparagus is crisp-tender. (Do not overcook.)

With frozen asparagus: Use 2 packages (10 ounces each) frozen asparagus cuts; melt the butter with seasonings and omit the ⅓ cup water.

6 servings.

BEANS—GREEN AND WAX

Amount for 4 servings: 1 pound.

Season available: All year (peak—summer).

When shopping: Look for bright, good color; firm, crisp pods.

Ways to serve: Buttered, with salt and pepper. . . . Tossed with bacon or ham drippings or crumbled crisply fried bacon. . . . Seasoned with basil, dill, marjoram, nutmeg, savory or thyme. . . . Sprinkled with buttered bread crumbs.

TO PREPARE

Wash beans and remove ends. Leave beans whole, cut French style into lengthwise strips or crosswise into 1-inch pieces.

TO COOK

Place beans in 1 inch salted water (½ teaspoon salt to 1 cup water). Heat to boiling.

Green beans: Cook uncovered 5 minutes. Cover and cook until tender—10 to 15 minutes for whole or cut beans, 5 to 10 minutes for French style. Drain.

Wax beans: Cook covered 15 to 20 minutes for whole or cut beans, 10 to 15 minutes for French style. Drain.

GREEN BEANS DELUXE

Prepare and cook 1 pound fresh green beans, cut French style, as directed above.*

Heat oven to 350°. Stir together beans and 1 can (10½ ounces) condensed cream of mushroom soup.

*Or, use 2 packages (9 ounces each) frozen French-style green beans, cooked and drained.

Pour into ungreased 1-quart casserole. Bake uncovered 10 minutes.

Sprinkle top with 1 can (3½ ounces) French fried onion rings. Bake 5 to 10 minutes longer or until onion rings are heated through.

With canned beans: Use 2 cans (1 pound each) French-style green beans, drained; bake casserole uncovered 35 minutes before sprinkling top with onion rings.

6 servings.

GREEN BEANS CAESAR

1½ pounds fresh green beans*	2 tablespoons dry bread crumbs
2 tablespoons salad oil	2 tablespoons grated Parmesan cheese
1 tablespoon vinegar	
1 tablespoon instant minced onion	1 tablespoon butter or margarine, melted
¼ teaspoon salt	Paprika
1 clove garlic, crushed	
⅛ teaspoon pepper	

If using fresh beans, prepare and cook beans, cut into 1-inch pieces, as directed at left.

Heat oven to 350°. Toss beans with salad oil, vinegar, onion, salt, garlic and pepper. Pour into ungreased 1-quart casserole. Stir together bread crumbs, cheese and butter; sprinkle over beans. Sprinkle with paprika. Bake uncovered 15 to 20 minutes or until heated through.

With canned beans: Use 2 cans (1 pound each) cut green beans, drained; bake casserole 40 to 45 minutes or until heated through.

6 servings.

*Or, use 2 packages (9 ounces each) frozen cut green beans, cooked and drained.

ALMOND CRUNCH WAX BEANS

1 pound fresh wax beans	¾ teaspoon salt
½ cup water	3 tablespoons toasted slivered almonds
2 tablespoons butter or margarine	

Prepare fresh beans in 1-inch pieces as directed at left.

Cook and stir beans, water, butter and salt over medium heat until butter is melted. Cover; cook 20 to 25 minutes or until beans are tender. Stir in almonds.

With canned beans: Use 1 can (15½ ounces) cut wax beans, drained. Omit water; decrease salt to ¼ teaspoon and cook until heated through.

With frozen beans: Use 1 package (9 ounces) frozen cut wax beans. Omit water; decrease salt to ¼ teaspoon and cook 12 to 15 minutes.

4 servings.

BEANS—GREEN LIMAS

Amount for 4 servings: 3 pounds (unshelled).
Season available: July through November.
When shopping: Look for broad, thick, shiny pods that are plump with large seeds.
Ways to serve: Buttered, with salt and pepper. . . . Seasoned with snipped parsley, savory or sage. . . . In a cream or butter sauce.

TO PREPARE

Wash lima beans thoroughly. Shell just before cooking. To shell beans, remove thin outer edge of pod with sharp knife or scissors. Beans will slip out.

TO COOK

Heat 1 inch salted water (½ teaspoon salt to 1 cup water) to boiling. Add beans. Heat to boiling and cook uncovered 5 minutes. Cover and cook 15 to 20 minutes longer or until tender. Drain.

LIMA BEANS WITH MUSTARD SAUCE

3 pounds fresh lima beans*
½ cup salad dressing or
  mayonnaise
2 tablespoons milk
1 teaspoon prepared
  mustard
Paprika

If using fresh lima beans, prepare and cook as directed above.

Heat salad dressing, milk and mustard, stirring constantly. Turn hot beans into serving dish; pour hot sauce over beans. Sprinkle with paprika.

4 servings.

*Or, use 1 package (10 ounces) frozen baby lima beans, cooked and drained.

LIMA BEANS WITH MUSHROOMS

3 pounds fresh lima beans*
1 can (3 ounces) sliced
  mushrooms, drained

2 tablespoons soft butter
  or margarine

If using fresh lima beans, prepare and cook as directed above. Add mushrooms and butter; toss.
4 servings.

*Or, use 1 package (10 ounces) frozen baby lima beans, cooked and drained.

BEETS

Amount for 4 servings: 5 medium (about 1¼ pounds).
Season available: All year (peak—June and July).
When shopping: Look for firm, round, smooth beets of a deep red color; fresh tops.
Ways to serve: Buttered, with salt and pepper. . . . Seasoned with fresh dill, caraway seed, bay leaf, cloves, basil, savory, mint or nutmeg. . . . Tossed with orange peel or lemon peel. . . . Pickled or glazed.

TO PREPARE

Cut off all but 2 inches of beet tops. Wash beets and leave whole, with root ends attached.

TO COOK

Heat 6 cups water, 1 tablespoon vinegar (to preserve color) and 1 teaspoon salt to boiling. Add beets. Cover and heat to boiling; cook 35 to 45 minutes or until tender. Drain. Run cold water over beets; slip off skins and remove root ends. Slice, dice or cut into shoestring pieces.

HARVARD BEETS

5 medium fresh beets (about
  1¼ pounds)
1 tablespoon cornstarch
1 tablespoon sugar

¾ teaspoon salt
Dash pepper
⅔ cup water
¼ cup vinegar

Prepare and cook fresh beets as directed above. Cut beets into slices.
In small saucepan, stir together cornstarch, sugar,

salt and pepper. Gradually stir in water and vinegar. Cook, stirring constantly, until mixture thickens and boils. Boil and stir 1 minute. Stir in beets; heat through.

With canned beets: Use 1 can (1 pound) sliced beets, drained (reserve liquid). For the water, use reserved beet liquid plus enough water to measure ⅔ cup.

4 servings.

ORANGE BEETS

5 medium fresh beets*
(about 1¼ pounds)
1 tablespoon cornstarch
1 tablespoon brown sugar
1 teaspoon finely
shredded orange peel

¾ teaspoon salt
Dash pepper
¾ cup orange juice
1 tablespoon vinegar

Prepare and cook fresh beets as directed on page 679. Cut into slices.

In small saucepan, stir together cornstarch, brown sugar, orange peel, salt and pepper. Stir in orange juice and vinegar. Cook, stirring constantly, until mixture thickens and boils. Boil and stir 1 minute. Stir in beets; heat through.

4 servings.

*Or, use 1 can (1 pound) sliced beets, drained.

BEETS IN SOUR CREAM

5 medium fresh beets*
(about 1¼ pounds)
2 tablespoons butter or
margarine
2 teaspoons flour
2 tablespoons vinegar

1 tablespoon sugar
¼ teaspoon salt
¼ teaspoon dill weed
⅛ teaspoon pepper
½ cup dairy sour cream
3 tablespoons light cream

If using fresh beets, prepare and cook as directed on page 679; cut beets into shoestring pieces.

Melt butter in medium saucepan over low heat. Blend in flour. Cook over low heat, stirring until mixture is smooth and bubbly. Remove from heat; stir in vinegar and the next 4 seasonings. Heat to boiling, stirring constantly. Boil and stir 1 minute. Stir in beets; heat through. Stir together sour cream and light cream; heat through over low heat. Pour over hot beets.

4 servings.

*Or, use 1 can (1 pound) shoestring beets, drained.

BROCCOLI

Amount for 4 servings: 1½ pounds.
Season available: All year.
When shopping: Look for firm, compact dark green clusters. Avoid thick, tough stems.
Ways to serve: Buttered, with salt and pepper. . . . Topped with Glorified Butters (page 581), Hollandaise Sauce (page 572) or grated cheese. . . . Seasoned with nutmeg or oregano. . . . Creamed.

TO PREPARE

Trim off large leaves; remove tough ends of lower stems. Wash broccoli. If stems are thicker than 1 inch in diameter, make lengthwise gashes in each stem.

TO COOK

Heat 1 inch salted water (½ teaspoon salt to 1 cup water) to boiling. Add broccoli. Cover and heat to boiling; cook 12 to 15 minutes or until stems are tender. Drain.

ITALIAN BROCCOLI

Simply cooked broccoli with the added flavor excitement of olive oil and Parmesan cheese.

Prepare and cook 1½ pounds fresh broccoli as directed above.*

Place 3 tablespoons olive oil, butter or margarine in saucepan. Add broccoli; cook and stir until broccoli is a delicate brown. Sprinkle with 2 tablespoons grated Parmesan cheese.

4 servings.

*Or, use 1 package (10 ounces) frozen broccoli spears, cooked and drained.

Make gashes in thick broccoli stems for even cooking.

BRUSSELS SPROUTS

Amount for 4 servings: 1½ pounds.
Season available: Fall and winter.
When shopping: Look for unblemished bright green sprouts; compact leaves.
Ways to serve: Buttered, with salt and pepper. . . . Seasoned with garlic salt, basil, caraway seed, cumin, dill, marjoram, sage or savory. . . . Creamed or topped with Cheese Sauce (page 568).

TO PREPARE

Remove any discolored leaves. Cut off stem ends; wash sprouts thoroughly.

TO COOK

Heat 1 inch salted water (½ teaspoon salt to 1 cup water) to boiling. Add Brussels sprouts. Cover and heat to boiling; cook 8 to 10 minutes or until tender. Drain.

BRUSSELS SPROUTS PARISIENNE

Elegant saucery for these little cousins of the cabbage. Remember these when serving broiled chops or steaks.

1½ pounds fresh Brussels
    sprouts*
2 tablespoons butter or
    margarine
2 tablespoons flour
¼ teaspoon salt
⅛ teaspoon nutmeg

Dash pepper
1 can (13¾ ounces)
    chicken broth
2 egg yolks, well beaten
¼ cup toasted slivered
    almonds

If using fresh Brussels sprouts, prepare and cook as directed above.

Melt butter in large saucepan over low heat. Blend in flour and seasonings. Cook over low heat, stirring until mixture is smooth and bubbly. Remove from heat. Stir in broth. Heat to boiling, stirring constantly. Boil and stir 1 minute.

Gradually stir at least half the hot mixture into egg yolks; then blend into hot mixture in saucepan. Boil 1 minute longer, stirring constantly. Stir in toasted almonds and Brussels sprouts; heat through.

4 to 6 servings.

*Or, use 2 packages (10 ounces each) frozen Brussels sprouts, cooked and drained.

CABBAGE—CHINESE AND CELERY

Amount for 4 servings: 1 medium head.
Season available: All year.
When shopping: Look for crisp, green heads, either firm or leafy.
Ways to serve: Buttered, with salt and pepper. . . . Sprinkled with grated cheese or buttered bread crumbs. . . . Topped with Hollandaise Sauce (page 572) or Cheese Sauce (page 568).

TO PREPARE

Remove root ends; wash cabbage. Shred.

TO COOK

Heat ½ inch salted water (½ teaspoon salt to 1 cup water) to boiling. Add cabbage. Cover and heat to boiling; cook 4 to 5 minutes or until crisp-tender. Drain.

CABBAGE—GREEN, SAVOY AND RED

Amount for 4 servings: 1 head (about 1½ pounds).
Season available: All year.
When shopping: Look for firm, heavy heads of fresh, good color.
Ways to serve: *Green*—Buttered, with salt and pepper. . . . Seasoned with caraway or celery seed. . . . Topped with Cheese Sauce (page 568). . . . Wedges, cooked in water with ham or corned beef. . . . Shredded, creamed or scalloped; *Red*—Buttered, with salt and pepper. . . . Shredded, seasoned with caraway or celery seed or crumbled crisply fried bacon.

TO PREPARE

Discard outside leaves; wash. Cut into wedges and remove core, or shred and discard core.

TO COOK

Green or Savoy: Heat 1 inch (½ inch for shredded) salted water (½ teaspoon salt to 1 cup water) to boiling. Add cabbage. Cover and heat to boiling. Cook wedges 10 to 12 minutes or until crisp-tender; cook shredded cabbage 5 minutes. Drain.

Red: Heat 1 inch (½ inch for shredded cabbage) salted water (½ teaspoon salt to 1 cup water) and 2 tablespoons vinegar or lemon juice to boiling. Add cabbage. Cover and heat to boiling; cook wedges about 20 minutes or until crisp-tender; cook shredded cabbage about 10 minutes. Drain.

PHILADELPHIA CABBAGE

1 medium head green cabbage (about 1½ pounds)
1 package (3 ounces) cream cheese, softened

2 tablespoons milk
½ teaspoon celery seed
Dash pepper

Prepare and cook 4 cups shredded cabbage as directed on page 683.

Mix cream cheese and milk; stir in seasonings. Stir cheese mixture into hot cabbage.

4 servings.

CHINESE-STYLE VEGETABLE MEDLEY

1 small head green cabbage (about 1 pound)
1 tablespoon shortening
1 cup thin diagonal slices celery

1 medium green pepper, cut into thin diagonal slices
⅔ cup chopped onion
1 teaspoon salt
⅛ teaspoon pepper

Prepare 3 cups finely shredded cabbage as directed on page 683.

Heat shortening in medium skillet. Add vegetables and stir. Cover; steam 5 minutes or until crisp-tender, stirring several times. Add salt and pepper. If desired, stir in 1 tablespoon soy sauce.

4 servings.

CHEESE 'N BACON CABBAGE WEDGES

1 large head green cabbage (about 2 pounds)
1 can (10¾ ounces) condensed Cheddar cheese soup

½ teaspoon dry mustard
½ teaspoon celery seed
• 6 slices bacon, crisply fried and crumbled

Prepare and cook 6 cabbage wedges as directed on page 683.

Stir together soup, mustard and celery seed in saucepan; heat through. Pour soup mixture over hot cabbage wedges; sprinkle with bacon.

6 servings.

SWEET-SOUR RED CABBAGE

1 medium head red cabbage (about 1½ pounds)	½ cup water
4 slices bacon, diced	¼ cup vinegar
¼ cup brown sugar (packed)	1 teaspoon salt
2 tablespoons flour	⅛ teaspoon pepper
	1 small onion, sliced

Prepare and cook 5 cups shredded cabbage as directed on page 683 for red cabbage. (Be sure to add the 2 tablespoons vinegar or lemon juice to the salted water.)

Fry bacon until crisp; remove and drain. Pour off all but 1 tablespoon bacon drippings. Stir brown sugar and flour into bacon drippings in skillet. Add water, vinegar, the salt, pepper and onion. Cook, stirring frequently, about 5 minutes or until mixture thickens.

Add bacon and sauce mixture to hot cabbage; stir together gently and heat through. If desired, garnish with additional crisply fried diced bacon.

6 servings.

CARROTS

Amount for 4 servings: 1¼ pounds.

Season available: All year.

When shopping: Look for firm, nicely shaped carrots of good color.

Ways to serve: Buttered, with salt and pepper. . . . Sprinkled with snipped parsley, mint, chives or cut green onion. . . . Topped with Lemon Butter or Brown Butter (pages 580–581). . . . Seasoned with basil, chervil, ginger, rosemary, savory or thyme. . . . Creamed or mashed.

TO PREPARE

Scrape carrots and remove ends. Leave carrots whole, shred or cut lengthwise into ⅜-inch-wide strips or crosswise into ¼-inch slices.

TO COOK

Heat 1 inch salted water (½ teaspoon salt to 1 cup water) to boiling. Add carrots. Cover and heat to boiling; cook until tender—25 minutes for whole, 5 minutes for shredded, 18 to 20 minutes for lengthwise strips, 12 to 15 minutes for crosswise slices. Drain.

CHIVE-BUTTERED CARROTS

A flavor favorite . . . and oh, so fast. But if chives aren't one of your kitchen's staples, substitute finely minced onion. Especially good with meat loaf, lamb or roast beef.

1½ pounds fresh carrots*	⅛ teaspoon pepper
¼ cup butter or margarine	1 tablespoon snipped
¼ teaspoon seasoned salt	chives

If using fresh carrots, prepare and cook whole carrots as directed above.

Melt butter in medium skillet; add carrots. Sprinkle with salt, pepper and snipped chives. Heat carrots through, turning occasionally to coat with butter.

With frozen carrots: Use 2 packages (10 ounces each) frozen carrots in butter sauce, cooked; sprinkle with the salt, pepper and snipped chives and serve.

5 or 6 servings.

*Or, use 2 cans (1 pound each) whole carrots, drained.

SHREDDED CARROTS WITH BACON

Especially good with meat loaf, lamb or ham.

1½ pounds fresh carrots	Dash pepper
3 slices bacon	¼ cup snipped parsley
½ teaspoon salt	

Prepare and cook 4 cups shredded carrots as directed above.

In large skillet, fry bacon until crisp; remove and drain. Pour off all but 2 tablespoons bacon drippings. Stir in shredded carrots, salt and pepper; heat through. Turn into serving dish. Crumble bacon; sprinkle bacon and parsley over carrots.

5 or 6 servings.

GLAZED CARROTS

1½ pounds fresh carrots
⅓ cup brown sugar (packed)
½ teaspoon salt
½ teaspoon grated orange
peel

2 tablespoons butter or
margarine

Prepare and cook carrots, cut into lengthwise strips, as directed on pages 685–686.

In large skillet, cook and stir brown sugar, salt, orange peel and butter until bubbly. Add carrot strips; cook over low heat, stirring occasionally, about 5 minutes or until carrots are glazed and heated through.

5 or 6 servings.

CARROTS COSMOPOLITAN

1¼ pounds fresh carrots
¼ cup butter or margarine,
melted
¼ cup brandy or, if desired,
pineapple juice

1 teaspoon sugar
1 teaspoon salt

Heat oven to 375°. Scrape carrots; remove ends. Cut carrots into strips, 2½x¼ inch. Place in ungreased baking dish, 8x8x2 inches.

Stir together butter, brandy, sugar and salt. Pour over carrots. Cover; bake 40 minutes or until carrots are tender.

4 servings.

CAULIFLOWER

Amount for 4 servings: 1 medium head (about 2 pounds).

Season available: All year.

When shopping: Look for clean, non-spreading curds (the white portion); green "jacket" leaves.

Ways to serve: Buttered, with salt and pepper. . . . Topped with buttered crumbs, grated cheese or Cheese Sauce (page 568). . . . Seasoned with basil, curry powder, nutmeg, celery seed or poppy seed. . . . Creamed. . . . Raw, as a relish.

TO PREPARE

Remove outer leaves and stalk. Cut off any discoloration on flowerets; wash cauliflower thoroughly. Leave whole or separate into flowerets.

TO COOK

Heat 1 inch salted water (½ teaspoon salt to 1 cup water) to boiling. Add cauliflower. Cover and heat to boiling; cook until tender—20 to 25 minutes for whole, 10 to 20 minutes for flowerets. Drain.

GLORIFIED CHEESE CAULIFLOWER

1 medium head cauliflower (about 2 pounds)
2 tablespoons butter or margarine
2 tablespoons flour
1 teaspoon dry mustard
¼ teaspoon each salt and pepper
1 cup milk
1 cup shredded process sharp American Cheese (about 4 ounces)
5 drops red pepper sauce

Prepare and cook whole cauliflower as directed above. Melt butter in saucepan over low heat. Blend in flour and seasonings. Cook over low heat, stirring until mixture is smooth and bubbly. Remove from heat. Stir in milk. Heat to boiling, stirring constantly. Boil and stir 1 minute. Stir in cheese and red pepper sauce. Cook and stir over low heat until cheese is melted. Pour sauce over hot cauliflower. If desired, sprinkle with paprika.

4 servings.

VARIATION

■ *Curried Cauliflower:* Substitute 1 teaspoon curry powder for mustard; omit red pepper sauce.

CELERY

Types: Pascal (green), Golden (bleached).
Amount for 4 servings: 1 medium bunch.
Season available: All year.
When shopping: Look for crisp, unblemished stalks; fresh leaves.

Ways to serve: Buttered, with salt and pepper. . . . Creamed or braised. . . . Seasoned with mustard. . . . Raw, as a relish.

TO PREPARE

Remove leaves and trim off root ends. Remove any coarse strings. Wash celery thoroughly. Cut stalks into 1-inch pieces (about 4 cups).

TO COOK

Heat 1 inch salted water (½ teaspoon salt to 1 cup water) to boiling. Add celery pieces. Cover and heat to boiling; cook 15 to 20 minutes or until tender. Drain.

GOLDEN CELERY

Introduce the family to this attractive change-of-pace vegetable.

1 medium bunch golden celery
¼ cup chopped onion
1 tablespoon butter or margarine
1 tablespoon flour
¼ teaspoon salt
⅛ teaspoon pepper

1 cup milk
1 cup shredded process American cheese (about 4 ounces)
1 teaspoon dry mustard
1 jar (2 ounces) sliced pimiento, drained

Prepare and cook 4 cups celery pieces as directed above.

In large skillet, cook and stir onion in butter until tender. Remove from heat. Stir in flour and seasonings. Cook over low heat, stirring until mixture is bubbly. Remove from heat. Stir in milk. Heat to boiling, stirring constantly. Boil and stir 1 minute.

Stir in cheese and mustard. Cook and stir over low heat until cheese is melted. Stir in celery and pimiento; heat through.

4 servings.

CELERY ROOT (CELERIAC)

Amount for 4 servings: 1½ pounds.
Season available: October through April.
When shopping: Look for firm, clean roots.

Ways to serve: Buttered. . . . Marinated in French dressing (as a salad). . . . Raw, as a relish.

TO PREPARE

Cut off leaves and root fibers. Scrub; do not pare.

TO COOK

Heat enough salted water to cover celery root (½ teaspoon salt to 1 cup water) to boiling. Add celery root. Heat to boiling; cook 40 to 60 minutes or until tender. Drain; pare and slice.

CHINESE PEA PODS

Amount for 4 servings: ½ pound.
Season available: All year.
When shopping: Look for flat, crisp, bright pods.
Ways to serve: Buttered. . . . With water chestnuts, almonds or mushrooms.

TO PREPARE

Wash pods; remove tips and strings.

TO COOK

Heat ½ inch salted water (½ teaspoon salt to 1 cup water) to boiling. Add pea pods. Heat to boiling; cook uncovered 2 to 3 minutes or until crisp-tender. Drain.

POLYNESIAN PEA PODS

½ pound fresh Chinese   1 can (8¾ ounces) pineapple
    pea pods*   tidbits, drained
2 tablespoons butter   ¼ teaspoon salt

If using fresh Chinese pea pods, prepare and cook as directed above.

Melt butter in medium saucepan; stir in pineapple. Cook and stir until heated through. Add pea pods and salt; toss and heat through.

4 servings.

*Or, use 1 package (7 ounces) frozen Chinese pea pods, cooked and drained.

CORN

Amount for 4 servings: 4 to 8 ears.
Season available: May through December.
When shopping: Look for bright green husks, fresh-looking silk, plump but not too large kernels.
Ways to serve: On the cob—with butter, salt and pepper. . . . Seasoned with basil, cayenne red pepper, celery seed, chili powder or rosemary.

TO PREPARE

Refrigerate unhusked corn until ready to use. Corn is best when eaten as soon after picking as possible. Husk ears and remove all silk just before cooking.

TO COOK

Place corn in enough *unsalted* cold water to cover. (Salt toughens corn.) Add 1 tablespoon sugar and 1 tablespoon lemon juice to each gallon of water. Heat to boiling; boil uncovered 2 minutes. Remove from heat; let corn stand about 10 minutes before serving.

CORN SESAME SAUTE

A delightful combination.

3 ears fresh corn*
3 tablespoons butter or
   margarine
1 clove garlic, crushed
2 tablespoons sesame seed

2 tablespoons chopped
   green pepper
½ teaspoon salt
¼ teaspoon basil leaves
⅛ teaspoon pepper

If using fresh corn, husk and remove silk; cut enough kernels from ears to measure 1½ cups.

Cook and stir all ingredients over medium heat until butter is melted. Cover; cook over low heat 15 minutes or until corn is tender.

With canned corn: Use 1 can (12 ounces) vacuum-packed whole kernel corn with peppers, drained; decrease butter to 1 tablespoon and omit green pepper. Cook and stir all ingredients except corn over medium heat until sesame seed is toasted. Stir in corn; heat through and serve.

4 servings.

*Or, use 1 package (10 ounces) frozen whole kernel corn and cook, stirring occasionally, 7 minutes or until corn is tender.

SCALLOPED CORN

A rich, colorful vegetable casserole.

4 ears fresh corn*
¼ cup chopped onion
¼ cup chopped green pepper
2 tablespoons butter or margarine
2 tablespoons flour
1 teaspoon salt
½ teaspoon paprika
¼ teaspoon dry mustard
Dash pepper
¾ cup milk
1 egg, slightly beaten
⅓ cup cracker crumbs
1 tablespoon butter or margarine, melted

If using fresh corn, prepare and cook ears as directed on page 691; cut enough kernels from ears to measure 2 cups.

Heat oven to 350°. Cook and stir onion and green pepper in 2 tablespoons butter until onion is tender. Remove from heat. Stir in flour and seasonings. Cook over low heat, stirring until mixture is bubbly. Remove from heat. Gradually stir in milk. Heat to boiling, stirring constantly. Boil and stir 1 minute. Stir in corn and egg. Pour into ungreased 1-quart casserole.

Combine cracker crumbs and the 1 tablespoon melted butter; sprinkle evenly over corn mixture. Bake uncovered 30 to 35 minutes.

4 servings.

*Or, use 1 package (10 ounces) frozen whole kernel corn, cooked and drained, or 1 can (1 pound) whole kernel corn, drained.

VARIATION

■ *Cheese Scalloped Corn:* Fold ½ cup shredded natural Cheddar cheese into the sauce mixture.

ROAST CORN ON THE GRILL

Better allow for two, even three, ears per person.

Select tender, young sweet corn. Remove large outer husks; turn back inner husks and remove silk. Spread corn with soft butter. Pull husks back over corn; tie with fine wire.

Place on grill 3 inches from hot coals; cook 20 to 30 minutes, turning frequently. Serve at once with salt, pepper and butter.

TOMATOED CORN

What a wonderful treat with garden-fresh corn and tomatoes. And quick, too.

4 ears fresh corn*	2 teaspoons sugar
¼ cup butter or margarine	½ teaspoon salt
¼ cup chopped onion	¼ teaspoon ground cumin
¼ cup chopped green pepper	1 large tomato, cut up

If using fresh corn, husk and remove silk; cut enough kernels from ears to measure 2 cups.

Cook and stir all ingredients except tomato over medium heat until butter is melted. Cover; cook over low heat 10 minutes. Stir in tomato. Cover; cook 5 minutes longer.

With canned corn: Decrease butter to 3 tablespoons; stir in 1 can (1 pound) whole kernel corn, drained, with the tomato.

4 servings.

*Or, use 1 package (10 ounces) frozen whole kernel corn.

SUCCOTASH

A typically American vegetable combination. Our recipe offers you the freedom to mix fresh, canned and frozen varieties.

3 pounds fresh lima beans*	½ teaspoon salt
4 ears fresh corn**	¼ teaspoon pepper
½ cup light cream	
2 tablespoons butter or margarine	

If using fresh lima beans, prepare and cook as directed on page 678.

If using fresh corn, prepare and cook ears as directed on page 691; cut enough kernels from ears to measure 2 cups.

In medium saucepan, combine cooked beans and corn with remaining ingredients. Heat through, stirring occasionally.

6 servings.

*Or, use 1 package (10 ounces) frozen baby lima beans, cooked and drained, or 1 can (1 pound) lima beans, drained.

**Or, use 1 package (10 ounces) frozen whole kernel corn, cooked and drained, or 1 can (1 pound) whole kernel corn, drained.

EGGPLANT

Amount for 4 servings: 1 medium (about 1½ pounds).

Season available: All year (peak—July, August, September).

When shopping: Look for smooth, firm eggplants of an even, dark purple.

Ways to serve: Buttered, with salt and pepper. . . . Sprinkled with Parmesan cheese, snipped chives or parsley. . . . Seasoned with allspice, chili powder, curry powder, garlic, oregano or rosemary. . . . Panfried, French fried, stuffed or scalloped.

TO PREPARE

Just before cooking, wash eggplant and, if desired, pare. Cut eggplant into ½-inch cubes, strips or ¼-inch slices.

TO COOK

To Boil: Heat small amount salted water (½ teaspoon salt to 1 cup water) to boiling. Add eggplant. Cover and heat to boiling; cook 5 to 8 minutes or until tender. Drain.

To Fry: Cook and stir eggplant in butter or bacon drippings 5 to 10 minutes.

INDIAN FRIED EGGPLANT

1 medium eggplant (about 1½ pounds)	1 teaspoon turmeric
1 cup all-purpose flour*	2 teaspoons curry powder
1 teaspoon baking powder	1 cup milk
1 teaspoon salt	1 egg
	¼ cup salad oil

Wash eggplant. Beat remaining ingredients with rotary beater until smooth. Heat fat or oil (1 inch deep) to 375° in large skillet.

Cut eggplant into ¼-inch slices. Dip slices into batter, letting excess drip into bowl. Fry in hot fat until golden brown, turning once. Drain. If desired, salt to taste.

4 servings.

If using self-rising flour, omit baking powder and salt.

Note: To keep fried eggplant slices warm and crisp, place in 300° oven until ready to serve.

MUSHROOM-STUFFED EGGPLANT

1 medium eggplant (1½ to
  2 pounds)
1 jar (4½ ounces) sliced
  mushrooms, drained
¼ cup all-purpose flour
¼ cup butter or margarine
2 tablespoons finely
  chopped green pepper
2 tablespoons finely
  chopped onion

1 clove garlic, crushed
1 teaspoon salt
⅛ teaspoon pepper
¼ cup light cream
1 jar (2 ounces) chopped
  pimiento, drained
1 tablespoon grated
  Parmesan cheese or 2
  tablespoons buttered
  bread crumbs

Heat oven to 350°. Wash eggplant; cut a large slice
lengthwise. Remove and cube enough eggplant from
shell to measure 3 cups.

In large skillet, stir together all ingredients except
cream, pimiento and Parmesan cheese. Cook and stir
over medium heat until mixture is brown. Remove from
heat; stir in cream and pimiento. Fill eggplant shell with
mixture; sprinkle with Parmesan cheese. Bake 40 to 45
minutes or until eggplant is tender.

4 to 6 servings.

RATATOUILLE

1 medium eggplant (about
  1½ pounds)
2 small zucchini (about ½
  pound)
1 cup finely chopped
  green pepper
1 medium onion, finely
  chopped (about ½ cup)

4 medium tomatoes, peeled
  and quartered
¼ cup salad oil
1 clove garlic, crushed
2 teaspoons salt
¼ teaspoon pepper

Prepare 5 cups cubed pared eggplant as directed at
left. Prepare 2 cups sliced zucchini as directed on page
717.

Cook and stir all ingredients until heated through.
Cover; cook over medium heat, stirring occasionally,
about 10 minutes or until vegetables are crisp-tender.

6 to 8 servings.

GREENS

Types: Mild-flavored—Beet tops, Chicory (outer
leaves), Collards, Escarole, Lettuce (outer leaves),

Spinach; Strong-flavored—Kale, Mustard Greens, Swiss Chard, Turnip Greens.

Amount for 4 servings: 2 pounds.

Season available: All year.

When shopping: Look for tender, young, unblemished leaves of bright green color.

Ways to serve: Buttered, with salt and pepper. . . . Seasoned with dill weed, marjoram, mint, nutmeg, rosemary or minced onion. . . . With lemon juice or vinegar, crumbled crisply fried bacon, horseradish, chili sauce or grated Parmesan cheese. . . . Wilted, molded or in soufflés. . . . Raw, in salads.

TO PREPARE

Remove imperfect leaves and root ends. Wash greens several times in water, lifting out of water each time so sand sinks to bottom. Drain.

TO COOK

Place greens with just the water which clings to leaves in saucepan. Cover and cook 3 to 10 minutes for spinach; 5 to 15 minutes for beet tops; 15 to 20 minutes for chicory, escarole and lettuce; 10 to 15 minutes for collards; 15 to 20 minutes for Swiss chard and mustard greens; 15 to 25 minutes for turnip greens and kale. Drain.

SPINACH GOURMET

1 pound fresh spinach or Swiss chard
1 can (4 ounces) button mushrooms, drained
1 teaspoon instant minced onion

1 small clove garlic, crushed
½ teaspoon salt
⅓ cup dairy sour cream
1 tablespoon light cream (20%) or milk

Prepare and cook fresh spinach or Swiss chard as directed above; chop and drain thoroughly.

Stir together spinach, mushrooms and seasonings in saucepan. Blend sour cream and light cream; pour over spinach mixture. Heat just to boiling.

With frozen spinach: Use 1 package (10 ounces) frozen chopped spinach, cooked and drained; add 2 tablespoons butter to ingredients in saucepan.

4 servings.

SPINACH SOUFFLÉ

1 pound fresh spinach or Swiss chard	1 teaspoon instant minced onion
¼ cup butter or margarine	1 teaspoon salt
¼ cup all-purpose flour	⅛ teaspoon nutmeg
¼ teaspoon salt	3 eggs, separated
⅛ teaspoon pepper	¼ teaspoon cream of tartar
1 cup milk	

Prepare and cook spinach or Swiss chard as directed at left; chop and drain thoroughly.

Heat oven to 350°. Butter 1½-quart soufflé dish or casserole. Melt butter in saucepan over low heat. Blend in flour, ¼ teaspoon salt and the pepper. Cook over low heat, stirring until mixture is smooth and bubbly. Remove from heat. Stir in milk. Heat to boiling, stirring constantly. Boil and stir 1 minute. Remove from heat. Stir in onion, 1 teaspoon salt and the nutmeg.

In large mixer bowl, beat egg whites and cream of tartar until stiff; set aside. In small mixer bowl, beat egg yolks until very thick and lemon colored; stir into white sauce mixture. Stir in spinach. Stir about ¼ of egg whites into sauce mixture; gently fold into remaining egg whites.

Carefully pour into casserole. Set casserole in pan of water (1 inch deep). Bake 50 to 60 minutes or until puffed and golden and until a silver knife inserted halfway between edge and center comes out clean. Serve immediately.

4 to 6 servings.

VARIATION

■ *Broccoli Soufflé:* Substitute 1 pound broccoli, prepared and cooked as directed on page 681, or 1 package (10 ounces) frozen broccoli, cooked and drained, for the spinach.

SALADS MADE SPECIAL A touch of the unexpected—Swiss chard, spinach, turnip greens, escarole—makes a mixed green salad something spectacular. (See pages 584–586 for more about salad greens.)

SWISS CHARD BAKE

2 pounds fresh Swiss chard
   or spinach
1 can (5 ounces) water
   chestnuts, drained and
   thinly sliced

1 can (10½ ounces)
   condensed cream of celery
   soup

Prepare and cook Swiss chard or spinach as directed on pages 695–696. Chop and drain thoroughly.

Heat oven to 350°. Place Swiss chard in ungreased baking dish, 10x6x1½ inches. Arrange water chestnuts over Swiss chard; spread soup over top. Bake 25 minutes or until heated through.

6 servings.

LEEKS

Amount for 4 servings: 2 pounds.

Season available: All year (peak—October through May).

When shopping: Look for bright green tops and white bulbs.

Ways to serve: Buttered, with salt and pepper. . . . Sprinkled with grated Parmesan cheese. . . . Seasoned with basil, ginger, rosemary or thyme. . . . Raw, in salads.

TO PREPARE

Remove green tops to within 2 inches of white part; peel outside layer of bulbs. Wash leeks.

TO COOK

Heat 1 inch salted water (½ teaspoon salt to 1 cup water) to boiling. Add leeks. Cover and heat to boiling; cook 12 to 15 minutes or until tender. Drain.

GOURMET LEEKS

1½ pounds leeks
  2 tablespoons butter or
   margarine
 ½ teaspoon salt

1 teaspoon lemon juice
2 tablespoons shredded
   Parmesan cheese

Prepare and cook leeks as directed above.

Melt butter in saucepan; stir in salt and lemon juice.

Add leeks; heat through. Turn into serving dish; sprinkle with cheese.

2 or 3 servings.

MUSHROOMS

Amount for 4 servings: 1 pound.
Season available: All year.
When shopping: Look for creamy white to light brown caps, closed around the stem; if slightly open, gills should be light pink or tan.
Ways to serve: Sautéed, as a hot vegetable or meat accompaniment. . . . Seasoned with marjoram, oregano, rosemary, savory or tarragon. . . . Creamed, scalloped or combined with other hot cooked vegetables—peas, green beans, limas.

TO PREPARE

Wash and trim off stem ends of mushrooms. Do not peel. If desired, slice parallel with stem.

TO COOK

In large skillet, heat 1 tablespoon butter or margarine until bubbly. Cook about ¼ of the mushrooms at a time about 4 minutes or until golden, turning once. Repeat with remaining mushrooms, using 1 tablespoon butter each time. Season with salt.

ORIENTAL MUSHROOMS

Vegetable with a party flair. Serve glamorously from a chafing dish as the perfect accompaniment for beef or pork roast.

1 pound fresh mushrooms*
¼ cup chopped onion
¼ cup butter or margarine
2 teaspoons flour
½ cup water
1 beef bouillon cube or 1 teaspoon instant beef bouillon
1 tablespoon soy sauce
Toasted slivered almonds

If using fresh mushrooms, prepare as directed above, slicing parallel with stem.

In large skillet, cook and stir onion in butter until ten-

*Or, use 2 jars (4½ ounces each) sliced mushrooms, drained.

der. Stir in mushrooms. Sprinkle flour over mixture; stir until mushrooms are coated.

Add water, bouillon cube and soy sauce, stirring until bouillon cube is dissolved. Cook over medium heat about 3 minutes. Sprinkle with slivered almonds.

4 to 6 servings.

OKRA

Amount for 4 servings: 1 pound.

Season available: June through November.

When shopping: Look for tender, unblemished, bright green pods, less than 4 inches long.

Ways to serve: Buttered, with salt and pepper. . . . Varied with dash of vinegar or lemon juice. . . . In soups and casseroles. . . . Combined with tomatoes.

TO PREPARE

Wash okra; remove ends and cut okra into ½-inch slices.

TO COOK

Heat 1 inch salted water (½ teaspoon salt to 1 cup water) to boiling. Add okra. Cover and heat to boiling; cook about 10 minutes or until tender.

ONION-FRIED OKRA

1 pound fresh okra	⅛ teaspoon pepper
½ cup white cornmeal	½ cup salad oil
½ teaspoon onion salt	

Prepare okra as directed above.

Before slicing okra, be sure to remove the ends.

Stir together cornmeal, onion salt and pepper. Add okra and toss until thoroughly coated. Heat oil in large skillet; cook and stir okra in oil until brown.

4 servings.

ONIONS

Types: Dry, small white (for whole-cooked); yellow or red (domestic, for seasoning); Spanish, Bermuda, Italian (sweet, for raw or French fried slices).

Amount for 4 servings: 1½ pounds.

Season available: All year.

When shopping: Look for firm, well-shaped onions with unblemished papery skins.

Ways to serve: Buttered, with salt and pepper. . . . Seasoned with basil, ginger, oregano or thyme. . . . Creamed, scalloped, au gratin, fried, baked, stuffed or sliced and French fried.

TO PREPARE

Peel onions under cool running water (to prevent tears).

TO COOK

To Boil: Heat several inches salted water (½ teaspoon salt to 1 cup water) to boiling. Add onions. Cover and heat to boiling; cook until tender—15 to 20 minutes for small onions, 30 to 35 minutes for large ones. Drain.

To Bake: Place peeled large onions in ungreased baking dish. Pour water into dish to ¼-inch depth; cover with aluminum foil. Bake in 350° oven 40 to 50 minutes or until tender.

CLOVED ONIONS

1½ pounds small white onions*	⅛ teaspoon cloves
	⅓ cup brown sugar (packed)
3 tablespoons butter or margarine	

If using fresh onions, prepare and boil whole onions as directed above.

In medium skillet, melt butter with cloves over me-

*Or, use 1 can (1 pound) whole onions, drained.

dium heat, stirring occasionally. Add onions; stir gently until coated.

Sprinkle brown sugar over onions. Cook, turning frequently, about 5 minutes or until golden and glazed.

4 servings.

DELUXE CREAMED ONIONS

1½ pounds small white onions*	½ teaspoon salt
	⅛ teaspoon pepper
2 tablespoons butter or margarine	1½ cups light cream (20%)
	1½ cups shredded carrots
2 tablespoons flour	

If using fresh onions, prepare and boil whole onions as directed on page 701.

Melt butter in saucepan over low heat. Blend in flour and seasonings. Cook over low heat, stirring until mixture is smooth and bubbly. Remove from heat.

Stir in light cream. Heat to boiling, stirring constantly. Boil and stir 1 minute. Stir in carrots and cook about 5 minutes longer. Pour sauce over hot onions.

4 to 6 servings.

*Or, use 2 cans (1 pound each) whole onions, heated and drained.

FRENCH FRIED ONION RINGS

1 large Spanish or Bermuda onion	½ cup all-purpose flour*
	¾ teaspoon baking powder
⅔ cup milk	¼ teaspoon salt

Peel onion; cut into ¼-inch slices and separate into rings.

Heat fat or oil (1 inch deep) to 375° in large skillet. Beat remaining ingredients with rotary beater until smooth. Dip each onion ring into batter, letting excess drip into bowl.

Fry a few onion rings at a time in hot fat about 2 minutes or until golden brown, turning once. Drain.

3 or 4 servings.

*If using self-rising flour, omit baking powder and salt.

Note: To keep fried onion rings warm, place in 300° oven until ready to serve.

ONIONS—GREEN

Amount for 4 servings: 2 bunches.
Season available: All year.
When shopping: Look for crisp, green tops; 2 to 3 inches of white root.
Ways to serve: Buttered, with salt and pepper. . . . Sprinkled with Parmesan. . . . Raw, as a relish.

TO PREPARE

Wash onions; remove any loose layers of skin. Leave about 3 inches of stem.

TO COOK

Heat 1 inch salted water (½ teaspoon salt to 1 cup water) to boiling. Add onions. Cover and heat to boiling; cook 8 to 10 minutes or just until tender.

PARSNIPS

Amount for 4 servings: 1½ pounds (about 6).
Season available: All year.
When shopping: Look for firm, nicely shaped, unblemished parsnips that are not too wide.
Ways to serve: Buttered, with salt and pepper. . . . Sprinkled with parsley. . . . Baked or mashed.

TO PREPARE

Scrape or pare. Leave whole or cut in half, into quarters, slices or lengthwise into ¼-inch strips.

TO COOK

Heat 1 inch salted water (½ teaspoon salt to 1 cup water) to boiling. Add parsnips. Cover and heat to boiling; cook 30 minutes or until tender. Drain.

PINEAPPLE-BAKED PARSNIPS

1½ pounds parsnips (about 6 medium)	1 teaspoon salt
½ cup pineapple juice	½ teaspoon pepper
1 teaspoon sugar	3 tablespoons butter or margarine

Heat oven to 350°. Prepare parsnips in lengthwise strips as directed above.

Place strips in ungreased baking dish, 11½ x 7½ x 1½ inches. Mix juice, sugar, salt, and pepper; pour over parsnips. Dot with butter. Cover; bake 1 hour.

4 servings.

PEAS—GREEN

Amount for 4 servings: 3 pounds.

Season available: September to June (peak—April and May).

When shopping: Look for bright green pods, well filled and tender.

Ways to serve: Buttered, with salt and pepper. . . . Seasoned with allspice, basil, chervil, marjoram, mint, rosemary, savory, thyme or tarragon. . . . Creamed or topped with Lemon-Chive or Maître d'Hôtel Butter (page 581). . . . Combined with vegetables such as carrots, onions or mushrooms.

TO PREPARE

Shell and wash peas just before cooking.

TO COOK

Heat 1 inch salted water (½ teaspoon salt to 1 cup water) to boiling. Add peas. Heat to boiling; cook uncovered 5 minutes. Cover and cook 3 to 7 minutes or until tender. If desired, add ½ teaspoon sugar and a few pods or leaf of lettuce to boiling water for added flavor. Drain.

CURRIED PEAS

Do you recall the days of shelling plump pods on the back porch —and sneaking a taste of the tender fresh peas in their raw state? But here they are cooked and treated to a delicately curried cream sauce.

3 pounds fresh green peas*
2 tablespoons chopped onion
2 tablespoons butter or margarine
2 tablespoons flour
½ teaspoon curry powder
¼ teaspoon salt
1½ cups milk

If using fresh peas, prepare and cook as directed above.

In medium skillet, cook and stir onion in butter until

*Or, use 1 package (10 ounces) frozen green peas, cooked and drained, or 1 can (1 pound 1 ounce) green peas, drained.

tender. Remove from heat. Stir in flour and seasonings. Cook over low heat, stirring until mixture is bubbly. Remove from heat. Stir in milk. Heat to boiling, stirring constantly. Boil and stir 1 minute. Gently stir in peas and heat through.

4 servings.

MINTED PEAS

Prepare and cook 3 pounds fresh green peas as directed at left.*

* Melt 1 tablespoon mint jelly in medium saucepan over low heat. Add hot peas and toss. Season to taste.

4 servings.

*Or, use 1 package (10 ounces) frozen green peas, cooked and drained.

PEAS, FRENCH STYLE

The classic of pea cookery. Lettuce provides the moisture and helps retain the spring flavor of tender new peas.

3 pounds fresh green peas*	⅛ teaspoon pepper
Lettuce leaves	⅛ teaspoon nutmeg
½ teaspoon salt	2 tablespoons butter

If using fresh peas, prepare as directed at left.

Line medium saucepan with lettuce leaves; add peas. Sprinkle salt, pepper and nutmeg; dot with butter. Cover peas with more lettuce leaves. Cover; cook over low heat 15 to 18 minutes or until peas are tender. Discard lettuce leaves.

4 servings.

*Or, use 1 package (10 ounces) frozen green peas, partially thawed and broken apart.

PEPPERS—GREEN BELL

Amount for 4 servings: 4 (1 per serving).

Season available: April through December.

When shopping: Look for well-shaped, shiny, medium to dark green peppers with firm sides.

Ways to serve: Stuffed and baked. . . . Fried or cooked in seasoned sauce.

TO PREPARE

Remove stems, seeds and membranes from peppers. Leave whole to stuff and bake; cut into thin slices or rings to fry.

TO COOK

To Bake: Parboil peppers 3 to 5 minutes; stuff and bake.

To Fry: Fry pepper slices or rings in small amount of butter 3 to 5 minutes or until crisp-tender and light brown.

SPANISH PEPPERS

Pepper strips with a zesty tomato sauce and a crunchy topping of garlic croutons team up to create a real flavor impact.

3 medium green peppers
1 cup ¼-inch diagonal slices celery
¼ cup finely chopped onion
2 tablespoons salad oil
½ teaspoon basil leaves
1 teaspoon salt
Dash pepper
1 can (15 ounces) tomato sauce
Garlic Croutons (below)

Remove stems, seeds and membranes from peppers. Cut peppers into strips.

In large skillet, cook and stir pepper strips, celery and onion in oil over medium heat until onion is tender. Stir in basil, salt, pepper and tomato sauce.

Cover; cook over medium heat 10 minutes or until pepper strips are tender. Turn into serving dish; sprinkle with Garlic Croutons.

4 to 6 servings.

GARLIC CROUTONS

Melt 2 tablespoons butter in small saucepan; stir in ¼ teaspoon garlic powder. Add 1 cup toasted bread cubes; toss.

POTATOES—NEW

Amount for 4 servings: 1½ pounds (10 to 12 small).
Season available: Spring and summer.
When shopping: Look for nicely shaped, smooth, firm

potatoes with unblemished skins, free from discoloration.

Ways to serve: Buttered, with salt and pepper. . . . Seasoned with snipped parsley, chives or green onion, paprika or lemon juice. . . . Creamed and often combined with peas.

TO PREPARE

Wash potatoes lightly and leave whole. If desired, pare narrow strip around center.

TO COOK

Heat 1 inch salted water (1 teaspoon salt to 1 cup water) to boiling. Add potatoes. Cover and heat to boiling; cook 20 to 25 minutes or until tender. Drain.

PARSLEYED NEW POTATOES

1½ pounds new potatoes (10   1 tablespoon snipped
    to 12 small)   parsley
  3 tablespoons butter or
    margarine, melted

Prepare and cook new potatoes as directed above. Just before serving, toss with butter and sprinkle with parsley.

  4 servings.

LEMON-BUTTERED NEW POTATOES

1½ pounds new potatoes (10   1 tablespoon lemon juice
    to 12 small)   2 teaspoons snipped chives
  2 tablespoons butter or   ½ teaspoon salt
    margarine   ⅛ teaspoon pepper
  ½ teaspoon grated lemon   Dash nutmeg
    peel

Prepare and cook new potatoes as directed above. Keep potatoes warm.

In small saucepan, heat remaining ingredients just to boiling. Turn hot potatoes into serving dish; stir lemon butter and pour over potatoes.

  4 servings.

POTATOES—WHITE

Amount for 4 servings: 2 pounds (about 6 medium).
Season available: All year.
When shopping: Look for well-shaped, smooth, firm potatoes with unblemished skins, free from discoloration.
Ways to serve: Buttered, with salt and pepper. . . . Seasoned with bay leaf, caraway seed, dill, mint, poppy seed or sage. . . . Baked, creamed, fried, scalloped or mashed.

TO PREPARE

For Boiling: Wash potatoes. Leave skins on whenever possible or pare thinly and remove eyes. Leave whole or cut into large pieces.
For Baking: Scrub potatoes and, if desired, rub with shortening for softer skins. Prick with fork to allow steam to escape.

TO COOK

To Boil: Heat 1 inch salted water (½ teaspoon salt to 1 cup water) to boiling. Add potatoes. Cover and heat to boiling; cook until tender—30 to 35 minutes for whole potatoes, 20 to 25 minutes for cut. Drain.
To Bake: Bake potatoes in 375° oven 1 to 1¼ hours, in 350° oven 1¼ to 1½ hours.

POTATO PANCAKES

Serve as a tasty side dish with steaks, a roast, ham slice or your favorite barbecued meat.

2 pounds potatoes (about 6 medium)	3 tablespoons flour
1 egg	1 teaspoon salt
⅓ cup finely chopped onion	¼ cup butter or margarine

Wash potatoes; pare thinly and remove eyes. Shred enough potatoes to measure 4 cups. Drain potatoes thoroughly.

In small mixer bowl, beat egg until thick and lemon colored. Mix in potatoes, onion, flour and salt. Melt butter in large skillet over low heat. Shape potato mixture into 8 patties; place in skillet. Cook over medium heat, turning once, about 5 minutes or until golden brown.

8 servings.

HASHED BROWNS

Often the specialty of the man who likes to cook. And most likely, he does it in one piece.

1½ pounds potatoes (about 4 medium)	⅛ teaspoon pepper
2 tablespoons finely chopped onion	2 tablespoons butter or margarine
½ teaspoon salt	2 tablespoons salad oil or bacon drippings

Prepare and cook pared potatoes as directed at left. Cool slightly. Shred enough potatoes to measure 4 cups.

Toss potatoes with onion, salt and pepper. Heat butter and oil in 9- or 10-inch skillet. Pack potato mixture firmly in skillet, leaving a ½-inch space around edge.

Cook over low heat 10 to 15 minutes or until bottom crust is brown. Cut potato mixture into fourths; turn each portion. Add 1 tablespoon salad oil if necessary. Cook 12 to 15 minutes longer or until brown.

4 to 6 servings.

Note: Potato mixture can be kept in one piece, if desired. To turn, invert onto plate and slide back into skillet.

COTTAGE FRIED POTATOES

Sometimes called Country Fried or Fried Cooked Potatoes— more often than not, made from precooked potatoes.

2 tablespoons butter or margarine	1 teaspoon salt
2 tablespoons shortening	⅛ teaspoon pepper
6 cooked pared medium potatoes	

Melt butter and shortening in large skillet over low heat. Slice potatoes into hot shortening. Season potato slices with salt and pepper. Cook over low heat until bottom crust is brown. Turn potatoes and cook until brown.

4 to 6 servings.

■ *Lyonnaise Potatoes:* Sprinkle ⅓ cup finely chopped onion over potato slices in skillet before cooking.

RAW FRIES

The secrets here are a heavy skillet, steady heat and the patience not to turn the potatoes until they're browned.

Pare about 6 medium potatoes. Cut into thin slices to measure about 4 cups.

Melt 2 tablespoons butter or margarine in large heavy skillet. Spread potato slices in 3 layers, each one slice thick, sprinkling each layer with ½ teaspoon salt and dash pepper. Dot top layer with 2 tablespoons butter.

Cover; cook over medium heat 20 minutes. Uncover; cook until potatoes are brown, turning once.

4 to 6 servings.

FRENCH FRIED POTATOES

Prepare 1½ pounds potatoes (about 4 medium) as directed on page 708 except—cut potatoes into lengthwise strips, ¼ to ⅜ inch wide.

Fill deep fat fryer or deep saucepan ½ full with salad oil or shortening; heat to 375°. Fill basket ¼ full with potatoes. Lower slowly into hot fat. If fat bubbles excessively, raise and lower basket several times. Use long-handled fork to keep potatoes separated. Fry 5 to 7 minutes or until potatoes are golden. Drain; repeat. Salt to taste.

4 servings.

MASHED POTATOES

2 pounds potatoes (about 6 medium)	½ teaspoon salt
	Dash pepper
⅓ to ½ cup milk	
¼ cup soft butter or margarine	

Prepare and cook pared potatoes as directed on page 708. Gently shake pan over low heat to dry potatoes.

Mash potatoes until no lumps remain. Add milk in small amounts, beating after each addition. (Amount of milk needed to make potatoes smooth and fluffy depends on kind of potatoes.) Add butter, salt and pepper; beat vigorously until potatoes are light and fluffy. If desired, dot with butter or sprinkle with paprika, snipped parsley, watercress or chives.

4 to 6 servings.

VARIATIONS

■ *Mashed Potatoes (Ricing Method):* Put potatoes through ricer instead of mashing. Add milk, butter, salt and pepper; whip until fluffy.

■ *Duchess Potatoes:* Heat oven to 425°. Beat 2 eggs; add to mashed potatoes and beat until blended. Drop mixture by spoonfuls into mounds on greased baking sheet, or form rosettes or pipe border around meat or fish using decorators' tube with tip. Brush mounds, rosettes or border with melted butter; bake 15 minutes or until potatoes are light brown. 9 or 10 mounds or rosettes.

SOUR CREAM MASHED POTATOES

Heat oven to 400°. Prepare instant mashed potato puffs as directed on package for 8 servings. Stir in 1 envelope (1½ ounces) sour cream sauce mix. Turn into ungreased 1-quart casserole. If desired, sprinkle with paprika or add one of the Variations (below). Bake uncovered 10 minutes.

8 servings.

VARIATIONS

■ *Almond Topping:* Sprinkle top with ¼ cup toasted slivered almonds and 1 tablespoon butter or margarine, melted.

■ *Blue Cheese:* Stir in 2 tablespoons crumbled blue cheese.

■ *Cheddar Cheese Topping:* Sprinkle top with 1 cup shredded Cheddar cheese (about 4 ounces).

■ *Herb:* Stir in ⅛ to ¼ teaspoon thyme, marjoram or basil.

IRISH MASHED POTATOES

The addition of another vegetable to mashed potatoes is called "champ" by the Irish.

1 medium head green cabbage (about 1½ pounds)
Instant mashed potato puffs

½ cup thinly sliced green onions
⅛ teaspoon pepper

Prepare and cook 4 cups shredded cabbage as directed on page 683.

Prepare potato puffs as directed on package for 8 servings. Stir in onions and pepper. Fold hot cabbage into potatoes.

8 to 10 servings.

CHEESE-POTATO BALLS

Instant mashed potato puffs
1½ cups water
2 tablespoons butter or margarine
1 teaspoon salt

½ cup milk
16 half-inch cubes process American cheese
3 tablespoons butter or margarine, melted

Heat oven to 400°. Measure ½ cup of the potato puffs (dry); set aside. Heat water, 2 tablespoons butter and the salt to boiling in large saucepan. Remove from heat; stir in milk and the remaining potato puffs. (Potatoes will be stiff). Form into 16 balls, shaping each heaping tablespoonful of potato around a cube of cheese.

Stir reserved potato puffs into the melted butter. Roll balls in buttered potato puffs; place on ungreased baking sheet. If desired, sprinkle with paprika. Bake 10 to 15 minutes or until light brown.

8 servings.

Note: Potatoes can be prepared, shaped and stored in refrigerator several hours ahead of serving time. Roll in buttered potato puffs just before baking.

SCALLOPED POTATOES

No sauce to make! Only a mix could be faster.

2 pounds potatoes (about 6 medium)	1 teaspoon salt
¼ cup finely chopped onion	¼ teaspoon pepper
3 tablespoons flour	¼ cup butter or margarine
	2½ cups milk

Heat oven to 350°. Wash potatoes; pare thinly and remove eyes. Cut potatoes into thin slices to measure about 4 cups.

In greased 2-quart casserole, arrange potatoes in 4 layers, sprinkling each of the first 3 layers with 1 tablespoon onion, 1 tablespoon flour, ¼ teaspoon salt, dash pepper and dotting each with 1 tablespoon butter. Sprinkle top with remaining onion, salt and pepper and dot with remaining butter. Heat milk just to scalding; pour over potatoes. Cover; bake 30 minutes. Uncover; bake 60 to 70 minutes longer or until potatoes are tender. Let stand 5 to 10 minutes before serving.

4 to 6 servings.

CREAMY SCALLOPED POTATOES

2 pounds potatoes (about 6 medium)	Salt and pepper
	2½ cups milk
3 tablespoons butter or margarine	¼ cup finely chopped onion
3 tablespoons flour	1 tablespoon butter or margarine

Heat oven to 350°. Wash potatoes; pare thinly and remove eyes. Cut potatoes into thin slices to measure about 4 cups. Melt 3 tablespoons butter in saucepan over low heat. Blend in flour and seasonings. Cook over low heat, stirring until mixture is smooth and bubbly. Remove from heat. Stir in milk. Heat to boiling, stirring constantly. Boil and stir 1 minute.

In greased 2-quart casserole, arrange potatoes in 2 layers, topping each with half the onion and ⅓ of the white sauce. Top with remaining potatoes and sauce. Dot with 1 tablespoon butter. Cover; bake 30 minutes. Uncover; bake 60 to 70 minutes longer or until potatoes are tender. Let stand 5 to 10 minutes before serving.

6 servings.

TOMATOED POTATOES

Quickly sauced with canned tomatoes.

1 package (5.5 ounces) scalloped potatoes	1 can (1 pound) tomatoes
2 cups water	¼ teaspoons basil, if desired

Heat oven to 400°. Place potatoes and seasoned sauce mix in ungreased 2-quart casserole. Heat water, tomatoes and basil to boiling; stir into potatoes. Cover; bake 35 to 40 minutes. If desired, garnish with snipped parsley.

4 to 6 servings.

GOURMET AU GRATIN POTATOES

Prepare 1 package (5.5 ounces) au gratin potatoes as directed except—stir in one of the following before baking:

½ cup chopped pimiento-stuffed olives	½ cup chopped green pepper
1 can (8 ounces) small white onions, drained, and 1 jar (2 ounces) sliced pimiento, drained	1 can (3 ounces) sliced mushrooms, drained

TWICE-BAKED POTATOES

Prepare and bake 2 pounds baking potatoes (about 4 large) as directed on page 708.

Increase oven temperature to 400°. Cut thin slice from top of each potato; scoop out inside, leaving a thin shell. Mash potatoes until no lumps remain. Add ⅓ to ½ cup milk in small amounts, beating after each addition. (Amount of milk needed to make potatoes smooth and fluffy depends on kind of potatoes.) Add ¼ cup soft butter or margarine, ½ teaspoon salt and dash pepper; beat vigorously until potatoes are light and fluffy.

Fill potato shells with mashed potatoes. If desired, sprinkle with finely shredded cheese. Bake 20 minutes or until filling is golden.

4 servings.

VARIATION

■ *Pepper or Pimiento Potatoes:* Stir ¼ cup finely chopped green pepper or ¼ cup drained chopped pimiento into mashed potato mixture.

BAKED POTATOES WITH TOPPERS

Prepare and bake 4 to 6 large baking potatoes as directed on page 708.

To serve, cut crisscross gash in tops; squeeze gently until some potato pops up through opening. Accompany with one of the toppers below:

BUTTER TOPPERS

Parsley Butter: Stir 1 tablespoon snipped parsley into ½ cup soft butter or margarine.

Thyme Butter: Stir ½ teaspoon thyme leaves into ½ cup soft butter or margarine.

SOUR CREAM TOPPERS

Cheesy Sour Cream: Stir ¼ cup shredded Parmesan cheese into 1 cup dairy sour cream.

Curried Sour Cream: Stir 1 teaspoon curry powder and ½ teaspoon salt into 1 cup dairy sour cream.

Sour Cream and Chives: Stir 2 tablespoons snipped chives and 1 teaspoon salt into 1 cup dairy sour cream.

CREAM CHEESE TOPPERS

Cream Cheese and Bacon: Beat 1 package (8 ounces) cream cheese, softened, and 5 tablespoons milk until fluffy. Stir in 4 slices bacon, crisply fried and crumbled.

Peanutty Cream Cheese: Beat 1 package (8 ounces) cream cheese, softened, and 5 tablespoons milk until fluffy. Stir in ¼ cup chopped peanuts.

FOIL-GRILLED POTATOES

Select medium white baking potatoes, sweet potatoes or yams. Scrub potatoes; rub skins with salad oil or butter. Wrap each potato securely in heavy-duty aluminum foil.

Place on grill 3 inches from hot coals; cook about 1 hour, turning frequently. Or place directly on medium coals and cook 45 to 60 minutes, turning frequently. Potatoes are done when soft to the touch (with abestos-gloved thumb).

To serve, make crosswise slits through foil and into potato; fold back foil and squeeze until potato pops up through opening. Pass butter, salt and pepper.

SQUASH—SUMMER

Types: White—Cymling, Pattypan and Scalloped; Yellow—Straightneck or Crookneck; Light green—Chayote; Dark green—Zucchini.

Amount for 4 servings: 2 pounds.

Season available: All year (peak—summer).

When shopping: Look for firm, well-shaped squash with shiny, smooth skins. Should be heavy for size.

Ways to serve: Buttered, with salt and pepper. . . . Seasoned with basil, marjoram, oregano or rosemary. . . . Sprinkled with Parmesan or mozzarella cheese. . . . Baked, mashed or fried. . . . Topped with Cheese or Chive-Parsley Butter (page 581).

TO PREPARE

Wash squash; remove stem and blossom end but do not pare. Cut into ½-inch slices or cubes.

TO COOK

Heat 1 inch salted water (½ teaspoon salt to 1 cup water) to boiling. Add squash. Cover and heat to boiling; cook until tender—12 to 15 minutes for slices, 7 to 8 minutes for cubes. Drain.

GINGERED VEGETABLE MÉLANGE

1 pound yellow summer squash

2 tablespoons butter or margarine

1 medium onion, thinly sliced

1 medium green pepper, cut into ¼-inch strips

3 medium tomatoes, peeled and quartered

1 teaspoon salt

1 teaspoon ginger

Prepare squash slices as directed above.

Melt butter in large skillet. Add squash, onion and green pepper; cook and stir over medium heat until vegetables are slightly brown. Cover; cook until squash is tender, about 6 minutes, stirring occasionally.

Stir in remaining ingredients. Cover; cook 2 to 3 minutes longer or until tomatoes are heated through.

4 to 6 servings.

BROILED ZUCCHINI

Wash 2 pounds (about 8 small) zucchini; remove stem and blossom ends. Cut each zucchini in half lengthwise.

Brush each cut side with melted butter or margarine; season with salt and pepper. Set oven control at broil and/or 550°. Broil 5 to 6 inches from heat 10 to 12 minutes or until tender.

4 servings.

HARVEST ZUCCHINI

1¼ pounds zucchini (about 5 small)
⅓ cup finely chopped onion
¼ cup butter or margarine
½ cup dairy sour cream
2 tablespoons milk
1 teaspoon salt
2 teaspoons paprika
2 teaspoons poppy seed

Prepare 4 cups sliced zucchini as directed at left.

In large skillet, cook and stir zucchini and onion in butter until butter is melted. Cover; cook, stirring occasionally, until zucchini is tender. Mix remaining ingredients; gently stir into zucchini and heat through.

4 servings.

CONTINENTAL ZUCCHINI

1 pound zucchini (about 4 small)
1 can (12 ounces) vacuum-packed whole kernel corn, drained
1 jar (2 ounces) chopped pimiento, drained
2 medium cloves garlic, crushed
2 tablespoons salad oil
1 teaspoon salt
¼ teaspoon pepper
½ cup shredded mozzarella cheese

Prepare 3 cups cubed zucchini as directed at left.

In large skillet, stir together all ingredients except

cheese. Cover; cook over medium heat, stirring occasionally, about 10 minutes or until squash is crisp-tender. Stir in cheese; heat through.

4 to 6 servings.

SQUASH—WINTER

Types: Medium—Acorn (Table Queen), Butternut; Large—Banana, Buttercup, Hubbard.

Amount for 4 servings: 3 pounds.

Season available: October through February.

When shopping: Look for good yellow-orange color, hard, tough rinds; squash that is heavy.

Ways to serve: Buttered, with salt and pepper. . . . Removed from rind and mashed with cream, nutmeg, brown sugar, crumbled crisply fried bacon, candied ginger, grated orange peel or orange juice.

TO PREPARE

Large: Cut squash into serving pieces; remove seeds and fibers. For boiling, cut into slices or cubes.

Medium: Cut in half; remove seeds and fibers.

TO COOK

To Bake: Place squash in ungreased baking dish, 13½x9x2 inches. Season cut sides with salt and pepper; dot with butter or margarine. Pour water into dish to ¼-inch depth; cover with aluminum foil. Bake in 400° oven 30 minutes or until tender.

To Boil (for large squash): Heat 1 inch salted water (½ teaspoon salt to 1 cup water) to boiling. Add squash. Cover and heat to boiling; cook 15 to 20 minutes or until tender. Drain.

SQUASH AND APPLE BAKE

2 pounds butternut or buttercup squash	1 tablespoon flour
½ cup brown sugar (packed)	1 teaspoon salt
¼ cup butter or margarine, melted	½ teaspoon mace
	2 baking apples, cored and cut into ½-inch slices

Heat oven to 350°. Cut each squash in half. Remove seeds and fibers; pare squash. Cut into ½-inch slices.

Stir together remaining ingredients except apple slices. Arrange squash in ungreased baking dish, 11½ x 7½ x 1½ inches; top with apple slices. Sprinkle sugar mixture over top; cover with foil. Bake 50 to 60 minutes or until squash is tender.

6 servings.

GOURMET GOLDEN SQUASH

3 pounds Hubbard squash*
2 tablespoons butter or margarine
1 cup dairy sour cream
½ cup finely chopped onion
1 teaspoon salt
¼ teaspoon pepper

If using fresh squash, prepare and boil cubed squash as directed at left.

Heat oven to 400°. Mash squash; stir in remaining ingredients. Turn mixture into ungreased 1-quart casserole. Bake uncovered 20 to 30 minutes.

6 servings.

*Or, use 2 packages (12 ounces each) frozen cooked squash, thawed.

NUTTY BAKED SQUASH

2 acorn squash (1 pound each)
⅔ cup cracker crumbs
⅓ cup coarsely chopped pecans
⅓ cup butter or margarine, melted
3 tablespoons brown sugar
½ teaspoon salt
¼ teaspoon nutmeg

Cut each squash in half; remove seeds and fibers. Stir together remaining ingredients; spoon ¼ of mixture into each half. Bake as directed at left.

4 servings.

SWEET POTATOES—JERSEY SWEETS, YAMS

Amount for 4 servings: 2 pounds (about 6 medium).

Season available: All year.

When shopping: Look for smooth, even colored skins; potatoes that are firm and nicely shaped.

Ways to serve: Buttered, with salt and pepper. . . . Mashed or candied. . . . In soufflés.

TO PREPARE

Wash sweet potatoes but do not pare.

TO COOK

Heat enough salted water to cover potatoes (½ teaspoon salt to 1 cup water) to boiling. Add potatoes. Cover and heat to boiling; cook 30 to 35 minutes or until tender. Drain. Slip off skins. Leave potatoes whole, slice or mash.

ORANGE-GLAZED SWEET POTATOES

2 pounds sweet potatoes (about 6 medium)
⅔ cup sugar
1 tablespoon cornstarch
1 teaspoon salt
½ teaspoon grated orange peel
1 cup orange juice
2 tablespoons butter or margarine

Heat oven to 400°. Pare sweet potatoes; cut each lengthwise in half. Arrange in ungreased 1½-quart casserole.

In small saucepan, stir together sugar, cornstarch, salt and orange peel. Slowly stir orange juice into sugar mixture. Add butter. Cook, stirring constantly, until mixture thickens and boils. Boil and stir 1 minute.

Pour hot orange juice mixture over sweet potatoes in casserole. Cover; bake 1 hour, basting occasionally.

4 to 6 servings.

CANDIED YAMS OR SWEET POTATOES

What's the difference between yams and sweet potatoes? Yams are more moist and orange colored—they're also sweeter than the "sweets."

2 pounds sweet potatoes or yams* (about 6 medium)
½ cup brown sugar (packed)
3 tablespoons butter or margarine
3 tablespoons light cream or milk
½ teaspoon salt

If using fresh sweet potatoes, prepare and cook as

*Or, use 1 can (1 pound 1 ounce) vacuum-packed sweet potatoes; cut each into ½-inch slices.

directed on page 720. Cut each potato crosswise into ½-inch slices.

In medium skillet, combine brown sugar, butter, cream and salt; cook over medium heat, stirring constantly, until smooth and bubbly. Add sweet potato slices; stir gently until glazed and heated through.

4 to 6 servings.

VARIATION

■ *Pineapple-Sweet Potatoes:* Omit cream and add 1 can (8¾ ounces) crushed pineapple, drained.

SWEET POTATO MALLOW

A classic recipe. Marshmallows form a snow-capped topping on the colorful casserole. It's a natural teammate for ham or the Thanksgiving turkey.

1 pound sweet potatoes or yams* (about 3 medium)	¼ teaspoon mace
½ cup dairy sour cream	¾ cup miniature marshmallows or cut-up large marshmallows
1 egg yolk	
½ teaspoon salt	

If using fresh sweet potatoes, prepare and cook as directed on page 720.

Heat oven to 350°. In small mixer bowl, combine sweet potatoes, sour cream, egg yolk, salt and mace; beat on medium speed until smooth.

Pour sweet potato mixture into buttered 1-quart casserole; top with marshmallows. Bake 30 minutes or until marshmallows are puffed and golden brown.

4 servings.

Or, use 1 can (1 pound 1 ounce) vacuum-packed sweet potatoes.

TOMATOES

Amount for 4 servings: 2 pounds (about 6 medium).
Season available: Summer and fall.
When shopping: Look for nicely ripened, well-shaped

tomatoes; fully ripe tomatoes should be slightly soft, have a rich red color.

Ways to serve: Buttered, with salt and pepper. . . . Seasoned with allspice, basil, bay leaf, chives, fennel, marjoram, oregano, sage or tarragon. . . . Fried, broiled or baked.

TO PREPARE

Wash tomatoes; cut into quarters or ¾-inch slices. If desired, peel tomatoes before cutting. To remove skin easily, dip tomato into boiling water ½ minute, then into cold water. Or scrape surface of tomato with blade of knife to loosen; peel.

TO COOK

Cook tomatoes covered *without water* over low heat 8 to 10 minutes, stirring occasionally, or until tender.

BAKED STUFFED TOMATOES

6 medium tomatoes (about 2 pounds)	⅓ cup croutons
¼ cup finely chopped green pepper	1 teaspoon salt
¼ cup grated Parmesan cheese	Parsley sprigs or crumbled crisply fried bacon

Heat oven to 350°. Wash tomatoes; remove stem ends. Remove pulp from each tomato, leaving a ½-inch wall; chop pulp to measure ⅓ cup.

Stir together tomato pulp and remaining ingredients except parsley. Fill tomatoes with tomato-cheese mixture. Place filled tomatoes in ungreased baking dish, 11½x7½x1½ inches. Bake 20 to 25 minutes or until tomatoes are heated through. Garnish with parsley.

6 servings.

CRUNCHY FRIED TOMATOES

4 firm ripe or green medium tomatoes (about 1½ pounds)	1 cup dry bread crumbs
1 egg, beaten	⅓ cup butter or margarine
	Salt and pepper

Prepare tomato slices as directed on page 722.
Dip slices into egg and then into crumbs. Melt butter

in large skillet. Add tomato slices; cook, turning once, until golden brown. Season to taste.

4 servings.

EASY PANFRIED TOMATOES

4 firm ripe or green medium tomatoes (about 1½ pounds)	1 teaspoon salt
	¼ teaspoon pepper
½ cup all-purpose flour*	⅓ cup butter or margarine

Prepare tomato slices as directed on page 722.

Stir together flour, salt and pepper. Dip tomato slices into flour mixture. Melt butter in large skillet. Add tomato slices and cook, turning once, until golden brown.

4 servings.

*If using self-rising flour, omit salt.

STEWED TOMATOES

3 large ripe tomatoes* (about 1½ pounds)	1 tablespoon sugar
	½ teaspoon salt
⅓ cup finely chopped onion	⅛ teaspoon pepper
2 tablespoons chopped green pepper	1 cup soft bread cubes

If using fresh tomatoes, remove stem end from each; peel tomatoes and cut into small pieces.

In medium saucepan, stir together all ingredients except bread cubes. Cover and heat to boiling; reduce heat and simmer 8 to 10 minutes. Stir in bread cubes.

4 or 5 servings.

*Or, use 1 can (1 pound) peeled tomatoes.

BROILED TOMATOES

Wash 4 medium tomatoes (about 1½ pounds). Remove stem end from each; cut tomatoes in half.

Set oven control at broil and/or 550°. Dot each half with ½ teaspoon butter or margarine. Season with salt, pepper, basil leaves, oregano leaves or ground savory.

Broil tomato halves cut side up 3 to 5 inches from heat 5 minutes or until tops are golden brown.
4 servings.

■ *Cheesy Broiled Tomatoes:* Dot tomatoes with butter but omit seasonings. Broil tomato halves cut side up 4 to 6 inches from heat 5 minutes. Sprinkle cut sides with ⅓ cup shredded Parmesan cheese. Broil 1 to 2 minutes longer or until cheese begins to melt.

SAUTÉED CHERRY TOMATOES

A surprise vegetable garnish.

Wash 1 pint cherry tomatoes; drain and remove stem ends. Prick each tomato several times.

Melt 2 tablespoons butter or margarine in medium skillet. Cook and stir tomatoes in butter over medium heat until heated through, about 3 minutes.
4 servings.

TURNIPS, RUTABAGAS (YELLOW TURNIPS) AND KOHLRABI

Amount for 4 servings: Turnips—2 pounds (about 6 medium); Rutabagas—1 large or 2 medium; Kohlrabi—4 to 6 medium.

Season available: Turnips—All year; Rutabagas—fall through early spring; Kohlrabi—summer and fall.

When shopping: Look for turnips that are smooth, round and firm, with fresh tops; look for rutabagas that are heavy, well shaped (round or elongated) and smooth.

Ways to serve: Buttered, with salt and pepper. . . . Seasoned with dill, poppy seed, thyme. . . . Mashed and seasoned, if desired, with cream and nutmeg. . . . Varied with snipped onion or chives and dash Worcestershire sauce. . . . Raw, as a relish.

TO PREPARE

Turnips: If necessary, cut off tops. Wash turnips and pare thinly; leave whole or cut into cubes.

Rutabagas: Wash rutabaga and pare thinly. Cut into ½-inch cubes or 2-inch pieces.

Kohlrabi: Trim off root ends and vinelike stems. Wash kohlrabi and pare. Cube or cut into ¼-inch slices.

TO COOK

Heat 1 inch salted water (½ teaspoon salt to 1 cup water) to boiling. Add turnip, rutabaga or kohlrabi. Cover and heat to boiling; cook until tender—*turnips:* 25 to 30 minutes for whole, 15 to 20 minutes for cubes; *rutabagas:* 20 to 25 minutes for cubes, 30 to 40 minutes for pieces; *kohlrabi:* 25 minutes. Drain.

MASHED RUTABAGA WITH GREEN PEAS

Remember this for a festive Christmas dinner.

1 large or 2 medium rutabagas (about 2 pounds)	Instant mashed potato puffs
1 package (10 ounces) frozen green peas	½ teaspoon salt
	⅛ teaspoon pepper

Prepare and cook cubed rutabagas as directed at left. Cook peas as directed on package. Prepare potato puffs as directed on package for 2 servings except— omit milk and butter. Combine rutabagas and potatoes. Add salt and pepper; mash. Spoon into bowl or onto platter, leaving an indentation in center. Fill center with drained hot peas.

With canned rutabaga: Use 2 cans (15½ ounces each) diced rutabaga, drained; omit salt and heat through after mashing.

4 to 6 servings.

MUSTARD KOHLRABI

4 to 6 medium kohlrabi	1 tablespoon prepared mustard
2 tablespoons butter or margarine	½ teaspoon salt

Prepare and cook sliced kohlrabi as directed at left. Melt butter in medium skillet. Stir in mustard and salt. Add kohlrabi and toss. Cook, turning slices, until golden brown.

4 servings.

Special Helps

Menus for Every Occasion

What's the secret ingredient that marks the difference between mere food and a meal that evokes murmurs of anticipation from an appreciative family or guests?

The answer is a *well-planned* meal. And what makes for a well-planned meal? Variety—foods that vary in shape and size, food textures that contrast (smooth vs. crunchy); food flavors that blend; food colors that combine harmoniously or spark an otherwise colorless dish; food garnishes that add the artist's touch to a perfectly prepared dish. All these add up to meals that bring the family to the table almost before you can call them.

To insure that your meals are nutritiously balanced as well as pleasing to the eye, check your plans with the chart on page 738. Then set an attractive, colorful table (see pages 730 to 733). There will be kudos for the cook and empty plates back for "seconds."

FOR A HOLIDAY DINNER

The Traditional
Roast Turkey
Stuffing **Cranberry Sauce**
Mashed Potatoes **Giblet Gravy**
Deluxe Creamed Onions **Buttered Broccoli**
Hot Rolls **Assorted Relishes**
Sweet Potato Pie

Start Your Own Tradition
Duckling à l'Orange with Fruit Wreath
Squash and Apple Bake
Dilled Green Beans Relish
Caraway Puffs
Eggnog Cake

FOR A BRUNCH

Everyone's Favorites
Chilled Orange Juice
Scrambled Eggs and Bacon
Assorted Cereals
Popovers
Cocoa and Coffee

Something Different
Spiced Cranberry Cider
Eggs on Corned Beef Hash
Saint Lucia Crown
International Coffee

FOR A BUFFET DINNER

The Classic Touch
Baked Ham with Brown Sugar Glaze
Scalloped Potatoes
Buttered Green Beans
Tossed Salad
Cherry Berries on a Cloud

With an Exotic Air
Lamb Curry and Accompaniments
Fluffy White Rice
Baked Bananas
Avocado-Citrus Salad
Coconut Pudding Pie

FOR AN EASY COMPANY DINNER

Before the Theater
Pow!
California Onion Dip
with Crackers and Chips
Pepper Steak with Rice
Peas, French Style
Peaches Flambé

Saturday Night
Quick French Onion Soup
Chicken Casserole Deluxe
Bulgur Pilaf
Mustard-glazed Fruits
Date-Peach Crumble

FOR A QUICK AND EASY FAMILY DINNER

After a Shopping Spree
Frankfurters
Speedy Baked Beans
Spinach-Apple Toss
Chocolate Deluxe Pudding

PTA Tonight
Salmon and Noodles Romanoff
Broiled Tomatoes
Wilted Lettuce Salad
Fruit Shortcake

FOR A SPECIAL OCCASION DINNER

The Boss Is Coming
Celery Victor
Steak Diane
Twice Baked Potatoes
Fried Zucchini
Apple Pie

Happy Birthday
Sparkling Red Rouser
Avery Island Deviled Shrimp
Oriental Asparagus
Zucchini Toss
Williamsburg Orange Cake

FOR A CROWD-SIZE SUPPER

After the Game
Italian Spaghetti
Easy-do Salade Provençal
Carrot and Celery Curls
Hot French Bread with Garlic Butter
Lemon Cheesecake

Reunion Time
Arroz con Pollo
Perfection Salad
Butter Dips
Gourmet Olives and Tomatoes
Chocolate Delight

FOR A BACKYARD BARBECUE

Family Favorites
Charcoal-grilled Steak
Roast Corn
Sliced Tomatoes   Relishes
French Vanilla Ice Cream
Chocolate Chip Cookies

When Company Comes
Charcoal-grilled Sugared Ham
Foil-grilled Sweet Potatoes
Vegetable Salad Plate
Hickory French Bread
Grapes and Pineapple in Sour Cream

FOR A DESSERT BRIDGE

In the Afternoon
Angel Food Waldorf
Tea
or
Maple Chiffon Cake with Ice Cream
Coffee

In the Evening
Dessert Cheese and Fruit Tray
Espresso
or
Chocolate Fondue
Coffee

Recipes can be found in the book; refer to the index.

Table Service

A carefully planned and well-prepared meal deserves an attractive setting. So, whether you are entertaining guests or feeding the family, set a table that beckons.

Start by mixing or matching colors for eye-appeal—in place mats or table linens, in china, in a centerpiece. Flowers are always lovely but don't think you can't have a centerpiece without them. Try a compote of fresh fruit, a pottery mug filled with sprays of autumn leaves or a brandy snifter brimming with seashells.

The Traditional Place Setting

The silver, placed 1 inch from the edge of the table, is arranged so that the pieces to be used first are farthest from the plate. The forks are placed to the left of the plate, the knife and spoons to the right. The butter plate is set above the forks with the butter knife lying across it, in either a horizontal or a vertical position. If salad is to be served *with* the main course, the salad plate is placed to the left of the forks, the salad fork either to the right or left of the dinner fork. Glasses are set above the knife, with wine glasses to the right of the water glass.

The napkin is folded and placed on the plate, unless the first course is to be on the table when the guests are seated; in that case, the napkin should lie to the left of

Traditional buffet service—the perfect opportunity to mix and match your china, linens, serving pieces and other accessories.

A dessert-and-coffee party is one of the nicest and most relaxed ways to entertain informally. And, for a pleasant change of pace, serve dessert and coffee on your living room coffee table after dinner.

Buffet service adapts readily to limited space—a sideboard or small chest can provide an offbeat and convenient substitute table.

If you have the space, use small, pre-set tables when entertaining a crowd. Your guests serve themselves at the buffet, then sit to eat at the tables—no juggling of plates.

A tea cart is a versatile vehicle for hostessing—here an easy and attractive way to serve post-buffet dessert and coffee.

Color plays the major role in this ultra-feminine luncheon setting. The crossed eyelet runners offer an unexpected accent surprise.

Straw mats, colorful dishes and a napkin centerpiece set the scene for good-morning cheer at breakfast.

1 2

1. Embroidered linen place mats set off the traditional elegance of this dinner party setting; they offer a striking alternative to the tablecloth.

2. For more formal meals, service plates are often used. They are replaced by heated dinner plates following the appetizer and soup courses. Thus, place settings are never empty.

3. A new start-the-day centerpiece gives every morning its own special brightness—all it takes is imagination.

4. A simple switch of linens and a few new accessories and the same china and silver take on a bold, new, up-to-the-minute personality.

3 4

the forks. Dessert service may be on the table throughout the meal, or brought to the table with the dessert course. If coffee or tea is to be served with the meal, the cup and saucer go slightly above and to the right of the spoons.

A sit-down meal is correctly served either entirely by the host from his place, with plates passed to the left; or with the meat course served by the host and other dishes by the hostess; or even arranged on plates in the kitchen and taken to the table two at a time.

Buffet

For a small buffet, the table should be moved against the wall. The centerpiece is placed at center-back with plates, napkins and silver arranged as shown in the photograph on page 730. A large buffet requires two arrangements of plates, utensils and food on opposite sides of the table. The table is moved away from the wall and the centerpiece placed in the middle of the table. For dessert, the buffet is reset with dessert plates, cups, silver and coffee service. Or dessert may be passed to the guests.

SETTING THE TABLE FOR A TEA

Tea

The simple elegance of a tea demands your finest damask, your best china and silver, and tall candles to glimmer in the dusk. Small napkins that match the tea cloth are folded and placed on the plates as they are stacked. The tea service graces the end of the table farthest from the door; the coffee or chocolate service is placed at the end near the door. See the diagram at left.

Guide to a Well-Balanced Diet

To keep your family healthy and alert, your meals must provide a daily selection of all the food nutrients essential to well-being.

To insure a well-balanced diet, simply follow the recommendations of the "basic four" food groups and the sample daily menu plan on page 738.

Calories Do Count

BEVERAGES

Coffee (1 cup)	0
with cream and sugar	35
Cola-type (8 ounces)	95
Ginger ale (8 ounces)	70
Lemonade (1 cup)	110
Milk (1 cup)	
skim	90
2%	140
whole	160
Orange juice (½ cup)	55
Tomato juice (½ cup)	20

BREADS

Biscuit (1 medium)	140
Graham cracker (1 medium)	30
Pancake (4″ diameter)	60
Saltine (1 square)	20
Sweet roll	135
Waffle (4½x5½ inches)	210
White, whole wheat, raisin, rye (1 slice)	60

CEREALS

Fortified whole wheat flakes cereal (1 cup)	101
Oatmeal, cooked (½ cup)	65
O-shaped puffed oat cereal (1 cup)	98
Whole wheat flakes cereal (1 cup)	101

CHEESE AND EGGS

American cheese (1 slice)	105
Cottage cheese (¼ cup)	60
Egg (1 large)	80
Fried or scrambled egg	110
Omelet (2 eggs)	215

DESSERTS

Brownie (2-inch square)	145
Cookie (3-inch diameter)	120
Cake (2-inch sector)	
angel food, unfrosted	110
chocolate, with chocolate frosting	445
Gelatin, flavored (½ cup)	70
Ice cream (½ cup)	140
Ice milk (½ cup)	140
Pie (1/7)	
apple	345
cherry	355
lemon meringue	305
Sherbet (½ cup)	130

FISH AND SEAFOOD

Fish sticks (4)	160
Salmon, canned (3 ounces)	120
Shrimp, canned (3 ounces)	100
Tuna, water packed (3 ounces)	110

FRUITS

Apple (2½-inch diameter)	70
Banana (6x1½ inches)	85
Grapefruit (½, 4¼-inch diameter)	60
Orange (3-inch diameter)	70

Peach (2-inch diameter)	35
Pear (3x2½ inches)	100

MEAT

Bacon (2 slices)	100
Baked ham (3 ounces)	245
Beef (3 ounces)	
hamburger, broiled	245
liver, fried	195
T-bone steak, broiled	400
Frankfurter (2)	310
Lamb chop (3 ounces), broiled	300
Pork chop (3 ounces), broiled	320
Spareribs (6 medium)	245

POULTRY

Chicken breast (3 ounces), broiled	100
Chicken drumstick (3 ounces meat), broiled	110
Turkey (3 ounces)	160

VEGETABLES

Asparagus (½ cup)	20
Beets (½ cup)	30
Broccoli (½ cup)	20
Cabbage (½ cup)	20
Carrots (½ cup)	30
Cauliflower (½ cup)	10
Celery (1 stalk)	5
Corn (5-inch ear)	70
Green beans (½ cup)	20
Lettuce, iceberg (¼ head)	15
Peas (½ cup)	60
Potatoes	
baked (medium)	90
French fried (10 pieces)	155
mashed, with milk and butter (½ cup)	95
Spinach (½ cup)	20
Tomato (1 small)	30

Note: These caloric values are averages not specifically calculated for the recipes in this book.

SAMPLE DAILY MENU PLAN

BREAKFAST

Citrus Fruit or Juice
Cereal with Milk
Egg or Meat
Toast, Quick Bread or Grits
Tea, Coffee or Milk

LUNCH

Meat, Fish, Poultry or Cheese*
Vegetable and/or Salad
Breads, Noodles or Rice
Fruit   Milk
Tea or Coffee (if desired)
*Legumes (dried peas or beans)
or peanut butter can be used

DINNER

Meat, Fish, Poultry or Cheese
Green or Yellow Vegetable and
  Salad (or two vegetables)
Breads, Noodles or Rice
Fruit or Dessert (if desired; or
  as a snack)
Milk
Tea or Coffee (if desired)

Note: Butter or margarine and sweets can be added to meet calorie needs.

Note: Fats and sugars provide additional calories for energy.

MILK
2 to 3 cups for children under
9 years
3 or more cups for children
9-12 years
4 or more cups for teen-agers
2 or more cups for adults

BREADS AND CEREALS
(whole grain, enriched or
restored)
4 or more servings every day.

VEGETABLES AND FRUITS
4 or more servings every day.
One citrus fruit daily and one
dark green or yellow vegetable every other day.

MEATS
2 or more servings every day.

Cooking Help for High Altitudes

People who live in a high-altitude area face some unique cooking problems. Certain foods and methods of preparation are affected by the pressure of high altitude, and recipes must be adapted to meet the needs.

If you're new to a high-altitude area, call the Home Service Department of the local utility company or the State Extension Office for recipe booklets and help in solving specific problems. Recipes for high-altitude cooking are also available from Colorado State University, Fort Collins, Colorado.

Here are a few guidelines to help you:

Vegetables—Because the boiling point of water is lower at high altitudes, vegetables (fresh or frozen) take longer to become tender, and cooking time must be increased.

Eggs—Again because water boils at a lower temperature, the cooking time for eggs in the shell must be increased. Keep a record for the future.

Meats—Meats cooked in boiling liquid or steam take longer to cook than at sea level, sometimes quite a bit longer. Meats cooked in the oven, however, are not affected by high altitude.

Deep-fried Foods—To prevent food from becoming too dark before it is cooked through, the temperature of the fat should be lower than at sea level. Fry several pieces at a lower temperature, then check doneness in the middle.

Candy and Cooked Frosting—The mixture should be cooked to a lower temperature. If you use a thermometer, first check the boiling temperature of water in your area then subtract this temperature from from 212°. Subtract the same number of degrees from the temperatures cited in the recipe. (Or, use the cold water tests for candy.)

Yeast Breads—At high altitudes, dough tends to rise more rapidly, and it is possible to overproof easily. Allow dough to rise for a shorter time (*just* until doubled)—or use less yeast than the recipe calls for.

Mixes—Most mixes that require adjustment for high altitude have specific directions right on the package. Be sure to look for them.

Cakes—Use recipes especially developed for high altitudes. Your best source is the Home Service Department of your local utility company. Here, however, are two basic recipes for your files.

COCOA FUDGE CAKE

For altitudes of 4,000 to 6,000 feet.

1¾ cups all-purpose flour*	1⅔ cups buttermilk
1⅓ cups sugar	½ cup shortening
⅔ cup cocoa	2 eggs
1¼ teaspoons soda	1 teaspoon vanilla
1 teaspoon salt	

Heat oven to 375°. Grease and flour baking pan, 13x 9x2 inches, or 2 round layer pans, 9x1½ inches. Measure all ingredients into large mixer bowl. Blend ½ minute on low speed, scraping bowl constantly. Beat 3 minutes high speed, scraping bowl occasionally. Pour into pan(s).

Bake oblong about 35 minutes, layers 25 to 30 minutes or until wooden pick inserted in center comes out clean. Cool.

*Do not use self-rising flour in this recipe.

GOLDEN LAYER CAKE

For altitudes of 4,000 to 6,000 feet.

2⅓ cups cake flour	1 cup plus 2 tablespoons
1⅓ cups sugar	milk
2 teaspoons baking powder	1½ teaspoons vanilla
1 teaspoon salt	2 eggs
½ cup shortening	

Heat oven to 375°. Grease and flour baking pan, 13x9x2 inches, or 2 round layer pans, 9x1½ inches. Measure all ingredients into large mixer bowl. Blend ½ minute on low speed, scraping bowl constantly. Beat 3 minutes high speed, scraping bowl occasionally. Pour into pan(s).

Bake layers 25 to 30 minutes, oblong about 30 minutes or until wooden pick inserted in center of cake comes out clean. Cool.

Facts About Freezing

An individualized supermarket. That's what your freezer can be—if you know what to freeze and how to freeze it. The following recommendations—general and specific—will help you. For any food not covered here, consult the booklet that comes with your freezer, one of the many books about freezing or your local utility company.

In general . . .

■ Select top-quality foods. The freezing process can only retain the quality of the food; it cannot improve it.

■ Cool cooked foods quickly.

■ Use good packaging and wrapping materials. Select them on the basis of convenience of use, space occupied in the freezer and cost. Freezer wraps and containers should be airtight, moisture- and vapor-proof. Among the best materials for freezing are heavy-duty aluminum foil, heavy-weight plastic wrap and freezer bags or containers.

■ Wrap securely to create an airtight package—unless directions specify otherwise.

■ Do not refreeze foods. Freeze in family-size portions.

■ Label each package with the date, contents and number of servings. Rotate food in freezer so as not to exceed expiration date.

■ Use a storage temperature of 0° or lower for most foods.

CANDIES

Special Instructions: Be sure to use moisture-proof wrap. Marshmallows freeze well; spun candy chips, chocolate-covered nuts and candies with hard centers may crack or split.

Storage Time: 12 months.

To Thaw: Leave in moisture-proof wrap and let stand at room temperature 4 to 8 hours.

COOKIES

Cookies can be frozen either baked or unbaked. See page 203 for specific instructions.

FOOD PREPARATION TIPS

Peeling Tomatoes: Place in boiling water 1 minute; plunge into cold water. Slip off skin with point of knife.

Deveining Shrimp: Make a shallow cut lengthwise down back of each shrimp; remove sand vein with point of knife.

Making Bread Crumbs: For soft crumbs, pull bread into pieces. For dry crumbs, dry bread in low oven; crush.

Adding Food Color: Add liquid color drop by drop. Add paste color (from specialty stores) sparingly.

Making Croutons: Trim bread and cut into cubes; toast in 300° oven. Add cubes to melted butter and toss.

Tinting Coconut: Add a few drops of liquid food color to coconut in a jar; shake until evenly tinted.

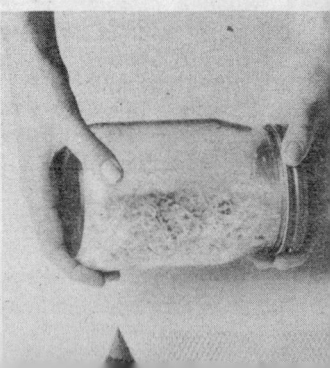

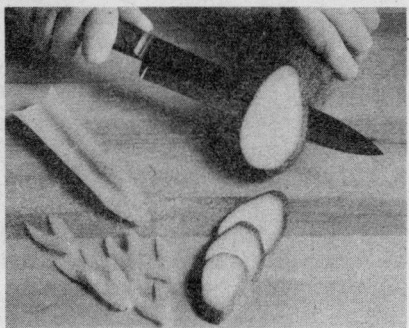

Cutting on the Diagonal: Use a very sharp knife, keeping blade angle almost parallel to the cutting surface.

Coating Chicken: Place seasonings, crumbs or flour in plastic or paper bag. Shake a few pieces at a time.

Melting Chocolate: Place in small heatproof bowl or in top of double boiler over hot (not boiling) water.

Mallet: Use to crush (candy, ice) or to pound thin (meat, poultry).

Wire Whip or Whisk: Use to blend (sauces, gravies) or to whip (cream).

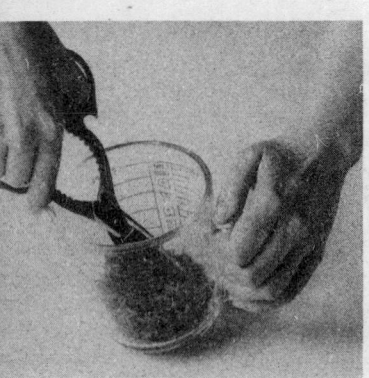 

Kitchen Shears: Use to snip (parsley, chives) or to cut (candied fruits).

Decorating Tube: Use for decorating tasks or to stuff (celery, eggs).

Scoops: Use to serve foods; use small size to shape (meatballs, cookies).

Apple Corer: Use to core (apples, pears). Some corers also slice.

 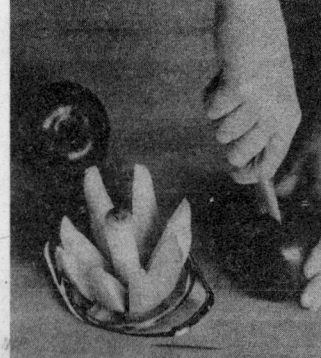

Sieve or Wire Strainer: Use to drain foods. Use colander for large amounts.

French Knives: Use two knives to chop finely; hold tips down, moving handles.

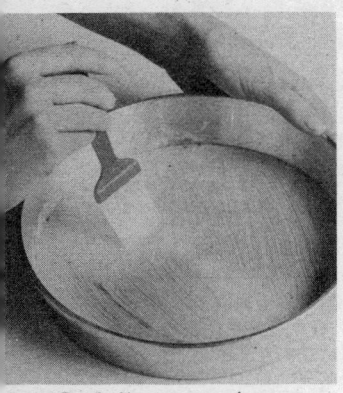 

Pastry Brush: Use to grease (pans, baking sheets) or to brush on glazes.

Vegetable Parer: Use to pare (fruits, too) or to make chocolate curls.

Garlic Press: Use to crush whole garlic cloves or to extract garlic juice.

Nut and Meat Grinders: Use for many foods. Some have choice of blades.

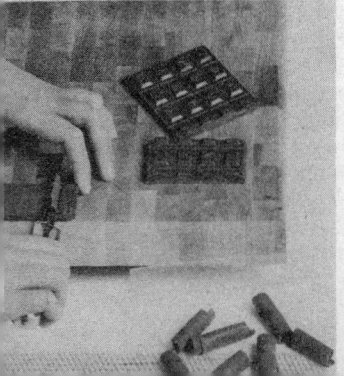 

QUICK BREADS

Biscuits, Muffins, Nut Breads, Waffles

Special Instructions: Best to bake before freezing—unbaked products may become tough and of poor texture and volume. Stack waffles but separate with wrap.

Storage Time: 2 to 3 months.

To Thaw: Leave in original wrap and let stand at room temperature, or warm in 325 to 350° oven. Heat waffles in toaster.

YEAST BREADS

Loaves

Special Instructions: Bake before freezing. (Slice for quick thawing.) Overwrap bakery bread if it is to be stored longer than 3 months.

Storage Time: 9 to 12 months.

To Thaw: Leave in original wrap and let stand at room temperature; if sliced, use toaster. A 1-pound loaf of bread thaws completely in about 3 hours.

Coffee Cakes, Sweet Rolls, Dinner Rolls

Special Instructions: Bake before freezing. (Unbaked dough loses some rising capacity—the texture is tougher and the volume smaller.) See also recipe for Brown 'n Serve Rolls on page 88.

Storage Time: 9 months; Brown 'n Serve Rolls, 2 to 3 months.

To Thaw: Leave in original wrap and heat in 350° oven 20 to 25 minutes. Or let stand (in original wrap) at room temperature 2 to 3 hours.

CAKES AND CUPCAKES

Frosted

Special Instructions: Some frostings and fillings do not freeze well. (The frostings change texture; fillings make the cake soggy.) Confectioners' sugar and fudge frostings freeze best. Boiled frostings are difficult to store—freeze before wrapping. Or insert wooden picks around the top of the cake to prevent the frosting from touching the wrapping.

Storage Time: 2 to 3 months.

To Thaw: Keep loosly covered in the refrigerator.

Unfrosted

Special Instructions: Bake before freezing; cook completely. For added protection, pack wrapped angel food and chiffon cakes in rigid boxes after freezing.

Storage Time: 4 to 6 months—fruitcakes can be stored longer.

To Thaw: Leave in original wrap (to prevent moisture formation on the cake surface) and let stand at room temperature 2 to 3 hours. Or place in 250 to 300° oven for a short time, but watch closely.

EGGS

See page 320—storing leftover egg yolks and whites. To improve texture of mixed whites and yolks, add 1 tablespoon sugar or corn syrup or ½ teaspoon salt per cup before freezing. For egg yolks, add two times the salt or sweetener recommended for whole eggs. Whites need no additions—put through a sieve for uniform texture.

FISH AND SEAFOOD

Special Instructions: Clean as for table use; wash and drain. For small fish, place in waterproof container and cover with water. Shrimp can be frozen cooked. Shrimp cocktail and shrimp creole can also be frozen, but no longer than 6 weeks.

Storage Time: 3 to 4 months.

To Thaw: Leave in original wrap and place under running cold water. Cook while still chilled. If only partially thawed, allow additional cooking time at a lower temperature.

MAIN DISHES

Rice, Pasta, Baked Beans

Special Instructions: Cook only partially; cool quickly. Freeze in casserole or freezer container.

Storage Time: 3 months.

To Thaw: Heat in covered saucepan (with small amount of butter in the bottom) over medium heat. Or place casserole in 350° oven until center is bubbly, about 45 minutes; add small amounts of liquid if food seems dry.

Creamed Dishes, Stews, Sauces

Special Instructions: Do not overcook. Cool promptly by partially submerging the saucepan of cooked food in a large pan of ice and water. Potatoes do not freeze well;

add when thawing. Keep spice level low. Cloves and garlic become stronger during storage—don't add before freezing. Onions gradually lose flavor; green peppers, sage and pimientos increase in strength; nutmeg and cinnamon don't change. Fats tend to separate but will usually recombine. Leave "headspace" in freezer container.

Storage Time: 3 to 4 months.

To Thaw: Partially thaw at room temperature to prevent scorching. Heat in double boiler 30 to 40 minutes. Add liquid if necessary; keep stirring to a minimum.

MEATS AND POULTRY

Special Instructions: Do not freeze fried foods—they become rancid and develop a warmed-over flavor when heated. Leftover roasts (beef, pork, ham, chicken and turkey) and Swiss steak freeze satisfactorily.

Storage Time: 4 months. See pages 361 and 440 for more information.

To Thaw: Let stand in refrigerator.

PIES AND PASTRY

Shells

Special Instructions: Wrap both baked and unbaked shells. Stack rounds of dough but separate with wrap.

Storage Time: Unbaked shells and rounds of dough, 2 months; baked shells, 4 months.

To Thaw: Let rounds of dough stand at room temperature. Unwrap baked shells and let stand at room temperature or place in 350° oven about 6 minutes. Bake unbaked shells in frozen state.

Baked Pies

Special Instructions: Best to freeze baked pies—the bottom crust of an unbaked pie may absorb juices from filling and become soggy. Cool quickly; freeze, then wrap. Deep dish pies (with top crust only) can be frozen unbaked, but store them only 2 to 3 months. Do not freeze custard, cream or meringue-topped pies.

Storage Time: 4 to 6 months. (Chiffon pies only 1 month; if stored longer, they toughen.)

To Thaw: Unwrap and let stand at room temperature 2 to 4 hours. Or unwrap and let stand at room temperature a short time, then place on lower shelf in 350° oven; heat just until warm. If using lightweight aluminum pie pans, place on baking sheet. For chiffon pies, unwrap and let stand at room temperature 2 to 4 hours.

Outdoor Cooking

There's something irresistible about a meal prepared over the glowing coals of a barbecue fire. It doesn't matter whether the food is cooked on a simple grill or on the most expensive rotisserie—as long as it's handled properly, it's a feast for the happy diners. (See the entry for Outdoor Cooking in the index for specific recipes.)

The secret of successful barbecuing lies in knowing how to build the fire and how to handle it. Here are some points to keep in mind when building your fire:

■ Follow the directions that come with your grill or rotisserie. Even specific recipe directions should be changed slightly for some grills.

■ If you find you have to add more fuel to a well-established fire, add it at the edges; then, when it is well kindled, gently rake it into the other coals. (Fresh fuel added to the center of a fire reduces the heat rapidly.) Better yet, if you know you're going to need additional fuel—when cooking a roast, for example—have a small brazier or hibachi with glowing coals ready and waiting beside the grill.

■ Allow plenty of time for the fire to reach its proper cooking temperature. Figure on half an hour to 45 minutes for charcoal briquets.

■ Once your fire is under way, disturb it as little as possible. Constant poking and raking breaks up pockets of heat and lowers the temperature.

■ Locate your fire in a spot where any breeze will blow the smoke away from the eating area—and the neighbors. And *always* build your fire at a safe distance from shrubs, trees or dry grass.

What Kind of Fuel?

Charcoal is by far the most popular form of outdoor-cooking fuel used today. It comes in compact units and is easy to store, transport and use. Furthermore, it produces a bed of bright coals more quickly and reliably than wood—and without the danger of flying sparks.

Charcoal is available in both lump and in briquets, briquets being preferable since they maintain a steady, consistent heat for a longer period of time.

Starting the Fire

Most barbecuers light their fire with one of the commercial liquid starters. They are especially effective with briquets and, unlike kerosene, leave no lingering flavor. *Never* use gasoline for a starter. It is much too dangerous. Follow the directions carefully when using a liquid starter.

When Is the Fire Ready?

Don't expect immediate results. At first, the briquets will just lie there, stubbornly black except for a few whitish-gray specks. Resist the temptation to add more starter fluid. The spots of ash mean the fire is on its way. After 10 or 15 minutes you can begin to turn the briquets that have a good covering of ash; this helps the others to catch. In another 15 to 30 minutes, all the coals will have a red glow and a covering of gray ash. When the fire reaches this point, arrange the coals as needed for cooking, then check the temperature. Use a grill thermometer attached to the grid or turnspit to determine the temperature at *food level,* where it matters. Or test with your hand, seeing how long you can hold it near the grid.

TEMPERATURE GUIDE AT GRID LEVEL

Coals	Thermometer Registers	Hand Withdrawn
Low	about 300°	between 4 and 5 seconds
Medium	about 350°	between 3 and 4 seconds
Hot	about 400°	in less than 3 seconds

Controlling the Heat

The marvelous flavor of properly barbecued food does not come from just any kind of fire, as many barbecuers believe. Rather, it is the result of *controlled* charring of the exterior over smokeless, high heat.

To control the heat when grilling, adjust the distance between the food and the fire to maintain an even cooking temperature. All but the most simple grills are equipped with grids that can be raised or lowered. Or use tongs to move the food away from, or toward, the hot center of the fire.

The coals are usually spread evenly over the firebed for grilling. But changing that shape can change the temperature—separate the coals to lower the heat; rake them closer together to raise it. (Remember this when cooking two courses at different temperatures.)

To control the temperature when cooking on a rotisserie, simply add or remove fuel to maintain a steady, even heat.

Cooking on a Grill

Grilling is perhaps the quickest way to cook over a charcoal or wood fire. Practically any cut of meat suitable for broiling, panbroiling or panfrying can be successfully cooked over the coals.

A few pieces of equipment are all you really need to produce successful results: two pairs of long-handled tongs (one for handling food, the other for handling coals) a long-handled basting brush, a pair of protective gloves and, of course, the grill of your choice.

An occasional flare-up is a necessary evil in grilling. The fats and juices that drip onto the hot coals may cause the flame to flare up, giving the meat the flavor of burned

---

GREAT FOR THE GRILL

Beef: Steaks of all kinds; tenderloin; ground; cubed (for kabobs)

Pork and Ham: Chops; tenderloin; Canadian-style bacon; canned ham; fully cooked ham slice; spareribs; back ribs

Lamb: Chops; cubed (for kabobs); ground; ribs

Miscellaneous Meats: Frankfurters and other sausages; canned luncheon meats

Poultry: Chicken halves, quarters, pieces; small turkey pieces; Rock Cornish hen halves

Fish and Seafood: Whole, fillets or steaks; lobster; lobster tails; shrimp; scallops; oysters

fat. To avoid this, prepare the meat carefully before placing it on the grill. Cut off most of the outside fat from steaks and chops and score the remaining fat with a sharp knife to keep the meat from curling. Leaving a ½- to 1-inch space between the briquets also helps cut down on flare-ups. (A water pistol comes in handy for putting out a flare-up. But use water sparingly; otherwise, your food will be steamed, not broiled.)

Cooking on a Rotisserie

When the main course of your outdoor meal is to be a roast, a whole chicken or turkey or any meat that contains a large amount of fat, wheel out the rotisserie.

Rotisseries range in price and style from expensive ones equipped with electrically driven spits to those designed for use over a simple brazier.

The ideal fire for cooking any sizable piece of meat on a revolving spit should be a little lower than that used for broiling. (For best results, start with medium-hot coals; the spit thermometer should read about 300°.) The coals should never be placed directly under the meat; instead, arrange them at the back of the firebox and make sure they give off an even heat for the entire cooking period. Place a foil drip pan under the spit to catch all of the meat's fat and juices.

Spit-cooked meat bastes itself as it turns. But the spit will not turn easily nor will the meat baste properly if it is not mounted correctly. To mount meat for spit-cooking, spear it on the main rod and hold it firmly in place with adjustable holding forks. Check the balance

---

JUST RIGHT FOR THE ROTISSERIE

Beef: Rib roasts; rolled rump roast (high quality); tip roast (high quality); cubed (for kabobs)

Pork and Ham: Boneless fresh pork roasts; smoked boneless ham; spareribs; back ribs; Canadian-style bacon

Veal: Boned and rolled roasts (shoulder, sirloin, leg)

Lamb: Boned and rolled roasts (shoulder, loin, sirloin, leg); rib roast

Miscellaneous Meats: Bologna (whole or cut) and other sausages

Poultry: Chicken, small turkey, Rock Cornish hens

by holding the ends of the spit rod across your palms. If the spit and meat do not rotate easily, remove the forks and rod and remount. Also, make sure that the spit turns away from you at the top of the turn. This allows the fat to drip off on the up-turn farthest from the fire.

Remember, a meat thermometer is the safest guide to the doneness of any roast, especially one cooked over a charcoal fire.

Special Food Terms

Antipasto: A course of assorted appetizers and relishes, such as olives, anchovies, sliced sausage, artichoke hearts. (Italian)

Appetizer: A small portion of a food or drink served before or as the first course of a meal.

Bisque: Thick soup of pureed shellfish, game or poultry, usually in cream.

Blintzes: Thin pancakes folded or rolled around a filling of cheese or fruit, then fried or baked.

Bouillon: A clear, usually seasoned broth made by straining the water in which chicken, beef or other meat has been cooked. Also made by dissolving commercially prepared bouillon cubes or instant bouillon in hot water.

Canapé: A thin piece of bread, toast, etc., spread or topped with cheese, caviar, anchovies or other foods.

Caviar: The roe (eggs) of sturgeon or other fish, usually served as an appetizer.

Chutney: A sauce or relish of East Indian origin containing both sweet and sour ingredients, with spices and other seasonings.

Compote: Fruit stewed or cooked in a syrup, usually served as a dessert.

Consommé: A clear, strong soup made by boiling meat and bones long and slowly in order to extract their nutritive properties.

Coquille: A shell or small dish made in the shape of a shell. Used for baking and serving various fish or meat dishes prepared with a sauce.

Creole: A dish made with tomatoes and peppers; usually served over rice.

Crêpes: Thin, light, delicate pancakes.

Demitasse: A small cup or serving of very strong black coffee.

Drippings: Fats and juices that come from meat as it cooks.

En papillote: Cooked and served in a wrapping of foil or oiled paper. Usually meat or fish is cooked this way. (French)

Flambé: Food served in flaming liquor (usually brandy).

Fricassee: To cook by braising. Meat, especially chicken or veal, browned lightly, stewed and served in a white sauce made with its own stock.

Giblets: The heart, liver, gizzard and neck of a fowl, often cooked separately.

Hors d'oeuvre: An appetizer (either a relish or a more elaborate preparation) served before or as the first course of a meal. Usually a finger food.

Legumes: Vegetables which bear their fruit or seeds in pods—for example, peas, beans or lentils.

Mocha: Flavoring obtained from coffee or from a combination of chocolate and coffee.

Mousse: Preparation with whipped cream as a base; often stabilized with gelatin and chilled.

Nesselrode: A mixture of preserved fruits, nuts and the like; used as a sauce or in puddings, pies, ice cream and other desserts.

Paella: Main dish of rice, chicken, shellfish, vegetables, saffron and other seasonings. Often includes sausage. (Spanish)

Pasta: A thin, dried dough produced in a variety of forms: spaghetti, macaroni, ravioli. (Italian)

Prosciutto: Spiced ham, often smoked, that has been cured by drying; always sliced paper-thin for serving. (Italian)

Scallop: A type of seafood. Also, to bake in a sauce (usually a white or cream sauce).

Score: To cut ridges or lines into meat or fish with shallow slashes, usually in a diamond pattern, before cooking.

Stroganoff: Meat browned with onion and cooked in sauce of sour cream, seasonings, and usually mushrooms.

Sukiyaki: Main dish made with thin slices of beef, and usually containing soy sauce, bean curd and greens. (Japanese)

Sweetbread: The pancreas or the thymus gland of a calf or lamb.

Tripe: Stomach tissue of beef or lamb.

Vinaigrette: A sauce made with vinegar or a combination of oil, vinegar and seasonings.

EMERGENCY SUBSTITUTIONS

An emergency is the only excuse for using a substitute ingredient—recipe results will vary. Following are some stand-ins for staples.

For	Use
1½ teaspoons cornstarch	1 tablespoon flour
1 whole egg	2 egg yolks plus 1 tablespoon water (in cookies) or 2 egg yolks (in custards and similar mixtures)
1 cup fresh whole milk	½ cup evaporated milk plus ½ cup water or 1 cup reconstituted nonfat dry milk plus 2 tablespoons butter
1 ounce unsweetened chocolate	3 tablespoons cocoa plus 1 tablespoon fat
1 cup honey	1¼ cups sugar plus ½ cup liquid

EQUIVALENT MEASURES

3 teaspoons = 1 tablespoon	2 pints = 1 quart
16 tablespoons = 1 cup	4 quarts (liquid) = 1 gallon
2 cups = 1 pint	4 tablespoons = ¼ cup
4 cups = 1 quart	5⅓ tablespoons = ⅓ cup

COMMON FOOD EQUIVALENTS

	Amount	Approximate Measure
Butter or other shortening	1 pound	2 cups
Cheese		
Cheddar or American	4 ounces	1 cup shredded
cottage	1 pound	2 cups
cream	3-ounce package	6 tablespoons
	8-ounce package	1 cup (16 tablespoons)
Chocolate		
chips	6-ounce package	1 cup
unsweetened	8-ounce package	8 square (1 ounce each)
Coconut, shredded or flaked	4-ounce can	about 1⅓ cups
Coffee, ground	1 pound	80 tablespoons
Cream		
whipping	½ pint	1 cup (2 cups whipped)
sour	8 ounces	1 cup

COMMON FOOD EQUIVALENTS

	Amount	Approximate Measure
Flour		
all-purpose	1 pound	about 3½ cups
cake	1 pound	about 4 cups
Lemon		
juice	1 medium	2 to 3 tablespoons
peel, lightly grated	1 medium	1½ to 3 teaspoons
Marshmallows	1 large	10 miniature
	about 11 large or 110 miniature	1 cup
Nuts		
almonds	1 pound in the shell	1 to 1¾ cups nutmeats
	1 pound shelled	3½ cups
pecans	1 pound in the shell	2¼ cups nutmeats
	1 pound shelled	4 cups
peanuts	1 pound in the shell	2¼ cups nutmeats
	1 pound shelled	3 cups
walnuts	1 pound in the shell	1⅔ cups nutmeats
	1 pound shelled	4 cups
Orange		
juice	1 medium	⅓ to ½ cup
peel, lightly grated	1 medium	1 to 2 tablespoons
Sugar		
brown	1 pound	2¼ cups (firmly packed)
confectioners'	1 pound	about 4 cups
granulated	1 pound	2¼ cups

Approximate Metric Equivalents

Quantity	Multiplied by	Equals
Teaspoons	5	Milliliters
Tablespoons	15	Milliliters
Fluid Ounces	30	Milliliters
Fluid Ounces	0.03	Liters
Cups	240	Milliliters
Cups	0.24	Liters
Pints	0.47	Liters
Quarts	0.95	Liters
Ounces	28	Grams
Pounds	454	Grams
Pounds	0.45	Kilograms
Inches	2.5	Centimeters
Fahrenheit temperature	5/9 (after subtracting 32)	Celsius temperature (exact)

HERBS AND SPICES

	ALLSPICE	BASIL	CHILI POWDER
SOUPS, STEWS AND SAUCES	Potato Soup Oyster Stew Barbecue Sauce Brown Sauce Tomato Sauces	Manhattan Clam Chowder Tomato Soup Vegetable Soup Beef Stew Spaghetti Sauce	Pea Soup Beef Stew Chili con Carne Cheese Sauces Gravy
FISH, POULTRY AND GAME	Poached Fish Chicken Fricassee	Crabmeat Fish Shrimp Tuna Fried Chicken	Shrimp Barbecued Chicken Fried Chicken
MEATS AND MAIN DISHES	Ham Meatballs Meat Loaf Pot-roasts	Beef Lamb Pork Pizza Spaghetti	Hamburgers Meat Loaf
VEGETABLES	Eggplant Parsnips Spinach Squash Turnips	Asparagus Green Beans Squash Tomatoes Wax Beans	Cauliflower Corn Lima Beans Onions Peas
SALADS AND SALAD DRESSINGS	Cabbage Cottage Cheese Fruit	Tomato Aspic Cucumber Seafood Tomato French Dressing Russian Dressing	Cottage Cheese Potato French Dressing Guacamole
DESSERTS	Chiffon Pie Fruitcake Mince Pie Pumpkin Pie Steamed Pudding Tapioca Pudding	Fruit Compotes	
MISCELLANEOUS	Egg Dishes Coffee Cakes Sweet Rolls Cranberry Sauce	Creamed Eggs Omelets Soufflés Seafood Cocktails	Cheese Fondue Scrambled Eggs Welsh Rabbit Biscuits French Bread

Use caution. Start with a small amount, especially if you're using dried herbs. If the taste is too delicate, you can always add more.

Spices are derived from the bark, root, fruits or berries of perennial plants. Herbs are the leaves of annual or perennial shrubs.

CINNAMON	CLOVES	DILL SEED AND WEED	GINGER
Fruit Soup Beef Stew	Bean Soup Onion Soup Pea Soup Tomato Sauces	Borsch Split Pea Soup Lamb Stew Drawn Butter Gravy	Bean Soup Onion Soup Potato Soup Cocktail Sauce
Sweet-sour Shrimp Stewed Chicken	Baked Fish Chicken à la King Roast Chicken	Salmon Shellfish Chicken	Fish Roast Chicken Roast Cornish Hens Roast Duckling
Ham Pork Chops Sauerbraten	Corned Beef Ham Tongue Baked Beans	Beef Steaks Lamb Chops Lamb Steaks	Beef Roasts Beef Steaks Baked Beans
Carrots Onions Spinach Squash Sweet Potatoes	Beets Carrots Onions Squash Sweet Potatoes	Cabbage Carrots Cauliflower Peas Potatoes Sauerkraut	Beets Carrots Squash Sweet Potatoes
Fruit	Spiced Fruit Fruit Salad Dressings	Cottage Cheese Potato Seafood French Dressing Sour Cream Dressings	French Dressing Fruit Salad Dressings
Apple Desserts Chocolate Pudding Fruit Compotes Rice Pudding	Applesauce Chocolate Cake Chocolate Sauce Gingerbread Pears	Green Apple Pie	Broiled Grapefruit Pears Steamed Pudding Stewed Dried Fruit
Biscuits Nut Bread Sweet Rolls Tea, Coffee Chocolate	Coffee Cakes Nut Bread Sweet Rolls Fruit Punch	Deviled Eggs Rice Dishes Seafood Cocktails Onion Rolls	Macaroni and Cheese Rice Dishes Cookies Nut Bread

	MACE	MARJORAM	NUTMEG
SOUPS, STEWS AND SAUCES	Vegetable Soup Oyster Stew Veal Stew	Chicken Soup Onion Soup Potato Soup Brown Sauce Gravy	Oyster Stew Mushroom Sauce
FISH, POULTRY AND GAME	Baked Fish Shrimp Creole Chicken Fricassee	Salmon Loaf Shellfish Chicken Turkey Venison	Fish Fried Chicken
MEATS AND MAIN DISHES	Meatballs Meat Loaf Veal	Beef Hamburgers Lamb Pork Veal	Meatballs Meat Loaf Pot-roasts
VEGETABLES	Broccoli Brussels Sprouts Cabbage Succotash	Celery Eggplant Greens Potatoes Zucchini	Beans Carrots Cauliflower Corn Onions
SALADS AND SALAD DRESSINGS	Fruit	Chicken Egg Green Seafood French Dressing	Sweet Salad Dressings
DESSERTS	Chocolate Desserts Citrus Desserts Cottage Pudding Custards	Cooked Fruits Fruit Cup	Apple Pie Custards Hard Sauce Pumpkin Pie Vanilla Ice Cream
MISCELLANEOUS	Quiche Lorraine Welsh Rabbit Banana Bread Doughnuts	Omelets Scrambled Eggs Soufflés Fruit Juice	Coffee Cakes Nut Bread Sweet Rolls

OREGANO	SAGE	THYME
Beef Soup Bouillon Stews Butter Sauces Mushroom Sauce	Chicken Soup Consommé Tomato Soup Stews Cheese Sauces	Borsch Clam Chowder Stews Bordelaise Sauce
Broiled Fish Shellfish Chicken Pheasant	Fish Chicken Duckling Turkey Poultry Stuffing	Tuna Fried Chicken Roast Duckling Poultry Stuffing
Hamburgers Liver Swiss Steak Veal Pizza Spaghetti	Cold Roast Beef Lamb Pork Veal	Roasts Variety Meats
Broccoli Cabbage Mushrooms Onions Tomatoes	Brussels Sprouts Eggplant Lima Beans Squash Tomatoes	Artichokes Carrots Green Beans Mushrooms Peas Potatoes
Egg Seafood Vegetable	Chicken French Dressing	Chicken Cottage Cheese Green Tomato Tomato Aspic
	Custards	
Boiled Eggs Egg Sandwich Spread Guacamole Dip Cheese Spreads	Cheese Fondue Omelets Biscuits Corn Bread Hot Milk Tea	Omelets Scrambled Eggs Soufflés Biscuits Corn Bread

Index

A

Acorn squash, 718
  nutty baked, 719
Alamo tamale supper, 469
Allemande sauce, 579
Allspice, 758
Almond(s)
  cream filling, 200
  crunch wax beans, 677
  fluff, 199
  garlic, 14
  gingered, 14
  loaf cake, 156
  peach angel food cake, 165
  ting-a-lings, 261
  torte, 149
  velouté sauce, 578
Ambrosia
  balls, 225
  honey bee, 267
  tapioca, 291
Ambrosial salad, triple-orange, 604
Anchovy
  open-face sandwiches, 659
  pizza, 480
  velouté sauce, 578
Angel food cakes, 165-167. *See also Cake(s); Dessert(s), cake*
Anise loaf cake, 156
Anniversary cake, 184
Appetizer(s), 1-35. *See also Canapé(s); Dip(s); Snack(s).*
  antipasto platter, vegetable, 592
  asparagus with curried mayonnaise, 611
  beverages, 51-53
  caviar classic, 16
  celery root-grape salad, 612
  celery Victor, 611
  clams on the half shell, 24
  cocktail
    buns, 18
    meatballs, 16
  deep-fried, 68
  escargots (snails), 28
  fruit compote, sparkling, 23
  fruit cup
    spring grapefruit, 21
    Tahitian, 22
  gazpacho, 631
  grapefruit-seafood cocktail, 23
  hibachi, 21
  London broil, 32
  Lorraine tarts, quick, 32
  melon and prosciutto, 23
  mushrooms royale, 17
  oysters
    on the half shell, 25
    Parmesan, 27
    Rockefeller, 26

  Parmesan
    appetizer loaf, 30
    fans, 19
  pâté
    appetizer, 10
    frosted liverwurst, 11
    salad loaf, 609
  pickled mushrooms, 558
  rumaki, 15
  salads, first course, 611
  seafood coquille, 27
  serving suggestions, 7, 21, 630
  shrimp
    cocktail, 24
    nippy, 15
    remoulade, 25
  soups, 630-633
  spreads
    gouda burst, 11
    party cheese ball (and variations), 12
Apple(s)
  baked (and variation), 271
  caramel, 257
  cider
    punch, hot, 49
    spiced cranberry, 53
  crisp, 274
  dumplings, 275
  muffins, 62
  'n cheese slaw, 593
  pancakes, 78
  pie (and variations), 510-512
    cran-apple, 512
    cranberry, fresh, 513
    crumble pizza, 514
    deep dish, 513
    mincemeat, 524
  raisin stuffing, 445
  salad
    spinach toss, 599
    Waldorf, 599
Applesauce, 272
  cake, 154
  jumbles, 207
Apricot(s)
  balls, 264
  glazed petits fours, 144
  mint sauce, 576
  nut
    balls, 264
    bread, 70
  refrigerator dessert, 312
  spiced, 563
Arroz con pollo, 500
Artichokes
  French, 670, 674
  Jerusalem, 673, 674
  with onion dip, 1
Asparagus, 673
  Oriental, 675

KITCHEN POWER!

- [ ] PUTTING FOOD BY—Hertzberg, Vaughan & Green   2030 • $2.50
- [ ] AMERICAN HERITAGE COOKBOOK   2220 • $1.95
- [ ] CROCKERY COOKERY—Mable Hoffman   2400 • $1.95
- [ ] ORIENTAL COOKING—Myra Waldo   6482 • $1.25
- [ ] THE ART OF JEWISH COOKING—Jennie Grossinger   7033 • $1.25
- [ ] COMPLETE BOOK OF WINE COOKERY—Waldo   7080 • $1.25
- [ ] THE COMPLETE BOOK OF PASTA—Jack Denton Scott   8064 • $1.25
- [ ] THE ART OF ITALIAN COOKING—Mario LoPinto   8298 • $1.25
- [ ] MADAME WU'S ART OF CHINESE COOKING   8642 • $1.50
- [ ] BETTER HOMES & GARDENS HOME CANNING COOKBOOK   10246 • $1.75
- [ ] BETTY CROCKER'S COOKBOOK   10477 • $2.25
- [ ] AMERICA'S FAVORITE RECIPES FROM BETTER HOMES & GARDENS   10538 • $1.50
- [ ] BETTER HOMES & GARDENS CASSEROLE COOKBOOK   10539 • $1.50
- [ ] THE ART OF FRENCH COOKING—Fernande Garvin   10682 • $1.50
- [ ] FANNIE FARMER BOSTON COOKING SCHOOL COOKBOOK —Wilma Perkins   10919 • $2.25

Buy them wherever Bantam Bestsellers are sold or use this handy coupon:

Bantam Books, Inc., Dept. KP, 414 East Golf Road, Des Plaines, Ill. 60016

Please send me the books I have checked above. I am enclosing $_____ (please add 35¢ to cover postage and handling). Send check or money order —no cash or C.O.D.'s please.

Mr/Mrs/Miss_____

Address_____

City_____ State/Zip_____

KP—3/77

Please allow three weeks for delivery. This offer expires 3/78.

Bantam Book Catalog

It lists over a thousand money-saving best-sellers originally priced from $3.75 to $15.00 —bestsellers that are yours now for as little as 60¢ to $2.95!

The catalog gives you a great opportunity to build your own private library at huge savings!

So don't delay any longer—send us your name and address and 25¢ (to help defray postage and handling costs).